Research Methods
in the
Social Sciences

FOURTH EDITION

Research Methods
in the
Social Sciences

FOURTH EDITION

Chava Frankfort-Nachmias
University of Wisconsin, Milwaukee

David Nachmias
University of Wisconsin, Milwaukee

St. Martin's Press ■ New York

Acquisitions editor: Louise H. Waller
Development editor: Douglas Bell
Software editor: Kim Richardson
Production supervisor: Alan Fischer
Text design: Gene Crofts
Cover design: Tom McKeveny

Library of Congress Catalog Card Number: 90-63540

Manufactured in the United States of America.

65432
fedcb

For information, write:
St. Martin's Press, Inc.
175 Fifth Avenue
New York, NY 10010

ISBN: 0-312-06275-3

To our daughters, Anat and Talia

PREFACE

The goal of the Fourth Edition of *Research Methods in the Social Sciences*, as in the previous editions, is to offer a comprehensive, systematic treatment of the scientific approach. We emphasize the relationship between theory, research, and practice, and integrate various research activities in an orderly framework so that the reader can more easily comprehend research in the social sciences.

Social science research is, in our view, a cyclical, self-correcting process consisting of seven major interrelated stages: the research problem, the hypothesis, the research design, measurement, data collection, data analysis, and generalization. Each of these stages is interrelated with theory in that it both affects and is affected by it. The text leads the reader through each stage of this process.

The New Edition

The Fourth Edition incorporates a number of significant revisions—most notably, a fully updated section on the recent 1990 U.S. Census, including a discussion of census history, procedures, technical advances in data collection and coverage, population sampling, ongoing census surveys, and available census products; a totally revised chapter on data preparation and analysis; a revision of Appendix A that includes an introduction to SPSS, and a new appendix for SAS. Both appendixes serve to assist students in preparing and executing computerized data analysis utilizing these widely available and often-used software packages.

The revision also includes the addition of chapter previews that present an outline at the beginning of each chapter of the material to be studied, that compliment the existing chapter summaries, lists of key terms, study questions, and additional readings; an expanded glossary that is now cross-referenced to the text; and computer software—available to all adopters in IBM- and Macintosh-compatible 3.5 and 5.25 formats—that can be both replicated and downloaded to a network. Previous users will notice that the text has been totally redesigned to incorporate a more user-friendly format that utilizes tints to highlight the pedagogical features offered in each chapter.

The new edition continues to blend a broad range of classic social science research studies with up-to-date examples of contemporary social science issues. These additions and changes reflect today's concerns and developments in the field that have surfaced since the publication of the previous edition. The text has also benefitted from the constructive criticism offered by instructors across the country, both users and nonusers, in research methods courses from a variety of disciplines.

The Plan of the Book

The book's organization progresses logically from the conceptual and theoretical building blocks of the research process to data analysis and computer applications offering students a comprehensive and systematic foundation that leads to insights into the breadth and depth of social science research. The book's self-contained yet integrated chapters promote flexibility in structuring the course, depending on an individual instructor's needs and interests. The text adapts easily to two kinds of courses: a basic methods course or one that covers methods and statistics sequentially.

Chapter 1 examines the foundations of knowledge, the objectives of scientific research, and the basic assumptions of the scientific approach. Chapters 2 and 3 discuss the basic issues of empirical research and the relationship between theory and research. Included are such topics as concept formation, the roles and types of theories, models, variables, and the various sources for research problems and for the construction of hypotheses. Chapter 4 focuses on ethical concerns in social science research and ways to ensure the rights and the welfare of research participants, including the right to privacy.

Chapters 5 and 6 present the research design stage. A research design is a strategy that guides investigators; it is a logical model for inferring causal relations. Experimental designs are discussed and illustrated in Chapter 5, and quasi- and preexperimental designs are examined in Chapter 6. Chapter 7 is concerned with measurement and quantification. The issues of validity and reliability—which are inseparable from measurement theory—are also discussed here, along with a new discussion of measurement error. In Chapter 8, we present the principles of sampling theory, the most frequently used sampling designs, and the methods for estimating sample size.

In Chapters 9 through 13, we present and exemplify the various methods of data collection available to social scientists. Observational methods, laboratory experiments, and field experimentation are the subjects of Chapter 9. Survey research—in particular the mail questionnaire, the personal interview, and the telephone interview—is examined in Chapter 10. Chapter 11 describes and illustrates methods of questionnaire construction: the content of questions, types of questions, question format, and the sequence of questions. Pitfalls of questionnaire construction address the issue of avoiding bias. Chapter 12 is devoted to the theory and practice of qualitative research, with a particular emphasis on participant observation and field research. In Chapter 13 we discuss major issues of secondary data analysis—the census, unobtrusive data such as private and public documents, and content analysis.

The next five chapters are concerned with data processing and analysis. In Chapter 14 we present the latest techniques of codebook construction, coding schemes and devices, ways to prepare data for computer processing, the use of computers in social science research, and linkages through communication networks. Chapter 15 introduces the univariate distribution, measures of central tendency and dispersion, and the various types of frequency distributions. Chapter 16 examines the central concept of bivariate analysis, specifically several measures of nominal, ordinal, and interval relationships which are discussed and compared. The major topics of multivariate analysis, statistical techniques of control and interpretation, causal inferences, and path analysis are the subjects of Chapter 17. Chapter 18 presents common techniques used in constructing indexes and scales; and in Chapter 19 we discuss strategies of hypothesis testing, the level of significance, the region of rejection, and several parametric and nonparametric tests of significance.

This text, together with the supporting materials, will help readers move through the major stages of the research process.

Included in the ancillary materials are the *Study Guide*, which lists chapter objectives, key terms and concepts, main points in the chapters, self-evaluation exercises, review tests, and exercises and projects; an *Instructor's Manual* and test bank that provides chapter-opening previews, objectives, lists of key terms, suggested research projects, and essay, discussion, and multiple-choice questions for each chapter; and *Computer Software*—a data bank taken from the 1980 and 1990 U.S. Census for the largest cities in two key states suitable for use with problems in the analysis of variables and levels of measurement.

Acknowledgments

Our literary debts are testified to throughout the text. Many students, instructors, reviewers, and colleagues have offered useful ideas and comments since the First Edition was published in 1976.

We are particularly grateful to Michael Baer, Bruce S. Bowen, Jeffery Brudney, Gary T. Henry, and Allen Rubin. We are also grateful to the Literary Executor of the late Sir Ronald A. Fisher, F.R.S., to Dr. Frank Yates, F.R.S., to Longman Group Ltd., London, for permission to reprint appendixes from their book *Statistical Tables for Biological, Agricultural, and Medical Research*, Sixth Edition (1974), and to the reviewers of the Fourth Edition: Lawrence R. Alschuler, University of Ottawa, Ottawa, Canada; Franklin J. Boster, Michigan State University; Robert X. Browning, Purdue University; Robert A. Ellis, University of Georgia; Glenn A. Harper, University of Maryland, College Park; Susan Hunter, West Virginia University; Curtis T. Langley, Norfolk State University; Kathryn L.

Malec, Indiana University, NW; and John M. Nickerson, University of Maine, Augusta.

We are also grateful to Claire L. Felbinger, Levin College of Public Administration, Cleveland State University, for her work in updating Chapter 14, "Data Preparation and Analysis," and, in collaboration with her assistant Stephen F. Schwelgien, for the preparation of the appendixes on SPSS and SAS. Our gratitude is also extended to Maria Morales-Harper, Information Services Specialist at the Bureau of the Census, for her valuable assistance in providing updates for the discussions of the U.S. Census.

Finally, we wish to extend our sincere thanks to Louise Waller, Douglas Bell, Richard Steins, Bruce Glassman, and Kim Richardson at St. Martin's Press for their patience and conscientious work on behalf of this edition.

Chava Frankfort–Nachmias
David Nachmias

CONTENTS IN BRIEF

Appendixes

DETAILED CONTENTS

Part III ▪ Data Collection

Appendixes

Research Methods
in the
Social Sciences

FOURTH EDITION

PART I

Foundations of Empirical Research

CHAPTER 1

The Scientific Approach

In this chapter, we define the scientific approach, first by its assumptions about nature and experience and then by its methodology relating to communication, reasoning, and intersubjectivity.

WHAT BENEFITS CAN THE SCIENTIFIC approach have to offer to people who take an interest in the problems of society? How can we acquire reliable knowledge about those aspects of the human experience that are considered "social," "political," "economic," and "psychological"? More specifically, how can the scientific approach be of value in understanding phenomena such as inflation, unemployment, democratic governance, bureaucracy, deviance, or self-actualization?

One way to answer these questions is first to define **science** and then to take a close look at the scientific approach, its assumptions, goals, and attributes and compare these with other approaches to knowledge. In this chapter, we first define *science* and then compare the scientific approach with three other approaches to knowledge. We discuss the assumptions of science, its aims, and the role of methodology in the scientific approach. We then present the ideas of scientific revolutions, discoveries, and scientific progress. The last section presents a model of the research process, the stages of which are discussed throughout this book.

What Is Science?

Unfortunately, *science* cannot be easily defined. Laypersons, journalists, policymakers, scholars, and scientists themselves define the term *science* in different ways and employ it in different contexts. To some, science connotes a prestigious undertaking; to others, science implies a body of true knowledge; to still others, it means an objective investigation of empirical phenomena.

The difficulty encountered in attempting to define *science* emerges primarily from the practice of confusing the content of science with its methodology. Although science has no particular subject matter of its own, we do not view every study of phenomena as science. For example, astrology studies the positions of the stars and various events in human life and tries to establish relations between them and to predict future events. These goals and activities do not qualify astrology for admission into the family of the various sciences. Even if a prestigious university would decide to establish a Department of Astrology, recruit faculty, develop a curriculum, and offer a Master of Science degree, astrology would not qualify as a scientific discipline. The reason that we reject astrology as a science is not because of its subject matter, but rather because the methodology used by astrologists is considered to be unscientific. Whenever a branch of supposed factual knowledge is rejected by scientists, it is always on the basis of its methodology. Furthermore, much of the content of science is constantly changing; knowledge regarded as scientific at present may become unscientific in the future. Science is not any general or particular body of knowledge; science is distinct because of its methodology. For these reasons we shall use the term *science* throughout this book to mean all knowledge collected by the means of the scientific methodology.

Approaches to Knowledge

The word *science* is derived from the Latin word *scire*, "to know." Throughout history, knowledge has been acquired in various ways. The scientific approach is by no means the only way by which people have attempted to understand their environment and themselves. Three other general modes have served the purpose of acquiring knowledge: the authoritarian mode, the mystical mode, and the rationalistic mode. Major distinctions among these modes is the way in which each vests credibility in the source or producer of knowledge (that is, *Who* says so?), the procedure by which knowledge is produced (*How* do you know?), and the effect of the knowledge produced (*What difference* does it make?)[1] A brief description of these modes pro-

---

1. Walter L. Wallace, *The Logic of Science in Sociology* (Hawthorne, N.Y.: Aldine, 1971), p. 11. See also, Anthony O'Hear, *An Introduction to the Philosophy of Science* (New York: Oxford University Press, 1989).

vides a comparative perspective for the evaluation of the scientific approach.

Authoritarian Mode.   In the authoritarian mode, knowledge is sought by referring to people who are socially or politically defined as qualified producers of knowledge. These may be oracles in tribal societies, archbishops in theocratic societies, kings in monarchical societies, and individuals occupying scientific positions in technocratic societies. Within any society, different authorities may be approached for knowledge about different phenomena. For devout Catholics, the pope possesses undisputed authority on matters viewed as religious. Similar authority was possessed by the Soviet Academy of Sciences, which in 1950 decreed that statistical theories based on probability are nonscientific; this decision was an abortive attempt to resolve the contradiction between the determinism of dialectical materialism and the theory of probability. In the authoritarian mode, laypersons attribute the ability to generate knowledge to the social, political or religious authority of the producer. The manner in which the layperson solicits this authority (e.g., prayer, ceremony) affects the nature of the authority's response but not the recipient's confidence in the response. Repeated refutations are required to delegitimize the authority of a knowledge producer and replace them.

Mystical Mode.   In the mystical mode, knowledge is obtained from supernaturally knowledgeable authorities such as prophets, divines, gods, and mediums. In this sense, the mystical mode is similar to the authoritarian mode. However, it differs in its dependence on manifestations of supernatural signs and on the psychophysical state of the knowledge consumer. For example, the rites surrounding the process of astrological prophecy are aimed at persuading the layperson of the astrologer's supernatural powers. The mystical mode depends, to a large extent, on using ritualistic and ceremonial procedures.

Moreover, under conditions of acute depression, helplessness, and intoxication, the knowledge consumer is most willing to accept knowledge produced by the mystical mode. The confidence in the knowledge produced in this manner decreases as the number of refutations increases or as the educational level of a society advances.

Rationalistic Mode.   **Rationalism** is a school of philosophy that holds that the totality of knowledge can be obtained by strict adherence to the forms and rules of logic. The underlying assumptions of rationalism are (1) that the human mind can understand the world independently of observable phenomena and (2) that forms of knowledge exist that are prior to our personal experiences. In other words, the concern of the rationalistic mode is what must be true in principle and what is logically possible and permissible.

To the rationalist, abstract formal logic is a normative master science that makes it possible to separate scientific propositions from unsound thinking. According to classical rationalists, Aristotle had explored once and for all the entire subject matter of logic and thus the structure of knowledge and truth. The German philosopher Immanuel Kant (1724–1804) declared of logic:

> Since Aristotle it has not had to retrace a single step, unless we choose to consider as improvements the removal of some unnecessary subtleties, or the clearer definition of its matter, both of which refer to the elegance rather than to the solidity of the science. It is remarkable also, that to the present day, it has not been able to make one step in advance, so that, to all appearances, it may be considered as completed and perfect.[2]

Kant elaborated the theory that our minds imprint a certain pattern on the observational world. This pattern is in terms of space, time, and certain "categories." The statements of logic and mathematics tell us something about our experiences. Such statements of knowledge are produced by pure reason, for it is the mind that relates them to reality.

The view that a priori knowledge exists and that it is independent of the human experience did not end with classical rationalism. The supreme embodiment of rationalism in contemporary social sciences is abstract, pure mathematics. Pure mathematics consists of statements that are universally valid, certain, and independent of the empirical world. For example, the statements of pure geometry are considered to be absolute and true by definition. Pure geometry says nothing about reality; its propositions are tautological, that is, true by virtue of their logical form alone. Although pure mathematics and formal logic are essential to the scientific approach, their value for the social sciences "exists only in so far as they serve as means to fruitful progress in the subject-matter, and they should be applied, as complex tools always should, only when and where they can help and do not hinder progress."[3]

The Assumptions of Science

The scientific approach is grounded on a set of fundamental **assumptions** that are unproven and unprovable. They are necessary prerequisites for the conduct of scientific discourse and represent issues in the area of the philosophy of science known as **epistemology**—the study of the foundations of knowledge. By examining these assumptions, we can better understand the scientific approach and its claim for superiority over other approaches to knowledge.

1. *Nature is orderly.* The basic assumption of the scientific approach is that there is a recognizable regularity and order in the natural world; events

2. Immanuel Kant, *Critique of Pure Reason*, trans. Max Muller (London: Macmillan, 1881), p. 688.
3. Kurt Lewin, *Field Theory in Social Science* (Westport, Conn.: Greenwood Press, 1975), p. 12.

do not occur randomly. Even within a rapidly changing environment, it is assumed that there is a degree of order and structure and that change itself is patterned and can be understood.

The concept of nature does not refer to omnipotent or supernatural forces. In science, nature encompasses all empirically observable objects, conditions, and phenomena that exist independent of human intervention and includes the human being as a biological system. The laws of nature do not prescribe, but rather describe, what actually is happening. Furthermore, order and regularity in nature are not necessarily inherent in the phenomena. For example, there is no logically compelling reason why spring should follow winter, winter follow autumn, autumn follow summer, and summer follow spring. But they do, and regularly so, and such regularities underly other observable phenomena.

2. *We can know nature.* The assumption that we can know nature is no more provable than the assumptions that nature is orderly and that there are laws of nature. It expresses a basic conviction that human beings are just as much part of nature as other natural objects, conditions, and phenomena and that, although we possess unique and distinctive characteristics, we can nevertheless be understood and explained by the same methods by which we study nature. Individuals and societal phenomena exhibit sufficient recurrent, orderly, and empirically demonstrable patterns to be amenable to scientific investigation. The human mind is not only capable of knowing nature but also of knowing itself and the minds of others.

3. *Knowledge is superior to ignorance.* Closely related to the assumption that we can know nature and ourselves is the belief that knowledge should be pursued both for its own sake and for improving human conditions. The argument that knowledge is superior to ignorance does not mean that everything in nature can or will be known. Rather, it is assumed that scientific knowledge is tentative and changing. Things that we did not know in the past we know now, and current knowledge might be modified in the future. Truth in science is always relative to the evidence, the methods, and the theories employed.

The belief that relative knowledge is better than ignorance is diametrically opposed to epistomologies based on absolute truth. As Gideon Sjoberg and Roger Nett put it:

> Certainly the ideal that human dignity is enhanced when man is restless, inquiring, and "soul searching" conflicts with a variety of belief systems that would strive toward a closed system, one based on absolute truth. The history of modern science and its clash with absolute systems bears testimony to this proposition."[4]

True believers already "know" all that there is to know. Scientific knowledge threatens the old ways of doing things; it is detrimental to tranquillity,

4. Gideon Sjoberg and Roger Nett, *A Methodology for Social Research* (New York: Harper & Row, 1968), p. 25.

stability, and the status quo. In exchange, the scientific approach can offer only tentative truth that is relative to the existing state of knowledge. These are both the strength and weakness of the scientific approach:

> It is a strength in the sense that rational man will in the long run act to correct his own errors. It is a weakness in that scientists, not being so confident of the validity of their own assertions as is the general public, may, in those frequent periods when social crises threaten public security, be overturned by absolutists. Science is often temporarily helpless when its bastions are stormed by overzealous proponents of absolute systems of belief.[5]

4. *All natural phenomena have natural causes.* The assumption that all natural phenomena have natural causes epitomizes the scientific revolution. It has placed the scientific approach in opposition to fundamentalist religion on the one hand and spiritualism and magic on the other. The assumption implies that natural events have *natural* causes or antecedents. It rejects the counterassumption that forces other than those found in nature operate to cause the occurrence of natural events. Moreover, until scientists can account for the occurrence of phenomena in natural terms, they reject the argument that some other supernatural explanation is necessary. The main function of this assumption is to direct scientific research away from omnipotent supernatural forces and toward the empirical regularities and order that underlie natural phenomena. Once delineated, such regularities can serve as evidence for cause-and-effect relationships.

5. *Nothing is self-evident.* Scientific knowledge is not self-evident; claims for truth must be demonstrated objectively. Tradition, subjective beliefs, and common sense could not be exclusively relied on in the verification of scientific knowledge. Possibilities for error are always present, and even the simplest claims call for objective verification. Therefore, scientific thinking is skeptical and critical.

6. *Knowledge is derived from the acquisition of experience.* If science is to help us understand the real world, it must be **empirical**; that is, it must rely on perceptions, experience, and observations. Perception is a fundamental tenet of the scientific approach, and it is achieved through our senses:

> Science assumes that a communication tie between man and the external universe is maintained through his own sense impressions. Knowledge is held to be a product of one's experiences, as facets of the physical, biological, and social world play upon the senses.[6]

This assumption should not be interpreted in the narrow definition of the five senses—touch, smell, taste, hearing, and seeing. Many phenomena cannot be directly experienced or observed. Observation is not "immedi-

---

5. Ibid., p. 26.
6. Ibid.

ately given" or entirely detached from scientific terms, concepts, and theories. As the British philosopher of science Sir Karl Popper wrote:

> The naïve empiricist . . . thinks that we begin by collecting and arranging our experiences, and so ascend the ladder of science. . . . But if I am ordered: "Record what you are experiencing," I shall hardly know how to obey this ambiguous order. Am I to report that I am writing; that I hear a bell ringing; a newsboy shouting; a loudspeaker droning; or am I to report, perhaps, that these noises irritate me? . . . A science needs points of view, and theoretical problems.[7]

Still, from a historical perspective, the assumption that scientific knowledge should be based upon empirical observations was a reaction against the belief that knowledge is innate in human beings or that "pure reason" alone is sufficient to produce verifiable knowledge.

Aims of the Social Sciences

Having examined the assumptions of science, we are now in a position to address the question raised earlier: What does science have to offer to people who take an interest in societal problems? The ultimate goal of the social sciences is to produce an accumulating body of reliable knowledge. Such knowledge would enable us to *explain, predict,* and *understand* empirical phenomena that interest us. Furthermore, a reliable body of knowledge could be used to improve the human condition. But what are scientific explanations? When can we make predictions? When are we justified in claiming that we understand empirical phenomena?

Scientific Explanation

Why are per capita government expenditures higher in Sweden than in the United States? "Because," some persons might respond, "Swedes want their government to spend more." Such an explanation might satisfy the layperson, but it would not satisfy social scientists unless they could employ the same reasoning to explain per capita government expenditures in other political systems. In fact, per capita government expenditures in Britain have decreased since the Conservative party won national elections in the 1980s, although most Britons are reported to want their government to spend more.

The social sciences aim to provide general explanations to "Why?" questions. When scientists ask for an explanation of why a given event or behavior has taken place, they ask for a systematic and empirical analysis of

---

7. Karl R. Popper, *The Logic of Scientific Discovery* (New York: Science Editions, 1961), p. 106.

the antecedent factors that are responsible for the occurrence of the event or behavior.

Ever since David Hume (1711–1776), such an application of the term **explanation** has been considered a matter of relating the phenomenon to be explained with other phenomena by means of *general laws*. General laws set the framework from which a particular explanation can be derived. In the words of Richard Braithwaite:

> The function of science . . . is to establish general laws covering the behavior of empirical events or objects with which the science in question is concerned, and thereby to enable us to connect together our knowledge of the separately known events, and to make reliable predictions of events as yet unknown. . . . If science is in a highly developed state, . . . the laws which have been established will form a hierarchy in which special laws appear as logical consequences of a small number of highly general laws. . . . If the science is in an early stage of development, . . . the laws may be merely the generalizations involved in classifying things into various classes.[8]

As scientific disciplines make progress, their forms of explanation change. Carl Hempel made an important distinction between two basic types of explanations: **deductive** and **probabilistic**. The classification is based on the kinds of generalizations that the explanation employs.[9]

Deductive Explanations.   A deductive explanation calls for a universal generalization, a statement of the conditions under which the generalization holds true, an event to be explained, and the rules of formal logic. In a deductive explanation, a phenomenon is explained by demonstrating that it can be deduced from an established universal law. For example, a scientific explanation for the return to earth of an object thrown into the air would be based on the law of gravitation. The scientist will point out that if *all* objects exercise a mutual attraction on one another, any particular object is expected to behave in the same way with reference to the earth. The essential condition for a universal law is that it includes all cases within its domain. In deductive reasoning, the premises lead necessarily to the conclusion; that is, if and only if the premises are true, the conclusion must be true. If, however, the premises are *not* true, the conclusion will not be true. For example, in democracies, elected officials seek reelection (untrue premise); John Brown is an elected official; therefore, John Brown seeks reelection (untrue conclusion). Deductive explanations are the most powerful type because their conclusions must be true if their premises are true and because they explain individual as well as general events and behavior.

Probabilistic Explanations.   Not all scientific explanations are based on laws of universal form. This is particularly the case in the social sciences

---

8. Richard B. Braithwaite, *Scientific Explanation* (New York: Harper & Row, 1960), p. 1.

9. Carl G. Hempel, *Philosophy of Natural Science* (Englewood Cliffs, N.J.: Prentice-Hall, 1966), ch. 5.

because few, if any, meaningful universal generalizations can be made. Social scientists use primarily probabilistic or inductive explanations. For example, a particular increase in government expenditures in the United States might be explained by suggesting that it happened in response to adverse economic conditions and that in the past increased expenditures followed severe economic conditions. This explanation links the phenomenon to be explained to an earlier occurrence—the country's economic conditions. The latter is suggested to provide an explanation because there is a relationship between economic conditions and government expenditures. The relationship, however, cannot be expressed by a law of universal form because not every case of adverse economic conditions brings an increase in government expenditures. What can be suggested is only that there is a high probability that severe economic conditions will bring increases in government expenditures or that in a high percentage of all cases that were investigated, severe economic conditions led to increases in government expenditures. General explanations of this type are referred to as *probabilistic* or *inductive* explanations, and they derive from probabilistic generalizations. In other words, a probabilistic explanation makes use of generalizations that express an arithmetic ratio between phenomena or generalizations that express tendencies. For example, a probabilistic generalization can take the form "*n* percent of *X* is *Y*," or "*X* tends to cause *Y*."

The major limitation of probabilistic or inductive generalizations, in comparison to universal laws, is that certain conclusions cannot be drawn about specific cases. If, for instance, one has the information that 70 percent of the members of an ethnic group voted for the Democratic party for the past 20 years, one still cannot conclude with certainty that the probability that a particular member of the group voted Democratic is 7/10. Other factors besides membership in the given group of which the generalization is true may influence the behavior in question. The particular person may also be a member of a social club with a long tradition of Republican political attachment, and this may outweigh the influence of his or her ethnic identification.

Prediction

Deductive and probabilistic explanations constitute one important component of scientific knowledge. **Prediction** constitutes the other. In fact, the ability to make correct predictions has been regarded as the foremost quality of science. If knowledge is deficient, prediction is impossible. For example, if one knows that 2 times 6 is 12, one can predict the outcome of a count of two combined groups of six objects. If one knows that the freezing point of water is 32°F or 0°C, one can predict what will happen to one's car if an antifreeze treatment is not applied to the water in the radiator during the freezing season. If one knows that governments increase their spending in economic recessions, one can predict that future recessions will bring in-creases in government spending. If one knows that job placement programs solve unemployment problems, one can predict that high rates of unemploy-ment are temporary and unemployment is bound to drop.

The expectation that scientific knowledge should lead to accurate pre-dictions is based on the argument that *if* it is known that X causes Y and that X is present, *then* the prediction that Y will occur can be made. Under-lying this argument is the assumption that if a universal law or a probabilis-tic generalization is *both* known and true—that the antecedent conditions are sufficient for predicting the outcome—then the only reasons for failure in prediction can be (1) that the law or the generalization is not true or (2) that the antecedent conditions are incorrectly perceived. Thus if, say, the problem of unemployment remains unsolved, it is either because the gener-alization that job placement programs solve unemployment problems is not true or because the activities aimed at solving unemployment are errone-ously perceived as job placement programs.

Recalling the deductive mode of explanations, we can see that the pro-cess of prediction is, logically speaking, the *reverse* of the process of expla-nation. The antecedent observations merely point out that the initial condi-tions are present. Universal laws or probabilistic generalizations are used to justify the prediction that if the initial conditions are present, the conse-quence must follow.

The logical structure of scientific explanations and predictions can now be explained.[10] This structure consists of the following parts:

1. A statement E describing the specific phenomena or event to be ex-plained.
2. A set of statements A_1 to A_n describing specific relevant conditions that are antecedent or causally related to the phenomenon to be de-scribed by E.
3. A set of universal laws or probabilistic generalizations L_1 to L_n that state: "Whenever events of the kind described by A_1 to A_n take place, an event of the kind described by E occurs."

For these three parts to constitute an explanation of the event or the phenomenon, they must fulfill at least two conditions:

1. The E statement must be deducible from the A and L statements to-gether but not from either set of statements alone.
2. The A and L statements must be true.

The following is a symbolic presentation of the logical structure of sci-entific explanations and predictions.

---

10. The following discussion draws on Richard S. Rudner, *Philosophy of Social Science* (Englewood Cliffs, N.J.: Prentice-Hall, 1966), p. 60.

$$L_1, \ldots, L_n$$
$$\underline{A_1, \ldots, A_n}$$
Therefore, E

The logical structure of explanation is identical to that of prediction. The only difference between them is the vantage point of the scientist. In the case of explanation, E is a past event relative to the scientist's present vantage point, and he or she seeks the appropriate L's and A's under which to deduce it; in the case of prediction, the scientist already knows the L's and A's and seeks a future event that the former imply.

Understanding

The third component of social scientific knowledge is a sense of understanding. The meaning of the term *understanding* is used in two radically different senses—*Verstehen* (or empathic understanding) and predictive understanding. These different usages evolved because the social sciences are both humanistic and scientific and because social scientists are observers as well as participants in the subject matter of their disciplines. In the words of Hans Zetterberg:

> Symbols are the stuff out of which cultures and societies are made. . . . For example, a sequence of conception, birth, nursing and weaning represents the *biological* reality of parenthood. But in analyzing human parenthood we find, in addition to the biological reality, a complex of symbols dealing with the license to have children, responsibilities for their care and schooling, rights to make some decisions on their behalf, obligations to launch them by certain social rituals. . . . Our language thus contains codifications of what parents are and what they shall do and what shall be done to them, and all these sentences in our language represent the *social* reality of parenthood. Social reality, in this as in other cases, consists of symbols.[11]

But are symbols and, by implication, human behavior amenable to investigation by the same scientific methodology that is used in the natural sciences? Is the subject matter of the social sciences so complex and distinct that a unique scientific methodology ought to be developed? Do social scientists, unlike natural scientists, have to "get inside" their subject matter in order to understand it?

The **Verstehen** *Tradition.*   According to the *Verstehen* (German for "empathy") tradition, the natural and social sciences are distinctive bodies of knowledge because of the divergence in the nature of their subject matter.

11. Hans L. Zetterberg, *On Theory and Verification in Sociology*, 3d enlarged ed. (Totowa, N.J.: Bedminster Press, 1965), pp. 1–2. See also Kenneth J. Gergen, *Toward Transformation of Social Knowledge* (New York: Springer-Verlag, 1982).

Thus natural scientists and social scientists must employ different methods of research. For example, the social scientist must understand both the historical dimension of human behavior and the subjective aspects of human experience. The German sociologist Max Weber (1864–1930) argued that if social scientists are to understand the behavior of individuals and groups, they must learn to "put themselves into the place of the subject of inquiry." They must gain an understanding of the other's view of reality: his or her symbols, values and attitudes.[12]

More recently, the **interpretive approach** emerged as an offspring of the *Verstehen* tradition. Kenneth Gergen, a proponent of the approach, states:

> A fundamental difference exists between the bulk of the phenomena of concern to the natural as opposed to the sociobehavioral scientist. There is ample reason to believe that the phenomena of focal concern to the latter are far less stable (enduring, reliable, or replicable) than those of interest to the former. . . . To place the matter squarely, it may be ventured that with all its attempts to emulate natural science inquiry, the past century of sociobehavioral research and theory has failed to yield a principle as reliable as Archimedes' principle of hydrostatics or Galileo's law of uniformly accelerated motion.[13]

Predictive Understanding.   In contrast to the *Verstehen* tradition, **logical empiricists** take the position that social scientists can attain objective knowledge in the study of the natural as well as the social world. The social and the natural sciences can be investigated by the same scientific methodology. Furthermore, logical empiricists see empathic understanding as a helpful route to discovery. But discoveries must be verified if they are to be integrated into the scientific body of knowledge. (The idea of discovery versus verification is discussed in greater detail later in this chapter.)

The Role of Methodology

Science is not united by its subject matter but rather by its methodology. What sets the scientific approach apart from other modes of acquiring knowledge are the assumptions on which it is based and its methodology.

The scientific **methodology** is a system of explicit rules and procedures on which research is based and against which claims for knowledge are evaluated. This system is neither closed nor infallible. Rather, the rules and procedures are constantly being improved; scientists look for new means of observation, inference, generalization, and analysis. As these are developed and found to be congruent with the underlying assumptions of the scientific approach, they are incorporated into the system of rules that govern the sci-

12. Max Weber, *The Theory of Social and Economic Organization*, trans. A. M. Henderson and Talcott Parsons (New York: Free Press, 1964).
13. Gergen, *Toward Transformation of Social Knowledge*, p. 12.

entific methodology. The scientific methodology is first and foremost self-correcting:

> Science does not desire to obtain conviction for its propositions in *any* price. [A] proposition must be supported by logically acceptable evidence, which must be weighed carefully and tested by the well-known canons of necessary and probable inference. It follows that the *method* of science is more stable, and more important to men of science, than any particular result achieved by its means. In virtue of its method, the scientific enterprise is a self-corrective process. It appeals to no special revelation or authority whose deliverances are indubitable and final. It claims no infallibility, but relies upon the methods of developing and testing hypotheses for assured conclusions. The cannons of inquiry are themselves discovered in the process of reflection, and may themselves become modified in the course of study. The method makes possible the noting and correction of errors by continued application of itself.[14]

The methodology of the social sciences has evolved slowly. In this evolution, criticism has always performed an important function. Through the continuous interchange of ideas, information, and criticism, it became possible to institutionalize commonly accepted rules and procedures and to develop corresponding methods and techniques. This system of rules and procedures is the *normative* component of the scientific methodology. It defines the "rules of the game," and these in turn enable communication, constructive criticism, and scientific progress.

Methodology as Rules for Communication

Anatol Rapoport illustrated the general problem of communication between two people who have not shared a common experience with the following anecdote:

> A blind man asked someone to explain the meaning of "white."
> "White is a color," he was told, "as, for example, white snow."
> "I understand," said the blind man. "It is a cold and damp color."
> "No, it doesn't have to be cold and damp. Forget about snow. Paper, for instance, is white."
> "So it rustles?" asked the blind man.
> "No indeed, it need not rustle. It is like the fur of an albino rabbit."
> "A soft, fluffy color?" the blind man wanted to know.
> "It need not be soft either. Porcelain is white, too."
> "Perhaps it is a brittle color, then," said the blind man.[15]

A major function of methodology is to facilitate communication between scientists who either shared or want to share a common experience.

14. Morris R. Cohen and Ernest Nagel, *An Introduction to Logic and Scientific Method*, (Orlando, Fla.: Harcourt Brace Jovanovich, 1962), pp. 395–396.
15. Anatol Rapoport, *Operational Philosophy* (New York: Wiley, 1969), p. 12.

Furthermore, by making the rules of methodology explicit, public, and accessible, the framework for replication and constructive criticism is set forth. **Replication**—the repetition of the same investigation in exactly the same way either by the same scientist or other scientists—is a safeguard against unintentional error or deception. Constructive criticism implies that as soon as one makes claims for knowledge, we can ask questions: "Does the explanation (prediction) follow logically from the assumptions?" "Are the observations correct?" "What were the methods of observation?" "Was the testing valid?" "Did other factors interfere in drawing conclusions?" "Should the findings be taken as evidence that another explanation is correct?" and so forth. We shall see throughout this book that such questions form the criteria for evaluating claims for scientific knowledge.

Methodology as Rules for Reasoning

Although empirical observations are fundamental to the scientific approach, they must be ordered and related into systematic logical structures. Empirical observations or facts don't "speak for themselves." The scientific methodology explains the logical foundations of reasoned knowledge. The essential tool of the scientific approach, along with factual observations, is logic—the system of valid reasoning about factual observations that permits reliable inferences to be drawn from them. That logic, as the study of the foundations and principles of reasoning, is crucial to the scientific approach can be seen in the vestige of its Latin root in the terms for many areas of study—for example, bio*logy*, anthropo*logy*, socio*logy*, crimino*logy*, and geo*logy*.

The scientific methodology requires competence in logical reasoning and analysis. Rules for definition, classification, and forms of deductive and probabilistic (inductive) inferences; theories of probability; sampling procedures; systems of calculus; and rules of measurement, as discussed in the following chapters, constitute the methodological tool kit of the social scientist. Furthermore, through the use of logic, science progresses in a systematic and revolutionary way. Logical procedures take the form of closely interdependent series of propositions that support each other, and in this way the scientific methodology enhances the internal consistency of claims for knowledge.

Methodology as Rules for Intersubjectivity

Logic is concerned with valid reasoning, not with empirical truth or verified facts. A fact is either certainly or probably true when objective evidence exists to support it. By contrast, a claim for knowledge is valid when an inference logically derives from prior assumptions. Thus scientists can make an erroneous inference from verified facts (truth statements) if they reason incorrectly. However, they can also make an erroneous inference by reasoning correctly (logically valid reasoning) but not employing verified facts: "The truth of an assertion is related to experience; the validity of an assertion is related to its inner consistency or its consistency with other assertions."[16]

Recall the forms of deductive and probabilistic explanations (predictions) discussed earlier. It should now be obvious that they relate only to logically valid reasoning. The validity of their conclusions follows strictly from their antecedent assumptions. Their truth cannot be established or verified solely on logical grounds. Truth has to be verified with empirical evidence. As the following syllogism demonstrates, strict adherence to logical reasoning without studying the empirical facts can lead to absurdities:

> All human beings are power-motivated organisms.
> All power-motivated organisms are destructive.
> Therefore, all human beings are destructive.

The scientific methodology explains the *accepted criteria* for empirical objectivity (truth) and the methods and techniques for verification. These are highly interdependent; empirical objectivity depends on verification so much that the scientist cannot make claims for objectivity until verification has been carried out.

Given that the criteria for empirical objectivity and the methods for verification are products of the human mind (in contrast to the belief that truth is an absolute given), the term **intersubjectivity** is more appropriate than *objectivity*. To be intersubjective, knowledge in general—and the scientific methodology in particular—has to be transmissible. Thus if one scientist conducts an investigation, another scientist can replicate it and compare the two sets of findings. If the methodology is correct and (we assume) the conditions have not changed, we would expect the findings to be similar. Indeed, conditions might change and new circumstances emerge. But the significance of intersubjectivity is that one scientist can understand and evaluate the methods of others and conduct similar observations so as to verify empirical facts. The methodological requirement for intersubjectivity is the evidence that empirical observations are uncontaminated by any factors save those common to all observers: "The methodological question is always limited to whether what is reported as an observation can be used in subsequent inquiry even if the particular observer is no longer a part of the context."[17]

Scientific Revolution

Scientific knowledge is knowledge provable by *both* reason and the evidence of the senses (experience). The importance of the scientific methodology is primarily to be found in institutionalizing a language for communication,

16. Ibid., p. 18.
17. Abraham Kaplan, *The Conduct of Inquiry* (New York: Harper & Row, 1968), p. 128.

rules for reasoning, and procedures and methods for observation and verification. In this sense, methodology demands conformity: claims for knowledge are rejected if they do not conform to the rules and procedures explained by the methodology. But does not methodological conformity hinder new discoveries and, by implication, scientific progress? Furthermore, scientists are members of scientific communities governed by conventions, norms, rituals, and power relations that may be incompatible with the objective pursuit of knowledge. Could scientific communities hinder scientific progress?

Philosophers of science and social theorists have long been concerned with the dangers of conformity and dogma in science. As Scott Greer put it, "If we are lucky and our scientific knowledge accumulates, it may spiral upward; it may also revolve at the same level, a merry-go-round of fashion; or it may spiral downward, from theory to doctrine to dogma."[18] Among the various attempts to describe scientific revolutions from a sociological-political perspective, Thomas Kuhn's thesis is provocative and worth outlining in some detail.

Normal versus Revolutionary Science

Basic to Kuhn's theory of the scientific enterprise is the distinction between *normal science* and *revolutionary science*. **Normal science** is the routine verification of the dominant theory in any historical period; verification and testing become part of a puzzle-solving activity. In Kuhn's words:

> "Normal science" means research firmly based upon one or more past scientific achievements, achievements that some particular scientific community acknowledges for a time as supplying the foundation of its practice. Today such achievements are recounted, though seldom in their original form, by science textbooks, elementary and advanced. These textbooks expound the body of accepted theory, illustrate many or all of its successful applications, and compare these applications with exemplary observations and experiments.[19]

Such works socialize students and practitioners into the scientific community. They define the kinds of research problems to be investigated, the kinds of assumptions and concepts to be employed, and the kinds of research methods to be used. Historically such works

> were able to do so because they shared two essential characteristics. Their achievement was sufficiently unprecedented to attract an enduring group of adherents away from competing modes of scientific activity. Simulta-

18. Scott Greer, *The Logic of Social Inquiry* (New Brunswick, N.J.: Transaction Books, 1989), pp. 3–4.
19. Thomas S. Kuhn, *The Structure of Scientific Revolutions*, 2d ed. (University of Chicago Press, 1970), p. 10.

neously, it was sufficiently open-ended to leave all sorts of problems for the redefined group of practitioners to resolve."[20]

Kuhn terms achievements that share these two attributes **paradigms** and suggests that they are closely related to the idea of normal science:

> By choosing [the term *paradigm*], I mean to suggest that some accepted examples of actual scientific practice—examples which include law, theory, application, and instrumentation together—provide models from which spring particular coherent traditions of scientific research. . . . The study of paradigm . . . is what mainly prepares the student for membership in the particular scientific community with which he will later practice.[21]

Furthermore, because scientists join a scientific community whose mentors learned the same conceptual and methodological foundations of their discipline from the same sources, their subsequent research will rarely evoke disagreement or criticism over fundamentals. Scientists whose research is grounded in a shared paradigm are psychologically committed to the same rules, norms, and standards for scientific practice: "That commitment and the apparent consensus it produces are prerequisites for normal science, [that is], for the genesis and continuation of a particular research tradition."[22]

Instead of neutral scientists, normal science views scientific communities as groups of partisans advocating and defending the established order of the paradigm. Yet adherence to a paradigm should not necessarily arrest scientific progress. Paradigms are necessary; without them, scientific research could not take place as a collective enterprise, for science needs an organizing principle: "Acquisition of a paradigm and of the more esoteric type of research it permits is a sign of maturity in the development of any given scientific field."[23]

Revolutionary Science

In contrast to normal science, Kuhn views **revolutionary science** as the abrupt development of a *rival paradigm* that can be accepted only gradually by a scientific community. Paradigm change is revolutionary in science. For example, the paradigm that human intelligence is a product of both the sociocultural environment and genetic processes transformed the paradigm that intelligence is determined entirely by genetic processes. This in turn revolutionized the study of personality and human behavior and has been the cornerstone of many social, educational, and economic public policies.

20. Ibid.
21. Ibid.
22. Ibid., pp. 10–11.
23. Ibid., p. 11.

The process of rejecting a dominant paradigm begins, according to Kuhn, as the paradigm is verified; for as scientists empirically test the various dimensions and implications of a dominant paradigm, its congruence with research findings becomes tenuous. Kuhn terms such incongruences *anomalies* and proposes that anomalies become more noticeable as verification or problem-solving activities proceed. At some point a rival candidate for a paradigm is constructed. Conflict emerges between the supporters of the old paradigm and the supporters of the new, ending in the acceptance of the new paradigm and reestablishment of the normal science. The period of transition from old to new paradigms produces uncertainty and cleavages in the scientific community. The transition period is characterized by random research, aimless verification, and accidental discoveries.

Scientific revolutions are rare. Scientists devote most of their time to normal science. They are *not* trying to refute dominant paradigms; they do not perceive anomalies right away. Perceptions are easily stored in mental categories established long before verification procedures. Scientists see what they come to see: a dominant paradigm tends to remain the accepted paragidm long after it fails to be congruent with empirical findings.

A Logic of Discovery?

In Kuhn's view, there can be no *logic* of discovery, only a *sociopsychology* of discovery: anomalies and inconsistencies always abound in science, but a dominant paradigm secures puzzle-solving activities until it is overthrown by a crisis. Is there a rational cause for the appearance of crisis? What makes scientists suddenly aware of one? How is a rival paradigm constructed? Kuhn's thesis does not address these questions; there is no logic of discovery but rather group struggle within scientific communities.

In sharp contrast to Kuhn's descriptive view of science is Karl Popper's prescriptive theory. Popper maintains that the scientific community ought to be, and to a considerable degree actually is, an *open society* in which no dominant paradigm is ever sacred. Science ought to be a revolution in permanence, and criticism should be the heart of the scientific enterprise. Refutations of claims for knowledge constitute revolutions:

> In my view the "normal" scientist, as Kuhn describes him, is a person one ought to be sorry for. . . . The "normal" scientist . . . has been badly taught. He has been taught in a dogmatic spirit: he is a victim of indoctrination. He has learned a technique which can be applied without asking for the reason why. . . .[24]

---

24. Karl R. Popper, "Normal Science and Its Dangers," in *Criticism and the Growth of Knowledge,* ed. Irme Lakatos and Alan Musgrave (New York: Cambridge University Press, 1970), p. 53.

Popper admits that at any moment scientists are "prisoners" caught in their paradigms, expectations, past experiences, and language—with an important qualification:

> We are prisoners in a Pickwickian sense: if we try, we can break out of our framework at any time. Admittedly, we shall find ourselves again in a framework, but it will be a better and roomier one; and we can at any moment break out of it again."[25]

It is helpful at this point to distinguish two contexts of scientific activities: discovery and justification.[26] The **context of justification** refers to the activities of scientists as they attempt logically and empirically to verify claims for knowledge. The scientific methodology establishes the logic of justification. Methodology is indifferent to how scientists arrive at their insights but asks only whether they are justified in reaching claims for knowledge. The activities of the scientist within the *context of discovery*, however, are not constrained by methodology. The scientific methodology may facilitate activities that lead toward discovery, but for the present no formalized rules or logic for discovery can be enunciated. Creativity, insight, imagination, and inspiration are of enormous importance in science. Although these can be nurtured, they cannot be reduced to rules: As John Stuart Mill (1806–1873) said, "There is no science which will enable man to bethink himself of that which will suit his purpose."[27]

The Research Process

Scientific knowledge is knowledge provable by both reason and experience (observation). Logical validity and empirical verification are the criteria employed by scientists to evaluate claims for knowledge. These two criteria are translated into the research activities of scientists through the **research process**. The research process can be viewed as the overall scheme of scientific activities in which scientists engage in order to produce knowledge; it is the paradigm of scientific inquiry.

As illustrated in Figure 1.1, the research process consists of seven main stages: *problem, hypothesis, research design, measurement, data collection, data analysis,* and *generalization*. Each stage affects *theory* and is affected by it as well. In this book, we will discuss extensively each stage and the transitions from one stage to the next. For the moment, we will limit ourselves to a general overview of the research process.

25. Ibid., p. 56.
26. See Kaplan, *Conduct of Inquiry*, pp. 12–18.
27. Ibid., p. 16.

Figure 1.1
The Main Stages of the Research Process

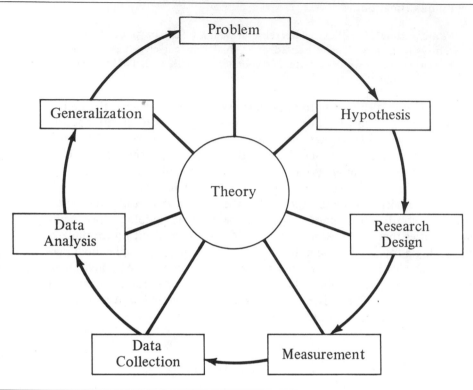

The most characteristic feature of the research process is its *cyclic nature*. It usually starts with a problem and ends in a tentative empirical generalization. The generalization ending one cycle is the beginning of the next cycle. This cyclic process continues indefinitely, reflecting the progress of a scientific discipline.

The research process is also *self-correcting*. Tentative generalizations to research problems are tested logically and empirically. If these generalizations are rejected, new ones are formulated and tested. In the process of reformulation, all the research operations are reevaluated because the rejection of a tentative generalization might be due not to its invalidity but to errors in the research operations. For example, a generalization that economic crises lead to increased government spending will be rejected if it cannot be logically validated and empirically verified. But the generalization might also be rejected, *even if it is true* if procedures for validation and verification (for example, research design, measurement, or data analysis) are deficient. To minimize the risk of rejecting true generalizations, one reexamines each of the stages in the research process prior to the formulation of new generalizations.

Finally, be aware that the research process as presented here is somewhat idealized; that is, it is a rational reconstruction of scientific practice:

> The reconstruction idealizes the logic of science only in showing us what it *would* be if it were extracted and refined to utmost purity. . . . [But] not even the greatest of scientists has a cognitive style which is wholly and perfectly logical, and the most brilliant piece of research still betrays its all-too-human divagations.[28]

In practice, the research process occurs

> (1) sometimes quickly, sometimes slowly; (2) sometimes with a very high degree of formalization and vigor, sometimes quite informally, unself-consciously, and intuitively; (3) sometimes through the interaction of several scientists in distinct roles (of, say, "theorist," "research director," "interviewer," "methodologist," "sampling expert," "statistician," etc.), sometimes through the efforts of a single scientist; and (4) sometimes only in the scientist's imagination, sometimes in actual fact.[29]

Thus our idealized reconstruction of the research process is not intended to be rigid but rather to convey the underlying themes of social science research.

The Plan of This Book

This book is organized along the major stages of the research process. Chapters 2 and 3 cover the conceptual foundations of empirical research and the relationships between theory and research. They focus on the ideas of concepts, definitions, the functions and structures of theories, models, relations, variables, and the construction of research hypotheses.

Chapter 4 is concerned with ethical and moral questions involved in the conduct of social science research. Issues relating to the rights of research participants, the obligations of scientists, the interactions between participants and scientists, and professional codes of ethics, which have become increasingly important in planning research projects, are discussed in this chapter.

In Chapters 5 and 6, we focus on the research design stage. A research design is the strategy that guides the investigator throughout the process of research. It is a logical model of proof that allows the drawing of inferences concerning the causal relations among the phenomena under investigation. As you will see, there are various types of research designs, each of which explains the conditions for accepting or rejecting causal inferences.

Chapter 7 is concerned with the measurement stage. Measurement is the

28. Ibid., pp. 10–11.
29. Wallace, *Logic of Science in Sociology*, p. 19.

procedure of systematically assigning symbols (in particular, numbers) to empirical observations. These symbols are in turn amenable to quantitative analyses that reveal information and relations that otherwise could not have been revealed. Numbers can be added, subtracted, percentaged, correlated, and used for describing, explaining, and predicting phenomena.

Generalizations constitute a major stage in the research process. Typically, they are not based on all the observations that are defined by a research problem, but on a relatively small number of cases—a sample. In Chapter 8, we cover major topics in sampling theory, methods for choosing representative samples, sample size, and sample designs.

The five subsequent chapters cover the data collection stage. In this stage, empirical observations are being made and recorded. Data (observations) can be collected by various methods, including structured observation, nonstructured observation, personal interviews, impersonal surveys, public records, or private records. No data collection method is foolproof, nor will one method suit all research problems. Different problems call for different methods, and each method has advantages but also inherent limitations.

Chapter 14 focuses on major topics of data processing, which is the link between data collection and data analysis. Data processing involves the transformation of observations gathered in the data collection stage into a system of conceptual categories and the translation of these categories into coding schemes that lend themselves to quantitative analysis. These codes can then be recorded and processed by computer. The central issues involved in coding and automatic data processing are also covered in this chapter.

In the next stage of the research process, the concern is with quantitative, statistical analyses. We view statistics as numbers that can be used to summarize, evaluate, or analyze a body of information. It is useful to distinguish two categories of statistics with different functions: *descriptive statistics* and *inferential statistics*. Descriptive statistics procedures are used to organize, describe, and summarize data. Chapter 15 covers descriptive univariate distributions; Chapter 16, bivariate distributions; and Chapter 17, multivariate data analysis techniques. In Chapter 18, we present methods of index construction and scaling. Inferential or inductive statistics make possible generalizations beyond the data in hand, the evaluations of differences among groups, and the estimation of unknown values. These methods of inference are discussed in Chapter 19.

Summary

1. Science is united by its methodology, not by its subject matter. What sets the scientific approach apart from other ways of acquiring knowledge are the assumptions on which it is grounded and its methodology.

2. The assumptions of the scientific approach are these: nature is orderly, we can know nature, knowledge is tentative but superior to ignorance, natural phenomena have natural causes, nothing is self-evident, and knowledge is derived from the acquisition of experience.

3. The methodology of the scientific approach serves three major purposes: rules for communication, rules for logical and valid reasoning, and rules for intersubjectivity. These three systems of rules allow us to understand, explain, and predict our environments and ourselves in a manner that other systems for producing information (authoritarian, mystical, rationalistic) cannot allow us to do.

4. Scientific knowledge is knowledge provable by *both* reason and the evidence of the senses. The scientific methodology requires strict adherence to the rules of logic and observation. Such adherence should not be seen as encouraging dogma because the research process is cyclic and self-correcting. Rational criticism should be at the heart of the scientific enterprise, and science ought to be a revolution in permanence. Obviously, scientific communities, like other social communities, are involved in power struggles that are not always conducive to the progress of science. Perhaps such power struggles are inevitable. But claims for knowledge are accepted only insofar as they are congruent with the assumptions of science and its methodology.

Key Terms for Review

science	interpretive approach
rationalism	logical empiricists
assumptions of science	methodology
epistemology	replication
empirical	intersubjectivity
explanation	normal science
deductive explanations	paradigm
probabilistic explanations	revolutionary science
prediction	context of justification
Verstehen	research process

Study Questions

1. Compare and contrast the scientific approach with the authoritarian, mystical, and rationalistic modes of knowing.
2. Discuss the assumptions underlying the scientific approach.
3. What are the aims of science as a knowledge-producing system?
4. Describe the research process and its stages.
5. How is science actually carried out, both as a cyclic process of reasoning and observation and as a social institution?

Additional Readings

Agnew, Neil M., and Sandra W. Pyke. *The Science Game: An Introduction to Research in the Behavioral Science*. 4th ed. Englewood Cliffs, N.J.: Prentice-Hall, 1987.

Boulding, Kenneth E. "Science: Our Common Heritage." *Science*, 207 (1980), 831–836.

Cohen, Bernard I. *Revolution in Science*. Cambridge, Mass.: Belknap Press, 1985.

Fiske, Donald W., and Richard A. Shweder, eds. *Metatheory in Social Science: Pluralisms and Subjectivities*. Chicago: University of Chicago Press, 1986.

Hughes, John A. *A Philosophy of Social Research*. White Plains, N.Y.: Longman, 1980.

Kruskal, William H., ed. *The Social Sciences: Their Nature and Uses*. Chicago: University of Chicago Press, 1986.

Lakatos, Irme. *The Methodology of Scientific Research Programs*. Cambridge: Cambridge University Press, 1978.

O'Hear, Anthony. *An Introduction to the Philosophy of Science*. New York: Oxford University Press, 1989.

Popper, Karl R. *Realism and the Aim of Science*. London: Hutchinson, 1983.

Scheffler, Israel. *Science and Subjectivity*. 2d ed. Indianapolis: Hackett, 1982.

Taylor, Charles. *Philosophy and the Human Sciences*. New York: Cambridge University Press, 1985.

CHAPTER 2

Conceptual Foundations of Research

First we investigate the formation of concepts, which eventually become theoretical systems. Then we distinguish four levels of theory and delineate models that represent aspects of the real world. Finally, we explore the links between theory and research.

SCIENTIFIC KNOWLEDGE IS PROVABLE BY both reason and experience. This implies that social scientists operate at two distinct but interrelated levels—conceptual-theoretical and observational-empirical. Social science research is the outcome of the interaction between these two levels. This chapter covers the basics of the conceptual-theoretical level and the relationships of theory, models, and empirical research.

Concepts

Thinking involves the use of language, which is a system of communication composed of symbols and a set of rules permitting various combinations of these symbols. One of the most significant symbols in language, especially as it relates to research, is the **concept**. Science begins by forming concepts to describe the empirical world. A concept is an abstraction representing an object, a property of an object, or a certain phenomenon. For example, "social status," "role," "power," "bureaucracy," and "relative deprivation" are common concepts in political science and sociology. Concepts such as "intelligence," "perception," and "learning" are common among psychologists. Every scientific discipline develops its unique set of concepts; to scientists, this constitutes a language; outsiders call it a "jargon."

Functions of Concepts

Concepts serve a number of important functions in social science research. First and foremost, they are the foundation of communication. Without a set of agreed-on concepts, intersubjective communication is impossible. Concepts are abstracted from sense impressions and are used to convey and transmit perceptions and information. Recognize that concepts do not actually exist as empirical phenomena; a concept is not the phenomenon itself but rather a *symbol* of the phenomenon. Treating concepts as though they were the phenomena themselves leads to the **fallacy of reification**—the error of regarding abstractions as actual phenomena. For example, it is erroneous to regard a concept such as "power" as having drives, needs, or instincts.

Second, concepts introduce a *perspective*—a way of looking at empirical phenomena: "Through scientific conceptualization the perceptual world is given an order and coherence that could not be perceived before conceptualization."[1] The concept enables scientists to relate to some aspect of reality and give it a common quality:

> It permits the scientist, in a community of other scientists, to lift his own idiosyncratic experiences to the level of consensual meaning. It also enables him to carry on an interaction with his environment; he indicates to himself what a concept means and acts toward the designation of that meaning. The concept thus acts as a sensitizer of experience and perception, opening new realms of observation, closing others.[2]

Third, concepts are means for classification and generalization. Scientists categorize, structure, order, and generalize their experiences and observations in terms of concepts. As John McKinney puts it:

> All phenomena are unique in their concrete occurrence; therefore no phenomena actually recur in their concrete wholeness. The meaning of identity is always "identical for the purpose in hand." To introduce *order* with its various scientific implications, including prediction, the scientist necessarily ignores the unique, the extraneous, and [the] nonrecurring, and thereby departs from perceptual experience. This departure is the necessary price he must pay for the achievement of abstract generality. To conceptualize

1. Norman K. Denzin, *The Research Act*, 3d ed. (Englewood Cliffs, N.J.: Prentice-Hall, 1988), p. 38.
2. Ibid.

means to generalize to some degree. To generalize means to reduce the number of objects by conceiving of some of them as being identical.[3]

For example, we can overlook the ways in which pine, oak, spruce, fir, palm, and apple differ from each other and grasp their generic resemblance via the concept "tree." "Tree" is the general concept that enables us to grasp a multiplicity of unique aspects and comprehend them within an order. "Tree" is also an abstract concept in the sense that the unique attributes of pine, oak, spruce, fir, palm, and apple are lost in the conceptualization process. This process of abstraction and generalization enables scientists to delineate the essential attributes of empirical phenomena. However, once a concept is formed, it cannot be a perfect symbol of what it represents because its content is inevitably reduced to the attributes that the scientist considers essential.

Fourth, concepts serve as components of theories and thus of explanations and predictions. Concepts are the most critical elements in any theory because they define its shape and content. For example, the concepts "power" and "legitimacy" define the shape and content of theories of governance. The concepts "individualism" and "Protestantism" defined and shaped Durkheim's suicide theory, which predicts suicide rates in various situations as a function of the relationships between individualism and religion. The concept "relative deprivation" is central in theories of violence, and "supply" and "demand" are pillar concepts in economic theory. Such concepts, when linked in a systematic and logical way, lead to theories; concept formation and theory construction are closely related.

Definitions

If concepts are to serve the functions of communication, sensitization of experience, generalization, and theory construction, they have to be clear, precise, and agreed-on. The problem with everyday language is that it is often vague, ambiguous, and imprecise. Concepts such as "power," "bureaucracy," and "satisfaction" mean different things to different people and are used in different contexts to designate various things. Usually, this does not create major problems in everyday communication. But science cannot progress with ambiguous and imprecise language.

Any scientific discipline is necessarily concerned with its vocabulary. Social scientists have attempted to establish a clear and precise body of concepts (abstractions) to characterize their subject matter. Although in the process, many concepts were invented, used, refined, and discarded, many concepts remain ambiguous and inconsistent. This should not be too sur-

---

3. John C. McKinney, *Constructive Typology and Social Theory* (Norwalk, Conn.: Appleton & Lang, 1966), p. 9.

prising. Social scientists face the difficult problem of distinguishing their concepts from those commonly used by the public they want to study. But as the social sciences progress, so will their vocabulary. Clarity and precision in the use of concepts are achieved by definitions. Two types of definitions are important in social science research: *conceptual* and *operational*.

Conceptual Definitions

Definitions that describe concepts by using other concepts are **conceptual definitions**. For example, "power" has been conceptually defined as the ability of an actor (for example, an individual, a group, the state) to get another actor to do something that the latter would not otherwise do. The concept "relative deprivation" is defined as actors' perception of discrepancy between their "value expectations" and their "value capabilities." "Value expectations," in turn, are defined as the goods and conditions of life to which people believe they are rightfully entitled, and "value capabilities" are defined as the goods and conditions people think they are capable of getting and keeping.[4]

In these examples, a number of concepts were used to define other concepts. But the process of definition might not stop here. In the case of "relative deprivation," a person unfamiliar with the theory is likely to ask, "What are 'capabilities,' 'expectations,' and 'perceptions'?" These concepts call for further clarification. "Expectations," for instance, have been defined as a manifestation of the prevailing norms set by the immediate economic, social, cultural, and political environment. But what is meant by "norms," "immediate," "social," "cultural," "economic," and "political"? These concepts can be defined by still other concepts, and so on. At a certain point in this process, one encounters concepts that cannot be defined by other concepts. These are called **primitive terms**. For example, colors, sounds, smells, and tastes are primitive terms. Primitive terms are those on which there is a consensus on their meaning. Usually, their meaning is conveyed by indicating examples. Such demonstrative procedures are called **ostensive definitions**. They must be used in order to develop basic language terms.

Conceptual definitions consist of primitive terms and *derived terms*. Derived terms are those that can be defined by the use of primitive terms. Thus if there is an agreement on the primitive terms "individual," "interact," "two or more," and "regularly," we can define "group" (derived term) as two or more individuals that interact regularly. The main advantage of derived terms is that their use is more efficient; they require less effort than the set of the primitive terms that compose the definition of the derived term.[5]

4. Ted R. Gurr, *Why Men Rebel* (Princeton, N.J.: Princeton University Press, 1970), p. 24.
5. Paul D. Reynolds, *A Primer in Theory Construction* (New York: Macmillan, 1971), pp. 45–48.

Conceptual definitions are neither true nor false. As pointed out earlier, concepts are symbols that permit communication. Conceptual definitions are either useful for communication and research, or they are not. Indeed, one may criticize the intelligibility of a definition or question whether it is being used consistently. But there is no point in criticizing a conceptual definition for not being true; the definition is what the definer says it is. Conceptual definitions that enhance communication share the following essential attributes:

- A definition must point out the unique attributes or qualities of whatever is defined. It must be inclusive of all cases it covers and exclusive of all cases not covered.
- A definition should not be circular; that is, it must not contain any part of the thing being defined. Defining "bureaucracy" as an organization that has bureaucratic qualities or "power" as a quality shared by powerful people does not enhance communication.
- A definition should be stated positively. Defining "intelligence" as a property that lacks color, weight, and character obviously does not enhance communication because there are many other things that lack color, weight, and character.
- A definition should use clear terms. A term such as "conservative" means different things to different people, and unless there is an agreement on its meaning, it should not be used in a definition.

Operational Definitions

Often the empirical attributes or events that are represented by concepts cannot be observed directly. For example, the concepts "power," "relative deprivation," "intelligence," and "satisfaction" and, in general, nonbehavioral properties (such as, perceptions, values, and attitudes) cannot be observed directly. In such cases, the empirical existence of a concept has to be inferred. Inferences of this kind are made with operational definitions. Operational definitions provide concepts with empirical referents.

An **operational definition** is a set of procedures that describe the activities to perform to establish empirically the existence or degree of existence of a phenomenon described by a concept. Such definitions concretize the meanings of concepts; operational definitions lay out the measuring procedures that provide criteria for the empirical application of concepts. Thus operational definitions bridge the conceptual-theoretical and empirical-observational levels. They tell *what to do* and *what to observe* in order to bring the phenomenon defined within the range of the researcher's experience: "The thing or quality defined is not assumed to exist a priori. Rather its existence or reality follows from the operations performed and resides in the invariants observed."[6]

---

6. Anatol Rapoport, *Operational Philosophy* (New York: Wiley, 1969), p. 29.

The idea of operational definitions was developed by the operationist school of thought as exemplified in the works of the physicist P. W. Bridgman. His central idea is that the *meaning* of *every* scientific concept must be specifiable by means of an operation that tests a certain criterion for its application. The meaning of a concept is fully and exclusively determined by its operational definition. Bridgman explains:

> The concept of length is therefore fixed when the operations by which length is measured are fixed: that is, the concept of length involves as much as and nothing more than the set of operations by which length is determined. In general, we mean by any concept nothing more than a set of operations; *the concept is synonymous with the corresponding set of operations.*[7]

Thus an operational definition of "length" would specify a procedure involving the use of a ruler for determining the distance between two points. An operational definition of "weight" would specify *how* weight is determined by means of an appropriate instrument, for instance, a scale. Similarly, the term "harder" as applied, say, to minerals might be operationally defined as follows: "To determine whether mineral m_1 is harder than mineral m_2, draw a sharp point of a piece of m_1 under pressure across the surface of a piece of m_2 (test operation); m_1 will be said to be harder than m_2 only if a scratch is produced (specific test result)."[8] An operational definition of "intelligence" could consist of a test to be administered according to specifications; the test results are the responses of the individuals tested or a quantitative summary of their responses.

The structure of operational definitions is straightforward. If a given stimulus (S) is applied to an object, consistently producing a certain reaction (R), the object has the property (P), this being an operational definition. In the last example, an intelligence test (stimulus) is administered to respondents producing test scores (R); intelligence (P) is inferred from, or defined by, the test scores.

Many concepts used by social scientists are operationally defined solely on the strength of reactions to specific stimuli, conditions, or situations because the physical manipulation of individuals or events is either impracticable or unethical. Even if we could manipulate individuals through certain operations—say, induce severe anxiety in a laboratory situation—it would involve a number of critical ethical dilemmas, including the rights of scientists to do so and the personal rights of the research subjects. (The ethical dilemmas involved in social science research are discussed in Chapter 4.) In such cases, concepts are operationally defined by reactions to stimuli such as tests, questionnaires, and aggregate indicators, which will be discussed in later chapters.

7. Percy W. Bridgman, *The Logic of Modern Physics* (New York: Ayer, 1980), p. 5.

8. Carl G. Hempel, *Philosophy of Natural Science* (Englewood Cliffs, N.J.: Prentice-Hall, 1966), p. 89 (edited slightly).

Example: The Definitions of Alienation

Let's see how the very abstract and complex concept "alienation" has been empirically researched. In a pioneering study, Melvin Seeman argued that alienation was conceptualized in the literature as "a sense of the splitting asunder of what was once held together, the breaking of the seamless mold in which values, behavior, and expectations were once cast into interlocking forms."[9] This conceptualization, he suggested, attributes five meanings to alienation, and thus five conceptual definitions are called forth:

1. *Powerlessness*—the expectation of individuals that their behavior cannot determine the occurrence of outcomes or reinforcements they seek.
2. *Meaninglessness*—perception by individuals that their minimal standards for clarity in decision making are not met.
3. *Normlessness*—high expectancy that socially unapproved behaviors are required to achieve certain goals.
4. *Isolation*—assignment of low reward value to goals and beliefs that are typically highly valued in society.
5. *Self-estrangement*—the degree of dependence of a given behavior on anticipated future rewards that lie outside the activity itself.

In later research, these five concepts, or dimensions of alienation, were operationally defined by constructing questionnaire items for each dimension; the responses of individuals to the entire questionnaire defined the empirical existence of each dimension. As a means of operationalizing "powerlessness," the following question was used: "Suppose your town was considering a regulation that you believed to be very unjust or harmful. What do you think you could do?" Individuals who responded that they could do nothing were categorized as powerless. Other questions used to define powerlessness operationally are these: (1) If you made an effort to change this regulation, how likely is it that you would succeed? (2) If such a case arose, how likely is it that you would actually do something about it? (3) Would you ever try to influence a local decision? (4) Suppose Congress were considering a law that you believed to be very unjust or harmful. What do you think you could do? (5) Would you ever try to influence an act of Congress?[10]

Figure 2.1 illustrates the process of transformation from the conceptual to the observational level, using the example of alienation. The concept "alienation" cannot be directly observed; its empirical existence can, however, be inferred. To establish its empirical existence, we first delineate its conceptual components or dimensions. There are five distinct dimensions of

9. Melvin Seeman, "On the Meaning of Alienation," in *Continuities in the Language of Social Research*, ed. Paul Lazarsfeld, Ann Pasanella, and Morris Rosenberg (New York: Free Press, 1972), pp. 25–34.

10. David Nachmias, "Modes and Types of Political Alienation," *British Journal of Sociology*, 24 (1976): 478–493.

Figure 2.1
Transition from the Conceptual to the Observational Level:
The Case of Alienation

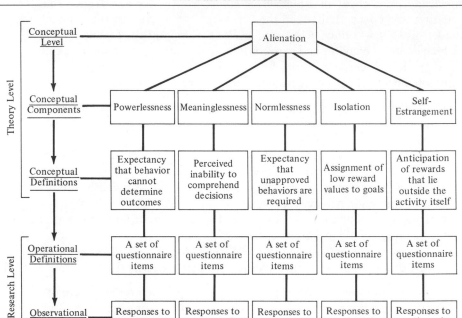

alienation, each of which is conceptually defined; the conceptual definitions indicate that the dimensions refer to different empirical aspects. Next, operational definitions are constructed; in this example, they are questionnaire items. The questionnaire items serve the purpose of transforming the conceptual definitions into the observational level. Finally, the questionnaire items (operational definitions) are administered; from the responses to the questionnaire we infer the extent to which the five dimensions of alienation exist at the empirical level.

The Congruence Problem

Two important issues arise with the transition from the conceptual level to the empirical-observational level. The first is the degree of congruence between conceptual definitions and operational definitions. If "intelligence" is defined conceptually as "the ability to think abstractly" and operationally by an intelligence test, what is the degree of congruence between the two definitions? Does the score achieved by a certain individual in an intelligence test represent everything that the conceptual definition of "intelligence" conveys? The degree of congruence between a conceptual definition and an operational definition can be evaluated with the aid of validity tests, such as those discussed in Chapter 7. At this stage, it should be pointed out that there is no absolute criterion for checking congruence, and there may indeed be situations in which an operational definition does not contain all the aspects of a conceptual definition. Improving operational definitions and extending the degree of congruence between them and conceptual definitions constitute important challenges to social scientists.

Theoretical Import

The second issue involved in the transformation from the conceptual to the observation level arises when concepts cannot be defined operationally; that is, they cannot be observed either directly or indirectly. For example, "ego," "Oedipus complex," "dialectical materialism," "subconscious," "marginal utility," and "public interest" are concepts for which no satisfactory operational definitions have yet been constructed.

According to the orthodox operational approach, a concept that cannot be operationally defined (at least in principle) should not be used in scientific research because it is not amenable to intersubjective verification; such a concept necessarily leads to meaningless research. The scientific meaning of a concept can be established only by constructing a set of operations (instruments of observation); to know these operations is to understand a concept and to be able to investigate empirically the phenomenon that it represents. Historically, this approach fulfilled the important function of stressing the empirical concern of science—of demarcating the physical from the metaphysical. But when carried to its extreme, the orthodox operational approach becomes problematic.

Scientific concepts should not be evaluated only in terms of their observability but also in terms of their **theoretical import**; that is, some concepts gain meaning only in the context of the theory in which they are introduced. For example, the concept "anomie" becomes meaningful in the context of Durkheim's suicide theory, the concept "ego" gains meaning in the context of psychoanalytic theory, and "public interest" cannot be viewed independently from a theory of democracy. Carl Hempel's idea of "systematic import" has influenced current practice:

> Scientific systematization requires the establishment of diverse connections, by law or theoretical principles, between different aspects of the empirical world, which are characterized by scientific concepts. Thus, the concepts of science are the knots in a network of systematic interrelationships in which laws and theoretical principles form the threads. . . . The more threads converge upon, or issue from, a conceptual knot, the stronger will be its systematizing role, or its systematic import.[11]

11. Hempel, *Philosophy of Natural Science*, p. 94.

Not only are scientific concepts to be evaluated with reference to their observability, but their theoretical import must also be considered:

> Empirical import as reflected in clear criteria of application, on which operationalism rightly puts much emphasis, is not the only desideratum for scientific concepts: systematic import is another indispensable requirement—so much so that the empirical interpretation of theoretical concepts may be changed in the interest of enhancing the systematic power of the theoretical network. In scientific inquiry, concept formation and theory formation must go hand in hand.[12]

In other words, concepts gain empirical meaning from operational definitions and gain theoretical meaning within the context of the theory within which they are employed. Theory, as indicated in Figure 1.1, plays a vital and central role in the research process. It is not only an important source for the generation of problems and hypotheses, as discussed in Chapter 3, but the meaning and significance of key concepts are interpreted in the context of a theory.

Theory: Functions and Types

Having discussed concepts, conceptual and operational definitions, and the idea of theoretical import, we now turn to the place of theory in empirical research. Although social scientists are in agreement that one of the most important functions of empirical research is to contribute to the development and refinement of theory and that theory enhances the goals of science, there is little agreement on what theory is. George Homans made the following critical observation on the state of theory in sociology:

> Contemporary sociologists have been preoccupied with "theory," yet have seldom tried to make clear what theory *is*. . . . We sociologists show our confusion about the nature of theory both by what we say about theory in general and by what kinds of theories we actually produce.[13]

Since then, similar statements have been made by social scientists in other disciplines.

Theory means different things to different people. Some social scientists would identify theory with any kind of conceptualization. Such concepts as "power," "social status," "democracy," "bureaucracy," and "relative deprivation," when defined and used in interpretations of empirical phenomena, are equated with theory. In this broad sense, any conceptualization, as opposed to observation, is theory. Other social scientists equate theory with the "history of ideas." Still others view theory in a narrow

---

12. Ibid., pp. 96–97.
13. George C. Homans, "Contemporary Theory in Sociology," in *Handbook of Modern Sociology*, ed. R. E. L. Faris (Chicago: Rand McNally, 1964), p. 951.

sense: a *logical-deductive* system consisting of a set of interrelated concepts from which testable propositions can be deductively derived. Before we discuss what theory is and what types of theory are common in the social sciences, it is useful to point out three common misconceptions of theory.

What Theory Is Not

The layperson usually contrasts "theory" and "practice." The adage that something is "all right in theory but won't work in practice" conveys the idea that theory is impractical. As Arnold Brecht put it, "The relation between practice and theory is well indicated in the popular saying that we learn best through 'trial and error.' Trial is practice; error refers to theory. When theory miscarries in practical trials it needs correction."[14] But theory is *of* practice, and in this sense it will be accepted or rejected by scientists with its practicality provided only that the method and contexts of its application (practice) are logically and explicity pointed out. In principle, there is no contrast between theory and practice. A sound theory is the conceptual foundation for reliable knowledge; theories help us to explain and predict phenomena of interest to us and, therefore, to make intelligent practical decisions.

Another misconception of theory results from the substitution of "theory" for "philosophy." Thus the writings of classical scholars such as Plato, Aristotle, Locke, Marx, and Pareto are identified as "theory." In fact, prior to World War II, theory in the social sciences almost exclusively implied philosophy in its various forms, with particular emphasis on moral philosophy—that is, how things *ought* to be. Plato's presentation of the ideal, just polity in which the absolute knowledge of the philosopher-king is the guide for political and social behavior is a familiar example.

Moral philosophies state value judgments. They are neither true nor false because they are not empirically verifiable. If one strongly believes that socialism is the best economic system, no amount of empirical evidence can prove or disprove that belief. Unlike philosophical works, scientific theories are abstractions representing certain aspects of the empirical world; they are concerned with the *how* and *why* of empirical phenomena.

Types of Theories

There is no one simple definition of theory on which all social scientists would agree. This is because there are many different kinds of theories, serving different purposes. David Easton, for example, suggested that theories can be classified according to their *scope*—whether they are macro or micro theories; according to their *function*—whether they seek to deal with statics or dynamics, with structure or process; according to their *structure*—

14. Arnold Brecht, *Political Theory* (Princeton, N.J.: Princeton University Press, 1959), p. 19.

whether they are postulational systems of thought with closely knit, logical interrelations or whether they constitute a more loosely defined set of propositions; or according to their *level*—"by the relationship of the behavioral systems to which they refer as ranked on some hierarchical scale."[15] Our classification is based on the Parsons and Shils distinction among four *levels* of theory: ad hoc classificatory systems, taxonomies, conceptual frameworks, and theoretical systems.[16]

Ad Hoc Classificatory Systems.   The lowest level of theorizing is the **ad hoc classificatory system**. It consists of arbitrary categories constructed in order to organize and summarize empirical observations. For example, the classification of individuals' responses to the questionnaire item "All groups can live in harmony in this country without changing the system in any way" into the four categories "Strongly Agree," "Agree," "Disagree," and "Strongly Disagree" constitutes an ad hoc classificatory system.

Taxonomies.   The second level of theory is the *categorical system*, or **taxonomy**. It consists of a system of categories constructed to fit the empirical observations so that relationships among categories can be described. Often the categories are interdependent. A taxonomy is closely related to the empirical world: the categories reflect the reality described. Parsons's analysis of social action exemplifies this level of theory. He suggested that behavior has four attributes: it is goal-oriented, occurs in situations, is normatively regulated, and involves an expenditure of energy. When behavior is so organized, it constitutes a social system. Furthermore, social systems take three forms: personality systems, cultural systems, and social structures.[17] Parsons carefully defined these seven categories and then explained their logical interrelations. Eventually, empirical observations have been fitted to the categories.

Taxonomies perform two important functions in social science research. Their careful definitions specify the unit of empirical reality to be analyzed and indicate how the unit may be described (in Parsons's taxonomy, social systems). The goal of a taxonomy

> is an orderly schema for classification and description. . . . When faced with any subject of research, [one] can immediately identify its crucial aspects or variables by using his taxonomy as a kind of a "shopping list." To "test" his taxonomy, he takes a fresh look at subject X and shows that the general terms defining his dimensions have identifiable counterparts in X.[18]

15. David Easton, "Alternative Strategies in Theoretical Research," in *Varieties of Political Theory*, ed. David Easton (Englewood Cliffs, N.J.: Prentice-Hall, 1966), pp. 1–13.

16. Talcott Parsons and Edward A. Shils, *Toward a General Theory of Action* (New York: Harper & Row, 1962), pp. 50–51.

17. Ibid., pp. 247–275.

18. Hans L. Zetterberg, *On Theory and Verification in Sociology,* 3d enlarged ed. (Totowa, N.J.: Bedminster Press, 1965), p. 26.

Figure 2.2
A Conceptual Framework of Political Systems

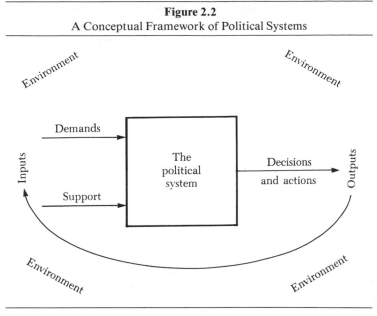

The second function of the taxonomy is to "summarize and inspire descriptive studies,"[19] such as those concerned with the empirical distributions of one or more categories of the taxonomy. Taxonomies, however, do not provide explanations; they only describe empirical phenomena by fitting them into a set of categories. To know the concepts that represent phenomena (for example, "government spending") and their distributions (for example, how much is being spent on various programs) is not to explain or predict phenomena (for example, why our government spends more on defense than on education).

Conceptual Frameworks.   The third level of theory is the **conceptual framework**. Descriptive categories are systematically placed in a broad structure of explicit, assumed propositions. Easton's conceptualization of politics is a fruitful example of a conceptual framework. By defining politics as the "authoritative allocation of values,"[20] Easton identified the major functions of political systems. All political systems, no matter what their form of government (democracies as well as dictatorships) allocate values authoritatively. Concepts such as "inputs," "outputs," "environment," and "feedback" (Figure 2.2) are used to describe and explain empirical observations. These concepts are interrelated, with "feedback" performing the functions of continuity and change. Easton offers a variety of proposi-

---

19. Ibid.

20. David Easton, *A System Analysis of Political Life* (Chicago: University of Chicago Press, 1979), pp. 21–32; see also David Easton, *A Framework for Political Analysis* (Chicago: University of Chicago Press, 1979).

tions to explain how "inputs" (differentiated into "demands" and "supports") are generated, how political decision makers react to "inputs," how the "environment" influences "inputs" and decision makers, and how "outputs" (differentiated into "decisions" and "actions") change through "feedback" the nature of "inputs."

This conceptual framework stands above taxonomy because its propositions summarize and provide explanations and predictions for vast numbers of empirical observations. Much of what is considered theory in the social sciences consists of conceptual frameworks that direct systematic empirical research. However, the propositions derived from conceptual frameworks are not established deductively. This limits their explanatory and predictive powers and impairs their usefulness for future research.

Theoretical Systems.   **Theoretical systems** combine taxonomies and conceptual frameworks by relating descriptions, explanations, and predictions in a systematic manner. At this level, theory meets its most rigorous definition: a system of propositions that are interrelated in a way that permits some to be derived from others. When such a theoretical system exists, social scientists can claim to have explained and predicted the phenomenon at hand.

A theoretical system is one that provides a structure for a complete explanation of empirical phenomena; its scope is not limited to a particular aspect. It consists of a set of concepts, some of which are *descriptive*, showing what the theory is about (for example, "relative deprivation," "suicide," "political participation"), and others that are *operative* or empirical properties (for example, "the *extent* of relative deprivation," "suicide *rate*," "*incidence* of political participation"). These empirical properties are termed *variables*. (A detailed discussion of variables and their types is found in Chapter 3.) A theoretical system also consists of a set of *propositions*, statements of relationships between two or more empirical properties that can be verified or refuted. Such a set of propositions forms a *deductive system*. In other words, the set of propositions forms a *calculus*, and according to the rules for the manipulation of the calculus, some propositions are deduced from others. When propositions are so deduced, they are said to be explained as well as to provide predictions. Finally, some of the propositions of a theoretical system must be *contingent* in the sense that "experience is relevant to their truth or falsity or to that of propositions derived from them."[21] Indeed, acceptance of theoretical systems depends on whether their propositions have been empirically verified.

Durkheim's theory of suicide, as presented by George Homans, provides a classic example of a theoretical system:[22]

21. Homans, "Contemporary Theory in Sociology," p. 959.
22. Ibid.

1. In any social grouping, the suicide rate varies directly with the degree of individualism (egoism).
2. The degree of individualism varies with the incidence of Protestantism.
3. Therefore, the suicide rate varies with the incidence of Protestantism.
4. The incidence of Protestantism in Spain is low.
5. Therefore, the suicide rate in Spain is low.

In this example, proposition 3 is deduced from propositions 1 and 2, and proposition 5 is deduced from 3 and 4. Furthermore, if, for example, one did not know what the suicide rate in Bulgaria was but did know that the incidence of Protestantism was low, this observation, together with proposition 3, would allow one to predict that the suicide rate was also low. Thus the theoretical system provides both an explanation and a prediction of suicide rates.

Axiomatic Theory

One theoretical system that deserves special mention is the *formal* or **axiomatic theory**. An axiomatic theory contains the following:

1. A set of concepts and definitions—conceptual and operational.
2. A set of statements describing the situations in which the theory can be applied.
3. A set of relational statements, divided into
    a. Axioms—untestable statements or assumptions assumed to be true. For example, the axioms in geometry need not apply to the empirical world.
    b. Theorems—propositions *deduced* from the axioms and amenable to empirical verification.
4. A logical system employed to
    a. Relate *all* concepts within statements.
    b. Deduce theorems from axioms, combinations of axioms, and theorems.

Hans Zetterberg's reformulation of Durkheim's theory is an early and often cited example of axiomatic theory. Zetterberg explicated the following ten propositions:[23]

1. The greater the division of labor, the greater the consensus.
2. The greater the solidarity, the greater the number of associates per member.
3. The greater the number of associates per member, the greater the consensus.

23. Zetterberg, *On Theory and Verification*, pp. 159–160.

4. The greater the consensus, the smaller the number of rejections of deviants.

5. The greater the division of labor, the smaller the number of rejections of deviants.

6. The greater the number of associates per member, the smaller the number of rejections of deviants.

7. The greater the division of labor, the greater the solidarity.

8. The greater the solidarity, the greater the consensus.

9. The greater the number of associates per member, the greater the division of labor.

10. The greater the solidarity, the smaller the number of rejections of deviants.

He then selected the last four propositions as axioms and argued that the remainder can be deduced from this combination of axioms: 7 and 8 generate theorem or proposition 1; 7 and 9 render 2; 8 and 2 render 3; 8 and 10 lead to 4; 7 and 10 generate 5; and 9 and 5 render 6. Thus with the four axioms, all the theorems were deduced.

The most difficult problem in axiomatic theory involves the choice of axioms. What criteria should be used to choose certain propositions and treat them as axioms? Why did Zetterberg choose the last four propositions and not others to constitute his set of axioms? One criterion of selection is *consistency*: axioms should not lead to contradictory theorems. Another criterion is to select the smallest set of axioms from which *all* other theorems can be deduced. This criterion reflects the preference of scientists for *parsimony* or simplicity when constructing substantive theories. The third criterion for the selection of axioms—and the one that makes the construction of axiomatic theory in the social sciences most difficult—is to choose as axioms only propositions that have achieved the status of laws. However, propositions that become laws must have considerable empirical support before they are considered laws. At present, very few propositions in the social sciences have achieved such status.

In recent research, the practice has been to select as axioms the set of independent propositions that makes the substantive theory explicit and easiest to understand. This is achieved when the propositions that describe a *direct causal* relationship between two concepts are employed as axioms. As Hubert Blalock put it, ''An axiom might be stated somewhat as follows: An increase in X will produce (cause) an almost immediate increase in Y; this increase in Y will, in turn, result in further increase in X, but with a delayed reaction.''[24] Using the rule of direct causal relationships, Blalock restated Zetterberg's four axioms in the following way:[25]

24. Hubert M. Blalock, Jr., *Theory Construction* (Englewood Cliffs, N.J.: Prentice-Hall, 1969), p. 18.
25. Ibid., p. 19.

1. An increase in the number of associates per member will produce an increase in the division of labor.
2. An increase in the division of labor will produce an increase in solidarity.
3. An increase in solidarity will produce an increase in consensus.
4. An increase in solidarity will produce a decrease in the number of rejections of deviants.

These causal axioms in turn lead to the generation of empirically testable theorems or propositions.

Advantages of Axiomatic Theory.   Given that only very few propositions in the social sciences have achieved the status of laws, why construct axiomatic theories?

There are several advantages to axiomatic theory. First, it calls for a careful description of substantive theory, for the explanation of the central concepts and assumptions used in a theory. Second, each concept has to be clearly defined, using both primitive and derived terms and operational definitions. Third, axiomatic theory can provide a parsimonious summary of actual and anticipated research. Instead of having a large number of independent propositions, an axiomatic theory presents only the essential ones. Fourth, an axiomatic theory can be used "to coordinate research so that many separate findings support each other, giving the highest plausibility to the theory per finding."[26] Because the theory consists of a set of interrelated propositions, empirical support for any one proposition tends to provide support for the entire theory. Fifth, the axiomatic form allows researchers to examine *all* the consequences of their axioms; this in turn helps to determine which parts of the theory are verified and which call for further research. This is particularly useful when we want to study research topics that will contribute most to theory.[27] Finally, the axiomatic form is compatible with causal analysis, described in Chapter 17.

Models

Closely related to the idea of theory as a systematic conceptual organization is the notion of **models**. Often conceptual organization is attempted by models. A model can be viewed as a likeness of something. For example, an engineer might have a model of a machine such as a space shuttle. The model is a miniature reproduction of the real space shuttle including scale representation of some of the real space shuttle's features—its structure— but omitting other aspects, such as its control instruments. The model serves as a physical, visual representation of the structure and features of the space shuttle. The model can be used in place of the real space shuttle

---

26. Zetterberg, *On Theory and Verification*, p. 163.
27. For an excellent application of these advantages, see Gerald Hage, *Theories of Organizations: Forms, Process, and Transformation* (New York: Wiley-Interscience, 1980).

for experimentation and testing. For example, the engineer might subject the model to the effects of a wind tunnel (itself a model) to determine the space shuttle's performance.

In the social sciences, models usually consist of symbols rather than physical matter; that is, the characteristics of some empirical phenomenon, including its components and the relationships between the components, are represented in logical arrangements among concepts. Thus we can more formally define a model as an abstraction from reality that serves the purpose of ordering and simplifying our view of reality while still representing its essential characteristics:

> A characteristic feature in the construction of a model is abstraction; certain elements of the situation may be deliberately omitted because they are judged irrelevant, and the resulting simplification in the description of the situation may be helpful in analyzing and understanding it. In addition to abstraction, model-building sometimes involves a conceptual transference. Instead of discussing the situation directly, it may be the case that each element of the real situation is simulated by a mathematical or physical object, and its relevant properties and relations to other elements are mirrored by corresponding simulative properties and relations . . .; a city's traffic system may be simulated by setting up a miniature model of its road net, traffic signals, and vehicles.[28]

A model, then, is a representation of reality; it delineates certain aspects of the real world as being relevant to the problem under investigation, it makes explicit the significant relationships among the aspects, and it enables the formulation of empirically testable propositions regarding the nature of these relationships. After testing, a better understanding of some part of the real world could be achieved. Models are also used to gain insight into phenomena that cannot be observed directly. In policy analysis, for example, models of the structures and processes of decision making are constructed, and propositions relating to the behavior of the decision makers are deduced. These propositions are then evaluated with empirical data. Also in policy analysis, models are used to estimate the consequences of various alternative courses of action that a decision maker might select. The models provide a more systematic basis for policy choices than subjective judgments.

Example: A Model of Policy Implementation

Thomas Smith's model of the policy implementation process provides an interesting example of modeling complex and directly nonobservable aspects of the real world.[29] Many laypersons believe that once a public policy has

---

28. Olaf Helmer, *Social Technology* (New York: Basic Books, 1966), pp. 127–128.

29. Thomas B. Smith, "The Policy Implementation Process," *Policy Sciences*, 4 (1973): 197–209.

been decided (for example, through passage of a bill by Congress), implementation will follow naturally and even automatically to achieve the goals desired by the policymakers. This rarely happens. Problems of implementation are widespread, and policies are almost never implemented in the manner originally intended. Public bureaucrats, interest groups, and affected individuals and organizations often attempt to force changes in policy during the implementation process.

The model developed by Smith abstracts certain aspects of the implementation process and focuses on four components:

1. The idealized policy, that is, the idealized patterns of interaction that the policymakers are attempting to induce.
2. The target group, defined as the people that the policy obliges to adopt new patterns of interaction. They are the individuals most directly affected by the policy and who must change to meet its demands.
3. The implementing organization, usually a government agency, responsible for implementation of the policy.
4. The environmental factors influenced by implementation of the policy. The general public and various special-interest groups are included here.

These four components and their postulated relations are diagrammed in Figure 2.3. The policymaking process produces public policies; these serve as a tension-generating force in society: implementation causes tensions, strains, and conflicts among both the implementers of the policy and the people affected by it. Tensions lead to *transactions*, Smith's term for the responses to these tensions and conflicts. The feedback produced by transac-

Figure 2.3
A Model of the Policy Implementation Process

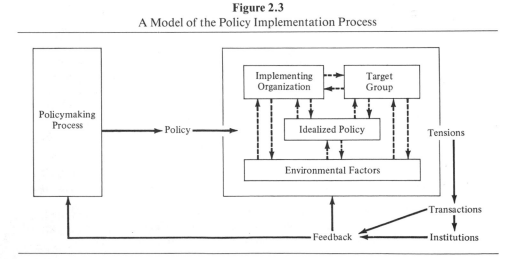

tions and institutions influences future policymaking as well as the four components of the implementation process.

Models, then, are tools for explanation and prediction. If well designed, they approximate reality, but the models themselves are never the reality. Indeed, models are often changed to represent reality more accurately and to incorporate new knowledge. The critical attribute of a scientific model is that it can be tested empirically; that is, it can be falsifiable.

Theory, Models, and Empirical Research

The social sciences as scientific disciplines rest on two major components: theory and empirical research. Social scientists, as scientists, operate in two "worlds"—the world of observation and experience and the world of ideas, theories, and models. Establishing a systematic connection between these two worlds enhances the goals of the social sciences. But how should this connection be achieved? Should we first construct our theories and models and then move to the world of empirical research? Or should theory *follow* empirical research?

Theory before Research

According to one major school of thought, theory should come first, to be followed by research; this is often referred to as the **theory-then-research strategy**. Karl Popper has developed this strategy most systematically. He argues that scientific knowledge would advance most rapidly through the development of ideas (conjectures) and attempts to refute them through empirical research (refutations).[30] Popper denies the systematic bearing of empirical research on theorizing; research seldom generates new theories, nor does it serve as a logical method for theory construction. Theories "can only be reached by intuition, based upon something like an intellectual love of the objects of experience."[31] A similar position was taken by Watson:

> At first we operate only with thought abstractions, mindful of our task only to construct inner representation-pictures. Proceeding in this way, we do not as yet take possible experiential facts into consideration, but merely make the effort to develop our thought-pictures with as much clarity as possible and to draw from them all possible consequences. Only subsequently, after the entire exposition of the picture has been completed, do we check its agreement with experiential facts.[32]

30. Karl R. Popper, *Conjectures and Refutations: The Growth of Scientific Knowledge* (New York: Harper & Row, 1968).
31. Karl R. Popper, *The Logic of Scientific Discovery* (New York: Science Editions, 1961), p.
32. W. H. Watson, "On Methods of Representation," in *Philosophy of Science*, ed. Arthur Danto and Sidney Morgenbesser (New York: Harper & Row, 1974), pp. 226–244.

Although somewhat simplified, the theory-then-research strategy involves the following five stages:[33]

1. Construct an explicit theory or model.
2. Select a proposition derived from the theory or model for empirical investigation.
3. Design a research project to test the proposition.
4. If the proposition derived from the theory is rejected by the empirical data, make changes in the theory or the research project (for example, research, design, measurement; see Figure 1.1) and return to stage 2.
5. If the proposition is not rejected, select other propositions for testing or attempt to improve the theory.

Research before Theory

In sharp contrast to the theory-then-research strategy, Robert Merton, a proponent of the **research-then-theory strategy**, argued as follows:

> It is my central thesis that empirical research goes far beyond the passive role of verifying and testing theory; it does more than confirm or refute hypotheses. Research plays an active role: it performs at least four major functions which help shape the development of theory. It initiates, it reformulates, it deflects, and it clarifies theory.[34]

Empirical research suggests new problems for theory, calls for new theoretical formulations, leads to the refinement of existing theories, and serves the function of verification. The research-then-theory strategy consists of the following:[35]

1. Investigate a phenomenon and delineate its attributes.
2. Measure the attributes in a variety of situations. (Measurement and measuring procedures are discussed in Chapter 7.)
3. Analyze the resulting data to determine if there are systematic patterns of variation.
4. Once systematic patterns are discovered, construct a theory. The theory may be of any of the types discussed earlier, although a theoretical system is preferred.

Clearly, both strategies regard theory as a manifestation of scientific progress. The dilemma is over the place of theory in the research process. It is our contention that no dogmatic commitment to either strategy is neces-

---

33. Reynolds, *Primer in Theory Construction*, pp. 140–144.
34. Robert K. Merton, *Social Theory and Social Structure,* rev. and enlarged ed. (New York: Free Press, 1968), p. 103.
35. Reynolds, *Primer in Theory Construction*, pp. 140–144.

sary in the conduct of research. The social sciences have progressed in spite of this controversy, and scientific undertakings are being pursued under both strategies. In fact, theory and research interact continuously, as suggested in Chapter 1 in Figure 1.1. Furthermore, as Ernest Nagel maintains, the contrast between the two strategies is more apparent than real:

> Distinguished scientists have repeatedly claimed that theories are "free creations of the mind." Such claims obviously do not mean that theories may not be *suggested* by observational materials or that theories do not require support from observational evidence. What such claims do rightly assert is that the basic terms of a theory need not possess meanings which are fixed by definite experimental procedures, and that a theory may be adequate and fruitful despite the fact that the evidence for it is necessarily indirect.[36]

Summary

1. One of the most significant symbols in science is the concept. Science begins by forming concepts to describe the empirical world and advances by relating these concepts into theoretical systems. Concepts enable effective communication, introduce a point of view, are means for classification and generalization, and serve as the building blocks of propositions, theories, and hypotheses, which will be discussed in Chapter 3.

2. To serve their functions effectively, concepts have to be clear, precise, and agreed-on. This is achieved by conceptual and operational definitions. A conceptual definition describes concepts using primitive and derived terms. Operational definitions point out the set of procedures and activities that one should perform in the empirical observation of the phenomena represented by concepts. Operational definitions connect the conceptual-theoretical level with the empirical-observational level.

3. Although social scientists are in agreement that theory is the ultimate achievement of scientific undertakings, there are divergent views concerning the meaning and structure of theory. At present, four levels of theory can be distinguished: ad hoc classificatory systems, taxonomies, conceptual frameworks, and theoretical systems. One form of theoretical system is the axiomatic theory. It contains a set of concepts and definitions, a set of existence statements, a set of relational statements divided into axioms and theorems, and a logical system used to relate concepts with statements and to deduce theorems from axioms.

4. Models are often used by social scientists to represent certain aspects of the real world systematically. Models are abstractions from reality that serve the purpose of ordering and simplifying our view of reality while still representing its essential attributes. Models are also used to gain insight into phenomena that cannot be observed directly, such as an economic system.

36. Ernest Nagel, *The Structure of Science* (New York: Heckett, 1979), p. 86.

5. The establishment of systematic links between the empirical and the conceptual worlds has been achieved with the aid of two general strategies: theory-then-research and research-then-theory. Although there is a lively controversy as to which strategy most fruitfully enhances scientific progress, our position is that theory and research should interact constantly and that the contrast between the two strategies is more apparent than real.

Key Terms for Review

concept

fallacy of reification

conceptual definition

primitive term

ostensive definition

operational definition

theoretical import

ad hoc classificatory system

taxonomy

conceptual framework

theoretical system

axiomatic theory

model

theory-then-research strategy

research-then-theory strategy

Study Questions

1. Discuss the four functions of concepts in social science research.
2. Distinguish between conceptual definitions and operational definitions.
3. Discuss three common misconceptions of theories.
4. Describe and explain the use of models in social science research.
5. Discuss the controversy of theory before research versus research before theory.

Additional Readings

Bartholomew, David J. *Mathematical Models in Social Science.* New York: Wiley, 1981.

Blalock, Hubert M., Jr. *Basic Dilemmas in the Social Sciences.* Newbury Park, Calif.: Sage, 1984.

Braithwaite, Richard B. "Models in Empirical Science." In *Readings in the Philosophy of Science,* ed. Baruch A. Grody. 2d ed. Englewood Cliffs, N.J.: Prentice-Hall, 1989, pp. 268–293.

Isaak, Alan C. *Scope and Methods of Political Science.* 4th ed. Homewood, Ill.: Dorsey Press, 1985.

Krathwohl, David R. *Social and Behavioral Science Research.* San Francisco: Jossey-Bass, 1985.

Lave, Charles A., and James G. March. *An Introduction to Models in the Social Sciences*. New York: Harper & Row, 1975.

Rubinstein, Moshe F., and Kenneth Pfeiffer. *Concepts in Problem Solving*. Englewood Cliffs, N.J.: Prentice-Hall, 1980.

Simon, Herbert A. *The Science of the Artificial*. 2d ed. Cambridge, Mass.: MIT Press, 1981.

Stinchcombe, Arthur L. *Constructing Social Theories*. Orlando, Fla.: Harcourt Brace Jovanovich, 1968.

CHAPTER 3

Basic Elements of Research

In this chapter, we examine the formulation of problems amenable to research and consider two fallacies. We then define types of variables and explore the relations between them. Next we trace hypotheses and their derivations. Finally, we review major guides to published research, including online databases.

I N SOCIAL SCIENCE RESEARCH, WHETHER carried out under the theory-then-research or the research-then-theory strategy, the terms *research problem, variable, relation,* and *hypothesis* crop up with great frequency. They are the basic elements of research; they help transform an idea into concrete research operations. In this chapter, we define, discuss, and exemplify the use of these basic terms in the context of the research process.

Research Problems

In the beginning is the problem. **A research problem** is an intellectual stimulus calling for an answer in the form of scientific inquiry. For example, "Who rules America?" "What incentives lead to energy conservation?" "How can inflation be contracted?" or "Does social class influence voting behavior?" are all problems amenable to scientific research.

Not all intellectual stimuli can be studied empirically, and not all human behavior is guided by scientific knowledge. In fact, we saw in Chapter 1 that the assumptions of science themselves are empirically nonresearchable; they are neither proven nor provable. Similarly, questions such as "Will Western civilization disappear?" "Is blue nicer than green?" or "Is Impressionism the most advanced form of art?" cannot be investigated empirically. In general, problems that cannot be empirically grounded or that are concerned with subjective preferences, beliefs, values, or tastes are not amenable to empirical research.

The observation that our subjective preferences cannot be studied scientifically should not, of course, imply that social scientists in their roles as concerned citizens, parents, friends, and so on do not have subjective preferences about many things, just as nonscientists do. However, such preferences are not empirically verifiable and are thus beyond the realm of scientific knowledge.

Certain subjective preferences or biases can be studied in the same way that scientists approach empirical phenomena—as factual problems to be investigated by means of the scientific approach. For example, one could study why some people believe that Western civilization will disappear and why others do not share this view or whether the preference for Impressionism is related to social class or to personality characteristics.

In addition to being empirically grounded, research problems have to be clearly and specifically articulated. For example, the problem "What incentives lead to energy conservation?" is too general and too ambiguous. It means different things to different people. It does not specify the types of incentives (e.g., economic, social, patriotic) or the sources of energy (crude oil, gasoline, natural gas, coal). It also fails to distinguish between industrial and residential conservation. The lack of clarity and specificity may lead to ambiguous findings that can be interpreted in contradictory ways.

Units of Analysis

In the formulation of a research problem, serious consideration must also be given to the **units of analysis**, which influence research design, data collection, and data analysis decisions. Does the research problem call for the study of perceptions, attitudes, or behavior? Should we concentrate on individuals or groups? Institutions or societies? Abraham Kaplan called selecting the units of analysis the "locus problem":

> The locus problem may be described as that of selecting the ultimate subject-matter for inquiry in behavioral science, the attribute space for its description, and the conceptual structure within which hypotheses about it are to be formulated. Quite a number of alternatives present themselves, and have been selected in various inquiries: states of conscious acts, actions

(segments of meaningful behavior), roles, persons, personalities, interpersonal relations, groups, classes, institutions, social traits or patterns, societies, and cultures. With respect to each of these, there is the associated problem of unit, *that is, of what constitutes the identity of the element selected. Are legal institutions, for example, quite distinct from the institution of the state or part of it, and if so, in what sense of "part"?*[1]

In principle, there are no limitations on the selection of units to be analyzed in a research project. However, once a selection has been made, subsequent research operations, in particular the scope and the level of generalization and theorizing, are to be congruent with the units of analysis chosen. Units of analysis have unique attributes; thus it is often misleading to shift from one unit to another. Generalizations based on individuals as units of analysis and generalizations based on groups can be quite different.

A major reason for such disparities is that similar concepts are often used to refer to attributes of different units. For example, the concept "survival" is being used to explain the behavior of individuals, groups, formal organizations, and countries. But "survival" means different things when applied to these different units. There is no a priori reason to assume that the relationships between "survival" and other concepts will be identical across units of analysis. The behavioral consequences of survival can be similar for individuals, but they certainly differ when organizations or nations are considered.

The Ecological Fallacy

The specification of units of analysis is important for methodological reasons as well. When relationships are estimated at one level of analysis (e.g., collectivities) and then extrapolated to another level (e.g., individuals) distortions are likely to result. This kind of distortion is termed the **ecological fallacy**.

In a classic study, William Robinson effectively demonstrated the consequences of the ecological fallacy.[2] Focusing on the relationship between literacy and place of birth in the 1930s, Robinson compared the geographical regions of the United States. He found that regions with higher percentages of foreign-born people had higher literacy rates than regions with lower percentages of foreign-born persons. But when he subsequently examined the same relationships at the *individual* level, he came up with the *opposite* results: native-born individuals were more literate than foreign-born. What explains the reversal of the findings? Two possibilities are significant differences in the quality of public education from region to region and the tend-

---

1. Abraham Kaplan, *The Conduct of Inquiry* (New York: Harper and Row, 1968), p. 78.
2. William S. Robinson, "Ecological Correlations and the Behavior of Individuals," *American Sociological Review,* 15 (1950): 351–357.

ency for immigrants to settle in regions that happened to have better public education.

The Individualistic Fallacy

The converse of the ecological fallacy is the reductionist or *individualistic fallacy.* This results when inferences about groups, societies, or nations are drawn from individuals. For example, to count the percentage of individuals who agree with particular statements on democracy and to take this as an indicator of the degree to which a political system is democratic is to commit the individualistic fallacy. A political system can have an authoritarian regime even if most of its citizens share democratic values. Furthermore, the term *democratic* does not mean the same thing on the two levels of analysis. Applied to the individual, it refers to values, attitudes, and behavior; applied to the political system, it refers to the structure and institutions of the system. We cannot explain or predict the political system's structure or behavior only from knowledge of its individual members.

Variables

Research problems are conveyed with a set of concepts. We saw in Chapter 2 that concepts are abstractions representing empirical phenomena. In order to move from the conceptual to the empirical level, concepts are converted into *variables.* It is as variables that our concepts will eventually appear in hypotheses and be tested.

Concepts are converted into variables by *mapping* them into a set of values. For example, assigning numbers (one type of values) to objects is a mapping of a set of objects into a set of numbers. A variable is an empirical property that takes two or more values. If a property can change in value or kind, it can be regarded as a variable. For example, "social class" is a variable because it can be differentiated by at least five distinct values: lower, lower middle, middle, upper middle, and upper. Similarly, "expectations" is a variable because it can be assigned at least two values: "high" and "low." A variable that can have only two values is called a *dichotomous variable.* For purposes of research, it is important to make an analytic distinction among dependent, independent, and control variables and between continuous and discrete variables.

Dependent and Independent Variables

The variable that the researcher wishes to explain is the **dependent variable**. The variable expected to explain change in the dependent variable is referred to as the **independent variable**. The independent variable is the explanatory variable; it is the presumed cause of changes in the values of the dependent variable; the dependent variable is the expected outcome of the independent variable. (Dependent variables are also called *criterion variables*; independent variables are also called *predictor variables.*)

In the language of mathematics, the dependent variable is the variable that happens to appear on the left-hand side of an equation. For example, if we write $Y = f(X)$, we are considering Y to be the dependent and X the independent variable. In this case, we say that Y is a *function* of X—that changes in the values of X are associated with changes in the values of Y or that X yields Y (via f). For example, a researcher might want to explain why some people participate in politics more than others. Based on the theory of social stratification, the researcher may deduce that the higher an individual's social class, the more likely that person is to participate in politics. In this case, political participation is hypothesized to be the *outcome* of social class; social class is presumed to cause variations in political participation. Accordingly, political participation is the dependent variable, and social class is the independent variable.

It should be stressed that the distinction between dependent and independent variables is analytic and relates *only* to the research purpose. In the real world, variables are neither dependent nor independent; the researcher decides how to view them, and that decision is based on the research objective. An independent variable in one investigation may be a dependent variable in another, and the same researcher in different projects may classify the same variables in different ways. If one wants to explain variations in political participation, the latter will be the dependent variable. One variable that explains variations in political participation is social class, and this will be regarded as an independent variable. But if one wants to explain variations in social class (for example, why some individuals are in the lower class and others in the middle), the latter will be now regarded as a dependent variable. One variable that may be hypothesized to explain variations in social class is educational attainment, which will now be regarded as an independent variable.

Most of the phenomena investigated by social scientists call for the assessment of the effects of several independent variables on one or more dependent variables. This happens because of the complexity of phenomena. One independent variable usually explains only a certain amount of the variation in the dependent variable, and more independent variables have to be introduced in order to explain more variation. For example, when political participation is studied as a dependent variable, social class explains why some people participate in politics more than others. This explanation, however, is incomplete because there are reasons in addition to social class that explain variations in political participation. Among these additional independent variables are age, gender, interest in politics, and political efficacy (the extent to which individuals believe that their participation will affect political outcomes).

Control Variables

The function of **control variables** in empirical research is to reduce the risk of attributing explanatory power to independent variables that in fact are not responsible for the occurrence of variation in the dependent variable. Control variables are used to test the possibility that an empirically observed relation between an independent and a dependent variable is *spurious*. A **spurious relation** is a relation that can be explained by other variables. In other words, if the effects of all relevant variables are eliminated (or controlled for) and the empirical relation between the independent variable and the dependent variable is maintained, then the relation is nonspurious. It implies that there is an inherent, causal link between the variables, that the observed relation is not based on an accidental connection with some other related phenomenon.

Suppose that one observes that the number of firefighters is related to the amount of fire damage. The more firefighters at the fire site, the greater the amount of fire damage. Obviously, firefighters are not the cause of the damage. Accordingly, the amount of fire damage should not be explained by the number of firefighters at the site but by another variable, namely, the size of the fire. Large fires call forth more firefighters and also cause more damage. Thus the original observed relation between the number of firefighters at the fire site and the amount of fire damage is spurious because a third factor, the size of the fire, explains it. In this case, the size of the fire is a control variable. Without the influence of the control variable, no relation would have been observed between the number of firefighters (the independent variable) and the amount of fire damage (the dependent variable). This is illustrated in Figure 3.1.

Another example illustrating the significance of control variables is the empirical relation observed between political participation and government expenditure. Is the amount of government expenditure (dependent variable)

Figure 3.1
Importance of a Control Variable

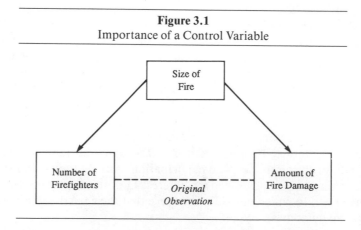

caused by the extent of political participation (independent variable)? Seemingly yes. But when Hayward Alker, in a critical study, examined economic development as a control variable, he found that the empirical relation between political participation and government expenditure vanished.[3] The level of economic development influences *both* government expenditure and political participation. Without the influence of economic development, no relation would have been observed between political participation and government expenditure. Control variables thus serve the purpose of testing whether the observed relations between independent and dependent variables are nonspurious.

Continuous and Discrete Variables

One other important attribute of variables is their being either continuous or discrete. This attribute, as we shall see in later chapters, affects subsequent research operations, particularly measurement procedures, data analysis, and methods of inference and generalization.

A **continuous variable** does not have a minimum-sized unit. Length is an example of a continuous variable because there is no minimum unit of length. A particular object may be 10 inches long, it may be 10.5 inches long, or it may be 10.5431697 . . . inches long. In principle, we can speak of a tenth of an inch, a ten-thousandth of an inch, or a ten-trillionth of an inch. Although we cannot measure all possible length values with absolute accuracy (some values will be too small for any measuring instrument to register), it is possible for objects to exist at an infinite number of lengths.

Unlike continuous variables, **discrete variables** do have a minimum-sized unit. The amount of money in your bank at this moment is an example of a discrete variable because currency has a minimum unit. One can have $101.21 or $101.22 but not $101.21843. Different amounts of money cannot differ by less than the minimum-sized unit. The number of children per family is another example of a discrete variable because the minimum unit is one child. Families may have three or four children but not 3.5 children. If some quantity of a variable cannot be subdivided, the variable is discrete.

Relations

In earlier chapters, we saw that scientific explanations and predictions involve *relating* the phenomena to be explained (dependent variable) to other explanatory phenomena (independent variables) by means of general laws or theories. But what is a relation?

A **relation** in research always means a relation between two or more variables. When we say that variable X and variable Y are related, we mean that

---

3. Hayward R. Alker, *Mathematics and Politics* (New York: Macmillan, 1965).

Table 3.1
Relation between Education and Income

Observations	Years of Schooling	Income
Dan	16	$35,000
Ann	15	30,000
Marie	14	27,000
Jacob	13	19,000
Phillip	12	15,000
Suzanne	11	12,000

there is something *common* to both variables. For example, if we say that education and income are related, we mean that the two "go together," that they covary. The **covariation** is what education and income have in common: individuals with higher education have higher incomes. Establishing a relation in empirical research consists of determining which values of one variable covary with values of one or more other variables. The researcher systematically pairs values of one variable with values of other variables. For example, the two sets of observations given in Table 3.1 report the values of education (operationally defined by years of schooling) and income of six individuals. The table expresses a relation because the two sets of values have been paired in an orderly way; they covary: higher education is paired with higher income and lower education with lower income.

Kinds of Relations

We say that two variables are related when changes in the values of one systematically bring changes in the values of the other. In the last example, changes in years of schooling brought changes in income. Two properties of relations are always of concern in empirical research: direction and magnitude.

Direction. When we speak of *direction*, we mean that the relations between variables are either positive or negative. A **positive relation** means that as values of one variable increase, values of the other also increase. For example, the relation between education and income is positive because increases in years of schooling lead to higher income. There is also a positive relation between interest in politics and political participation: as individuals become more interested in politics, they tend to participate more in political activities. A positive relation has also been found between economic development and government expenditures, as pointed out earlier.

A **negative** (or *inverse*) **relation** indicates that as values of one variable increase, values of the other decrease. High values for one variable are associated with low values for the other. For instance, the interest rate for a

Table 3.2
Number of Hours of Study per Day and Number of
Excellent Grades (Hypothetical Data)

Number of Hours of Study per Day (X)	Number of Excellent Grades (Y)
8	5
7	5
6	4
5	3
4	2
4	1
3	1
2	0
1	2

house mortgage is inversely related to the number of new home loans: as the interest rate increases, the number of new home loans decreases. There is also an inverse relation between education and racial prejudice: people with higher levels of education tend to be less prejudiced. An inverse relation was also found between bureaucratization and political participation: as political systems become more bureaucratized, the level of political participation declines.

The relation between an independent variable and a dependent variable can be illustrated with the aid of orthogonal axes. Following mathematical custom, X, the independent variable, is represented by the horizontal axis, and Y, the dependent variable, by the vertical axis; X values are laid out on the X axis, Y values on the Y axis. A very common way to observe and interpret a relation is to plot the pairs of XY values, using the X and Y axes as a frame of reference. Let us suppose that in a study of academic achievement we have two sets of measures: X measures the number of hours a student devotes to studying each day, and Y measures the number of excellent grades attained by a student in a given semester. Hypothetical data of nine students on the two measures are presented in Table 3.2, and the measures are plotted in Figure 3.2.

The relation between the number of daily hours of study (independent variable) and the number of excellent grades (dependent variable) can now be made visible: high values on the X axis are related to high values on the Y axis, medium values on the X axis are related to medium values on the Y axis, and low values on the X axis are related to low values on the Y axis. The relation between the independent variable (X) and the dependent variable (Y) is depicted by the joint distribution of values. The straight line passing through the points representing pairs of values indicates the direction of the relation. Furthermore, with the aid of information about the characteristics of the straight line (its slope and the intercept), one can pre-

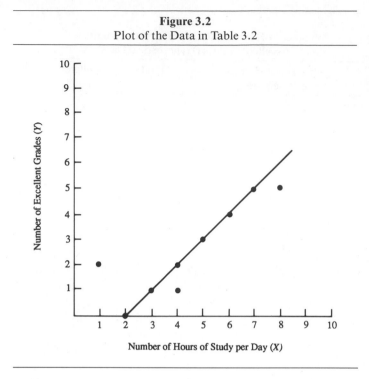

Figure 3.2
Plot of the Data in Table 3.2

Number of Hours of Study per Day (X)

dict the values of the dependent variable according to the values of the inde-pendent variable. (For methods of calculating the slope and the intercept, see Chapter 16.) For example, if the slope of the straight line and the value of the point at which it intersects the *Y* axis are known, it is possible to pre-dict how many daily hours of study will produce how many excellent grades.

   Magnitude.   Relations between variables are characterized not only by direction but also by *magnitude.* The **magnitude of a relation** is the extent to which variables covary positively or negatively. The highest magnitude of relation is a *perfect relation,* in which knowledge of the value of one or more independent variables determines exactly the value of the dependent vari-able. Physical laws such as $E = mc^2$ (Einstein's mass-energy law) are almost perfect relations because there are few exceptions to the rule. The hypotheti-cal example in Table 3.1 displays a perfect relation: there are no exceptions to the rule that increases in years of schooling bring increases in income.

   At the other extreme is the lowest magnitude of relation, the *zero rela-tion.* No systematic covariation between the values of an independent vari-able and a dependent variable can be discerned; that is, the variables are not related; changes in the values of one variable do not affect the values of the other.

   The relations studied in the social sciences range in magnitude between zero and perfect. The relation between education and income is positive but

not perfect: individuals who have higher education *tend* to have higher income, but there are many exceptions. The relation between education and
racial prejudice is inverse but not perfect: not all highly educated persons
are nonprejudiced, and not all persons with lower education are prejudiced.
(Precise measures of magnitude such as coefficients of correlations are presented in Chapters 16 and 17.)

Having discussed variables and relations, we are now in a position to
elaborate more fully on the idea and the characteristics of hypotheses.

Hypotheses

A **hypothesis** is a tentative answer to a research problem, expressed in the
form of a relation between independent and dependent variables. Hypotheses are *tentative* answers because they can be verified only *after* they have
been tested empirically. When proposing a hypothesis, the researcher does
not know whether it will be verified or not. A hypothesis is constructed and
tested; if it is rejected, another one is put forward; if it is accepted, it is incorporated into the scientific body of knowledge.

Hypotheses can be derived deductively from theories, directly from observations, intuitively, or in a combination of these approaches. The sources
from which researchers derive their hypotheses are of little significance in
comparison with the way in which they reject or fail to reject them. For example, some theorists believe that an apple falling from a tree led Newton to
propose his hypothesis about gravitation. However, it was not this episode
that convinced scientists to accept the hypothesis but the empirical data.

Research hypotheses share four common characteristics. They are *clear,
value-free, specific,* and *amenable to empirical testing* with the available research methods. Examining these characteristics in greater detail will help
you construct your own hypotheses and evaluate the hypotheses of others.

1. *Hypotheses must be clear.* Conceptual and operational definitions as
discussed in Chapter 2 help clarify hypotheses. In order to test a hypothesis
empirically, one has to define all the variables in the hypothesis operationally. The professional literature and experts' opinions can be of great help
when constructing hypotheses and defining the variables. For example, if
the hypothesis is that alienation is inversely related to political participation, the independent variable is alienation and the dependent variable is
political participation. An examination of the professional literature will reveal how other researchers defined the variables. Among these definitions,
one is likely to find a definition suitable to one's research hypothesis. If not,
the investigator can always build on others' experience while defining the
variables in a more appropriate way. In any case, operational definitions
must be specific and precise so that observation and replication are made
possible.

2. *Scientific hypotheses are value-free.* In principle, the researcher's own values, biases, and subjective preferences have no place in the scientific approach. However, given that research in the social sciences is to a certain extent a social activity whose problems are affected by its milieu, the researcher must be aware of personal biases and make them as explicit as possible. As Myrdal wrote in a classic investigation of racial relations:

> The attempt to eradicate biases trying to keep out the valuations themselves is a hopeless and misdirected venture. . . . There is no other device for excluding biases in the social sciences than to face the valuations and to introduce them as explicitly stated, specific, and sufficiently concretized value premises.[4]

3. *Hypotheses are specific.* The investigator has to point out the expected relations among the variables in terms of direction (positive or negative) and the conditions under which the relations will hold. A hypothesis stating that X is related to Y is too general. The relation between X and Y can be positive or negative. Furthermore, relations are not independent of time, space, or the unit of analysis. As we saw earlier, the observed relations between variables may vanish when the unit of analysis changes (for example, the ecological fallacy). Thus the relations between, say, education and political participation can be studied at the individual, group or district level; these different levels of analysis require different conceptualizations and different operational definitions. The hypothesis will express the expected relations between the variables as well as the conditions under which the relations will be observed. Here theory becomes especially important in generating researchable and fruitful hypotheses.

4. *Hypotheses are testable with available methods.* One can arrive at clear, value-free, and specific hypotheses and find that there are no research methods to test them. How, for example, are we to test the hypothesis that object A is 3 inches longer than object B without a ruler? Or how are we to test the hypothesis that the excretions of microbe C have a positive relation to disease D without an instrument permitting the identification of the microbe? Or how are we to test the relation between education and political participation without instruments to observe these variables?

The simplicity of these examples should stress the point that the evaluation of hypotheses depends on the existence of methods for testing them. Indeed, progress in science is dependent on the development of new research methods, methods of observation, data collection, and data analysis.

Some social scientists attach little value to methods for fear of being captivated by them. It is, of course, possible to become confined to a method of research if one employs it dogmatically, without regard to the research problem at hand or if the method is regarded as an end rather than a

---

4. Gunnar Myrdal, *The American Dilemma* (New York: Harper, 1944), p. 1043.

means. Even hypotheses that lack methods of testing may have a place in the scientific approach if they are innovative. However, their verification depends on the ability to test them, which in turn depends on the availability of methods of research.

Problems and Hypotheses: Some Examples

Problems are questions about relations among variables, and hypotheses are tentative, concrete, and testable answers. A few examples will further clarify the distinction between problems and hypotheses and illustrate how hypotheses are constructed and expressed.

Problems are general questions. The following are examples of research questions.

- Who rules America?
- What causes inflation?
- Why does bureaucracy threaten democracy?
- Are affirmative action programs achieving their objectives?
- Does school integration enhance educational attainment?
- What factors determine urbanization?
- What causes political violence?

Such general questions are operationalized into a series of hypotheses. For example, the question on political violence has been answered by Ted Gurr with a series of hypotheses, including the following:[5]

- The potential for group violence increases as the intensity and scope of relative deprivation among members of a group increases.
- The potential for political violence varies strongly with the intensity and scope of normative justifications for political violence among members of a group.
- The potential for political violence varies strongly with the intensity and scope of utilitarian justifications for political violence among members of a group.
- The potential for specifically political violence varies strongly with the potential for group violence generally.
- The magnitude of political violence varies strongly with the potential for political violence.
- The intensity of relative deprivation varies strongly with the average degree of perceived discrepancy between value expectations and value capabilities.

5. Ted R. Gurr, *Why Men Rebel* (Princeton, N.J.: Princeton University Press, 1970), pp. 360–367.

Another example of hypothesis construction is from Gibbs and Martin's often-cited study on the causes of urbanization.[6] The authors advanced these hypotheses:

- The degree of urbanization in a society varies directly with the dispersion of objects of consumption.
- The degree of urbanization in a society varies directly with the division of labor.
- The division of labor in a society varies directly with the dispersion of objects of consumption.
- The degree of urbanization in a society varies directly with technological development.
- Technological development in a society varies directly with the dispersion of objects of consumption.

Gerald Hage's attempt to synthesize theory and research in the field of complex organizations is an excellent illustration of hypotheses arrived at deductively.[7] Hage translated some key ideas in Max Weber's theory of bureaucracy into variables. For example, the concept of "hierarchy of authority" was translated as the degree of organizational centralization, and the concept of "rules and procedures" was translated into the variable degree of formalization (how much the behavior of each job is codified into rules and regulations). This enabled the construction of three major hypotheses:

- The greater the centralization in organizations, the greater the volume of production, and vice versa.
- The greater the centralization, the greater the efficiency, and vice versa.
- The greater the centralization, the greater the formalization, and vice versa.

Weber's evolutionary perspective on bureaucracies is expressed in the "vice versa" parts of the hypotheses. Hage also used Chester Barnard's theory of organization, translating the idea of "status system" into the variable *stratification*—the concentration of rewards and the amount of upward mobility in organizations. This led to three more significant hypotheses:

- The higher the stratification, the lower the morale.
- The higher the stratification, the higher the production.
- The higher the stratification, the lower the innovation.

From these six basic hypotheses, Hage deduced some 20 more, synthesizing major ideas in theories of organizations in an empirically testable way.

6. Jack P. Gibbs and Walter T. Martin, "Urbanization, Technology, and the Division of Labor: International Patterns," in *Urbanism, Urbanization and Change,* ed. Paul Meadows and Ephraim H. Mizruchi, 2d ed. (Reading, Mass.: Addison-Wesley, 1976), pp. 132–145.

7. Gerald Hage, *Theories of Organizations: Forms, Process, and Transformation* (New York: Wiley–Interscience, 1980), pp. 36–40.

Sources of Research and Hypotheses

Research problems and hypotheses can be derived in many ways—from theories, directly from observation, intuitively—singly or in combination. Probably the greatest source of problems and hypotheses is the professional literature. A critical review of the professional literature familiarizes the researcher with the current state of knowledge; with problems and hypotheses that others have studied; with concepts, theories, major variables, and conceptual and operational definitions; and with the research methods used. This also contributes to the cumulative nature of scientific knowledge.

Since thousands of articles and books in the social sciences are published every year, it is best to begin any search with one of the guides to published literature. These guides are increasingly computerized and include bibliographies, indexes, and abstracts.

Bibliographies, Indexes, and Abstracts

The following are useful reference books, bibliographies, and indexes for published professional literature in the social sciences:

- Sheehy, Eugene P., ed. *Guide to Reference Books*. 10th ed. Chicago: American Library Association, 1986.
- The library card catalog and subject guide. (Many universities have computerized their card catalogs with online database programs. One can use a terminal to check bibliographic information and to find out whether the library owns the item.)
- The following reference works list the complete publication information necessary to find the literature being sought.

Biography Index	*National Union Card Catalogue*
Book Review Index	*Public Affairs Information Service Bulletin*
Cumulative Book Index	
Education Index	*Social Science Citation Index (SSCI)*
Index of Economic Journals	
International Bibliography of the Social Sciences	*Social Sciences Index*

- Abstracts contain short summaries of the works cited.

Current Contents in the Social Behavioral Sciences	*Psychological Abstracts*
	Public Administration Abstracts
Dissertation Abstracts International	*Public Policy: A Guide to Information Services*
Historical Abstracts	*Resources in Education*
International Political Science Abstracts	*SAGE Urban Studies Abstracts*
Journal of Economic Abstracts	*Social Work Research and Abstracts*
Political Science Abstracts	*Sociological Abstracts*

Professional Journals

Today there are so many social science journals that one must use abstracts, indexes, and other guides to locate the literature of interest. These are some of the major journals, arranged by discipline.

Political Science

American Journal of Political Science
American Political Science Review
American Politics Quarterly
British Journal of Political Science
Canadian Journal of Political Science
Canadian Journal of Political and Social Theory
Comparative Political Studies
Comparative Politics
European Journal of Political Research
International Studies Quarterly

Journal of Political Psychology
Journal of Politics
Policy Sciences
Policy Studies Journal
Policy Studies Review
Political Science Quarterly
Polity
Public Interest
Public Opinion Quarterly
Public Policy
Urban Affairs Quarterly
Western Political Quarterly
World Politics

Sociology

American Journal of Sociology
American Sociological Review
British Journal of Sociology
Canadian Review of Sociology and Anthropology
Human Relations
International Journal of Comparative Sociology

Journal of Mathematical Sociology
Journal of Social Issues
Social Forces
Social Problems
Social Science Quarterly
Sociological Quarterly
Sociometry

Psychology

American Behavioral Scientist
Canadian Journal of Psychology
Journal of Applied Behavioral Research
Journal of Applied Psychology

Journal of Applied Social Psychology
Journal of Personality and Social Psychology
Psychological Bulletin
Psychological Reviews

Public Administration and Management

Academy of Management Journal
Administrative Science Quarterly
Administration and Society
Advanced Management Journal

American Public Administration Review
Canadian Journal of Administrative Sciences

Decision Sciences
Evaluation
Evaluation Quarterly
Harvard Business Review

Management Science
Personnel Administration
Public Administration Review

Economics and Business

American Economic Review
Bell Journal of Economics and
  Management Science
Econometrica
Economic Journal
Fortune

Journal of Political Economy
Quarterly Journal of Economics
Review of Economics and Statis-
  tics
Socioeconomic Planning Sciences

Social Work

Criminology
Social Work
Social Service Review

Social Work Research and Ab-
  stracts
Journal of Social Service Research

Statistical Sourcebooks

The following are useful statistical sourcebooks and government publications.

- U.S. Bureau of the Census. *Historical Statistics of the United States: Colonial Times to 1970.* Washington, D.C.: U.S. Government Printing Office, 1975. Arranged in 26 chapters: population; vital statistics and health and medical care; migration; labor; prices and price indexes; national income and wealth; consumer income and expenditures; social statistics; land, water, and climate; agriculture; forestry and fisheries; minerals; construction and housing; manufactures; transportation; communication; power; distribution and services; foreign trade and other international transactions; business enterprise; productivity and technological development; banking and finance; government; colonial statistics. Index of names and subjects.

- U.S. Bureau of the Census. *Statistical Abstract of the United States.* Washington, D.C.: U.S. Government Printing Office. Published annually. Arranged in 33 sections: population; vital statistics, health, and nutrition; immigration and naturalization; education; law enforcement, federal courts, and prisons; area, geography, and climate; public lands, parks, recreation, and travel; labor force, employment, and earnings; national defense and veterans affairs; social insurance and welfare services; income, expenditures, and wealth; prices; elections; federal government finances and employment; state and local government finances and employment; banking, finance, and insurance; business enterprise; communications; power; science; transportation—land; transportation—air and water; agriculture—farms, land, and finances; agriculture—production, marketing, and trade; forests and forest products; fisheries; mining and mineral products; construction and housing; manufactures; distribution and services; foreign commerce and aid; outlying areas under the jurisdiction of the United States; comparative international statistics. Six appendixes. Index of names and subjects.

- U. S. Bureau of the Census. *United States Census of Population by States*. Washington, D.C.: U.S. Government Printing Office. Published every ten years. Contains the following information for most urban places of 2,500 inhabitants or more: population by sex; major occupational groups by sex; color of population by sex; age of population by sex; years of school completed; marital status of males and females, 14 years of age and older; country of birth of foreign-born whites.

- Zarozny, Sharon and Monica Horner. *The Federal Data Base Finder: A Directory of Free and Fee-based Data Bases and Files Available from the Federal Government*. Chevy Chase, Md.: Information USA, 1987.

- U.S. Superintendent of Documents. *Monthly Catalog to U.S. Government Publications*. Washington, D.C.: U.S. Government Printing Office. Published monthly.

- Taylor, Charles L., and David Jodice. *World Handbook of Political and Social Indicators*. 3d ed. New Haven, Conn.: Yale University Press, 1983. An extensive compilation of 75 variables for 133 countries based on indexes covering human resources, government and politics, communication, wealth, health, education, family and social relations, distributions of wealth and income, and religion.

- City directories. Often useful in giving a wide range of information about industries and social organizations of the community. Contain alphabetical lists of persons and typically list occupation and address of each adult.

- *The County and City Date Book*. Washington, D.C.: U.S. Government Printing Office. Lists numerous tables for each county and cities with 25,000 inhabitants or more. Contains tables on such areas as labor force, income, elections, banking and finance, business enterprises, and education.

- *The Municipal Year Book*. Chicago: International City Managers' Association. Published annually. Authoritative reference book on municipal governments. Facts available about the role of city governments (including education, housing, welfare, and health) make it possible to compare any city with other cities on hundreds of varibles.

- *American Statistics Index.* A comprehensive index of statistical publications from more than 400 agencies of the U.S. government.
- *Statistical Reference Index.* Information on state government publications, and on statistical studies by universities and independent research organizations.

Handbooks

There are several excellent handbooks that describe in great detail the sources of problems, hypotheses, and data available to social scientists. These include the following:

- Bart, Pauline, and Linda Frankel. *The Student Sociologist Handbook.* 4th ed. New York: McGraw-Hill, 1986.
- Holler, Fredrick. *Information Sources of Political Science.* 4th ed. Santa Barbara, Calif.: American Bibliographical Center/Clio Press, 1986.
- Miller, Delbert C. *Handbook of Research Design and Social Measurement.* 4th ed. White Plains, N.Y.: Longman, 1983.
- Murphy, Thomas P., ed. *Urban Indicators: A Guide to Information Sources.* Detroit: Gale Research, 1980.
- Wasserman, Paul, and Jacqueline O'Brien. *Statistics Sources.* Detroit: Gale Research, 1982.

Summary

1. Research problems are intellectual stimuli calling for an answer in the form of a scientific inquiry. Problems amenable to research are empirically grounded, clear, and specific. In the problem formation stage, one should also give serious consideration to the units of analysis. Analyzing certain units but making inferences to other units can lead to two fallacies, the ecological and the individualistic.

2. To move from the conceptual to the observational level, concepts are converted into variables by mapping them into a set of values. A variable is an empirical property that takes two or more values. For purposes of research, a distinction is made between independent, dependent, and control variables. An independent variable is the presumed cause of the dependent variable, and a dependent variable is the presumed outcome of the independent variable. Control variables serve the purpose of testing whether the observed relations between independent and dependent variables are spurious. Variables can also be continuous or discrete. A discrete variable has a minimim-sized unit; a continuous variable does not have a minimum-sized unit.

3. A relation in empirical research always means an association between two or more variables. When we say that two variables are related, we mean that there is something common to them. Establishing a relation consists of determining which values of one variable covary with values of other variables. Two properties of relations should be stressed: direction and magnitude. When we speak of direction, we mean that the relation between the variables is either positive or negative. The magnitude of a relation is the extent to which variables covary positively or negatively.

4. Hypotheses are tentative answers to research problems. They are expressed in the form of a relation between dependent and independent variables. Research hypotheses have to be clear, value-free, specific, and amenable to empirical testing with the available research methods.

5. Research problems and hypotheses can be derived from theories, directly from observation, or intuitively, or from a combination of these. But the greatest source of problems and hypotheses is the professional literature. One should stay informed of the major guides to published research, including reference books, bibliographies, indexes, abstracts, journals, and statistical sourcebooks. Most university libraries now offer online database search services.

Key Terms for Review

research problem
units of analysis
ecological fallacy
dependent variable
independent variable
control variables
spurious relation
continuous variables

discrete variables
relation
covariation
positive relations
negative relations
magnitude of a relation
hypothesis

Study Questions

1. Identify two empirical social science problems.
2. What is the ecological fallacy?
3. Write three researchable hypotheses and identify independent, dependent, and control variables.
4. Describe hypotheses in terms of their magnitude and direction.
5. What are some major sources of research problems?

Additional Readings

Alker, Hayward R. "A Typology of Ecological Fallacies." In *Quantitative Analysis in the Social Sciences,* ed. Mattei N. Dogan and Stein Rokkam. New York: Cambridge University Press, 1969.

Bailey, Kenneth D. *Methods of Social Research.* 3d ed. New York: Free Press, 1987.

Bronowski, Jacob. *The Origins of Knowledge and Imagination.* New Haven, Conn.: Yale University Press, 1978.

Gilreath, Charles L. *Computerized Literature Searching: Research Strategies and Data Bases.* Boulder, Colo.: Westview Press, 1984.

Harris, Cooper M. *Integrating Research: A Guide to Literature Review.* Newbury Park, Calif.: Sage, 1989.

Johnson, Janet B. *Political Science Research Methods.* Washington, D.C.: CQ Press, 1986.

Kramer, Jerald H. "The Ecological Fallacy Revisited: Aggregate versus Individual Level Findings on Economics and Elections and Sociotropic Voting." *American Political Science Review,* 77 (1983): 92–111.

Reason, Peter, and John Rowan, eds. *Human Inquiry: A Sourcebook of New Paradigm Research.* New York: Wiley, 1981.

Williams, Martha E., Lawrence Lannon, and Carolyn G. Robins, eds. *Computer-readable Databases: A Directory and Data Sourcebook.* Chicago: American Library Association, 1985.

CHAPTER 4

Ethics in Social Science Research

In this chapter, we discuss the dilemma of individual rights (e.g., informed-consent and privacy) in relation to research in terms of values and costs. We then examine professional and personal codes of ethics and evaluate responsibility for ethical decision making.

I N CHAPTER 1, WE ARGUED THAT THE social sciences are both scientific and humanistic and that social scientists are observers as well as participants in the subject matter of their disciplines. Social science research is not conducted in isolation. Researchers are constantly interacting with a complex and demanding sociopolitical environment that formally and informally influences their research decisions. A central dimension of this environment is the ethics of research.

This chapter discusses the ethics of conducting social science research and ways to ensure the rights and welfare of persons and communities that are the subjects of the studies of social scientists. First, we review the reasons for recent concerns with research ethics. Next, we present three case studies—on obedience to authority, police behavior, and the characteristics of college students—to exemplify some central ethical concerns. We then discuss the ethical dilemma of social scientists—the conflict between the right to research and the right of research participants to self-determination, privacy, and dignity. We also suggest a cost-benefit framework for making ethical decisions in particular situations. Informed consent and the right to privacy are important ethical issues; we discuss them next. Finally, we examine professional codes of ethics and present a composite code for social scientists.

Why Research Ethics?

As the scope of the social sciences has expanded and as our methods of research and analysis have become more penetrating and more sophisticated, concern over the ethics of conducting social science research has been growing. Issues related to research participants' rights and welfare and researchers' obligations have been discussed in each of the social science professions, and most scientific societies have adopted ethical codes that cover their particular domains.

Obviously, conducting research that may violate the rights and welfare of research participants is neither the intent nor the major interest of social scientists. The underlying objective of research is to contribute to the development of systematic, verifiable knowledge. The research process, as discussed earlier (see Figure 1.1), is the overall scheme of activities in which scientists engage in order to produce systematic and verifiable knowledge. However, each of the stages of the research process may involve ethical considerations in addition to the purely scientific ones.

Ethical issues arise from the kinds of problems social scientists investigate and the methods used to obtain valid and reliable data. They may be evoked by the research problem itself (e.g., genetic engineering, determinants of intelligence, program evaluation), the setting in which the research takes place (hospital, prison, public school), the procedures required by the research design (exposure of the experimental group to conditions that may have negative effects on the participants), the method of data collection (covert participant observation), the kinds of persons serving as research participants (the poor, children, politicians, mental patients, people with AIDS), and the type of data collected (sensitive, personal information). To exemplify these arguments more concretely, let us examine three studies.

Obedience to Authority Study

The Milgram study is an important and controversial case worth describing in some detail. Stanley Milgram conducted a controlled laboratory experiment to find the conditions under which individuals would fail to obey instructions from a person in a position of authority.[1]

---

1. The following discussion is based on Stanley Milgram, *Obedience to Authority* (New York: Harper & Row, 1975).

Two people came to a psychology laboratory to work together in a study of learning processes. One was to be a "teacher" and the other a "learner." The real experimental participant was the teacher, who was told that the objective of the experiment was to study the effect that punishment would have on learning. However, the learner, who was seated in a chair with his arms strapped to prevent movement and an electrode attached to his wrist, had been instructed beforehand on how to react. The individual conducting the experiment told the learner that he was to learn a list of pairs of words. If he made an error, he would receive a shock. The teacher observed all this and was then taken into the main experimental room and instructed how to use an impressive-looking shock generator that had an array of 30 switches labeled from 15 to 450 volts. The switches were also labeled from "slight shock" to "danger—severe shock"; at level 28 (420 volts), the label indicated "XXX" in red.

The teacher was then told that he would "teach" the person in the other room by reading to him paired words, such as "*nice—day*" or "*blue—box.*" The teacher read a stimulus word and then four possible responses. The learner indicated which of the possible responses was correct by pressing one of four switches. If the response was correct, the teacher went on to the next set. If the response was incorrect, he was to administer a shock to the learner. The teacher was also instructed to move one level higher on the shock generator whenever a wrong response was given. However, *no actual shocks were ever given to the learner.*

The primary dependent variable in these experiments was obedience— the refusal of the teacher to follow the instructions of the person in authority, the investigator, who encouraged him to continue to administer increasingly severe shocks to the learner, who continued to make errors or failed to respond. The instructions took the form of statements, such as "You must go on. The experiment requires that you go on. I'll take the responsibility." The learner continues to give the same set of reactions to the experimental procedure. He indicated no discomfort until the 75-volt shock, at which time he gave a little grunt. The same was true for the 90-volt and the 105-volt shocks, but at the 120-volt shock, the learner shouted that the shocks were painful. At 135 volts he groaned loudly, and at 150 volts he shouted that he wanted to be released and refused to continue. He gave similar responses but with greater intensity to subsequent shocks, and at 180 volts he cried out that he couldn't stand the pain. At 270 volts he screamed in agony, and at 300 volts he refused to continue giving answers. After 330 volts, the learner was no longer heard from.

The findings of these experiments defied common morality: many research participants were obedient and continued to administer quite painful and dangerous shocks to the learner in compliance with the experimenter's instructions. In one experiment, 26 of the 40 research participants continued the shocks to the maximum of 450 volts, 5 gave 300 volts before quitting, and 8 gave between 315 and 360 volts.

Another important finding in this study was the extent to which the experimental experience induced a high level of stress for the *teacher* rather than for the learner, who was never actually shocked. According to Milgram, "Subjects were observed to sweat, bite their lips, groan, and dig their fingernail into their flesh. These were characteristic, rather than exceptional, responses to the experiment."[2] There was substantial evidence that the stress for the research participants, usually those who were obedient, was extreme. Such stress was acknowledged by both the teachers and the experimenters. Aware of the possibility that the research procedures might have long-term negative consequences on the participants, the investigator took two measures. First, all participants were later provided with a complete, true description of the purposes and the mechanics of the experiment, and a friendly encounter between the teacher and the learner took place. Second, one year after the experiment, a psychiatric interview was conducted with a sample of the participants; no negative effects were detected.

A number of ethical criticisms have been raised concerning these experiments. First, the teachers were under the impression that they were inflicting pain on another individual. Thus their right to full and truthful information about the experiment had been denied. The participants were *initially deceived* about the true purpose of the research. Second, the participants suffered extreme stress; they became seriously upset and nervous, and some even had uncontrollable seizures. Third, some critics charged that as the results were made known, participants might be overwhelmed with guilt when they realized what the results might have been had they really administered electric shocks. Fourth, the experiment was criticized on the grounds that "it could easily effect an alteration in the subject's . . . ability to trust adult authorities in the future," to undermine the participants' trust in authority. Finally, it was maintained that because the participants derived no benefit from being in the obedience study, the experiments should not have been carried out.[3] Although Milgram has responded to these ethical concerns, the issues raised by the critics are indeed valid and important.[4]

Police Behavior Study

In the 1960s, charges of police brutality were frequent in communities throughout the United States. Such charges and actual police behavior toward the public in general had not until then been studied systematically. Albert Reiss decided to observe how police treated citizens. He knew, however, that had the true purpose of the study been known to the individual po-

---

2. Stanley Milgram, "Behavioral Study of Obedience," *Journal of Abnormal and Social Psychology,* 67 (1963): 375.

3. For a more detailed discussion of these criticisms, see Diana Baumrind, "Some Thoughts on Ethics of Research: After Reading Milgram's Behavioral Study of Obedience," *American Psychologist*, 19 (1964): 421–423.

4. For Milgram's responses, see his *Obedience to Authority,* pp. 193–202.

lice officers who were being observed, it would have curtailed police brutality. Reiss, therefore, led the officers to believe that the study mainly concerned the reactions of citizens to the police. In the course of the study, Reiss recorded a substantial amount of mistreatment and brutality on the part of the police.[5]

This study raised three important ethical issues. First, deception had been used to gain access to observations that the researcher would otherwise have been denied. (The individual police officers had not known the true purpose of the study, nor had they known that *they* were the primary units of observation and analysis.) Second, and relatedly, the police officers had not agreed to participate in the study. They had not exercised fully informed consent because they had not known that they were being researched. And third, studies of this type could generate distrust in research participants to the extent that future investigators would find it difficult to obtain information and to gain the cooperation of participants such as police officers.

Characteristics of College Students Study

A study that had a considerable impact on the development of ethical issues in survey research was the American Council of Education project on the characteristics of college students.[6] Designed during the period of student unrest on college campuses in the 1960s, its purpose was to provide information on the attitudes and behavior of college undergraduates during and after their college years. This longitudinal study involved repeated measures of the same individuals and of hundreds of thousands of respondents. Controversy over the project was heightened when questions related to political orientation and activism were included in the survey questionnaire. Substantial attention was drawn to the questions of the possible uses of the data and to the suspicion that school administrators or government agencies might be able to identify activist students by having access to the questionnaire. In this case, the major ethical issue was the participants' anonymity and the confidentiality of the data. These, in turn, are closely related to concerns over participants' rights and welfare, as will be discussed shortly.

Balancing Costs and Benefits

These three studies illustrate that important ethical issues arise before and after the conduct of research. The issues raised by these studies are common and frequent. Research that employs **deception** as a part of the experiment

5. Albert J. Reiss, *The Police and the Public* (New Haven, Conn.: Yale University Press, 1971), and "Police Brutality: Answers to Key Questions," *Transaction*, 5 (1968): 10–19.

6. See Robert F. Boruch, "Education Research and the Confidentiality of Data: A Case Study," *Sociology of Education,* 44 (1971): 59–85, and J. Walsh, "A.C.E. Study on Campus Unrest: Questions for Behavioral Scientists," *Science*, 165 (1969): 1243–1245.

has become commonplace because it offers methodological and practical advantages. Some data are collected without the knowledge of the observed individuals, and the confidentiality of survey data has not always been maintained.

In many cases, social scientists face a conflict between two rights: the right to research and to acquire knowledge and the right of individual research participants to self-determination, privacy, and dignity. A decision not to conduct a planned research project because it interferes with the participants' welfare is a limit on the first of these rights. A decision to conduct research despite an ethically questionable practice (for example, deception) is a limit on the second right. This is the **ethical dilemma** of social science research.

There are no absolute right or wrong answers to this dilemma. The values people attach to the benefits and costs of social science research depend heavily on their background, convictions, and experience. For example, whereas policy analysts emphasize the benefits that can result from accurately predicting the effects of public policies, civil libertarians are always alert to possible dangers to individual freedom, privacy, and self-determination. They tend to doubt that the benefits of any study justify taking even small risks of invading individual rights.

In planning a research project, researchers have the obligation to weigh carefully the potential benefits or contributions of a proposed project against the costs to individual participants. Such costs may include affronts to dignity, anxiety, embarrassment, loss of trust in social relations, loss of autonomy and self-determination, and lowered self-esteem. The benefits of a study are potential advances in theoretical or applied knowledge, gains to the research participant (including monetary compensation), satisfaction in making a contribution to science, and better understanding of the researched phenomena.

The process of balancing potential benefits against possible costs is necessarily subjective. Scientists make decisions about research procedures in accordance with professional and personal values. Our choices are related to our values, and we should weigh these values carefully when making ethical decisions. Furthermore, ethical decisions are to be made individually in each case because the process by which decisions are made is as important as the final choice. The ethical researcher "is educated about ethical guidelines, carefully examines moral alternatives, exercises judgment in each situation, and accepts responsibility for his choice."[7] Within the context of costs versus benefits, two central problems that most often concern investigators are those of informed consent and privacy.

---

7. Eduard Diener and Rick Crandall, *Ethics in Social and Behavioral Research* (Chicago: University of Chicago Press, 1978), pp. 4–5.

Informed Consent

There is a wide consensus among social scientists that research involving human participants should be performed with the **informed consent** of the participants. Informed consent is absolutely essential whenever participants are exposed to substantial risks or are asked to forfeit personal rights. In fact, the U.S. Department of Health and Human Services guidelines governing research supported under its grants require that a signed consent form should be completed if research participants are placed "at risk."[8] Major universities have voluntarily agreed to comply with federal guidelines in reviewing all research conducted in their institutions, whether funded by the federal government or not. The informed consent policy does not preclude the conduct of social science research that involves risk, but it does require the use of informed participants. When research participants are to be exposed to pain, physical or emotional injury, invasion of privacy, or physical or psychological stress or when they are asked to surrender their autonomy temporarily (for example, in drug research), informed consent must be fully guaranteed. Participants should know that their involvement is voluntary at all times, and they should receive a thorough explanation beforehand of the benefits, rights, risks, and dangers involved as a consequence of their participation in the research project.

Reasons for Informed Consent

The idea of informed consent derives from both cultural values and legal considerations. It is rooted in the high value we attach to freedom and to self-determination. People should be free to determine their own behavior because freedom is a good in itself. Advocates of this view might even argue, like John Locke, that being free is a natural right, and restrictions on freedom must be carefully justified and agreed to. When persons involved in research risk a limitation of their freedom, they must be asked to agree to this limitation.

Furthermore, asking individuals whether they wish to participate in a research project reflects a respect for the right of self-determination and shifts part of the responsibility to the participants for any negative effects that might occur in the course of the study. Another reason for consent is based on the argument that mature individuals are best able to promote their own well-being. Because people will protect their own interests, allowing them freedom of choice about participation in research builds into the

8. U.S. Department of Health, Education and Welfare, Public Health Service and National Institutes of Health, *The Institutional Guide to D.H.E.W. Policy on Protection of Human Subjects,* DHEW Publication (NIH): 72-102 (December 2, 1971). See also, Arturo Gandara, *Major Federal Regulations Governing Social Science Research* (Santa Monica, Calif.: Rand, 1978).

situation a safeguard against hazardous research procedures.[9] Finally, from the researchers' perspective, informed consent reduces their legal liability because participants will have voluntarily agreed to take part in the research project.

The Meaning of Informed Consent

Although the principle of informed consent has enjoyed widespread acceptance, its implementation is still inconsistent. This is mainly a result of disagreements about what informed consent means in particular cases. Questions like these—"What is an informed participant?" "How do we know that a person understands the information that is given?" "How much information should be given?" "What if it is extremely important that participants do not know whether they are in the experimental or control group?"—are obviously difficult, and there are no standard answers to them. It is possible and useful, however, to clarify the intent of the informed consent principle in general terms, to point out its major elements, and to discuss some issues involved in its implementation.

Eduard Diener and Rick Crandall define informed consent as "the procedure in which individuals choose whether to participate in an investigation after being informed of facts that would be likely to influence their decision."[10] This involves four elements: competence, voluntarism, full information, and comprehension.

Competence.   The underlying assumption of the principle of informed consent is that any decision made by a responsible, mature individual *who is given the relevant information* will be the correct decision. That is the assumption of **competence**. However, because there are many persons who are not mature and responsible, the problem becomes one of systematically identifying them.

In general, persons are incapable of providing consent if they have impaired mental capacity or a questionable ability to exercise self-determination. Persons considered incompetent include young children, comatose medical patients, and mental patients. When such participants may receive direct benefits from their involvement in a research project (for example, therapeutic treatment), it is considered appropriate for the guardians, parents, and others responsible for such participants to make decisions for them. When direct benefits are not expected and there is some risk of negative effects, many would suggest that the research be prohibited altogether.[11]

Voluntarism.   Compliance with the principle of informed consent will ensure the freedom of participants to choose whether or not to take part in a research project and will guarantee that exposure to known risks is undertaken voluntarily. But establishing the conditions under which an individual

9. Diener and Crandall, *Ethics,* p. 36.
10. Ibid., p. 34.

is considered to be deciding on the basis of free will is a complex task. In research situations that involve institutional settings such as prisons, mental institutions, hospitals, or public schools, substantial influence from persons in positions of authority is involved. For example, a patient in care of a physician-researcher may consent to a treatment because he or she is physically weak or in other ways under the influence of the physician. In fact, the ethics of medical experimentation emphasize voluntary consent, but until recently, researchers have not realized the subtle nature of some infringements on that **voluntarism**. The context for the careful explanation of the need for truly voluntary consent has been set forth in the Nuremberg Code:

> This means that the person involved should have legal capacity to give consent; [the person] should be so situated as to be able to exercise free power of choice, without the intervention of any element of force, fraud, deceit, over-reaching, or other ulterior form of constraint or coercion.[12]

In order to establish conditions conducive to voluntary consent, some observers have suggested that the researcher create an egalitarian relationship with the participants and view the research endeavor as a joint adventure in an exploration of the unknown.[13] Other scientists suggest that the presence of a neutral third party during the informed consent procedure will minimize possibilities for coercion. Still others advise that participants be allowed to consult with others after a request for consent is made and before a decision is reached.

Full Information.   To be satisfactory, consent must be *voluntary* and *informed*. Consent may be uninformed yet given voluntarily or fully informed yet involuntary.

In practice, it is impossible to obtain fully informed consent, which would require the communication of numerous technical and statistical details. Furthermore, in many situations scientists themselves do not have full information on the consequences associated with research projects. If, in Paul Reynolds's words, "there were full information, there would be no reason to conduct the research—research is only of value when there is ambiguity about a phenomenon."[14] This, however, should not imply that the entire informed consent philosophy is inapplicable. Instead, the strategy of **reasonably informed consent** has been adopted.

The federal guidelines are based on the idea of reasonably informed consent. The guidelines call for six basic elements of information to be communicated for consent to be reasonably informed:[15]

11. Paul D. Reynolds, *Ethical Dilemmas and Social Science Research* (San Francisco: Jossey-Bass, 1979), p. 91.
12. Ibid., p. 436.
13. Ibid., p. 93.
14. Ibid., p. 95.
15. HEW, *Institutional Guide to DHEW Policy,* p. 7.

1. A fair explanation of the procedures to be followed and their purposes.
2. A description of the attendant discomforts and risks reasonably to be expected.
3. A description of the benefits reasonably to be expected.
4. A disclosure of appropriate alternative procedures that might be advantageous to the participant.
5. An offer to answer any inquiries concerning the procedures.
6. An instruction that the person is free to withdraw consent and to discontinue participation in the project at any time without prejudice to the participant.

Some of the elements of information included in these guidelines are obviously controversial. For example, disclosure of the research purpose could invalidate the findings; this was the case in the Milgram experiments and the Reiss study. There is also disagreement over how much information must be disclosed. In fact, a study by Resnick and Schwartz illustrates a situation in which giving complete information was found to be undesirable. These researchers told the participants in the study everything about a verbal conditioning experiment before it began, giving them a lengthy, detailed explanation about the research procedures. Many participants never showed up for the study. Contrary to the findings in most verbal conditioning studies, those who did come were not positively conditioned. The study showed that giving participants too much information has destructive effects on the research outcomes.[16]

Questions concerning the criteria for deciding what information should be given to participants have taken on crucial importance. One criterion is the legal framework of what a "reasonable and prudent person" would want to know. There must be full disclosure of all aspects that a person concerned about his or her own welfare would need to know before making a decision. Research participants should always be informed of any potential danger or of any rights to be lost during the study.

A more operationally applicable criterion to determine what information may be relevant to participants is to let a committee representative of potential participants or of both investigators and participants make a selection. Another procedure is to interview surrogate participants systematically and allow them to determine what is relevant information.[17]

Comprehension.   The fourth element of informed consent, **comprehension**, refers to "confidence that the participant has provided knowing consent when the research procedure is associated with complex or subtle

---

16. H. J. Resnick and T. Schwartz, "Ethical Standards as an Independent Variable in Psychological Research," *American Psychologist*, 28 (1973): 134–139.
17. For this and other procedures, see Reynolds, *Ethical Dilemmas*, pp. 95–96.

risks.''[18] Clearly, an elaborate description of the project, even if it is provided in nontechnical language, may be difficult to comprehend fully.

A number of suggestions have been made for ways to ensure that participants comprehend. They include the use of highly educated participants who are most likely to understand the information, the availability of a consultant to discuss the study with the participant, and a time lag between the request for participation and the decision to take part in the study. A common procedure is to provide an independent measure of comprehension by questioning the participants or by asking them to respond to questionnaires that test whether they know the information.[19]

The Responsibility of the Scientist

The practice of informed consent is the most general solution to the problem of how to promote social science research without encroaching on individual rights and welfare. If all the conditions associated with informed consent— competence, voluntarism, full information, and comprehension—are present, the scientist can be relatively confident that the rights and welfare of research participants have been given appropriate attention.

The principle of informed consent should not, however, be made an absolute requirement of all social science research. Although usually desirable, it is not absolutely necessary in studies where no danger or risk is involved. The more serious the risk to research participants, the greater becomes the obligation to obtain informed consent. At the same time, investigators remain responsible for possible negative effects for participants, even if the latter consented to take part in the research. Informing participants does not totally shift responsibility from investigators to research participants.

Privacy

Invasions of privacy are of great concern to all, especially in a time when information is easy to obtain. The **right to privacy**—"the freedom of the individual to pick and choose for himself the time and circumstances under which, and most importantly, the extent to which, his attitudes, beliefs, behavior, and opinions are to be shared with or withheld from others"[20]—may easily be violated during an investigation or after its completion.

In the study of the American Council on Education on the characteristics of college students, we saw that respondents were requested to give pri-

18. Ibid., p. 97.
19. Ibid.
20. M. O. Ruebhausen and Oliver G. Brim, "Privacy and Behavioral Research," *American Psychologist*, 21 (1966): 432.

vate, sensitive information that could have been used by campus administrators and government authorities to identify campus activists. The data were placed in computer storage and made available to anyone willing to pay a small user's fee. To protect their research participants, the researchers separated the identification of the participants from their responses in the data bank. But there still existed the possibility that the authorities might subpoena the information. In this study, the researchers requested private information from students, but they could not guarantee confidentiality in the political climate of the time. Subsequently, the sensitive information was made "subpoena-free" by storing the code that linked the data to individual respondents abroad.

Dimensions of Privacy

Privacy has been considered from three different perspectives: the sensitivity of information being given, the setting being observed, and dissemination of the information.[21] Before discussing a few methods for safeguarding privacy, it is useful to discuss the three perspectives of privacy.

Sensitivity of Information.   **Sensitivity of information** refers to how personal or potentially threatening the information is that is being collected by the researcher. Certain kinds of information are more personal than others and may be potentially more threatening. As a report by the American Psychological Association states, "Religious preferences, sexual practices, income, racial prejudices, and other personal attributes such as intelligence, honesty, and courage are more sensitive items than 'name, rank, and serial number.'"[22] The greater the sensitivity of the information, the more safeguards are called for to protect the privacy of the research participants.

Settings Being Observed.   The setting of a research project may vary from very private to completely public. For example, the home is considered one of the most private settings in our culture, and intrusions into people's homes without their consent are forbidden by law. However, the extent to which a particular setting is public or private is not always self-evident and thus may lead to ethical controversies. For example, to study the nature of the activities of male homosexuals engaging in brief, impersonal sexual encounters in public locations (restrooms), Laud Humphreys assumed the role of a covert participant. He adopted the voyeuristic role of a "watch queen" (warning participants of approaching police, teenagers, or heterosexual males), thus gaining the confidence of the participants and access to their behavior. The license plates of 134 vehicles used by the participants were re-

21. Diener and Crandall, *Ethics*, pp. 55–57.

22. American Psychological Association, *Ethical Principles in the Conduct of Research with Human Subjects* (Washington, D.C.: Ad Hoc Committee on Ethical Standards in Psychological Research, American Psychological Association, 1973), p. 87.

23. Laud Humphreys, *Tearoom Trade: Impersonal Sex in Public Places* (Hawthorne, N.Y.: Aldine, 1975).

corded, and 50 of these people were interviewed in their homes as part of a legitimate social health survey one year later.[23] Critics charged that although the study was conducted in a public restroom, the participants did not initiate sexual activities ("private acts") until they were assured that the setting was temporarily "private."

Dissemination of Information. The third aspect of privacy concerns the ability to match personal information with the identity of research participants. Information about income remains relatively private if only a single investigator is informed of it. But when information is publicized with data and names through the media, privacy is seriously invaded. The more people who can learn about the information, the more concern there must be about privacy.

It is not uncommon for a whole town or a small community to be able to identify participants in a research project even when fictitious names are used. For example, in *Small Town in Mass Society*, Arthur Vidich and Joseph Bensman described the intimate and sometimes embarrassing details of the lives of the residents in a small town in upstate New York.[24] Although the town and the residents were given fictitious names, the individual descriptions in the book were easily recognizable by those involved. Not only was this aspect of the study severely criticized,[25] but the townspeople staged a parade in which each wore a mask on which was written the fictitious name given to him or her by the researcher—a clear indication that the whole town knew the identity of the participants in the book. At the end of the parade came a manure spreader, with an effigy of the researcher looking into the manure.[26]

Researchers must consider all three aspects—sensitivity of the information, the setting of the project, and the extent of the dissemination of information obtained—when deciding how private certain information is and what safeguards must be used to protect research participants.

Like most rights, privacy can be voluntarily relinquished. Research participants may voluntarily give up their right of privacy by either allowing a researcher access to sensitive topics and settings or by agreeing that the research report may identify them by name. In the latter case, the informed consent of participants is necessary.

Anonymity and Confidentiality

Two common methods to protect participants are anonymity and confidentiality. The obligation to protect the anonymity of research participants and to keep research data confidential is all-inclusive. It should be fulfilled at all

24. Arthur J. Vidich and Joseph Bensman, *Small Town in Mass Society* (Garden City, N.Y.: Doubleday, 1960).

25. Urie Bronfenbrenner, "Freedom and Responsibility in Research: Comments," *Human Organization*, 18 (1959): 49–52.

26. Diener and Crandall, *Ethics*, p. 62.

costs unless arrangements to the contrary are made with the participants in advance.

Anonymity

Anonymity requires that the identity of individuals be separated from the information they give. A participant is considered anonymous when the researcher or other persons cannot identify particular information with a particular participant. If the information is given anonymously, with the researcher unable to associate a name with the data, then the privacy of the participant is secured even though sensitive information may be revealed. For example, anonymity is maintained in a mail survey (discussed in Chapter 10) in which no identification numbers are placed on the questionnaires before their return. On the other hand, a respondent to a personal interview cannot be considered anonymous because the respondent is identifiable to the interviewer.

One procedure for ensuring anonymity is simply not to acquire names and other means of identifying participants in a research project. Alternatively, participants may be asked to use an alias of their own creation or to transform well-remembered data (for example, by subtracting their birthday from their social security number). Anonymity may be enhanced if names and other identifiers are linked to the information by a code number. Once the data have been prepared for analysis, anonymity can be maintained by separating identifying information from the research data. Further safeguards include the prevention of duplication of records, passwords to control access to data, and automatic monitoring of the use of files.[27]

Confidentiality

Participants in social science research are often told that the information they provide will be treated as confidential, that is, that even though researchers are able to identify a particular participant's information, they would not reveal it publicly. Although investigators have a strict moral and professional obligation to keep the promise of **confidentiality**, there are circumstances in which it may be difficult or even impossible to do so. One of the most important of such situations is when information is subpoenaed by judicial authorities or legislative committees.

In the data collection stage, participants should be given clear, accurate statements about the meaning and limits of confidentiality. The greater the jeopardy posed by the information itself and the greater the chances of subpoena or audit of individual data, the more explicit the explanation given to participants should be. Donald Campbell and coauthors offer suggestions

27. For an excellent discussion of these and other procedures, see Reynolds, *Ethical Dilemmas*, pp. 167–174.

for possible explanations. Where the material solicited involves no obvious jeopardy to respondents a general promise of confidentiality is sufficient, for example:

> These interviews will be summarized in group statistics so that no one will learn of your individual answers. All interviews will be kept confidential. There is a remote chance that you will be contacted later to verify the fact that I actually conducted this interview and have conducted it completely and honestly.[28]

Where full and honest answers to research questions could jeopardize a respondent's interests in the case of subpoena, the respondent should be so informed, for example:

> These interviews are being made to provide average statistical evidence in which individual answers will not be identified or identifiable. We will do everything in our power to keep your answer completely confidential. Only if so ordered by Court and Judge would we turn over individually identified interviews to any other group or government agency.[29]

In order to assure outsiders' access to data without compromising the confidentiality requirement, a number of techniques have been developed. These include the following:[30]

1. *Deletion of identifiers*—for example, deleting the names, social security numbers, and street addresses from the data released on individuals.
2. *Crude report categories*—for example, releasing county rather than census-tract data, year of birth rather than date, profession but not speciality within profession, and so on.
3. *Microaggregation*—that is, construction of "average persons" from data on individuals and the release of these data, rather than data on individuals.
4. *Error inoculation*—deliberately introducing errors into individual records while leaving the aggregate data unchanged.

Professional Codes of Ethics

Regulations guiding social science research now exist at several levels. Legal statutes, ethics review committees in research universities and institutions, the personal ethics of the individual researcher, and ethical codes of the pro-

28. Donald T. Campbell et al., "Protection of the Rights and Interests of Human Subjects in Program Evaluation, Social Indicators, Social Experimentation, and Statistical Analyses Based upon Administrative Records: Preliminary Sketch." Northwestern University, mimeographed, 1976.

29. Ibid.

30. See Henry W. Riecken and Robert F. Boruch, *Social Experimentation* (Orlando, Fla.: Academic Press, 1979), pp. 258–269.

fessional associations are all important regulatory mechanisms. Here we explore the issue of professional codes of ethics and present a composite ethical code for social scientists.

The major professional societies of social scientists have developed **codes of ethics** to assist their members. These codes comprise the consensus of values within the profession. They help the individual researcher because they state and explain what is required and what is forbidden. Ethical codes are written to cover the specific problems and issues that are frequently encountered in the types of research carried out within a particular profession. Codes sensitize the researcher to obligations and to problem areas where there is agreement about proper ethical practice.

Paul Reynolds has put together a useful composite code of ethics based on statements appearing in 24 codes related to the conduct of social science research. Most represent codes adopted by national associations of social scientists. This composite code is reported in Exhibit 4.1. (The figure after each item indicates how many of the 24 ethical codes included that statement.)

Exhibit 4.1
A Code of Ethics for Social Scientists

Principles

General Issues Related to the Code of Ethics

1. The social scientist(s) in charge of a research project is (are) responsible for all decisions regarding procedural matters and ethical issues related to the project whether made by themselves or subordinates (7).

2. Teachers are responsible for all decisions made by their students related to ethical issues involved in research (1).

3. All actions conducted as part of the research should be consistent with the ethical standards of both the home and host community (1).

4. Ethical issues should be considered from the perspective of the participant's society (2).

5. If unresolved or difficult ethical dilemmas arise, assistance or consultation should be sought with colleagues or appropriate committees sponsored by professional associations (2).

6. Any deviation from established principles suggests: (a) that a greater degree of responsibility is being accepted by the investigator, (b) a more serious obligation to seek outside counsel and advice, and (c) the need for additional safeguards to protect the rights and welfare of the research participants (2).

Decision to Conduct the Research

7. Research should be conducted in such a way as to maintain the integrity of the research enterprise and not to diminish the potential for conducting research in the future (3).

8. Investigators should use their best scientific judgment for selection of issues for empirical investigation (1).

9. The decision to conduct research with human subjects should involve evaluation of the potential benefits to the participant and society in relation to the risks to be borne by the participant(s)—a risk-benefit analysis (2).

10. Any study which involves human subjects must be related to an important intellectual question (4).

11. Any study which involves human subjects must be related to an important intellectual question with humanitarian implications, and there should be no other way to resolve the intellectual question (2).

12. Any study which involves human participants must be related to a very important intellectual question if there is a risk of permanent, negative effects on the participants (2).

13. Any study involving risks as well as potential therapeutic effects must be justified in terms of benefits to the client or patient (2).

14. There should be no prior reason to believe that major permanent negative effects will occur for the participants (1).

15. If the conduct of the research may permanently damage the participants, their community, or institutions within their community (such as indigenous social scientists), the research may not be justified and might be abandoned (2).

Conduct of the Research

16. All research should be conducted in a competent fashion, as an objective, scientific project (4).

17. All research personnel should be qualified to use any procedures employed in the project (7).

18. Competent personnel and adequate facilities should be available if any drugs are involved (4).

19. There should be no bias in the design, conduct, or reporting of the research— it should be as objective as possible (4).

Effects on and Relationships with the Participants

Informed Consent

General

20. Informed consent should be used in obtaining participants for all research; investigators should honor all commitments associated with such agreements (10).

21. Participants should be in a position to give informed consent; otherwise it should be given by those responsible for the participant (2).

22. Informed consent should be used if the potential effects on participants are ambiguous or potentially hazardous (7).

23. If possible, informed consent should be obtained in writing (1).

24. Seek official permission to use any government data, no matter how it was obtained (1).

Provision of Information

25. Purposes, procedures, and risks of research (including possible hazards to physical and psychological well-being and jeopardization of social position) should be explained to the participants in such a way that they can understand (7).

Exhibit 4.1 *(continued)*

---

26. Participants should be aware of the possible consequences, if any, for the group or community from which they are selected in advance of their decision to participate (1).

27. The procedure used to obtain the participant's name should be described to him or her (1).

28. Sponsorship, financial and otherwise, should be specified to the potential participants (2).

29. The identity of those conducting the research should be fully revealed to the potential participants (2).

30. Names and addresses of research personnel should be left with participants so that the research personnel can be traced subsequently (1).

31. Participants should be fully aware of all data gathering techniques (tape and video recordings, photographic devices, physiological measures, and so forth), the capacities of such techniques, and the extent to which participants will remain anonymous and data confidential (2).

32. In projects of considerable duration, participants should be periodically informed of the progress of the research (1).

33. When recording videotapes or film, subjects should have the right to approve the material to be made public (by viewing it and giving specific approval to each segment) as well as the nature of the audiences (1).

Voluntary Consent

34. Individuals should have the option to refuse to participate and know this (1).

35. Participants should be able to terminate involvement at any time and know that they have this option (3).

36. No coercion, explicit or overt, should be used to encourage individuals to participate in a research project (6).

Protection of Rights and Welfare of Participants

General Issues

37. The dignity, privacy, and interests of the participants should be respected and protected (8).

38. The participants should not be harmed; welfare of the participants should take priority over all other concerns (10).

39. Damage and suffering to the participants should be minimized through procedural mechanisms and termination of risky studies as soon as possible; such effects are justified only when the problem cannot be studied in any other fashion (8).

40. Potential problems should be anticipated, no matter how remote the probability of occurrence, to ensure that the unexpected does not lead to major negative effects on the participants (1).

41. Any harmful aftereffects should be eliminated (4).

42. The hopes or anxieties of potential participants should not be raised (1).

43. Research should be terminated if danger to the participants arises (3).

44. The use of clients seeking professional assistance for research purposes is justified only to the extent that they may derive direct benefits as clients (1).

Deception

45. Deceit of the participants should only be used if it is absolutely necessary, there being no other way to study the problem (3).

46. Deception may be utilized (1).

47. If deceit is involved in a research procedure, additional precautions should be taken to protect the rights and welfare of the participants (2).

48. After being involved in a study using deception, all participants should be given a thorough, complete, and honest description of the study and the need for deception (5).

49. If deception is not revealed to the participants, for humane or scientific reasons, the investigator has a special obligation to protect the interests and welfare of the participants (1).

Confidentiality and Anonymity

50. Research data should be confidential and all participants should remain anonymous, unless they (or their legal guardians) have given permission for release of their identity (15).

51. If confidentiality or anonymity cannot be guaranteed, the participants should be aware of this and its possible consequences before involvement in the research (4).

52. Persons in official positions (studied as part of a research project) should provide written descriptions of their official roles, duties, and so forth (which need not be treated as confidential information) and provided with a copy of the final report on the research (1).

53. Studies designed to provide descriptions of aggregates or collectivities should always guarantee anonymity to individual respondents (1).

54. "Privacy" should always be considered from the perspective of the participant and the participant's culture (1).

55. Material stored in data banks should not be used without the permission of the investigator who originally gathered the data (1).

56. If promises of confidentiality are honored, investigators need not withhold information on misconduct of participants or organizations (1).

57. Specific procedures should be developed for organizing data to ensure anonymity of participants (1).

Benefits to Participants

58. A fair return should be offered for all services of participants (1).

59. Increased self-knowledge, as a benefit to the participants, should be incorporated as a major part of the research design or procedures (1).

60. Copies or explanations of the research should be provided to all participants (2).

61. Studies of aggregates or cultural subgroups should produce knowledge which will benefit them (1).

Effects on Aggregates or Communities

62. Investigators should be familiar with, and respect, the host cultures in which studies are conducted (1).

63. Investigators should cooperate with members of the host society (1).

64. Investigators should consider, in advance, the potential effects of the research

---

Exhibit 4.1 *(continued)*

---

on the social structure of the host community and the potential changes in influence of various groups or individuals by virtue of the conduct of the study (1).

65. Investigators should consider, in advance, the potential effects of the research and the report on the population or subgroup from which participants are drawn (1).

66. Participants should be aware, in advance, of potential effects upon aggregates or cultural subgroups which they represent (1).

67. The interests of collectivities and social systems of all kinds should be considered by the investigator (1).

Interpretations and Reporting of the Results of the Research

68. All reports of research should be public documents, freely available to all (4).

69. Research procedures should be described fully and accurately in reports, including all evidence regardless of the support it provides for the research hypotheses; conclusions should be objective and unbiased (14).

70. Full and complete interpretations should be provided for all data and attempts made to prevent misrepresentations in writing research reports (6).

71. Sponsorship, purpose, sources of financial support, and investigators responsible for the research should be made clear in all publications related thereto (3).

72. If publication may jeopardize or damage the population studied and complete disguise is impossible, publication should be delayed (2).

73. Cross-cultural studies should be published in the language and journals of the host society, in addition to publication in other languages and other societies (2).

74. Appropriate credit should be given to all parties contributing to the research (9).

75. Full, accurate disclosure of all published sources bearing on or contributing to the work is expected (8).

76. Publication of research findings on cultural subgroups should include a description in terms understood by the participants (2).

77. Whenever requested, raw data or other original documentation should be made available to qualified investigators (1).

78. Research with scientific merit should always be submitted for publication and not withheld from public presentation unless the quality of research or analysis is inadequate (1).

Reprinted with permission from Paul Davidson Reynolds, *Ethical Dilemmas and Social Science Research* (San Francisco: Jossey-Bass, 1979), pp. 443–448.

Summary

1. Since the social sciences are both scientific and humanistic, a fundamental ethical dilemma exists: How are we to develop systematic, verifiable knowledge when research procedures may infringe on the rights and welfare

of individuals? There are no absolute right or wrong answers to this dilemma.

2. The values that we attach to the potential benefits and costs of social science research depend on our backgrounds, convictions, and experience. Nonetheless, a broad consensus has been emerging as is evident from the ethical codes of professional societies. These codes state what is required and what is forbidden. Although they sensitize researchers to their obligations and to problem areas where there is agreement about proper ethical practice, there is no substitute for the personal code of ethics of the individual investigator. The ethical researcher is educated about ethical guidelines, thoroughly examines the costs and potential benefits of the research project, exercises judgment in each situation, and accepts responsibility for his or her choice.

3. Within this ethical decision-making framework, two common issues are informed consent and privacy. Informed consent is the most general solution to the problem of how to promote social science research without encroaching on individual rights and welfare. It is the procedure whereby individuals choose whether to participate in a research project after being informed of the facts that would be likely to influence their decision. Informed consent involves four basic aspects: competence, voluntarism, full information, and comprehension. The more serious the risk to research participants, the greater the obligation to obtain informed consent becomes.

4. The right to privacy can be easily violated during an investigation or after its completion. In deciding how private given information is, one should consider three criteria: the sensitivity of the information, the setting being observed, and the extent of dissemination of the information. Two common ways to protect the privacy of research participants are to maintain their anonymity and to keep the data confidential.

Key Terms for Review

deception	comprehension
ethical dilemma	right to privacy
informed consent	sensitivity of information
competence	anonymity
voluntarism	confidentiality
reasonably informed consent	codes of ethics

Study Questions

1. Why do ethical concerns often arise in the conduct of research?
2. List several costs and benefits of research that an investigator must weigh in deciding whether the benefits of a research project outweigh its costs to participants.

3. Discuss in detail the nature of informed consent.
4. How can we protect the privacy of individuals without avoiding sensitive research topics?
5. Distinguish between the guarantees of anonymity and confidentiality for research participants.

Additional Readings

Beauchamp, Tom L., et al., eds. *Ethical Issues in Social Science Research.* Baltimore: Johns Hopkins University Press, 1982.

Bermant, Gordon, Herbert C. Kelman, and Donald P. Warwick, eds. *The Ethics of Social Intervention.* New York: Wiley, 1978.

Boruch, Robert F., and Joe S. Cecil. *Assuring the Confidentiality of Social Research Data.* Philadelphia: University of Pennsylvania Press, 1979.

Faden, Ruth R. *A History and Theory of Informed Consent.* New York: Oxford University Press, 1986.

Gubrium, Jaber F., and David Silverman, eds. *The Politics of Field Research.* Newbury Park, Calif.: Sage, 1989.

Kelman, Herbert C. *A Time to Speak: On Human Values and Social Research.* San Francisco: Jossey-Bass, 1968.

Kimmel, Allan J. *Ethics and Values in Applied Social Research.* Newbury Park, Calif.: Sage, 1988.

Lappe, M. "Accountability in Science." *Science*, 187 (1975): 696–698.

Punch, Maurice. *The Politics and Ethics of Field Work.* Newbury Park, Calif.: Sage, 1986.

Sieber, Joan E., ed. *The Ethics of Social Research.* New York: Springer-Verlag, 1982.

PART II

Design and Structure
of Research

CHAPTER 5

Research Designs: Experiments

In this chapter, we take the classic experimental design as a general model of proof. We then address issues of internal and external validity as they pertain to various designs. Finally, we examine experimental designs to study effects extended in time, as well as factorial designs.

ONCE THE RESEARCH OBJECTIVES HAVE been determined, the hypotheses explained, and the variables defined, the researcher confronts the problem of constructing a research design that will make it possible to test the hypotheses. A research design is the program that guides the investigator in the process of collecting, analyzing, and interpreting observations. It is a logical model of proof that allows the researcher to draw inferences concerning causal relations among the variables under investigation. The research design also defines the domain of generalizability, that is, whether the obtained interpretations can be generalized to a larger population or to different situations.

In this chapter, we first discuss the research design as a logical model of causal inference and then distinguish among several research designs. First, we give an example of how an experimental research design is implemented. In the second section, we explain the structure of experimental designs. The third section examines the four components of research designs: comparison, manipulation, control, and generalizability. Finally, we present some commonly used experimental designs.

The Research Design: An Example

Any researcher who is about to test a hypothesis faces some fundamental problems that must be solved before the project can be started: Whom shall we study? What shall we observe? When will observations be made? How will the data be collected? The **research design** is the "blueprint" that enables the investigator to come up with solutions to these problems. It is a logical model of proof that guides the investigator in the various stages of the research.

Our purpose here is to describe the processes involved in designing a study and to demonstrate how a decision to adopt a specific research design helps to structure the collection, analysis, and interpretation of data. We will describe research based on an experimental design summarized in the book *Pygmalion in the Classroom*.[1] This study was an attempt to test the effect that others' expectations have on a person's behavior. The central idea of the study was that one person's expectations for another's behavior may serve as a self-fulfilling prophecy. This is not a new idea, and we can find many anecdotes and theories to support it. The most notable example is George Bernard Shaw's play *Pygmalion* (1916). To use Shaw's own words:

> You see, really and truly, apart from the things anyone can pick up (the dressing and the proper way of speaking, and so on), the difference between a lady and a flower girl is not how she behaves, but how she's treated. I shall always be a flower girl to Professor Higgins, because he always treats me as a flower girl, and always will; but I know I can be a lady to you, because you always treat me as a lady, and always will.

Many studies on animal behavior support Shaw's shrewd observations. In these studies, when experimenters expected their animal subjects to be genetically inferior, these animals performed poorly. However, when the experimenters expected the animals to be genetically superior, the animals excelled in their performance. In reality, there were no genetic differences between the two groups of animals.

Rosenthal and Jacobson, who conducted the *Pygmalion in the Classroom* study, argued that if animal subjects believed to be brighter actually became brighter because of their trainers' expectations, then it might also be true that schoolchildren believed by their teachers to be brighter would indeed become brighter because of their teachers' expectations.

To test this hypothesis, the investigators selected one school—Oak School—as a laboratory in which the experiment would be carried out. Oak was a public elementary school in a lower-class community. On theoretical

1. Robert Rosenthal and Lenore Jacobson, *Pygmalion in the Classroom* (New York: Holt, Rinehart and Winston, 1968); see also Babad, E. Y., J. Inbar, and R. Rosenthal, "Pygmalion, Galatea, and the Golem: Investigations of Biased and Unbiased Teachers," *Journal of Educational Psychology*, 74 (1982): 459–474.

grounds, the study had to examine the effects of teachers' favorable or unfavorable expectations on their pupils' intellectual competence. However, on ethical grounds, only the hypothesis that teachers' favorable expectations will lead to an increase in intellectual competence was tested.

The independent variable of the study was the expectations held by the teachers. The expectations were manipulated by the investigators by using the results of a standard nonverbal test of intelligence. This test was presented to the teachers as one that would predict intellectual "blooming." At the beginning of the school year, following schoolwide pretesting, the teachers were given the names of about 20 percent of Oak School's children, in their respective classrooms, who in the academic year ahead would supposedly show dramatic intellectual growth. These predictions were allegedly made on the basis of these children's scores on the "intellectual blooming" test. However, the names of the potential bloomers were actually chosen randomly. Thus the difference between the potential bloomers and the ordinary children was only in the mind of the teacher.

The dependent variable was the intellectual ability of the children. It was measured by using the standard IQ test that allegedly predicted intellectual growth. All the children of Oak School were retested with the same test after a full academic year. (The tests were given after one semester and after two academic years, but we will refer here only to the first retest.) Gains in IQ from the first to the second testing were computed for the potential bloomers, and for all the other children. Advantage resulting from positive teachers' expectations was defined by the degree to which IQ gains by the "special" children exceeded gains by all other children. After the first year of the experiment, a significant gain was observed among the potential bloomers, especially those in the first and second grades.

In interpreting the results of the experiment, Rosenthal and Jacobson concluded that the teachers' favorable expectations for the potential bloomers accounted for their significant gain in IQ. In summarizing their results, the investigators attempted to account for this process:

> We may say that by what she said, by how and when she said it, by her facial expression, postures, and perhaps by her touch, the teacher may have communicated to the children of the experimental group that she expected improved intellectual performance. Such communications together with possible changes in teaching techniques may have helped the child learn by changing his self-concept, his expectations of his own behavior, and his motivation, as well as his cognitive style and skills.[2]

Let us now introduce some of the terms employed in discussions on experimental research designs while looking at the *Pygmalion* experiment as an example of a classic experimental design.

---

2. Rosenthal and Jacobson, *Pygmalion in the Classroom*, p. 180.

The Classic Experimental Design

The **classic research design** consists of two comparable groups: an **experimental group** and a **control group**. These two groups are equivalent except that the experimental group is exposed to the independent variable (also termed the treatment) and the control group is not. Assignment of cases to either the experimental or the control group is based on chance—cases are randomly assigned to either group. To assess the effect of the independent variable, researchers take measurements on the dependent variable, designated as scores, twice from each group. One measurement, the **pretest**, is taken prior to the introduction of the independent variable in the experimental group; a second, the **posttest**, is taken after exposure has taken place. The difference in measurements between posttest and pretest is compared in each of the two groups. If the difference in the experimental group is significantly larger than in the control group, it is inferred that the independent variable is causally related to the dependent variable.

The classic design is often diagrammed as in Table 5.1, where X designates the independent variable; O_1, . . ., O_4, the measurements on the dependent variable; R, the random assignment of subjects to the experimental group and the control group; and d_e and d_c, the difference between the posttest and the pretest in each group.

Why Study Experiments?

The classic experimental design is usually associated with research in the biological and physical sciences. We are used to associating experiments with scientific study rather than with the study of group behavior or voters' political preferences. Why, then, do we spend considerable time discussing experiments in the social sciences? The reasons are twofold. First, the classic experimental design helps us understand the logic of *all* research designs; it is a model against which we can evaluate other designs. Second, the significance of the experiment is that it allows the investigator to draw causal inferences and observe, with relatively little difficulty, whether or not the independent variable caused changes in the dependent variable. With other research designs, this cannot be easily determined. Thus when we understand the structure and logic of the classic experimental design, we can also understand the limitations of other designs.

Table 5.1
The Classic Experimental Design

		Pretest		Posttest	Difference
Experimental group	R	O_1	X	O_2	$O_2 - O_1 = d_e$
Control group	R	O_3		O_4	$O_4 - O_3 = d_c$

The experiment is used less widely in the social sciences, primarily because its rigid structure often cannot be adapted to social science research. Thus social scientists frequently use designs that are weaker for drawing causal inferences but are more appropriate to the type of problems they examine. Designs identified as quasi-experiments (discussed in Chapter 6) are more common.

Yet, as we see from the examples in this discussion, experiments certainly are used in the social sciences. As a matter of fact, in some social science fields, such as social psychology, experiments are the predominant design. Moreover, the use of experiments has become more widespread in policy analysis and evaluation research.

The Structure of the Classic Experimental Design

To illustrate the application of the classic experimental design in a social setting, let us examine again the Rosenthal and Jacobson study on the self-fulfilling prophecy. All the Oak School children participated in the experiment. The children defined by the investigator as potential bloomers were in the *experimental group*, and all the other children were in the *control group*. The decision as to who would be in either group was determined randomly (designated R in Table 5.1). Children were randomly assigned to the experimental group or the control group. Twenty percent of the Oak School children were in the experimental group, and all the rest were in the control group. All the children were pretested (designated O_1 and O_3) with the standard nonverbal test of intelligence. Following the pretest, each of the participating teachers was given the names of the children purportedly expected to show intellectual growth. These predictions were allegedly made on the basis of an intellectual blooming test and generated the teachers' expectations, the independent variable in the study (designated X in Table 5.1). All the children in the two groups were retested (posttested) with the same intelligence test after one year (O_2 and O_4), and gains in intelligence were measured. The changes in intelligence were defined as the dependent variable. A significant difference between the pretest and the posttest was found only among the children of the experimental group. This finding led the investigators to conclude that the positive expectations of teachers accounted for the intellectual growth of the children in the experimental group.

Another interesting example based on an experimental design, in the area of policy research, is the Manhattan Bail Project, initiated by the Vera Institute in New York City.[3] The Vera Institute sought to furnish criminal court judges with evidence that many persons could be safely released prior to trial and without bail provided they had strong links to the community

---

3. This account draws on Bernard Botein, "The Manhattan Bail Project: Its Impact in Criminology and the Criminal Law Process," *Texas Law Review,* 43 (1965): 319–331.

through employment, family, residence, and friends. The population examined included persons accused of felonies and misdemeanors; individuals charged with more serious crimes were excluded from the experiment. New York University law students and Vera staff members reviewed the defendants' records of employment, families, residences, references, current charges, and previous records to decide whether a pretrial release without bail should be recommended to the court. The total group of recommendees was split randomly into experimental and control groups, and recommendations were made to the judge only for persons in the experimental group. The independent variable was pretrial releases granted, and the dependent variable was the default rate.

The recommendation for pretrail release without bail for the experimental group was accepted by the judges in the majority of the cases. The results of the experiment were clear-cut. Between 1961 and 1964, when the experiment ended, less than 1 percent of the experimental group failed to show up in court for trial—a rate considerably lower than that for similarly charged defendants who had posted bail, suggesting that the relaxation of the bail requirement did not result in unacceptable default rates. Following this experiment, the New York Probation Department extended this program to criminal courts in all five boroughs of the city.

Causal Inferences

Both the *Pygmalion* experiment and the Manhattan Bail Project are tests of causal hypotheses. Indeed, at the heart of all scientific explanations is the idea of causality; that is, an independent variable is expected to produce a change in the dependent variable in the direction and of the magnitude specified by the theory. However, an observation that whenever the independent variable varies, the dependent variable varies too does not necessarily mean that a cause-and-effect relationship exists.

Consider, for instance, crime control policies. A major objective of such policies is to deter crime. Now, does the observation that a person does not commit a crime imply that he or she has been effectively deterred from doing so by a government policy? Obviously, the answer depends on whether the individual was inclined to engage in criminal behavior. Furthermore, even if the person were inclined to commit a crime, was he or she deterred by the possibility of apprehension and punishment or by other factors such as the lack of opportunity or peer group influence? Accordingly, even if researchers observe that with the enactment of more aggressive crime control policies the frequency of crimes actually committed declines, they cannot safely conclude that the two are causally related.

In practice, the demonstration of causality involves three distinct operations: demonstrating covariation, eliminating spurious relations, and establishing the time order of the occurrences.

Covariation

Covariation simply means that two or more phenomena vary together. For example, if a change in the level of education is accompanied by a change in the level of income, one can say that education covaries with income, that is, that individuals with higher levels of education have higher incomes than individuals with lower levels of education. Conversely, if a change in the level of education is not accompanied by a change in the level of income, education does not covary with income. In scientific research, the notion of covariation is expressed through measures of relations commonly referred to as correlations or associations. Thus a correlation between phenomena is necessary evidence for a causal interpretation. For example, if relative deprivation is not correlated (does not covary) with violence, it cannot be the cause of violence.

Nonspuriousness

The second operation requires the researcher to demonstrate that the observed covariation is *nonspurious.* As explained in Chapter 3, a nonspurious relation is a relation between two variables that is not explained by a third variable in the analysis. In other words, if the effects of all relevant variables are controlled for and the relation between the original two variables is maintained, the relation is nonspurious. A nonspurious relation implies that there is an inherent causal link between variables and that the observed covariation is not based on an accidental connection with some associated phenomena. As we saw in Figure 3.1, the observed covariation between the number of firefighters at a fire and the amount of fire damage is spurious because a third variable—the size of the fire—explains the covariation.

Time Order

The third operation, *time order,* requires the researcher to demonstrate that the assumed cause occurs first or changes prior to the assumed effect.

For example, in a number of studies it has been shown that the covariation between urbanization and democratic political development is nonspurious. To establish that urbanization is causally related to democratic development, one must also demonstrate that the former precedes the latter. The implicit assumption here is that phenomena in the future cannot determine phenomena in the present or the past. In many cases, there is little difficulty in determining the time order of phenomena. Thus the status of parents influences the educational expectations of their children, and not vice versa; an interest in politics precedes political participation; and depression precedes suicide. In other cases, the time order is harder to determine. Does urbanization precede political development, or does political development occur prior to urbanization? Does achievement follow motivation, or does a change in the level of motivation follow achievement? We shall discuss the methods employed to determine the time order of events, but at this point we merely want to stress the significance of the time order criterion when formulating causal explanations.

Components of a Research Design

The classic research design consists of three components: comparison, manipulation, and control. All three are necessary to establish that the independent and dependent variables are causally related. Comparison allows us to demonstrate covariation, manipulation helps in establishing the time order of events, and control enables us to determine that the observed covariation is nonspurious. Here we shall discuss each of these components separately.

Comparison

The process of comparison underlies the concept of covariation or correlation. A **comparison** is an operation required to demonstrate that two variables are correlated. Let us say that we wanted to demonstrate a correlation between cigarette smoking and lung cancer: that the smoking of cigarettes is associated with a greater risk of getting lung cancer. To examine this, one may compare the frequency of cancer cases among smokers and nonsmokers or, alternatively, compare the number of cancer cases in a population of smokers before and after they started smoking. Or suppose that we believe that television viewing contributes to sexist views of the roles of men and women among adolescents. We should then expect to find covariation of television viewing with sexist attitudes. That is, adolescents who spend more time watching television will exhibit traditional sex role stereotypes. To estimate the covariation of television viewing and sex roles conceptions, we could compare groups of light and heavy viewers, or we could compare one group's sex role conception before and after viewing a television program that portrays traditional sex role images. In other words, to assess covariation, one evaluates the adolescents' scores on the dependent variables before and after the introduction of the independent variable, or one compares a group that is exposed to the independent variable with one that is not. In the former case, a group is compared with itself; in the latter case, an experimental group is compared with a control group.

Manipulation

The notion of causality implies that if Y is caused by X, then an induced change in X will be followed by a change in Y. It is hypothesized that the relations are asymmetrical: that one variable is the determining force and the other is a determined response. For this to be established, the induced change in X would have to occur prior to the change in Y, for what follows cannot be the determining variable. For example, if participating in an alcohol treatment group is said to decrease denial of drinking problems, it has to be demonstrated that a decrease in denial took place after participation in the treatment group. This can be accomplished by some form of control over (**manipulation** of) the assignment to the treatment group so that the researcher can measure the level of denial of drinking problems before and after participation in the group. In experimental settings, especially in laboratory experiments, researchers can introduce the experimental treatment themselves; in natural settings, however, this is not always possible. In both cases, the major evidence required to determine the time sequence of events, that is, that the independent variable precedes the dependent variable, is that a change occurred only after the activation of the independent variable.

Control: The Internal Validity of Research Designs

Control, the third criterion of causality, requires that other factors be ruled out as rival explanations of the observed association between the variables under investigation. Such factors could invalidate the inference that the variables are causally related. Donald Campbell and Julian Stanley have termed this the problem of **internal validity**, which is the sine qua non of research; it refers to the question of whether the independent variable did, in fact, cause the dependent variable.[4]

The factors that may jeopardize internal validity can be classified as those that are extrinsic to the research operation and those that are intrinsic and impinge on the results during the study period.

Extrinsic Factors.   **Extrinsic factors** account for possible biases resulting from the differential recruitment of research participants to the experimental and control groups. These selection factors produce differences between the experimental and control groups *prior to* the research operation. For example, in an evaluation of the effectiveness of employment programs for welfare recipients, the Manpower Demonstration Research Corporation compared welfare recipients who participated in federal job programs with other welfare recipients. They found that these programs increased the employment and earnings of participants and reduce welfare costs for taxpayers. However, a rival explanation for the observed changes in employment and earnings is that the program participants were initially different from other welfare recipients; perhaps they differed in their motivation to seek employment, and this initial difference could have accounted for their high level of employment and earnings.

4. Donald T. Campbell and Julian C. Stanley, *Experimental and Quasi-experimental Designs for Research* (Skokie, Ill.: Rand McNally, 1963), p. 3.

Selection effects are especially problematic in cases in which the individuals themselves decide whether to participate in an experiment. In such cases, the investigator cannot tell whether the independent variable itself caused the observed differences between the experimental and control groups or whether other factors related to the selection procedures were responsible for the observed effects. In fact, many social programs are available on a self-selection basis to a larger target population. Assessment of the effectiveness of such programs is difficult because of the selection effects, among other things. Selection factors must be controlled before the investigator can rule them out as rival explanations. Later we shall discuss methods for controlling selection factors.

Intrinsic Factors.   **Intrinsic factors** account for changes in the individuals or the units studied that occur during the study period, changes in the measuring instrument, or the reactive effect of the observation itself. The following are the major intrinsic factors that might invalidate a causal interpretation given to research findings.[5]

1. *History.* **History** refers to all events occurring during the time of the study that might affect the individuals studied and provide a rival explanation for the change in the dependent variable. For example, in a study attempting to assess the effect of an election campaign on voting behavior, the hypothesis might be that propaganda to which voters are exposed during the campaign is likely to influence their voting. The voting intentions of individuals are compared before and after exposure to propaganda. Differences in voting intentions of the two groups—one that has been exposed to propaganda and another that has not—could result from differential exposure to the propaganda or, alternatively, from events that occurred during this period, for example, additional taxes levied, governmental conflicts, international crises, or rapid inflation. The longer the time lapse between the pretest and the posttest, the higher the probability that events other than the independent variable will become potential rival hypotheses.

2. *Maturation.* **Maturation** involves biological, psychological, or social processes that produce changes in the individuals or units studied with the passage of time. These changes could possibly influence the dependent variable and lead to erroneous inferences. Suppose that one wants to evaluate the effect of a specific teaching method on student achievement and records the students' achievement before and after the method was introduced. Between the pretest and the posttest, students have gotten older and perhaps wiser; this change, unrelated to the teaching method, could possibly explain the difference between the two tests. Maturation, like history, is a serious threat to the validity of causal inferences.

3. *Experimental mortality.* **Experimental mortality** refers to dropout problems that prevent the researcher from obtaining complete information

---

5. Ibid.

on all cases. When individuals drop out selectively from the experimental or control group, the final sample on which complete information is available may be biased. In a study on the effect of the media on prejudice, for instance, if most dropouts were prejudiced individuals, the impression rendered could be that exposure to media reduced prejudice, whereas in fact it was the effect of experimental mortality that produced the observed shift in opinion.

4. *Instrumentation.* **Instrumentation** designates changes in the measuring instruments between the pretest and the posttest. To associate the difference between posttest and pretest scores with the independent variable, one has to show that repeated measurements with the same measurement instrument under unchanged conditions will yield the same result. If this cannot be shown, observed differences could be attributed to the change in the measurement instrument and not necessarily to the independent variable. The stability of measurement is also referred to as *reliability,* and its absence can be a threat to the validity of experiments (see Chapter 7). For example, if a program to improve cognitive skills were evaluated by comparing preprogram and postprogram ratings by psychologists, any changes in the psychologists' standard of judgment that occurred between testing periods would bias the findings.

5. *Testing.* The possible reactivity of measurement is a major problem in social science research. The process of testing may itself change the phenomena being measured. The effect of being pretested might sensitize individuals and improve their scoring on the posttest. A difference between posttest and pretest scores could thus be attributed not necessarily to the independent variable but rather to the experience gained by individuals while taking the pretest. It is known, for example, that individuals may improve their scores on intelligence tests by taking them often. Similarly, through a pretest, individuals may learn the socially accepted responses either through the wording of the questions or through discussing the results with friends. They might then answer in the expected direction on the posttest.

6. *Regression artifact.* The **regression artifact** is a threat that occurs when individuals have been assigned to the experimental group on the basis of their extreme scores on the dependent variables. When this happens and measures are unreliable, individuals who scored below average on the pretest will appear to have improved on retesting. Conversely, individuals who scored above average on the pretest would appear to have done less well on retesting. The most familiar example of this problem is taken from our own experience in test taking. Most of us have sometimes performed below our expectations on an academic test because of factors beyond our control that had nothing to do with our academic ability. For example, we may have had a sleepless night just before taking the test or were distracted by some serious personal problems. These factors, which do not reflect true ability, are defined as errors. It is very likely that the next time the test would be taken,

our performance would improve without any additional studying. Viewed more generally, regression artifact can become a threat to the validity of a study whenever the treatment is expected to produce a change in individuals whose scores on the dependent variable are extreme to begin with.

For example, the Job Corps is considered a successful program for disadvantaged out-of-school youth, providing remedial education, vocational training, and health care. But if enrollees were chosen to participate in the program on the basis of their low scores, it is possible that they will show improvement even without being directly affected by the program simply because they cannot get any worse. There is a risk, then, that their improvement will be erroneously attributed to the effect of the program.

7. *Interactions with selection.* Many of the intrinsic factors that pose a threat to the internal validity of experiments can interact with selection and present added threats to the validity of the study. The factors that are most commonly cited are *selection-history* and *selection-maturation.*

Selection-history interaction results when the experimental group and the control group are selected from different settings so that each might affect their response to the treatment. Suppose, for example, that a study is designed to test the effect of personnel training on the transition of the hardcore unemployed into nonsubsidized jobs. Participants in the program (the experimental group) were inadvertently selected from regions where several industrial plants had closed down just when the training program terminated, making it very difficult for program graduates to obtain employment. Thus it would seem that the program had no effect, whereas it was the interaction of the specific economic condition in the region and the selection of participants from that region that produced these results.

Selection-maturation interaction occurs when the experimental group and the control group mature at a different rate. For example, suppose that the cognitive development of males and females is compared at pretest and posttest. It is possible that the rate of development for females is faster than for males, and this might account for their better performance on the posttest.

Procedures of Control

Extrinsic and intrinsic factors that threaten the internal validity of causal inferences may be controlled by several procedures. Two methods of control are employed to counteract the effect of extrinsic factors. The first, matching, controls for variables that are known to the investigator prior to the research operation. The second, randomization, helps to offset the effect of unforeseen factors. Using a control group helps counteract the effects of intrinsic factors. We shall review each of these procedures.

Matching.   **Matching** is a way of equating the experimental and control groups on extrinsic factors that are known to be related to the research hypothesis. Two methods can be used to match the experimental and control groups: *precision matching* and *frequency distribution*. With the first method (also known as pairwise matching), for each case in the experimental group, another one with identical characteristics is selected for the control group. As a means of controlling the effect of age, for example, for every individual in a specific age category in one group, there should be one in the same category in the second group. Having matched on the extrinsic variables, the investigator can conclude that any difference found between the experimental and control groups cannot be due to the matched variables.

The main drawback in this method is the difficulty in matching a large number of factors. For example, if we wanted to control for age, gender, race, and education, for every Asian male 30 years old with a college degree in the experimental group, we would have to find an individual with the same combination of characteristics for the control group. Therefore, when there are many relevant characteristics that need to be controlled, it is difficult to find matching pairs. Indeed, precision matching often causes a loss of about 90 percent of the cases for which an appropriate match cannot be found.

An alternative and more efficient method of matching is frequency distribution. With this method, the experimental and control groups are made similar for each of the relevant variables *separately* rather than in combination. Thus instead of a one-to-one matching, the two groups are matched on central characteristics. For example, when one is matching for age, the average age of one group should be equivalent to that of the other. If gender is controlled, care should be taken that the two groups have the same proportion of males and females. Thus the two groups are matched separately for each extrinsic factor. Although somewhat less precise, frequency distribution matching is much easier to execute than precision matching and enables the investigator to control for several factors without having to discard a large number of cases.

The most basic problem in using matching as a method of control is that ordinarily the investigator does not know which of *all* the relevant factors are critical in terms of explaining the independent-dependent variable relationship. Furthermore, one is never certain that *all* the relevant factors were considered.

Randomization.   Matching is a method of controlling for a limited number of predefined extrinsic factors. However, even if it were possible to eliminate the effects of all the factors, one can never be sure that all of them have been isolated. There may be other factors that the investigator is unaware of that may lead to erroneous causal interpretations. This problem can be avoided by resorting to **randomization**, a process whereby cases are assigned to the experimental and control groups. Randomization can be accomplished, for example, by flipping a coin, by using a table of random digits, or by any other method that ensures that any of the cases has an equal probability of being assigned to either the experimental group or the control group.

Suppose that a researcher is examining the hypothesis that the participation of workers in the decision-making process of their place of work is conducive to production. Workers are divided into experimental and control groups; the experimental group is allowed to participate in decisions concerning the work schedule and its organization. The production level of both groups is measured at the beginning and at the end of the experiment. The objective is to see whether workers who took part in the decisions are significantly more productive than workers in the control group. However, a difference in the production level can be accounted for by numerous factors other than participation in the decision-making process, whose effect is directly examined. Obviously, a number of personal factors, such as age, physical fitness, intelligence, and motivation, could account for the difference. The highly motivated, the more intelligent, the more physically fit, and the younger workers could be more productive. Without a controlled assignment of the workers to the groups, perhaps the most motivated, intelligent, and fit among the younger participants would volunteer for the experimental group, a fact that might account for the improved production level.

One way to counteract the effect of these variables is by pairwise matching. Another is to randomize the groups by flipping a coin or using a table of random digits (see Appendix D) to decide which workers are assigned to the experimental group and which to the control group. The latter process ensures similar distributions of all prior characteristics of the workers in both groups. It is expected that motivation, intelligence, physical fitness, and average age will have similar distributions in the two groups. Consequently, any difference in production between them can be attributed to participation in the decision-making process of the experimental group. In other words, randomization cancels out the effect of any systematic error due to extrinsic variables that may be associated with either the dependent or the independent variable. The advantage of this method is that it controls for numerous factors simultaneously even without the researcher's awareness of what they are. With this method, the investigator can equalize the experimental and control groups on *all* initial differences between them.

The Control Group.   Intrinsic factors are controlled by using a control group from which the experimental stimulus is withheld. Ideally, the control and experimental groups are selected randomly or by matching so that they will have the exact same characteristics and are also under identical conditions during the study except for their differential exposure to the independent variable. Thus features of the experimental situation or external events that occur during the experiment are likely to influence the two groups equally and will not be confounded with the effect of the independent variable.

We will discuss briefly the way in which each of the intrinsic factors is controlled by the use of a control group. First, history cannot remain a rival hypothesis, for the control and experimental groups are both exposed to the same events occurring during the experiment. Similarly, maturation is neutralized because the two groups undergo the same changes. The inclusion of a control group does not necessarily avoid the mortality problem because the loss of cases might be differential and bias the results. However, the acceptable procedure is to include in the final sample only cases for which complete information is available. The influence of instrument change can be avoided by a control group; if the change between posttest and pretest scores is a result of the instrument's unreliability, this will be reflected in both groups. Yet only when the groups are exposed to identical testing conditions does this method of control provide a solution to the instrumentation problem. Using a control group is also an answer to the matter of testing. The reactive effect of measurement, if present, is reflected in both groups and leaves no grounds for misinterpretation.

The use of a control group will help in counteracting effects of factors that interact with selection (selection-maturation, selection-history, and other interactions) only if it is used in conjunction with methods that control for extrinsic factors, such as matching and randomization. Such methods assure that the group being treated and the control group have the same properties and that they experience identical conditions during the experiment.

Generalizability: External Validity

Internal validity is indeed a crucial aspect of social research. An additional significant question concerns the extent to which the research findings can be generalized to larger populations and applied to different social or political settings. Surely, most research is concerned not only with the effect of one variable on another in the particular setting studied but also with its effect in a natural setting and on a larger population. This concern is termed the **external validity** of research designs. The two main issues of external validity are the representativeness of the sample and the reactive arrangements in the research procedure.

Representativeness of the Sample.   Randomization contributes to the internal validity of a study. However, it does not necessarily ensure the representativeness of the population of interest. Results that prove to be internally valid might be specific to the group selected for the particular study. This possibility becomes likely in situations where the recruitment of cases to the study is difficult. Consider an experiment on college students that is carefully planned yet is based on volunteers. This group cannot be assumed to be representative of the student body, let alone the general population. To make possible generalizations beyond the limited scope of the specific study, one should take care to select the sample using a sampling method that assures representation. Probability methods such as random sampling would make generalizations to larger and clearly defined populations possible, as discussed in Chapter 8. In theory, the experimental and control groups should each constitute a probability sample of the population. In practice, however, drawing a probability sample for an experiment often involves problems such as high cost and high rate of refusal to cooperate.

Reactive Arrangements.   The results of a study are to be generalized not only to a larger population but also to a real-life setting. This cannot always be accomplished, especially when a study is carried out in a highly artificial and contrived situation such as a laboratory. For example, Muzafer Sherif's well-known study on group influences on the formation of norms was designed to assess the influence of the group on individuals placed in an unstable situation in which all external bases of comparison were absent.[6] Sherif created an unstable situation experimentally by using the autokinetic effect, which can be produced in complete darkness. The autokinetic effect is produced when a single ray of light introduced to the room cannot be localized; it seems to move erratically in all directions and to appear at different places in the room each time. The investigator examined the norms as to the movement of the light that were evolving in this context of uncertainty. However, it can be claimed that an experimental situation in which persons are placed in a dark room and are required to respond to a moving ray of light does not represent ordinary social situations and that the observed results might very well be specific to the artificial situation alone.

Various other features in the setting might be reactive and affect the external validity of the study. For example, the pretest may influence the responsiveness of individuals to the experimental stimulus; its observed effect would thus be specific to a population that has been pretested.

Design Types

Research designs can be classified by the extent to which they meet the criteria we have discussed so far. Some designs allow for manipulation but fail to employ methods of control or to provide an adequate sampling plan; others may include control groups but have no control over the manipulation of the independent variable. Accordingly, major design types can be distinguished: *experimental, quasi-experimental, correlational,* and *preexperimental.* In experimental designs, individuals or other units of analysis are randomly assigned to the experimental and control groups and the independent variable is introduced only to the experimental group. Such designs allow for comparison, control, manipulation, and, usually, generalizability. Quasi-experimental and correlational designs ordinarily include combinations of some of these elements but not all of them. Typically, these designs lack possibilities for manipulation and randomization. Preexperimental designs include

6. Muzafer Sherif, "An Experimental Approach to the Study of Attitudes," *Sociometry*, 1 (1937): 90–98.

even fewer safeguards than quasi-experimental and correlational designs, and in this sense they provide the least credibility as to whether two or more variables are causally related. Some commonly used experimental designs are discussed in this chapter; preexperimental, quasi-experimental, and correlational designs will be presented in Chapter 6.

Controlled Experimentation

The classic experimental design presented in Table 5.1 is one of the strongest logical models for inferring causal relations. The design allows for pretest, posttest, and control group–experimental group comparisons; it permits the manipulation of the independent variable and thus the determination of the time sequence; and most significant, by including randomized groups, it controls for most sources of internal validity. However, this design is weak on external validity and does not allow for generalizations to be made to nontested populations. Two variations of this design are stronger in this respect: the Solomon four-group design and the posttest-only control group design.

The Solomon Four-Group Design

The pretest in an experimental setting has advantages as well as disadvantages. Although it provides an assessment of the time sequence as well as a basis of comparison, it can have severe reactive effects. By sensitizing the sampled population, a pretest might in and of itself affect posttest scores. For example, measuring public attitudes toward a government policy prior to its implementation may sensitize individuals to respond differently from nonpretested persons. Furthermore, there are circumstances under which a premeasurement period is not practical. In education, for instance, entirely new methods for which pretests are impossible are often experimented with.

The Solomon four-group design, presented in Table 5.2, contains the same features as the classic design plus an additional set of control and experimental groups that are not pretested. Therefore, the reactive effect of testing can be directly measured by comparing the two experimental groups (O_2 and O_5) and the two control groups (O_4 and O_6). These comparisons will

	Table 5.2		
	The Solomon Four-Group Design		
	Pretest		Posttest
R	O_1	X	O_2
R	O_3		O_4
R		X	O_5
R			O_6

indicate whether X has an independent effect on groups that were not sensitized by a pretest. If it can be shown that the independent variable had an effect even with the absence of the pretest, the results can be generalized to populations that were not measured prior to exposure to X. Moreover, as Campbell and Stanley suggest,

> not only is generalizability increased, but in addition, the effect of X is replicated in four different fashions: $O_2 > O_1$, $O_2 > O_4$, $O_5 > O_6$, and $O_5 > O_3$. The actual instabilities of experimentation are such that if these comparisons are in agreement, the strength of the inference is greatly increased.[7]

An Example: The Selling of the Pentagon.   An interesting application of the four-group design was a study on the effect of public affairs television in politics.[8] Throughout the early 1960s, most political scientists clung to the theory of minimal consequences, which relegated television and all mass media to a position of relative impotence. This position was beginning to change late in the decade when, during the war in Vietnam and the student revolution, television journalism became a new focus. This study addressed the issue of public television and politics. It asked several questions: Does public affairs television affect the national political ethos? Has it fostered cynicism, feelings of inefficacy? Has it influenced a national election?

The researcher adopted the Solomon four-group design to test the impact of a CBS documentary, *The Selling of the Pentagon*, on individual opinions about the military, the administration, and the media. (Actually, there were two sets of experiments—one set for testing effects of the program, the other set for testing effects of the commentary presented at the end of the program. We shall discuss only the first set of experiments.)

To test the program effects, the design included two experimental groups and two control groups. A pretest was administered to some, but not all, of the participants. Posttests were administered to the experimental groups immediately following presentation of *The Selling of the Pentagon*. Control groups were tested just prior to exposure. A follow-up test was administered to all groups two months later. The design is presented in Table 5.3. The pretest and posttest were in the form of a questionnaire, which tapped opinions about the behavior and credibility of (1) social and political institutions, (2) public officials, (3) private citizens, and (4) new organizations. The follow-up questionnaire tapped similar dimensions but was shorter.

The analysis of the results demonstrates some of the practical realities involved in social science research. The Solomon design was originally selected because it provides unusually greater power for controlling virtually all potential factors that might provide alternative explanations for the

---

7. Campbell and Stanley, *Experimental and Quasi-experimental Designs*, p. 25.

8. Michael J. Robinson, "Public Affairs Television and the Growth of Political Malaise: The Case of 'The Selling of the Pentagon,'" *American Political Science Review,* 70 (1976): 409–432.

Table 5.3
The *Selling of the Pentagon* Experiment

	Pretest (Nov. 1971)	Mode of Exposure	Posttest (Dec. 1971)	Follow-up (Feb. 1972)
Group A	Yes	Program	Yes	Yes
Group B	No	Program	Yes	Yes
Group C	Yes	Control	Yes	Yes
Group D	No	Control	Yes	Yes

Adapted from Michael J. Robinson, "Public Affairs Television and the Growth of Political Malaise: The Case of 'The Selling of the Pentagon,'" *American Political Science Review*, 70 (1976): 412.

results. Yet the inclusion of an experimental and a control group that were not pretested raised some serious problems. It turned out that group B and group D, which were not pretested, were far less likely to arrive and participate later on than those who had been questioned earlier. Thus the dropout rate from these two groups was so serious that the investigator had to rely on only the pretested group for the analysis of the results.

The results confirmed that *The Selling of the Pentagon* changed beliefs about the behavior of the American military, rendering those beliefs less positive. The experimental groups perceived the military as more likely to get involved in politics and more likely to seek special political advantage than these subjects had previously believed. The control group showed no significant change on any of the items. The experimentally induced change is significant because it was in the direction of "disloyalty," that is, change in beliefs about governmental misconduct.

The Posttest-Only Control Group Design

Although the Solomon four-group design is a strong experimental design, it is often impractical to implement or too costly, or the pretests might be reactive. The posttest-only control group design is a variation of both the classic design and the Solomon design; it omits the pretested groups altogether. The design is diagrammed in Table 5.4. It is identical to the last two groups of the Solomon four-group design, which are not pretested. Individuals are randomly assigned to either the experimental or the control group and are measured during or after the introduction of the independent variable.

For example, suppose that a researcher examining the effects on attitude change of an educational session about the AIDS virus selects a sample of people who are randomly assigned to either of the two groups. One group participates in a four-hour-long educational program on AIDS; later both groups are interviewed and their responses are compared. Attitudes about safer sex in the experimental group are compared with attitudes in the control group. A significant difference will indicate that the educational session

		Posttest
R	X	O_1
R		O_2

Table 5.4
The Posttest-only Control Group Design

had an effect on changing attitudes. The time order can be inferred from the randomization process used to assign the individuals to the different groups. This procedure removes any initial differences between the groups, and it can therefore be inferred that any observed difference was caused by the educational program.

The posttest-only control group design controls for all intrinsic sources of invalidity. With the omission of the pretest, testing and instrumentation become irrelevant sources of invalidity. It can also be assumed that the remaining intrinsic factors are controlled, for both groups are exposed to the same external events and undergo the same maturation processes. In addition, the extrinsic factor of selection is controlled by the random assignment of individuals, which removed an initial bias in either group.

Experimental Designs to Study Effects Extended in Time

In all the experimental designs described so far, it was assumed that the effect of the independent variable on the dependent variable can be observed immediately or within a very short period of time. But sometimes we can expect long-range effects that are spread out over time. This is particularly evident in policy studies and in research in which the dependent variable is an attitude.

Suppose that we want to study the integration of race and gender into the curriculum and its effect on sexism and racism among students. It is likely that the effect of a curriculum integration project will not be immediately observed and thus the observation of possible changes in attitudes should be spread out over a long period of time. Or say that we wanted to examine the effect of restricting abortion on voting for pro-choice political candidates. The central concern in research on this topic would be to test and specify the conditions under which persons change their voting behavior as a response to more restrictive abortion policies. Yet the change cannot be expected to occur immediately, and thus the assessment of changes in voting behavior will have to be of longer duration.

One solution to a delayed-effect study would be to introduce additional posttest periods, for example, six months or a year later. This is a convenient solution in research taking place in school settings, for instance, where posttest measures such as grades would be collected anyway. However, as Campbell and Stanley have indicated,

Table 5.5
An Experimental Design for Delayed Effect

	Pretest		Posttest	Posttest
R	O_1	X	O_2	
R	O_3		O_4	
R	O_5	X		O_6
R	O_7			O_8

when the posttest measures are introduced by the investigator, the repeated measurements on the same subjects could have the same invalidating effect as the pretest would. Therefore, a better solution would be to set up separate experimental and control groups for each time delay for the posttest.[9]

An illustration is presented in Table 5.5.

The same duplication of the experimental group can be incorporated into other research designs.

Factorial Designs

In all the designs discussed until now, there was only one independent variable (the treatment), which was introduced in the experimental group and withheld from the control group. For example, the independent variables have been an educational program, a film, and a social policy, and the effect of only a single variable was observed systematically. Often, more insight might be gained if the effect of two or more independent variables were studied simultaneously. For example, research on organizations suggests that the size of the organization is related to the members' morale. Larger organizations are more likely to present their members with situations that lead to stress and lowered morale. However, although size is an important determinant of morale, it cannot be considered independently of other organizational variables. The effect of size will be different in different types of organizations. Large organizations vary in structure, and the negative effects of size can be minimized through decentralization.

Examining the effect of more than one independent variable requires a large number of experimental groups and a **factorial design**. Suppose that we use size and decentralization as our independent variables and morale as the dependent variable. If each independent variable had only two possible values (dichotomous variables), four experimental groups are necessary to study all combinations of these two variables. We can diagram the combinations as in Table 5.6.

The four experimental groups have four different "treatments" representing all possible combinations of values of the two variables: (1) large

---

9. Campbell and Stanley, *Experimental and Quasi-experimental Designs*, p. 32.

Table 5.6

Possible Combinations in a Two-Independent-Variable Design

	Size	
Decentralization	Large	Small
High	1	2
Low	3	4

size and high decentralization, (2) small size and high decentralization, (3) large size and low decentralization, and (4) small size and low decentralization. Any of the designs discussed previously can be applied to this problem. For example, in Table 5.7, the posttest-only control group design is applied. The four different treatments illustrated in Table 5.6 are represented by X_1 to X_4, and O_1 to O_4 are posttest measures on morale. As usual, the cases have been randomly assigned to the four groups.

External Validity of Factorial Designs.   The chief advantage of factorial designs is that they may considerably broaden the range of generalizability. Instead of "controlling for everything," as in single-variable experiments, additional relevant variables are introduced, each at two or more different levels. Consequently, the researcher is not restricted by some constant level of each of these relevant variables when generalizing on the effect of an independent variable. Rather, the investigator is in a position to infer that the effect occurs similarly across several levels of the variables or, alternatively, that the effect is different at different levels of one or another of these variables. Factorial designs, then, increase the external validity of experiments because, as R. A. Fisher has suggested:

> Any conclusion . . . has a wider inductive basis when inferred from an experiment in which the quantities of other ingredients have been varied than it would have from any amount of experimentation in which these had been kept strictly constant. The exact standardization of experimental conditions, which is often thoughtlessly advocated as a panacea, always carries

Table 5.7

A Factorial Design to Test the Effects of Size and
Decentralization on Morale

		Posttest
R	X_1	O_1
R	X_2	O_2
R	X_3	O_3
R	X_4	O_4

with it the real disadvantage that a highly standardized experiment supplies direct information only in respect of the narrow range of conditions achieved by standardization. Standardization, therefore, weakens rather than strengthens our ground for inferring a like result, when, as is invariably the case in practice, these conditions are somewhat varied.[10]

Interaction Effects in Factorial Designs.   Another advantage of the factorial design is that it allows us to assess systematically how two (or more) independent variables interact. Interaction is present when the effect of one independent variable on the dependent variable depends on the value of the second independent variable.

For example, if large organizational size is associated with low morale of members *only* in organizations that are low on decentralization, it means that size and decentralization interact. Conversely, if large size leads to lowered morale whether or not the organization is more or less decentralized, the effect of size on morale is independent of decentralization, and there is no interaction. The test for interaction makes it possible to expand greatly our understanding of the effect of independent variables on the dependent variable. It allows us to qualify the conclusion on their effects in an important way because we study the simultaneous operation of the two independent variables.

Summary

1. The research design is the program that guides the investigator in the process of collecting, analyzing, and interpreting observations. It allows inferences concerning causal relations and defines the domain of generalizability.

2. The classic research design consists of four components: comparison, manipulation, control, and generalization. Comparison is an operation required to demonstrate that the independent and dependent variables are related. Manipulation involves some form of control over the introduction of the independent variables, so that the time order of the variables can be determined. Control requires that other factors be ruled out as rival explanations of the observed associations between the independent and dependent variables.

3. The process of control is related to the internal validity of the research design. Factors that may jeopardize internal validity are intrinsic or extrinsic to the research operation. Extrinsic factors are called selection effects. They are biases resulting from the differential recruitment of respondents to the experimental and control groups. Intrinsic factors are history,

---

10. Ronald A. Fisher, *The Design of Experiments,* 8th ed. (New York: Hafner Press, 1971), p. 106.

maturation, experimental mortality, instrumentation, testing, regression artifact, and factors that interact with differential assignment of subjects to the experimental and control groups.

4. Two methods of control are employed to counteract the effect of extrinsic factors. Matching controls for variables that are known to the investigator prior to the research operation, and randomization helps to offset the effects of foreseen as well as unforeseen factors. Intrinsic factors are controlled by using a control group.

5. Generalization addresses the problem of the external validity of research designs. It concerns the extent to which the research findings can be generalized to larger populations and applied to different settings.

6. Experimental research designs are the strongest models of proof in that they permit the manipulation of the independent variables and provide maximum control over intrinsic and extrinsic factors. Two variations of the classic experimental design are the Solomon four-group design and the posttest-only control group design. Other designs allow the study of effects extended in time, and factorial designs permit examination of the effects of more than one independent variable. The advantage of factorial designs is that they strengthen the external validity of the study and allow the assessment of interaction between the independent variables.

Key Terms for Review

research design
classic research design
experimental group
control group
pretest
posttest
comparison
manipulation
control
internal validity
extrinsic factors

intrinsic factors
history
maturation
experimental mortality
instrumentation
regression artifact
matching
randomization
external validity
factorial design

Study Questions

1. Describe the elements of the classic experimental design.
2. Distinguish between external and internal validity.
3. What operations are involved in the demonstration of causality?
4. List and describe the different methods of controlling threats to the internal validity of research.

5. What are three important variants of the classic experimental design? What are their advantages?

Additional Readings

Aronson, Elliot, Marilyn Brewer, and James Carlsmith. "Experimentation in Social Psychology." In *The Handbook of Social Psychology*, ed. Lindzey Gardner and Elliot Aronson. New York: Random House, 1985.

Berkowitz, L., and E. Donnerstein. "External Validity Is More than Skin Deep: Some Answers to Criticisms of Laboratory Experiments." *American Psychologist*, 37 (1982): 245–257.

Brewer, Marilynn B., and Barry E. Collins, eds. *Scientific Inquiry and the Social Sciences*. San Francisco: Jossey-Bass, 1981.

Brinberg, David, and Joseph McGrath. *Validity and the Research Process*. Newbury Park, Calif.: Sage, 1985.

Campbell, Donald T., and Thomas D. Cook. *Quasi-experimentation*. Skokie, Ill.: Rand McNally, 1979.

Davis, J. A. *The Logic of Causal Order*. Newbury Park, Calif.: Sage, 1985.

Kirk, R. E. *Experimental Design: Procedures for the Behavioral Sciences*. 2d ed., Pacific Grove, Calif.: Brooks/Cole, 1982.

Martin, David W. *Doing Psychology Experiments*. Pacific Grove, Calif.: Brooks/Cole, 1985.

Miller, Stephen H. *Experimental Design and Statistics*. 2d ed. New York: Methuen, 1989.

Monk, Melvin M., and Thomas D. Cook. "Design of Randomized Experiments and Quasi-experiments." In *Evaluation Research Methods,* ed. Leonard Ruttman. Newbury Park, Calif.: Sage, 1984.

Ray, William, and Richard Ravizza, *Methods toward a Science of Behavior and Experience*. Belmont, Calif.: Wadsworth, 1985.

CHAPTER 6

Research Designs: Correlational and Quasi-experimental Designs

In this chapter, we discuss designs more common in the social sciences—preexperiments, correlational designs, and quasi-experiments.

THE CONTROLLED EXPERIMENT ALLOWS the most unequivocal evaluation of causal relations between two or more variables. However, many phenomena that are of interest to social scientists are not amenable to the straightforward application of experimental designs. Furthermore, social, political, and ethical considerations may discourage or prevent the conducting of controlled experiments. For example, although we can induce fear in laboratory situations and experimentally manipulate individuals, the question of whether we have the right to do so, even for the sake of science, is extremely important. In general, the experimental design cannot be employed if randomization and experimental control cannot be guaranteed.

Taking the experimental design as the strongest model of logical proof, we shall present a number of designs that are more common in the social sciences. These designs are generally weaker on internal validity, and their causal inferential powers are consequently impaired. They are often referred to as quasi-experiments, correlational designs, or preexperiments. Before we discuss these designs, let us look at the relation between the types of variables we study and the research designs we employ.

Types of Relations and Designs

In Chapter 5, we discussed research examples in which the independent variables could be manipulated by the researcher. Unfortunately, we cannot manipulate many of the variables we study in the social sciences. We cannot manipulate the race or gender of our subjects, nor can we make them younger or older when we wish to study the effect of these variables on some dependent variables. In the social sciences, we usually study the relationships between some *property* and a corresponding *disposition*, for example, the relation between social class and an attitude such as political tolerance or between race and prejudice. In contrast, in fields characterized more often as experimental, the relationships studied are of the *stimulus-response* type. **Stimulus-response relationships** are characterized by an independent variable that can be manipulated by the researcher, for example, the inducement of stress or the exposure of subjects to an advertising campaign. The dependent variable would then be a direct response to the independent variable; for example, it could be a certain psychological reaction to stress or an increase in consumption patterns following the advertising campaign.

Whereas stimulus-response relationships are well suited for experimental investigation, property-disposition relationships are not. The reason lies in the inherent differences between them on four issues: time interval, degree of specificity, the nature of comparison groups, and the time sequence of events.[1]

1. *Time interval.* The first difference relates to the time interval between the effect of the independent variable and the response to it. In a stimulus-response relationship, the time interval is relatively short, whereas with the property-disposition type it can extend over a long period. For example, the response to a drug or an advertising campaign can be observed within a short period, but the effects of properties such as age, race, and social class are not of such an immediate nature.

2. *Degree of specificity.* The second difference is the degree of specificity of the independent variable. A stimulus is usually easy to isolate and identify, and its effect can be concretely delineated. However, a property such as social class is more general and incorporates various factors, including prestige, occupation, and education, each exerting its relative influence. Therefore, it is often difficult with this type of variable to define the relevant causes and to manipulate them experimentally.

3. *Nature of comparison groups.* The nature of the comparison group is the third difference between stimulus-response and property-disposition relationships. In the first, comparisons can be made of two similar groups, one that has been exposed to the stimulus and one that has not, or the same group both before and after exposure to the stimulus. In the second kind of

1. Morris Rosenberg, *The Logic of Survey Analysis* (New York: Basic Books, 1968), Chap. 1.

relationship, a before-after comparison is practically impossible, especially with properties that do not change, such as gender and race. Similarly, it is difficult to assume that two groups having different properties are comparable in any other respect. Indeed, a lower-class group and an upper-class group differ in various aspects other than class: values, orientations, child-rearing practices, voting behavior, and so on.

4. *Time sequence of events.* With the stimulus-response kind of relation, the direction of causation is relatively clear, especially when the research design allows for before-after comparisons. But the time sequence is harder to establish with some properties. With fixed properties such as race and gender, there are more difficulties because these can only be the determining factors, not the determined effects. However, this is not the case with properties that are acquired, including intelligence, education, and political orientation. These properties can both determine and be determined by other factors. All the same, the time order cannot be easily established.

Owing to these difficulties, the components of research designs—comparison, manipulation, and control—cannot be applied to property-disposition relations in the pure experimental sense. Not all the phenomena that are of interest to social scientists can be experimentally manipulated by them. Moreover, units of analysis cannot always be randomly assigned to experimental and control groups, and many social, political, and economic processes can be studied only after a relatively long period of time. Yet social scientists have been trying to approximate the experimental model by employing specialized data analysis techniques that compensate for the limitations inherent in studying property-disposition relations.

Correlational Designs

The **correlational design**, often referred to as the *cross-sectional study*, is perhaps the most predominant design employed in the social sciences. This design is often identified with survey research, a method of data collection common in many social science fields. Survey research (discussed in more detail in Chapters 10 and 11) usually involves asking a random sample of individuals to respond to a set of questions about their backgrounds, past experiences, and attitudes. In most cases, survey research yields data that are used to examine relationships between property and dispositions; and although numerous studies are concerned with establishing causal relations between these properties and dispositions, an important component in many others is simply to describe the pattern of relation before any attempt at causal inference is made.

As an example of a typical problem to be examined by using a correlational design, consider the question of supporting nuclear power production. Attitudes toward nuclear power have important implications for the

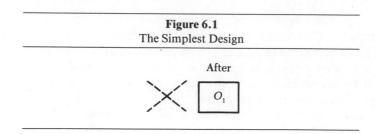

Figure 6.1
The Simplest Design

After

environment and human safety.[2] A consistent finding in many studies is the existence of a large "gender gap" in attitudes toward nuclear power production, with females less supportive than males.

A cross-sectional study would involve obtaining a representative random sample of males and females and asking them to respond to a number of questions about their attitudes toward nuclear power production. This research problem can be classified as a property-disposition type, and as such it is not amenable to experimental investigation. The reason lies in the nature of the variables being investigated, especially the independent variable, gender. Obviously, gender cannot be manipulated by the researcher; hence a before-after comparison typical of experimental studies cannot be made. Moreover, the time interval in which attitudes toward nuclear power are shaped by gender extends over a relatively long period. Because of these limitations, it would be difficult to incorporate into a research design components like manipulation and control, which are necessary to establish causality. This such design may be diagrammed as in Figure 6.1, where the dotted X indicates gender and O_1 indicates attitudes toward nuclear power production. Obviously, such a design would suffer from serious methodological limitation, especially with regard to its internal validity. However, statistical analysis allows us to approximate some of the operations that are naturally built into an experimental design. As a first step, we would want

Table 6.1
Gender and Attitudes toward Nuclear Power

	Male	Female
Support	59%	29%
Oppose	41	71
	100%	100%

Adapted from Lawrence S. Solomon, Donald Tomaskovic-Devey, and Barbara J. Risman, "The Gender Gap and Nuclear Power: Attitudes in a Politicized Environment," *Sex Roles*, 21 (1989): 407.

2. This example is drawn from Lawrence S. Solomon, Donald Tomaskovic-Devey, and Barbara J. Risman, "The Gender Gap and Nuclear Power: Attitudes in a Politicized Environment," *Sex Roles*, 21 (1989): 401–414.

Figure 6.2
The Correlational Design

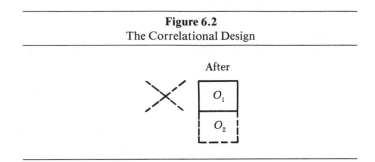

After

to establish that gender and attitudes toward nuclear power are interrelated. Table 6.1 presents the results of analysis designed to assess the relationship between these two variables. We can see that 59 percent of men but only 29 percent of women support nuclear power, giving a gender gap of 30 percent. This observation is based on data analysis techniques called *cross-tabulation* and *bivariate percentage analysis*, which will be discussed in detail in Chapter 16.

By using these techniques, we have improved our design to approximate the posttest-only control group design. This improved correlational design is diagrammed in Figure 6.2. The dotted cell indicates extra information we obtained during the data analysis stage, which allowed us to make a number of comparisons between the different groupings.

Though the correlational design as presented in Figure 6.2 would allow us to assess the relation (or correlation) between gender and support for nuclear power production, we cannot conclude that these two variables are causally related, nor do we understand why females are less likely than males to support nuclear power production. There are a number of explanations for the gender gap; for example, the women in the study may have been less knowledgeable about technological matters and therefore more reluctant to support nuclear power. Or perhaps women's greater concern with safety would lead them to oppose nuclear power more than men. Whereas with experimental design these factors are controlled for by randomization and by employing a control group, with a correlational design these factors must be controlled for statistically. (For further elaboration on this issue, see Chapter 17.)

The most common alternative to experimental methods of control and the drawing of causal inference in correlational designs are multivariate methods of statistical analysis, such as elaboration by cross-tabulation, multiple regression, and path analysis. These methods are discussed in Chapter 17. With cross-tabulation, the original relationship between the independent and dependent variable is reexamined in subcategories of the control variable. Thus to control for degree of knowledge, we would divide our sample into homogeneous groups by degree of knowledge and perform the original analysis, as in Table 6.1, separately for each of the groups. This operation is similar to matching; however, as with matching, its main draw-back is that only known and predetermined factors can be controlled for.

Another statistical technique that provides a substitute for experimental methods is path analysis. This method allows the researcher to analyze more complex systems involving a number of independent, intervening, and dependent variables.

Note, however, that in correlational design, one cannot establish the time order of the variables by performing statistical analyses. The time sequence has to be established by the researcher on the basis of theoretical and logical considerations. The main advantage of correlational studies is that they are carried out in natural settings and permit the employment of random probability samples. This allows statistical inferences to be made to broader populations and permits generalization to real-life situations, thereby increasing the external validity of the study.

Quasi-experimental Designs

Keeping the classic experimental design as a model of logical proof, scientists have developed a number of quasi-experimental designs. These designs are weaker on internal validity than experimental designs, and like correlational designs, they depend on data analysis techniques as a method of control and do not require randomization. They are superior, however, to correlational designs because they usually involve the study of more than one sample, often over an extended period of time. We shall explore the most important quasi-experimental designs in current use.

Contrasted Groups Designs

A common problem in social science research is that in many cases the researcher cannot randomly assign individuals or other units of analysis to experimental and comparison groups. At times, intact comparison groups are used either at the pretest phase only or at the posttest phase. Causal inferences concerning the independent variables are especially vulnerable when groups are compared that are known to differ in some important attributes, as when comparing poor communities with relatively well-to-do ones, groups from different ethnic backgrounds, or males with females. If a posttest-only design is used with such contrasted groups, differences on the posttest measures are likely to be due to initial differences between the groups rather than to the impact of the independent variable. Nevertheless, when differences among such contrasted groups are to be assessed, several elaborations in the research design are possible that can be regarded as safeguards against the intrusion of influences other than the independent variable.

The least elaborate design for **contrasted groups** is one in which individuals or other units of analysis are regarded as members of categoric groups.

(Categoric group members share some attribute that assigns them to an identifiable category, such as males, Democrats, or Catholics.) Members of each group are measured with respect to the dependent variables. For example, one can compare the reading performance of children residing in different communities. This design can be symbolized in the following way, where $O_1 \ldots O_k$ represent measures on the dependent variable:

$$O_1$$
$$O_2$$
$$O_3$$
$$O_4$$

.

.

.

$$O_k$$

Differences in measurement scores obtained for the k groups are amenable to straightforward comparative statistical analyses (for example, difference between means). However, because such contrasted groups differ from one another in many ways, difficulties arise when attempts are made to assess the causes for the observed differences. Relatedly, the groups might differ because of artifacts in the measurement procedures rather than because of any real differences among them. For instance, it has been repeatedly shown that measurements based solely on personal interviews are affected by the interviewers' backgrounds and that black and white interviewers elicit different answers from black respondents. (A more detailed discussion of this and other problems with interviews appears in Chapter 10.)

One way to reduce the risk of being wrong when making causal inferences based on contrasted groups designs is to obtain supplementary evidence over time regarding the hypothesized differences. If the same finding is obtained in other settings and comparisons are made on a number of measures concerning the dependent variables, such supplementary evidence can increase the inferential powers of a contrasted groups design.

A more elaborate design for contrasted groups is one in which two or more intact groups are compared before and after the introduction of the treatment variable. In this design—the nonequivalent control group design—statistical techniques are used to test for comparability between the contrasted groups before causal inferences are drawn.

A recent study evaluating an undergraduate course on AIDS exemplifies this design.[3] The researchers set out to evaluate the impact of a college course on AIDS, AIDS-relevant knowledge, attitudes, and behavior. Two

---

3. Paul R. Abramson, Joan C. Sekler, Richard A. Berk, and Monique Y. Cloud, "An Evaluation of an Undergraduate Course on AIDS," *Evaluation Review*, 13 (1989): 516–532.

	Table 6.2	
	A Nonequivalent Control Group Design	
Pretest		Posttest
O_1	X	O_2
O_3		O_4

groups of subjects were studied. The experimental group consisted of students recruited from the course, "AIDS: The Modern Plague." The control group consisted of students recruited from a different course, "Astronomy: The Nature of the Universe."

A pretest and a posttest were administered: students were asked to fill out a self-administered questionnaire in both classes, at the beginning and at the end of each course. The design used in this study is shown in Table 6.2. Since random assignment to experimental and control groups was impossible, evaluating the course's impact had important methodological limitations. A critical issue, for example, was the fact that both groups were constituted by self-selection. If students in the experimental group had preexisting concern about AIDS, they might have been more likely to adopt safer sexual practices whether or not they took the AIDS course. Therefore, special efforts had to be made to approximate comparability between the experimental and comparison groups. One strategy was to pick a comparison group that would be as similar as possible to the experimental group. Relevant criteria for selecting the control group included (1) cohort effect (both courses were offered during the same quarter), (2) discipline (both courses were listed in the science curriculum), (3) open enrollment, and (4) popularity (both courses had popular appeal on campus).

In addition, using multivariate statistical techniques, the researchers equated the experimental and control groups on age, gender, ethnicity, class, and the pretest, ruling out the alternative explanation that preexisting differences of these factors accounted for differences between the two groups on the posttest. The results of the study suggest that the course on AIDS had a beneficial impact on attitudes, knowledge, and behavior relevant to the transmission of the AIDS virus. At the same time, we stress again the design's limitation: internal validity is jeopardized by the absence of random assignment to the experimental and control groups.

In some cases in which contrasted groups are compared, measures are available on a number of occasions before and after the introduction of the independent variable. In such cases, multiple measures can be obtained before and/or after exposure. Such supplementary data provide a measure of the amount of normal variation in the dependent variable from time to time, irrespective of the independent variable's impact. Suppose that researchers wish to evaluate the effectiveness of a new approach to teaching reading implemented through the fifth grade in school E. They can compare achievement test scores in reading for children in the third through seventh grades

Figure 6.3
Comparison of Two Contrasted Groups Indicating That the
Independent Variable Had a Definite Effect

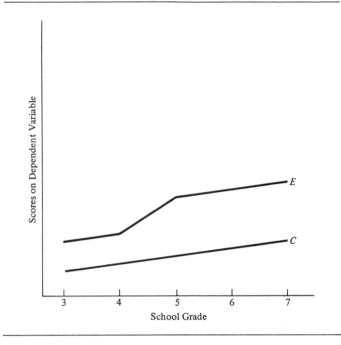

in that school and in another school (C) in the same community that did not use the new approach. The study is conducted retroactively for students who are currently in the seventh grade and have remained in school from the third grade up to that time. Because schools administer achievement tests each year, the researchers can obtain comparable measures for each of the five years. Evidence for a program effect when there are multiple measures over time consists of a sharp interaction from before to after implementation of the program for the units being compared, as illustrated in Figure 6.3.

Unlike the hypothetical results in Figure 6.3, the findings shown in Figure 6.4 indicate that the independent variable had no effect at all on the individuals in group E beyond what could be expected from the usual course of events, as evidenced in group C. The apparent change in group E is illusory because it is matched by a proportional change in group C.

Planned Variation Designs

Planned variation designs involve exposure of individuals to systematically varying kinds of stimuli to assess their causal effects. The Head Start Planned Variation (HSPV) study exemplifies such designs. HSPV was a

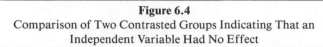

Figure 6.4
Comparison of Two Contrasted Groups Indicating That an
Independent Variable Had No Effect

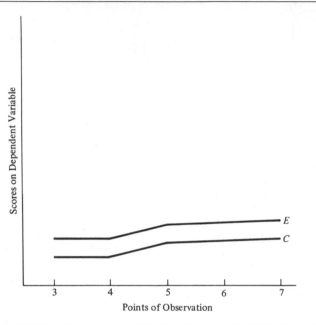

three-year investigation designed to compare the effects that different kinds of Head Start centers were having on the development of the academic skills of children from relatively poor families. The study was developed on the assumption that by selecting "sponsors" for different types of programs and by systematically varying the kinds of programs offered to children, one could discover which kinds of programs most benefited which kinds of children.[4]

Sponsors selected to participate in the investigation had a substantial amount of variation in their goals and their teaching structures. During the 1971–1972 academic year, 11 sponsors were distributed over a total of 28 sites. For purposes of comparison, 11 of the 28 sites also had "nonsponsored" Head Start classrooms. In addition, three sites had comparison group children who were not enrolled in any program. Children for this comparison group were contacted by direct recruitment and from Head Start waiting lists. Each sponsor had two, three, or four sites. Within each site were variable numbers of classrooms run by the appropriate sponsor.

---

4. The following account draws on Herbert I. Weisberg, *Short-Term Cognitive Effects of Head Start Programs: A Report on the Third Year of Planned Variation, 1971–1972* (Cambridge, Mass.: Huron Institute, 1973).

Some sites contained both sponsored classrooms and regular, nonsponsored Head Start classrooms; other sites had only sponsored classrooms.

One major shortcoming of this research design was that a number of important variables were not equally distributed across the sponsors. Herbert I. Weisberg points out that race, age of children, prior preschool experience, and socioeconomic background were all unequally distributed. For example, one sponsor had almost no black children at his site, whereas another sponsor had almost no white children. In spite of this serious source of invalidity, three general inferences were drawn: (1) overall, both the sponsors' programs and the regular Head Start programs tended to accelerate certain kinds of specific academic performance, such as number and letter recognition; (2) pooling the 11 sponsored sets of classrooms and comparing them with the regular, nonsponsored Head Start classrooms showed no large differences; and (3) when the sponsored sets of classrooms were compared among themselves, some differences in performance emerged on the several cognitive tests the children were given. In other words, certain types of curricula seemed to enhance different kinds of cognitive development.

Obviously, these conclusions are suggestive at best because of the unequal distributions of important variables across the sponsors. The confidence in findings obtained with planned variation designs can be increased to a certain extent if the distribution of important variables is equal among the various groups and if measures of the dependent variable are taken on a number of occasions before and after exposure to an independent variable.

Panels and Time-Series Designs

Some quasi-experiments are extended over time to allow for the examination of changes in the dependent variable. We shall discuss two major designs that incorporate time: *panels* and *time-series designs*.

Panels.   A more rigorous solution to the time dilemma in cross-sectional studies and correlational designs is the **panel**, in which the same sample is examined at two or more time intervals. Panel studies offer a closer approximation to the before-after condition of experimental designs by studying a group at two or more points in time before and after exposure to the independent variable.

An illustration of the panel design is a recent study that investigated the effects of children leaving home on parental well-being.[5] Most studies on the effects of the child-leaving phase rely on cross-sectional designs, which limit the analysis of change in parental well-being associated with launching. This research is based on a national sample interviewed in 1980 and again in 1983 and 1988. The investigators followed a sample of 402 parents of older chil-

---

5. Lynn White and John N. Edwards, "Emptying the Nest and Parental Well-being: An Analysis of National Panel Data," *American Sociological Review*, 55 (1990): 235–242.

dren and compared changes in marital happiness and life satisfaction between those who did and did not empty their nest. The main advantage of such a study plan was that it enabled the determination of the direction of causation. With comparison of the measures of parental well-being of the same respondents taken before and after the children leave home, the time order could be determined.

The main problem of panels is obtaining an initial representative sample of respondents who are willing to be interviewed at set intervals over an extended period. Moreover, even if a researcher succeeds in obtaining the commitment of respondents, there are subsequent dropouts, owing to refusals to continue cooperating and difficulties in tracing respondents who move or change jobs. A serious consequence is that those who drop out may change in a different way from the rest of the panel, thus affecting the findings. Another problem with repeated interviews with the same group is *panel conditioning*—the risk that repeated measurements may sensitize the respondents. For example, members of a panel may try to appear consistent in the views they express on consecutive occasions. In such cases, the panel becomes atypical of the population it was selected to represent. One possible safeguard to panel conditioning is to give members of a panel only a limited panel life and then to replace them with persons taken randomly from a reserve list.[6]

Time-Series Designs. In some cases when no comparison group is available for assessing cause-and-effects relations, **time-series designs**—research designs in which pretest and posttest measures are available on a number of occasions before and after the activation of an independent variable—can be used. Usually the investigator attempts to obtain at least three sets of measures before and after the introduction of the independent variable. A typical time-series design can be represented as follows:

$$O_1 \quad O_2 \quad O_3 \quad X \quad O_4 \quad O_5 \quad O_6$$

Employment of a time-series design makes it possible to separate reactive measurement effects from the effects of an independent variable. A time-series design also enables the researcher to see whether an independent variable has an effect over and above the reactive effects. The reactive effect shows itself at O_3; this can be compared with O_4. An increase at O_4 above the increase at O_3 can be attributed to the independent variable. A similar argument applies for the maturation source of invalidity.

A classic study that illustrates the advantages as well as the problems involved with time-series designs is the evaluation of the Connecticut crackdown on speeding following a record number of traffic fatalities in 1955.[7]

6. For a detailed analysis of the advantages and disadvantages of panels, see Robert F. Boruch and Robert W. Pearson, "Assessing the Quality of Longitudinal Surveys" *Evaluation Review*, 12 (1988): 3–58.

7. Donald T. Campbell, "Reforms as Experiments," *American Psychologist*, 24 (1969): 409–429.

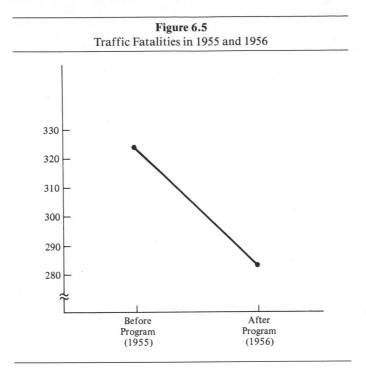

Figure 6.5
Traffic Fatalities in 1955 and 1956

At the end of 1956 there had been 284 traffic deaths, compared with 324 the year before, a reduction of 12.3 percent. The results are graphed in Figure 6.5, with the intent to magnify differences. Referring to these data, the authorities concluded that "the program is definitely worthwhile." As this inference is based on a sort of pretest-posttest design, a number of plausible rival interpretations could also be advanced. For instance, 1956 might have been a particularly dry year, with fewer accidents due to rain or snow.

    A more valid causal inference can be made if the data are presented as part of an extended time series, as illustrated in Figure 6.6. This time-series design controls for maturation. The data permit the rejection of a rival interpretation suggesting that traffic death rates were already going down year after year, which could be a plausible interpretation if the measures were carried out only one year before and after implementation of the program.

    Although the **extended time-series design** takes into account four observations before introduction of the program and three observations after its implementation, it nevertheless fails to control for the effects of other potential sources of invalidity; for example, history remains a plausible rival explanation. In such a case, one strategy for strengthening the credibility of the inference is to make use of supplementary data if these are available. For example, weather records can be examined to evaluate the rival interpretation that weather conditions were responsible for the decline in traffic deaths.

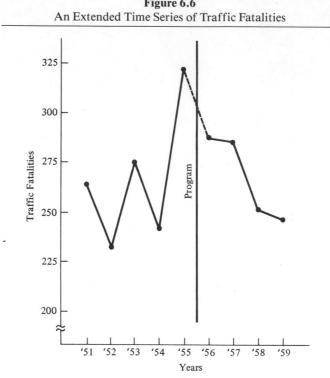

Figure 6.6
An Extended Time Series of Traffic Fatalities

But time series are unstable even when no independent variables are being introduced. The degree of this normal instability is, according to Campbell, "the crucial issue, and one of the main advantages of the extended time-series is that it samples this instability."[8] In the Connecticut case, the authorities had in fact implied that all the change from 1955 to 1956 was due to the crackdown policy. However, as Figure 6.6 indicates, the relatively high preprogram instability makes the policy look ineffective: "The 1955–1956 shift is less than the gains of both 1954–1955 and 1952–1953. It is the largest drop in the series, but it exceeds the drops of 1951–1952, 1953–1954, and 1957–1958 by trivial amounts."[9] Accordingly, one can legitimately advance the argument that the 1955–1956 drop is merely a manifestation of series instabilities. Notwithstanding this plausible interpretation, it can be observed that after the crackdown there are no year-to-year gains, suggesting that the character of the time series has changed.

Regression artifacts also present a serious threat to the validity of time-series designs, especially when these are characterized by instabilities. As a

8. Ibid., p. 413.
9. Ibid.

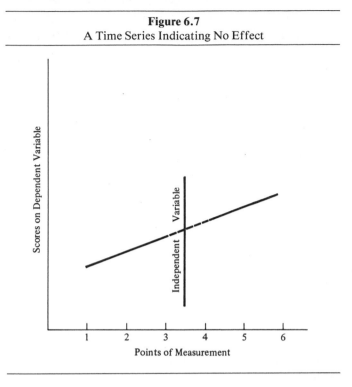

Figure 6.7
A Time Series Indicating No Effect

rule, it is maintained that with any highly variable time series, if one selects a point that is the "highest so far," the next point, on the average, will be lower or nearer to the general trend. In the Connecticut example, the most dramatic shift in the whole series is the upward shift just prior to the crackdown. Thus it is plausible that this caused the implementation of the program rather than, or in addition to, the program's causing the 1956 decline in traffic fatalities. Therefore, at least part of the 1956 drop is an artifact of the 1955 extremity.

Figure 6.7 illustrates a case from which it can be concluded that an independent variable had no effect on the dependent variable. The curve goes up from before the introduction of the independent variable to after its implementation. However, the curve was going up at the same rate before the introduction and continues up at the same rate after implementation.

Interpretation of the hypothetical data in Figure 6.8 is more problematic. The curve goes up from the introduction of the independent variable to after its implementation. However, the great variations before introduction, as well as those observed after its introduction, provide no confidence concerning causal effects.

Figures 6.7 and 6.8 illustrate but two different types of findings that could be obtained from a time-series study. They do, however, demonstrate again that time-series designs, like other quasi-experimental designs without

Figure 6.8
A Time Series Illustrating an Illusory Causal Effect

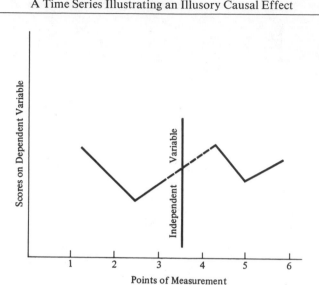

any comparison group, provide only partial evidence concerning cause-and-effects relations.

Control-Series Designs

We already pointed out that one of the major obstacles in constructing experimental designs is the difficulty of applying random selection procedures in assigning individuals or other units of analysis to experimental and comparison groups. Procedures for matching might also be vulnerable when evidence concerning significant external factors is unavailable. However, nonequivalent comparison groups used in time series provide more reliable evidence on causal effects. Such designs are called **control-series designs** because they attempt to control the aspects of history, maturation, and test-retest effects that are shared by the experimental and comparison groups.

Figure 6.9 illustrates these points for the Connecticut speeding crackdown, adding evidence from the fatality rates of neighboring states (the comparison group). To make the two series of comparable magnitude, Campbell presented the data as population-based fatality rates. The control-series design shows that downward trends were present in the neighboring states for 1955–1956 owing to history and maturation (weather, automative safety devices, and so on). However, the data are also indicative of a general trend for Connecticut to rise relatively closer to the other states prior to 1955 and to drop steadily and more rapidly than other states from

Figure 6.9
A Control-Series Design Comparing Connecticut Traffic
Fatalities with Those of Four Other States

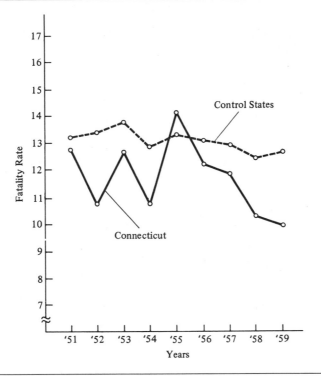

From Donald T. Campbell, "Reforms as Experiments," *American Psychologist*, 24 (1969): 419. Reprinted by permission.

1956 onward. From such evidence one can infer that the program had some effect over and above the regression artifact.

Combined Designs

We have so far focused on the weakest and the strongest of the many possible quasi-experimental designs.[10] The stronger designs control in more effective ways for more intrinsic factors (e.g., history, maturation, regression artifacts) that might invalidate causal inferences, whereas the weakest

10. For other types of quasi-experimental designs, see Thomas D. Cook and Donald T. Campbell, *Quasi-experimentation: Design and Analysis Issues for Field Settings* (Skokie, Ill.: Rand McNally, 1979), and E. A. Suchman, *Evaluation Research*, (Englewood Cliffs, N.J. Prentice-Hall, 1987).

quasi-experimental designs introduce a greater measure of ambiguity of inference.

Each of these designs can provide valid information, but they differ both in the kind of data that they generate and in the limitation they impose on inferring causation. The multimethod approach has systematically elaborated possibilities for combining two or more designs in a single study.[11]

Perhaps one of the most instructive field investigations that used **combined designs** to assess causal effects is that of the Salk vaccine—a preventive medication for paralytic poliomyelitis first experimented with in 1954.[12] In the initial design the idea was to give the vaccine only to second graders whose parents volunteered them for study and not to give it to first and third graders. Presumably, the comparison of results for the experimental group and the comparison groups would be indicative of the vaccine's effectiveness. Such a research design was most vulnerable, however, because polio occurred more frequently in more sanitary neighborhoods than in unsanitary ones, and the more sanitary neighborhoods are associated with higher socioeconomic status. People of higher socioeconomic status tend to volunteer more than people of lower socioeconomic status. Consequently, it could have been expected that more volunteers in the second grade would have been prone to have the disease in the first place than second graders in general and the average of the first and third graders. This bias could have invalidated the comparison. Furthermore, if only second graders were vaccinated, physicians might have suspected that some of them had caught paralytic polio because of exposure to the vaccine itself, so that there might have been significant frequency differences in diagnoses in the volunteer and nonvolunteer groups.

Realizing these problems, some state public health officials recommended a controlled field experiment that randomized the vaccine among volunteers from all grade groups. Half the volunteers received the vaccine and half a saltwater injection (placebo), so that the "blindness" of the diagnoses could be protected and physicians could be shielded from their expectations for the outcome in making a diagnosis. In other words, the self-selection source of invalidity would be balanced between the vaccinated and unvaccinated groups of volunteers.

Some states applied the original design; others, the randomized controlled design. The results of the latter conclusively showed a reduction in the paralytic polio rate from about 57 per 100,000 among the comparison groups to about 16 per 100,000 in the experimental group. In the states

11. John Brewer and Albert Hunter, *Multimethod Research: A Synthesis of Styles.* (Newbury Park, Calif.: Sage, 1989).

12. The following account draws on Paul Meier, "The Biggest Health Experiment Ever," in *Statistics: A Guide to the Unknown,* ed. Judith M. Tamur et al. (Oakland Calif.: Holden Day, 1972), pp. 2–13, and K. A. Brownlee, "Statistics of the 1954 Polio Vaccine Trials," *Journal of the American Statistical Association,* 50 (1955): 1005–1013.

where only the second-grade volunteers were vaccinated, the experimental group had about the same rate (17 per 100,000) as those vaccinated in the placebo comparison neighborhoods. The expected bias of an increased rate for volunteers compared with nonvolunteers appeared among the whole group. Among the placebo comparisons, the volunteers who were not vaccinated had the highest rate (57 per 100,000), and those who declined to volunteer had about 36 per 100,000. In the states using the initial quasi-experimental design, the first and third graders, who were not asked to volunteer and were not vaccinated, had a rate between the two extremes, 46 per 100,000.

In the Salk vaccine investigation, the two research designs were used simultaneously, and they supported each other. However, in many other situations, the use of a quasi-experimental design alone does not provide sufficient confidence in the results. Moreover, when complex problems are studied, one or more of their major components can frequently be studied experimentally and the remaining components with quasi-experimental designs.

Preexperimental Designs

Preexperimental designs are not suitable for experimental manipulations and do not allow for the random allocation of cases to an experimental group and a control group. In fact, most often these designs do not include a comparison group. In addition, in preexperimental studies, respondents are not randomly selected from a larger representative population, nor are multivariate statistics used as a substitute for experimental control. Preexperiments are the weakest research designs since most of the sources of internal and external validity are not controlled for. The risk of drawing causal inferences from preexperimental designs is extremely high, and they are primarily useful as a basis for pretesting some research hypotheses and for exploratory research. An example of a preexperimental design is the one-shot case study.

The One-Shot Case Study

A **one-shot case study** involves an observation of a single group or event at a single point in time, usually subsequent to some phenomenon that allegedly produced change. For example, the study might be an observation of a community after an urban renewal program, a political system after general elections, or a school after it has been exposed to an innovative teaching method.

The case of Head Start vividly illustrates the pitfalls of the one-shot case study. In January 1965, President Lyndon B. Johnson informed the public that a preschool program named Head Start would be established as part of the Community Action Program. Initially, $17 million would be committed for the summer of 1965 to enable 100,000 children to participate.[13] The publicity given Head Start generated a large volume of demands for funds from numerous localities. The Office of Economic Opportunity (OEO) met these demands by committing $103 million to provide places for 560,000 children during the summer of 1965. Later in the year, Head Start was made a permanent part of the antipoverty program. According to President Johnson, Head Start had been "battle-tested" and "proven worthy," and as a result, it was expanded to include a full-year program. In 1968, $330 million was allocated to provide places for 473,000 children in summer programs and another 218,000 in full-year programs, turning Head Start into the largest single component of the Community Action Program.

As late as mid-1967, no reliable evidence existed regarding the effectiveness of the program. Members of Congress, the Bureau of the Budget, and OEO officials were pressing for evidence. Consequently, the evaluation division of the Office of Research, Plans, Programs and Evaluations (RPP&E) proposed a study design for Head Start in which children who had participated in the program and were currently in the first, second, and third grades of school would be observed through a series of cognitive and affective tests. Performance on these tests would serve as evidence of the effectiveness of Head Start.

Head Start officials opposed the proposed study on the grounds that such a design cannot provide solid evidence for inferring causality. Numerous rival explanations and hypotheses can explain differential performance in cognitive and affective tests. Observations made only at the testing period would have no meaningful basis of comparison, and comparison is an essential component of making causal inferences. Furthermore, this design fails to provide any evidence of whether the program had *any* impact on the children. For drawing valid causal inferences, it is necessary to have observations made *prior to* implementation of the program. The design has no control over extrinsic and intrinsic factors. It also does not allow for before-after or control group–experimental group comparison. The one-shot case study cannot be used for testing causal relations.

The one-shot case study is useful in exploratory research. It may lead to insights that could in turn be studied as research hypotheses. But in the case of Head Start, this weak design was used to test the effectiveness of the program, and when the research findings were made available they were ignored precisely because of "problems in research design."[14]

---

13. This account draws on Walter Williams and John W. Evans, "The Politics of Evaluation: The Case of Head Start," *Annals of the American Academy of Political and Social Science*, 385 (September 1969): 118–132.

14. David Nachmias and Gary T. Henry, "The Utilization of Evaluation Research: Problems and Prospects," in *The Practice of Policy Evaluation*, ed. David Nachmias (New York: St. Martin's Press, 1980), pp. 461–476.

Despite these limitations, for many policy questions, especially on controversial issues, when it is difficult to implement a quasi-experimental or experimental design, the one-shot case study may be the only available technique.

As the number of case studies on a certain topic grows, it is important to attempt to integrate the findings of the various studies, to overcome the limitation of a single-case study. Recently, a method of integrating case studies has been suggested. This technique, the case survey method, involves analyzing the content of case studies, aggregating the various case experiences, and then making generalizations about the studies as a whole.[15]

A Comparison of Designs

In Chapter 5 and this chapter, we have focused on two basic problems of scientific research: inferring causation and generalizing the findings. These problems pose a basic dilemma: to secure unambiguous evidence about causation, one frequently sacrifices generalizability. This is the problematic relation between internal and external validity. Designs that are strong on internal validity tend to be weak on external validity, whereas designs that are weak on internal validity are, by definition, weak on external validity. Without internal validity, no generalizations can be made.

Perhaps the most serious threat to the internal validity of research designs is adequate control of extrinsic and intrinsic factors. In generalizability, the main issues are the representation of the research population and of a real social situation. External validity is sometimes increased by increasing the heterogeneity of the sample and of the experimental situation. These issues are juxtaposed; as one increases realism and heterogeneity, one may frequently sacrifice control.

This is the point where the weaknesses and advantages of the various designs can be compared. Whereas experiments are strong on control and weak on representation, quasi-experiments and correlational designs are strong on representation but weak on control. Experiments have several advantages. First and foremost, they enable valid causal inferences to be made by exerting a great deal of control, particularly through randomization, over extrinsic and intrinsic variables. The second advantage is their control over the introduction of the independent variable, thus permitting the direction of causation to be determined. These advantages are the shortcomings of quasi-experiments and correlational designs and more so of preexperiments. Lack of adequate control over rival explanations and difficulties in manipulating the independent variable prevent the researcher from drawing unambiguous inferences.

15. Michael A. Berger, "Studying Enrollment Decline (and Other Timely Issues) via the Case Survey," *Evaluation Studies*, 11 (1986): 720–730.

However, although the experiment is accepted as the scientific method par excellence, it has several shortcomings. The most frequent criticism lodged at experiments, especially laboratory experiments, is that they are artificial and removed from real-life situations. It is maintained, as we shall see in Chapter 9, that reality cannot be replicated in experimental settings and hence that important issues cannot be analyzed there. A second problem concerns the sample design. In experimental designs, it is difficult to represent a specified population, for many experiments include volunteers or have an incidental sample at best. Nonrepresentative samples prevent the investigator from generalizing to populations of interest and limit the scope of the findings. Conversely, most correlational designs are carried out in natural settings and permit the employment of probability samples. This allows statistical inferences to be made to broader populations and permits generalizations to real-life situations.

Given that no design can solve the problems of control and representation simultaneously, the investigator faces a difficult choice. Although in practice the nature of the study dictates this choice, it is generally accepted that the attainment of internal validity is more crucial than the attainment of external validity. Still, experiments, correlational studies, and quasi-experiments can be improved. Experiments can increase external validity by clearly defining the population to be studied and by drawing sampling units from this population following a probability sample design. Correlational studies and quasi-experiments can greatly improve their internal validity by including auxiliary information as a control against rival hypotheses. Moreover, with recent statistical techniques such as path or causal analysis, the quality of causal inferences can be greatly improved.

Summary

1. Randomization, together with careful experimental control, gives scientific research strength and persuasiveness that cannot ordinarily be obtained by other means. However, property-disposition relations are not readily amenable to experimentation, and social, political, and ethical considerations may discourage or prevent experiment with stimulus-response relations.

2. Traditionally, preexperimental research designs, such as the one-shot case study, were used when experimentation was impossible. Preexperiments are the weakest research designs since most of the sources of internal and external validity are not controlled for. Correlational designs, most predominant in survey research, are considered superior to preexperimental designs. In many cases, they are used to examine relations between property and disposition and attempt to approximate the posttest-only control group design by using data analysis techniques.

3. Quasi-experimental designs are similar to correlational designs in that they are weaker on internal validity than experimental designs and depend on data analysis techniques as a method of control. They are superior to correlational designs, however, because they usually involve the study of more than one sample, often over an extended period of time. Contrasted groups designs and planned variation designs are quasi-experiments; panel and time-series designs are quasi-experiments that are extended over time.

Key Terms for Review

stimulus-response relationship
correlational design
contrasted groups
planned variation
panel

time-series design
extended time-series design
control-series design
combined designs
one-shot case study

Study Questions

1. Describe the kinds of relationships that lend themselves to study with experimental or quasi-experimental designs.
2. Discuss the limitations of preexperimental designs.
3. Develop a quasi-experimental design to study the effect of sex education programs on teenage pregnancy rates. Be sure to explain your logic and the advantages and disadvantages of your research design.
4. Differentiate among combined designs, correlational designs, and panel designs in terms of their strengths and weaknesses.
5. Discuss why designs with high internal validity tend to have low external validity.

Additional Readings

Berk, Richard A., et al. "Social Policy Experimentation." *Evaluation Review*, 9 (1985): 387–429.

Brewer, John, and Albert Hunter. *Multimethod Research: A Synthesis of Styles.* Newbury Park, Calif.: Sage, 1989.

Coleman, James S. *Longitudinal Data Analysis.* New York: Basic Books, 1981.

Cook, Thomas D. "Quasi-experimentation: Its Ontology, Epistemology and Methodology." In *Beyond Method: Strategies for Social Research*, ed. G. Morgan. Newbury Park, Calif.: Sage, 1983.

Cook, Thomas D., and Donald T. Campbell. *Quasi-experimentation.* Skokie, Ill.: Rand McNally, 1979.

Cronbach, Lee J. *Designing Evaluations of Educational and Social Programs*. San Francisco: Jossey-Bass, 1982.

Feinberg, Stephen. B., and Judith M. Tamur. "The Design and Analysis of Longitudinal Surveys: Controversies and Issues of Costs and Continuity." In *Designing Research with Scarce Resources*, ed. Robert F. Boruch and Robert W. Pearson. New York: Springer-Verlag, 1987.

Hausman, Jerry A., and David A. Wise. *Social Experimentation*. Chicago: University of Chicago Press, 1985.

Kish, Leslie. "Some Statistical Problems in Research Design." *American Sociological Review*, 24 (1959): 328–338.

Lazarsfeld, Paul F. "Some Episodes in the History of Panel Analysis." In *Longitudinal Research on Drug Abuse*, ed. D. B. Kandel. New York: Hemisphere, 1978.

McCleary, Richard, and Richard A. Hay. *Applied Time-Series Analysis for the Social Sciences*. Newbury Park, Calif.: Sage, 1980.

Nachmias, David. *Public Policy Evaluation*. New York: St. Martin's Press, 1979. See especially Chapter 3.

Rossi, Peter H., and H. Freeman. *Evaluation: A Systematic Approach*. 3d ed. Newbury Park, Calif.: Sage, 1985.

Suchman, E. A. *Evaluation Research*. Englewood Cliffs, N.J.: Prentice-Hall, 1987.

Trochim, William M. K. *Research Design for Program Evaluation: Regression-Discontinuity Approach*. Newbury Park, Calif.: Sage, 1984.

CHAPTER 7

Measurement

In this chapter, we explore the structure of measurement and its various levels of measurement. We also discuss validity and reliability.

W HEN INVESTIGATORS DECIDE ON A research problem and begin to specify the hypotheses to be examined, they are immediately confronted with the problem of how to design the study and how to measure the variables. In Chapters 5 and 6, we discussed issues of research design. This chapter focuses on measurement, its nature and structure, levels of measurement, and the validity and reliability of measuring instruments. The major point to recognize about measurement is that, in the classic words of Norbert Wiener, "things do not . . . run around with their measures stamped on them like the capacity of a freight car: it requires a certain amount of investigation to discover what their measures are."[1] In some cases, this investigation will take the form of a search for a measure developed and reported in the professional literature; in other cases, the investigator has to develop measures that will render empirical observations in the form required by the research problem and the research design. Researchers must provide evidence that the measures are valid and reliable.

1. Norbert Wiener, "A New Theory of Measurement: A Study in the Logic of Mathematics," *Proceedings of the London Mathematical Society*, 19 (1920): 181. Quoted in *Research Methods: Issues and Insights*, ed. Billy J. Franklin and Harold W. Osborne (Belmont, Calif.: Wadsworth, 1971), p. 118.

The Nature of Measurement

Measurement is closely tied to the idea of operational definitions discussed in Chapter 2. Operational definitions are measurement procedures bridging the conceptual-theoretical level with the empirical-observational level. More specifically, measurement is a procedure in which one assigns numerals—numbers or other symbols—to empirical properties (variables) according to rules.[2] Suppose that you intend to purchase a new car. Having found that the difference in price among the various compact cars is minute, you decide to make the purchase on the basis of which model best meets the following requirements: design, economical operation, and service. These three features vary. For example, one model may be well designed and economical to operate, but the service supplied by the manufacturer may be unsatisfactory. Accordingly, you decide to rank each of the three features by five numbers: 10, 11, 12, 13, and 14. Number 10 indicates total dissatisfaction, and number 14 stands for the highest degree of satisfaction. Numbers 11, 12, and 13 indicate increasing degrees of satisfaction with the feature being examined. You examine five models. Table 7.1 summarizes the evaluation of each model according to the three criteria that were set. After examining the scores, you decide to purchase car C because it received the highest score on all three counts, indicating the highest degree of satisfaction.

This is an extremely simplified instance of measurement, but it conveys the basic idea expressed in the definition. You assigned numerals to properties according to rules. The properties or variables, the numerals, and the rules for assignment were contained in the instructions that you specified. The numerals, which are the end product of measurement, might be used for comparison, evaluation, and the assessment of relations between the various properties. For example, you can compute measures of relation between design and economy or between design and service.

Table 7.1
Preference Ranking

	Design	Economy	Service
Car A	10	11	10
Car B	13	14	12
Car C	14	14	14
Car D	14	12	13
Car E	10	12	14

2. S. S. Stevens, "Mathematics, Measurement and Psychophysics," in *Handbook of Experimental Psychology*, ed. S. S. Stevens (New York: Wiley, 1951), p. 8.

Defining Measurement

Further clarification of the three basic concepts used to define measurement—numerals, assignments, and rules—is called for. A *numeral* is a symbol of the form I, II, III, . . ., or 1, 2, 3, ... A numeral has no quantitative meaning unless one gives to it such a meaning. Numerals can be used to identify phenomena, objects, or persons such as months, driving licenses, streets, books, variables, or football players. Numerals that are given quantitative meaning become numbers; these enable the use of mathematical and statistical techniques for purposes of description, explanation, and prediction. In other words, numbers are amenable to quantitative analyses, which may in turn reveal new information about the items being studied.

In the definition of measurement, the term *assignment* means mapping. Numerals or numbers are mapped onto objects or events. Figure 7.1 illustrates the mapping idea in measurement: in the assortment of circles and squares, 1 is mapped onto the circles, and 2 is mapped onto the squares.

The third concept used to define measurement is that of *rules*. A rule specifies the procedure according to which numerals or numbers are to be assigned to objects or events. A rule might say: "Assign the numerals 10 through 15 to political systems according to how democratic the systems are. If a political system is very democratic, let the number 15 be assigned to it. If a political system is not at all democratic, let the number 10 be assigned to it. To political systems between these limits, assign numbers between the limits." Or suppose that a group is composed of three Democrats and two Republicans and that one uses the following mapping rule: "If an individual is a Democrat, assign a 1; if a Republican, assign a 2." The application of this rule is illustrated in Figure 7.2.

Figure 7.1
Assignment or Mapping

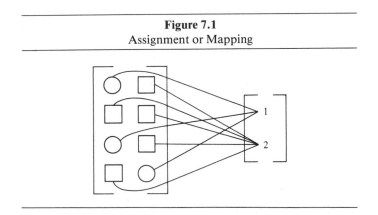

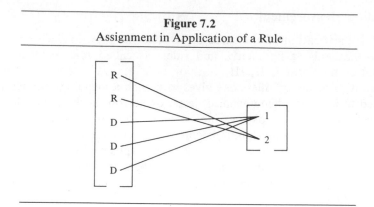

Figure 7.2
Assignment in Application of a Rule

Structure of Measurement

Measurement, then, is the assignment of numerals or numbers to objects, events, or variables according to rules. Rules are the most significant component of the measurement procedure because they determine the quality of measurement. Poor rules make measurement meaningless. Measurement is meaningless when it is not tied to reality, and the function of rules is to tie the measurement procedure to reality. Meaningful measurement is achieved only when the measurement procedure has an empirical correspondence with reality. For example, suppose that someone is measuring the softness of three objects. If object A can scratch B and not vice versa, then B is softer than A. Similarly, if A can scratch B and B can scratch C, then A can probably scratch C, and one can deduce that object C is softer than object A. These are observable propositions, and numbers indicating degrees of softness can be assigned to each of those objects after performing a few scratch tests. In this case, the measurement procedure and the number system are isomorphic to reality.

Isomorphism means "similarity or identity of structure." In measurement, the crucial question to be asked is whether the numerical system is similar in structure to the structure of the concepts being measured. Are the two similar in some structural aspect? To the physical scientist, the problem of isomorphism is often of secondary concern because the relation between the concepts being observed and the numbers assigned to the observations is quite direct. The social scientist, in contrast, must almost always be alert to this fact:

> In order for him to be able to make certain operations with numbers that have been assigned to observations, the structure of his method of mapping numbers to observations must be isomorphic to some numerical structure which includes these operations.[3]

If two systems are isomorphic, their structures are the same in the relations and operations they allow for. Thus a researcher who assigns numbers to objects and then manipulates these numbers by, say, adding them, is implying that the structure of this measurement is isomorphic to the numerical structure of arithmetic.

Frequently, social scientists measure **indicators** of concepts. Concepts such as democracy, motivation, hostility, and power cannot be observed directly; one must infer them from the measurement of indicators of the concepts. If elections are held regularly in a political system, one may infer that this is one indicator of democracy. If someone achieves a certain score in a motivation test, one may infer something about this person's level of motivation. In these examples, some identifiable behavior is an indicator of an underlying concept. Often, multiple indicators must be developed to represent abstract concepts. For example, democracy entails much more than elections. Fairness of elections, freedom of the press, freedom to organize, and the rights of minorities are other essential attributes. Indicators should not be selected arbitrarily. They are to be grounded in both theory and the empirical world. The indicators used to measure democracy in the previous example derive from both democratic theory and the actual behavior of political systems. Important concepts in the social sciences are multifaceted and thus require the use of multiple indicators, each reflecting a distinct aspect of the concept involved. Although the process of measuring directly observable concepts is identical to the one for measuring indicators of concepts, the rules in the latter are more difficult to formulate because a larger degree of inference is called for. Thus indicators are specified by operational definitions; after observation of the indicators, numerals or numbers are substituted for the values of the indicators, and quantitative analyses are performed. The numerical structure that substitutes indicators must be similar, in its relations and operations, to the structure of indicators; that is, the two must be isomorphic.

Levels of Measurement

The requirement of isomorphism between numerical systems and empirical properties (or indicators) leads to a distinction among different ways of measuring, that is, to distinct levels of measurement. (The term *scales of measurement* is sometimes used instead of *levels of measurement*. A scale may be thought of as a tool for measuring; a speedometer is a scale, as is a ruler or a questionnaire.) The mathematical and statistical operations permissible on a given set of numbers are dependent on the level of measurement attained. Here we will discuss four levels of measurement—nominal, ordinal, interval, and ratio—and the rationale of the operations that are permitted with each level.

3. Sidney N. Siegel, *Nonparametric Statistics for the Behavioral Sciences* (New York: McGraw-Hill, 1988), p. 22.

Nominal Level

The lowest level of measurement is the **nominal level**. At this level, numbers or other symbols are used to classify objects or observations. These numbers or symbols constitute a nominal, or classificatory, scale. By means of the symbols 1 and 2, for instance, it is possible to classify a given population into males and females, with 1 representing males and 2 standing for females. The same population can be classified by religion; Christians might be represented by the numeral 6, Jews by 7, and Muslims by 8. In the first case, the population was classified into two categories; in the second, into three. As a rule, when a set of objects can be classified into categories that are exhaustive (that is, that include all the objects) and mutually exclusive (that is, with no case in more than one category) and when each category is represented by a different symbol, a nominal level of measurement is attained. Gender, nationality, ethnicity, religion, marital status, place of residence (e.g., urban or rural), and party identification are all nominal variables.

Mathematically, the basic property of the nominal level of measurement is that the properties of objects in one category are equal to each other, but not to anything else in their identical aspect. The logical properties of equivalence are reflexivity, symmetry, and transitivity. Reflexivity means that every object in one of the categories is equal to itself—for example, $a = a$ in the "Christians" category. "If $a = b$, then $b = a$" defines symmetry, and "if $a = b$ and $b = c$, then $a = c$" expresses transitivity. These three logical properties are operative among objects within the same category, but not necessarily between categories. For instance, these relations will apply to all persons classified as "Christian" but not between "Christians" and "Jews."

At the nominal level, the classification of objects may be carried out with any set of symbols. The symbols may also be interchanged without altering any information, if this is done consistently and completely. Accordingly, only statistics that would remain unchanged by such transformation are permissible at the nominal level. These include the mode, measures of qualitative variation, and appropriate measures of associations; these statistics are presented in Chapters 15 and 16.

Ordinal Level

Many variables studied by social scientists not only are classifiable but also exhibit some kind of relation. Typical relations are "higher," "greater," "more desired," "more difficult," and so on. Such relations may be designated by the symbol >, which means "greater than." In reference to particular properties, > may be used to designate "is higher than," "is greater than," "is more desired than," and so on. For instance, it can be hypothesized that France is more democratic than the Soviet Un-

ion but less so than England or that socialist political parties are less dogmatic than communist parties but more so than religious parties. In general, if (in addition to equivalence) the relation $>$ holds for all pairs of
observations generating a complete ranking of objects, an **ordinal level** of
measurement is attained. The equivalence relation holds among cases of
the same rank, whereas the $>$ relation holds between any pair of ranks.

The $>$ relation is irreflexive, asymmetrical, and transitive. Irreflexivity
is a logical property wherein it is not true that for any a, $a > a$. Asymmetry
means that if $a > b$, then $b \not> a$. Transitivity means that if $a > b$ and $b > c$,
then $a > c$. In other words, if a variable such as "conservatism" is measured on the ordinal level, one can infer that if person A is more conservative than person B, and if B is more conservative than C, then A is more
conservative than C, and that the $>$ relation is maintained with regard to all
the individuals in the group.

To exemplify measurement at the ordinal level, consider the following
common practice of measuring attitudes. Attitudes are measured by means
of a series of questions, with the alternative answers being ranked in ascend-
ing or descending order. For instance, one of the questions used to measure
political alienation is "People like me have a lot of influence on government
decisions." The respondent is asked to mark the number representing his or
her degree of agreement or disagreement with this statement. The correspondence between the numbers and the answers might be made as in Table
7.2. Other questions on the same attitude are presented to the respondent,
who can then be ranked according to his or her responses to all the questions. Suppose that a researcher employs ten statements in all, each permitting four alternative answers: 1 standing for "agree strongly," 2 for
"agree," 3 for "disagree," and 4 for "disagree strongly." The highest score
that can be achieved in this case is 40 (that is, a score of 4 on each of the ten
questions), and the lowest is 10. To simplify matters, we assume that the respondents answered all questions. A respondent whose score is 40 will be regarded as the most alienated and will be ranked first. Another, whose score
is nearest to 40—say, 36—will be ranked second, and so on for each individual in the group. The ranking process ends when all the respondents are
ranked by their scores on the political alienation questionnaire. Table 7.3
displays hypothetical scores and rankings of seven respondents. An exami-

Table 7.2
Ordinal Ranking Scale

Rank	Value
1	Agree strongly
2	Agree
3	Disagree
4	Disagree strongly

Table 7.3
Individuals Ranked by Their Scores on a
Test of Political Alienation

Respondent	Score	Rank
S_1	10	7
S_2	27	3
S_3	36	2
S_4	25	4
S_5	20	5
S_6	40	1
S_7	12	6

nation of the table reveals that respondent S_6 is the most alienated and respondent S_1 the least.

The ordinal level of measurement is unique up to a monotonic transformation; that is, any order-preserving transformation does not change the information obtained. It does not matter what numbers one assigns to a pair of objects or to a category of objects so long as one is consistent. It is a matter of convenience whether to use lower numbers for the "higher" ranks, although we usually refer to superior performance as "first class" and to progressively inferior performances as "second class" and "third class." Besides attitudes, other ordinal variables are social class, school grades, military ranks, hierarchical positions in organizations, and political party participation.

The numbers assigned to ranked objects are called *rank values*. Rank values are assigned to objects according to the following rule: the object at one extreme (largest or smallest) is assigned 1; the next in size, 2; the third in size, 3; and so on to the object at the other extreme, which is assigned the last number in the series. In the example in Table 7.3, S_6 was assigned 1, S_3 was assigned 2, S_2 was assigned 3, S_4 was assigned 4, S_5 was assigned 5, S_7 was assigned 6, and S_1 was assigned 7. It is important to stress that ordinal numbers indicate rank order and nothing more. The numbers do not indicate that the intervals between them are equal, nor do they indicate absolute quantities. It cannot be assumed that because the numbers are equally spaced, the properties they represent are also equally spaced. If two respondents have the ranks 7 and 5 and two others are ranked 4 and 2, one cannot infer that the differences between the two pairs are equal.

Transformations that do not change the order of properties are permissible at the ordinal level. Accordingly, mathematical operations and statistics that do not alter the order of properties are also permissible. For example, a statistic that describes the central tendency of ordinal numbers is the median. The median is not affected by changes in any numbers above or below it so long as the number of ranked observations above and below remains the same. Other statistics appropriate for the ordinal level discussed in Chapters 15 and 16 are the range, gamma, and tau-*b*.

Interval Level

If, in addition to being able to rank a set of observations in terms of the > relation, one also knows the exact distance between each of the observations and this distance is constant, then an **interval level** of measurement has been achieved. In addition to saying that one object is greater than another, one can also specify by how many units the former is greater than the latter. For example, with interval measurement it is possible to say not only that Sue earns more than Mike but also that Sue earns, say, $5,000 more than Mike. To make these quantitative comparisons, one must have a unit of measurement; if a unit of measurement has been established, an interval level of measurement has been achieved. Examples of variables measured at the interval level are income, intelligence quotient (IQ), SAT scores, voter turnout, and crime rates. An interval level of measurement, then, is characterized by a common and constant unit of measurement that assigns a real number to all pairs of objects in the ordered set. In this kind of measurement, the ratio of any two intervals (distances) is independent of the unit of measurement.

The structure of the interval level of measurement is such that the differences between observations are isomorphic to the structure of arithmetic. Numbers may be assigned to the positions of the objects so that several arithmetic operations may be meaningfully applied to the differences between these numbers. The following formal properties characterize the interval level of measurements:

1. Uniqueness: if a and b stand for real numbers, then $a + b$ and $a \times b$ represent one and only one real number.
2. Symmetry: if $a = b$, then $b = a$.
3. Commutation: if a and b denote real numbers, then $a + b = b + a$, and $ab = ba$.
4. Substitution: if $a = b$ and $a + c = d$, then $b + c = d$; and if $a = b$ and $ac = d$, then $bc = d$.
5. Association: if a, b, and c stand for real numbers, then $(a + b) + c = a + (b + c)$, and $(ab)c = a(bc)$.

Any change in the numbers assigned to the observations must preserve not only their ordering but also their relative differences. In more formal language, the interval level of measurement is unique up to a linear transformation. Thus the information obtained at this level is not altered if each number is multiplied by a positive constant and then a constant is added to this product. All the descriptive and inferential statistics are applicable to interval data.

Table 7.4
Levels of Measurement and Their Characteristic Properties

Level	Equivalence	Greater Than	Fixed Interval	Natural Zero
Nominal	Yes	No	No	No
Ordinal	Yes	Yes	No	No
Interval	Yes	Yes	Yes	No
Ratio	Yes	Yes	Yes	Yes

Ratio Level

Variables that have natural zero points can be measured on the **ratio level** of measurement. Variables such as weight, time, length, and area have natural zero points and are measured at the ratio level. At this level, the ratio of any two numbers is independent of the unit of measurement. The interval and the ratio levels are similar, and the rules by which numbers are assigned are the same, with one exception. For a ratio level of measurement, we apply the operations and the numbers to the total amount measured from an absolute zero point; for an interval level, we apply the operation to differences from one arbitrary point. A ratio level of measurement, most commonly encountered in the physical sciences, is achieved only when all four of these relations are operationally possible to attain: (1) equivalence, (2) greater than, (3) known distance of any two intervals, and (4) a true zero point.[4]

Data Transformation

Variables that can be measured at the ratio level can also be measured at the interval, ordinal, and nominal levels. As a rule, properties that can be measured at a higher level can also be measured at lower levels, but not vice versa. A variable such as party affiliation can be measured only at the nominal level. The formal properties characterizing each level of measurement are summarized in Table 7.4. For example, whereas the equivalence property exists at each of the four levels, a natural zero characterizes only the ratio level.

Earlier we pointed out the kinds of numerical operations and statistics that are, in a strict sense, legitimate and permissible with each level. Some researchers tend to deemphasize this question. The problem, however, is significant enough to warrant a few additional comments.

Mathematics and statistics are contentless languages. They deal with numbers and are not concerned with whether the numbers represent the empirical world. Their foremost advantage is their precision and their enabling

---

4. For more details on levels of measurement, see Siegel, *Nonparametric Statistics*, which informed much of our discussion.

researchers to reveal information about phenomena that cannot otherwise be revealed. A question such as "To what extent are a series of variables related?" can be meaningfully and precisely answered by computing measures of relations. With numbers, any kind of statistical operation can be performed. Social scientists are concerned with empirical phenomena, and numbers are used chiefly to gain a better understanding of the relations between these phenomena. Employing numerical systems and statistics that are not isomorphic to the structure of empirical phenomena is of little use in advancing our knowledge.

Measurement Error

Measurement procedures lead to the assignment of numerals, numbers, or scores to properties. Differences in the scores can be attributed to two sources. One is the extent to which the properties exhibit *real differences* in the aspects of the property being measured. The other source of difference in the scores is the extent to which the measure itself or the setting in which it takes place influences the scores. In this case, the measures are showing unreal differences. Perfect measures reveal only real differences between the properties. However, measures are seldom perfect and often reflect not only real differences but also artifact differences produced by the measuring procedure itself. Differences that are due to anything other than real differences are termed **measurement errors**. They are not real differences between the properties but differences due to the imperfection of the measuring procedure.

There are several common sources of measurement errors. First, the scores obtained may be related to an associated attribute. For example, a question measuring moral development may require a certain level of intelligence and social awareness to be interpreted and answered. The responses of individuals to this question will reflect not only real differences in moral development but also differences in intelligence and social awareness. The effects of associated attributes are measurement errors. Second, measurement errors may result because of differences in temporary conditions, such as health or mood, that may affect a person's responses to a questionnaire or a person's behavior. Third, measurement errors may also result when different people interpret the measuring instrument in different ways. Fourth, differences in the setting in which the measure is used contribute to measurement errors. For example, the age, race, and gender of interviewers influences the answers of survey respondents. Fifth, differences in the administration of the measuring instrument (e.g., poor lighting, noise, tired interviewers) lead to measurement errors. The last major source of distortion is differences in processing (e.g., different coders code similar answers to a question differently) and analyzing data.

The errors that arise from these sources are either systematic or random errors. *Systematic errors* are produced whenever the measuring instrument is used, and they are constant between cases and studies. They introduce a measure of invalidity to the findings. *Random errors*, by contrast, affect each usage of the measuring instrument in a different way. Validity and reliability are concerned with techniques for reducing measurement errors.

Validity

The problem of validity arises because measurement in the social sciences is, with very few exceptions, indirect. Under such circumstances, researchers are never completely certain that they are measuring what they intend to measure. **Validity** is concerned with the question "Is one measuring what one intends to measure?" For example, does voter turnout measure political development? Is agreement with the statement "This world is run by a few people in power, and there is not much the little guy can do about it" an indicator of the variable "alienation"? To answer such questions, the researcher must provide supporting evidence that a measuring instrument does, in fact, measure what it appears to measure.

Three basic kinds of validity can be distinguished, each of which is concerned with a different aspect of the measurement situation: content validity, empirical validity, and construct validity. Each includes several kinds of evidence and has special value under certain conditions.

Content Validity

There are two common varieties of content validity: face validity and sampling validity. **Face validity** rests on the investigator's subjective evaluation as to the validity of a measuring instrument. In practice, face validity does not relate to the question of whether an instrument measures what the researcher wishes to measure; rather, it concerns the extent to which it measures what it appears to measure according to the researcher's subjective assessment. For example, an investigator intends to measure the variable "liberalism" by a questionnaire consisting of ten statements. After constructing the questionnaire, the researcher reviews each statement to assess the extent to which it is related to "liberalism." To do so, the researcher might consult a number of specialists (judges). If there is agreement among the judges, the researcher will propose that the questionnaire has face validity and that, consequently, it measures "liberalism." Disagreement among the judges would impair the face validity of a measuring instrument.

The main problem with face validity is that there are no replicable procedures for evaluating the measuring instrument, so one has to rely entirely on subjective judgments.

The primary concern of **sampling validity** is whether a given population of situations or behavior is adequately sampled by the measuring instrument in question; that is, does the content of the instrument adequately represent the content population of the property being measured? The underlying assumption of sampling validity is that every variable has a content population consisting of a large number of items (statements, questions, or indicators) and that a highly valid instrument constitutes a representative sample of these items. In practice, problems arise with the definition of a content population, for this is a theoretical, not an empirical, construct. (These problems are discussed in Chapter 8, in which sampling techniques are presented.) These problems impair the effectiveness of sampling validity as a test of an instrument's validity. However, sampling validity serves an important function: it requires familiarity with all the items of the content population. Sampling validity is especially common in exploratory research, where investigators attempt to construct instruments and employ them for the first time. After the instrument has been used, its validity can be evaluated with other tests.

Empirical Validity

The concern of empirical validity is with the relations between a measuring instrument and the measurement outcomes. It is assumed that if a measuring instrument is valid, there should be strong relations between the results produced by the instrument and other variables. Evidence to support the existence of a relation is obtained by measures of correlation appropriate to the level of measurement. (A correlation coefficient is an index of the degree of relation between two measures; details can be found in Chapter 16.) Of the various tests designed to evaluate empirical validity, predictive validity is the most widely used. For this reason, we shall discuss it at some length.

Predictive validity is estimated by a prediction to an external measure referred to as a *criterion* and by checking a measuring instrument against some outcome. In other words, predictive validity is the correlation coefficient between the results of a given measurement and an external criterion. For example, one can validate an intelligence test by first obtaining the test scores of a group such as college students and by then obtaining the grade point averages that these students achieved in their first year of college. A correlation coefficient is then computed between the two sets of measurements. This correlation coefficient is called the *validity coefficient*. Other criteria that one could use to validate intelligence tests are social outcomes of adjustment tests and ratings of performance.

The process by which the predictive validity of an instrument is evaluated is illustrated in Figure 7.3. A variable (V) is measured by a certain measuring instrument (I), and the researcher desires to evaluate the predictive

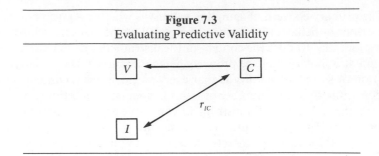

Figure 7.3
Evaluating Predictive Validity

validity of the instrument. To assess its predictive validity, a criterion (C) whose validity is agreed on is used. The measurements obtained by I are correlated with the measurements obtained by C. The size of the validity coefficient (r_{IC}) measures the predictive validity of the instrument.

Two general issues are to be considered when using the predictive validity test. One relates to the validity of the criterion, and the other concerns the reasons for using a measuring instrument instead of the criterion itself; for example, why not measure grade point averages directly? In regard to the second point, in some cases the criterion is technically difficult or too expensive to use, and in other cases investigators have to measure a variable before they can make use of the criterion. For example, the scholastic abilities of students have to be determined prior to admitting them to universities.

With regard to the validity of the criterion, two common methods are used. One method relies on agreement among researchers that a certain criterion is valid to evaluate a measuring instrument. The agreement is subject to tests of face validity and sampling validity. A somewhat different method is to express the relationship between the instrument and the criterion in terms of the percentage of individuals (or other units of analysis) who would be correctly classified by the instrument according to their known group membership.[5]

Suppose that one has to evaluate the validity of an instrument designed to measure political conservatism. If there are theoretically sound reasons for arguing that people in the lower class are more conservative than people in the middle class, the two classes can be compared as a check of predictive validity. In this case, social class serves as an indirect criterion for the predictive validity of the instrument. If the findings reveal that persons in the lower-class group are as conservative as persons in the middle-class group, the instrument lacks predictive validity. Conversely, a relatively high correlation between social class and conservatism would validate the instrument. However, a high correlation is a necessary but not a sufficient condition to

---

5. C. G. Helmstadter, *Research Concepts in Human Behavior* (Englewood Cliffs, N.J.: Prentice-Hall, 1970).

the predictive validity of an instrument because the indirect criterion (social class) may also be related to variables other than political conservatism (e.g., education). The instrument might measure other variables instead of political conservatism. An indirect criterion, then, is more useful for disvalidating than for validating a measuring instrument.

Construct Validity

Construct validity involves relating a measuring instrument to a general theoretical framework in order to determine whether the instrument is tied to the concepts and theoretical assumptions that are employed. Lee J. Cronbach, an early proponent of construct validity, observed that "whenever a tester asks what a score means psychologically or what causes a person to get a certain test score, he is asking what concepts may properly be used to interpret the test performance."[6] Theoretical expectations about the variable being measured lead the investigator to postulate various kinds and degrees of relationships between the particular variable and other specified variables. To demonstrate construct validity of a measuring instrument, an investigator has to show that these relationships do in fact hold. We shall illustrate the utility of construct validity through Milton Rokeach's famous research on dogmatism.[7]

On the basis of theoretical reasoning, Rokeach constructed a dogmatism questionnaire. This instrument consisted of statements assumed to measure closed-mindedness, a way of thinking associated with any belief system or ideology regardless of content. Rokeach argued that individuals' ideological orientations are related to their personalities, thought processes, and behavior. Consequently, he predicted, among other things, that dogmatism is related to opinionation. Rokeach conducted a number of studies aimed at testing his theory and the construct validity of the measuring instruments. In one study, he used the **known-groups technique**. In this method, a measuring instrument is administered to groups of people with known attributes, and the direction of differences is predicted. Rokeach asked college professors and graduate students to select friends who they thought to be open-minded or closed-minded. The dogmatism questionnaire clearly differentiated the two groups. This finding provided supporting evidence of the construct validity of the dogmatism measure.

Cronbach and Meehl describe the logical process of construct validation in the following way: first, a proposition that an instrument measures a certain property—say, property A—is set forth; second, the proposition is inserted into the present theory of property A; third, working through the theory, one predicts other properties that should be related to the instrument

---

6. Lee J. Cronbach, *Essentials of Psychological Testing*, 4th ed. (New York: Harper & Row, 1984), p. 121.

7. Milton Rokeach, *The Open and the Closed Mind* (New York: Basic Books, 1960).

and properties that should exhibit no relation to the instrument; finally, one collects data that empirically confirm or reject the predicted relations. If the anticipated relationships are found, the instrument is considered valid. If the predictions fail, there are three possibilities: (1) the instrument does not measure property A, (2) the theoretical framework that generated the predictions is flawed, or (3) the research design failed to test the predictions properly. The researcher must then make a decision as to which of these three conditions has occurred. Such a decision is based on a careful reconstruction of each of the four steps constituting the validation process.[8]

Campbell and Fiske suggested another method of construct validation involving correlation matrices.[9] This is the *convergent-discriminant* conception of validity, or the *multitrait-multimethod matrix* technique. This method derives from the idea that different methods of measuring the same property should yield similar results, whereas different properties should yield different measurement results regardless of the measuring instrument. Operationally, this means that correlation coefficients among scores for a given property measured by different instruments should be higher than correlations among different properties measured by similar instruments. Evidence of the construct validity of an instrument must therefore make use of both a convergent principle—that is, two measures of the same property should correlate highly with each other even though they represent different methods—and a discriminant principle, which implies that two measures should not correlate highly with each other if they measure different properties even though a similar instrument is used. Thus the validation process calls for the computation of intercorrelations among measuring instruments that represent at least two properties, each measured by at least two different instruments.

In view of the distinctions among the three types of validity, which test should we use when evaluating the validity of a given measuring instrument? There is no simple solution to this problem. Its significance led a team of experts from different disciplines to recommend that thorough examination of a measuring instrument include information about the three types of validity.[10] Thus in the first phase of the construction of a measure, one might evaluate theories that would serve as a foundation for the instrument; next a content population of items from which a representative sample is to be drawn might be defined; and finally, the predictive validity of the instrument might be assessed by correlating it with an external criterion.

8. Lee J. Cronbach and Paul Meehl, "Construct Validity in Psychological Tests," *Psychological Bulletin*, 52 (1955): 281–302.

9. Donald T. Campbell and Donald W. Fiske, "Convergent and Discriminant Validation by the Multitrait-Multimethod Matrix," *Psychological Bulletin*, 56 (1959): 81–105.

10. See American Psychological Association Committee on Psychological Tests, "Technical Recommendations for Psychological Tests and Diagnostic Techniques," *Psychological Bulletin Suppl.*, 51 (1954), pt. 2: 1–38, and Donald T. Campbell, "Recommendations for APA Test Standards Regarding Construct, Trait, or Discriminant Validity," *American Psychologist*, 15 (1960): 546–553.

Reliability

Reliability is of central concern to social scientists because measuring instruments are rarely completely valid. In many cases, validity evidence is almost entirely lacking; one has to evaluate the measuring instrument with respect to other characteristics and assume its validity. A frequently used method for evaluating an instrument is its degree of reliability.

Reliability refers to the extent to which a measuring instrument contains *variable errors*, that is, errors that differed from observation to observation during any one measuring instance or that varied from time to time for a given unit of analysis measured twice or more by the same instrument. For example, if one measures the length of a desk at two points in time with the same instrument—say, a ruler—and gets slightly different results, the instrument contains variable errors. Because of the indirect nature of measurements in the social sciences, the errors that occur when social variables are measured tend to be greater than those occurring when physical variables are measured. Factors such as momentary distraction when completing a questionnaire, ambiguous instructions, and technical difficulties (a pencil breaks while the respondent is filling in a questionnaire) may cause the introduction of variable (measurement) errors. These errors are called variable errors because the amount of error varies from one observation to the next and also because the amount of error is different for a given observation each time it is measured.

Each measurement, then, consists of two components: a *true component* and an *error component*. Reliability is defined as the ratio of the true-score variance to the total variance in the scores as measured.[11] (The variance is a measure of the spread of observations, or scores; it is a description of the extent to which the observations differ from each other; that is,

$$\sigma^2 = \frac{\sum_{i=1}^{N} (x_i - \bar{x})^2}{N}$$

See Chapter 15 for a detailed presentation.) Algebraically, each person's observed score can be represented as

$$x_i = t_i + e_i \tag{7.1}$$

where x_i = score actually obtained by person i

  t_i = true score for person i

  e_i = amount of error that occurred for person i at the time the measurement was made

---

11. This definition and the following presentation are based on C. G. Helmstadter, *Research Concepts*, pp. 169–176.

Expressed in variance terms, we get

$$\sigma_x^2 = \sigma_t^2 + \sigma_e^2$$

where σ_x^2 = variance of observed scores

$\quad \sigma_t^2$ = variance of true scores

$\quad \sigma_e^2$ = variance of errors

Reliability, defined as the ratio of true-score variance to observed-score variance, can be expressed as

$$\text{Reliability} = \frac{\sigma_t^2}{\sigma_x^2} = \frac{\sigma_x^2 - \sigma_e^2}{\sigma_x^2} \qquad (7.2)$$

From Equation (7.2) we can see that if the measurement involves nothing but error, then $\sigma_x^2 = \sigma_e^2$ and the reliability is zero. However, when there is no variable error at all, $\sigma_e^2 = 0$, and the ratio defined as reliability becomes

$$\frac{\sigma_x^2}{\sigma_x^2} = 1$$

The **reliability measure** varies on a scale from 0 to 1, having the former value when the measurement involves nothing but error and reaching 1 when there is no variable error at all in the measurement.

In practice, it is impossible to compute the true score independently of the amount of error that occurs in any particular measurement. Consequently, the ratio σ_t^2 / σ_x^2 has to be estimated. There are three common ways of estimating reliability: the test-retest method, the parallel-forms technique, and the split-half method.

Test-Retest Method

The **test-retest method** derives directly from the conceptual definition of reliability. A measuring instrument is administered to the same group of persons at two different times, and the correlation between the two sets of observations (scores) is computed. The obtained coefficient is the *reliability estimate*. With this method, error is defined as anything that leads a person to get a different score on one measurement from what that person obtained on another measurement. Symbolically,

$$r_{xx'} = \frac{S_t^2}{S_x^2} \qquad (7.3)$$

where x = performance on the first measurement

$\quad x'$ = performance on the second measurement

$\quad r_{xx'}$ = correlation coefficient between x and x'

$\quad S_t^2$ = estimated variance of the true scores

$\quad S_x^2$ = calculated variance of the observed scores

The correlation $r_{xx'}$ provides an estimate of reliability defined as a ratio of the true variance to the observed variance. (For methods of computing the correlation coefficient, see Chapter 16.)

The test-retest method has two main limitations. First, measurement on one occasion may influence measurements on subsequent occasions. If, for example, the instrument is a questionnaire, a respondent may remember specific questions and answer the same way as on the first occasion, thus yielding a high but overstated reliability estimate. Second, many phenomena change all the time. It is possible that changes may have occurred in the measured variable during the measurement interval, thus lowering the estimate of reliability. The test-retest method, then, may either overestimate or underestimate the true reliability of the instrument, and in many cases it is difficult to determine which has occurred.

Parallel-Forms Technique

One way to counter the two limitations of the test-retest method is to use the **parallel-forms technique**. This technique requires two forms of a measuring instrument that are parallel. The two forms are then administered to a group of persons, and the two sets of measures (scores) are correlated to obtain an estimate of reliability. With this technique, there is the problem of determining whether the two forms of an instrument are in fact parallel. Although statistical tests have been developed to determine whether the forms are parallel in terms of statistical measures, evaluation of the content of the forms is made judgmentally.[12]

Split-Half Method

The **split-half method** estimates reliability by treating each of two or more parts of a measuring instrument as a separate scale. Suppose that the measuring instrument is a questionnaire. The questionnaire is separated into two sets, using the odd-numbered questions for one set and the even-numbered questions for the other. Each of the two sets of questions is treated separately and scored accordingly. The two sets are then correlated, and this is taken as an estimate of reliability. To correct the correlation coefficient obtained between the two halves, the following formula, known as the Spearman-Brown prophecy formula, may be applied:

$$r_{xx'} = \frac{2r_{oe}}{1 + r_{oe}} \tag{7.4}$$

where $r_{xx'}$ = the reliability of the original test

r_{oe} = the reliability coefficient obtained by correlating the scores of the odd statements with the scores of the even statements

12. See Harold Gulliksen, *Theory of Mental Tests* (New York: Wiley, 1962).

This correction assumes that an instrument that is $2n$ questions long will be more reliable than an instrument that is n questions long and that because the length of the instrument has been halved by dividing it into odds and evens, the full instrument will have a higher reliability than either half would.

Cronbach, Rajaratnam, and Glesser introduced a revision to the traditional concept of reliability.[13] These authors maintain that the chief concern of reliability theory is to answer the question "To what universe of potential measurements do we wish to generalize?" Thus instead of reliability, the idea of generalizability is introduced. **Generalizability** implies that what one really wants to know about a set of measurements is to what extent and with respect to what properties are they like other sets of measurements that one might have taken from a given universe of potential measurements? And to what extent and with respect to what properties do they differ from other measurements that one might have drawn from that universe of potential measurements? If one asks the likeness and difference questions of potential measurements, one is asking about the limits of generalizability of the results of one's set of measurements. Whether we consider a particular relation among measurements to be evidence of reliability or generalizability depends on how we choose to define likeness and difference of conditions and measures. The construction of what is the same and what is different in sets of measurements depends, in turn, on the research problem.[14]

Summary

1. Measurement is the assignment of numerals to variables, properties, or events according to rules. The most significant concept in this definition is "rules." The function of a rule is to tie the measurement procedure to reality; to establish isomorphism between a certain numerical structure and the structure of the variables being measured. On establishing isomorphism, researchers can perform quantitative analyses with the numerals that stand for the properties. Isomorphism between numerical systems and empirical properties leads to a distinction among four levels of measurement: nominal, ordinal, interval, and ratio. In general, the quantitative analyses permissible on a given set of numbers are dependent on the level of measurement obtained.

13. Lee J. Cronbach, Nageswars Rajaratnam, and Goldine C. Glesser, "A Theory of Generalizability: A Liberalization of Reliability Theory," *British Journal of Statistical Psychology*, 16 (1963): 137–163.

14. For the statistical expression of the generalizability index, see ibid., and Goldine C. Glesser, Lee J. Cronbach, and Nageswars Rajaratnam "Generalizability of Scores Influenced by Multiple Scores of Variance," *Psychometrika*, 30 (1965): 395–418.

2. The ideas of validity and reliability are inseparable from measurement theory. Validity is concerned with the question of whether one is measuring what one thinks one is measuring. Traditionally, three basic types of validity have been distinguished, each of which relates to a different aspect of the measurement situation: content validity, empirical validity, and construct validity. To validate a certain measuring instrument, one must look for information about these three types. Reliability indicates the extent to which a measure contains variable errors. Operationally, it is assumed that any measure consists of a true component and an error component and that the proportion of the amount of variation in the true component to the total variation measures reliability. This measure can be estimated by one or more of the following methods: test-retest, parallel-forms, and split-half. The notion of generalizability implies that the main concern of reliability is with the extent to which a set of measurements is like other sets of measurements that might have been drawn from a given universe of potential measurements.

Key Terms for Review

measurement	sampling validity
isomorphism	predictive validity
indicator	construct validity
nominal level	known-groups technique
ordinal level	reliability
interval level	reliability measure
ratio level	test-retest method
measurement errors	parallel-forms technique
validity	split-half method
face validity	generalizability

Study Questions

1. Define measurement and explain why measurement is important to scientific research.
2. What are the various levels of measurement? Why are the differences between the levels of measurement important?
3. Define the concept ''validity'' and explain how to distinguish among the three major types of validity.
4. Define the concept ''reliability'' and discuss the ways of assessing it.

Additional Readings

Achen, Christopher H. "Toward Theories of Data: The State of Political Methodology." In *Political Science: The State of the Discipline*, ed. Ada Finifter. Washington, D.C.: American Political Science Association, 1983.

Allen, Mary J. *Introduction to Measurement Theory*, Pacific Grove, Calif.: Brooks/Cole, 1979.

Blalock, Hubert M., Jr. *Conceptualization and Measurement in the Social Sciences.* Newbury Park, Calif.: Sage, 1982.

Bohrnstedt, George W., and Edgar F. Borgatta, eds. *Social Measurement.* Newbury Park, Calif.: Sage, 1981.

Carley, Michael. *Social Measurement and Social Indicators.* Boston: Allen & Unwin, 1981.

Ghiselli, Edwin E., John P. Campbell, and Sheldon Zedeck. *Measurement Theory for the Behavioral Sciences.* New York: Freeman, 1981.

Kidder, Louise H. "Face Validity from Multiple Perspectives." In *New Directions for Methodology of Social and Behavioral Science: Forms of Validity*, ed. David Brimberg and Louise Kidder. San Francisco: Jossey-Bass, 1982.

Shively, Philip W. *The Craft of Political Research.* 3d ed. Englewood Cliffs, N.J.: Prentice-Hall, 1990.

Sullivan, John L., and Stanley Feldman. *Multiple Indicators.* Newbury Park, Calif.: Sage, 1979.

Zeller, Richard A., and Edward G. Carmines. *Measurement in the Social Sciences.* New York: Cambridge University Press, 1980.

CHAPTER 8

Sampling and Sample Designs

In this chapter, we discuss the fundamentals of sampling theory—sample size, standard error, and confidence intervals—and we explain how to draw a random sample. Four basic probability samples are considered and summarized. Finally, we examine bias introduced by nonresponse.

ONCE THE MEASURING INSTRUMENTS have been constructed, data pertinent to the research problem can be collected. Data are collected to test hypotheses; to provide empirical support to explanations and predictions. Explanations and predictions must be general to be of scientific value. In Chapter 1 (Figure 1.1), we emphasized that generalizations constitute a major stage of the research process. Generalizations are important not only for testing hypotheses but also for descriptive purposes. For example, questions such as "What is the level of political trust among Americans?" or "Are voters more conservative now than they were a decade ago?" call for descriptive generalizations.

Typically, generalizations are not based on data collected from *all* the observations, *all* the respondents, or *all* the events that are defined by the research problem. A relatively small number of cases (a sample) is used as the basis for inferences to all the cases (a population). A familiar example is elections polls. Pollsters forecast from the responses of a relatively small group of respondents how the entire population of voters would vote if **169** the election were held at the time the poll was taken, and they also attempt to predict how the population of voters will vote when the actual election is held. How do pollsters select their samples? What considerations are involved? How are inferences from a sample to a population made? We shall soon find out.

In this chapter, we cover the fundamentals of sampling theory. In the first section we discuss the aims of sampling. We then move to definitions and discussions of central concepts—population, the sampling unit, sampling frame, and the sample—as well as procedures of probability and nonprobability sampling designs. Next, we discuss the considerations involved in determining the sample size. Finally, we present procedures for estimating nonsampling errors.

Aims of Sampling

Empirically supported generalizations are usually based on partial information. This is the case because often it is impossible, impractical, or extremely expensive to collect data from all the potential units of analysis encompassed in the research problem. Yet precise inferences on all the units (a set) based on a relatively small number of units (a subset) can be drawn when subsets accurately represent the relevant attributes of the whole set. In marketing research, the preferences of a small subset of households are used to target new products to millions of customers. The Environmental Protection Agency uses a small number of automobiles of various kinds to obtain data on performance. The data collected from the subset are used to regulate the performance of all automobiles.

When the data are partial and used to make generalizations on the whole, the subset is called a **sample**, and the whole is called a **population**. A particular value of the population, such as the median income or the level of formal education, is called a **parameter**; its counterpart in the sample is termed a **statistic**. The major objective of sampling theory is to provide accurate estimates of unknown parameters from sample statistics that can be easily calculated.

To estimate unknown parameters accurately from known statistics, three major problems have to be dealt with effectively: (1) the definition of the population, (2) the sample design, and (3) the size of the sample.

Population

A population is the "aggregate of all cases that conform to some designated set of specifications."[1] For example, by the specifications "people" and "residing in Britain," we define a population consisting of all people who reside in Britain. Similarly, by the specifications "students" and "enrolled

---

1. Isidor Chein, "An Introduction to Sampling," in Claire Selltiz et al., *Research Methods in Social Relations*, 4th ed. (New York: Holt, Rinehart and Winston, 1981), p. 419.

in state universities in the United States,'' we define a population consisting of all students enrolled in state universities in the United States. One may similarly define populations consisting of all the households in a given community, all the registered voters in a particular precinct, or all the books in a public library. A population may be a group of people, houses, records, legislators, and so on. The specific nature of the population depends on the research problem. If one is studying voting behavior in a presidential election, the population would be defined as all citizens who registered to vote. If one is investigating consumer behavior in a particular city, the population might be all the households in that city.

One of the first problems facing a researcher who wishes to estimate a population value from a sample value is the determination of the population involved. If one is interested in voting behavior in Britain and wishes to draw a sample so as to predict how the election will turn out, the sample should exclude individuals under 18. The population of voters in Britain is not the same as the entire British population. Even ''all British subjects 18 years of age or older'' is not an adequate definition of the population of voters because individuals have to meet certain legal requirements before the election is held. Individuals who do not meet such criteria are ineligible to vote; hence they should be excluded from the sampling population. The population, then, has to be defined in terms of (1) content, (2) extent, and (3) time—for example, (1) all residents over 18 years of age living in private dwelling units, (2) in England, (3) on May 1, 1992.

The Sampling Unit

A single member of a sampling population (e.g., a voter, a household, an event) is referred to as a **sampling unit**. Usually, sampling units have numerous attributes, one or more of which are relevant to the research problem. For example, if the population is defined as all third graders in a given town attending public schools on a particular day, the sampling units are all third graders. Third graders, however, have many traits (variables), including grades, habits, opinions, and expectations. A research project may examine only one variable, such as arithmetic grades, or relations among several variables, for example, arithmetic grades, IQ scores, and formal education of parents.

A sampling unit is not necessarily an individual. It may be an event, a university, a city, or a nation. For example, in a study of conflict behavior within and between nations, Rudolph J. Rummel collected data on 22 measures of foreign and domestic conflict behavior (such as assassinations, guerrilla warfare, purges, riots, revolutions, military actions, wars) for 77 nations over a three-year period.[2] In his study, the sampling units were na-

2. Rudolph J. Rummel, ''Dimensions of Conflict Behavior within and between Nations,'' in *Macro-quantitative Analysis: Conflict, Development and Democratization,* ed. J.V. Gillespie and B.A. Nesvold (Newbury Park, Calif.: Sage, 1971).

tions. The sampling units had to meet two criteria to be included in the study: (1) sovereign statehood for at least two years, as evidenced by diplomatic relations with other countries and the existence of a foreign ministry, and (2) a minimum population of 800,000.

Finite and Infinite Populations

A population may be finite or infinite, depending on whether the sampling units are finite or infinite. By definition, a *finite population* contains a countable number of sampling units, for example, all registered voters in a particular city in a given year. An *infinite population* consists of an endless number of sampling units, such as an unlimited number of coin tosses. Sampling designed to produce information about particular characteristics of a finite population is usually termed *survey sampling*.

Sampling Frame

Once the population has been defined, a sample is drawn that adequately represents the population. The actual procedures involve a selection of a sample from a complete list of sampling units called a **sampling frame**. Ideally, the sampling frame should include all sampling units in the population. In practice, a physical list rarely exists, and an equivalent list is substituted for it. For example, in large national studies, it is impossible to obtain a complete and accurate listing of all individuals residing in the United States, a difficulty encountered even by a large research organization such as the Census Bureau, which counts the entire nation every decade. For example, the 1990 census cost an estimated $2.6 billion and required 277 million forms. An estimated 3.3 billion individual answers were collected and processed by nearly 480,000 census workers over a period from 1988-1991. These workers compiled and checked address lists, and gathered and processed vital information on approximately 250 million people and 106 million housing units in the United States and its territories. The Census Bureau also hired 35,000 temporary employees during 1988-1989 to go door-to-door compiling a list of about 43 million address of housing units, many outside metropolitan areas. In addition, the Census Bureau purchased about 55 million residential addresses in large metropolitan areas from commercial mailing list companies. Census and Postal Service workers checked and updated the address lists before the Census Bureau produced mailing labels for the questionnaire envelopes.[3] Yet for all its efforts, it is estimated that the census missed approximately 5 million of the nation's residents. As in the 1980 census, an increasingly transient lifestyle in the United States made the compilation of mailing lists difficult.

3. From *Census '90 Basics* (U.S. Department of Commerce, Bureau of the Census, December 1985), p. 1.

In smaller-scale studies, the sampling frame may be based on telephone directories, city directories, or membership lists that are held by many private and public organizations.

There should be a high degree of correspondence between a sampling frame and the sampling population. The accuracy of a sample depends on the sampling frame. Indeed, every aspect of the sample design—the population coverage, the stages of sampling, and the actual selection process—is influenced by the sampling frame. Prior to the selection of a sample, the sampling frame has to be evaluated for potential problems. Leslie Kish provides a useful classification of typical problems in sampling frames: incomplete sampling frames, clusters of elements, and blank foreign elements.[4]

Incomplete Frames.   The problem of incomplete sampling frames occurs when sampling units included in the population are missing from the list. For example, if the population includes all new residents in a community, a sampling frame based on the real estate multiple-listing service in the community would be incomplete because it consists only of new homeowners (sellers and buyers) and does not include renters.

When the sampling frame is incomplete, supplemental lists could be used. For example, it may be possible to compile a list of all new renters in the community by using the city directory, which sometimes identifies new residents in the community as homeowners or renters.

Clusters of Elements.   The second potential problem of a sampling frame is clusters of elements. This problem occurs when sampling units are listed in clusters rather than individually. For example, the sampling frame may consist of city blocks, whereas the study focuses on individuals, heads of households. A possible solution to this problem would be to take a sample of blocks and then to list all the individual households in each of the selected blocks. The selection of individuals from each household (most households include more than one individual) would be according to prespecified criteria, such as any individual over 18 or only heads of households.

Blank Foreign Elements.   The problem of blank foreign elements is quite common and occurs when the sampling units of the sampling frame are not included in the original population, for example, when the population is defined as consisting only of eligible voters whereas the frame contains some individuals who are too young to vote. This is often a problem when the listing used as a frame is outdated. Another example, often encountered with the use of city directories, is the failure to list residents when an address in the directory is given. This does not necessarily mean that nobody lives at that address, but possibly the residents have recently moved to a new address and could not be located. These cases should be treated as blanks and simply omitted from the sample. It is a good practice to select a slightly larger sample initially in order to compensate for such omissions.

4. Leslie Kish, *Survey Sampling* (New York: Wiley, 1965), sect. 2.7.

Errors in Sampling Frames: The 1936 Presidential Election

The discussion of errors in sampling frames could not be complete without mentioning the best-known example of sampling failure, the 1936 *Literary Digest* poll. In 1936, Franklin Delano Roosevelt, completing his first term of office as president of the United States, was running against the Republican candidate Alfred Landon of Kansas. The *Literary Digest* magazine, in the largest poll in history, consisting of about 2.4 million individuals, predicted a victory for Landon by 57 percent to 43 percent. Despite this decisive prediction, Roosevelt won the election by a huge landslide—62 percent to 38 percent.[5]

The error was enormous, the largest ever made by any polling organization, despite the very large sample size. The major reason for the error was found in the sampling frame. The *Digest* had mailed questionnaires to 10 million people, names and addresses coming from various sources such as telephone directories and club membership lists. In 1936, however, few *poor* people had telephones, nor were they likely to belong to clubs. Thus the sampling frame was incomplete and systematically excluded the poor. This omission was of particular significance in 1936 because in that year the poor voted overwhelmingly for Roosevelt, whereas the well-to-do voted mainly for Landon.[6] Thus the sampling frame did not accurately reflect the actual voter population.

Sample Designs

We have just discussed sampling problems in relation to the definition of the population and the sampling frame. The second sampling problem arises in connection with the method of securing a **representative sample**. The essential requirement of any sample is that it be as representative as possible of the population from which it is drawn. A sample is said to be representative if the analyses made on its sampling units produce results similar to those that would be obtained had the entire population been analyzed.

Probability and Nonprobability Sampling

In modern sampling theory, a basic distinction is made between probability and nonprobability sampling. The distinguishing characteristic of **probability sampling** is that one can specify for each sampling unit of the population the probability that it will be included in the sample. In the simplest case, each of the units has the same probability of being included in the sample.

5. David Freedman, Robert Pisani, and Roger Purves, *Statistics* (New York: Norton, 1978), pp. 302–307.
6. Ibid.

In **nonprobability sampling,** there is no way of specifying the probability of each unit's inclusion in the sample, and there is no assurance that every unit has some chance of being included. If a set of units has no chance of being included in the sample, a restriction on the definition of the population is implied; that is, if the traits of this set of units are unknown, then the precise nature of the population also remains unknown.[7] For example, in the 1936 election forecast, the voting intentions of the poor were unknown. Accordingly, only probability sampling makes representative sampling designs possible.

A well-designed sample ensures that if a study were to be repeated on a number of different samples drawn from a given population, the findings would not differ from the population parameters by more than a specified amount. A probability sample design makes it possible to estimate the extent to which the findings based on one sample are likely to differ from what would have been found by studying the entire population. With a probability sample design, it is possible to attach estimates of the population's parameters from the sample statistics.

Although accurate estimates of the population's parameters can be made only with probability samples, social scientists do employ nonprobability samples. The major reasons for this practice are convenience and economy, which, under certain circumstances (e.g., exploratory research), may outweigh the advantages of using probability sampling. Nonprobability samples are also used when a sampling population cannot be precisely defined and when a list of the sampling population is unavailable. For example, there is no list of drug addicts or of illegal residents in the United States.

Nonprobability Sample Designs

Three major designs of nonprobability samples have been used by social scientists: convenience samples, purposive samples, and quota samples.

Convenience Samples. A convenience sample is obtained when the researcher selects whatever sampling units are conveniently available. Thus a college professor may select students in a class; or a researcher may take the first 200 people encountered on the street who are willing to be interviewed. There is no way of estimating the representativeness of convenience samples and thus of estimating the population's parameters.

Purposive Samples. With purposive samples (occasionally referred to as judgment samples), the sampling units are selected subjectively by the researcher, who attempts to obtain a sample that appears to be representative of the population. The chance that a particular sampling unit will be selected for the sample depends on the subjective judgment of the researcher. Because it is impossible to determine why different researchers judge each

7. Chein, "An Introduction to Sampling," p. 421.

sampling unit they select to contribute to the representativeness of the sample, it is impossible to determine the probability of any specific sampling unit's being included in the sample. Purposive samples have been used with some success in attempts to forecast election turnout. In the United States, for example, a number of small election districts in each state are selected, their election returns in previous years having approximated the overall state returns. All the eligible voters in the selected districts are interviewed on their voting intentions, and the forecast is based on these reports. The underlying (and indeed risky) assumption is that the selected districts remain representative of their respective states.

Quota Samples.   The chief aim of a quota sample is the selection of a sample that is as similar as possible to the sampling population. For example, if it is known that the population has equal numbers of males and females, the researcher selects an equal number of males and females in the sample. If it is known that 15 percent of the population is black, 15 percent of the total sample would be black. In quota sampling, interviewers are given an assignment of quota groups specified by variables such as gender, age, place of residence, and ethnicity. For example, an interviewer may be instructed to interview 15 individuals, of whom 6 live in the suburbs and 7 in the central city. Seven have to be men and 6 women; of the 7 men (and the same quota for women), exactly 3 should be married and 4 single. It is obvious that disproportions between the sample and the population are likely to occur in variables that have not been specified in the interviewers' quotas. As with other nonprobability samples, we cannot estimate the parameters of the population accurately from quota samples.

Quota samples were frequently used by pollsters until the presidential election of 1948, when the polls incorrectly predicted that Thomas E. Dewey would be elected president.[8] Three major polls predicted the outcome of the election, and all three had declared Dewey the winner. Yet on election day President Harry S Truman won with almost 50 percent of the popular vote, whereas Dewey got just over 45 percent.

All three polls used quota samples, taking into consideration variables that they assumed influenced voting such as place of residence, gender, age, ethnicity, and income. Although this is a sensible assumption, many factors influence voting besides the ones considered in the 1948 election. Moreover, no quota was set on Republican or Democratic votes because the distribution of political opinion was exactly what these polling organizations did not know and were trying to find out. Finally—and perhaps the most serious problem—within the assigned quotas, the interviewers were free to choose anybody they liked. This left a lot of room for discretion, which in turn created a significant bias.[9]

8. Freedman et al., *Statistics,* pp. 302–307.
9. Ibid., pp. 305–307.

Probability Sample Designs

Earlier we pointed out that in contrast to nonprobability sampling, probability sample designs permit the specification of the probability of each sampling unit's being included in the sample in a single draw from the population. Here we present four common designs of probability samples: simple random sampling, systematic sampling, stratified sampling, and cluster sampling.

Simple Random Samples. **Simple random sampling** is the basic probability sampling design, and it is incorporated into all the more elaborate probability sampling designs. Simple random sampling is a sampling procedure that gives each of the *N* sampling units of the population an equal and known nonzero probability of being selected. For example, when you toss a perfect coin, the probability that you will get a head or a tail is equal and known (50 percent), and each subsequent outcome is independent of previous outcomes. Scientists usually use computer programs or tables of random digits to select random samples. A table of random digits is reproduced in Appendix D. The use of such a table is quite simple. Each sampling unit of the population is listed and given a number from 1 to *N*. The table of random digits is entered at some random starting point. Each digit that appears in the table is read in order (up, down, or across; the direction does not matter, as long as it is consistent). Whenever a digit that appears in the table of random digits corresponds to the number of a sampling unit in the list, that sampling unit is selected for the sample. This process is continued until the desired sample size is reached. The selection of any given sampling unit is independent of the selection of previous sampling units. Consequently, bias in the selection procedure is eliminated, and estimates of parameters can be made.

Random selection procedures ensure that every sampling unit of the population has an equal and known probability of being included in the sample; this probability is n/N, where *n* stands for the size of the sample and *N* for the size of the population.[10] For example, if the population consists of 50,389 eligible voters in a town and a simple random sample of 1,800 is to be drawn, the probability of each sampling unit of the population's being included in the sample is 1,800/50,389, or .0357. (See Exhibit 8.1.)

Systematic Samples. **Systematic sampling** consists of selecting every *K*th sampling unit of the population after the first sampling unit is selected at random from the first *K* sampling units. Thus if one desires to select a sample of 100 persons from a population of 10,000, one takes every hundredth individual ($K = N/n = 10,000/100 = 100$). The first selection is determined by some random process, such as the use of a table of random digits. Suppose that the fourteenth person were selected; the sample would then consist of individuals numbered 14, 114, 214, 314, 414, and so on.

---

10. For the mathematical proof, see Kish, *Survey Sampling,* pp. 39–40.

Exhibit 8.1
How to Draw a Random Sample

The Problem

In a cost containment study of a regional hospital, patients' records are to be examined. There are $N = 100$ patients' records from which a simple random sample of $n = 10$ is to be drawn.

　　1. We can number the accounts, beginning with 001 for the first account and ending with 100 representing the hundredth account. Notice that we have three-digit numbers in our population. If the total number of records were 1,250, we would need four-digit numbers. In our case, we need to select three-digit random numbers in order to give every record the same known chance of selection.

　　2. Now refer to Appendix D and use the first column. You will notice that each column has five-digit numbers. If we drop the last two digits of each number and we proceed down the column, we obtain the following three-digit numbers

104	854	521	007*
223	289	070*	053*
241	635	486	919
421	094*	541	005*
375	103	326	007
779	071*	293	690
995	510	024*	259
963	023*	815	097*
895	010*	296	

The last number listed is 097 from line 35 (column 1). We do not need to list more numbers since we already have ten different numbers that qualify for our sample (007 appears twice but is selected only once). The starred numbers are the records chosen for our sample. These are the only numbers that fall between the range we specified, 001–100.

　　We now have ten records in our simple random sample. Let us list them:

094	070	005
071	024	097
023	007	
010	053	

　　3. We need not start with the first row of column 1. We can select any starting point, such as the seventh row of column 2. We can also choose to progress in any way we want down the columns, across them, or diagonally as long as we decide ahead of time what our plan will be.

　　Systematic sampling is more convenient than simple random sampling. When interviewers who are untrained in sampling are to execute the sampling in the field, it is much simpler to instruct them to select every Kth person from a list than to have them use a table of random digits. Systematic

---

Exhibit 8.2
How to Draw a Systematic Sample

The Problem

A social scientist is interested in investigating the relationship between parents' occupations and the grade point average of students on a large urban campus
($N = 35,000$). As the information needed can be obtained from the students' records,
a sample of say $n = 700$ records must be selected. Although a simple random sample
could be selected (see Exhibit 8.1), this would require a great deal of work. Alternatively, we could use the following procedure.

1. The first step is to determine the sampling interval, K. As $N = 35,000$ and the
sample size $n = 700$, K is 35,000/700; that is, $K = 50$.

2. We now select the first record at random from the first $K = 50$ records listed
and then select every fiftieth record thereafter until a sample size of 700 is selected.
This method is called a 1-in-50 systematic sample.

---

samples are also more convenient to use with very large populations or
when large samples are to be selected. (See Exhibit 8.2.)

With systematic sampling, each sampling unit in the population has a
$1/K$ probability of being included in the sample. However, there may be a
systematic pattern in the data occurring at every Kth unit, and this will bias
the sample. For example, if single houses or blocks are selected and the first
chosen is a corner house, every Kth element may also be a corner house.
This may introduce a bias since corner houses tend to be larger. If one is
aware of a systematic pattern in the population, and if one can shuffle the
list thoroughly first, one can minimize problems.[11]

Stratified Samples.   **Stratified sampling** is used primarily to ensure that
different groups of a population are adequately represented in the sample so
that the level of accuracy in estimating parameters is increased. Furthermore, all other things being equal, stratified sampling reduces the cost of ex-
ecution considerably. The underlying idea in stratified sampling is that available information on the population is used "to divide it into groups such
that the elements within each group are more alike than are the elements in
the population as a whole."[12] If a series of homogeneous groups can be sampled in such a way that when the samples are combined, they constitute a
sample of a more heterogeneous population, increased accuracy will result.
For example, suppose that it is known that there are 700 whites, 200 blacks,
and 100 Mexican-Americans in a given population. If a random sample of

---

11. For some other procedures for avoiding problems caused by systematic patterns in populations, see William Cochran, *Sampling Techniques,* 3d ed. (New York: Wiley, 1977).

12. Morris H. Hansen, William N. Hurwitz, and William G. Madow, *Sample Survey Methods
and Theory* (New York: Wiley, 1953), p. 40.

100 persons were drawn, one would probably not get exactly 70 whites, 20 blacks, and 10 Mexican-Americans; the proportion of Mexican-Americans, especially, might be relatively too small. A stratified sample of 70 whites, 20 blacks, and 10 Mexican-Americans would ensure better representation of these groups. Stratification does not violate the principle of random selection because a probability sample is subsequently drawn within each stratum.

The necessary condition for division into homogeneous strata is that the criteria for division be related to the variable being studied. A second consideration is that the criteria used not require too many subsamples that would increase the size of the sample over that required by a simple random sample. Suppose that you want to estimate the median family income in a small town and you know the traits of the families in the population. Since it has already been established that income correlates with occupation, education, ethnicity, age, and gender, these would become logical bases for stratification. However, if all these bases were used, the value of stratified sampling would diminish, for the number of subsamples would become enormous. Consider what would happen if there were four categories of occupation, three of education, three of ethnicity, three of age, and two of gender. The number of subsamples would then equal $4 \times 3 \times 3 \times 3 \times 2$, or 216. Because a statistically satisfactory frequency in the smallest cell cannot be less than ten cases, this would require a minimum of 2,160, assuming that the frequencies in all cells were equal. No one would consider such a number as a sample of a small town. To solve this problem, we assume that many such stratification bases occur as associated factors. Thus if social status is chosen to stand for occupation, education, and ethnicity, the number of subsamples can be reduced to 4 (social-status groups) $\times$ 3 (age groups) $\times$ 2 (gender groups) = 24 subsamples. This is a more usable sample design, and it would represent the population better than a simple random sample.

Sampling from the different strata can be either proportional or disproportional. If one draws into the sample the same number of sampling units from each stratum, or a uniform sampling fraction (n/N), the sample is known as a *proportionate stratified sample*. The sample size from each stratum is proportional to the population size of the stratum. However, if there are variable sampling fractions (that is, if the total number in each stratum is different), the sample is a *disproportionate stratified sample*. Disproportionate stratified samples are used either to compare two or more particular strata or to analyze one stratum intensively. When a disproportionate stratified sample is used, the population's parameters have to be weighted by the number of each stratum.[13] (See Exhibit 8.3.)

Cluster Samples.   The fourth type of probability sampling used by social scientists is **cluster sampling**. It is frequently used in large-scale studies

---

13. See Kish, *Survey Sampling,* pp. 77–82, for methods of weighting.

Exhibit 8.3
How to Draw a Stratified Sample

The Problem

In a study of revitalization in an urban neighborhood, the attitudes of new residents toward their community is to be examined. It is anticipated that the attitudes of homeowners may differ from those of renters. Therefore, as a means of ensuring proper representation of both groups, it is decided to use a proportional stratified random sample with two strata: homeowners and renters.

1. The population consists of $N = N_1 + N_2$, with N_1 denoting new homeowners and N_2 new renters. $N_1 = 200$ and $N_2 = 300$. Therefore, $N = 500$. It is decided to select a proportional sampling fraction of $1/10$ from each stratum. Thus $N_1 = 20$ homeowners and $N_2 = 30$ renters will be included in the sample.

2. The procedure of simple random sampling (see Exhibit 8.1) is applied separately to the homeowner and renter lists.

---

because it is the least expensive sample design. Cluster sampling involves first selecting larger groupings, called clusters, and then selecting the sampling units from the clusters. The clusters are selected by a simple random sample or a stratified sample. Depending on the research problem, all the sampling units in these clusters can be included in the sample, or a selection from within the clusters can be made using simple or stratified sampling procedures.

Suppose that the research objective is to study the political attitudes of adults in the various election districts of a city in which no single list containing all the names is available, and it is too expensive to compile such a list. However, a map of the election districts exists. We can randomly select election districts from the list (first-stage cluster sampling). Within each of the districts, we can then select blocks at random (second-stage cluster sampling) and interview all the persons on these blocks. We may also use a simple random sample within each block selected, in which case a three-stage cluster sample will be obtained. (This sampling method is also called *area probability sampling* or just *area sampling*.) Similarly, a survey of urban households may take a sample of cities; within each city that is selected, a sample of districts; and within each selected district, a sample of households. (See Exhibit 8.4.)

The choice of clusters depends on the research objectives and the resources available for the study. Households, blocks, schools, districts, and cities have all been used as clusters. In fact, as Leslie Kish points out:

> The population of the United States may be alternatively regarded as an aggregate of units which are entire counties; or of cities, towns, and townships; or of area segments and blocks; or of dwellings; or, finally, as indi-

Exhibit 8.4
How to Draw a Cluster Sample

The Problem

The purpose of the study is to interview residents of an urban community. No list of resident adults is available, and thus cluster sampling is used as the sampling design.

Stage 1

1. The area to be covered is defined using an up-to-date map. Boundaries are defined, and areas that do not include dwelling units are excluded.
2. The entire area is divided into blocks. Boundary lines should not bisect dwellings and should be easily identifiable by fieldworkers.
3. Blocks are numbered, preferably serially and in serpentine fashion.
4. A simple random or systematic sample of blocks is selected, using the appropriate procedure.

Stage 2

1. All dwelling units in each of the selected blocks are listed and numbered. The delineation sometimes requires fieldworkers to ensure that all new constructions are listed.
2. A simple random or systematic sample of dwelling units is selected.
3. Selected individuals within each selected dwelling unit are interviewed. The selection usually follows the investigator's guidelines.

Based in part on Matilda White Riley, *Sociological Research: Exercises and Manual* (Orlando, Fla.: Harcourt Brace Jovanovich, 1963), vol. 2, p. 172.

Table 8.1
Description of Four Probability Samples

Type of Sampling	Description
Simple random	Assign to each sampling unit a unique number; select sampling units by use of a table of random digits.
Systematic	Determine the sampling interval (N/n); select the first sample unit randomly; select remaining units according to the interval.
Stratified	
Proportionate	Determine strata; select from each stratum a random sample proportionate to the size of the stratum in the population.
Disproportionate	Determine strata; select from each stratum a random sample of the size dictated by analytical considerations.
Cluster	Determine the number of levels of clusters; from each level of clusters select randomly; ultimate units are groups.

Based on Russell Ackoff, *The Design of Social Research* (Chicago: University of Chicago Press, 1953).

vidual persons. Indeed, all those sampling units are employed in turn for area samples of the United States.[14]

Probability Sampling: A Summary

The four designs of probability sampling that we have described do not exhaust the range of probability sampling procedures, and you are advised to consult the additional reading listing at the end of this chapter. However, these are the basic designs most commonly used by social scientists. By way of a summary, a brief description of the four designs is given in Table 8.1.

Probability Sampling: An Example

To illustrate the entire sampling process, we shall examine the procedures employed by the Institute for Social Research (ISR) at the University of Michigan in its national surveys.[15] The sampling procedure involves three sampling designs: cluster sampling, stratified sampling, and simple random sampling.

ISR is among the largest university-based social science research organizations in the United States. Research projects conducted by the institute are sponsored by governmental organizations, private business, and public service organizations. Many of the studies involve large nationwide samples. Listed here are the steps roughly followed by the center in drawing a national sample.[16] (See Figure 8.1.)

1. The entire geographic area of the United States is divided into small areas each called a *primary sampling unit* (PSU). The PSUs are generally counties or metropolitan areas. Out of the entire list of PSUs, 74 are selected by stratified random sampling to ensure adequate representation of rural areas, large and middle-sized cities, and regions.

2. Each of the 74 selected PSUs is further subdivided into a smaller area. For example, a hypothetical PSU consisting of two large cities, six medium-sized towns, and the rural remainder of the county would be divided into three strata: (1) large cities, (2) smaller cities and towns, and (3) rural areas. Units within these strata are called *sample places*. One or more sample places are selected within each stratum.

3. Each sample place is further divided into *chunks*. A chunk is defined as an area having identifiable boundaries: for example, in urban areas, a chunk is equivalent to a block; in rural areas, it is bounded by roads or county lines. Within each sample place, chunks are selected randomly.

4. At this stage, the interviewers play a major role in the sampling process. They visit each chunk, listing all the dwelling units, and suggest how

14. Ibid., p. 150.
15. Survey Research Center, *Interviewer's Manual*, rev. ed. (Ann Arbor: Institute for Social Research, University of Michigan, 1976), Chapter 8.
16. Ibid.

Figure 8.1
Drawing a National Sample

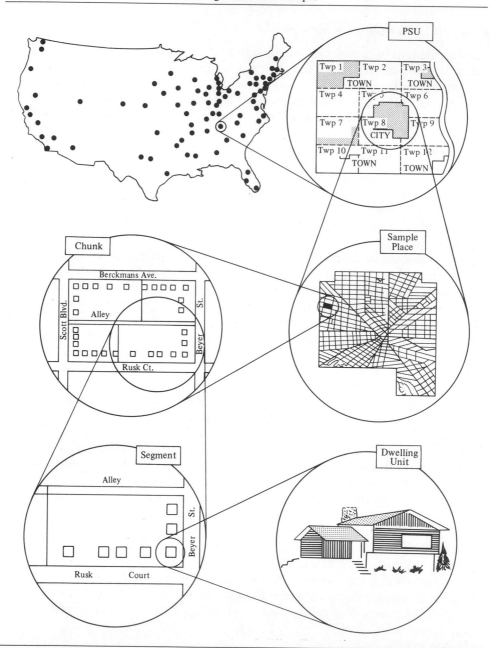

From Survey Research Center, *Interviewer's Manual*, rev. ed. (Ann Arbor: Institute for Social Research, University of Michigan, 1976), p. 8–2.

the chunk can be divided into areas each containing 4 to 12 dwelling units. These areas are called *segments*. Segments are then randomly selected from each chunk.

5. At the last stage, dwelling units are selected from each segment to be included in the final sample. The selection of dwelling units varies. When a segment includes only a few dwelling units, all are included in the study. If the segment contains more dwelling units, only a specified fraction of the dwellings in that segment will be included in the study.

Sample Size

A *sample* is any subset of sampling units from a population. A subset is any combination of sampling units that does not include the entire set of sampling units that has been defined as the population. A sample may be one sampling unit, all but one sampling unit, or any number in between. How do we determine the size of a sample?

There are several popular notions about the necessary size of a sample. One is that the sample size must be a certain proportion (often put at 5 percent) of the population; another is that the sample should total about 2,000; still another is that any increase in the sample size will increase the precision of the sample results. These are faulty notions because they do not derive from sampling theory. The adequate size of the sample is properly estimated by deciding what level of accuracy is expected; that is, how large a standard error is acceptable.

Standard Error

The idea of **standard error** (some people use the terms *error margin* or *sampling error*) is central to sampling theory and to determining the size of a sample. We will illustrate the idea of standard error by examining a small hypothetical population from which simple random samples are drawn.

The population consists of five students earning $500, $650, $400, $700, and $600 per month, so the population's mean monthly income (denoted by μ) is $570.[17] Say that we draw a sample of two with the purpose of estimating μ and that the draw results in the selection of two persons earning $500 and $400. The sample mean ($\bar{x}$) is therefore ($500 + $400)/2 = $450, which we take as the estimate of μ, the population mean. Since we already know that the population mean is $570, the estimate of $450 is inaccurate. Had we selected the two students earning $650 and $700, the sample mean would have been $675, which is also an inaccurate estimate of the population mean. We can draw all the samples of size $n = 2$ from this population. Table

---

17. See Chapter 15 for a discussion of the mean and the standard deviation.

Table 8.2
Estimates of the Population's Mean

Possible Samples of $n=2$ (incomes of students selected, in $)	$\bar{x}$ (estimate of μ, in $)
500 and 650	575
500 and 400	450
500 and 700	600
500 and 600	550
650 and 400	525
650 and 700	675
650 and 600	625
400 and 700	550
400 and 600	500
700 and 600	650
Total	5,700

8.2 presents the ten possible samples and the estimates of μ derived from each. None of these samples accurately estimates μ. However, some sample means (for example, $500 and $650) are closer to the population mean than others. If we continue indefinitely to draw samples of $n=2$, each of the samples in Table 8.2 would be selected more than once. We can then plot the distribution of all sample means. The distribution that results from the value of the sample mean ($\bar{x}$) derived from an *infinite* number of samples is termed the *sampling distribution of the mean*. In our example, each of the ten samples has an equal chance of being drawn (it is a simple random sample), and if we continue the selection indefinitely, samples would be drawn an equal number of times. Consequently, the mean of the estimates derived from *all* the possible samples is $5,700/10 = 570$, which equals the population mean.

In general, the mean distribution of an infinite number of samples is assumed to equal the mean of the population. The more dispersed the distribution of samples about its mean, the greater will be the variability of findings obtained by samples, and the greater the risk in making a large error in estimating a parameter from a sample statistic.

In our hypothetical example, we knew the population mean and could compare it with the means obtained from the samples. In reality, the population mean is unknown, and a single sample (not an infinite number of samples) is drawn in order to estimate the population parameter. The distribution obtained from a single sample serves as an indicator of the entire sampling distribution, and the dispersion within the single sample is measured by the standard deviation (s). The distribution of all samples about the mean of the samples is the standard error ($S.E.$). We can calculate the standard deviation and then estimate the $S.E.$ The $S.E.$ cannot be calculated directly because we do not draw the infinite number of samples necessary for its calculation. It is assumed that the dispersion within a single randomly selected and representative sample indicates the dispersion within the sampling population.

The standard deviation of the sampling distribution in our example is

$$[(575-570)^2 + (450-570)^2 + (600-570)^2 + (550-570)^2$$
$$+ (525-570)^2 + (675-570)^2 + (625-570)^2 + (550-570)^2$$
$$+ (500-570)^2 + (650-570)^2]/10 = \sqrt{4,350} = 65.95$$

The *S.E.* can be estimated by dividing the standard deviation of the sample by the square root of the sample size (*n*):

$$S.E. = \frac{s}{\sqrt{n}}$$

If the population is small, the factor $1-n/N$, called the finite population correction, has to be included in the equation:

$$S.E. = \frac{s^2}{n}\left(1-\frac{n}{N}\right)$$

In this formula, *n* refers to the sample size and *N* stands for the size of the population. In our example, $N=5$ and $n=2$, so

$$s^2 = \frac{(500-570)^2 + (650-570)^2 + (400-570)^2 + (700-570)^2 + (600-570)^2}{4}$$

$$= \frac{58,000}{4} = 14,500$$

Therefore,

$$S.E.(\bar{x}) = \sqrt{\left(\frac{14,500}{2}\right)\left(\frac{5-2}{5}\right)} = \sqrt{4,350} = 65.95$$

which is identical to the previous result.

Confidence Intervals

We need to discuss one more concept, **confidence interval,** before presenting the method for determining the sample size. We have pointed out that the population mean equals the mean of all the sample means that can be drawn from a population and that we can compute the standard deviation of these sample means. If the distribution of sample means is normal or approximates normality, we can use the properties of the normal curve to estimate the location of the population mean.[18] If we knew the mean of all sample

18. See pages 361–362 for a detailed discussion of the normal curve and its properties.

means (the population mean) and the standard deviation of these sample means (standard error of the mean), we could compute Z scores and determine the range within which any percentage of the sample means can be found. Between $-1Z$ and $+1Z$, we would expect to find 68 percent of all sample means; between $-1.96Z$ and $+1.96Z$, we would expect to find 95 percent of all sample means; and between $-2.58Z$ and $+2.58Z$, we would expect to find 99 percent of all sample means. However, it is this mean of the population that is unknown and that we have to estimate on the basis of a single sample.

The normal curve can be used for this purpose. A sample mean that is $+1.96Z$ scores (or standard errors of the mean) above the population mean has a .025 probability of occurrence; 97.5 percent of all sample means will be smaller than $+1.96$ standard errors of the mean. If it is a rare event for a sample mean to be 1.96 or more standard errors of the mean above the population mean, it is just as rare for the population mean to be 1.96 standard errors of the mean below a given sample mean. But we do not know whether the sample mean is larger or smaller than the true mean of the population. Nevertheless, if we construct an interval of -1.96 to $+1.96$ about the sample mean, we can be confident that the population mean is located in that interval. We do not expect that the sample mean will in fact be as far as ±1.96 standard errors of the mean away from the population mean, and we are confident that the population mean is no farther than this from the sample mean. If we construct an interval of ±1.96 standard errors of the mean

Figure 8.2
Normal Curve: Percent Areas from the Mean to Specified
Standard Error Distances

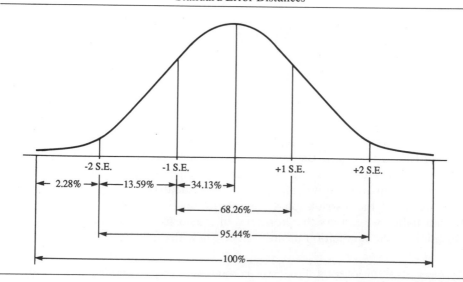

about the sample mean, we expect the population mean to be within this interval with 95 percent confidence. There is a 5 percent chance that we are wrong, that is, that the population mean is not within the interval (see Figure 8.2). If you do not wish to run a 5 percent risk of being incorrect, you can use a different confidence interval. The chance that the population mean will be within $+2.58$ and -2.58 standard errors of the sample mean is 99 out of 100, and this is the 99 percent confidence interval. The width of the confidence interval around the sample mean is decided by the researcher. The confidence interval can be narrow if the researcher is willing to run a large risk of being wrong. The researcher could use an interval of $\pm.68$ standard errors of the mean and have only a 50 percent chance of being correct in assuming that the population mean is within the interval.

To sum up, if a given sampling distribution is known to be approximately normal, one can infer that about 68 percent of the sample estimates of which it is comprised will lie between its mean and one standard error, about 95 percent between its mean and twice the standard error.

Determining the Sample Size

Now we can estimate the size of samples. If cost and other practical limitations do not enter into the decision about sample size, there is no difficulty in determining the desired size. Recall the formula for the standard error of the mean:

$$S.E. = \frac{s}{\sqrt{n}}$$

where s is the standard deviation of the variable under study in the population. Inverting, we then have

$$n = \frac{s^2}{(S.E.)^2}$$

To calculate the sample size, n, we have to have some idea of the standard deviation in the population and must also decide how big a standard error can be tolerated. If, for example, a random sample is to be drawn from a population consisting of 10,000 sampling units, $s^2 = .20$, and the desired $S.E. = .016$, the estimated sample size is

$$n = \frac{.20}{.000256} = 781.25$$

If the sample size is too large relative to the population, the finite population correction is added. In such cases, the final sample size is calculated by

$$n' = \frac{n}{1 + (n/N)}$$

where N is the population size. In our example, if $N = 10,000$, then

$$n' = \frac{781.25}{1 + \dfrac{781.25}{10,000}} \cong 725$$

In practice, decisions concerning the sample size are more complicated. The first difficulty relates to the precision required. Researchers must decide how precise they want their sample results to be, that is, how large a standard error is acceptable. Second, the decision on a sample size also depends on the way the results are analyzed. Third, if more than one variable is to be studied, a sample that is adequate for one variable may be unsatisfactory for another.[19]

Nonsampling Errors

Sampling theory is concerned with the error introduced by the sampling procedure. In a perfect design, this error is minimized for an individual sample. The error in estimates refers to what is expected in the long run if a particular set of procedures is followed. However, even if the sampling error is minimized, there are other sources of error, for example, measurement error (see Chapter 7). In survey research, the most pervasive error is the **nonresponse error**. Nonresponse is defined as observations that are not carried out because of reasons such as refusal to answer, absence, and lost forms. Nonresponse can introduce a substantial bias into the findings.

Recall the *Literary Digest* poll of 1936. We discussed the errors made by the *Digest* in the sampling frame selection process. The *Digest* failed not only at this stage but also later on when it based its estimates on a very low response rate. The results of the poll were based on the response of 2.4 million people, out of 10 million originally selected to be included in the sample.[20] This biased the results considerably because there was evidence showing that the nonrespondents tended to vote for Roosevelt whereas, among the respondents, over half favored Landon.

Generally, the amount and kind of bias is related to the following conditions:

1. The greater the nonresponse proportion, the greater the biasing effects. The response proportion can be computed as follows:

$$R = 1 - \frac{n-r}{n}$$

For example, if the original sample size is 1,200, and 1,000 responses are actually obtained, the response rate is $1 - (1,200 - 1,000)/1,200 = .83$, and the nonresponse rate is .17, or 17 percent.

2. The seriousness of the nonresponse bias depends on the extent to which the population mean of the nonresponse stratum differs from that of the response stratum.[21] In symbols,

19. For further details, see Kish, *Survey Sampling*; and C. A. Moser and Graham Kalton, *Survey Methods in Social Investigation*, 2d ed. (New York: Basic Books, 1972).

20. Freedman et al., *Statistics*, pp. 302–307.

21. Moser and Kalton, *Survey Methods in Social Investigation*, pp. 166–167.

$$\mu_1 - \mu = \mu_1 - (R_1\mu_1 + R_2\mu_2)$$
$$= \mu_1(1 - R_1) - R_2\mu_2$$
$$= R_2(\mu_1 - \mu_2)$$

where N_1 is a "response stratum," N_2 a "nonresponse stratum," $N_1/N = R_1$, and $N_2/N = R_2$.

3. Each of the following nonresponse types influences the sample results in a different way. (These types apply to entire interview schedules as well as to parts of an interview or questionnaire or to single questions.)[22]

- *Uninterviewables:* people who are ill, illiterate, or have language barriers.
- *Not found:* people who have moved and are inaccessible, for instance, who cannot make an appointment.
- *Not-at-homes:* people who are out when the interviewer calls but are reached later.
- *Refusals:* people who refuse to cooperate or to answer survey questions. Refusals may also vary with the type of question being asked.

The proportion of nonrespondents depends on factors such as the nature of the population, the data collection method, the kinds of questions being asked, the skill of the interviewers, and the number of callbacks that can be made. A poorly designed and administered interview will result in a very low response rate.

To estimate the effect of nonresponse, one can collect information about the nonrespondents on callbacks. Based on such information, estimates can be made. Suppose that voters in a small community are surveyed to estimate the proportions that identify with one party or another and that the survey has a 10 percent nonresponse rate. This can be corrected with additional information on the education or income of the nonrespondents. Suppose that 10 percent amounts to 300 voters and that of these, 70 percent have incomes of about $25,000 a year. If one knew that, in general, 90 percent of the people in this income level are Democrats, one might estimate that $.70 \times 300 \times .90 = 189$ are Democrats. However, there is no way of computing the possible error of this estimate. Such estimates can be used to correct for nonresponse only if the response rate is relatively low.

Summary

1. In this chapter, we focused on drawing population estimates from sample statistics. To arrive at accurate estimates of parameters, the researcher has to deal effectively with three problems: (1) definition of the

22. Dennis J. Palumbo, *Statistics in Political and Behavioral Science*, rev. ed. (New York: Columbia University Press, 1977), p. 296.

population, (2) selection of a representative sample, and (3) determination of the sample size.

2. A population has to be defined in terms of content, extent, and time. A sample is any subset of sampling units from the population. A sample may be one sampling unit, all but one sampling unit, or any number in between. The determination of a sample size is essentially dependent on the value of the standard error and on the width of the confidence interval that is set by the researcher. The confidence interval can be made extremely narrow if the researcher is willing to run a large risk of being wrong or extremely wide if the researcher opts to run a negligible risk.

3. After the definition of a population and the estimation of the size of the sample, a representative sampling design has to be selected. A sample is representative if the analyses made on its units produce results equivalent to those that would be obtained had the entire population been analyzed. Most often, researchers use probability sampling designs because they can specify the probability of each unit of the population's being included in the sample. The characteristics of four basic probability samples—simple random, systematic, stratified, and cluster—were summarized in Table 8.1.

4. In survey research, in addition to sampling error, nonresponse error is pervasive. Nonresponse is defined as measurements that are not carried out because of refusal to answer, absence, lost forms, and so on. Nonresponse can introduce a substantial bias into the findings, and techniques exist for estimating bias.

Key Terms for Review

sample	nonprobability sample
population	simple random sample
parameter	systematic sample
statistic	stratified sample
sampling unit	cluster sample
sampling frame	standard error
representative sample	confidence interval
probability sample	nonresponse error

Study Questions

1. How are samples used to describe populations?
2. Discuss the idea of sampling error and how it allows researchers to construct confidence intervals around their sample estimates.
3. Distinguish between probability and nonprobability sampling, and explain the advantages and disadvantages of each.

4. Discuss the major types of probability sampling, cite their strengths and weaknesses, and explain how to select a sample using each method.
5. What factors could introduce nonsampling error into a survey?

Additional Readings

Alreck, Pamela L., and Robert B. Settle. *The Survey Research Handbook*. Homewood, Ill.: Irwin, 1985.

Granovettes, Mark. "Network Sampling: Some First Steps." *American Journal of Sociology*, 81 (1976): 1287–1303.

Hess, Irene. *Sampling for Social Research Surveys*. Ann Arbor: Institute for Social Research, University of Michigan, 1985.

Jaeger, Richard M. *Sampling for Education and the Social Sciences*. White Plains, N.Y.: Longman, 1984.

Kalton, Graham. *Introduction to Survey Sampling*. Newbury Park, Calif.: Sage, 1983.

Kruskal, William H., and Frederick Mosteller. "Ideas of Representative Sampling." In *New Directions for Methodology in Social and Behavioral Science*, ed. Donald W. Fiske. San Francisco: Jossey-Bass, 1981, pp. 3–24.

Stuart, Alan. *The Ideas of Sampling*. 3d ed. New York: Oxford University Press, 1987.

Wainer, Howard. *Drawing Inferences from Self-selected Samples*. New York: Springer-Verlag, 1986.

Yates, Frank. *Sampling Methods for Censuses and Surveys*. 4th ed. London: Griffin, 1981.

PART III

Data
Collection

CHAPTER 9

Observational Methods

In this chapter, we first discuss and exemplify the idea of triangulation. Next we discuss the varied roles of observation in social science research. We then present the strategies for conducting direct observations, followed by a discussion of controlled observation in the laboratory and the field.

HAVING DECIDED ON THE *WHAT* AND the *how* of an investigation, we proceed to the data collection stage. Social science data are obtained when investigators or others record observations about the phenomena being studied. Four general forms of data collection may be distinguished: observational methods, survey research, secondary data analysis, and qualitative research. Each form employs a number of particular methods, the most common of which are discussed in the following chapters. It should be emphasized at the outset, however, that each of these four forms has certain unique advantages but also some inherent limitations. For example, asking respondents to report who is the most influential member in their work group (survey research) may yield findings quite different from the ones obtained from data collected by direct observation. There is a certain degree of "method specificity" in each of the forms of data collection used by social scientists. Consequently, there is a great advantage in triangulating methods whenever feasible, that is, using more than one form of data collection to test the same hypothesis.

Triangulation

Data in the social sciences are obtained in either formal or informal settings and involve either verbal (oral and written) or nonverbal acts or responses. A variety of combinations of these two settings for data collection and the two types of acts results in the four major forms of data collection: observational methods, survey research (personal interviews and questionnaires as discussed in Chapters 10 and 11), secondary data analyses (for example, analysis of existing documents as discussed in Chapter 13), and qualitative research (discussed in Chapter 12). At the one extreme, where the concern is nonverbal actions in informal settings, participant observation—a form of qualitative research—is a common data collection method. At the other extreme, where the research focuses on verbal (oral and written) acts in formal, structured settings, the most common forms of data collection are laboratory experiments and structured questionnaires.

As we pointed out, each of these data collection methods has certain advantages but also some inherent limitations. For example, if we observe behavior as it occurs (direct observation), we may miss the reasons for its occurrence (which may be understood from structured questionnaires). Similarly, if we ask respondents to report on their behavior verbally (interviewing), we have no guarantee that their actual behavior (studied by direct observation or existing records) is identical to their reported behavior. For example, in a study on the validity of welfare mothers' interview responses to questions on voting, Weiss reported:

> On the voting and registration questions, 82 percent of the welfare mothers answered accurately. Sixteen percent overreported their registration and 2 percent underreported. The amount and direction of response error are similar to those of the largely middle-class populations whose voting self-reports have been validated in previous studies.[1]

In voting behavior as well as in other behavior, there is often a discrepancy between people's verbal reports and their actual behavior.

To a certain degree, research findings are affected by the nature of the data collection method used. Findings that are very strongly affected by the method used could be artifacts rather than empirical facts. As Donald Fiske points out:

> Knowledge in social science is fragmented, is composed of multiple discrete parcels. . . . The separateness or specificity of those bodies of knowledge is a consequence, not only of different objects of inquiry, but also of method specificity. Each method is one basis for knowing, one discriminable way of knowing.[2]

1. Carol Weiss, "Validity of Welfare Mothers' Interview Responses," *Public Opinion Quarterly*, 32 (1968): 622–633.
2. Donald W. Fiske, "Specificity of Method and Knowledge in Social Science," in Donald W. Fiske and Richard A. Shweder, *Metatherapy in Social Science* (Chicago: University of Chicago Press, 1986), p. 62.

To minimize the degree of specificity in bodies of knowledge, a researcher can use two or more methods of data collection to test hypotheses and measure variables; this is the essence of **triangulation**. For example, a structured questionnaire could be supplemented with in-depth interviewing, existing records, or field observation. Consistent findings among different data collection methods increase the credibility of research findings. And as a research strategy, triangulation raises social scientists "above the personal biases that stem from single methodologies. By combining methods and investigators in the same study, observers can partially overcome the deficiencies that flow from one investigator or one method."[3]

Roles of Observation

Social science research is rooted in observation. Political scientists observe, among other things, the behavior of occupants of political roles; anthropologists observe rituals in simple societies; and social psychologists observe interactions in small groups. In a sense, all social science research begins and ends with observations.

The main advantage of observation is its *directness*; it makes it possible to study behavior as it occurs. The researcher does not have to ask people about their own behavior and the actions of others; he or she can simply watch them do and say things. This in turn enables the collection of first-hand data that are uncontaminated by factors standing between the investigator and the object of research. For example, when people are asked to report their past behavior, distortions in memory may significantly contaminate the data, whereas memory has no effect at all on behavioral data collected through observational methods.

Moreover, data collected by observation may describe the observed phenomena as they occur in their *natural settings*. Other data collection methods introduce elements of artificiality into the research environment. An interview, for instance, is a form of face-to-face interaction, subject to peculiar problems because of the lack of consensus surrounding the roles of researcher and respondent. In such an interaction, the respondents might behave in a way that is not characteristic of their typical behavior (see Chapter 10). Artificiality can be reduced in observational studies, especially when the subjects are not aware of their being observed or when they become accustomed to the observer and do not regard him or her as an intruder.

Some studies focus on individuals who are unable to give verbal reports or to articulate themselves meaningfully. For example, it is necessary to use observation in studies of children because it is difficult for children to introspect, to verbalize, and to remain attentive to lengthy tasks. David Riesman

---

3. Norman K. Denzin. *The Research Act: A Theoretical Introduction to Sociological Methods*, 3d ed. (Englewood Cliffs, N.J.: Prentice-Hall, 1989), p. 236.

and Jeanne Watson, in an intriguing sociability study, used observational methods because the people studied "had no language for discussing sociable encounters, no vocabulary for describing parties except to say that they were 'good' or 'bad,' no way of answering the question 'What do you do for fun?' "[4]

Observational methods might also be used when persons are unwilling to express themselves verbally. Observation demands less active involvement on the part of the individuals being studied than verbal reports do. Furthermore, verbal reports can be validated and compared with actual behavior through observation. Finally, the relationship between a person and his or her environment is not altered in observational studies. Opportunities for analyzing the *contextual background* of behavior are improved by the researcher's ability to observe the environment's impact on the researched individuals.

Observation takes many forms. It includes casual experiences as well as sophisticated laboratory devices such as one-way-vision screens and video cameras. The many forms of observation make it a suitable method for a variety of research purposes. It might be used in exploratory research to gain insights that will subsequently be tested as hypotheses. Observational methods might also be used to collect supplementary data that may help interpret or qualify findings obtained by other methods, or they might be used as the primary methods of data collection in descriptive studies.

Observation may take place in natural settings or in the laboratory. A research problem such as patterns of learning may be studied as it occurs in a real-life situation (e.g., classroom or playground) or in the laboratory room. Observational procedures may range from complete flexibility, guided only by a general problem, to the use of structured instruments designed in advance. Researchers may themselves participate in the activities of the group they are observing; they may be viewed as members of the group but minimize their participation; they may assume roles of observers without being part of the group; or their presence might be concealed from the people being observed. Whatever the purpose of the study and the observational procedure used, three major considerations must be dealt with if the data obtained are to be systematic and meaningful: what to observe, when to observe and how to record, and how much inference is required.

Types of Behavior

The first significant consideration concerns *what should be observed*. Suppose that someone interested in studying the relation between frustration and aggression hypothesizes that frustration leads to aggression. To test this

4. David Riesman and Jeanne Watson, "The Sociability Project: A Chronicle of Frustration and Achievement," in *Sociologists at Work*, ed. Phillip E. Hammond (New York: Basic Books, 1964), p. 313.

hypothesis, frustration and aggression are to be observed. This requires clear and precise operational definitions of the two variables. The measurement of the variables "frustration" and "aggression," as well as of all other variables, may be based on nonverbal, spatial, extralinguistic, or linguistic behavior.[5]

Nonverbal Behavior

Nonverbal behavior is "the body movements of the organism" and "consists of motor expressions . . . [that] may originate in various parts of the body."[6] Nonverbal behavior has been studied extensively, and it has been repeatedly shown to be a valid indicator of social, political, and psychological processes. Paul Ekman suggests that observations of nonverbal behavior generate data that can serve "to repeat, contradict, or substitute for a verbal message, as well as accent certain words, maintain the communicative flow, reflect changes in the relationship in association with particular verbal messages and indicate a person's feeling about his verbal statement."[7] Facial expressions, in particular, convey a whole range of emotions, including fear, surprise, anger, disgust, and sadness.

Spatial Behavior

Spatial behavior refers to the attempts of individuals to structure the space around them. For example, people move toward, move away from, maintain closeness, and maintain distance. The range, frequency, and outcomes of such movements provide significant data for a variety of research purposes.

For example, there are distinct patterns in the way people use the space that immediately surrounds them when interacting with others. In different cultures there are unwritten customs regulating how close individuals approach each other: Latin Americans have closer personal spaces than do Americans, Germans, and the English. Cultural variations in personal space can have serious implications in culturally heterogeneous societies or cities. An individual from a German background may find it uncomfortable to interact with a Latin American because they have difficulty establishing satisfactory interpersonal spacing. Friction may develop between the two, since

5. The following discussion draws from Karl E. Weick, "Systematic Observational Methods," in *The Handbook of Social Psychology*, 3d ed., ed. Gardner Lindzey and Elliot Aronson (New York: Random House, 1985).

6. Paul Ekman, "A Methodological Discussion of Nonverbal Behavior," *Journal of Psychology*, 43 (1957): 14, 136.

7. Paul Ekman, "Communication through Nonverbal Behavior: A Source of Information about Interpersonal Relationship," in *Affect, Cognition, and Personality*, ed. Silvan S. Tomkins and Carroll E. Izard (New York: Springer, 1965), p. 441, and Paul Ekman and W. Friesen, "The Repertoire of Nonverbal Behavior: Categories, Origins, Usage and Coding," *Semiotica*, 1 (1969): 1–20.

each may view the other as rude. Actually, they are both attempting to establish spacing that is comfortable and acceptable in their respective cultures. Even within one society there are differences in personal space norms. Aiello and Thompson found that at young ages, blacks interact more closely than whites. However, adolescent blacks interact at greater distance than adolescent whites.[8] A common response to violations of personal space is stress. People whose personal space is violated report feeling tense and anxious. Physiological functions such as galvanic skin response, heart rate, and blood pressure increase when personal space is violated.[9]

Extralinguistic Behavior

Words, or linguistic content, make up only a small portion of behavior. Noncontent behaviors such as rate of speaking, loudness, tendency to interrupt, and pronunciation peculiarities constitute a fruitful source of data and are generally referred to as *extralinguistic behavior*, or *paralanguage*. The significance of paralanguage in the study of human behavior has been documented in numerous studies. For example, a vocal characteristic such as pitch accurately measures emotional states.[10] The average unit length of spontaneous speech increases as the size of the group increases.[11] Frequency of interruption reflects differences in personal power. Passive emotions such as sadness are expressed through slow speech and lower volume and pitch, and active emotions such as anger are communicated by fast, loud, and high-pitched speech. These examples only hint at the range of applications of extralinguistic indicators in the study of behavior and demonstrate the potential significance of noncontent behavior to social research.

Linguistic Behavior

Linguistic behavior is the manifest content of speech and the structural characteristics of talking. Measures of linguistic behavior have been widely used in studies on social interaction. Robert Bales, for example, developed a well-known system for organizing and coding the process of interaction in groups involved in problem-solving activities. Bales's system, Interaction Process Analysis, or IPA, contains 12 kinds of distinctive behavior within which the interaction of group members can be coded and analyzed. The IPA code of categories is shown in Exhibit 9.1.

8. A. J. Aiello and E. D. Thompson, "Personal Space, Crowding, and Spatial Behavior in a Cultural Context," in *Human Behavior and Environment*, ed. I. Altman et al. (New York: Plenum, 1980).

9. S. Worchel, and C. Teddlie, "The Experience of Crowding: A Two-Factor Theory," *Journal of Personality and Social Psychology*, 34 (1976): 30–40.

10. William F. Soskin and Paul E. Kauffman, "Judgment of Emotion in Word-free Voice Samples," *Journal of Communication*, 11 (1961): 73–80.

11. William F. Soskin and John P. Vera, "The Study of Spontaneous Talk," in *The Stream of Human Behavior*, ed. Roger C. Baker (Norwalk Conn.: Appleton & Lang, 1963).

Exhibit 9.1
IPA Code of Categories

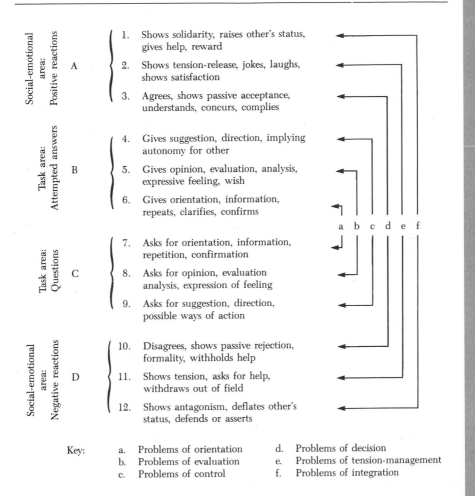

Key:
a.	Problems of orientation	d. Problems of decision
b.	Problems of evaluation	e. Problems of tension-management
c.	Problems of control	f. Problems of integration

Timing and Recording

The second major consideration in observational studies concerns the timing and the recording of observations. Obviously, it is impossible to make an infinite number of observations, so a decision must be made about when to observe. An acceptable approach to this problem is to follow a **time-sampling schedule**. *Time sampling* refers to the selection of observation units at different points in time. Observation units can be selected in sys-

tematic ways so as to ensure representation of a defined population of behavior. For example, one might make one's observations for a 15-minute period of each hour randomly selected after stratification by day of the week
and hour of the day. Time samples ensure the representativeness of ongoing
occurrences. Another useful sampling procedure is *individual sampling*, also
referred to as *specimen records*. The researcher selects one individual and
records all behavior and events centering on that individual. For example,
the observer selects a child and records all instances of physical aggression
between the child and other classmates. Every 30 minutes a different child is
selected. The collected data then represent the behavior of all the children in
the class.

   In addition to developing a time-sampling design, the researcher must
develop a coding system for recording the observations. Categorization is
necessary to transform the complexity of ongoing events into data that can
be expressed numerically or quantified. Such a coding system can be constructed by either a deductive approach or an inductive approach. A deductive approach implies that the researcher begins with a conceptual definition, then specifies indicators of the behavior to be observed, and then
standardizes and validates the resulting instrument. The deductive approach
is implemented when observations are assigned to categories at the time the
record is made. By contrast, the inductive approach requires first the selection of indicators and postpones definitions until some pattern is identified.
Each approach involves some risk. With the deductive approach, it is difficult to foresee whether the conceptual definition is precise. The empirical
approach poses difficulties in interpreting the observations (see also Chapter 14). The ideal way to reduce these risks is to combine the two approaches. Karl Weick suggests that

> in the ideal sequence, the observer would start with the empirical approach,
> obtain extensive records of natural events, induce some concepts from the
> records, and then collect a second set of records which are more specific
> and pointed more directly at the induced concept.[12]

   Regardless of whether a deductive or an inductive approach is used, the
categories to which observations are assigned must exhibit certain characteristics. A *category system* must

> limit the observation to one segment or aspect of . . . behavior, and con-
> struct a finite set of categories into one and only one of which every unit
> observed can be classified. The record obtained purports to show, for each
> period of observation, the total number of units of behavior which oc-
> curred and the number classifiable in each category.[13]

12. Weick, "Systematic Observational Methods," p. 102.
13. Donald M. Medley and Harold E. Mitzel, "Measuring Classroom Behavior by Systematic
Observation," in *Handbook of Research on Teaching*, ed. Nathaniel L. Gage (Skokie, Ill.:
Rand McNally, 1963), p. 298.

In other words, the categories must be explicit, exhaustive, and mutually exclusive. An explicit category is specified in terms of the occurrence to be observed, the situation in which the occurrence takes place, and the event that precedes or follows the observed occurrence. For instance, Edgar Borgatta specified a "shows tension increase" category in his interaction process scores observational system in the following way:

> In this category are scored the periods of tenseness that grow largely out of impasses or bankruptcy of conversation. Most of the scores that fall into this category are the awkward pauses, which are usually punctuated by clearing of throats, looking around by one person or another, etc. For the whole group, however, it is sometimes noted that the level of participation grows more tense because of the general personal involvement of the group.[14]

Inference

The third major consideration in structured observational studies relates to the degree of inference made by the observer. Most records in observation involve inferences. An investigator observes a certain act or behavior and must process this observation and make an inference that the behavior measures a certain variable. Some observational systems require a low degree of observer inference, for example, such straightforward acts as "asks a question," "suggests a course of action," and "interrupts another group member." Many acts, however, require a higher degree of inference. Suppose that one observes an adult striking a child. An inference has to be made whether this act represents "aggression," "aggressive behavior," "hostility," "violence," or some other variable. The correctness of such an inference depends to a large extent on the competence of the observer. Well-trained observers are likely to make more reliable inferences, other things being equal.

As a means of increasing the reliability of inferences, training programs applicable to various observational situations were designed. Typically, a program begins with an exposition of the theory, the research hypotheses involved in a given study, and an explanation of the category system constructed to record the observations. After the trainees have had an opportunity to raise questions, they apply the category system in a real-life situation, and only then does the actual data collection begin.

14. Edgar F. Borgatta, "A Systematic Study of Interaction Process Scores, Peer and Self-assessments, Personality and Other Variables," *Genetic Psychological Monographs*, 65 (1962): 219–291.

Types of Observation

The extent to which decisions regarding behavior, timing, recording, and inference are systematically and rigorously implemented is a criterion by which we can distinguish between controlled and noncontrolled observational systems. A controlled observational system is typified by clear and explicit decisions on what, how, and when to observe; a noncontrolled system is considerably less systematic and allows great flexibility. For example, in **controlled observation**, a time sample is usually drawn prior to observation; in **noncontrolled observation**, samples are rarely taken. The choice between controlled and noncontrolled observation depends to a large extent on the research problem and research design; that is, controlled observation is most frequently used with experimental research designs and seldom with preexperimental designs or qualitative studies. Controlled observational systems are discussed in this chapter; noncontrolled observation (qualitative research) is presented in Chapter 12.

Controlled Observations

Controlled observations are carried out either in the laboratory or in the field. In both settings, the investigator wishes to infer causality by maximizing control over extrinsic and intrinsic variables while employing one of the various experimental research designs and systematically recording observations.

Laboratory Experimentation

The most controlled method of data collection in the social sciences is *laboratory experimentation*. It involves the creation of conditions in a controlled environment (the laboratory) that simulates certain features of a natural environment, and a supervised manipulation of one or more independent variables at a time to observe the effects produced.

Classic examples of laboratory experimentation are Solomon Asch's experiments on interpersonal influence. Asch's objective was to examine the social and personal conditions that induce individuals to yield to or resist group pressures when such pressures are perceived to be contrary to fact. Asch developed a procedure for placing individuals in intense disagreement with their peers and for measuring the effect of this relationship on them. Eight individuals were instructed to match the length of a given line with one of three unequal lines. Group members were asked to announce their judgments aloud. In the middle of the test, one individual would suddenly be contradicted by the entire group, because Asch had instructed the seven other members to respond at certain points with wrong judgments. The errors of the majority were large, ranging between ½ inch and 1¾ inches. The eighth individual confronted a situation in which the group unanimously contradicted the evidence of his or her senses. This individual, commonly referred to as the *critical subject*, was the object of investigation. Asch also used a control group in which the errors introduced by the majority were not of the same order encountered under experimental conditions. One of the interesting findings was a marked movement toward the majority:

> One third of all the estimates in the critical group were errors identical with or in the direction of the distorted estimates of the majority. The significance of this finding becomes clear in the light of the virtual absense of errors in the control group.[15]

The Asch experiment exemplifies the two major advantages of laboratory experimentation: it allows rigorous control over extrinsic and intrinsic factors, and it provides unambiguous evidence about causation. Asch eliminated the effects of many variables that might have caused critical subjects to yield to or to resist group pressure; this increased the possibility of observing existing differences due to their experimental treatment. Moreover, Asch could unambiguously specify what caused the movement of his critical subjects toward the majority because he himself controlled and manipulated the independent variable—the seven members of the group who were told when to respond with wrong judgments. Furthermore, Asch varied the experimental treatment in a systematic way, thus allowing for the precise specification of important differences. Finally, the experiment was constructed in a way that enabled a clear detection of the effects of the experimental treatment: the critical subjects had to state their judgments aloud. They had to declare themselves and to take a definite position vis-à-vis their peers. They could not avoid the dilemma by pointing to conditions external to the experimental situation.

Laboratory experiments vary in complexity and design, depending on the research problem and the ingenuity of the experimenter. Experimenters have to construct a set of procedures that capture the meaning of their conceptualization and that enable the testing of hypotheses. This in turn demands the invention of a method of measuring the effect this has on the behavior of the researched individual and the construction of a setting within which the basic manipulations of the independent variables make sense and the measurements are valid and reliable.

Experimental and Mundane Realism

You may perhaps question the meaningfulness of laboratory experimentation, since it does not represent a real-world situation. In the Asch experiment, critical subjects were judging a very clear physical event (the length of

15. Solomon E. Asch, "Effects of Group Pressure upon the Modification Distortion of Judgments," in *Readings in Social Psychology*, ed. Eleanor Maccoby, Theodore Newcomb, and Eugen Hartley (New York: Holt, Rinehart and Winston, 1958), p. 177.

lines) and were contradicted by their peers. However, in everyday life, a situation where the unambiguous evidence of one's senses is contradicted by the unanimous judgments of one's peers is unlikely.

This problem has led to a distinction between two senses in which any given experiment can be said to be realistic.[16] In one sense, an experiment is realistic if the situation is realistic to the research participants, if it involves them and affects them. This kind of realism is commonly termed **experimental realism**. In the Asch experiment, the critical subjects exhibited signs of tension and anxiety. The subjects were reacting to a situation that was as real for them as any of their experiences outside the lab.

The second sense of realism refers to the extent to which events occurring in a laboratory setting are likely to occur in the real world. This type of realism is called **mundane realism**. An experiment that is high on mundane realism and low on experimental realism does not necessarily yield more meaningful results than one that is high on experimental realism and low on mundane realism. Were Asch to observe interpersonal influences in the real world, he probably would not have found a situation so clearly structured for observing the effects of group pressure on individual members. Moreover, if we assume that such a situation could have been found, the effects of intrinsic and extrinsic factors could not have been controlled for, and the obtained findings would have been ambiguous and inconclusive. Experimental realism enables the experimenter to increase the internal validity of the experiment by producing a significant effect within the experimental situation.

Sources of Bias in Laboratory Experiments

Notwithstanding the advantages of laboratory experiments, they have certain inherent limitations. These can be classified into three types: bias due to the demand characteristics of the experimental situation itself, bias due to the unintentional influence of the experimenters, and measurement artifacts.

Demand Characteristics.   Bias due to **demand characteristics** may occur when individuals know that they are in an experimental situation, are aware that they are being observed, and believe that certain responses are expected from them. Consequently, they may not respond to the experimental manipulation at face value but rather to their interpretation of the responses that these manipulations are intended to elicit. Even if the experimenter announces that there are no right or wrong responses, subjects will

---

16. The following discussion is based on Elliot Aronson, Marilynn B. Brewer, and James Carlsmith, "Experimentation in Social Psychology," in *The Handbook of Social Psychology*, 3d ed., ed. Gardner Lindzey and Elliot Aronson (New York: Random House, 1985), pp. 481–483.

nevertheless assume that certain behaviors are expected and will try to present as positive an image as possible.[17] Subjects may discover the research hypothesis and respond in a manner consistent with it in an attempt to please the experimenter. One practice commonly used to counteract this source of bias is to reduce participants' awareness of being observed in a research situation. Another strategy is to discuss only general rather than specific research objectives with the participants. The thinking is that if various subjects modify their behavior so as to support or refute an erroneous hypothesis, the results relating to the true hypothesis might not be affected, at least not systematically.[18]

Experimenter Bias.   Behavior of the part of the experimenter that is not intended to be part of the experimental manipulation but nevertheless influences participants is termed **experimenter bias** or the *experimental expectancy effect*. Experimenters who are conscious of the effects they desire from individuals may unintentionally communicate their expectations in various ways, for example, by showing tension or relief on occasion or by nodding the head. Robert Rosenthal and his colleagues found that when 8 of 12 experimenters testing individuals on the same assignment received biased data from their first two subjects (who were accomplices of Rosenthal and his coinvestigators), these early returns influenced the data they collected from subsequent true research participants. The four experimenters who received hypothesis-confirming data from their first two participants record the strongest confirming data from naïve participants who followed the planted participants. The four experimenters who received disconfirming data from their first two participants obtained the most disconfirming data from the naïve participants who followed the plants. The comparison group of experimenters, who tested only naïve participants, obtained values between those obtained by the other two groups of experimenters. Accordingly, the authors concluded that early returns bias subsequently obtained data.[19] Experimenter bias is thus the outcome of observers' motivations.

Using tape recorders, television cameras, or other automated procedures to minimize interactions between experimenter and research participants can minimize unintentional experimenter bias and eliminate the communication of expectations. Bias effects have also been mitigated by using experimenters with differing expectations for the outcome of the investigation. In one study, experiments with different expectations about the effects

17. M. T. Orne, "Demand Characteristics and the Concept of Quasi-controls," in *Artifacts in Behavioral Research*, ed. Robert Rosenthal and R. L. Rosnow (Orlando, Fla.: Academic Press, 1969).

18. For a comprehensive discussion of bias-reducing methods, see Aronson et al., "Experimentation in Social Psychology."

19. Robert Rosenthal et al., "The Effects of Early Data Returns on Data Subsequently Obtained by Outcome-biased Experimenters," *Sociometry*, 26 (1963): 487–493.

of the manipulated variables were included as one of the variables in the experimental design. In this case, the researchers assessed whether their own differing expectations produced different outcomes.[20] The use of more than one observer or data gatherer has also been recommended in order to estimate the effect of researchers' personality traits and physical characteristics and subtle differences in the treatment of participants.

Measurement Artifacts.   Measurement is a crucial part of the research process. In laboratory experiments, where the effects of an independent variable may be small, short, and sensitive, precise measurement is needed to detect such effects. Moreover, measurement procedures are not independent of research design problems, as measurement procedures may create additional interpretations of the data obtained by giving experimental participants additional ideas about what is going on, by giving individuals the opportunity to make a favorable impression and so on.

Measuring instruments may be reactive in the sense that they may change the phenomenon being measured. For instance, the use of cameras in the presence of experimenters may cause the individuals being studied to behave atypically. Exposure to the measuring instrument in a pretest may sensitize individuals and affect their posttest scores. Even the time of measurement may produce misleading results, in that a researcher may measure for the effects of independent variables before they have time to affect the dependent variable or after their effects have already waned, thus concealing their actual effect. Carl Hovland and his coauthors found, in their pioneering study, that discredited speakers have no immediate persuasive effect on their listeners but may have a significant effect a month later, unless the listeners are reminded of the source.[21]

Recording Observations

Observations in the laboratory are recorded on the spot during the experimental session. Often mechanical devices such as motion pictures, tape recordings, and television are used to obtain an overall view of the occurrences. Next the units of observation are assigned to a well-structured category system such as the one reproduced in Exhibit 9.1. Categorization may also take place during the experimental session if the system of recording is prepared and pretested well in advance. With a well-prepared system of recording and trained observers, the degree of inference required of the observers is minimal.

20. J. Merrill Carlsmith, Barry E. Collins, and Robert L. Helmreich, "Studies in Forced Compliance: I. The Effect of Pressure for Compliance on Attitude Change Produced by Face-to-Face Role Playing and Anonymous Essay Writing," *Journal of Personality and Social Psychology*, 4 (1966): 1–13.

21. Carl I. Hovland, Irving L. Janis, and Harold H. Kelley, *Communication and Persuasion* (New Haven, Conn.: Yale University Press, 1953).

Field Experimentation

The major difference between laboratory experimentation and experiments in the field is, as the terms imply, the setting. Laboratory experimentation involves the introduction in a controlled environment of conditions that simulate certain features of a natural environment. **Field experimentation,** by contrast, consists of a research study in a *natural* situation in which one or more independent variables are manipulated by the investigator under as carefully controlled conditions as the situation permits. In terms of research designs, the contrast between the laboratory experiment and the field study is not sharp (see Chapter 5). However, the difficulties involved in controlling intrinsic and especially extrinsic factors are considerably greater in field experiments.

An intriguing example of field experimentation is the oft-cited Piliavin, Rodin, and Piliavin study on helping behavior—altruism.[22] A field experiment was conducted to research the effects of several variables on helping behavior, using the express trains of the New York Eighth Avenue Independent Subway as a laboratory on wheels. Four teams of students, each consisting of a victim, a model, and two observers, staged standard collapses in which type of victim (ill or drunk), race of victim (black or white), and presence or absence of a model were varied. Data were recorded on number and race of observers, latency of the helping response and race of helper, number of helpers, movement out of the "critical area," and spontaneous comments. Figure 9.1 illustrates the setting of this field experiment.

The researchers found that (1) an apparently ill person is more likely to receive assistance than one who appears to be drunk, (2) race of victim has

Figure 9.1
Scheme of the Field Experiment

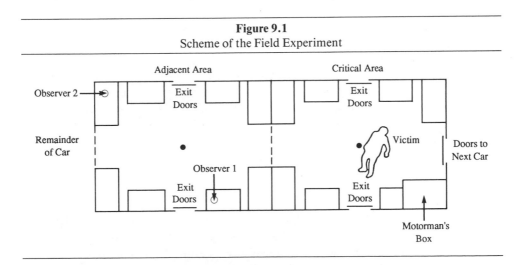

22. Irving M. Piliavin, Judith Rodin, and Jane Allyn Piliavin, "Good Samaritanism: An Underground Phenomenon?" *Journal of Personality and Social Psychology*, 13 (1969): 289–299.

little effect on race of helper except when the victim is drunk, (3) men are considerably more likely to help than women, and (4) the longer the emergency continues without help being offered, the more likely it is that someone will leave the area of the emergency.

In this study, the investigators relied primarily on systematic observation within a naturally occurring system. The experimenters did not control their setting but introduced a systematic variation into existing conditions: the behavior of an experimental accomplice was varied in the largely uncontrolled context of a subway train in order to study bystander helping behavior in that setting. In other cases, the researcher constructs experimental situations as well as experimental variations. In yet other cases, the researcher does not manipulate the independent variables directly but rather selects among natural stimulus situations that represent the theoretical concept of interest.

As we pointed out earlier, the main appeal of field experiments is that they permit the investigation of complex interactions, processes, and change in a natural setting. Their major weakness is that of control: intrinsic and extrinsic sources of validity cannot be controlled for as systematically as in laboratory experiments. Participant self-selection is a pervasive problem; randomization is often impossible. Pilot research is useful in such situations. The investigator has to make a convincing case that the research participants are not likely to differ systematically on any relevant factors other than the causal process of interest.[23]

Ethical issues are of a major concern in field experiments. Is it ethical to expose bystanders to someone who collapses and pretends to be seriously ill? In laboratory experiments, the rights of the participants are protected by informed consent and by debriefing; research participants are aware that they are taking part in research. Even if the participants enter the experimental session with no information of the experiment's objective, they know that they will be informed by the time the session is over. In field experiments, individuals are often unaware that they are participating in research. In such situations, the researcher has to ensure that the privacy of the researched individuals is not violated and that they will be protected from undue embarrassment or distress. (Methods for ensuring privacy and confidentiality are discussed in Chapter 4.)

Summary

1. Observation is considered the archetypical method of scientific research. If one wishes to understand, explain, and predict what exists, one can simply go and observe it. But if one's findings are to be systematic, the

---

23. For other methods used to minimize validity problems, see Aronson et al., "Experimentation in Social Psychology."

observations must be carried out with reference to three crucial issues: what to observe, where and when to observe, and how much to infer when recording observations.

2. Decisions concerning these issues depend on the research problem and the research design. When the researcher's objective is to test a hypothesis experimentally, the units of observations are explicitly defined; a setting is chosen—laboratory or field; a time sample is drawn; and the observations are systematically recorded with as little observer inference as possible. These operations typify controlled observations.

3. It is helpful to distinguish between experimental realism—the extent to which an experimental situation is real to the research participants—and mundane realism—the relevance of an experimental situation to the real world. Systematic bias may be introduced in experiments as a result of demand characteristics, experimenter bias, and measurement artifacts. The credibility of findings can be further enhanced by triangulation, the use of two or more data collection methods to study the same phenomenon.

Key Terms for Review

triangulation	experimental realism
nonverbal behavior	mundane realism
time-sampling schedule	demand characteristics
controlled observation	experimenter bias
noncontrolled observation	field experimentation

Study Questions

1. Why would a researcher choose to triangulate?
2. Describe the kinds of behavior and research purposes to which observation can be fruitfully applied.
3. Discuss the strengths and weaknesses of the laboratory experiment as a mode of observation.
4. Describe the major techniques for timing and recording observations.
5. List the advantages and drawbacks of field experimentation.

Additional Readings

Bales, Robert F., and Stephen P. Cohen. *SYMLOG: A System for the Multiple Level Observation of Groups.* New York: Free Press, 1979.

Bonacich, Philip, and John Light. "Laboratory Experimentation in Sociology." *Annual Review of Sociology*, 4 (1978): 145–170.

Brewer, John, and Albert Hunter. *Multimethod Research: A Synthesis of Styles.* Newbury Park, Calif.: Sage, 1989.

Emerson, Robert M. "Observational Field Work." *Annual Review of Sociology*, 7 (1981): 351–378.

Iyengar, Shanto, Mark D. Peters, and Donald R. Kinder. "Experimental Demonstrations of the 'Not-So-Minimal' Consequences of Television News Programs." *American Political Science Review*, 76 (1982): 848–888.

Rosenthal, Robert. *Experimenter Effects in Behavioral Research.* New York: Irvington, 1976.

Saxe, Leonard. *Social Experiments: Methods for Design and Evaluation.* Newbury Park, Calif.: Sage, 1981.

Suen, Hoi K. *Analyzing Quantitative Behavioral Observation Data.* Hillsdale, N.J.: Erlbaum, 1989.

Vargas, Marjorie F. *Louder Than Words: An Introduction to Nonverbal Communication.* Ames: Iowa State University Press, 1986.

CHAPTER 10

Survey Research

In this chapter, we explore survey design, considering three types of survey—mail questionnaires, personal interviews, and telephone interviewing—in detail.

O BSERVATIONAL METHODS OF DATA collection are suitable for investigating phenomena that can be observed directly by the researcher. However, not all phenomena are accessible to the investigator's direct observation; very often, therefore, the researcher must collect data by asking people who have experienced certain phenomena to reconstruct these phenomena. The researcher approaches a sample of individuals presumed to have undergone certain experiences and interviews them concerning these experiences. The obtained responses constitute the data on which the research hypotheses are examined. Three major survey research methods are used to elicit information from respondents: the mail questionnaire, the personal interview, and the telephone survey.

Mail Questionnaire

The **mail questionnaire** is an impersonal survey method. Under certain conditions and for a number of research purposes, an impersonal method of data collection can be useful. Let us examine the advantages and disadvantages of this method.

Advantages of the Mail Questionnaire

1. *Low cost*. Economy is one of the most obvious appeals of mail questionnaires. The mail questionnaire does not require a trained staff of interviewers; all it entails is the cost of planning, sampling, duplicating, mailing, and providing stamped, self-addressed envelopes for the returns. Processing and analysis are usually also simpler and cheaper than for other survey methods. The lower cost in the administration of a mail questionnaire is particularly evident when the population under study is widely spread geographically. Under such circumstances, the cost of interviewing could become prohibitive, and the mail questionnaire may be the only practicable instrument.

2. *Reduction in biasing error*. The mail questionnaire reduces *biasing errors* that might result from the personal characteristics of interviewers and variability in their skills. Personal interview situations are fraught with possibilities for bias due to the nature of the interaction between the interviewer and the respondent. This can be completely avoided with a mail questionnaire.

3. *Greater anonymity*. The absence of an interviewer also provides greater anonymity. The assurance of anonymity with mail questionnaires is especially helpful when the survey deals with sensitive issues, such as sexual behavior or child abuse. On such matters, a mail questionnaire may elicit a higher response rate than a personal interview.

4. *Considered answers and consultations*. Mail questionnaires are also preferable when questions demand a considered (rather than an immediate) answer or if answers require consulting personal documents or other people.

5. *Accessibility*. Finally, the mail questionnaire permits wide geographic contact at minimal cost. For example, when a survey requires wide coverage and addresses a population that is dispersed geographically, interviewing would involve high travel costs and time investments.

Disadvantages of the Mail Questionnaire

1. *Requires simple questions*. The mail questionnaire can be used as an instrument for data collection only when the questions are straightforward enough to be comprehended solely on the basis of printed instructions and definitions.

2. *No opportunity for probing*. The answers have to be accepted as final; there is no opportunity to probe beyond the given answer, to clarify ambiguous answers, or to appraise the nonverbal behavior of respondents.

3. *No control over who fills out the questionnaire*. With a mail questionnaire, researchers have no control over the respondent's environment; hence they cannot be sure that the appropriate person completes the questionnaire. An individual other than the intended respondent may complete it.

4. *Low response rate*. The final disadvantage of a mail questionnaire—and perhaps its most serious problem—is that it is often difficult to obtain an adequate **response rate**. For many mail surveys, the reported response rates are much lower than for personal interviews. The typical response rate for a personal interview is about 95 percent, whereas that for a mail survey without follow-up is between 20 and 40 percent. Researchers who use mail questionnaires must almost always face the problem of how to estimate the effect the nonrespondents may have on their findings. (The response rate is of great significance when making generalizations; see Chapter 19.) The nonrespondents are usually quite different from those who answer the questionnaire. Often they are the poorly educated who may have problems understanding the questions, the elderly who are unable to respond, or the more mobile who cannot be located. Consequently, the group of respondents is not likely to constitute the representative group originally defined by the investigators, and this will undoubtedly introduce bias into the study.

Factors Affecting the Response Rate of Mail Questionnaires

The difficulty of securing an acceptable response rate to mail questionnaires requires the use of various strategies that can be taken to increase the response rate. Let us review these strategies.

Sponsorship.   The sponsorship of a questionnaire has a significant effect in motivating a respondent to fill it out and return it. Therefore, information on sponsorship must be included, usually in the cover letter accompanying the questionnaire. Sponsorship affects the response rate by convincing the respondent of the study's legitimacy and value as well as the perceived sanctions of a failure to reply. For example, the U. S. Bureau of the Census is successful in obtaining a near 95 percent response rate on its National Health Interview Survey. At the other extreme, in some mail surveys only 5 percent of the sample responds.[1] In general, government-sponsored questionnaires obtain high responses and relatively little known commerical organizations get low ones.

Inducement to Respond.   Researchers must appeal to the respondents and persuade them that they should participate by filling out the questionnaires and mailing them back. Several methods can be used, but they vary in their degree of effectiveness. One is to appeal to the respondents' goodwill, telling them that the researchers need their help. For example, a student conducting a survey for a class project may mention that his or her grade may be affected by the response to the questionnaire.[2]

Another widely used method is offering the respondent a reward, such as a prize or a nominal sum of money. The problem with offering money is

1. Floyd J. Fowler, Jr., *Survey Research Methods* (Newbury Park, Calif.: Sage, 1989), p. 48.
2. Kenneth D. Bailey, *Methods of Social Research* (New York: Free Press, 1987), p. 156.

that some respondents will be indignant that the researchers consider the respondent's time worth so little and thus may not respond at all.[3] However, most often the reward is seen as a symbolic gesture, and the respondents cooperate because they consider the study worthwhile.

Perhaps the most effective strategy is to appeal to the respondents' altruistic sentiments and to convince them of the study's significance. In the following example, the importance of the study and the respondents' potential contribution to its success are expressed in the cover letter accompanying the questionnaire:

> As you know, public service employment is a major part of the federal, state, and local strategy to overcome the employment and income problems of economically disadvantaged unemployed people. There is no question that the program is needed throughout the country. . . . You are probably also aware . . . that public service employment programs are quite controversial and their future may be in jeopardy. Part of the reason that these programs are so controversial is that no systematic evaluation of the benefits of these programs for the individuals employed and the communities served has been conducted.
>
> Because this specific evaluation has significant national implications, I strongly urge you to give this enclosed questionnaire your prompt attention and thank you for your cooperation in this evaluation.[4]

Questionnaire Format and Methods of Mailing.   Several considerations are involved in designing a mail questionnaire: typography, color, and length and type of cover letter. A slightly larger investment in format and typography (e.g., high-quality paper and adequate spacing) will pay off in a higher response rate. Note that the use of unusual colors is not recommended because it may have a negative effect.[5]

Cover Letter.   Another factor to be considered in designing the questionnaire is the cover letter. The cover letter must succeed in convincing the respondents to fill out the questionnaire and mail it back. It should therefore identify the sponsor of the study, explain its purpose, tell the respondents why it is important that they fill out the questionnaire, and ensure them that the answers will be held in strict confidence. The investigator must choose between a formal or a semipersonal letter. It has been shown that a semipersonal letter generates a slightly higher response rate than a formal form letter.

Type of Mailing.   An important consideration is the type of mailing to be used. Questionnaires not accompanied by a postpaid return envelope ob-

3. Ibid., p. 157.

4. Mickey L. Burnim, *An Evaluation of the Public Service Employment Projects in Florida Created under Title VI of the Comprehensive Employment and Training Act of 1973* (Tallahassee: Florida Department of Community Affairs, 1978), p. 164.

5. Pamela L. Alreck and Robert B. Settle, *The Survey Research Handbook* (Homewood, Ill.: Irwin, 1985).

Table 10.1
Average Cumulative Response Rates to Four Mailings

Mailing	Time	Average Response Rate
1. First mailing	Week 1	23.8%
2. Postcard follow-up	Week 2	42.0
3. First replacement questionnaire	Week 4	59.0
4. Second replacement sent by certified mail	Week 7	72.4

Adapted from Donald A. Dillman, James A. Christensen, Edward H. Carpenter, and Ralph M. Brooks, "Increasing Mail Questionnaire Response: A Four-State Comparison," *American Sociological Review*, 39 (1974): 755, and Donald A. Dillman and D. E. Moore, "Improving Response Rates to Mail Surveys: Results from Five Surveys," paper presented at the annual meeting of the American Association for Public Opinion Research, Hershey, Pa., 1983.

tain few responses. It is unreasonable to expect the respondent not only to fill out the questionnaire but also to find an envelope and then go to the post office to have it weighed and stamped. Hence it is a common practice to enclose a stamped, self-addressed envelope. (An official-looking business reply envelope tends to reduce the response rate.)

The Total Design Method (TDM). In recent years, data collection with mail surveys has improved considerably through application of the *total design method*, a standardized set of step-by-step procedures[6] that is divided into two parts: questionnaire construction and survey implementation.

The principles followed in constructing TDM questionnaires includes particular attention to details such as the outside of the envelope that contains the questionnaire, the front cover of the questionnaire, and the order of the questions. TDM tries to make sure that the questionnaire will be immediately differentiated from junk mail.

The TDM implementation approach focuses primarily on **follow-up** procedures. The most common follow-up strategy is to send a reminder postcard one week after the first mailing to respondents who have not yet replied. The second follow-up consists of another reminder letter and a replacement questionnaire with a return envelope sent at the end of the third week. After seven weeks, another letter with a replacement questionnaire is sent, preferably by certified mail, to all who have not yet responded by that time.

The effectiveness of these follow-up methods was tested on large statewide samples of the general population in four states. Table 10.1 shows the average response rates of the four mailings used in the study. The results obtained by this study reveal the importance of a *multiwave follow-up*. Ob-

6. Donald A. Dillman, "Mail and Other Self-administered Questionnaires," in *Handbook of Survey Research*, ed. Peter H. Rossi, James D. Wright, and Andy B. Anderson (Orlando, Fla.: Academic Press, 1983), and Anton J. Nederhof, "Effects of a Final Telephone Reminder and Questionnaire Cover Design in Mail Surveys," *Social Science Research*, 17 (1988): 353–361.

serve that the final wave increased the response rate by more than 13 percent. Indeed, "with a mail methodology available which will consistently provide a high response, poor return rate can no more be excused than can inadequate theory or inappropriate statistics."[7] Recently, it has been suggested that the use of certified mail has some important drawbacks.[8] The requirement of signing for receipt may seem coercive, and the cost in time and money may be even larger if the respondent has to go to the post office to retrieve the questionnaire. The final follow-up by certified mail may be replaced by a telephone reminder, which is as effective as certified mail in reducing nonresponse.

Although follow-up is clearly an important mechanism in raising the response rate, it raises several problems. First, because follow-up letters and questionnaires are sent only to respondents who have not replied, it is necessary to identify all respondents; thus anonymity cannot be maintained. A way to get around this difficulty is to ensure respondents that the replies will be held in strict confidence. Another limitation of the follow-up is that the quality of the response rate declines with successive mailings. Respondents who do not respond the first time might be less likely to take the study seriously and thus may send in an incomplete questionnaire, or their answers may be unreliable. Bias due to this reason can be studied by comparing those who respond immediately with those who respond after one or more follow-up steps are taken.[9]

Selection of Respondents. The selection of the respondents is largely determined by the nature of the study and the characteristics of the population. Thus beyond the definition of the sampling population, there is very little one can do in the selection process to increase the response rate. However, recognizing that certain characteristics of the respondents are associated with a high or low response rate will help determine whether to use a mail questionnaire to begin with or whether other strategies should be used to increase the response rate. The most significant dimension in selecting the respondents is whether they consist of a heterogeneous or a homogeneous group. Heterogeneous groups could consist of individuals from various ethnic and racial backgrounds, different levels of income, or both urban and rural locations. Homogeneous groups, by contrast, consist of individuals with similar characteristics. Heterogeneous groups are typically used in opinion polls, whereas in more specialized studies, questionnaires are sent to more select groups, for example, to physicians, legislators, city managers, university professors, or members of the local chamber of commerce. The

---

7. Donald A. Dillman, James A. Christensen, Edward H. Carpenter, and Ralph M. Brooks, "Increasing Mail Questionnaire Response: A Four-State Comparison." *American Sociological Review*, 39 (1974): 755.

8. Nederhof, "Effects," p. 354.

9. Fowler, *Survey Research Methods*, p. 54.

response rate for select groups is usually higher than it is for the general population because members of these groups are more likely to identify with the goals of the study and thus will be more motivated to respond. Beyond this distinction, certain background characteristics are associated with differentials in response rate. Respondents who are more educated are more likely to fill out and return questionnaires. Interest in or familiarity with the topic under investigation is another important factor in determining the rate of return. Finally, in general, professionals tend to have the highest response rate among all occupations.

Table 10.2 ranks the various procedures discussed so far according to their relative effectiveness in increasing the rate of return. The ranks were determined on the basis of various studies estimating the possible increase of total return of each procedure. Rank could not be determined for the last three procedures.

Evaluating the Response Rate

What is an acceptable response rate for a mail questionnaire? Most investigators attempt to maximize the response rate by using some or all of the strategies just discussed. Yet despite these efforts, many mail surveys achieve a response rate no larger than 50 percent. Nonresponse is a serious problem because nonrespondents differ considerably from respondents. For example, it has been shown that mail questionnaires addressed to the general population result in an upward bias in education: better-educated people are more likely to respond more quickly to mail questionnaires.[10] The bias resulting from the nonresponse may limit the ability to make generalization to the entire population.

The question of what constitutes an acceptable response rate cannot easily be answered because there is no agreed standard for a minimum response rate. For example, surveys done under contract to the federal government are expected to yield a response rate higher than 75 percent. But whereas academic survey organizations are usually able to achieve that level, the response rates for surveys conducted by more obscure organizations are considerably lower.

Finally, there is some evidence that response rates on mail questionnaires have been improving with more standardization of follow-up techniques.[11]

Indeed, in recent years, survey research has become a widely used tool, not only of research and marketing organizations but also of national and local government. Some citizens, though dedicated and loyal to the goals of

10. Ibid., pp. 355–356.
11. Nederhof, "Effects," p. 356.

Table 10.2
Techniques for Increasing Response Rate

Method	Rank (High to Low)	Optimal Conditions
Follow-up	1	More than one follow-up. Telephone could be used for follow-up.
Inducement	2	Questionnaires containing a token monetary reward produce better results than ones without. However, the population and the type of the questionnaire have to be considered.
Sponsorship	3	People the respondent knows produce the best result.
Introductory letter	4	An altruistic appeal seems to produce the best results.
Method of return	—	A regular stamped envelope produces better results than a business reply envelope.
Format	—	Aesthetically pleasing cover; a title that will arouse interest; an attractive page format.
Selection of respondents	—	• Nonreaders and nonwriters are excluded from participation. • Interest in or familiarity with the topic under investigation is a major factor in determining the rate of return. • The better educated are more likely to return the questionnaires. • Professionals are more likely to return questionnaires.

Adapted from Delbert C. Miller, *Handbook of Research Design and Social Measurement* (New York: McKay, 1977), pp. 77–78; Pamela L. Alreck and Robert B. Settle, *The Survey Research Handbook* (Homewood, Ill.: Irwin, 1985), and Anton J. Nederhof, "Effects of a Final Telephone Reminder and Questionnaire Cover Design in Mail Surveys," *Social Science Research*, 17 (1988): 353–361.

research, may find themselves facing a unique decision as to which and how many of the questionnaires they receive each year they should respond to. An attempt to sensitize the questioners to this problem is presented in the satirical questionnaire for questioners reprinted in Exhibit 10.1.

Exhibit 10.1
Questionnaire for Questioners

Dear Questioner:

You are no doubt aware that the number of questionnaires circulated is rapidly increasing, whereas the length of the working day has, at best, remained constant. In order to resolve the problem presented by this trend, I find it necessary to restrict my replies to questionnaires to those questioners who first establish their *bona fide* by completing the following questionnaire.

1. How many questionnaires, per annum, do you distribute? ____
2. How many questionnaires, per annum, do you receive? ____
3. What fraction of the questionnaires you receive do you answer? ____
4. What fraction of the questionnaires you distribute are answered? ____
5. Do you think the ratio of the fraction 3:4 should be greater than 1, less than 1, any other value? (Please explain.) ____
6. What fraction of your time (or effort) do you devote to:
    a. Compiling questionnaires? ____
    b. Answering questionnaires? ____
    c. Examining the replies to your own questionnaires? ____
    d. Examining the replies to other people's questionnaires? ____
    e. Drawing conclusions from questionnaires? ____
    f. Other activities? ____
    (a + b + c + d + e + f should add up to 100 percent. If not, please explain.)
7. Do you regard the ratio of (a + b + c + d + e)/f as:
    a. too small? ____
    b. too large? ____
    c. any other ____ (check one only)
8. Do you ever distribute questionnaires exclusively to people who you know distribute questionnaires? ____
9. Do you expect answers to questionnaires from people who themselves distribute questionnaires about questionnaires? ____
10. Do you consider it would be of value to distribute a questionnaire regarding answers to questionnaires to those individuals who receive questionnaires about the distribution of questionnaires?
    Yes ____
    No ____ (check one only)
    Any other answer? please explain.

Replies to this questionnaire *must* be signed. As you may surmise, they are not suitable, nor will they be used for statistical purposes.

From Samuel Devons, "A Questionnaire for Questioners," *Public Opinion Quarterly*, 39 (1975): 255–256.

Personal Interview

The personal interview is a face-to-face interpersonal role situation in which an interviewer asks respondents questions designed to elicit answers pertinent to the research hypotheses. The questions, their wording, and their sequence define the structure of the interview.

The Schedule-structured Interview

The most structured form is the **schedule-structured interview**, in which the questions, their wording, and their sequence are fixed and are identical for every respondent. This is done to make sure that any variations between responses can be attributed to the actual differences between the respondents and not to variations in the interview. The researcher attempts to reduce the risk that changes in the wording of questions, for example, might elicit differences in responses. The schedule-structured interview is based on three crucial assumptions:

1. That for any research objective "the respondents have a sufficiently common vocabulary so that it is possible to formulate questions which have the same meaning for each of them."[12]
2. That it is possible to phrase all questions in a form that is equally meaningful to each respondent.
3. That if the "meaning of each question is to be identical for each respondent, its context must be identical and, since all preceding questions constitute part of the contexts, the sequence of questions must be identical."[13]

The Focused Interview

The second basic form is the *non-schedule-structured* or **focused interview**. This form has four characteristics:[14]

1. It takes place with respondents known to have been involved in a particular experience.
2. It refers to situations that have been analyzed prior to the interview.
3. It proceeds on the basis of an interview guide specifying topics related to the research hypotheses.
4. It is focused on the subjects' experiences regarding the situations under study.

12. Stephen Richardson, Barbara S. Dohrenwend, and David Klein, *Interviewing: Its Forms and Functions* (New York: Basic Books, 1965), p. 40.
13. Ibid., p. 43.
14. Robert K. Merton and Patricia L. Kendal, "The Focused Interview," *American Journal of Sociology*, 51 (1946): 541–557.

Although the encounter between the interviewer and respondents is structured and the major aspects of the study are explained, respondents are given considerable liberty in expressing their definition of a situation that is presented to them. For example, in her study of women's best friends and marriage, Stacey Oliker employed a focused interview that was "malleable enough to follow emergent leads and standardized enough to register strong patterns."[15] The focused interview permits the researcher to obtain details of personal reactions, specific emotions, and the like. The interviewer, having previously studied the situation, is alert and sensitive to inconsistencies and omissions of data that may be needed to clarify the problem.

The Nondirective Interview

The least structured form of interviewing is the *nonstructured* or **nondirective interview**. Here no prespecified set of questions is employed, nor are the questions asked in a specified order. Furthermore, no schedule is used. With little or no direction from the interviewer, respondents are encouraged to relate their experiences, to describe whatever events seem significant to them, to provide their own definitions of their situations, and to reveal their opinions and attitudes as they see fit. The interviewer has a great deal of freedom to probe various areas and to raise specific queries during the course of the interview. For example, Eleanor Miller's study of female street hustlers is based on such nondirective interviews:[16]

> Seventy women agreed to taped interviews with me during which they shared with me the details of their lives. Special attention was paid to the initiation of these women into street hustling and the development of a career line as a street hustler. Although the same broad topics were introduced during each interview, many of my questions changed over time. Initial taped interviews were played again and again after being recorded. Tentative hypotheses and emergent behavior categories arose out of these hours of listening. During subsequent interviews, . . . I would introduce questions to test these tentative hypotheses.[17]

The differences in interviewing styles in the three types of interviews are illustrated in Exhibits 10.2, 10.3, and 10.4, all concerned with the same research problem. The purpose of the study is to discover the types of conflict between parents and teenagers and their relationship to juvenile crime. The interviews are conducted with two groups of children. One consists of teenagers who have committed no crimes, and the second consists of teenagers who have been known to commit several juvenile crimes.

---

15. Stacey J. Oliker, *Best Friends and Marriage* (Berkeley: University of California Press, (1989), p. xvi.

16. Eleanor M. Miller, *Street Woman* (Philadelphia: Temple University Press, 1986).

17. Ibid, p. 26.

Exhibit 10.2
The Schedule-structured Interview

Interviewer's explanation to the respondent: We are interested in the kinds of problems teenagers have with their parents. We need to know how many teenagers have conflicts with their parents and what those conflicts are. We have checklist here of some of the kinds of things that happen. Think about your own situation, and put a check mark to show which conflicts you have had and about how often they have happened. Be sure to put a check in every row. If you have never had such a conflict, put the check in the first column, where it says, "Never."

(Hand respondent the first card dealing with conflicts over the use of the automobile, saying, "If you don't understand any of the things listed or have some other things you would like to mention about how you disagree with your parents over the automobile, let me know and we'll talk about it.")

AUTOMOBILE	Never	Only Once	More Than Once	Many Times
1. Wanting to learn to drive				
2. Getting a driver's license				
3. Wanting to use the family car				
4. Using it too much				
5. Keeping the car clean				
6. Repairing the car				
7. Driving someone else's car				
8. Want to own a car				
9. The way you drive your own car				
10. Other				

(When the respondent finishes all rows, hand him or her card number 2, saying, "Here is a list of types of conflicts teenagers have with their parents over their friends of the same sex. Do the same with this as you did with the last list.")

Adapted from Raymond L. Gorden, *Interviewing: Strategy, Techniques, and Tactics*, 2d ed. (Homewood, Ill.: Dorsey, 1975), pp. 63–65.

An interview may be completely structured or nonstructured, as illustrated in the exhibits. Alternatively, an interview may combine structured and nonstructured elements, depending on the purpose of the study. For example, a researcher may use the schedule-structured interview for most questions but rely on the nondirective format for questions that are particularly sensitive.

Exhibit 10.3
The Focused Interview

Instructions to the interviewer: Your task is to discover as many specific kinds of conflicts and tensions between child and parent as possible. The more *concrete* and detailed the account of each type of conflict, the better. Although there are four areas of possible conflict that we want to explore (listed in question 3 below), you should not mention any area until after you have asked the first two questions in the order indicated. The first question takes an indirect approach, giving you time to build up rapport with the respondent.

1. What sorts of problems do teenagers have in getting along with their parents? (Possible probes: Do they always agree with their parents? Do any of your friends have "problem parents"?)
2. What sort of disagreements do you have with your parents? (Possible probes: Do they cause you any problems? In what way do they try to restrict you? Do they like the same things you do?)
3. Have you ever had any disagreement with either of your parents over:
    a. using the family car?
    b. friends of the same sex?
    c. dating?
    d. smoking?

Adapted from Raymond L. Gorden, *Interviewing: Strategy, Techniques, and Tactics*, 2d ed. (Homewood, Ill.: Dorsey, 1975), pp. 63–65.

Personal Interview versus Mail Questionnaire

Advantages of the Personal Interview

1. *Flexibility*. The interview allows great flexibility in the questioning process, and the greater the flexibility, the less structured the interview. The interview allows the interviewer to determine the wording of the questions, to clarify terms that are unclear, to control the order in which the questions are presented, and to probe for additional information and detail.

Exhibit 10.4
The Nondirective Interview

Instructions to the interviewer: Discover the kinds of conflicts that the teenager has had with the parents. Conflicts should include disagreements; tensions due to past, present, or potential disagreements; outright arguments; and physical conflicts. Be alert for as many categories and examples of conflicts and tensions as possible.

Adapted from Raymond L. Gorden, *Interviewing: Strategy, Techniques, and Tactics*, 2d ed. (Homewood, Ill.: Dorsey, 1975), pp. 63–65.

2. *Control of the interview situation*. One major advantage of the interview is that it allows greater control over the interviewing situation. An interviewer can ensure that the respondents answer the questions in the appropriate sequence or that they answer certain questions before they are asked subsequent questions. Moreover, in an interview situation, it is possible to standardize the environment in order to ensure that the interview is conducted in private; thus respondents would not have the opportunity to consult one another before giving their answers. It is also possible to record the exact time and place of the interview; this allows the researcher to interpret the answers more accurately, especially in cases in which an event occurring around the time of the interview could have influenced the respondent's answers.[18]

3. *High response rate*. The personal interview results in a higher response rate than the mail questionnaire. Answers from respondents who would not ordinarily reply to a mail questionnaire can easily be obtained in an interview. This is likewise true of persons who have difficulties in reading or writing, do not fully understand the language, or are simply unwilling to take the time to write out their answers and mail the questionnaire.

4. *Collection of supplementary information*. An interviewer can collect supplementary information about respondents. This may include background information about the respondents' personal characteristics and their environment that can aid the researcher in the interpretation of the results. Moreover, an interview situation often yields spontaneous reactions that the interviewer can record and that might be useful in the data analysis stage.

Disadvantages of the Personal Interview

1. *Higher cost*. The cost of interview studies is significantly higher than that of mail surveys. There are costs involved in selecting, training, and supervising interviewers, in paying them, and in the travel and time required to conduct interviews. Furthermore, the cost of recording and processing the information obtained in nonstructured interviews is especially high.

2. *Interviewer bias*. The very flexibility that is the interview's chief advantage leaves room for the interviewer's personal influence and bias. The lack of standardization in the data collection process also makes interviewing highly vulnerable to the interviewer bias. Although interviewers are instructed to remain objective and to avoid communicating personal views, they nevertheless often give cues that may influence respondents' answers.[19] Even when verbal cues are avoided, nonverbal communication can escape the interviewer's control. Sometimes even the interviewer's race or gender

18. Bailey, *Methods of Social Research*, p. 174.
19. John B. Williamson, David A. Konk, and John R. Dalphin, *The Research Craft* (Boston: Little, Brown, 1977).

can influence respondents, who in an attempt to please the interviewer may give socially admirable but potentially misleading answers.

3. *Lack of anonymity.* The interview lacks the anonymity of the mail questionnaire. Often the interviewer knows all or many of the potential respondents (or at least their name, address, and telephone number). Thus the respondent may feel threatened or intimidated by the interviewer, especially if the topic or some questions are of a sensitive nature.

Principles of Interviewing

We now turn to a more detailed discussion of principles and procedures of interviewing. The first step in the interviewing process is getting the respondent to cooperate and to provide the desired information. Three factors help in motivating the respondent to cooperate.[20]

1. *The respondents need to feel that their interaction with the interviewer will be pleasant and satisfying.* It is up to interviewers to present themselves to respondents as being understanding and easy to talk to.

2. *The respondents need to see the study as being worthwhile.* The respondents should feel not only that the study may be beneficial to themselves but also that it deals with a significant issue and that their cooperation is important. Interviewers should interest the respondents in the study by pointing out its significance and the contribution that the respondents can make by cooperating.

3. *Barriers to the interview in the respondents' mind need to be overcome.* Interviewers must correct misconceptions. Some respondents may be suspicious of the interviewers, seeing them as salespeople or as representatives of the government. The interviewers should explain, in a friendly manner, the purpose of the study, the method of selecting respondents, and the confidential nature of the interview.

The Survey Research Center of the University of Michigan's Institute for Social Research provides some useful pointers on how the interviewer should introduce himself or herself to the respondent:[21]

1. Tell the respondent who you are and who you represent.
2. Tell the respondent what you are doing in a way that will stimulate his or her interest.
3. Tell the respondent how he or she was chosen.
4. Keep doorstep instructions brief.
5. Adapt your approach to the situation.
6. Try to create a relationship of confidence and understanding (rapport) between yourself and the respondent.

20. Survey Research Center, *Interviewer's Manual* (Ann Arbor, Mich.: Institute for Social Research, University of Michigan, 1969), p. 3–1.
21. Ibid. (edited slightly).

After the initial introduction, the interviewer is ready to begin the interview. There are specific techniques that the interviewer can use in this process:[22]

1. *The questionnaire should be followed, but it can be used informally.*

2. *The interview should be conducted in an informal and relaxed atmosphere, and the interviewer should avoid creating the impression that what is occurring is a cross-examination or a quiz.*

3. *The questions should be asked exactly as worded in the questionnaire.* This is of particular importance, for even slight changes in the way the questions are presented may change the response obtained. Various studies have shown that even small omissions or changes in the phrasing of questions can distort the results.

4. *Questions should be presented in the same order as in the questionnaire.* The question sequence has been planned by the researcher to provide continuity and make sure that the respondents' answers will not be influenced by their response to previous questions. Moreover, to standardize the interview, every interviewer should adhere to the same sequence as directed by the investigator.

5. *Questions that are misinterpreted or misunderstood should be repeated and clarified.* In most cases, respondents will not have any problem interpreting or understanding a question. At most, some people would need more time before they respond to a particular question. But occasionally, respondents who have language or hearing problems will have difficulties in understanding a question. The interviewer should then repeat the question. Only on rare occasions should the interviewer reword the question, and then only if convinced that otherwise the respondent would misinterpret the question.

Probing

In the *Interviewer's Manual* of the University of Michigan Survey Research Center, **probing** is defined as

> the technique used by the interviewer to stimulate discussion and obtain more information. A question has been asked and an answer given. For any number of reasons, the answer may be inadequate and require the interviewer to seek more information to meet the survey objectives. Probing is the act of getting this additional information."[23]

Probes have two major functions: they motivate the respondent to elaborate or clarify an answer or to explain the reasons behind the answer, and they help focus the conversation on the specific topic of the interview.

22. Ibid., p. 4–1 (edited slightly).
23. Ibid., p. 5–1.

In general, the less structured the interview, the more important probing becomes as an instrument for eliciting and encouraging further information.

The following is an illustration of probing used by the interviewer to elicit additional information by "repeating the respondent's statements without including a direct question."[24]

RESPONDENT: The main reason I came to Antioch College was because of the combination of high academic standards and the work program. It appealed to me a lot.

INTERVIEWER: It appealed to you a lot?

RESPONDENT: That's right.

INTERVIEWER: Could you tell me a little more exactly why it had this appeal for you?

RESPONDENT: I don't know—it was just that the place sounded less stuffy and straightlaced than a lot of places with just as good an academic program.

INTERVIEWER: You don't like places that are stuffy and straightlaced?

RESPONDENT: You can say that again. A lot of places spend most of their time trying to work out a way of controlling the students, assuming that they are completely incapable of self-control. . . .

INTERVIEWER: Why do you suppose Antioch has less supervision by the administration?

RESPONDENT: Well, it is part of the educational philosophy. . . .

INTERVIEWER: Let me see if I have grasped the whole picture—you like a school with high academic standards, but one that is not too straightlaced and operates on the assumption that college students can exercise self-control. . . .

RESPONDENT: That hits it on the head.

Telephone Interview

The telephone interview, also called the *telephone survey*, can be characterized as a semipersonal method of collecting information. Not too long ago, telephone surveys were viewed with skepticism or outright distrust. Some texts explicitly warned their readers to avoid them.[25] The primary reason for the reluctance to use telephone interviewing was the high likelihood of a serious sampling bias. When a substantial proportion of the population had no access to telephones, the sample tended to overrepresent those who were

---

24. Raymond L. Gorden, *Interviewing: Strategy, Techniques, and Tactics,* 2d ed. (Homewood, Ill.: Dorsey: 1975), p. 436.

25. William R. Klecka and Alfred J. Tuchfarber, "Random Digit Dialing: A Comparison to Personal Survey," *Public Opinion Quarterly,* 42 (1978): 105–114. Many details of our discussion derive from this source.

relatively well-off and could afford a telephone. More recently, however, telephone surveys have gained general acceptance as a legitimate method of data collection in the social sciences.

The main rationale for employing telephone surveys more extensively is that today coverage of more than nine-tenths of the population is likely. In 1958, only 72.5 percent of U.S. households had access to telephones; by the end of the 1980s, the figure was close to 98 percent. In addition, financial pressures have made the telephone survey more attractive. Increasing salaries and fuel costs made the personal interview extremely costly. In comparison, the telephone is convenient, and it produces a very significant cost saving. Moreover, the telephone interview results in a higher response rate than the personal interview. In some metropolitan areas, people are quite nervous about opening the doors to strangers. Finding respondents at home has also become increasingly difficult with the increased participation of married women in the labor force.

Technological changes and improvement in telephone equipment have also made telephone interviewing easier. It has become possible to draw a random sample of telephone numbers by a process called **random-digit dialing (RDD)**. This method requires the identification of all working telephone exchanges in the targeted geographic area. A potential telephone number is created by randomly selecting an exchange and then appending a random number between 0001 and 9999. Additional numbers are created by repeating these two steps. Nonresidential telephones and nonworking numbers are excluded during the interviewing process.

But beyond the obvious advantages of cost and speed that the telephone survey provides, there remains the question of whether telephone surveys are an alternative to face-to-face interviewing. In the first major experiment designed to answer this question, William Klecka and Alfred Tuchfarber replicated a large, personal interviewing survey by means of an RDD telephone survey.[26] The personal interview survey on crime victimization was conducted by the U.S. Bureau of the Census in 1974. The two samples were compared on demographic characteristic measures of crime victimization and attitudes toward crime and the police. The results were very similar, indicating that random-digit dialing is an accurate and cost-effective alternative to the personal interview. More recent studies that compared answers to the same questions in mail telephone and personal interviews likewise found little difference in their validity.[27]

Aside from its relative accuracy, telephone interviewing tends to increase the quality of the data. In most cases, telephone interviewers are working from a central office, and their work can be monitored constantly

26. Ibid.
27. Seymour Sudman and Norman M. Bradburn, *Asking Questions* (San Francisco: Jossey-Bass, 1982).

by the supervisory staff. This helps ensure that the questions are being asked correctly and that problems can be identified immediately and corrected.

One of the latest developments in telephone surveys is the use of computerized questionnaires. In **computer-assisted telephone interviewing (CATI),** the interviewer sits at a computer terminal and, as a question flashes on the screen, asks it over the telephone. Respondents' answers are typed and coded directly on a disk, and the next question comes up on the screen. Among the advantages of CATI are its speed and the use of complex instructions, programmed in advance. However, CATI is not suitable for open-ended questions.[28]

However, the weaknesses of the method cannot be ignored. Telephone interviewing has created a new kind of nonresponse—the "broken-off" interview. In about 4 percent of the calls, respondents terminate the interview before it is completed—a rare occurrence in personal interviews.[29] Telephone interviews also produce less information; interviewers cannot describe the respondents' characteristics or their environment in detail. Moreover, proportionately more telephone respondents indicate that they feel uneasy about discussing some topics, especially financial status and political attitudes, over the telephone.

In summary, telephone interviewing should be used as an alternative to personal interviewing under certain circumstances—especially when the interview schedule is relatively simple. However, the question of whether personal and telephone interviews are interchangeable remains to be answered. Surveys in the future may be conducted totally by telephone; others may combine telephone and personal interviews so that the two can complement each other and provide greater precision and increased response rate.

Comparing the Three Survey Methods

In deciding which survey method is best suited for one's research, one has to evaluate which criteria are most significant to the research objective. For example, if a researcher plans a long interview with a representative sample of the general population and wishes to control for nonverbal behavior, and if sufficient funds are available, a form of a personal interview is preferable.[30] Conversely, if the interview can be simplified, and if funds and speed are concerns, the telephone survey can be used to collect the information. If a rather lengthy questionnaire is to be used or one that includes threatening or sensitive questions, and especially if the population to be investigated is rel-

28. Ibid.

29. Institute for Social Research, University of Michigan, *Newsletter*, 4 (Autumn 1976).

30. A sample is representative if the measurements made on its units produce results equivalent to those that would be obtained had the entire population been measured. See Chapter 8.

Table 10.3
Evaluation of Three Survey Methods

Criterion	Personal Interview	Mail	Telephone
Cost	High	Low	Moderate
Response rate	High	Low	High
Control of interview situation	High	Low	Moderate
Applicability to geographically dispersed populations	Moderate	High	Moderate
Applicability to heterogeneous populations	High	Low	High
Collection of detailed information	High	Moderate	Moderate
Speed	Low	Low	High

atively dispersed geographically or is a selective population, the mail questionnaire can be considered as an alternative.

Table 10.3 presents some of the comparative advantages and limitations of the three methods of survey research.

Conclusion

The survey method is one of the most important data collection methods in the social sciences, and as such it is used extensively to collect information on numerous subjects of research. In recent years, with the public demands for government accountability, emphasis on survey instruments has increased. There are indications that survey research is becoming a widely used tool of various government organizations. Studies of local governments indicate that 50 percent of cities with populations over 100,000 and counties over 250,000 have used some form of survey. With the growth in the number of surveys conducted, the method has come in for increased criticism. Comments such as "Getting things right in social science research is not easy," "The sample of potential respondents was a hodgepodge of various procedures," and "I wouldn't trust any survey with a response rate like that," are typical. Although sometimes these remarks are justified, often they are not based on facts and are simply "lip service" to the spirit of criticism. Yet there is no denying that we need a set of criteria that will help us evaluate the usefulness of surveys, detect and control errors in them, and perhaps compensate for these errors wherever possible.[31]

Half a century ago, Edward Deming wrote an article, now a classic, called "On Errors in Surveys."[32] In this article, Deming lists 13 potential er-

---

31. Gregory Daneke and Patricia Klobus Edwards, "Survey Research for Public Administrators," *Public Administration Review*, 39 (1979): 421–426.
32. W. Edward Deming, *Some Theory of Sampling* (New York: Wiley, 1950).

rors that should be considered when planning a survey and when evaluating its results. The most important factors that might become potential errors in surveys were discussed in this chapter: interviewer bias, low response rate, and difficulty in asking sensitive questions. Reuben Cohen made the following remarks regarding these potential errors in his presidential address to the American Association for Public Opinion Research:

> Some 30 years ago, I was handed a reprint of W. Edward Deming's list of errors in surveys. The message was pretty obvious: Now that you know about them don't make them. With my relative inexperience, and my eternal optimism, I accepted the challenge. My first approach was to try to do the perfect survey. I am still trying, but I should know better. I quickly discovered Murphy's Law—if anything can go wrong, it probably will. But I also discovered something else. Even without the time and budget constraints that most of us complain about, there are no perfect surveys. Every survey has its imperfections. The world is not ideally suited to our work. The best we can do is think through the ideal approach to a survey design, or implementation, or analysis problem—what we would do if we had our druthers—then get as close to the ideal as we can within the constraints of time and budget which govern much of our work.[33]

And to readers who might be discouraged for these less than perfect goals, we offer the following advice:

> Practical work consists in good part of guessing what irregularities, where, and how much one can afford to tolerate. . . . The same is true for survey research. It should be done well. It can and should conform well, even if not perfectly, to an ideal approach.[34]

Summary

1. In this chapter, we discussed the survey as a method of data collection. Three methods were described: the mail questionnaire, the face-to-face interview, and the telephone interview.

2. The mail questionnaire is regarded as an impersonal survey method. Its major advantages are low cost, relatively small biasing error, anonymity, and accessibility. Its disadvantages are a low response rate, no opportunity for probing, and lack of control over who fills out the questionnaire.

3. The difficulty of securing an acceptable response rate to mail questionnaires calls for the use of various strategies that are known to affect the response rate. Among those, the most effective are the use of follow-up mailings, sponsorship of the survey, and the appeal of the questionnaire.

---

33. Reuben Cohen, "Close Enough for All Practical Purposes," *Public Opinion Quarterly*, 43 (1979): 421–422.

34. Ibid., p. 424.

The questionnaire's format and the methods of mailing used will also affect the response rate.

4. The personal interview is a face-to-face situation in which an interviewer asks respondents questions designed to obtain answers pertinent to the research hypotheses. The most structured form of interview is the schedule-structured interview, in which the questions, their wording, and their sequence are fixed and are identical for every respondent. The focused interview follows an interview guide specifying topics related to the research hypothesis and gives considerable liberty to the respondents to express their views. Finally, nondirective interviews are the least structured, employing no prespecified set of questions. The interviewer has a great deal of freedom to probe various areas and to raise specific queries during the course of the interview.

5. Telephone interviewing has gained general acceptance as a substitute for personal interviewing. The telephone survey is convenient and cost-effective. In addition, it sometimes results in a higher response rate than the personal interview. Furthermore, technological change and improvement in telephone equipment have also made telephone interviewing easier, especially when using random-digit dialing and computer-assisted telephone interviewing.

Key Terms for Review

mail questionnaire
response rate
follow-up
schedule-structured interview
focused interview

nondirective interview
probing
random-digit dialing (RDD)
computer-assisted telephone
    interviewing (CATI)

Study Questions

1. Describe the basic techniques of survey data collection.
2. Discuss the advantages and disadvantages of mail questionnaires, telephone interviews, and personal interviews.
3. List and describe the basic principles of interviewing.
4. What type of survey research would you use to study drug users? Defend the logic of your choice.
5. Suppose that you are engaged in a research project to determine the attitudes in a small town toward welfare. A mailed questionnaire is to be used, and a sample has been chosen. Write the cover letter.

Additional Readings

Backstrom, Charles, and Gerald Hursh. *Survey Research*. 2d ed. New York: Wiley, 1981.

Bainbridge, William Sims. *Survey Research: A Computer-assisted Introduction*. Belmont, Calif.: Wadsworth, 1989.

Banaka, William H. *Training in Depth Interviewing*. New York: Harper & Row, 1971.

Call, Vaughn, Luther B. Otto, and Kenneth I. Spenner. *Tracking Respondents: A Multimethod Approach*. Lexington, Mass.: Lexington Books, 1982.

Cannell, Charles F., P. V. Miller, and L. Oksenberg. "Research on Interviewing Techniques." In *Sociological Methodology*, ed. Reinhardts. San Francisco: Jossey-Bass, 1981.

Cunverse, Jean M. *Survey Research in the United States*. Los Angeles: University of California Press, 1987.

De Vaus, D. A. *Survey in Social Research*. London: Allen & Unwin, 1986.

Fowler, Floyd J., Jr. *Survey Research Methods*. Newbury Park, Calif.: Sage, 1989.

Frey, James H. *Survey Research by Telephone*. Newbury Park, Calif: Sage, 1983.

Gorden, Raymond L. *Interviewing: Strategy, Techniques, and Tactics*. 3d ed. Homewood, Ill.: Dorsey, 1980.

Jolliffe, F. R. *Survey Design and Analysis*. London: Ellis Horwood, 1986.

Marsh, Catherine. *The Survey Method*. London: Allen & Unwin, 1982.

Schuman, Howard, and Graham Kalton. "Survey Method." In *The Handbook of Social Psychology*, 3d ed., ed. Gardner Lindzey and Elliot Aronson. New York: Random House, 1985.

Sonquist, John A., and William C. Dunkelberg. *Survey and Opinon Research: Procedures for Processing and Analysis*. Englewood Cliffs, N.J.: Prentice-Hall, 1977.

Tucker, C. "Interviewer Effects in Telephone Surveys." *Public Opinion Quarterly*, 47 (1983): 84–95.

CHAPTER 11

Questionnaire Construction

In this chapter, we discuss the formulation of specific types of questions and question formats in survey design. Wording of questions and pitfalls in questionnaire construction are detailed.

I N THIS CHAPTER, WE FOCUS ON THE questionnaire as the main instrument in survey research. We start by discussing the foundation of all questionnaires—the question. We then look at the content of questions and differentiate between open-ended, closed-ended, and contingency-type questions and analyze their format and sequencing. Next we explore possible biases in the wording of questions, as well as leading, double-barreled, and threatening questions. Finally, we give important pointers on the cover letter accompanying the questionnaire and the instructions included in it.

The Question

The foundation of all questionnaires is the **question**. The questionnaire must translate the research objectives into specific questions; answers to such questions will provide the data for hypothesis testing. The question must also motivate the respondent to provide the information being sought. The major considerations involved in formulating questions are their content, structure, format, and sequence.

Content of Questions

Survey questions may be concerned with facts, opinions, attitudes, respondents' motivation, and their level of familiarity with a certain subject. Most questions, however, can be classified in either of two general categories: factual questions and questions about subjective experiences.

Factual Questions

Factual questions are designed to elicit objective information from the respondents regarding their background, environment, habits, and the like. The most common type of factual question is the background question, which is asked mainly to provide information by which respondents can be classified, such as gender, age, marital status, education, or income. Such classifications may in turn aid in explaining differences in behaviors and attitudes. The following is an example of such a question:

> What was the last grade you completed in school? (Please check one.)
> _____ 8th grade or lower
> _____ 9th or 10th grade
> _____ 11th or 12th grade: high school graduate? __Yes __No
> _____ 1 to 2 years of college
> _____ 3 to 4 years of college: college graduate? __Yes __No
> _____ 5 or more years of college

Other kinds of factual questions are intended to provide information on the respondents' social environment ("Would you please tell me, who are the people living in your household?"), means of transportation ("How do you generally get to work?"), or leisure activities ("How often do you go to the movies?").

Factual questions are thought to be easier to design than other types of questions. However, even factual questions can present the researcher with problems. How accurately people report depends on what and how they are being asked. There are four reasons why respondents give less than accurate anwers to factual questions:[1]

1. They do not know the information.
2. They cannot recall the information.
3. They do not understand the question.
4. They are reluctant to answer.

The researcher can take several steps to increase accuracy, including encouraging respondents to consult other members of the household, asking more than one question about the matter, repeating questions, and making respondents feel comfortable when asking about events that the respondents may find embarrassing.

---

1. Floyd J. Fowler, Jr., *Survey Research Methods* (Newbury Park, Calif.: Sage, 1989), p. 91.

Questions about Subjective Experiences

Subjective experience involves the respondents' beliefs, attitudes, feelings, and opinions.[2] Questions about attitudes are often included in surveys conducted in the social sciences. **Attitudes** are general orientations that can incline a person to act or react in a certain manner when confronted with certain stimuli. Here is an example of a question about attitudes toward abortion:

> On the issue of abortion, how would you describe your personal position?
>
> 1. Favorable
> 2. Neutral
> 3. Opposed

An individual's attitudes are expressed, in speech or behavior, only when the object of the attitude is perceived. A person may have strong attitudes for or against abortion, but these are aroused and conveyed only when that person encounters some issue connected with abortion or is confronted with a stimulus such as a question in an interview.

Attitudes can be described by their content (what the attitude is about), their direction (positive, neutral, or negative feelings about the object or issue in question), and their intensity (an attitude may be held with greater or lesser vehemence). To one person, abortion may be of but passing interest; to another, it may be of great significance and lead that person to join a pro-choice organization. One would expect the latter person to agree or disagree more strongly than the former on questions dealing with, say, the passage of a constitutional amendment that would make abortion illegal.

In general, we are interested in measuring attitudes because they account for the respondent's general inclination. The study of opinion is of interest only insofar as it is a symbol of an attitude. The main difference between asking for opinions and measuring attitudes is that an **opinion** is generally measured by estimating what proportion of the surveyed population say they agree with a single opinion statement. Attitudes are measured by attitude scales consisting of five to two dozen or more attitude statements, with which the respondent is asked to agree or disagree. An essential requirement of attitude measurement is that such attitude statements be scaled, that is, that the statements be selected and put together from a much larger number of attitude statements according to certain techniques. These techniques are discussed in Chapter 18.

Survey questions about opinions and attitudes present more problems in construction than questions about facts. It is relatively simple to obtain accurate information on, for example, whether or not a person is married or single. One may reasonably assume that the respondent knows whether he

2. Royce Singleton, Jr., Bruce C. Straits, Margaret M. Straits, and Ronald J. McAllister, *Approaches to Social Research* (Oxford: Oxford University Press, 1988), p. 272.

or she is married or not. With opinions or attitudes, the assumption that the respondents know cannot always be made. Respondents may not have an attitude toward making abortions illegal, or if they do, it might be latent. Moreover, given that many attitudes have numerous aspects or dimensions, the respondent may agree with one aspect and disagree with another. This is why attitudes cannot be measured by a single question. For example, if a person strongly disagrees with the statement ''Abortions should be available to any woman who wants one,'' this does not imply a broad antiabortion attitude.

This person's view may be different if the woman's life is in danger, if the pregnancy resulted from incest or rape, or if a doctor said that the baby will be severely deformed. By using several attitude statements, one can reduce the effects of one-sided responses.

Finally, answers to opinion and attitude questions are more sensitive to changes in wording, emphasis, and sequence than answers to factual questions. This reflects, in part, the multidimensionality of many attitudes. Questions presented in different ways sometimes reflect different aspects of the attitude and thus result in different answers.

Types of Questions

The content of the question is only one important aspect in the construction of survey questionnaires. The researcher must also consider the structure of the question and the format of the response categories accompanying the questions. Three types of question structures can be distinguished and will be discussed: open-ended questions, closed-ended questions, and contingency questions.

Open-ended and Closed-ended Questions

Questions in a questionnaire can be either open-ended or closed-ended. In a **closed-ended question**, respondents are offered a set of answers and asked to choose the one that most closely represents their views. For example, to measure the degree of satisfaction with family life the General Social Survey, a public opinion poll conducted yearly by the National Opinion Research Council, the following closed-ended question was used:

Tell me the number that shows how much satisfaction you get from your family life.

1. A very great deal
2. A great deal
3. Quite a bit
4. A fair amount
5. A little

6. Very little
7. None
8. Don't know
9. No answer

Answers to closed-ended questions can be more elaborate, like the following question taken from a survey about women's and men's attitudes about a woman's place and role.[3]

> Suppose both a husband and wife work at good and interesting jobs and the husband is offered a very good job in another city. Assuming they have no children, which one of these solutions do you think they should seriously consider?
>
> - Husband should turn down the job
> - Wife should quit and relocate with husband
> - Husband should take new job and move/wife should keep her job and stay

Closed-ended questions are easy to ask and quick to answer; they require no writing by either respondent or interviewer, and their analysis is straightforward. Their major drawback is that they may introduce bias, either by forcing the respondent to choose from given alternatives or by making the respondent select alternatives that might not have otherwise come to mind.

Open-ended questions are not followed by any kind of specified choice, and the respondents' answers are recorded in full. For instance, the question "What do you personally feel are the most important problems the government in Washington should try to take care of?" is an open-ended question used frequently in questionnaires designed to study public opinion. The virtue of the open-ended question is that it does not force the respondent to adapt to preconceived answers: having understood the intent of the question, one can express one's thoughts freely, spontaneously, and in one's own language. If the answers to open-ended questions are unclear, the interviewer may probe by asking the respondent to explain further or to give a rationale for something stated earlier; such open questions enable the interviewer to clear up misunderstandings, and they encourage rapport. However, open-ended questions are difficult to answer and still more difficult to analyze. The researcher has to design a coding frame in order to classify the various answers; in this process, the details of the information provided by the respondent might get lost (see Chapter 14).

The appropriateness of either open-ended or closed-ended questions depends on a number of factors. Some years ago, Paul Lazarsfeld suggested the use of the following considerations to determine appropriateness:[4]

1. *The objectives of the questionnaire.* Closed-ended questions are suitable when the researcher's objective is to lead the respondent to express

3. Rita J. Simon and Jean M. Landis, "Report: Women's and Men's Attitudes about a Woman's Place and Role," *Public Opinion Quarterly*, 53 (1989): 265–276.

4. Paul F. Lazarsfeld, "The Controversy over Detailed Interviews: An Offer for Negotiation," *Public Opinion Quarterly*, 8 (1944): 38–60.

agreement or disagreement with an explicit point of view. When the researcher wishes to learn about the process by which the respondent arrived at a particular point of view, an open-ended question is likely to be more appropriate.

2. *The respondent's level of information about the topic in question.* Open-ended questions provide opportunities for the interviewer to ascertain lack of information on the part of the respondent, whereas closed-ended questions do not. Obviously, it is futile to raise questions that are beyond the experiences of respondents.

3. *The extent to which the topic has been thought through by the respondent.* The open-ended question is preferable in situations where the respondents have not yet crystallized their opinions. The use of a closed-ended question in such situations involves a risk that in accepting one of the alternatives offered, the respondent may make a choice that is quite different from an opinion that would have otherwise been expressed had he or she gone through the process of recall and evaluation of past experience.

4. *The ease with which the content of the answer can be communicated by the respondent or the extent to which the respondent is motivated to communicate on the topic.* The closed-ended question requires less motivation to communicate on the part of the respondent, and the response itself is usually less revealing (and hence less threatening) than in the case of the open-ended question. The researcher who uses closed-ended questions tends to encounter less frequent refusals to respond.

Sometimes there may be good reasons for asking the same question in both open-ended and closed-ended form. For example, an open-ended answer to the question "Who rules America?" will provide a clear idea of the respondent's perception of the political system and the significance that the person attaches to different power groups. Although this datum is most valuable, it might not allow comparison of one group of respondents with another. Furthermore, one cannot be sure that all information of importance to the respondent has been mentioned; factors such as the inability to articulate thoughts or a momentary lapse of memory may cause omission of significant points. Therefore, the researcher can ask the same question again, later in the interview, but this time in closed-ended form.

Contingency Questions

Frequently, questions that are relevant to some respondents may be irrelevant to others. For example, the question "Check the most important reasons why you are going to college" obviously applies only to high school students who are planning to go to college. It is often necessary to include questions that might apply only to some respondents and not to others. Some questions may be relevant only to females and not to males, others will apply only to respondents who are self-employed, and so on.

A **contingency question**—a special-case closed-ended question—is one that applies only to a subgroup of respondents. The relevance of the question to this subgroup is determined by the answer of all respondents to a preceding **filter question**. For example, in a news media survey, the filter question might read, "Do you regularly follow the news in the papers?" The contingency question could be, "What recent event do you remember reading about? (Give a brief description.)" The relevance of the second question to the respondent is contingent on his or her response to the filter question. Only respondents who responded "Yes" to the filter question will find the contingency question relevant. Therefore, the response categories of the filter questions will be "1. Yes (answer the following question); 2. No (skip to question 3)."

The formats for filter and contingency questions vary. One alternative is to write directions next to each response category of the filter question. Another common format is to use arrows to direct the respondent either to skip to another question or to answer the contingency question, as in the following example:

Is this the first full-time job you have held since you graduated from college?

1. Yes
2. No ⟶
   What happened to the job you had before—were you promoted, laid off, or what? (Check one.)

   1. Company folded
   2. Laid off or fired
   3. Job stopped; work was seasonal
   4. Quit voluntarily
   5. Promoted; relocated
   6. Other

Another format is to box the contingency question and to set it apart from the ordinary questions to be answered by everybody. An example of such a format appears in Exhibit 11.1. When there are several subgroups to which the questionnaire is addressed and when several contingency questions apply to each subgroup, it is useful to indicate by number which questions the respondent should answer. The instructions are written next to the appropriate response categories in the filter question. This is demonstrated in the following example:

22. Are you looking for another job at this time?

    —— yes
    —— no
    —— don't know   } Go to question 25.
    —— inappropriate

Exhibit 11.1
Contingency Question

ANSWER QUESTIONS BELOW IF YOU ARE A SENIOR PLANNING TO GO TO COLLEGE NEXT FALL. NONSENIORS SKIP TO QUESTION 144.

137. Did you take the College Entrance Board Exams?
    ____ yes
    ____ no

138. Do you definitely know yet which college you will attend?
    ____ yes
    ____ no

139. If "yes," how does this school compare to the others you were considering, in each of the following ways?

1. ☐ 2. ☐ 3. ☐ 4. ☐   Offering the course
                               of study you want.
1. ☐ 2. ☐ 3. ☐ 4. ☐   General reputation
                               of the school.

SKIP TO QUESTION 151 ON THE NEXT PAGE.

With computer-assisted telephone interviewing (CATI), the computer is preprogrammed to do the skipping automatically. If a respondent answered "no," "don't know," or "inappropriate" to the preceding question, question 25 would automatically appear on the screen.

Question Format

We will now discuss some of the common techniques for structuring the response categories of closed-ended questions. The general format is to present all possible answers and have the respondents check the appropriate categories. The respondents can either circle or write the number of the answer or check a box or a blank, as here:

What is your marital status?

__	Married		☐	Married	1.	Married
__	Single	*or*	☐	Single	*or* 2.	Single
__	Divorced		☐	Divorced	3.	Divorced
__	Widowed		☐	Widowed	4.	Widowed

Of course, specific directions should be provided as to whether the respondent is to circle a number or check a blank or a box. Among the three methods shown, the least recommended is the one with blanks because respondents may check between the blanks, making it difficult to tell which category was intended. Circling a code number is preferable because the code number can be easily transferred to a computerized storage device.

Rating

One of the most common formats for questions asked in social science surveys is the rating scale. The **rating** scale is used whenever respondents are asked to make a judgment in terms of sets of ordered categories, such as "strongly agree," "favorable," or "very often"; for example:

> Police should be allowed to conduct a full search of any motorist arrested for an offense such as speeding.
>
> 1. Agree strongly
> 2. Agree
> 3. Disagree
> 4. Disagree strongly
> 5. No opinion

The response categories of such questions are termed **quantifiers**; they reflect the *intensity* of the particular judgment involved. The following sets of response categories are quite common:

1. Strongly agree	1. Too little	1. More
2. Agree	2. About right	2. Same
3. Depends	3. Too much	3. Less
4. Disagree		
5. Strongly disagree		

The numerical codes that accompany these categories are usually interpreted to represent the intensity of the response categories, so that the higher the number, the more intense the response. Yet it should be emphasized that though we assume that the quantifiers involved are ordered by intensity, it does not imply that the distance between them is equal. Indeed, rating scales such as these are most often measured on ordinal levels of measurement, as discussed in Chapter 7.

Despite the difficulty in estimating intensities, we cannot typically ask respondents for exact estimates because most would have a great deal of difficulty with the task. Although it would seem relatively easy to report how many hours in the past week a person watched television, most people have greater difficulty in estimating precisely events of relatively low salience, such as attitudes about foreign policy.[5]

---

5. Norman M. Bradburn and Seymour Sudman, *Improving Interview Method and Questionnaire Design* (San Francisco: Jossey-Bass, 1974), pp. 152–162.

Matrix Questions

The **matrix question** is a method for organizing a large set of rating questions that have the same response categories. The following is an example of such a device:

Indicate your reaction to each of the following statements.

	I strongly agree.	I agree.	It depends.	I disagree.	I strongly disagree.
My vote gives me all the power I want in governmental affairs.	( )	( )	( )	( )	( )
If I complained to the people at a city agency, they would fix up whatever was wrong.	( )	( )	( )	( )	( )
I've sometimes wished that government officials paid more attention to what I thought.	( )	( )	( )	( )	( )

Card Sort

Another way to measure intensities of judgments is the **card sort**. The respondent is handed a set of cards, each bearing a statement, and is asked to sort them into one of seven boxes, depending on his or her degree of agreement with the statement. The following is an example of such a device:

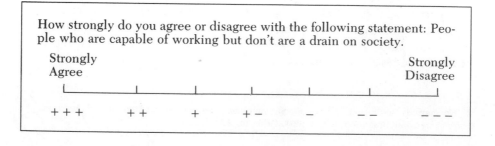

Semantic Differential

The **semantic differential** is another type of rating scale. It measures the respondent's reaction to some object or concept in terms of rating on bipolar scales defined with contrasting adjectives at each end:[6]

$$\text{Good} \underset{3}{\underline{\quad}} \underset{2}{\underline{\quad}} \underset{1}{\underline{\quad}} \underset{0}{\underline{\quad}} \underset{1}{\underline{\quad}} \underset{2}{\underline{\quad}} \underset{3}{\underline{\quad}} \text{Bad}$$

The zero marks the *neutral position* on the scale, and the positions 1–3 measure the intensities in either direction, with 1 being the slightest reaction and 3 the most intense.

Examine this example of an application of the semantic differential:[7]

> Here is a list of pairs of words you might use to describe civil servants. Between each pair is a measuring stick of seven lines. Taking the first pair of words—i.e., "good/bad"—as an example, the line on the extreme left would mean that the civil servant is very good, the next line would mean he or she is fairly good, and so on. The words at the top of your card will help you choose the line you think is appropriate.
>
> Now will you tell me which line you would use to describe civil servants?

	Very	Fairly	Slightly	Neither	Slightly	Fairly	Very	
Good	__:	__:	__:	__:	__:	__:	__:	Bad
Honest	__:	__:	__:	__:	__:	__:	__:	Dishonest
Efficient	__:	__:	__:	__:	__:	__:	__:	Inefficient
Deep	__:	__:	__:	__:	__:	__:	__:	Shallow
Active	__:	__:	__:	__:	__:	__:	__:	Passive

Ranking

We use **ranking** in questionnaires whenever we want to obtain information regarding the degree of importance or the priorities that people give to a set of attitudes or objects. For instance, in a survey on the quality of life, respondents were asked to rank various dimensions they consider important in life.

> "I would like you to tell me what you have found important in life. Please look at this card and tell me which of these is most important to *you* as a goal in *your* life, which comes next in importance, which is third, and which ranks fourth."

6. David R. Heise, "The Semantic Differential and Attitude Research," in *Attitude Measurement*, ed. Gene F. Summers (Skokie: Ill.: Rand McNally, 1970), p. 235.

7. David Nachmias and David H. Rosenbloom, *Bureaucratic Culture: Citizens and Administrators in Israel* (New York: St. Martin's Press, 1978), pp. 110–115.

	Rank			
A prosperous life (having a good income and being able to afford the good things in life)	1	2	3	4
A family life (a life completely centered on my family)	1	2	3	4
An important life (a life of achievement that brings me respect and recognition)	1	2	3	4
A secure life (making certain that all basic needs and expenses are provided)	1	2	3	4

Ranking is a useful device in providing some sense of relative order among objects or judgments. This is particularly important given that many properties measured in the social science (for example, "quality of life," "status") cannot be given any precise numerical value. However, with the use of ranking we can at least obtain information regarding their relative order. It should be emphasized, however, that ranking does not provide any information about the distance between the ranks. The difference between, say, rank 1 and rank 2 may not be the same as the difference between rank 2 and rank 3.

Sequence of Questions

After question format has been determined, the order in which the questions are placed in the questionnaire should be considered. Two general patterns of question sequence have been found to be most appropriate for motivating respondents to cooperate: the *funnel sequence* and the *inverted funnel sequence*.

Funnel Sequence

In the funnel sequence, each successive question is related to the previous question and has a progressively narrower scope. For example, if one were interested in finding out how respondents' views of political, economic, and social problems are related to the newspapers they read, one might want to know what sorts of things the respondents think of as problems, what the perceived relative significance of each problem is, how much information they have on the topic, what their sources of information are, and whether certain newspapers have influenced their thinking on the problem. The following questions form a funnel sequence:

1. What do you think are some of the most important problems facing the nation?
2. Of all the problems you have just mentioned, which do you think is the most important one?
3. Where have you obtained most of the information about this problem?
4. Do you read the *Washington Post*?

When the objective of the survey is to obtain detailed information and when the respondent is motivated to supply the information, the funnel approach helps the respondent recall details more efficiently. Furthermore, by asking the broadest questions first, the interviewer can avoid imposing a frame of reference before obtaining the respondent's perspective. When the objective of the survey is to discover unanticipated responses, broader questions should be pursued first.[8]

Inverted Funnel Sequence

In the inverted funnel sequence, narrower questions are followed by broader ones. When the topic of the survey does not strongly motivate the respondents to communicate—either because the topic is not important to them or because their experiences are not recent enough to be vivid in their memory—it may be helpful to begin with the narrow questions, which are easier to answer, and reserve the broader (and more difficult) ones until later. If the purpose is to obtain a generalization in the form of a judgment regarding a concrete situation and if the interviewer is unfamiliar with the facts but the respondent knows them, narrower questions aimed at establishing specific facts should precede questions requiring an overall judgment.[9]

In the following example, the attempt is to obtain the respondents' judgment regarding the effectiveness of rescue operations during a disaster. To help people make an unbiased judgment, the researcher felt that it was better to deal with the specifics first, asking for the generalization later.[10]

1. How many people were killed in the tornado?
2. How many do you suppose were injured so seriously that they had to go to the hospital?
3. How long was it before most of the injured got to the hospital?
4. Did you see anyone administer first aid by giving artificial respiration or stopping bleeding? Who was it?
5. In general, how well do you think the first aid and rescue operations were carried out?

The order in which the questions are presented has been shown to affect the type of response given. For example, there is evidence that answers to attitude questions in surveys can vary markedly, depending on the preceding items in the questionnaire. In a recent study, more than 1,100 respondents were asked about target issues such as abortion, defense spending, and welfare.[11] In one version of the questionnaire, target questions were preceded

8. Raymond L. Gorden, *Interviewing: Strategy, Techniques, and Tactics*, 3d ed. (Homewood, Ill.: Dorsey, 1980), pp. 415–416.

9. Ibid.

10. Ibid.

11. Roger Tourangeau, Kenneth A. Rasinski, Norman M. Bradburn, and Roy D'Andrade, "Carryover Effects in Attitude Surveys," *Public Opinion Quarterly*, 53 (1989): 495–524.

by related context questions; in others, the target questions were preceded by neutral questions. For example, the abortion target question "Do you favor or oppose the Supreme Court's decision that legalized abortion?" was preceded in the first version by a number of context questions about traditional values and about rape. Respondents were generally affected by related context questions, especially when they held conflicting beliefs about the target issue. There is also evidence that the position of an item in a list has a significant impact on its being chosen, with items appearing first being endorsed more often.[12] It has been shown too that when respondents are asked to assign numerical values to a set of items (for example, according to their degree of importance), the items appearing first tend to receive a higher rank.

In the following question, respondents are more likely to assign the first rank to the first category than to the last one simply because it is listed first.

> Among the items below, what does it take to get to be important and looked up to by the other students here at school? (Rank from 1 to 6.)
>
> —— Coming from the right family
> —— Leader in activities
> —— Having a nice car
> —— High grades, honor roll
> —— Being an athletic star
> —— Being popular

This problem may arise especially in situations where the questions are subjective statements like attitudes, which are not central or salient to the respondent. In such situations, the item appearing first tends to form a point of reference for all items that follow. This problem can be overcome by acquainting respondents with the list of items before evaluations are to be made. Alternatively, the order of presentation could be randomized so that the order effects will be randomized, too, and will not result in any systematic bias.[13]

Finally, it should be pointed out that questions that are presented first in the questionnaire should put the respondent at ease; those in an interview should help create rapport between the interviewer and the respondent. Thus the opening question should be easy to answer, interesting, and non-controversial. For example, questions about the respondent's drinking habit or sex life, if placed at the beginning, will in all likelihood increase the refusal rate. It is also recommended that open-ended questions be placed later, for they usually require more time and thought and thus may reduce the respondent's initial motivation to cooperate.

12. William A. Belson, "The Effects of Reversing the Presentation Order on Verbal Rating Scales," *Journal of Advertising Research*, 6: 4 (1966): 30–37.
13. Edwin H. Carpenter and Larry G. Blackwood, "The Effects of Question Position on Responses to Attitudinal Questions," *Rural Sociology*, 44 (1979): 56–72.

Avoiding Bias:
Pitfalls in Questionnaire Construction

Wording

The question must be worded so that the respondent understands it. For example, the researcher's vocabulary might include a word such as *charismatic* that might not be understood by most other people. If the respondents come from all walks of life, the interviewer should use words understandable by the average eighth grader. Furthermore, words that are open to interpretation should be either avoided or qualified. For example, asking whether someone is a liberal might refer to the person's education, politics, profession, or sex life. But a question such as "Do you consider yourself liberal? Politically, I mean," instructs the respondent to use the political frame of reference in answering the question. Questions should be worded so that the respondent understands the question and so that the question has the same meaning to each respondent.

Response Set

A *response set* is the tendency to answer all questions in a specific direction regardless of their content.[14] This may be a problem when a set of questions is presented together with the same response format, especially when the questions all refer to the same topic. For example, if a set of questions reflects a pro-choice attitude regarding abortion, respondents who are against abortion may check all the same response categories (for example, all "strongly disagree," or all "strongly agree") simply because they assume that these categories all express objection to abortion. A response set can be avoided by changing the question format, either by varying the response categories for each question or by avoiding the lumping together of questions referring to the same topic.

Leading Questions

A **leading question** is a question phrased in such a manner that it seems to the respondent that the researcher expects a certain answer. A question designed to elicit general attitudes toward legal abortions might read, "Do you favor or oppose legal abortions?" The same question phrased in leading form might read, "You wouldn't say that you were in favor of legal abortion, would you?" A more subtle form of leading question might be, "Would you say that you are not in favor of legal abortions?" This last question makes it easier for respondents to answer yes than no because most

14. Kenneth D. Bailey, *Methods of Social Research* (New York: Free Press, 1987), p. 133.

people feel more comfortable agreeing with the language of the question and not contradicting the interviewer.

Respondents also tend to agree with questions that support accepted norms or that are perceived as socially desirable. Questions that reflect socially undesirable behavior or attitudes are endorsed less frequently than those high on the scale of social desirability. Similarly, issue labeling and enhancement can have a substantial effect on public support for some issues. Analyses of variations in question wording in the General Social Survey showed significant differences in responses. For example, when a question on welfare spending read "Are we spending too much, too little, or about the right amount on welfare?" 23 percent said too little. But when the question was worded "Are we spending too much, too little, or about the right amount on assistance to the poor," almost 63 percent said too little.[15]

Leading questions are to be avoided if one is looking for undistorted responses. Under certain circumstances, however, leading questions may serve the research objective. The question "Would you favor sending food overseas to feed the starving people of India?" was used to determine the number of people who were so strongly opposed to shipping food to other countries that they rejected the idea even within the strong emotional context of "starving people."[16]

Threatening Questions

Often it is necessary to include questions on topics that the respondent may find embarrassing and thus difficult to answer. Such **threatening questions** are, according to Norman Bradburn and coauthors, "anxiety-arousing questions about, for example, behaviors that are illegal or contra-normative or about behaviors that, though not socially deviant, are not usually discussed in public without some tension."[17] Threatening questions may inquire, for example, about the respondents' gambling habits, drinking, or sexual preferences.

There is considerable empirical evidence that threatening questions lead to response bias, either denial of the behavior in question or underreporting. In general, the reporting of certain behaviors decreases as questions increase in their degree of threat. When presented with a threatening question, respondents are caught in a conflict between the role demands of the "good respondent," who responds truthfully to all the questions, and the tendency to present oneself positively. The conflict is usually resolved not by refusing

15. Kenneth A. Rasinski, "The Effect of Question Wording on Public Support for Government Spending," *Public Opinion Quarterly*, 53 (1989): 388–394.

16. Robert I. Kahn and Charles F. Cannell, *The Dynamics of Interviewing* (New York: Wiley, 1957), p. 129.

17. Norman M. Bradburn, Seymour Sudman, Ed Blair, and Carol Stocking, "Question Threat and Response Bias," *Public Opinion Quarterly*, 42 (1978): 221–222.

to answer but by reporting that one did not engage in the particular activity when one in fact did.[18]

Because threatening questions may elicit biased responses, it is important that researchers first identify whether or not certain questions are threatening. Norman Bradburn and Seymour Sudman suggest that the best method to determine the relative threat of questions is to ask respondents to rate question topics as to how uneasy they thought most people would feel in talking about them.[19] One could also ask about the respondents' own reactions to the questions or rate the degree of difficulty the topics caused in the interview.

Once threatening questions have been identified, what should be done about them? In a comprehensive study dealing with response effects to threatening questions in survey research, Bradburn and Sudman determined that the construction of questions makes a great deal of difference.[20] Perhaps their most significant finding was the discovery that the accuracy of the response is considerably increased by using a long introduction to the question rather than asking short questions, by employing an open-ended rather than a closed-ended format, and, to a lesser extent, by letting the respondents choose their own words when talking about sensitive topics. Their questionnaire contained an item about the number of times in the past year the respondent had become intoxicated. In the short, closed form, the item read: "In the past year, how often did you become intoxicated while drinking any kind of beverage?" Respondents were asked to classify their response into one of the following categories: never, once a year or less, every few months, once a month, every few weeks, once a week, several times a week, and daily. In the open-ended, long form, the respondents were first asked to provide their own word for intoxication: "Sometimes people drink a little too much beer, wine, or whiskey so that they act different from usual. What word do you think we should use to describe people when they get that way, so that you will know what we mean and feel comfortable talking about it?" The intoxication item then read: "Occasionally people drink on an empty stomach or drink a little too much and become (respondent's word). In the past year, how often have you become (respondent's word) while drinking any kind of alcoholic beverage?" No response categories were provided for these questions.[21]

Double-barreled Questions

Double-barreled questions combine two or more questions in one. Here is an example from an opinion poll about domestic violence:

18. Ibid., pp. 221–234.
19. Bradburn and Sudman, *Improving Interview Method and Questionnaire Design*, p. 165.
20. Ibid., pp. 14–25.
21. Ibid., p. 18.

Domestic violence and AIDS are the most serious problems facing America
today.

— Agree   — Disagree
— Depends — Strongly disagree

The problem with such a question is that it might confuse respondents who
agree with one aspect of the question, say, domestic violence, but disagree
with the other, AIDS. Many questions that contain *and* are very likely dou-
bled-barreled. Questions with *and* can be used, however, if the dimensions
separated by *and* are mutually exclusive and the respondent is asked to select
one or to rank them according to some criterion, for instance:

At the present time, the country is facing with two major problems: the environment and domestic violence. Which of these two problems would you
say is the more important?

— The environment
— Domestic violence

Cover Letter

After the questionnaire has been constructed, the next step is to write an introductory statement (for a personal telephone interview) or a cover letter
(for a mail questionnaire) to explain the purpose of the survey to the respondents and to encourage a high response rate. This is of particular importance in mail questionnaires, where the difficulty of securing a high response rate, especially when one needs to ask more than a few simple
questions, is well documented (see Chapter 10).

A cover letter must succeed in overcoming any resistance or prejudice
the respondent may have against the survey. It should (1) identify the sponsoring organization or the persons conducting the study, (2) explain the purpose of the study, (3) tell why it is important that the respondent answer the
questionnaire, and (4) ensure the respondent that the information provided
will be held in strict confidence.

In general, the cover letter for a mail questionnaire needs to be more detailed than the introductory statement in a personal interview. In an interview, the interviewer is always there to explain or persuade the respondent
should that become necessary. With a mail questionnaire, the cover letter is
all there is, and thus its function is very significant.

Two examples of cover letters used in various mail surveys are shown
here. The first, presented in Exhibit 11.2, was used with a mail questionnaire designed by the Institute of Social Research at Florida State University
under the auspices of the State Department of Manpower Planning of Florida to evaluate the Public Service Employment and Training Act, Title VI
(CETA).[22]

22. Mickey L. Burnim, *An Evaluation of the Public Service Employment Projects in Florida
Created under Title VI of the Comprehensive Employment and Training Act of 1973* (Tallahassee: Florida State University, 1978), p. 164.

Exhibit 11.2
Florida Questionnaire Cover Letter

To Program Operators:

The Office of Manpower Planning, Department of Community Affairs, in conjunction with the State Manpower Services Council, has funded a special evaluation of public service employment projects authorized under Title VI of the Comprehensive Employment and Training Act. This evaluation is being conducted by Dr. M. L. Burnim in the Institute for Social Research at Florida State University. The purpose of the evaluation is to determine the impact of public service employment projects on unemployed persons in Florida and to measure the benefit of these projects to the communities in which they are conducted.

As you know, public service employment is a major part of the federal, state, and local strategy to overcome the employment and income problems of economically disadvantaged, unemployed people. There is no question that the program is needed throughout the country to create jobs and training opportunities for the large numbers of people who remain unemployed. You are probably also aware, however, that public service employment programs are quite controversial and their future may be in jeopardy. Part of the reason that these programs are so controversial is that no systematic evaluation of the benefits of these programs for the individuals employed and the communities served has been conducted.

Because this specific evaluation has significant national policy implications, I strongly urge you to assist the research team in compiling the necessary data. It is very important that you complete the survey questionnaire transmitted to you as as soon as possible.

Thank you for your cooperation.

Sincerely,

Edward A. Feaver, Director
Office of Manpower Planning

The second example, reprinted in Exhibit 11.3, is from a study on commitment to civil liberties, conducted by investigators at the University of Wisconsin at Milwaukee.[23] The letter emphasizes the confidentiality of the study and explains in detail how the individual responses will be used.

Finally, an important issue is the style used in the cover letter, that is, whether it is a formal or a semipersonal letter. In the two examples, a form letter was sent out to all respondents included in the sample. Alternatively, rather than addressing the letter to "Dear Friend" or "Dear Respondent,"

---

23. Richard D. Bingham and James L. Gibson, "Conditions of Commitment to Civil Liberties," unpublished (Milwaukee: Department of Political Science, University of Wisconsin, 1979).

Exhibit 11.3
Wisconsin Questionnaire Cover Letter

Dear Friend:

We are conducting a survey sponsored by the University of Wisconsin—Milwaukee and assisted by the American Civil Liberties Union (ACLU). Our purpose is to learn more about how people like yourself feel about certain aspects of civil liberties and how beliefs are related to behavior. You have been selected at random to participate in this survey—thus your opinions will represent the opinions of thousands of people much like yourself.

Enclosed find a copy of our questionnaire. While it is a bit lengthy and will require about 20 minutes to complete, we hope that you will take the time to complete it and return the questionnaire to us in the enclosed self-addressed envelope. The information you provide will contribute to an important study and may also be used to influence ACLU policy.

A bit about confidentiality. We promise you confidentiality under the academic ethics standards of the American Political Science Association. Your name will not be revealed or associated with your response nor will anyone outside of the project staff here at the University of Wisconsin—Milwaukee be allowed to see your response. Thus, while the ACLU may be interested in the policy implications of our study, they will not be furnished with any information which in any way identifies you as an individual. Please note the number in the upper right-hand corner of the questionnaire. This number allows us to temporarily identify you. By referring to this number we will know that you responded to the questionnaire and will not send you the follow-up mailing we will have to send to nonrespondents.

We appreciate your willingness to help us in our research effort. If you would like a copy of our completed study please indicate this on the last page of the questionnaire. We will make certain that you receive a copy of our results. We believe that you will find the questionnaire both interesting and provocative and look forward to receiving your reply.

Sincerely yours,

Richard D. Bingham   James L. Gibson
Associate Professor   Assistant Professor

Note: If by some chance you recently received and responded to this particular questionnaire, please return the blank questionnaire to us indicating "duplicate" on the first page.

the respondent's name and address may be inserted. It has been shown that a more personal letter generates a slightly higher response rate than a form letter.[24]

Instructions

Another element to be considered when constructing a questionnaire is the instructions that go with each question or with a set of questions. Instructions should be included with questions that are not self-explanatory; they may range from very simple ones such as "circle the appropriate category" to more complex instructions that explain how to rank a set of priorities. When the questionnaire is administered by an interviewer, the instructions are usually written for the interviewer and thus are often short and concise, instructing the interviewer what to do when the respondent provides a certain answer, when to probe for a more detailed answer, or how to clarify a certain question. The following is an example of instructions written for the interviewer:

Who was your employer on your last job?
(PROBE FOR CORRECT CATEGORY)

       Private
       City
       County
       State
       Federal
       Self-employed
       Public, nonprofit
       Other _____ (specify)
       Doesn't know

Whereas in an interview study the interviewer is available to answer any questions that the respondent may raise, this is not the case with mail questionnaires, where any questions that remain vague or unclear are likely to be answered incorrectly, if at all. Therefore, providing clear instructions is extremely important. They can vary from general instructions introducing the questionnaire or its subsections to specific details preceding individual questions.

The following is an example of general instructions given at the beginning of a questionnaire on attitudes toward civil liberties:[25]

---

24. Michael T. Matteson, "Type of Transmittal Letter and Questionnaire Color as Two Variables Influencing Response Rates in a Mail Survey," *Journal of Applied Psychology*, 59 (1974): 532–536.

25. Bingham and Gibson, "Conditions of Commitment to Civil Liberties."

INSTRUCTIONS: For each of the following questions please mark the answer that comes closest to the way you feel about the issue. There are no "right" or "wrong" answers—please answer the questions as honestly as possible. Answer each of the questions in the order in which it appears. If you wish to make additional comments on any of the specific questions or on the issues in general, use the space at the end of the questionnaire. Your opinions are extremely important for understanding these complex civil liberty issues—we greatly appreciate your cooperation!

The next example, from the same questionnaire, introduces a subsection, presented in a matrix format:

As you know, there are many groups in America that try to get the government or the American people to see things more their way. We would like to get your opinions toward what you perceive to be the aims, objectives, or ideas advocated by these groups. In particular, we would like your opinion on how significant the change in the American system of government would be if the ideas of the group were put into practice. Please rate each of the following groups in terms of the nature of the change in our system of government that would follow the implementation of their ideas.

Check only one answer in each column

	Communists	Nazis	Ku Klux Klan
The ideas, if implemented, would create a totally different and much worse system of government	☐	☐	☐
The ideas, if implemented, would significantly change our system of government for the worse	☐	☐	☐
I oppose the ideas, but they would not change our system of government if they were implemented	☐	☐	☐
I support the ideas, but they would not change our system of government if they were implemented	☐	☐	☐
The ideas, if implemented, would significantly change our system of government for the better	☐	☐	☐
The ideas, if implemented, would create a totally different and much better system of government	☐	☐	☐
No Opinion	☐	☐	☐

Finally, here is an example is of a specific instruction for replying to a single question.

> About how many states have you lived in during your life? (Count only those states that you lived in for at least one year.)

Constructing a Questionnaire: A Case Study

There are many stages involved in the construction of a questionnaire, beginning with the research problem and going through the process of formulating the questions and considering the format and the type of questions to be used. To illustrate these, we present in Exhibit 11.4 a questionnaire based on an actual study conducted by the Institute for Social Research at the University of Michigan.[26]

The study's objective was to explore the attitudes and perceptions related to urban problems and race relations in 15 northern cities in the United States. It sought to define the social and psychological characteristics as well as the aspirations of the black and white urban populations. A black sample and a white sample were selected in each of the cities in the study. Approximately 175 black and 175 white respondents were interviewed in each city. In addition, 366 whites were interviewed in two suburban areas. Altogether, 2,809 black respondents and 2,950 white respondents were interviewed. Individuals interviewed were between the ages of 16 and 69 and lived in private households.

The study used two questionnaire forms, one for whites and one for blacks. Questions about background characteristics were almost identical in the two forms. The attitudinal questions were also identical in both interview forms, but a greater number of questions were addressed exclusively to one racial group or to the other. The questionnaires contained attitudinal questions probing the respondents' satisfaction with neighborhood services, their feelings about the effectiveness of the government in dealing with urban problems, their interracial relationships, their attitudes toward integration, and their perception of the hostility between the races. The questionnaire in Exhibit 11.4 is a shortened version of the original questionnaire addressed to blacks.

You will notice that the questionnaire starts off with identification numbers for the person being interviewed as well as his or her location. There is also room to provide information on when the interviewer began. Question 1 is an example of an attitude question on degree of satisfaction with services provided by the city. The question was put in a matrix format.

---

26. Based on Angus Campbell and Howard Schuman, *Racial Attitudes in Fifteen American Cities* (Ann Arbor, Mich.: Social Science Archive, 1973).

Exhibit 11.4
Urban Problem Study Questionnaire

TIME INTERVIEW BEGAN: _____ A.M. P.M.

City
Number ☐☐ v.3

FOR OFFICE USE
ONLY

☐☐☐☐☐ v.2

Segment
Number ☐☐☐ v.9

DULS
Line
Number ☐☐☐☐ v.10

Person
Number ☐ v.19

1. First, I'd like to ask how satisfied you are with some of the main services the city is supposed to provide for your neighborhood. What about the quality of public schools in this neighborhhod—are you generally satisfied, somewhat dissatisfied, or very dissatisfied?

(CODE A BELOW, AND ASK B THROUGH E)

	Generally satisfied	Somewhat satisfied	Very dissatisfied	Don't know
A. Quality of public schools	1	2	3	8
B. Parks and playgrounds for children in this neighborhood	1	2	3	8
C. Sports and recreation centers for teenagers in this neighborhood	1	2	3	8
D. Police protection in this neighborhood	1	2	3	8
E. Garbage collection in this neighborhood	1	2	3	8

---

2. Thinking about city services like schools, parks, and garbage collection, do you think your neighborhood gets better, about the same, or worse services than most other parts of the city?

Better ....(ASK A) 1
About same 2
Worse ....(ASK A) 3
Don't know...........8

A. IF BETTER OR WORSE: What is the reason this neighborhood gets (better/worse) services?

---

3. If you have a serious complaint about poor service by the city, do you think RECODED you can get city officials to do something about it if you call them?   VALUES

Yes......(ASK A)......1
No......(ASK A)......5
Don't know ..(ASK A) ..8

A. Have you ever called a city official with a complaint about poor service?

Yes 1
No..........5

---

4. In general, do you think (CITY) city officials pay more, less, or the same attention to a request or complaint from a black as from a white person?

More 1   1
Less 2   3
Same 3   2
Don't Know 8   8

Now let's talk about the problems of (CITY) as a whole.

5. Do you think the Mayor of (CITY) is trying as hard as he/she can to solve the main problems of the city, or that he/she is not doing all he/she could to solve these problems?

Trying as hard as he/she can 1
Not doing all he/she could (ASK A) X
Don't know 8

A. IF NOT DOING ALL HE/SHE COULD: Do you think he/she is trying fairly hard to solve these problems, or not hard at all?

Fairly hard 2
Not hard at all 3

---

6. How about the state government? Do you think they are trying as hard as they can to solve the main problems of cities like (CITY), or that they are not doing all they could to solve these problems?

Trying as hard as they can 1
Not doing all they could (ASK A) . X
Don't know 8

A. IF NOT DOING ALL THEY COULD: Do you think they are trying fairly hard to solve these problems, or not hard at all?

Fairly hard 2
Not hard at all 3

---

7. How about the federal government in Washington? Do you think they are trying as hard as they can to solve the main problems of cities like (CITY), or that they are not doing all they could to solve such problems?

Trying as hard as they can 1
Not doing all they could (ASK A) . X
Don't know 8

A. IF NOT DOING ALL THEY COULD: Do you think they are trying fairly hard to solve these problems, or not hard at all?

Fairly hard 2
Not hard at all 3

---

8. A black mayor has been elected in Cleveland and also in Gary, Indiana. What effect do you think this will have on solving city problems in Cleveland and Gary? Do you think it will make things better, worse, or won't there be much change?

Better 1
Worse 2
Not much change 3
Don't know . . . . (ASK A) 8

A. IF DON'T KNOW: What would you *guess* the effect would be—to make things better, worse, or won't there be much change?

Better 1
Worse 2
Not much change 3

Exhibit 11.4 (*continued*)

Now I want to talk about some complaints people have made about the (CITY) police.

9. First, some people say the police don't come quickly when you call them for help. Do you think this happens to people in this neighborhood?

Yes	..........(ASK A)	1
No	.......(GO TO Q. 10)	5
Don't know	.......(ASK A)	8

A. IF YES OR DON'T KNOW: Has it ever happened to you?

Yes	........(ASK B & C)	1
No	..........(ASK C)	5

B. IF YES TO A: How long ago was that (the last time)?

_____ years ago

C. IF YES OR NO TO A: Has it happened to anyone you know?

Yes	1
No	5

---

10. Some people say the police don't show respect for people or they use insulting language. Do you think this happens to people in this neighborhood?

Yes	..........(ASK A)	1
No	.......(GO TO Q. 11)	5
Don't know	.......(ASK A)	8

A. IF YES OR DON'T KNOW: Has it ever happened to you?

Yes	........(ASK B & C)	1
No	..........(ASK C)	5

B. IF YES TO A: How long ago was that (the last time)?

_____ years ago

C. IF YES OR NO TO A: Has it happened to anyone you know?

Yes	1
No	5

RECODED VALUES

11. Some people say the police frisk or search people without good reason. Do you think this happens often to people in this neighborhood?

Yes	..........(ASK A)	1
No	.......(GO TO Q. 12)	5
Don't know	.......(ASK A)	8

A. IF YES OR DON'T KNOW: Has it ever happened to you?

Yes	........(ASK B & C)	1
No	..........(ASK C)	5

B. IF YES TO A: How long ago was that (the last time)?

_____ years ago

C. IF YES OR NO TO A: Has it happened to anyone you know?

Yes	1
No	5

---

12. Some people say the police rough up people unnecessarily when they are arresting them or afterwards. Do you think this happens to people in this neighborhood?

Yes . . . .(ASK A) 1
No . . . .(GO TO Q. 13) 5
Don't know . . . .(ASK A) 8

A. IF YES OR DON'T KNOW: Has it ever happened to you?

Yes . . . .(ASK B & C) 1
No . . . .(ASK C) 5

B. IF YES TO A: How long ago was that (the last time)?

_____ years ago

C. IF YES OR NO TO A: Has it happened to anyone you know?

Yes 1
No 5

---

13. Do you think black citizens are generally given better treatment by black police officers, by white police officers, or that it doesn't make much difference?

Black police officers (ASK A) 1	1
White police officers (ASK A) 2	2
Not much difference 3	2
Don't know 8	8

A. IF BLACK OR WHITE POLICE OFFICERS: Why do you think this is?

---

14. In general, do you think judges in (CITY) are usually harder on blacks, harder on whites, or that there is not much difference?

Harder on blacks 1	1
Harder on whites 2	3
Not much difference 3	2
Don't know 8	8

---

15. Do you personally feel safer from crime now than you did two or three years ago, or is there no change, or do you feel less safe?

Safer today 1
No change 2
Less safe 3

---

16. Here are some complaints you hear sometimes about stores and merchants. Would you tell me if these things ever happen *to you* when you shop in stores in or near this neighborhood?

Exhibit 11.4 (*continued*)

	Often	Sometimes	Rarely	Never	Don't shop in neighborhood

A. Do you think you are unfairly over-charged for goods often, sometimes, rarely, or never?

    1   2   3   4   5
                        (GO TO D)

B. Do you think you are sold spoiled or inferior goods often, sometimes, rarely, or never?

    1   2   3   4

C. In such stores, are you treated disrespectfully often, sometimes, rarely, or never?

    1   2   3   4

D. IF NEVER SHOP IN NEIGHBORHOOD: Why don't you shop around here?

FILL IN ITEMS BELOW IMMEDIATELY AFTER LEAVING RESPONDENT

A. Total length of interview:

_____ Minutes

B. Cooperativeness of respondent:

    Very cooperative 1
    Somewhat cooperative . . . 2
    Not cooperative 3

C. Interest of respondent in racial issues:

    Great interest 1
    Ordinary interest 2
    Little interest 3

D. Respondent's understanding of questions:

    Good understanding 1
    Fair understanding 2
    Poor understanding 3

E. What persons over 14 years of age were present during interview? CIRCLE *ALL* THAT APPLY.

v.63
    None 0
    Spouse 1
    Parent 2
    Child over 14 3
    Other relative or friend . . 4
    Other (SPECIFY) 5

F. Neatness of home interior:

v.64
    Very neat and clean 1
    Fairly neat and clean 2
    Fairly messy 3
    Very messy 4

G. Date of Interview: _____

v.69

H. Interviewer's Signature:

I. Please give here a brief description of the respondent, and of any special conditions that affected the interview.

Note also that instructions are provided both for the interviewer ("Code A below, and ask B through E") and the respondent.

Question 2 has a closed-ended and open-ended component (A). Item A is also a contingency question. Questions 3, 5, 6, and 7 are likewise contingency questions. The first part is the filter question, and the second is the contingency question, which applies only to respondents who have checked specific categories in the first part. All questions use a numerical code, which is checked off by the interviewer.

The final section of the questionnaire demonstrates the relative advantage of an interview over other modes of filling out questionnaires (mail, telephone). The interviewer can provide detailed information on the general attitude of the respondents, which can help in interpreting their response pattern.

Summary

1. The foundation of all questionnaires is the question. The questionnaire must translate the research objectives into specific questions. Answers to these questions will provide the necessary data for hypothesis testing.

2. Most questions can be classified as either factual questions or questions about subjective experiences. Factual questions are designed to elicit objective information from the respondent. Subjective questions are concerned with inclinations, preferences, prejudices, ideas, fears, and convictions. In general, subjective questions are much more complex to construct than questions about personal facts. Answers to these questions are more sensitive to changes in wording, emphasis, and sequence than are those to factual questions.

3. Four types of question structure can be distinguished: open-ended questions, closed-ended questions, contingency questions, and matrix questions. In closed-ended questions, respondents are offered a set of response categories from which they must choose the one that most closely represents their view. Open-ended questions are not followed by any kind of choice, and the respondnents' answers are recorded in full. A contingency question applies only to a subgroup of respondents. The relevance of the question to this subgroup is determined by the answer of all respondents to a preceding filter question. The matrix question is a method for organizing a large set of items that have the same response categories.

4. One of the most common formats for questions asked in surveys is the rating scale, whereby the respondent makes judgments in terms of sets of ordered categories. There are several types of rating scales, including the card sort and the semantic differential. Ranking is used in questionnaires when the objective is to obtain information regarding the degree of importance or the priorities that people apply to a set of attitudes or objects.

5. Questions must be worded so that they are comprehended by all respondents. A leading question is phrased in such a manner that it appears to the respondent that the researcher expects a certain answer. Threatening questions raise the anxiety level of the respondents. Both types of questions may lead to response bias. Leading questions should be avoided, and threatening questions must be constructed with great sensitivity, using special techniques, such as a long introduction to the question and an open-ended rather than a closed-ended format.

Key Terms for Review

question	quantifiers
factual question	matrix question
attitude	card sort
opinion	semantic differential
closed-ended question	ranking
open-ended question	leading question
contingency question	threatening question
filter question	double-barreled question
rating	

Study Questions

1. Discuss the various ways in which questions can be used to get factual information, opinions, and attitudes from respondents.
2. Explain the uses of open-ended, closed-ended, and contingency questions.
3. List and describe the formats used to ask questions for various purposes.
4. Discuss the importance of question sequencing in a questionnaire.
5. List the various problems that may arise while constructing questionnaires.

Additional Readings

Bailey, Kenneth D. *Methods of Social Research*. New York: Free Press. 1987.

Bishop, G. F., R. W. Oldendick, and Alfred J. Tuchfarber. "Effects of Filter Questions in Public Opinion Surveys." *Public Opinion Quarterly*, 47, (1983): 528–546.

———. "What Must My Interest in Politics Be If I Just Told You 'I Don't Know?'" *Public Opinion Quarterly*, 46 (1982): 510–519.

Gorden, Raymond L. *Interviewing: Strategy, Techniques, and Tactics*. 3d ed. Homewood, Ill.: Dorsey, 1980.

Kahn, Robert I., and Charles F. Cannell. *The Dynamics of Interviewing*. New York:
Wiley, 1957.

Schuman, Howard, and Stanley Presser. *Questions and Answers in Attitude Surveys*. Orlando, Fla.: Academic Press, 1981.

Singleton, Royce, Jr., Bruce C. Straits, Margaret M. Straits, and Ronald J. McAllister. *Approaches to Social Research*. Oxford: Oxford University Press, 1988.

Sudman, Seymour, and Norman M. Bradburn. *Asking Questions*. San Francisco:
Jossey-Bass, 1982.

Tourangeau, Roger, and Kenneth A. Rasinski. "Cognitive Processes Underlying
Context Effects in Attitude Measurement." *Psychological Bulletin*, 103 (1988):
299–314.

CHAPTER 12

Qualitative Research

In this chapter, we focus on field research for qualitative study, concentrating on participant observation and participant-as-observer roles. We explore both grounded theory and analytic induction and review the stages of field research. Finally, we consider the ethical and political dilemmas of field research.

S O FAR WE HAVE DISCUSSED METHODS of data collection designed primarily for quantitative analyses. In this chapter, we describe the prototype of qualitative research—field research. Qualitative research, as a method of data collection and analysis, derives from the *Verstehen* tradition described in Chapter 1. Scientists must gain an empathic understanding of societal phenomena, and they must recognize both the historical dimension of human behavior and the subjective aspects of the human experience. In his study of asylums, Goffman describes the process of actively participating in the daily life of the observed and the gaining of insights by introspection in the following way:

> My immediate object in doing field work at St. Elizabeth's was to try to learn about the social world of the hospital inmate, as this world is subjectively experienced by him. . . . It was then and still is my belief that any group of persons—prisoners, primitives, pilots, or patients—develop a life of their own that becomes meaningful, reasonable, and normal once you get close to it, and that a good way to learn about any

of these worlds is to submit oneself in the company of the members to the daily round of petty contingencies to which they are subject.[1]

Qualitative researchers attempt to understand behavior and institutions by getting to know the persons involved and their values, rituals, symbols, beliefs, and emotions. Applying such a perspective, one would, for example, study poverty by immersing oneself in the life of the poor rather than collecting data with a structured interview schedule.

Field Research

Field research is the most central strategy of data collection associated with qualitative methodology. In general terms, **field research** is defined as "the study of people acting in the natural courses of their daily lives. The fieldworker ventures into the worlds of others in order to learn firsthand about how they live, how they talk and behave, and what captivates and distresses them."[2] More explicitly, fieldwork is characterized by its location and by the manner in which it is conducted.[3] With respect to location, fieldwork is carried out in *natural* settings, for example, anthropologists living with remote tribes or sociologists sharing in and observing the daily life of a local community. Field research is also a way of empathizing and understanding the subjective meanings of the people being studied. Typically, fieldworkers attempt to incorporate these two characteristics in their studies.

Contemporary sociological fieldwork has its origins in the social reform movement of the turn of the twentieth century, in which description of the life and conditions of the urban poor was viewed as paving the way for change and improvement. The reform movement found its strongest academic expression in the Chicago School in the early 1920s. The Chicago School sociologists were intensely involved in the social reform movement centered outside the university. Robert Park, a leading figure in the Chicago School, law in the city a critical area for sociological research and urged his students to make firsthand observations of life in its various enclaves:

> Go and sit in the lounges of the luxury hotels and on the doorsteps of the flophouses; sit on the Gold Coast settees and on the slum shake-downs; sit in Orchestra Hall and in the Star and Garter Burlesk. In short, gentlemen, go get the seat of your pants dirty in real research.[4]

At that time, the methodology of qualitative research was limited to assembling a variety of personal documents, autobiographies, life histories, letters, and diaries, and it had only a limited conception of participation in the

1. Erving Goffman, *Asylums* (Garden City, N.Y.: Doubleday, 1961), pp. ix–x.
2. Robert M. Emerson, ed., *Contemporary Field Research* (Boston: Little, Brown, 1983), p. 1.
3. Ibid.
4. John C. McKinney, *Constructive Typology and Social Theory* (Norwalk, Conn.: Appleton & Lang, 1966) p. 71.

lives of the people being studied. During the following two decades, as field-work became a more established methodology in sociology, it came to emphasize more participation in the lives of those studied in order to share and consequently better understand their subjective perspectives.

Participant Observation

The method of data collection most closely associated with contemporary field research is **participant observation,** whereby the investigator attempts to attain some kind of membership or close attachment to the group that he or she wishes to study.[5] In doing so, the participant observer attempts to adopt the perspectives of the people in the situation being observed. The participant observer's role is that of "conscious and systematic sharing, insofar as circumstances permit, in the life activities, and on occasion, in the interests and effects of a group of persons."[6] The observer's direct participation in the activities of the observed often entails learning their language, their habits, their work patterns, their leisure activities, and the like. The researcher assumes either a complete participant role or a participant-as-observer role.

Complete Participant

In a **complete participant** role, the observer is wholly concealed; the research objectives are unknown to the observed, and the researcher attempts to become a member of the group under observation. The complete participant interacts with the observed "as naturally as possible in whatever areas of their living interest him and are accessible to him."[7]

For example, Festinger, Riecken, and Schachter studied a group of persons who predicted the destruction of the world. The nature of the group led the investigators to believe that if they presented themselves as researchers, they would be denied access to the group. Consequently, they posed as individuals interested in the activities of the group and became full-fledged members trying to be "nondirective, sympathetic listeners, passive participants who were inquisitive and eager to learn whatever others might want to tell us."[8] In another case study, Sullivan, Queen, and Patrick studied the motivations and attitudes of the personnel in a military training program. One of the researchers enlisted as a basic trainee and became a full member

5. Rosalie H. Wax, "Participant Observation," *International Encyclopedia of Social Sciences* (New York: Macmillan, 1968), p. 238.

6. Florence Kluckhohn, "The Participant-Observer Technique in Small Communities," *American Journal of Sociology*, 46 (1940): 331.

7. Raymond L. Gold, "Roles in Sociological Field Observation," *Social Forces*, 36 (1958): 219.

8. Leon Festinger, Henry Riecken, and Stanley Schachter, *When Prophecy Fails* (New York: Harper & Row, 1956), p. 234.

of the group. His identity, research objective, and role as a researcher remained unknown to members of the group, including his own commanding officer.[9]

Complete participation has been justified on the grounds that it makes possible the study of inaccessible groups or groups that do not reveal to outsiders certain aspects of their life. Presumably, the fieldworker is treated as just another member of the group. Despite this research advantage, the complete participant role has been severely criticized on methodological and ethical grounds. Kai Erikson, for example, rejects all field observations that do not make the role of the researcher and the intent of the study known beforehand because they constitute an invasion of privacy and may harm the observed:

> The sheer act of entering a human transaction on the basis of deliberate fraud may be painful to the people who are thereby misled; and even if that were not the case, there are countless ways in which a stranger who pretends to be something else can disturb others by failing to understand the conditions of intimacy that prevail in the group he has tried to invade.[10]

Erikson points to the difficulties that may arise when one takes on a complete participant role and considers an incident reported in the Festinger, Riecken, and Schachter study, *When Prophecy Fails:*

> At one point in the study, two observers arrived at one of the group's meeting places under instructions to tell quite ordinary stories about their experience in Spiritualism in order to create as little commotion as possible. A few days afterwards, however, the leader of the group was overheard explaining that the two observers had appeared upset, excited, confused, and unsure of their errand at the time of their original visit, all of which helped confirm her suspicion that they had somehow been "sent" from another planet. In one sense, of course, this incident offered the observers an intriguing view of the belief structure of the cult, but in another sense, the leader's assessment of the situation was very shrewd: after all, the observers *had* been sent from another world, if not another planet, and she may have been quite right to sense that they were a bit confused and unsure of their errand during their early moments in the new job. "In both cases," the report informs us, the visits of the observers "were given as illustrations that 'strange things are happening.'" Indeed, strange things *were* happening; yet we have no idea how strange they really were. It is almost impossible to evaluate the reaction of the group to the appearance of the pair of observers because we do not know whether they were seen as ordinary converts or as extraordinary beings. And it makes a difference, for in the first instance the investigators would be observing a response which fell

---

9. Mortimer A. Sullivan, Stuart Queen, and Ralph Patrick, "Participant Observation as Employed in the Study of a Military Training Program," *American Sociological Review*, 23 (1958): 660–667.

10. Kai T. Erikson, "A Comment on Disguised Observation in Sociology," *Social Problems*, 14 (1967): 368.

within the normal range of the group's experience, while in the second instance they would be observing a response which would never have taken place had the life of the group been allowed to run its own course.[11]

The complete participant role poses several methodological problems. First, observers may become so self-conscious about revealing their true selves that they would be handicapped when attempting to perform convincingly in the pretended role. Or they may "go native," that is, incorporate the pretended role into their self-conception and lose the research perspective.[12] Second, the decision what specifically to observe is most problematic because the researcher cannot evoke responses and behavior and must be careful not to ask questions that might raise the suspicions of the persons observed. Third, recording observations or taking notes is impossible on the spot; these have to be postponed until the observer is alone. However, time lags in recording observations introduce selective bias and distortions through memory.

Participant-as-Observer

In view of these limitations, contemporary fieldworkers most often assume the **participant-as-observer** role. This type of role makes the researcher's presence known to the group being studied. Researchers make long-term commitments to becoming active members and attempt to establish close relationships with members of the group who subsequently serve as both informants and respondents. Van Maanen's research on police training illustrates the process of taking this role.

> While a graduate student at the University of California . . ., I began contacting police officials across the country seeking permission to conduct a one-man field study inside a large, metropolitan law-enforcement agency. . . . Although I encountered some initial difficulties in locating a department willing to tolerate my planned foray into its organizational spheres, eventually I managed to gain access to one police organization. . . . Throughout the study I worked in the fashion of a traditional ethnographer or participant observer, made no attempt to disguise my scholarly aim or identity, and met with little overt hostility from the men whose everyday affairs were the explicit subject of my investigation. In most respects I felt my mode of inquiry approximated both the substance and spirit of Evans-Pritchard's classic formulation of the ethnographic technique: "to get to know well the persons involved and to see and hear what they do and say."[13]

11. Ibid., pp. 371–372.

12. Gold, "Roles in Sociological Field Observations," p. 220.

13. John Van Maanen, "The Moral Fix: On the Ethics of Fieldwork," in *Contemporary Field Research*, ed. Emerson, pp. 269–270.

As this example demonstrates, the participant-as-observer role differs from complete participation in that the research goal is explicitly identified. Yet membership and participation in the observed group is still an important dimension in this form of research. With this method, the fieldworker gains a deeper appreciation of the group and its way of life and may also gain different levels of insight by actually participating rather than only observing.[14]

The Practice of Field Research

Selecting a Research Topic

The first step in doing field research is to select a topic for investigation. Very often, the selection of a topic is influenced by personal interests or concerns. Such concerns may be related to one's job, personal relationships, family history, social class, or ethnic background. Lofland and Lofland, in their useful guide to doing qualitative research, describe this process as "starting where you are."[15] This practice originated in the 1920s with the Chicago School, where many well-known qualitative studies were conducted by students with little background in doing social research but with unique experiences that served as a start. Everett Hughes has described the beginning of this tradition in the following way:

> Most of these people didn't have any sociological background. . . . They didn't come in to become sociologists. They came in to learn something and Park picked up whatever it was in their experience which he could build on. . . . He took these people and he brought out of them whatever he could find there. . . . They might be Mennonites who were just a little unhappy . . . about wearing plain clothes . . ., girls who didn't like to wear long dresses and funny little caps; . . . or children of Orthodox Jews who really didn't like to wear beards anymore. . . . And he got hold of people and emancipated them from something that was inherently interesting but which they regarded as a cramp. And he turned this "cramping orthodoxy" into something that was of basic and broad human interest. And that was the case for a lot of these people. He made their pasts interesting to them, much more interesting than they ever thought they could be.[16]

The approach to social research exemplified here requires that the investigators first determine what they care about independent of scientific considerations. This emotional involvement in one's work provides a meaningful link between the personal and emotional life of the researchers and

---

14. Ibid., p. 270.

15. John Lofland and Lyn H. Lofland, *Analyzing Social Settings* (Belmont, Calif.: Wadsworth, 1984), p. 7.

16. Ibid., pp. 9–10.

the rigorous requirement of the social scientific endeavor; not only does this make the involvement in social research more personally rewarding but it helps in coping with problems that are inevitable in every research project.[17]

Choosing a Site and Gaining Access

Once a researcher has chosen a research topic, the next stage of field research is to select an appropriate research site and to gain access to it. To a large extent, the choice of a topic determines the range of appropriate sites. For example, Festinger and his colleagues were interested in how religious sects deal with prophetic failure.[18] This interest necessarily limited their choice to a contemporary research site where prophecies likely to fail had been made about events in the near future. They chose a religious sect that predicted a natural disaster on a given date. This allowed them to make observations *before* the predicted disaster and *after* the date of the failed prophecy. In this case, substantive and theoretical interest dictated the choice of setting.

Very often, geographic or other practical considerations will dictate the choice. Moreover, it is tempting to choose a site that is easily accessible, where a researcher has an influential contact or is a member. However, in situations where would-be observers are close to the group and thus have easy access, they must find ways for some distancing. Conversely, investigators who are outsiders to the research setting and may have more difficult access need to reduce the distance after entering the research site. Another important consideration in gaining access are the ascriptive attributes of the investigator. For example, the gender, age, race, or ethnicity of the observers, if different from the observed, may create serious barriers in gaining access or in communication.[19]

In the words of Rosalie Wax:

> Many tribal or folk societies not only maintain a strict division of labor between the sexes and ages, but the people who fall into these different categories do not converse freely or spontaneously with each other. . . . I, as a middle aged woman, was never able to converse openly or informally with either the old or the young Indian men at Thrashing Buffalo. The older men, even when I knew them fairly well, would tend to deliver lectures to me; the younger men, as was proper, were always too bashful or formally respectful to say much. With the Indian matrons, on the other hand, I could talk for hours.[20]

17. Ibid.
18. Festinger et al., *When Prophecy Fails.*
19. Lofland and Lofland, *Analyzing Social Settings.*
20. Rosalie H. Wax, "The Ambiguities of Fieldwork," in *Contemporary Field Research*, ed. Emerson, pp. 194–195.

On the basis of her experience in the field, Wax concluded that to avoid a biased view, research teams mixed in terms of personal attributes should undertake studies directed at "whole" cultures.

The problems that confront young female fieldworkers in gaining access to male-dominated settings were discussed by Easterday and her associates:

> One of us established rapport with the photographers of a special military photography programme by being a photographer and knowing their language. The relationship was sustained by insisting that the researcher not be photographed as a model, but rather that she be "one of the boys" on the other side of the lens. In an attempt to gain approval for the study from the programme's director, the researcher was denied full access with the statement, "It won't work. The men in the programme are a close bunch, and the talk is rough. They wouldn't be themselves if you are there."[21]

Whereas these examples demonstrate that status and gender categories may be a handicap in field research, there are situations where differences have definite advantages. Blanche Geer wrote about women:

> The most handicapped observer is the one doing people and situations he/ she is closest to. Hence, women are in luck in a male-run world. They can see how few clothes the emperor has on, question the accepted, what is taken for granted.[22]

In other words, being an outsider can sometimes seem less threatening, provide access to the field, and contribute to the perceptiveness that the researcher brings to the field.

Establishing Relations with Members

The ease with which relationships with members of a group are established depends to a large extent on the nature of the group and the skills of the researcher. Evans-Pritchard gives an example:

> Azande would not allow me to live as one of themselves; Nuer would not allow me to live otherwise. Among Azande I was compelled to live outside of the community; among Nuer I was compelled to be a member of it. Azande treated me as a superior; Nuer as an equal.[23]

The phase of establishing social relations has been emphasized by contemporary field researchers as perhaps the most central aspect of fieldwork: "Good fieldwork . . . depends crucially upon discovering the meaning of social relations, and not just those characterizing the natives' relations with

21. Lois Easterday, Diana Papedemas, Laura Schorr, and Catherine Valentine, "The Making of a Female Researcher: Role Problems in Fieldwork," in *Field Research: A Sourcebook and Field Manual*, ed. Robert G. Burgess (London: Allen & Unwin, 1982), pp. 63–64.

22. Ibid., p. 66.

23. Edward E. Evans-Pritchard, *The Nuer* (Oxford: Clarendon, 1940), p. 15.

each other. It depends equally upon discovering the meanings of anthropologists' relations with people they study.''[24]

One basic requirement, significant especially when studying subcultures, is understanding the jargon used by the particular group. Eleanor Miller, who studied ''street women,'' describes her frustration in her initial encounter with the women she interviewed:

> I remember very well my first visit to Horizon House. I had been invited to dinner after which I was to describe my study and recruit informants. Dinner was being served, so I sat down. There were, perhaps, eight others seated as well, mostly black women. . . . People talked and joked and occasionally sang along with the radio. I couldn't understand half of what was being said. With a sinking feeling I started to question whether or not I could ever be comfortable enough personally to do this study.[25]

There are several aspects to the kinds of social relations that develop between the observer and the observed. Rosalie Wax has noted that the identity that is chosen by the fieldworker and the role playing that takes place in the field are central to this social process. She suggests that in a well-balanced relationship, the fieldworker ''strives to maintain a consciousness and respect for what he is and a consciousness and respect for what his hosts are.''[26] The tendency to assume a ''native'' identity is one of the most serious errors that a fieldworker can commit. Polsky, in his study of criminals, stresses the danger of ''going native'':

> In doing field research on criminals you damned well better not pretend to be ''one of them,'' because they will test this claim out and one of two things will happen: either you will . . . get sucked into participant observation of the sort you would rather not undertake, or you will be exposed, with still greater negative consequences. You must let the criminals know who you are; and if it is done properly . . . it does not sabotage the research.[27]

There are no magic formulas for learning the ropes, and it is generally recommended that the research begin by participating in the daily life of the observed, a process described as ''hanging around.''[28] Learning the ropes and establishing relationships involve adopting a variety of roles. These roles are sometimes spontaneously invented and blend with the demands of the particular research setting. Rosalie Wax describes her experiences while

24. Ivan Karp and Martha B. Kendall, ''Reflexivity in Field Work,'' in *Explaining Human Behavior: Consciousness, Human Action, and Social Structure*, ed. Paul F. Secord (Newbury Park, Calif.: Sage, 1982), p. 250.

25. Eleanor Miller, *Street Woman* (Philadelphia: Temple University Press, 1986), pp. 221–222.

26. Wax, ''Ambiguities of Fieldwork,'' p. 197.

27. Ned Polsky, *Hustlers, Beats, and Others* (Hawthorne, N.Y.: Aldine, 1967) p. 124.

28. William B. Shaffir, Robert A. Stebbins, Allan Turowetz, eds., *Fieldwork Experience: Qualitative Approaches to Social Research* (New York: St. Martin's Press, 1980), p. 113.

conducting a fieldwork study of the Japanese relocation centers during the Second World War:

> I would not have been able to do field work in Gila and Tule Lake if my respondents and I had not been able, jointly, to invent and maintain many of these relationships. Some Japanese Americans felt more comfortable if they could treat me like a sympathetic newspaper reporter. I knew very little about how a reporter behaved (indeed, I had never seen or spoken with one), but I responded and we were able to converse more easily. In Tule Lake the superpatriots and agitators found it easier to talk to me once they convinced themselves that I was German *Nisei*, "full of the courageous German spirit." I found this fantasy personally embarrassing, but I did not make a point of denying my German ancestry. Finally, I was not a geisha, even though a shrewd Issei once suggested that it was because I functioned as one that I was able to find out so much of what happened at Tule Lake. His explanation was that Japanese men—and especially Japanese politicians—do not discuss their plans or achievements with other men or with their wives, but they are culturally conditioned to speak of such matters with intelligent and witty women.[29]

As this example shows, learning the ropes and adopting the range of research roles is a flexible process that requires ingenuity and the sensitivity of the fieldworker to the personalities and perceptions of the research participants.

Finding Resourceful and Reliable Informants

Once relationships with members of the group are established, participant observers are regarded as provisional members of the group. They learn how to behave in the group and "teach" the observed how to act toward them. Next observers are accepted as *categorical members* of the group. By this time, rapport will have been established, areas of observation will be agreed on, and **informants** will be providing information. William Whyte's experiences illustrate several phases in this process:

> I began with a vague idea that I wanted to study a slum district. . . . I made my choice on very unscientific grounds: Cornerville best fitted my picture of what a slum district should look like. . . . I learned early in my Cornerville period the crucial importance of having the support of the key individuals in any groups or organizations I was studying. Instead of trying to explain myself to everyone, I found I was providing far more information about myself and my study to leaders such as Doc than I volunteered to the average corner boy. I always tried to give the impression that I was willing and eager to tell just as much about my study as anyone wished to know, but it was only with group leaders that I made a particular effort to provide really full information. . . . Since these leaders had the sort of position in

---

29. Wax, "Ambiguities of Fieldwork," p. 200.

the community that enabled them to observe much better than the followers what was going on and since they were in general more skillful observers than the followers, I found that I had much to learn from a more active collaboration with them.[30]

Intimate relationships with informants may, however, bias their reports, as Whyte himself has observed:

> Doc found this experience of working with me interesting and enjoyable, and yet the relationship had its drawbacks. He once commented: "You've slowed me up plenty since you've been down here. Now, when I do something, I have to think what Bill Whyte would want to know about it and how I can explain it. Before, I used to do things by instinct.[31]

Leaving the Field

The social complexity of field research is not limited to gaining access and establishing relationships. Leaving the field is no less problematic. This stage depends on the agreement reached between the observer and the observed at the entrance phase and on the kind of social relationships that developed during the research process. The research requirement of "getting involved" during the fieldwork itself presents a problem when it is time to leave, as Wax notes:

> Being by that time experienced fieldworkers, Murray and I had planned to stay six months in the field and spend six months writing our report. But rough as life was, I had become so attached to some of my Indian friends that I talked Murray into staying an extra month—even at temperatures of 30 below zero. I did not want to leave but I had to.[32]

Another problem in leaving the field is how it affects the subjects themselves. "As they see it, they stand to gain little, if anything, from our research findings and may even lose. A related reason for their reluctance is their impression that our work will add little to their own lives."[33]

Field exit processes range from the quick and sharply defined to the gradual and drawn out. Leaving can be a recurring phenomenon when research needs require the researcher to leave and come back numerous times. In the end, the selected procedure is a function of the commitment the researcher made while conducting the research.[34]

30. William F. Whyte, *Street Corner Society*, 2d ed. (Chicago: University of Chicago Press, 1955), pp. 279–358.

31. Ibid., p. 301.

32. David R. Maines, William B. Shaffir, and Allan Turowetz, "Leaving the Field in Ethnographic Research: Reflections on the Entrance Exit Hypothesis," in *Fieldwork Experience*, ed. Shaffir, et al., p. 277.

33. Shaffir et al., *Fieldwork Experience*, p. 258.

34. Maines et al., "Leaving the Field," p. 273.

Recording Observations

In field research, the primary sources of data are what people say and do. These may be recorded by writing notes, tape recording, and on occasion photographing or videotaping. In most cases, unless the researcher is observing secretly, recording can be done on the spot, during the event. The documentation may take the form of a diary, or it may be a daily record of each event. When constant recording interferes with the quality of observation, devices for remembering things can be designed. For example, associating the first outstanding incident that occurs during the observation with a word beginning with *a*, the next incident with a word beginning with *b*, and so forth. These key words can guide the researcher later when writing up a fuller account of the occurrences.[35]

In notes not written on the spot but immediately after the observation, opportunities for distortion and misrepresentation increase. It is helpful to employ certain notational conventions to minimize distortions. For example, one could use quotation marks around recorded material to indicate exact recall; data with no quotation marks would be based on impressions or inferences. Such a recording practice is vulnerable because of observer inference. Lofland and Lofland suggest asking the following questions before the data is written up:[36]

1. Is the report firsthand?
2. What was the spatial location of the observer?
3. Did the research participant have any reason to give false or biased information?
4. Is the report internally consistent?
5. Can the report be validated by using other independent reports?

Although information gained from these questions does not guarantee that a report is true, it helps in the assessment of the reliability of the data.

Analyzing Data

Data analysis in qualitative field research is an ongoing process. Observers formulate hypotheses and note important themes throughout their studies. As the research progresses, some hypotheses are discarded, others are refined, and still others are formulated. Bogdan and Taylor give an example of such a process:

> In the job training program study, the observer had an early hunch that men trainees clearly differentiated "women's factory work" from "men's factory work." The hunch came after one of the staff personnel had re-

35. E. J. Lindgren, "Field Work in Social Psychology," *British Journal of Psychology*, 26 (1935): 174–182.

36. Lofland and Lofland, *Analyzing Social Settings*, p. 51.

ported the following to the observer: "When the men saw women doing the work (soldering) on the assembly line, they didn't want any part of it." Since this sex differentiation would have important implications for the potential success of the program and for the meanings of work, the researcher presented his hunch on later visits to the setting. He found that, although men and women differed in the types of work they valued, men did not reject certain work as "women's work." For example, they expressed little pride in doing physical labor and openly avoided jobs that were dangerous or "too hard." The observer dropped his earlier hypothesis and turned to the pursuit of others.[37]

An important, though technical, aspect of data analysis during the period of data collection is establishing files. Files can be established either by using the common file folder system or by using a word processor. In either case, the filing system is the physical record of the more abstract process of building codes, where the labels on the files are categories that guide the filing process.[38]

Becker and Geer, in their study of a medical school, have found it useful to prepare data for analysis by making a running summary of their field notes. They coded the data into separate incidents, summarizing for each incident their observation of a student's action. They tentatively identified the major areas or categories during the fieldwork process, and when going through a summarized incident, they marked it with a number standing for each area into which it could be classified. The following examples from their field notes and their subsequent analysis illustrates this process:

"Mann says that now that he and the other students have found out what Dr. Prince, the staff physician, is like, they learn the things they know he's going to try to catch them on and keep him stumped that way." This incident contains some reference to student-faculty relations and would accordingly be coded under that category. It also refers indirectly to the phenomenon of student cooperation on school activities and would be coded under that category as well. The next stage in the analysis would be to inspect the various items coded under one area, and formulate a more detailed statement of the content of this area or perspective citing examples of actions and statements that characterize it.[39]

Next the frequency of that perspective is assessed by comparing the number of items from the data that substantiate the perspective with the number of negative instances. In addition, the range of the perspective is checked, that is, how widely the items of data were distributed through a number of different situations. An important final step in the analysis of

---

37. Robert Bogdan and Steven J. Taylor, *Introduction to Qualitative Research Methods* (New York: Wiley, 1975), pp. 80–81.

38. Lofland and Lofland, *Analyzing Social Settings*, pp. 131–134.

39. Howard S. Becker and Blanche Geer, "Participant Observation: The Analysis of Qualitative Field Data" in *Field Research*, ed. Burgess, p. 245.

qualitative data is to consider all cases that run counter to the tentative hypothesis. A careful study of all negative cases may help in reformulating the original hypothesis or rejecting it altogether.

When analyzing qualitative data, it is useful to look for certain regularities or patterns that emerge from the numerous observations made during the fieldwork stage. In performing this task, a number of questions can be posed:[40]

1. What type of behavior is it?
2. What is its structure?
3. How frequent is it?
4. What are its causes?
5. What are its processes?
6. What are its consequences?
7. What are people's strategies?

The culmination of the study is writing the report. The final report describes the background for the study, the theoretical framework guiding it, the design and methodology of the study, and a detailed analysis of the data, its interpretation, and its implications for further analysis or public policy.

The Theory of Field Research

The goal of field research is to develop a theory that is "grounded," that is, closely and directly relevant to the particular setting under study. Using the **grounded-theory approach**, the researcher first develops conceptual categories from the data and then makes new observations to clarify and elaborate these categories:

> While in the field, the researcher continually asks questions as to fit, relevance and workability about the emerging categories and relationships between them. By raising questions at this point in time the researcher checks those issues while he still has access to the data. As a result, he continually fits his analysis to the data by checking as he proceeds.[41]

An alternative theoretical approach to field research is the method of **analytic induction**. Whereas with the grounded-theory approach, concepts and tentative hypotheses are developed from the data, with analytic induction, a researcher begins with a tentative hypothesis explaining the phenomenon observed and then attempts to verify the hypothesis by observing a small number of cases. If the hypothesis does not fit these cases, it is either

---

40. Lofland and Lofland, *Analyzing Social Settings*, p. 94.

41. Barney G. Glaser, *Theoretical Sensitivity* (Mill Valley, Calif.: Sociology Press, 1978), p. 39.

rejected or reformulated so that the cases account for it. Blanche Geer exemplifies this method in the following excerpt:

> My use of hypotheses falls roughly into three sequential types. The first operation consisted of testing a crude yes-or-no proposition. By asking informants or thinking back over volunteered information in the data . . . I stated a working hypothesis in the comments and began the second operation in the sequence: Looking for negative cases or setting out deliberately to accumulate positive ones. . . . Working with negatively expressed hypotheses gave me a specific goal. One instance that contradicts what I say is enough to force modification of the hypothesis. . . . The third state of operating with hypotheses in the field involves two-step formulations and eventually rough models. Hypotheses take the form of predictions about future events which may take place under specific conditions or changes in informants over time in conjunction with events.[42]

In its final stage of development, the hypothesis is not of the "*X* causes *Y*" type; rather, an inclusive set of propositions (a model) is developed to explain the totality of the phenomenon.

A classic instance of field research using analytic induction is Cressey's study of embezzlement.[43] Cressey defined embezzlement as the phenomenon of accepting a position of trust in good faith and then violating this trust by committing a crime. He initially formulated a hypothesis that these violations of trust occurred when thefts were conceived of as "technical violations" but rejected this hypothesis after finding embezzlers who said they knew their behavior had been wrong and illegal. Cressey next hypothesized that violators defined the illegal use of funds as an emergency that could not be met by legal means. But this hypothesis was revised again when he observed violators who did not report an emergency or who noted an even greater emergency in the past. Next Cressey noted that violators were individuals who felt they needed to use "secret means." But again, this hypothesis had to be reformulated upon discovering deviant cases. The final hypothesis, according to Cressey, is the one that accounts for all cases observed:

> Trusted persons became trust violators when they conceive of themselves as having a financial problem which is non-shareable, are aware that this problem can be secretly resolved by violation of the position of financial trust, and are able to apply to their own conduct in that situation verbalizations which enable them to adjust their conceptions of themselves as trusted persons with their conceptions of themselves as users of the entrusted funds or property.[44]

---

42. Blanche Geer, "The First Days in the Field," in *Sociologists at Work*, ed. Phillip Hammond (Garden City, N.Y.: Doubleday, 1967), pp. 389–390.

43. Donald R. Cressey, *Other People's Money: A Study in the Social Psychology of Embezzlement* (New York: Free Press, 1953).

44. Ibid. p. 273.

Blue-Collar Community:
An Example of Field Research

Before concluding our discussion of field research, it is useful to illustrate the various stages with one inclusive study, *Blue-Collar Community*, conducted by William Kornblum in South Chicago.[45] Kornblum used a variety of methods to gather data, including discussions with community residents, archival records, census data, interviewing, and attending community meetings. However, the study leans primarily on Kornblum's firsthand involvement and participation in the life of the community. As such, it is a good example of a field study employing participant observation as the main method of analysis.

Choosing the Research Topic and the Research Site.   The general topic was suggested to Kornblum by his professors in graduate school who were interested in sponsoring a study of Chicago's south Slavic ethnic groups. Kornblum conducted some research on local community organizations in Yugoslavian communities and was interested in the general question of how Yugoslav immigrants adapted in the United States. He decided to focus on the south Slavic settlement in South Chicago and on the Pulaski-Milwaukee section on the Northwest side and started interviewing Croatian and Serbian immigrants. He also visited the immigrant coffee shops, soccer clubs, and taverns and was gradually drawn toward the steel mill neighborhoods of South Chicago. Kornblum describes his choice of the community in the following way:

> South Chicago fascinated me. I had never seen such heavy industry at close range, and I was awed by the immensity of the steel mills and the complexity of the water and rail arteries which crisscrossed the area's neighborhoods. In the people's faces and in their neighborhoods I saw more of the spectrum of cultural groups which had settled and built the community. Thus, I was beginning to see that my study would have to concern itself as much with the larger community as it would with the cultural and social adaptations of Serbian and Croatian settlers.[46]

Kornblum found a Serbian immigrant restaurant where he was introduced to some of the regular patrons. The majority of them were Serbian immigrant men in their mid-thirties to early forties, most of whom were steelworkers. Although it was a congenial spot, the restaurant was socially peripheral because its patrons were mostly recent immigrants. At this point Kornblum wanted to make contacts with American-born Serbian and Croatian residents, so he began looking for a place to settle in the community.

---

45. William Kornblum, *Blue-Collar Community* (Chicago: University of Chicago Press, 1974).
46. Ibid., p. 232.

Gaining Access.   Soon after moving into the community, Kornblum started attending public meetings to identify local leaders and to arrange an introductory meeting with them. He identified himself as a researcher only to a few; to most residents he said he was teaching at the nearby University of Indiana while his wife was a student at the University of Illinois in the central city and that the neighborhood was a halfway point for both of them.

Gradually, Kornblum became friendly with a larger number of political activists and leaders, in particular with a group of steelworkers who ran the local union at one of the mills. He began to feel that it was necessary to make more of a commitment to South Chicago's lifestyle:

> I felt like a knowledgeable outsider who was missing some of the most important experiences of life in the community. . . . A friend whose opinion I highly valued, the Serbian president of a local steel union, confronted me with a serious challenge "How can you really understand what goes on here . . . if you've never spent any time inside a steel mill?"[47]

Subsequently, Kornblum was hired as a subforeman in the steel mill that became the focus of his study.

Establishing Relations with Members.   Kornblum's job as a subforeman proved to be an ideal position from a research perspective. As subforeman he had to understand how the work at his end of the mill fit with the overall division of labor in the entire plant. As a manager he could walk freely throughout the mill and converse informally with workers. This made him sensitive to the interactions that took place in the mill, especially to the meaning of unionism. He began to understand how steel production creates an occupational community inside the mill.

Kornblum was particularly interested in understanding the community's political leaders, especially unionist politicians. At that time, the community was involved in choosing the leaders to its central institutions. Therefore, many of his friends and informants were actively involved in politics and were sometimes members of opposing factions. This created a problem that is quite typical of field research. Kornblum notes:

> I began to feel that I could not remain aloof from political commitment when all the people I cared for had so much more at stake than I did. Aside from the personal aspect of this decision, there are very real limitations to what one can learn about political processes through informants. If one wishes actually to watch decisions being made in a competitive political system, it is often necessary to become part of the decision-making body itself. I did this by taking highly partisan although "behind the scenes" roles in most of the political campaign reported in this study. The liabilities of this strategy are numerous and deserve some attention. First, it is obvious

47. Ibid., pp. 235–236.

that the more committed one is to a particular faction, the less one can learn, at first hand, about others. . . . In consequence of this, whenever I committed myself to a given faction I attempted to function as much as possible in capacities which would require little public exposure. In order to keep up with events in opposing factions I attempted to explain my affiliations as frankly as possible to friends on opposite sides, in much the same terms as any other resident of the community would. In this way it was possible to act as a partisan and still communicate with friends in opposing factions who acted as my informants. . . . Another problem in taking on partisan roles as a researcher is that it almost inevitably causes bias in favor of those to whom one is committed. In my case, again, the answer to this problem was to maintain close informants on opposing sides, and to try, in the analysis of events, to be on guard against my own partialities so that I might correct them or use them knowingly.[48]

Leaving the Field.   Kornblum and his family moved from South Chicago to Seattle, where the study was written. Periodically, he returned to South Chicago to continue his involvement in local political life.

Ethical and Political Issues of Fieldwork

Because fieldwork is characterized by long-term and intimate participation in the daily life of the people being studied, it is associated with a number of ethical, legal, and political dilemmas. Two ethical issues are associated with fieldwork: the problem of potential deception and the impact the fieldwork may have on the lives of those studied.[49]

Earlier in this chapter, we saw that fieldworkers sometimes conduct their study under a false identity in order to gain access to the field and that this kind of fieldwork has generated considerable controversy and criticism. However, some field researchers defend the use of disguised observation; they claim that it is the only way to gain access to important research sites. Furthermore, they argue that covert methods have never directly harmed the people studied in any significant way.

Obviously, this is a serious controversy that cannot be easily resolved. It should be stressed, however, that anyone planning to use disguised identity in a field study should be aware of the serious ethical implications of doing so. If at all possible, the researcher should examine alternative ways of gaining access to the research site.

Another important ethical issue is the unanticipated effect that any kind of fieldwork may have on the people being studied. Very often the fieldworkers have more power than their hosts. They may be perceived as being able to allocate material resources, political connections, and social prestige. For example, in a study conducted in New Guinea, the Papuan set-

48. Ibid., pp. 240–241.
49. Emerson, *Contemporary Field Research,* p. 255.

tlers (mistakenly) credited the fieldworkers with getting the government to change certain land policies.[50] Obviously, such a perception could be very harmful to the relations between the researcher and the study population, especially if the fieldworker fails to perform in ways that the people expect.

The research community has become more concerned with the political issues associated with field research, as governments and other political groups have become increasingly interested in who gets studied and in what ways.[51] This has particular relevance in cases where the results of research dealing with disadvantaged groups may have political and social implications. In addition, many of these groups are now claiming the right to review both research proposals and prepublication drafts of research reports.

Summary

1. Field research is the most central strategy of data collection associated with the qualitative method. Field research is conducted in natural settings in an effort to understand subjectively the people being studied.

2. The method of data collection most closely associated with field research is participant observation, the process in which the investigator attempts to obtain membership in or a close attachment to the group he or she wishes to study. The researcher can assume either a complete participant role or a participant-as-observer role. Complete participants conceal their identities and do not make their research objectives known, whereas participants-as-observers make their presence known to the group being studied.

3. Field research is guided by either grounded theory or analytic induction. With grounded theory, conceptual categories are developed directly from the data. With analytic induction, analysis begins with a tentative hypothesis explaining the phenomenon being observed, and then attempts are made to verify the hypothesis by observing a small number of cases.

4. The practice of field research can be divided into the following distinct stages: selecting a research topic, choosing an appropriate research site and obtaining access, establishing relations with members of the group and finding reliable informants, and leaving the field and analyzing the data.

5. Fieldwork is associated with a number of ethical and political dilemmas. The first problem is the potential for deception, which is especially likely in studies in which observation is disguised. An important ethical issue is the unanticipated consequences of the research. Researchers may be perceived as being able to allocate material resources, political connections, and social prestige, resources that are unrelated to the research process or its objectives.

50. Ibid.
51. Ibid., p. 266.

Key Terms for Review

field research   informant
participant observation   grounded-theory approach
complete participant   analytic induction
participant-as-observer

Study Questions

1. Discuss the main differences between qualitative and quantitative research.
2. Compare and contrast *complete participant* and *participant-as-observer*.
3. Describe the difficulties associated with gaining access to a research site.
4. What is analytic induction?
5. What are the major ethical and political issues of fieldwork?

Additional Readings

Agar, Michael H. *Speaking of Ethnography*. Newbury Park, Calif.: Sage, 1986.

Berg, Bruce L. *Qualitative Research Methods*. Boston: Allyn & Bacon, 1989.

Burgess, Robert G., ed. *Field Research: A Sourcebook and Field Manual*. London: Allen & Unwin, 1982.

Emerson, Robert M., ed. *Contemporary Field Research*. Boston: Little, Brown, 1983.

Golde, Peggy, ed. *Women in the Field: Anthropological Experience*. 2d ed. Berkeley: University of California Press, 1986.

Gorden, Raymond, L. *Interviewing: Strategy, Techniques, and Tactics*. 3d ed. Homewood, Ill.: Dorsey, 1980.

Lofland, John, and Lyn H. Lofland. *Analyzing Social Settings*. Belmont, Calif.: Wadsworth, 1984.

McCracken, Grant. *The Long Interview*. Newbury Park, Calif.: Sage, 1988.

Miles, Matthew B., and Michael A. Huberman. *Qualitative Data Analysis*. Newbury Park, Calif.: Sage, 1983.

Shaffir, William B., Robert A. Stebbins, and Allan Turowetz, eds. *Fieldwork Experience: Qualitative Approaches to Social Research*. New York: St. Martin's Press, 1980.

Smith, Robert B., and Peter K. Manning, eds. *Handbook of Social Science Methods: Vol. 2. Qualitative Methods*. Cambridge, Mass.: Ballinger, 1982.

Strauss, Anselm L. *Qualitative Analysis for Social Scientists*. New York: Cambridge University Press, 1987.

Van Maanen, John. *Tales of the Field*. Chicago: University of Chicago Press, 1988.

————, ed. *Qualitative Methodology*. Newbury Park, Calif.: Sage, 1983.

Wax, Rosalie H. *Doing Fieldwork: Warnings and Advice*. Chicago: University of Chicago Press, 1971.

CHAPTER 13

Secondary Data Analysis

In this chapter, we first discuss the reasons for the increased use of secondary data; then we point out the advantages and inherent limitations of secondary data analysis. Next we examine the major sources of secondary data including the census, special surveys, simple observation, and archival data. Finally, we present content analysis as a method for systematically analyzing data obtained from archival records, documents, and newspapers.

THE DATA COLLECTION METHODS THAT we have discussed so far generate primary data. They take place in a contrived or a natural setting (for example, field experimentation) in which the research participants are aware of being studied and in which the researcher either collects the data personally or has trained observers or interviewers do so. Increasingly, however, social scientists are making use of data previously collected by *other* investigators, usually for purposes that *differ* from the original research objectives. *Secondary data analysis* refers to research findings based on data collected by others. For example, census data collected by governments for administrative and public policy purposes have been used by social scientists to investigate, among other things, the structures of households, income distribution and redistribution, immigration and migration patterns, characteristics of racial and ethnic groups, changes in family composition, occupational structures, social mobility, and attributes of rural, urban, and metropolitan areas. Data collected by Gallup and other national survey research organizations have been used to study a variety of issues such as changes in public opinion, political attitudes, and voting patterns and their determinants.

Why Secondary Data Analysis?

Secondary data analysis has a rich intellectual tradition in the social sciences. Emil Durkheim examined official statistics on suicide rates in different areas and found that the suicide rates in Protestant countries were higher than in Catholic countries.[1] Karl Marx used official economic statistics to document his "class struggle" thesis and argue for economic determinism.[2] Max Weber studied the official ideologies of early Protestant churches and other historical documents to rebut Marx's analysis by suggesting that religion was the source of sociopolitical behavior rather than economic determinism.[3]

Recently, social scientists have been increasingly using data that were previously collected by other investigators and institutions for research purposes different from the original reasons for collecting the data. Referring specifically to survey research, Norval Glenn has observed that

> an almost revolutionary change in survey research would seem to be occurring. Until recently, survey data were analyzed primarily by the persons who designed the surveys, but there seems to be a rather strong trend toward separation of survey design from data analysis. One can almost envision a time when some survey researchers will specialize in survey design and others will specialize in data analysis.[4]

There are three explanations for the increased use of secondary data: conceptual-substantive reasons, methodological reasons, and economic reasons.

Conceptual-substantive Reasons. From a conceptual-substantive point of view, secondary data may be the only data available for the study of certain research problems. Social and political historians, for example, must rely almost exclusively on secondary data.

In research on more contemporary issues, as Herbert Hyman points out, the investigator searches through a wide range of materials covering different areas and eras, which may result in greater scope and depth than is

1. Emil Durkheim, *Suicide* (New York: Free Press, 1966). Originally published 1897.
2. Karl Marx, *Capital* (New York: International Publishers, 1967). Originally published 1867.
3. Max Weber, *The Protestant Ethic and the Spirit of Capitalism,* trans. Talcott Parsons (New York: Scribner, 1977). Originally published 1905.
4. Norval D. Glenn, "The General Social Surveys: Editorial Introduction to a Symposium," *Contemporary Sociology,* 7 (1978): 532.

possible with a single primary data research project.[5] With such secondary analysis, we can better understand the historical context, and by analyzing data collected in different times on similar issues, we can also describe and explain change. For example, the Interuniversity Consortium for Political and Social Research (ICPSR) at the University of Michigan has systematic survey data on American national elections since 1952.[6] These have been used to describe and explain stability and change in ideology, trust, party identification, and voting over time.

Secondary data may also be used for comparative purposes. Within and between nations and societies, comparisons may enlarge the scope of generalizations and provide insights. For example, the ICPSR has data on election studies conducted in European democracies. Since many similar variables were measured in these studies, it was possible to compare issues such as political participation, ideologies and voting, party identification and voting, and the structures of conflict and consensus. As Hyman suggests in the context of survey research:

> Secondary analysis of a series of comparable surveys from different points in time provides one of the rare avenues for the empirical description of long-term changes and for examining the way phenomena vary under the contrasted conditions operative in one society at several points.[7]

Methodological Reasons. There are several methodological advantages to secondary analysis. First, secondary data provides opportunities for replication. A research finding gains more credibility if it appears in a number of studies. Rather than conduct several studies personally, a researcher can use data collected by others. Second, the availability of data over time enables the employment of longitudinal research designs. One can find baseline measurements in studies conducted decades ago and locate similar data collected more recently. Indeed, primary data can be compared with the data collected in earlier studies to provide a follow-up. Third, secondary analysis may improve measurement. In Hyman's words, the secondary analyst

> must examine a diverse array of concrete indicators, assorted specific manifestations of behavior or attitude. . . . He is likely to be more exhaustive in his definition of a concept, to think about it not only in his accustomed ways, but in all sorts of odd ways,[8]

---

5. Herbert H. Hyman, *Secondary Analysis of Sample Surveys* (Middletown, Conn.: Wesleyan University Press, 1987), Chapter 1.

6. Warren E. Miller et al., *American National Elections Studies Data Sourcebook, 1952–1978* (Cambridge, Mass.: Harvard University Press, 1980).

7. Hyman, *Secondary Analysis*, p. 17.

8. Ibid., p. 24.

thereby gaining new insights. Fourth, with secondary data we can increase the sample size, its representativeness, and the number of observations that could lead to more encompassing generalizations. Finally, secondary data can be used for triangulation purposes, increasing the credibility of research findings obtained with primary data.

Economic Reasons. Primary research is a costly undertaking. A survey of a national sample of 1,500 to 2,000 individuals can cost $125,000 or more. This is a prohibitive sum for university professors, independent researchers, and graduate students, particularly now that research support and funding opportunities have been retrenching. It is considerably cheaper to use existing data rather than to collect new data.

Public Opinion and Public Policy: An Example

What effects, if any, does public opinion have on government policy? To study this important question, Page and Shapiro examined several hundred surveys of national samples of Americans conducted between 1935 and 1979 by Gallup, the National Opinion Research Center, and the Center for Political Studies' Survey Center at the University of Michigan.[9] They archived 3,319 questionnaire items about policy preferences, of which some 600 were repeated in identical form at two or more points in time. Then the authors identified every instance in which there was a significant change in opinion from one survey to another (6 percent or more in samples of 1,500 with fairly even divisions of opinion). They found 357 such instances of significant change in Americans' policy preferences, encompassing a wide range of foreign and domestic issues, such as taxation, spending, regulation, trade, and military action.

For each of these instances of opinion change, indicators of policy outputs were measured beginning two years before the data of the initial opinion survey and ending four years after the final survey. Using these two sets of data, the authors coded agreements and disagreements between the instances of opinion change and the policy indicators. Upon analyzing the data, they found a great deal of congruence between changes in policy and changes in opinion during the half century they studied. Furthermore, congruence was more frequent when the policymaking process had time to react to change in public opinion. The author's concluded that "public opinion, whatever its sources and quality, is a factor that genuinely affects government policies in the United States."[10]

---

9. Benjamin I. Page and Robert Y. Shapiro, "Effects of Public Opinion on Policy," *American Political Science Review,* 77 (1983): 175–190.

10. Ibid., p. 189.

Limitations of Secondary Data Analysis

Like other data collection methods, secondary data analysis has certain inherent limitations. Perhaps the most serious problem in using secondary data is that often they only approximate the kind of data that the investigator would like to have for testing hypotheses. There is an inevitable gap between primary data collected by the investigator personally with specific research purposes and intentions and data collected by others for other purposes. Differences are likely in sample size and design, question wording and sequence, the details of interviews, and the setup of laboratory experiments.

A second problem in using secondary data is access to such data. Although thousands of studies are available in data archives, it may be difficult to find the ones with the variables of interest. Sometimes the relevant data may be inaccessible because the original investigator will not make them available. Researchers are not required to make their data available for secondary analysis. Indeed, creativity in locating relevant data and in measuring variables is important to secondary data analysis.

A third problem of secondary data analysis may emerge if there is insufficient information about the collection of the data to determine potential sources of bias, errors, or problems with internal or external validity. The ICPSR, for example, deals with this problem by classifying data into four classes according to the amount of information, documentation, and effort devoted by its staff and the original investigators to standardizing and checking the data (see Exhibit 13.1).

The Census

A *census* is defined as the recording of demographic data of a population in a strictly defined territory made by the government at a specific time and at regular intervals. The census enumeration should in principle be universal, including every person who lives in the designated area.[11]

There are some indications that censuses date back to 3800 B.C. in Babylonia, to about 3800 B.C. in China, and to 2500 B.C. in Egypt. Reports have also been cited of population enumerations made in ancient Greece and Rome and by the Incas. Modern censuses, however, began in Canada in 1666 and in the United States in 1790. In both countries, a decennial (every ten years) census has taken place since then.[12]

---

11. William Peterson, *Population* (New York: Macmillan, 1975).

12. Mortimer Spiegelman, *Introduction to Demography* (Cambridge, Mass.: Harvard University Press, 1968).

Exhibit 13.1
ICPSR Data Classes

Class I

Class I data sets have been checked, corrected if necessary, and formatted to ICPSR specifications. Also the data may have been recoded and reorganized in consultation with the investigator to maximize their utilization and accessability. A codebook, often capable of being read by a computer, is available. This codebook fully documents the data and may include descriptive statistics such as frequencies or means.

Class II

Class II studies have been checked and formatted to ICPSR standards. All non-numeric codes have been removed. The studies in this class are available on magnetic tape in either OSIRIS (a computer software package) or card image format. The documentation exists as either a machine readable codebook (which will be edited and updated as required by further processing), a multilithed draft version or a xeroxed copy of the investigator's codebook. Any peculiarities in the data will be indicated in the documentation. A copy of the documentation will be supplied when the data are requested.

Class III

Class III studies have been checked by the ICPSR staff for the appropriate number of cards per case and accurate data locations as specified by the investigator's codebook. Often frequency checks on these data have been made. Known data discrepancies and other problems, if any, will be communicated to the user at the time the data are requested. One copy of the codebook for these data will be supplied when the data are requested. The data themselves usually exist only in card image form.

Class IV

The Class IV studies are distributed in the form received by the ICPSR from the original investigator. Users of Class IV data should keep several considerations in mind.

Problems may exist which would not be known before processing begins, and thus the ICPSR can take no responsibility for the technical condition of the data. The requestor, therefore, must be prepared to accept some uncertainty as to the condition of the data. Requests for these studies will normally require a bit longer time to complete than more fully processed studies. In addition, staff assistance on problems encountered in the use of Class IV data will be limited. This policy is intended to ensure that staff resources are maximized while at the same time not preventing early access to data for those who must have them as soon as possible.

The documentation for Class IV studies is reproduced from the material originally received. One copy of the documentation will be supplied upon request. The majority of the studies in Class IV are available on magnetic tape. A few studies in this category are available only on cards because they contain multiple punches.

From Interuniversity Consortium for Political and Social Research, *Guide to Resources and Services, 1988–1989* (Ann Arbor: University of Michigan, Institute for Social Research Center for Political Studies, 1989) pp. 51–52.

The main reasons for population enumerations in early as well as in modern times was to collect data that would facilitate government activities such as taxation, military service, the appropriation of government aid, the apportioning of elected officials, and domestic public policies in general. The scope of the contemporary census has been enlarged. Data collected now also provide a source for research by government, industry, and by the academic community.[13]

The U.S. Census

Census taking in the United States dates back to 1790, when the first census was conducted by U.S. marshals under the supervision of Thomas Jefferson. In 1902, Congress established a permanent census office, the Bureau of the Census, which today is responsible for enumerating the population every ten years. In addition, the Census Bureau conducts numerous ongoing surveys of population, housing and construction, business and industry, federal, state, and local governments, and foreign trade.

The Census Bureau has introduced a number of statistical and technological innovations. Among the most important are population sampling, which increased the scope of the census; participation in the development of the first computer designed for mass data processing and, most recently, the development of the Topologically Integrated Geographic Encoding and Referencing (TIGER) system. TIGER is an automated geographic database that provides coordinate-based digital map information, including political and statistical area boundaries and codes, for the entire United States and its commonwealths and territories. Census and other statistical data can be obtained separately and added to the TIGER database with appropriate software to assist users in such tasks as drawing new political, administrative, and service-area boundaries, delineate highcrime areas, and plot projected population growth in their jurisdictions.[14]

The census of population and housing taken every ten years is called a **complete count census** and is intended to reach every household in the country. The complete count census includes only basic demographic information on each member of the household plus a few questions about the housing unit. In addition, a population sample consisting of 17 percent of all households surveyed, complete a longer questionnaire that includes additional questions on socioeconomic background and housing. The most recent complete count census of the United States was conducted in April, 1990.

The decennial census uses two questionnaires. A short form, that asks basic questions of *all* persons and their housing units, and a long form, or

---

13. Ibid.
14. For further discussion see *TIGER: The Coast-to-Coast Digital Map Data Base* (Washington, D.C.: U.S. Department of Commerce, Bureau of the Census, November, 1990).

sample questionnaire, which contains additional questions on socioeconomic status. This long form was sent to 17.7 million out of an estimated 106 million housing units.

A complete count of the population is necessary because the number of seats to which states are entitled in the U.S. House of Representatives is determined by census statistics. In addition, only a census provides information on small geographic areas such as a small town or a census block—the smallest geographic area where census data is collected. However, a complete count census is prohibitively expensive and its administration is complex, thus, it is used to collect only the most basic type of information. Population sampling (questions asked of only a sample of the surveyed population) has a number of advantages over a complete count census. It is more economical, more efficient, and faster to complete; therefore, it reduces the time between the collection of data and the publication of initial results. Moreover, the use of sampling allows the Census Bureau to expand the scope of its data gathering and to collect more detailed information regarding the population's housing and employment status. Some of the sample surveys conducted by the Census Bureau are designed to collect information regarding the population's attitudes toward a wide variety of issues.

Census data are generally provided for two types of geographic clusters: political units such as states, counties, or congressional districts; and statistical areas, which are groupings defined for statistical use. Among the most common statistical areas are **Metropolitan Statistical Areas (MSA), Census Designated Places (CDP),** and **Census tracts.** An MSA is defined as one or more counties, including a large population nucleus and nearby communities, that have a high degree of interaction.[15] CDPs are densely settled population centers without legally defined corporate limits or corporate powers.[16] Census tracts are small, locally defined statistical areas in metropolitan areas and some other counties with an average population of 4,000.[17]

Errors in Census Statistics

The modern census constitutes an important source of reliable statistical information. However, errors in census enumerations do occur, and users need to be aware of the methodological limitations of the data.

Census data are prone to two types of errors: errors in coverage and errors in content. *Errors in coverage* means that a person or group either is not counted or is counted twice. Duplicate counts are less serious than undercounts. Undercounting the population in decennial censuses has long been

---

15. From *Census '90 Basics* (Washington, D.C.: U.S. Department of Commerce, Bureau of the Census, December, 1985), p. 5.

16. Ibid.

17. Ibid.

of concern to elected officials, researchers, and the public because individuals (and especially groups) that are not counted often lose their representation in national, state, and local governments. Moreover, federal funds to state and local governments are distributed on the basis of decennial census data. One undercounted group consists of persons who cannot be located due to lack of a permanent address. Another is made up of people who deliberately avoid detection, such as illegal residents. Estimating error in this case is difficult because illegal residents are not likely to appear in other official records that could be used to verify census statistics.

Errors in content occur whenever information is incorrectly reported or tabulated. Apart from errors due to carelessness, errors in content often result because of a deliberate attempt by the persons surveyed to give an inaccurate response to questions measuring social standing. The misclassification of individuals into higher or lower income, occupation, or education categories is one such instance of errors in content.

Census Products

Census products are available from the Census Bureau in various formats: printed reports, computer tapes, microfiche, and more recently CD-ROM laser disks. Printed statistical reports are convenient and readily available. Data in printed reports are presented in the form of tables showing specific sets of data for a specified geographic area. The Census Bureau releases census reports in various series. In some, information is provided for the states, the nation as a whole, MSAs, urban areas, cities, and counties. The small area series presents block and census tract statistics. The subject reports series summarizes data on selected subjects at the national level.

Subject reports focus primarily on housing and on population subjects, but each publication centers on particular subjects within these general areas. For example, one report from the 1980 census titled "Journey to Work: Metropolitan Community Flows" contains statistics on local and national commuting patterns for each of the MSAs in the United States and presents information about the places where workers live and work. Another report, "Living Arrangements of Children and Adults," useful for studies of the American household, has national statistics about living arrangements for children and adults. It provides this information for children in various age groups according to relationship to householder and marital status of parents. The most recent data from the 1990 U.S. Census are currently being compiled and will be published in subject reports dealing with such topics as education, income, migration, the elderly population, and current language use.

For users needing census statistics in greater detail or for smaller geographic and statistical units than are available in the various printed reports, the Census Bureau provides census data on computer tapes in two forms— Summary Tape Files (STFs), which contain summary tables in greater detail than in the printed reports, and Public-Use Microdata Sample files (PUMS), consisting of a small sample of unidentified households and containing all census data collected about each person in the household. PUMS files enable users to prepare customized tabulations and cross tabulations of items on the census questionnaire and are of great interest to academic researchers who do their own tabulations in order to study some characteristics in more detail.[18]

Microfiche containing block statistics are also available as they were after the 1980 census. The microfiche will present a subset of the tabulations for blocks found in STF 1B. In 1990, for the first time, the entire nation is blocked. This will increase the number of blocks for which the Census Bureau provides data from 2.5 million in 1980 to about 7 million in 1990. The cost and storage of block data of this magnitude would be prohibitive if they were published in printed reports.[19]

CD-ROM, a compact disk-read only memory—a type of optical or laser disk—is the most recently developed technology for data storage and retrieval. One 4¾-inch CD-ROM can hold the contents of approximately 1,500 flexible diskettes, or three or four high-density tapes.[20] Special peripherals enable CD-ROMs to be used on personal computers.

Other Data Collected by the Census Bureau

The decennial census of population and housing, the main source of information about the American population, cannot cover many subjects of interest and after a few years may not be current enough for many purposes. Hence, the Census Bureau conducts a number of ongoing special censuses and sample surveys. Here we describe a few that may be of interest to social scientists.

Current Population Survey (CPS).   The Current Population Survey is a monthly sample survey of the civilian noninstitutional population of the United States. Its foremost aim is to produce statistics on unemployment and information on the personal characteristics of the labor force, such as age, sex, race, marital and family status, and educational background. The survey also provides information on other subjects that are periodically added to the survey. The Census Bureau publishes a number of reports based on these data under the title *Current Population Reports*.

American Housing Survey (AHS).   Every two years, as part of the AHS program, the Census Bureau interviews respondents in a representative sample of all housing units in the United States. The American Housing Survey includes extensive household-level data on housing quality, reasons

18. Ibid., p. 13.
19. Ibid., p. 16.
20. Ibid., p. 16.

for housing choices, and evaluation of public services and of the general quality of life in the neighborhood. This survey also helps to measure changes in the housing inventory resulting from losses, new construction, mobile home placement, and demographic characteristics of the occupants.[21]

Consumer Expenditure Survey. Consumer Expenditure Surveys are designed to monitor changes in prices paid for items by the public. Data from these surveys are essential in measuring the extent of the U.S. inflation rate and its impact on the cost of living. Data from this survey are also used by the Bureau of Labor Statistics to update the monthly Consumer Price Index (CPI). Consumer Expenditure Surveys take three forms: The Quarterly Interview Survey, The Diary Survey, and The Point of Purchase Survey.

The Quarterly Interview Survey is conducted monthly through household interviews and provides data on living expenses incurred during the three months prior to the interview.[22]

The Diary Survey, also conducted monthly, collects data on diary forms completed by persons living in a household. They record daily living expenses over two consecutive one-week periods.[23]

The annual Point of Purchase Survey is conducted to identify the kinds of stores and other establishments frequented by consumers as they purchase a variety of goods and services.

The Census Bureau publishes several useful guides: the *1990 Census User's Guide* is the primary guide for use of 1990 census data; *Census and You* is the Census Bureau's monthly newsletter for data users; and the *Census Catalog and Guide* provides a comprehensive list of all new publications, computer tape files, special tabulations, and products available from the bureau. In addition to its main headquarters in Washington, D.C., the Census Bureau operates 12 regional offices throughout the United States that are staffed by information services specialists who answer questions by telephone, in person, or through correspondence.

Searching for Secondary Data

With thousands of studies available in this country and abroad, how does one locate the precise data of interest? William Trochim offers some guidelines for data search:[24]

1. *Specification of needs:* examining subject indexes of archive holdings; identifying relevant keywords.

21. From *Census Surveys: Measuring America* (Washington, D.C.: U.S. Department of Commerce, Bureau of the Census, December, 1985), p. 6.

22. Ibid., p. 12.

23. Ibid.

24. William M. K. Trochim, "Resources for Locating Public and Private Data," in *Reanalyzing Program Evaluations,* ed. Robert F. Boruch (San Francisco: Jossey-Bass, 1981), pp. 57–67.

2. *Initial familiarization:* searching guides and catalogs and listing data archives or organizations that may have the desired data.
3. *Initial contacts:* contacting people familiar with the archive and obtaining information on the use of data.
4. *Secondary contacts:* verifying information and the details necessary to formally request the data.
5. *Accessibility:* obtaining information on possible problems from people who have used the data.
6. *Analysis and supplemental analyses:* obtaining additional data if needed.

The main resources available to would-be secondary data analysts searching for data are catalogs, guides, directories of archives, and organizations established to assist researchers. Useful catalogs of archives are *Encyclopedia of Information Systems and Services,* ed. A. T. Kruzas (Detroit: Gale Research Co., 1983); *Statistics Sources,* ed. P. Wasserman and J. Paskar (Detroit: Gale Research Co., 1977); and *Research Centers Directory,* 14th ed., ed. A. M. Palmer (Detroit: Gale Research Co., 1989). Major guides to government databases include *A Framework for Planning U.S. Federal Statistics* and *The Directory of Computerized Data Files and Related Software,* both published by the U.S. Department of Commerce; and *Federal Information Sources and Systems: A Directory for the Congress.*

The ICPSR at the University of Michigan and the Roper Center at the University of Connecticut are the largest archives of secondary data in the United States. The ICPSR publishes a yearly *Guide to Resources and Services.* The Association of Public Data Users publishes a *Data File Directory.* Other major organizations include the Bureau of Applied Social Research, Columbia University; the Laboratory for Political Research, Social Science Data Archive, University of Iowa; the National Opinion Research Center (NORC), University of Chicago; and the European Association of Scientific Information Dissemination Centers.[25]

Unobtrusive Measures

An **unobtrusive measure** (also known as a *nonreactive measure*) is any method of data collection that directly removes the researcher from the interactions, events, or behavior being investigated. For example, perusing public archival documents is an unobtrusive measure because the conditions under which the data are collected are not influenced by an intruding researcher. Unobtrusive measures avoid the contamination that might arise when investigators and research participants meet in data collection situa-

---

25. See also ibid., p. 65, and Catherine Hakim, *Secondary Analysis in Social Research: A Guide to Data Sources and Methods with Examples* (Boston: Allen & Unwin, 1982).

tions. With unobtrusive measures, the individual "is not aware of being tested, and there is little danger that the act of measurement will itself serve as a force for change in behavior or elicit role-playing that confounds the data."[26] These measures range from consulting private and public archives to simply observing people at work or play, from physical trace analysis to contrived observations. For example, physical traces and evidence left behind by a population are generated without the producer's knowledge of their future use by researchers.

Eugene Webb and coauthors make a distinction between two broad classes of physical evidence: erosion measures and accretion measures.[27] **Erosion measures** are the natural remnants of some population's activity that has selectively worn certain objects. For example, the wear on library books is an index of their popularity, and the number of miles accumulated by police officers in their patrol cars measures their daily activity. Thus one can cross-validate the verbal reports of police officers on their daily activities by checking the number of miles accumulated in their patrol cars.

Accretion measures constitute a population's deposit of materials. In this case, the researcher examines remnants that are suggestive of some human behavior. For example, the amount of dust on machines has been taken as an indicator of the frequency with which they are used. Samuel Wallace found that hotel clerks assess a person's relationship with legal authorities by the number of possessions the person leaves behind.[28] The popularity of various radio stations can be estimated by noting the settings on car radios when cars are brought in for servicing.

Both the time needed for collection and the dubious quality of the data make physical trace analysis problematic. Even more important, in many instances the researcher lacks sufficient information on the population from which the physical traces are drawn to make valid generalizations.

Simple Observation

Simple observations are another basic nonreactive measure. They are used in situations "in which the observer has no control over the behavior or sign in question, and plays an unobserved, passive and unobtrusive role in the research situation."[29] Although in all other respects simple observations take on the methodology of other observational methods, they are distinct because the researcher does not intervene in the production of the data. There are four basic types of simple observation: observation of exterior body and

---

26. Eugene J. Webb et al., *Nonreactive Measures in the Social Sciences* (Boston: Houghton Mifflin, 1981), p. 175.
27. Ibid., pp. 35–52.
28. Samuel E. Wallace, *Skid Row as a Way of Life* (Totowa, N.J.: Bedminster Press, 1965).
29. Webb et al., *Nonreactive Measures,* p. 112.

physical signs, analysis of expressive movement, physical location analysis, and observation of language behavior.

Observation of Exterior Body and Physical Signs.   This type of simple observation involves observation of the exterior body and physical signs as indicators of behavior or attitudes. Examples of such signs are tattoos, hairstyles, clothing, ornamental objects such as jewelry, and other possessions. Exterior signs in public places, such as the language of street and store signs, can serve as measures of social change, since as immigrant groups move into a neighborhood, exterior signs change.

Analysis of Expressive Movement.   A second type of simple observation is the analysis of expressive movement. Observation focuses on the self-expressive features of the body and the interpretation of social interactions. Many feelings are communicated through body language—by how close people stand, how much they look at each other, and how often they touch.

A major problem in the investigation of facial and body gestures is the determination of what a particular gesture conveys. For instance, a smile may mean relief or happiness. The meaning of a gesture has to be determined for both the person expressing it and the recipient. The situation in which the gesture is used must also be considered. A frown conveys different emotions in different situations.

Physical Location Analysis.   The main purpose of **physical location analysis** is to investigate the ways in which individuals use their bodies in a social space without the researcher's intervention in the conditions that elicit the behavior. To observers of Russian internal politics, for instance, who stood next to whom in Red Square while reviewing the May Day parade was for many years a clue of stability or change in the power elite. The proximity of a politician to the leader is a measure of status; physical position is interpreted as an indicator of other behavior that gave the politician the status position.

Observation of Language Behavior.   This fourth form of simple observation focuses on samples of conversations and the interrelationship of speech patterns to locale, to categories of persons present, and to time of day. The analysis combines the study of physical locations with that of expressive movements.

George Psathas and James Henslin examined the rules and definitions employed by cabdrivers as they located points of delivery and pickup on the basis of dispatcher messages. Both the information conveyed in the messages and the actions taken by the driver were analyzed. Each item of information was assigned a special code that represented specific directions for the cabdriver. For example, if a driver was told to ''drive up and get out,'' he must do more than merely drive up. His instructions involved getting out of the cab and actively looking for the passenger in a place where the passenger was presumed to be. The codes and their accompanying behavior represent a distinct system of social interaction meaningful only to group members.[30]

Problems with Simple Observations. The main advantage of simple observation is that the researcher has no part in structuring the observation situation and remains unobserved while observing. This eliminates bias that might otherwise be introduced. Simple observation, however, has some particular problems. First, the recorded observations may not represent a wider population, thus limiting the scope of generalizations. Second, bias might be introduced by the observer if he or she becomes more or less attentive, adept, or involved as time goes on. Third, if the observer remains unnoticed, then the settings most accessible to simple observation are public; private settings are inaccessible to simple observation. Fourth, much of the data collected by simple observation do not lead to explanations: "The data . . . don't offer the 'why,' but simply establish a relationship."[31] This relationship can be interpreted in different ways by different observers.

Archival Records

Another form of unobtrusive data are archival records. These data are collected from diverse sources such as actuarial records, political and judicial records, government documents, the mass media, and private records such as autobiographies, diaries, and letters. A large amount of data in the form of public and private archival records is readily available to social scientists. Some of these records have been compiled specifically for purposes of research, whereas others have been prepared for more general use.

Public Records

Four basic kinds of public records may be distinguished. First are **actuarial records** describing the personal demographic characteristics of the population served by the record-keeping agency, such as birth and death statistics and records of marriages and divorces. Second are political and judicial records concerning court decisions, legislators' activities, public votes, budget decisions, and the like. Third are governmental and quasi-governmental documents such as crime statistics, records of social welfare programs, hospitalization records, and weather reports. Fourth are the various reports, news items, editorials, and other communications produced by the mass media. Each of these four types contains information that has been used for

---

30. George Psathas and James N. Henslin, "Dispatched Orders and the Cab Driver: A Study of Locating Activities," *Social Problems,* 14 (1967): 424–443.

31. Webb et al., *Nonreactive Measures,* p. 127.

numerous and varied research purposes. We shall look at some examples of social science research that used the four kinds of public archival records.

Actuarial Records.   Most societies maintain records of births, deaths, marriages, and divorces. Such data have been used by social scientists for both descriptive and explanatory purposes. For example, Webb and colleagues report that Winston investigated the preference for male offspring in upper-class families by examining birth records. He noted the sex of each child in the birth order of each family. A preference for males was indicated if the male-female ratio of the last child born in families estimated to be complete was greater than that ratio for all children in the same families. The information contained in birth records enabled him to construct an upper-class sample of parents and to test his hypothesis.[32]

Russell Middleton examined fertility levels with two sets of data: fertility values expressed in magazine fiction and actuarial fertility levels at three different time periods. For 1916, 1936, and 1956, Middleton estimated fertility values by observing the size of fictional families in eight American magazines. A comparison with population data for the same years showed that shifts in the size of fictional families closely paralleled shifts in the actual United States fertility level.[33]

Death records were used in Lloyd Warner's original study on death and its accouterments in an American city. Warner investigated official cemetery documents to establish a history of the dead. He found the social structure of the city mirrored in the cemetery. For example, the father was most often buried in the center of the family plot, and headstones of males were larger than those of females. Moreover, a family that had raised its social status moved the graves of its relatives from less prestigious cemeteries to more prestigious ones.[34]

Political and Judicial Records.   Voting statistics have been used widely to study electoral behavior and the voting patterns of legislators. Collections such as *A Review of Elections of the World*, issued biennially by the Institute of Electoral Research in London, and *America at the Polls: A Handbook of American Presidential Election Statistics*, edited by Richard M. Scammon (Pittsburgh: University of Pittsburgh Press, 1965), provides useful historical data on voting. *The Congressional Quarterly Almanac* gives information on the U.S. Congress, including data on the backgrounds of members of Congress, information on major items of legislation, tabulations of roll-call votes, and a survey of political developments. In the *World Handbook of Political and Social Indicators* (New Haven, Conn.: Yale University Press, 1983), Charles L. Taylor and David Jodice report transnational data on 148

32. Ibid., p. 22.

33. Russell Middleton, "Fertility Values in American Magazine Fiction, 1916–1956," *Public Opinion Quarterly*, 24 (1960): 139–143.

34. Lloyd W. Warner, *The Living and the Dead: A Study of the Symbolic Life of Americans* (New Haven, Conn.: Yale University Press, 1965).

political and social measures, such as electoral participation, counts of riots by county per year, numbers of irregular government changes, and inequalities in income distribution. Harold W. Stanley and Richard G. Niemi, in *Vital Statistics on American Politics* (Washington, D.C.: Congressional Quarterly Press, 1988), present useful time-series data on political institutions, public opinion, and government policies.

The *Congressional Record* contains information that can be used to study the behavior not only of members of Congress but also of people outside Congress. For example, it is a common practice for members of Congress to insert in the *Record* newspaper columns that reflect their personal point of view. In an early study of political columnists, Webb employed these data for an estimate of conservatism and liberalism among Washington's columnists. Individual members of Congress were assigned a score on a liberal-conservative continuum by evaluating their voting record published by two opposing groups—the Conservative Americans for Constitutional Action and the Liberal Committee on Political Action of the AFL-CIO. Columnists were then ranked on the mean score of the members of Congress who placed their articles in the *Record*.[35]

Governmental Documents. Just as analyzing documents such as birth and death records can be fruitful, other governmental and quasi-governmental documents may also serve as a source of data. Lombroso used governmental documents to study the effect of weather and time of year on scientific creativity. He drew a sample of 52 physical, chemical, and mathematical discoveries and noted the time of their occurrence. His evidence showed that 22 of the major discoveries occurred in the spring, 15 in the autumn, 10 in the summer, and 5 in winter.[36]

City budgets were the data of Robert Angell's unique research on the moral integration of American cities. He constructed a "welfare effort index" by computing local per capita expenditures for welfare; he combined this with a "crime index" based on FBI data to get an "integration index."[37] Budgets have been used as indicators of policy commitments. The expenditure side of the budget shows "who gets what" in public funds, and the revenue side tells "who pays the cost." The budgetary process provides a mechanism for reviewing governmental programs, assessing their cost, relating them to financial sources, making choices among alternative expenditures, and determining the financial effort that a government will expend on these programs. Davis, Dempster, and Wildavsky in their classic study examined the federal budget in consecutive periods and identified two variables that explain the greatest portion of budgetary allocations in any year:

35. Eugene J. Webb, "How to Tell a Columnist," *Columbia Journalism Review,* 2 (1963): 20.

36. Webb et al., *Nonreactive Measures,* p. 72.

37. Robert C. Angell, "The Moral Integration of American Cities," *American Journal of Sociology,* 57 (1951): 1–140.

1. The agency request for a certain year is a fixed mean percentage of the Congressional appropriation for that agency in the previous year plus a random variable for that year. 2. The Congressional appropriation for an agency in a certain year is a fixed mean percentage of the agency's request in that year plus a variable representing a deviation from the usual relationship between the Congress and the agency for the previous year.[38]

The Mass Media.   The mass media constitute the most easily available source of social science data. Accordingly, research using data obtained from the mass media is voluminous, and only one example need be discussed here.[39] Oscar Grusky studied the relationship between administrative succession and subsequent change in group performance. From the sports pages, Grusky obtained data on the performance of various professional football teams, as well as the timing of changes in coaches and managers. He found that changing a manager makes a difference in the performance of a team.[40]

The mass media record people's verbal communications; these, in turn, have been analyzed to test a variety of propositions. With the introduction of content analysis, to be discussed later in this chapter, research using the mass media as a primary source of data has rapidly accelerated.

Private Records

Private records are more difficult to obtain than public records. Nevertheless, they can be of great value to researchers who wish to gain insights by inspecting an individual's own definition of a situation or an event. Private records include autobiographies, diaries, letters, essays, and the like. *Autobiographies* are the most frequently used private record; they reflect the author's interpretation of his or her personal experiences. The *diary* is a more spontaneous account, as its author is not constrained by task attitudes that control the production of autobiographies. Both autobiographies and diaries are initially directed to one person—the author. *Letters* have a dual audience—the writer and the recipient—and they often reflect the interaction between them.[41] These three main types of private records are written documents focusing on the author's personal experiences. They are usually produced on the author's own initiative and express his or her personal reflections.

38. Otto A. Davis, M. A. H. Dempster, and Aaron Wildavsky, "A Theory of the Budgetary Process," *American Political Science Review,* 60 (1966): 529–547.

39. For other studies using the mass media as a source of unobtrusive data, see Webb et al., *Nonreactive Measures.*

40. Oscar Grusky, "Managerial Succession and Organizational Effectiveness," *American Journal of Sociology,* 69 (1963): 21–31.

41. Norman K. Denzin, *The Research Act: A Theoretical Introduction to Sociological Methods,* 3d ed. (Englewood Cliffs, N.J.: Prentice-Hall, 1989), Chapter 8.

Autobiographies.   The uniqueness of the autobiography is that it provides a view of a person's life and experiences uncontaminated by the process of analysis. The investigator may gain an understanding of a person's life in its natural setting, thereby avoiding contamination in the process of problem conceptualization.

Gordon Allport distinguished three major types of autobiographies, each of which may serve different research objectives.[42] The first is the *comprehensive autobiography,* which covers a full cycle of the person's life from his or her earliest memory and integrates a large number of experiences. Helen Keller's accounts of her life as a blind deaf-mute exemplify the comprehensive autobiography. The second type is the *topical autobiography,* which focuses on a limited aspect of the person's life. For example, Edwin Sutherland studied only one phase of the life of a professional thief:

> The principal part of this book is a description of the profession of theft by a person who had been engaged almost continuously for more than twenty years in this profession. This description was secured in two ways: first, the thief wrote approximately two-thirds of it on topics and questions prepared by me; second, he and I discussed for about seven hours a week for twelve weeks what he had written, and immediately after each conference I wrote in verbatim form . . . all that he had said in the discussion.[43]

The third type is the *edited autobiography,* which is a monitored version of the person's account. The investigator selects only experiences that are relevant to the research purpose. Through editing one clarifies and organizes the material so that it illuminates the points relevant to the research hypotheses.

Diaries.   Diaries provide a firsthand account of the writer's life experiences. Written close to the occurrence of events, they convey immediate experiences undistorted by memory. Diaries are not inhibited by the fear of public showing; therefore, they reveal events and experiences that were considered significant at the time of their occurrence.

Diaries have been classified into three types. The *intimate journal* is a continuous record of one's subjective perception of one's experiences over a long period of time. The second type, the *memoir,* is rather impersonal and is written in a relatively short time; it resembles an objective record of the individual's affairs. The third type, the *log,* is also impersonal and contains a record of events, meetings, visits, and other activities of the individuals during a limited period of time.

Some social scientists find the intimate journal useful because it contains authentic expressions of one's perceptions over a prolonged period of

---

42. Gordon W. Allport, *The Use of Personal Documents in Psychological Research* (New York: Social Science Research Council, 1942).

43. Edwin H. Sutherland, *The Professional Thief* (Chicago: University of Chicago Press, 1988), p. v.

time. For example, one biography of the poet Dylan Thomas contains portions of his personal diary, notes he kept on poems he was writing, reflections on his financial status, and comments on his relations with the artistic world.[44] The intimate journal not only chronicles a person's subjective perceptions over an extended period but also allows the investigator to compare various time periods in a person's life and to note continuities and changes.

Letters. One of the earliest attempts to employ letters as a source of social data was William Thomas and Florian Znaniecki's study on the Polish peasant. The researchers collected letters sent between Poland and the United States from 1914 until 1989 to research the problems that arose when the writers moved from the old country to the new. The letters permitted the investigators to examine, among other things, the persons' personalities and the kinds of interactions they had with their correspondents.[45] Historians and literary critics make extensive use of letters as they attempt to reconstruct the lives of historical and literary figures.

Authenticity. One of the major problems in using private documents is the question of their **authenticity**. There are two possible kinds of unauthentic records: records that have been produced by deliberate deceit and records that have been unconsciously misrepresented by the author. Records may be falsified or forged for the sole purpose of gaining prestige or material rewards. For example, writers who claim to have an intimate knowledge of the subject's life can more easily sell an alleged biography to a publishing company; such was the case with a fake biography of the eccentric billionaire Howard Hughes, sold in 1972 to a reputable publisher under false pretenses. Several procedures can be used to check whether private records are genuine. First, authorship should be examined critically. Second, the date of the document has to be established, and dates that are mentioned in it must be verified. For instance, if the author refers to a particular event, say, a flood, this can be validated (for example, with newspapers). A reference to an event that had not yet happened at the time the document was purportedly written would of course be highly suspect.

The second kind of authenticity is much more difficult to detect. Documents may not be false yet misrepresent the truth nevertheless, for the following reasons: the authors of letters, diaries, or autobiographies may not remember the facts clearly, or they may try to please or amuse their readers by exaggerating, or perhaps they are constrained by norms and conventions and thus forced to present a somewhat distorted picture. Stuart Chapin has suggested that the following critical questions be answered before a document is accepted as an authentic record:[46]

44. Bill Read, *The Days of Dylan Thomas* (New York: McGraw-Hill, 1964).

45. William I. Thomas and Florian Znaniecki, *The Polish Peasant in Europe and America* (Champaign: University of Illinois Press, 1984).

46. Stuart F. Chapin, *Field Work and Social Research* (New York: Ayer, 1979), p. 37. Originally published 1920.

1. What did the author mean by a particular statement? Is its real meaning different from its literal meaning?
2. Was the statement made in good faith? Was the author influenced by sympathy or antipathy? By vanity? By public opinion?
3. Was the statement accurate? Was the author a poor observer because of mental defect or abnormality? Badly situated in time and place to observe? Negligent or indifferent?

With answers to these questions, the investigator is in a better position to evaluate records and accept only the credible ones.

Content Analysis

Data obtained from archival records and documents can be analyzed more systematically through content analysis. One can analyze the content of letters, diaries, newspaper articles, minutes of meetings, and the like. Content analysis is a method of data analysis as well as a method of observation. Instead of observing people's behavior directly or asking them about it, the researcher takes the communications that people have produced and asks questions of the communications. The content of communication serves as the basis of inference. For example, John Naisbitt in *Megatrends* analyzed the economic, social, and political currents in the United States to forecast new trends and directions.[47] Among other findings, Naisbitt reported that there are five states (California, Florida, Washington, Colorado, and Connecticut) in which most social invention occurs. The study analyzed the content of more than 2 million articles published in local newspapers about local events in the cities and towns throughout the country during a 12-year period.

Broadly defined, **content analysis** is "any technique for making inferences by systematically and objectively identifying specified characteristics of messages."[48] Objectivity in this context involves analysis carried out on the basis of explicit rules that enable different researchers to obtain the same results from messages or documents. In a systematic content analysis, the "inclusion or exclusion of content is done according to consistently applied criteria of selection; this requirement eliminates analyses in which only materials supporting the investigator's hypotheses are examined."[49]

---

47. John Naisbitt, *Megatrends: Ten New Directions Transforming Our Lives* (New York: Warner Books, 1984).
48. Ole R. Holsti, "Content Analysis," in *The Handbook of Social Psychology*, ed. Gardner Lindzey and Elliot Aronson (Reading, Mass.: Addison-Wesley, 1968), p. 601. The following discussion is based on this work.
49. Ibid., p. 598.

Applications of Content Analysis

Although content analysis is always performed on a message, it may also be used to answer questions about other elements of communication. Harold Lasswell formulated the basic question that can be raised by researchers: "Who says what, to whom, how, and with what effect?"[50] More explicitly, a researcher may analyze messages to test hypotheses about characteristics of the text, antecedents of the message, or effects of the communication. These three aspects differ with respect to the questions asked of the data, the dimension of communication analyzed, and the research design.

The most frequent application of content analysis has been to describe the attributes of the message. For example, the concern of one aspect of early research on revolution and the development of international relations was a survey of political symbols. Research designs were constructed to enable the testing of hypotheses on "world revolution" by identifying trends in the use of symbols that express major goal values of modern politics. Editorials from ten prestigious newspapers in the United States, England, France, Germany, and the Soviet Union were analyzed for the period 1890 to 1949. Editorials appearing on the first and the fifteenth day of each month were coded for the presence of 416 key symbols. These symbols included 206 geographic terms, such as names of countries and international organizations, and 210 ideological symbols, such as *equality*, *democracy*, and *communism*. When a symbol appeared, it was scored as present, and the expressed attitudes toward it were recorded in one of three categories: approval, disapproval, or neutrality. Data from 19,553 editorials were used to trace changing foci of attention and attitude. One of the many findings was that symbols of representative governments (for example, *freedom*) are used where the practice is in dispute, not where it is an accepted part of the traditions.[51]

In a study of a substantially different subject matter, Maher and colleagues examined the characteristics of schizophrenic language. The explicit research purpose was to identify the systematic differences between language evaluated to be thought-disordered and language free from thought disorder. To this end, the authors used documents produced by patients under conditions of spontaneity. The documents ranged from long-term sets of diaries to obscenities scrawled on matchbook covers. A sample of 50 words of text was drawn from each document. The samples were coded in accordance with a division of the text into simple thought sequences or simple units of thought. Each unit included a subject, a verb, and modifiers plus the source of the thought and the attributive subject. The text was divided into

50. Harold D. Lasswell, "Detection: Propaganda Detection and the Courts," in Harold D. Lasswell et al., *The Language of Politics: Studies in Quantitative Semantics* (Cambridge, Mass.: MIT Press, 1965), p. 12.

51. Ithiel de Sola Pool, *Symbols of Democracy* (Westport, Conn.: Greenwood Press, 1981). Originally published 1952.

these units, and each word was assigned to categories by its function in the text. Among other findings, the authors reported that (1) documents judged to be free from thought disorder used fewer objects per subject than those judged pathological and (2) documents judged normal contained more qualifiers per verb than those judged pathological.[52]

The second application of content analysis is that in which a text is analyzed in order to make inferences about the sender of the message and about the causes or antecedents of the message. A well-known attempt to determine the sender's identification is the Mosteller and Wallace study on who wrote *Federalist Papers,* 49–58, 62, and 63. The authors started with four sets of papers: those known to have been written by Madison, those thought to have been written by Madison or by Hamilton, and those thought to have been written by both. Upon examining the texts of the known set of papers, the investigators were able to select words that differentiated between the two authors. For example, the word *enough* tended to be used by Hamilton but not by Madison. These key differentiating words were then used in combination to attribute authorship of the disputed papers. The data strongly supported the claim of Madison's authorship.[53]

Content analysis has also been used to infer aspects of culture and cultural change. David McClelland tested his "need for achievement" theory by analyzing the content of literature in different cultures. An individual with high n-Achievement was viewed as someone who wants to succeed, who is nonconforming, and who enjoys tasks that involve elements of risk; n-Achievement is "a sum of the number of instances of achievement 'ideas' or images." The hypothesis that "a society with a relatively high percentage of individuals with high n-Achievement should contain a strong entrepreneurial class which will tend to be active and successful particularly in business enterprises so that the society will grow in power and influence" was tested by scoring samples of literature from different periods of Greek civilization.[54]

In another major application of content analysis, inferences are made about the effects of messages on the recipient. The researcher determines the effects of A's messages to B by content-analyzing B's messages. Alternatively, one can study the effects of communication by examining other aspects of the recipient's behavior. Content analysis helps to delineate the relevant independent variables that are related to the recipient's behavior.

---

52. Brendan A. Maher, Kathryn O. McKean, and Barry McLaughlin, "Studies in Psychotic Language," in Phillip J. Stone et al., *The General Inquirer: A Computer Approach to Content Analysis* (Cambridge, Mass.: MIT Press, 1968).

53. Frederick Mosteller and David L. Wallace, *Inference and Disputed Authorship: The Federalist* (Reading, Mass.: Addison-Wesley, 1964).

54. David C. McClelland, "The Use of Measures of Human Motivation in the Study of Society," in *Motives in Fantasy, Action and Society*, ed. John W. Atkinson (New York: Van Nostrand, 1966), p. 518.

Units and Categories

The content analysis procedure involves the interaction of two processes: *specification* of the content characteristics to be measured and *application of the rules* for identifying and recording the characteristics when they appear in the texts to be analyzed. The categories into which content is coded vary with the nature of the data and the research purpose. Before discussing general procedures for category construction, we must specify the various recording units used in research and make a distinction between recording units and context units. The **recording unit** is the smallest body of content in which the appearance of a reference is counted (a reference is a single occurrence of the content element). The **context unit** is the largest body of content that may be examined in characterizing a recording unit. For example, the recording unit may be a single term, but in order to decide whether the term is treated favorably, one has to consider the entire sentence in which the term appears (the context unit). Thus the sentence is taken into account when recording (and subsequently when coding) the term.

Five major recording units have been used in content analysis research: *words* or *terms*, *themes*, *characters*, *paragraphs*, and *items*. The word is the smallest unit generally applied in research. Its application results in a list of frequencies of selected words or terms. For many research purposes, the theme is a useful recording unit. In its simplest form, a theme is a simple sentence, that is, subject and predicate. Because in most texts themes can be found in clauses, paragraphs, and illustrations, it becomes necessary to specify which of these places will be searched when using the theme as a recording unit. For example, one may consider only the primary theme in each paragraph or count every theme in the text. Themes are most frequently employed in the study of propaganda, attitudes, images, and values.

In some studies, the character is employed as the recording unit. In this case, the researcher counts the number of persons rather than the number of words or themes. This in turn permits the examination of traits of characters appearing in various texts.

The paragraph is infrequently used as a recording unit because of difficulties in classifying and coding the various and numerous things implied in a single paragraph.

The item is the whole unit employed by the producer of a message. The item may be an entire article, a book, a speech, or the like. Analysis by the entire item is appropriate whenever the variations within the item are small and insignificant. For example, news stories can often be classified by subject matter such as crime, labor, or sports.

Eventually, recording units are classified and coded into *categories*. The problem of category construction, as Berelson points out, is the most crucial aspect of content analysis:

> Content analysis stands or falls by its categories. Particular studies have been productive to the extent that the categories were clearly formulated

and well adapted to the problem and to the content. Content analysis studies done on a hit or miss basis, without clearly formulated problems for investigation and with vaguely drawn or poorly articulated categories, are almost certain to be of indifferent or low quality as research productions. . . . Since the categories contain the substance of the investigation, a content analysis can be no better than its system of categories.[55]

Among the types of categories employed frequently in content analysis research are the following:[56]

"What Is Said" Categories

SUBJECT MATTER. What is the communication about?
DIRECTION. How is the subject matter treated (for example, favorably or unfavorably?
STANDARD. What is the basis on which the classification by direction is made?
VALUES. What values, goals, or desires are revealed?
METHODS. What methods are used to achieve goals?
TRAITS. What are the characteristics used in describing people?
ACTOR. Who is represented as undertaking certain acts?
AUTHORITY. In whose name are statements made?
ORIGIN. Where does the communication originate?
LOCATION. Where does the action take place?
CONFLICT. What are the sources and levels of conflict?
ENDINGS. Are conflicts resolved happily, ambiguously, or tragically?
TIME. When does the action take place?

"How It Is Said" Categories

FORM OR TYPE OF COMMUNICATION. What is the medium of communication (radio, newspaper, speech, television, etc.)?
FORM OF STATEMENT. What is the grammatical or syntactical form of the communication?
DEVICE. What is the rhetorical or propagandistic method used?

Categories must relate to the research purpose, and they must be exhaustive and mutually exclusive. Exhaustiveness ensures that every recording unit relevant to the study can be classified. Mutual exclusivity means that no recording unit can be included more than once within any given category system (see also Chapter 14). The researcher also has to specify explicitly the indicators that determine which recording units fall into each category. This enables replication, an essential requirement of objective and systematic content analysis.

Most content analysis research is quantitative in one form or another. Quantification may be performed by employing one of the following four

55. Bernard Berelson, *Content Analysis in Communication Research* (New York: Hafner, 1971), p. 147.
56. Holsti, "Content Analysis."

systems of enumeration: (1) a *time-space system* based on various measures of space (for example, column inches) or units of time (for example, minutes devoted to a news item on the radio) to describe the relative emphases of different categories in the analyzed material; (2) an *appearance system* that calls for searching the material for appearance of a certain attribute; the size of the context unit determines the frequency with which repeated recording units occurring in close proximity to each other are counted separately; (3) a *frequency system* in which every occurrence of a given attribute is recorded; (4) an *intensity system*, generally employed in studies dealing with attitudes and values. Methods of quantifying for intensity are based on the construction of scales (see Chapter 18). For example, using the paired-comparison technique developed by Thurstone, raters decide which of a possible pair of intensity indicators ranks higher on a scale of attitudes. The judgments are then used to construct categories into which recording units are placed.[57]

Summary

1. Secondary data analysis is performed on data collected by others. Secondary data may be the only source available to study certain research problems. It may also be used for comparative purposes. There are several methodological advantages to using secondary analysis: it provides opportunity for replication, it permits longitudinal research designs, it may improve measurement of certain variables, and it often allows for an increased sample size. And secondary data are considerably cheaper to obtain than primary data.

2. A widely used source of secondary data is the census—data collected by governments for administrative and public policy purposes. Census data are also used by researchers to investigate, among other things, the structure of households, neighborhood and housing characteristics, and changes in family composition. Printed statistical reports are the primary source of census data and are convenient and readily available. The Bureau of the Census provides census data on computer tapes for users needing census statistics in greater detail or for smaller geographic and statistical units than are available in the printed reports.

3. Another source of data that removes the investigator from the population being researched is unobtrusive measures. With unobtrusive mea-

---

57. The most recent development in content analysis is the programming of computers to process the variety of operations involved in textual analysis. It is beyond the scope of this book to survey these developments, but a good start would be Weber R. Philips, *Basic Content Analysis* (Newbury Park, Calif.: Sage, 1985).

sures, subjects are not aware of being researched, and there is little danger that the act of measurement will itself introduce a change in behavior or elicit role playing that might bias the data. We discussed three general types of unobtrusive measures: physical traces, simple observation, and archival records.

4. Individuals leave physical traces without any knowledge that they will be used. Two broad classes of physical traces are erosion measures and accretion measures. Erosion measures are the natural remnants of some population's activity that has selectively worn certain objects. Accretion measures constitute a population's deposit of materials.

5. Simple observation occurs in situations in which the observer has no control over the behavior in question and plays an unobserved role in the research. There are four types of simple observation: observation of exterior body and physical signs, analysis of expressive movement, physical location analysis, and observation of language behavior.

6. Another unobtrusive measure is the analysis of public and private archival records. These data are collected from diverse sources, such as actuarial records, political and judicial records, governmental documents, the mass media, and private records, including autobiographies, diaries, and letters. A major problem with private records is the question of their authenticity; they could have been consciously or unconsciously misrepresented by the author.

7. Content analysis permits systematic analysis of data obtained from archival records and documents. Instead of observing people's behavior or asking them about it, the investigator takes the communications that people have produced and asks questions of these communications. The content analysis procedure involves the interaction of two processes: specification of the content characteristics to be analyzed and application of the rules for identifying and recording the characteristics when they appear in the materials being analyzed. Obviously, the categories into which content is coded vary with the nature of the research problem and the data.

Key Terms for Review

complete count census	simple observation
Metropolitan Statistical Areas (MSA)	physical location analysis
	actuarial records
Census Designated Places (CDP)	authenticity
Census tract	content analysis
unobtrusive measures	recording unit
erosion measures	context unit
accretion measures	

Study Questions

1. What are the advantages of secondary data analysis?
2. How can secondary data relevant to one's research interest be located?
3. What is a complete count census?
4. What are the most common statistical units used by the census?
5. What are the primary forms of simple observation?
6. Discuss the major methodological issues in content analysis.

Additional Readings

Bertaux, Daniel, ed. *Biography and Society: The Life History Approach in the Social Sciences.* Newbury Park, Calif.: Sage, 1981.

Bloch, Marc. *The Historian's Craft.* New York: McGraw-Hill, 1964.

Bouchard, J. T. "Unobtrusive Measures: An Inventory of Uses," *Sociological Methods and Research,* 4 (1976): 267–300.

Denzin, Norman K. *Interpretive Biography.* Newbury Park, Calif.: Sage, 1989.

Felson, M. "Unobtrusive Indicators of Cultural Change: Neckties, Girdles, Marijuana, Garbage, Magazines, and Urban Sprawl," *American Behavioral Scientist*, 26 (1983): 534–542.

Hakim, Catherine. *Secondary Analysis in Social Research: A Guide to Data Sources and Methods with Examples.* Boston: Allen & Unwin, 1982.

Jacob, Herbert. *Using Published Data: Errors and Remedies.* Newbury Park, Calif.: Sage,1984.

Krippendorf, Klaus. *Content Analysis: An Introduction to Its Methodology.* Newbury Park, Calif.: Sage, 1980.

Stewart, David W. *Secondary Research: Information Sources and Methods.* Newbury Park, Calif.: Sage, 1984.

Weber, Robert P. *Basic Content Analysis.* Newbury Park, Calif.: Sage, 1984.

PART IV
Data Processing and Analysis

CHAPTER 14

Data Preparation and Analysis

In this chapter, we examine the common methods of preparing and coding data, and codebook construction. We then describe the use of computers in storing, processing, accessing, and analyzing data sets.

I T IS TAKEN FOR GRANTED THESE DAYS that data collected for analysis will be coded, stored, retrieved, and analyzed using computerized systems. Whether one is comfortable using a mainframe, minicomputer, or personal computer, the logic of the data handling and management is similar. The purpose of this chapter is to acquaint students with common methods for preparation of data, coding, and codebook construction and trade-offs for the use of various options to code and clean data for use in statistical analysis. The assignment of numeric codes increases the ability to retrieve data for computerized analysis.

Coding Schemes

As covered in Chapter 6, measurement consists of devising a system for the assignment of numbers to observations. These assignments may be purely arbitrary (as they are for nominal-level variables), or they may have ranked or interval interpretations. The number assigned to an observation is called a **code**. This code should be consistent across cases or units of analysis when the same condition exists. For example, if a code of 1 means "female," each female should receive a 1 on the variable associated with gender. The information regarding the substantive interpretation concerning a code should be found in the codebook that accompanies the data set. This section describes the process by which codes are assigned to observations.

Assignment of codes can also be used to group various classifications of a concept. Suppose that an investigator has gathered information on the occupation of several hundred individuals. The following are examples of the occupations listed:

Lawyer	*Practical nurse*
Barber	*Migrant farm laborer*
Carpenter	*Executive*
Broker	*High school teacher*
Elevator operator	*Electrician*
Veterinarian	*Advertising agent*

These data do not lend themselves to analysis without prior reduction into some system of categories. One acceptable way to classify them is according to the following categories:

1. *Professional and managerial*: lawyer, veterinarian, executive, high school teacher.
2. *Technical and sales*: advertising agent, broker.
3. *Service and skilled labor*: barber, elevator operator, practical nurse, electrician, carpenter.
4. *Unskilled labor*: migrant farm worker.

This system of categories allows for classification of occupations according to the level of income, prestige, and education that they have in common, permitting the researcher to handle four well-defined categories rather than several dozen specific occupations. Systems of categories such as this one, used to classify responses or acts that relate to a single item or variable, are referred to as **coding schemes.** The principles involved in constructing such schemes are discussed in the following sections.

Rules of Coding

Since coding is the process by which responses are classified into meaningful categories, the initial rule of coding is that the numbers assigned must make intuitive sense. For example, higher scores on a variable should result in the assignment of higher codes. This is most easily demonstrated with interval-level variables. A person who is older than another should receive a higher code on age. If a person is 28-year-old, the code would be 28 intuitively. A person who is 46 should receive a code higher than that for the 28-year-old—probably 46 if coded in years. Even if age categories are grouped ordinally, higher age should be associated with a higher grouping code. That makes intuitive sense.

However, for some variables (nominal ones), by definition there is no intuitively pleasing rationale for the assignment of numbers. Someone with a gender of 2 ("female") does not have more gender than one with 1 ("male"). Moreover, it would not make any difference whether you assigned the numbers 6 and 4, respectively, or even 4 and 6. However, when it comes to the reliability of coding, you would probably want to confine coding numbers to those starting with 0 or 1 and increasing by 1 over each category. Otherwise, you run the risk of miscodings like 4 and 7 (see "Editing and Cleaning the Data" later on).

Theory and Deductive Coding. Once intuitive sense has been satisfied, the factors of theory, mutual exclusivity, exhaustiveness, and detail must be factored into coding decisions. Linkage to **theory** assumes that the researcher has some idea from the literature of the types of responses to expect from a respondent. This drives the attention to mutual exclusivity and exhaustiveness but also dimensionality. For example, if the researcher is interested in examining "liberalism," theory would demonstrate that this concept is multidimensional. A person who is a social liberal (e.g., one who believes in a woman's right to birth choice) may not be a fiscal liberal (e.g., the same person does not believe that the government should fund contraception). In this case, a high score on social liberalism does not correlate with a high score on fiscal liberalism. Theory predicts that this may be the case.

Theory can be used to construct response categories before the instrument is administered to potential respondents. Thus **deductive coding** can be used. The respondents or those who administer the instrument can classify their responses in preestablished categories, as is the case with closed-ended questions. Pretesting the instrument can modify the expectations drawn from theory, especially when drawing data from a special population.

Inductive Coding. When a study is exploratory or when there is little theory informing the researcher about which responses to expect, **inductive coding** may be appropriate. In inductive coding, the coding scheme is designed on the basis of a representative sample of responses to questions (particularly open-ended questions), data from documents, or data collected through participant observation (see Chapter 12). Once a coding scheme is identified, it is applied to the remainder of the data set. Consider the responses to the following question, designed to determine women's reactions to being abused by a husband or a live-in partner.[1]

> In general, if a man physically abuses his wife or live-in partner, what do
> you think the woman should do?

---

1. Adapted from *Spouse Abuse in Texas: A Study of Women's Attitudes and Experiences* (Huntsville, Texas: Criminal Justice Center, 1983).

1. She should stay and try to work out the problem.
2. She should leave the house or apartment.
3. She should call a social service agency for advice.
4. She should call the police.
5. She should obtain a temporary restraining order against the abuser.
6. She should call a friend or relative for help.
7. Other (specify) _____
8. Don't know/refused to answer.
9. Missing.

In an inductive coding scheme, the responses mentioned most frequently are included in a coding scheme to analyze the data. In the preceding example, values 1 through 6 were mentioned frequently enough to merit their own categories. Values 7 through 9 were added once the inductive approach generated the first categories. In a final coding scheme, the "other" category is used for less frequently mentioned responses.

Categories are not always easily identified. Often the process of constructing a comprehensive coding scheme is a long one and involves switching back and forth between the raw data and the evolving scheme until the latter is applicable and ties in with the general purpose of the study. Paul Lazarsfeld and Alan Barton, examining some general principles of coding, illustrate this process by using some of the coding schemes constructed in the classic study *The American Soldier*.[2] In an attempt to determine which factors offset combat stress, the investigators of the American soldier drew up a preliminary list of categories on the basis of many responses:

1. Coercive formal authority.
2. Leadership practices (e.g., encouragement).
3. Informal group:
    a. Affectional support.
    b. Code of behavior.
    c. Provision of realistic security and power.
4. Convictions about the war and the enemy.
5. Desire to complete the job by winning war, to go home.
6. Prayer and personal philosophies.

These preliminary coding schemes enabled the investigators in this study to classify the raw data and substantially reduce the number of responses to be analyzed. A further modification was introduced after it was noted that formal sanctions are often more effective when channeled through informal group sanctions and internal sanctions. Conversely, the norms of the informal groups are influenced by formal sanctions as well as by individual conscience. On this basis, the responses were reanalyzed, and

2. Paul F. Lazarsfeld and Alan Barton, "Qualitative Measurement in the Social Sciences: Classification, Typologies, and Indices," in *The Policy Sciences*, ed. Daniel Lerner and Harold D. Lasswell (Stanford, Calif.: Stanford University Press, 1951), p. 160, and Samuel A. Stouffer, *The American Soldier* (New York: Wiley, 1965).

Table 14.1
How Norms Bear on Individual Behavior in Combat

Underlying Source of Norms	Channels
Norms of formal authorities	*Direct:* (a) Formal sanctions (b) Internal sanctions *Via group norms:* (c) Informal group sanctions (d) Internal sanctions
Norms of informal groups	(e) Formal group sanctions (f) Internal sanctions
Individual norms	(g) Internal sanctions

From Paul F. Lazarsfeld and Alan Barton, "Qualitative Measurement in the Social Sciences: Classification, Typologies, and Indices," in *The Policy Sciences*, ed. Daniel Lerner and Harold D. Lasswell (Stanford, Calif.: Stanford University Press, 1951), p. 161. Reprinted with permission.

additional information was obtained to produce a modified coding scheme (Table 14.1).

The following responses conform to the modified categories found in Table 14.1:

(a) I fight because I'll be punished if I quit.
(b) I fight because it's my duty to my country, the army, the government; it would be wrong for me to quit.
(c) I fight because I'll lose the respect of my buddies if I quit.
(d) I fight because it would be wrong to let my buddies down.
(e) You have to look out for your buddies even if it means violating orders, or they won't look out for you.
(f) You have to look out for your buddies even if it means violating orders because it would be wrong to leave them behind.
(g) I am fighting because I believe in democracy and hate fascism.

The chief advantages of the inductive approach are its flexibility and its richness, which enable the researcher to generate explanations from the findings. Moreover, it allows a variety of coding schemes to be applied to the same observation, and it often suggests new categories as well. The shortcoming of this method is that researchers may be bogged down by the mass of details they try to explain the data. Sometimes too little context is preserved for the coder to determine which details are trivial and can therefore be eliminated.

Mutual Exclusivity.   Under the rule of **mutual exclusivity**, the coding categories for each variable must be designed so that each case or unit of analysis would be coded in one and only one category of the variable. For example, in terms of religious preference, the use of Protestant and Methodist as categories would not be mutually exclusive as Methodists are considered to be a subset of Protestants. Methodists would thus erroneously be assigned to two categories. Theory should determine whether distinctions such as Methodists and Lutherans are more important than those between broader categories such as Protestant and Catholic, especially since Lutherans may be more like Catholics on some dimensions (e.g., fundamentalism) than Methodists.

Exhaustiveness.   The rule of **exhaustiveness** refers to the notion that the enumeration of categories is sufficient to exhaust all the relevant categories expected of respondents—each and every response or behavior can be classified without a substantial number being classified as "other." Again, this is driven by theory and knowledge of the expected sample. An example of a lack of exhaustiveness is the common classification of marital-relational status into four categories only: "married," "single," "divorced," and "widowed." For respondents who are "living together" but not legally married, the requirement of exhaustiveness is violated since they would not fit into the coding scheme. If the sample included only junior high school students, not only would the original coding scheme be exhaustive, but it would also be irrelevant (the variable would be a constant) since virtually all junior high school students are unmarried.

Detail.   The **detail** of categories in a coding scheme depends on the research question, but some general guidelines exist. First, when in doubt, add another category. One can always collapse categories to generalize responses (see Appendixes A and B for examples of how to do this with statistical computer packages); one cannot, however, disaggregate responses coded to a more general level. Second, let either theory or your knowledge of the sample modify the categories that would be dictated by theory or intuition. It would make no sense to ask medical doctors to report their incomes in the categories under $5,000, $5,000 to $10,000, $10,000 to $15,000, $15,000 to $20,000, and $20,000 and above, whereas those distinctions would be appropriate when surveying people living in poverty.

Codebook Construction

Once you have developed a coding scheme for each of the variables used in a research project, this information should be compiled in a **codebook**. Codebooks can vary in their detail; however, all good codebooks contain information regarding each variable's name or number, where each is located, the coding scheme, and codes for missing data. The codebook serves as a guide for the coders who will translate the raw data onto an input device for later use in computerized statistical analysis. It is also a reference for the principal researcher and any other researchers who wish to use the data set. For research involving the use of surveys, the actual survey question is often included in the codebook. A subset of the codebook used in Appendix A is reproduced in Exhibit 14.1.

Exhibit 14.1

A Codebook Format: Cleveland Poverty Survey

Variable Name		Column Numbers
IDNUMBER	Interviewee identification number	1–3
	Code Actual Number	
	(001-528)	
Q1	Highest Grade Completed	4
	1 = 1–8	
	2 = 9–11	
	3 = 12	
	4 = 13–15	
	5 = 16	
	6 = 17 +	
	.	
	.	
	.	
Q4	Gender	7
	1 = Male	
	2 = Female	
Q5	Weekly Take-Home Pay Current/Last Job	8–11
	Code in Actual Dollars	
Q6	Hours Worked per Week Current/Last Job	12–13
	Code in Actual Hours	
Q7	General Health Condition	14
	1 = Excellent	
	2 = Very Good	
	3 = Good	
	4 = Fair	
	5 = Poor	
	9 = DK/NA	
Q8	Good Education Way to Get Ahead	15
	1 = Strongly Agree	
	2 = Agree	
	3 = Somewhat Agree	
	4 = Somewhat Disagree	
	5 = Disagree	
	6 = Disagree Strongly	
	9 = DK/NA	
Q9	Reading Ability	16
	1 = Excellent	
	2 = Good	
	3 = Fair	
	4 = Poor	
	9 = DK/Na	

Note that each variable in Exhibit 14.1 is identified by its name, the coding scheme employed (values), the columns on the input device in which the values for the variable are found, which values stand for a missing value, and any other special coding rules employed on a variable-by-variable basis. Any researcher should be able to use the documentation to reconstruct the data set from the information contained in the codebook.

Coding Reliability and Data Entry Devices

Once the codebook is constructed, the data need to be "coded" or transferred to a form from which someone can enter them into a computer for storage and analysis. For instance, someone must translate a circled number on a questionnaire to the proper column or "field" represented by the variable (and defined in the codebook). Raw data can be coded in a number of ways to facilitate efficient computer entry. After dealing with human coder reliability, we shall consider reliability and the use of transfer sheets, edge coding, optical scanning, and direct data entry.

Coding Reliability

Studies with a well-constructed codebook, precoded, closed-ended questions, and proper coder training experience fewer problems with coder reliability than other studies, all things being equal. Coders for these studies do not have to exercise much of their own judgment in deciding what code to give a response. One of the biggest problems in these studies is making sure that the coders place the code in the correct column. It is standard practice to recheck or verify a sample of each coder's work to ensure that they have not become lax. The coding devices we will discuss demonstrate the tradeoffs for coder reliability based on choice of device.

However, in the coding of open-ended questions or other nonstructured material, coders are required to exercise more judgment in classifying responses. When given rules cannot be applied automatically, different coders may arrive at different interpretations. In such instances, the coding process becomes unreliable, a problem that is just as serious as the unreliability of interviewers or observers. Indeed, very often the coding phase of data analysis contributes the largest component of processing error. To increase coding reliability, keep the schemes as simple as possible and train coders thoroughly. The simplest solution is to compare the codings of two or more coders and resolve all differences by letting them decide on problematic items. An example of instructions to coders to ensure reliability is presented in Exhibit 14.2.

Another problem concerning discrepancies in interpretation of responses is much less frequently discussed in the literature. It has to do with differences between coder and respondent in interpreting the meaning of a

Exhibit 14.2
General Coding Instructions

A. Coding must be done in red *pencil*.

B. Never erase any interviewer-circled codes or comments. If the questionnaire must be corrected, draw a line through the code circled in error. Do not make it impossible to read what was done originally. Please note that green marks are field department corrections.

C. Every column must have a code, and no column may contain more than one clearly circled code.

D. For those questions noted *FLAG*: this instruction applies to questions where special coding problems have been anticipated. Coders will be provided with a supply of little clips (flags) to attach to the page where the problem occurs. Coders may also flag all other areas in the questionnaire where information is incomplete or unclear and requires the supervisor's attention.

E. For those questions noted *LIST*: record on an "OTHER" list form the questionnaire identification and all verbatim comments relating to the response to be listed. A separate list should be kept for each question. If, however, a question has more than one listed code, keep a separate list for each code. Record at the top of each form the study number, the question number, the deck and column number, and the listed code. In most surveys, all "Other (SPECIFY)" codes are listed.

F. The "no answer" (NA) and "refusal" code for this questionnaire is '9' in a one-column field, '99' in a two-column field, etc. NA is coded when the respondent does not give an answer, when the interviewer fails to ask a question or to record the answer, when the written information is contradictory or too vague to code, and when the coder needs to supply a code in order to resolve a tricky skip pattern. NA is allowed for every question except those specifically excepted in the codebook, such as race and sex.

G. The "not applicable" (NAP) code is "R," which means "reject" or "blank" to our keypunchers. NAP is coded when a question was not supposed to have been asked (i.e., because of directions to skip it).

H. If "don't know" (DK) is not a preprinted code, then DK is coded '8' in a one-column field, '98' in a two-column field, '998' in a three-column field, etc. If DK has been listed along with other responses in one question, edit out (or do not code) the DK response.

From Roper Center for Public Opinion Research, *General Social Survey, 1972–1989: Cumulative Codebook* (Storrs: University of Connecticut, 1989).

response. This question was formulated in a study that attempted to assess whether respondent and coder would reach agreement as to the meaning of the response.[3]

In other words, how would the research participants themselves code their answers within the set of categories provided by the researcher? If the research participants who provide the answers could also serve as coders, would their code differ from that of other coders, or would the research participants code their own responses as they are coded by others? Sixty-four college students were asked to complete a questionnaire that included fixed-alternative questions as well as open-ended ones. Later on, every research participant independently coded the questionnaires of several other participants as well as his or her own. A research participant's coding of his or her own response was compared with the way that response was coded by others. The comparison revealed significant differences, a consistent pattern indicating that the coding of a response deviated from the research participant's actual attitudes, the direction of this deviation being determined by the content of the item. The less structured the item, the larger the discrepancy between the respondent's interpretation and that of a coder. These findings raise some serious doubts regarding the process of coding nonstructured material. It is clear that such bias might affect relationships between variables investigated.

Coding Devices

Transfer Sheets.   Years ago, all data were key-punched onto computer cards and read into the computer. Although such cards are no longer used, data are often stored in lines containing up to 80 characters—the number of columns on the old computer card. **Transfer sheets** (or "coding sheets") traditionally resemble computer cards, each line being a separate "card image" with 80 columns across the horizontal axis (Figure 14.1). Coders then transfer the information from the data source to sets of columns or "fields" specified in the codebook.

Each line of data on the transfer sheet should begin with the unit's identification number. If more than one line of data is necessary, it is customary to begin the second line with the identification number and another variable field indicating that it is the second line of data for that case. Once the data are recorded on a transfer sheet, the lines of data are keyed onto a storage device such as a floppy disk, hard disk, or magnetic tape.

This two-step process usually involves different people at each stage—coding and keying. Every additional time the data are handled increases the

---

3. Kenneth C. W. Kammeyer and Julius A. Roth, "Coding Response to Open-ended Questions," in *Sociological Methodology*, ed. Herbert L. Costner (San Francisco: Jossey-Bass, 1971).

Figure 14.1
A Transfer Sheet

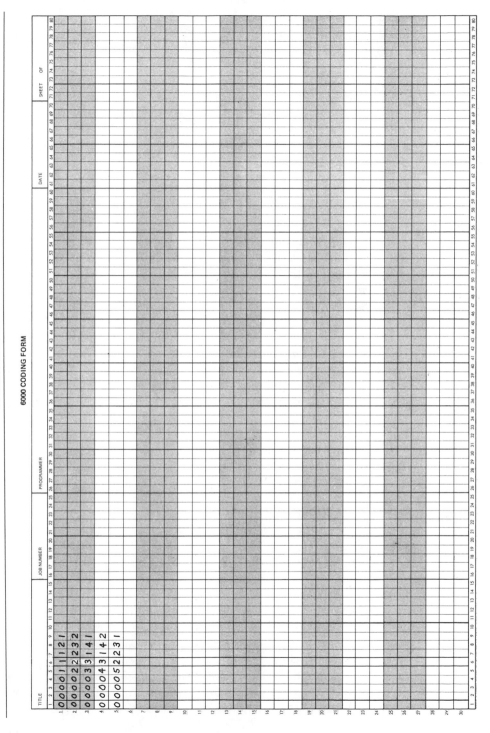

possibility of miscodings and threatens reliability. Verification at both steps enhances reliability. Coding via transfer sheets is useful with complex questionnaires and when gathering data from a number of sources.

Edge Coding.   The use of **edge coding** eliminates the need for transfer sheets. In this method, coders transfer questionnaire information directly onto spaces at the outside edge of the instrument. Note that in Figure 14.2 the column numbers associated with the variable are indicated. A data entry worker then keys the information from the edge directly to the data storage device. Reliability is enhanced as the coders' eyes do not have to leave the instrument, and they do not have to keep close track of column positions, as is the case with transfer sheets.

Optical Scanning.   Coders may also transfer data onto optical scanning sheets like the ones often used in computer-graded multiple-choice examinations. Scanning machines read black pencil marks and produce the data files automatically. This enhances reliability since it eliminates the data entry worker's handling of the data. However, poorly designed scanner sheets may affect the coder's ability to keep track of item numbers.

Since the use of **optical scanning** is so common, respondents may be asked directly to fill in scanning sheets with their responses. The scanning sheets should be designed specifically for the instrument to increase the ease and accuracy with which the respondents can complete the survey.

Direct Data Entry.   Perhaps the most important innovations in coding have come from **direct data entry**. There are two forms of direct data coding: coding from a questionnaire and coding by telephone interview. Both forms are based on computer programs that display each questionnaire item on a screen and prompt the coder-interviewer to input the response directly on the screen.

Material coded from questionnaires must be edited to ensure that missing responses have a designated code for the input. The coder than keys in the response. When a case is completed, the computer program adds the information directly into the raw data file. Again this reduces the number of data handlers, which enhances reliability.

Computer-assisted telephone interviewing (CATI) is a highly sophisticated system that greatly reduces miscoding. Interviewers read questionnaire items directly from the computer screen and input the respondent's response as it is given. If the coder keys in an inappropriate code (a value that is not designated for the particular variable), the coder is prompted to give a "real" value. CATI also automatically skips questions or jumps to others as a result of filter questions, thus avoiding having the interviewer flip through screens to access the appropriate next item. Therefore, not only does the program increase coder reliability, but it also ensures that respondents do not answer inappropriate questions. The sophistication of CATI technology has sharply reduced the use of mail surveys because of its high response rate and checks on reliability of data collection and coding.

Figure 14.2
An Edge-coded Questionnaire

THE UNIVERSITY OF WISCONSIN—MILWAUKEE
College of Letters and Science
Department of Political Science

N⁰   2 1 8 3

FOR PROJECT
USE ONLY

Civil Libertarian Project

INSTRUCTIONS: For each of the following questions please mark the answer that comes closest to the way you feel about the issue. There are no "right" or "wrong" answers — please answer the questions as honestly as possible. Answer each of the questions in the order in which it appears. If you wish to make additional comments on any of the specific questions or on the issues in general, use the space at the end of the questionnaire. Your opinions are extremely important for understanding these complex civil liberty issues — we greatly appreciate your cooperation!

We would like to begin with a few questions about your relationship with the American Civil Liberties Union (ACLU).

6 _1_

1a. About how many years have you been a member of ACLU? _____ years.

7 __ 8 __

1b. Why did you join the ACLU? That is, was there any particular cause that the ACLU was supporting or defending that prompted you to join the organization?
  ☐ Specific cause(s) – – → Which cause(s) _____
  ☐ No specific cause
  ☐ Don't remember _____

9 __

1c. Have you been very active in the affairs of the ACLU? For instance, have you done any of the following in the last five years?

		Yes	No	Don't Remember	
a. made financial contributions (beyond membership dues)		☐	☐	☐	10 __
b. written letters to ACLU leaders		☐	☐	☐	11 __
c. served in a leadership role		☐	☐	☐	12 __
d. attended local meetings of ACLU		☐	☐	☐	13 __
e. read ACLU newsletters and literature		☐	☐	☐	14 __
f. written letters to public officials at the urging of ACLU		☐	☐	☐	15 __
g. attended an ACLU party or benefit		☐	☐	☐	16 __
h. done volunteer work for ACLU (e.g., office assistance, phone calling, etc.)		☐	☐	☐	17 __
i. participated in a court case or public hearing at the urging of ACLU		☐	☐	☐	18 __

1d. The ACLU publishes a number of specialized newsletters and magazines that not all of the members receive. We would like to know if you have received any of these publications and, if so, how frequently you found the time to read them. For each of the following please check the most appropriate box.

	I have not received this publication	I received the publication and usually read it	I received the publication but rarely had time to read it	Don't Know	
a. Civil Liberties Review	☐	☐	☐	☐	19 __
b. Children's Rights Report	☐	☐	☐	☐	20 __
c. First Principles	☐	☐	☐	☐	21 __
d. Notes from the Women's Rights Project	☐	☐	☐	☐	22 __
e. Civil Liberties Alert	☐	☐	☐	☐	23 __
f. The Privacy Report	☐	☐	☐	☐	24 __
g. Civil Liberties	☐	☐	☐	☐	25 __

1e. Over the course of your membership, how satisfied have you been, in general, with the positions ACLU has taken on major issues?
  ☐ always in agreement   ☐ usually in disagreement   ☐ don't know
  ☐ usually in agreement   ☐ always in disagreement

26 __

2a. There are always some people whose ideas are considered bad or dangerous by other people. For instance, somebody who is against all churches and religion.

	Yes	No	No Opinion	
a. If such a person wanted to make a speech in your community against churches and religion, should he/she be allowed to speak or not?	☐	☐	☐	27 __
b. Should such a person be allowed to organize a march against churches and religion in your community?	☐	☐	☐	28 __
c. Should such a person be allowed to teach in a college or university, or not?	☐	☐	☐	29 __
d. If some people in your community suggested that a book he/she wrote against churches and religion should be taken out of your public library, would you favor removing the book, or not?	☐	☐	☐	30 __

Source: Reprinted by permission of Greenwood Publishing Group, Inc., Westport, CT, from *Civil Liberties and the Nazis* by James L. Gibson and Richard D. Bingham. Copyright © 1985, Praeger Publishers, New York, NY.

Editing and Cleaning the Data

Editing and cleaning the data are important steps in data processing that should always precede analysis of the collected information. **Data editing** occurs both during and after the coding phase. Some editing is performed by the coders themselves and involves checking for errors and omissions and making sure that all interview schedules have been completed as required. Most of the editing, however, especially in large-scale surveys, is performed by a supervisor who reviews each completed questionnaire to evaluate the interviews' reliability and check for inconsistencies in responses. For example, the National Opinion Research Center, which conducts the General Social Survey, instructs the supervisor to check that all filter (contingency) questions have been correctly marked so that the data will fit into the correct skip (or "go to") pattern. If more than one response is given to the filter question or if the filter question was left blank, the supervisor will determine what the code should be.

Data cleaning is the proofreading of the data to catch and correct errors and inconsistent codes. Most data cleaning of large-scale efforts is performed by special computer programs designed to test for logical consistency set up in the coding specification.[4] Though many questions are answered and coded independently, others are interconnected and must be internally consistent. For example, if a respondent has no children, all questions relating to children must be coded NA ("no answer") or left blank. Similarly, it would indicate an error to have a respondent who has two children to give her age as 5 years old.

Another function of data cleaning is checking for wild codes. For example, the question "Do you believe there is a life after death?" may have legitimate codes of 1 for "yes," 2 for "no," 8 for "undecided," and 9 for "no answer." Any code other than these four codes would be considered illegitimate. The simplest procedure to check for wild codes is to generate a frequency distribution (discussed in Chapter 15) for each variable. This method of data cleaning is also outlined in Appendixes A and B.

Using Computers in Social Science Research

By now everyone is affected by and familiar with the use of computers in many facets of life. Not only are our credit card bills produced by computers, but we can also call the credit card company and use our touch-tone phones to access its computer to learn our available credit amount. In fact, computers are calling our answering machines, alerting us that we have qualified for "valuable prizes"!

4. For example, Winona Ailkins, *EDIT: The NORC Cleaning Program: A Program to Develop Sequential Files* (Chicago: National Opinion Research Center, 1975).

Computers have been used in social science research for decades. Computer technology has changed drastically during that time. However, the rationale for their use has remained the same across the years. Computers are simply tools that allow us more easily to store, process, access, and analyze data sets. Once we understand the research methods and statistics discussed in this book, we can let a computer calculate statistics and provide printouts of the results. However, it is up to the researcher to supply correct and reliable data, choose statistics that are appropriate for the level of data, and interpret the results properly.

Types of Computers

There are currently three basic kinds of computers used to analyze social science data. **Mainframe computers** are large central-site computers that simultaneously handle the computing needs of many users. Users tend to "time-share" the capacity of the central processing unit so that the greatest number of users can access the computer at any given time. Mainframe sites also tend to have the capacity for reading magnetic data tapes like the type that data repositories send to members or clients. The Interuniversity Consortium for Political and Social Research at the University of Michigan is the largest repository for social science data. Besides storing academic research, it holds the data sets from national opinion firms like Roper, Harris, and NORC. Mainframes also support the major statistical packages used to analyze social science data. In that way individual researchers and students do not have to purchase multiple software packages.

Minicomputers are similar to mainframes in that they can support software packages, which are in turn accessed by multiple users. The number of users is smaller than is typical of mainframes. Dedicated terminals and networked **personal computers (PCs)** access the programs and data files in a miniature version of the time-share model.

Widespread social science research via PCs is a relatively recent phenomenon. As the price of PCs became affordable, the major statistical software supporters developed PC versions of the mainframe software used for years. For example, both SPSS and SAS (described in Appendixes A and B) have PC versions. This allowed researchers to make an easy transition to the PC. A large number of PC-only statistical packages have also been developed. The best explanation of what package a particular researcher will use is probably the one to which he or she is first introduced.

The major difference between the PC and the other computers is that the PC is self-contained. It is not necessary to have any physical linkage between the PC and any other unit. The simplest example of a PC is a keyboard, a screen, and a single floppy disk drive. However, most non-student-oriented versions of major statistical packages require a hard disk and the added capacity of a math coprocessor to enhance the researcher's ability to calculate complex statistics and manipulate larger data sets.

Linkages through Communication Networks

Not long ago, researchers felt the need to choose the medium (mainframe, mini, PC) by which they would do their computing or risk having to learn a variety of systems. The initial method to link up with computers from non-traditional remote sites was through **modems**, which allow terminals to access computers over regular telephone lines. The old acoustic coupler, a device within which a telephone receiver was inserted, has given way to modems that do not require the receiver itself to transmit. More typical now are "voice over data" telephone lines, which allow the simultaneous transmission of interaction with computers while conversations can take place on the phone without having to have multiple telephone lines. Modems for these types of lines are often within the telephone itself.

Another linkage that has occurred is between computing hardware. You can "upload" information from your PC to the mainframe or "download" information to your PC. The ability to accomplish this required that the different computer stations maintain input and output devices compatible with the larger or smaller system.

A third linkage has been between software programs. For example, statistical output generated by SPSS-PC+ can be directly input into various word processing files for generating reports and manuscripts. This compatibility has enhanced the interconnection between software packages used by researchers.

Linkage in the 1990s surpasses that of merely compatible software programs. Since the 1970s the technology has been available to link workstations through local area networks (LANs). Unfortunately, only one computer in a network can transmit data on the network at a time. In other words, the network partners share a common line of transmission. If one partner is transmitting a lot of information, the network can get bogged down and stall.

Newer technologies will speed transmissions, thus reducing congestion in networks. Other advances in switching technologies within networks will make the transmission routes more efficient in much the same way as long-distance phone calls are routed today. John Markoff reports that entirely new computer networks are being developed that will combine voice, data, and video transmissions simultaneously.[5] So-called multimedia computing will have a great impact on the form by which social scientists compute and communicate their findings in the future.

5. John Markoff, "Soon: Faster and Wiser Networks," *New York Times*, April 3, 1991, p. D6.

Summary

1. Data processing is a link between data collection and data analysis whereby observations are transformed into codes that are amenable to quantitative analysis. At the first stage of data processing, numerous individual observations are classified into a smaller number of categories so as to simplify the description and analysis of the data. Such systems are referred to as coding schemes.

2. Coding schemes must be linked to theory and the problem under study, which dictates the categories to be included. Other requirements of a coding scheme are that it be exhaustive and be mutually exclusive so that all observations can be classified, each only once. Coding schemes enable the translation of the data into a format that allows computer processing. The translation is usually guided by a codebook, which presents the schemes with their assigned values together with coding instructions.

3. A variety of coding devices are used to organize the raw data. These include transfer sheets, edge coding, optical scanning, and direct data entry. The choice of method depends on the format of the research and the technology available to the researcher. Each has implications for coding reliability; the direct data entry of data gathering through phone interviews ensures the greatest degree of reliability.

4. Social scientists have been using computers to organize the research process for many years. Technology is rapidly changing in this area, although students may encounter mainframe computers, minicomputers, and personal computers in the same class. Software compatibility and communications networking will be important features of future technological developments in computing.

Key Terms for Review

code

coding scheme

theory

deductive coding

inductive coding

mutual exclusivity

exhaustiveness

detail

codebook

transfer sheets

edge coding

optical scanning

direct data entry

data editing

data cleaning

mainframe computer

minicomputer

personal computer (PC)

modem

Study Questions

1. Discuss the differences between inductive and deductive coding schemes.
2. What are the main criteria of coding schemes?
3. Describe the steps involved in determining coding reliability.
4. What are the different types of data processing?

Additional Readings

Cozby, Paul C. *Using Computers in the Behavioral Sciences*. Mountain View, Calif.: Mayfield, 1986.

Flaherty, Douglas. *Humanizing the Computer*. Belmont, Calif.: Wadsworth, 1986.

Leff, S. Lawrence. *Data Processing: The Easy Way*. New York: Barron's, 1984.

Lefkowitz, Jerry M. *Introduction to Statistical Computer Packages*. North Scituate, Mass.: Duxbury Press, 1985.

CHAPTER 15

The Univariate Distribution

In this chapter, we explain the main characteristics of single-variable distributions. First we define and describe the frequency distribution; then we focus on measures of central tendency and measures of dispersion. Finally, we deal with the general form of distributions, emphasizing the normal curve.

S INCE THE 1950s, ALL SOCIAL SCIENCE disciplines have experienced a rapid increase in the use of statistics. They are essential to the field. Without statistics, we could not see the patterns and regularities in the phenomena we study. We need statistical methods to organize data, to display information in a meaningful manner, and to describe and interpret the observations in terms that will help us evaluate our hypotheses.

The word *statistics* has a dual meaning. Although it is used to refer to numbers—per capita income and batting averages and the like—it is also a field of study. We refer to the latter usage in our discussion, which will cover some of the basic applications of statistics in the social sciences.

The Role of Statistics

The field of statistics involves methods for describing and analyzing data and for making decisions or inferences about phenomena represented by the data. Methods in the first category are referred to as *descriptive statistics;* methods in the second are called *inferential statistics.*

Descriptive statistics enable the researcher to summarize and organize data in an effective and meaningful way. They provide tools for describing collections of statistical observations and reducing information to an understandable form.

Inferential statistics allow the researcher to make decisions or inferences by interpreting data patterns. The process involves noting whether an expected pattern designated by the theory and hypotheses is actually found in the observations. We might hypothesize, for example, that blue-collar workers are politically more conservative than professionals. To decide whether this hypothesis is true, we might survey blue-collar workers and professionals, asking them about their political views. We would then make comparisons between these groups, using descriptive statistics, and employ inferential statistics to determine whether the differences between the groups support our expectations.

Both descriptive and inferential statistics help in developing explanations for complex social phenomena that deal with relationships between variables. Statistics provides the tools to analyze, represent, and interpret those relationships.

Frequency Distribution

After data have been coded and prepared for automatic processing, they are ready for analysis. The first task is to construct frequency distributions to examine the pattern of response to each of the independent and dependent variables under investigation. (In the following discussion, *responses, answers, observations, cases, acts,* and *behavior* are used interchangeably.) A frequency distribution of a single variable, known as a *univariate frequency distribution*, is the frequency of observations in each category of a variable. For example, an examination of the pattern of response to the variable "religious affiliation" would involve a description of the number of respondents who claimed they were Protestants, Catholics, Jews, Muslims, and so on.

To construct a **frequency distribution**, the researcher simply lists the categories of the variable and counts the number of observations in each. Table 15.1 is an example of the standard form of a univariate frequency distribution. The table has five rows, the first four being the categories of the variable, which appear in the left-hand column, and the right-hand column shows the number of observations in each category. This number is called a *frequency,* and is usually denoted by the letter f. The last row (marked N) is the total of all frequencies appearing in the table. When the categories are mutually exclusive so that each observation is classified only once, the total

Table 15.1
General Form of a Univariate Frequency Distribution

Category	Frequency (f)
I	f
II	f
III	f
IV	f
Total	N

number of frequencies is equal to the total number of observations in the sample.

With nominal variables, the categories may be listed in any arbitrary order. Thus the variable "gender" may be described with the category "male" or the category "female" listed first. However, the categories of ordinal variables represent different rankings and are therefore arranged in order. As an illustration, consider the frequency distribution in Table 15.2, from a study that examined child abuse. The variable "child abuse" is listed by type of abuse—"physical," "sexual," "emotional."

Frequency Distributions with Interval Variables

When summarizing interval variables in frequency distributions, one must first decide on the number of categories to use and the cutting points between them. As interval variables are ordinarily continuous, the classification into distinct categories may be quite arbitrary. For example, age may be classified into one-year, two-year, or five-year groups. Similarly, income can be classified in a number of ways.

The intervals are usually of equal width, but the width depends both on the number of observations to be classified and the research purpose. The larger the number of observations, the wider the intervals become. However, wider categories also result in greater loss of detailed information. A general

Table 15.2
Distribution of Child Abuse, 1989

Category	f
Physical abuse	311,200
Sexual abuse	138,000
Emotional abuse	174,000
Total	623,200

From Mark E. Siegel, Nancy R. Jacobs, and Carol D. Foster (eds.), "Domestic Violence: No Longer behind the Curtains" (Wyle, Texas: Information Plus, 1989), p. 37.

| | | | Interval Midpoint |
Age in Years	f	Real Limits	(x)
1–2	6	.5–2.5	1.5
3–4	4	2.5–4.5	3.5
5–6	10	4.5–6.5	5.5
7–8	3	6.5–8.5	7.5

Table 15.3
A Frequency Distribution of Family Size

guideline to follow is that the intervals should not be so wide that two measurements included in it have a difference between them that is considered important. For example, if an age difference of one year is not of special significance for cognitive development but a difference of two is especially important, the intervals chosen could be 1–2, 3–4, 5–6. The intervals and their frequency for a hypothetical population are presented in the first two columns of Table 15.3.

The *real limits* express the interval boundaries that extend one-half of one year on either side of the interval. The interval width, expressed as w, is the difference between the real limits of the interval:

$$w = U - L$$

where U is the upper real limit and L is the lower real limit. For the last interval of Table 15.3, the width is

$$2 = 8.5 - 6.5$$

The midpoint of each interval, symbolized by x, is a single value, representing the class interval. It is obtained by adding half the interval width to the lower real limit of a class.

$$x = L + \frac{w}{2}$$

Thus for the second class interval of Table 15.3, the midpoint is

$$x = 2.5 + \frac{2}{2} = 3.5$$

Percentage Distributions

Summarizing the data by constructing frequency distributions of single variables is only the first step in data analysis. Next the frequencies must be converted into measures that can be interpreted meaningfully. An absolute frequency is meaningless in itself; it must be compared with other frequencies. For instance, the significance of 2,000 registered Democrats in one commu-

Table 15.4
Social-Class Distribution: Rural Population (in Absolute
Frequencies and Percentages)

Social Class	f	%
Upper middle	60	15
Middle	300	75
Lower	40	10
Total	400	100

nity can be assessed only in relation to the number of all registered voters, to the number of registered Republicans, or to the number of registered Democrats in other communities.

Frequencies expressed in comparable numbers are called *proportions* or *percentages*. A proportion is obtained by dividing the frequency of a category by the total number of responses in the distribution. When multiplied by 100, a proportion becomes a percentage. Proportions are usually expressed as f/N and percentages as $f/N \times 100$. Both proportions and percentages reflect the relative weight of a specific category in the distribution. For example, the relative weight of physical child abuse in Table 15.2 is expressed by the proportion $311,200/623,200 = .499$ or by the percentage $311,200/623,200 \times 100 = 49.9$ percent. These figures indicate that about one out of every two cases of child abuse involves physical abuse.

Proportions and percentages permit the comparison of two or more frequency distributions. Note, for instance, the social-class distribution of rural and urban populations displayed in Tables 15.4 and 15.5. Although there are more middle class respondents in rural areas (300 versus 200), a straightforward comparison of the absolute frequencies is misleading since the total N is different in each population. Instead, to assess the relative weight of the classes within each distribution, the frequencies should be expressed in percentages, which reveal that the impression gained from the absolute frequencies was indeed misleading. Whereas the middle class constituted 75 percent of the rural population, it was 80 percent of the urban group. The new figures make it easier to compare the two frequency distributions.

Table 15.5
Social-Class Distribution: Urban Population (in Absolute
Frequencies and in Percentages)

Social Class	f	%
Upper middle	20	8
Middle	200	80
Lower	30	12
Total	250	100

Measures of Central Tendency

When only a short summary of the data is required, the entire distribution need not be presented. A description of the educational level of Americans showing a frequency distribution of education in America could be rather cumbersome. Instead, one could point out that most Americans are high school graduates or that the average level of education in the United States is 12 years.

In most distributions, the observations tend to cluster around a central value. For instance, an income distribution can be characterized by the most common income or an average income. Similarly, attitude distributions cluster around a certain range. This property can be used when attempting to represent a distribution by a single value. The use of such a value not only allows for economy in describing the distribution but also facilitates comparison of different distributions. One is able to compare the average income in the United States with the average income in England or to contrast the average intelligence scores of Russian students with those of American students.

Statistical measures that reflect a "typical" or an "average" characteristic of a frequency distribution are referred to as *measures of central tendency*. The three most commonly used are the mode, the median, and the arithmetic mean.

Mode

The **mode** is the category or observation that appears most frequently in the distribution. It is used as a measure of central tendency mostly with distributions of nominal variables. To identify the mode, one singles out the category containing the largest number of responses. For example, consider the distribution of religious groups presented in Table 15.6. The distribution includes five categories; the first, the Protestant group, is the most predominant. This category is thus the mode of the distribution.

Table 15.6
Frequency Distribution of Religious Groups

Religious Group	f
Protestant	62
Catholic	52
Jewish	10
Muslim	12
Buddhist	2
Total	138

Most distributions are unimodal; that is, they include only one category in which most of the cases are concentrated. At times, however, the distribution is bimodal: it has two such maximum points. Such a pattern usually exists in distributions that combine two populations. For instance, the distribution of the heights of adults is bimodal; it comprises both men and women, and each gender is characterized by a different typical height.

The advantage of the mode is that it can be easily identified by inspection, and therefore it can be used as a first and quick indicator of the central tendency in a distribution. However, though easy to calculate, the mode is a sensitive indicator. Its position might shift whenever the manner of the distribution's division into categories is altered. Therefore, it is not a very stable measure of central tendency.

Median

The **median** is a positional measure that divides the distribution into two equal parts. It is defined as the observation that is located halfway between the smallest and the largest observations in the distribution. For example, in the series 1, 3, 4, 6, 7, the median is 4. The median can be calculated with observations that are ranked according to size, and as such it can be employed with variables that are at least ordinal.

The median is obtained for ungrouped data by identifying the middle observation. For an odd number of cases, it is the observation $(N+1)/2$, where N is the total number of cases. Consider the following set of nine observations:

$$6, 9, 11, 12, 16, 18, 21, 24, 30$$
$$\uparrow$$
$$\text{Median}$$

The fifth observation $[(9+1)/2]$ divides the distribution in half; the median is therefore the value of the fifth observation, 16. With an even number of observations, the median is located halfway between the two middle observations and is calculated as an average of the observations $N/2$ and $N/2+1$. For example, in the following set of observations

$$1, 3, 4, 5, 6, 7, 8, 9$$
$$\uparrow$$
$$\text{Median}$$

the median is the average of the fourth $(8/2)$ and the fifth $(8/2+1)$ observations: $(5+6)/2 = 5.5$.

For grouped data, the median is located by interpolating within the interval containing the middle observation. The formula for finding the median is

$$Md = L + \left[\frac{N(.5) - cf_{below}}{f}\right]w \qquad (15.1)$$

where Md = the median

L = the lower limit of the interval containing the median

cf_{below} = the cumulative sum of the frequencies below the interval containing the median

f = the frequency of the interval containing the median

w = the width of the interval containing the median

N = the total number of cases

To illustrate the computation of the median, consider the distribution in Table 15.7. The table shows the age distribution of 134 persons, divided into eight 10-year age groups. Because there are 134 observations ($N = 134$), the median has the value of the sixty-seventh observation [$134(.5) = 67$]. The cumulative frequency column shows that there are 60 observations preceding the interval 41–50. The interval 41–50 contains 25 more observations. Hence the sixty-seventh observation is located within that interval. It is necessary to find the exact age corresponding to the seventh case in this interval. These seven cases constitute $7/25 = 28$ percent of the cases in the interval. As the width of the interval is 10, we must add 28 percent of $10 = 2.8$ years to the lower limit of the interval containing the median. The median is therefore $40.5 + 2.8 = 43.3$. These steps can be summarized by employing Equation (15.1):

$$Md = 40.5 + \left[\frac{134(.5) - 60}{25}\right]10 = 40.5 + \left(\frac{7}{25}\right)10 = 40.5 + 2.8 = 43.3$$

Table 15.7
Age Distribution of 134 Cases (Hypothetical)

Age	Real Class Limits	f	Cumulative Frequency (cf)
1–10	0.5–10.5	10	10
11–20	10.5–20.5	12	22
21–30	20.5–30.5	17	39
31–40	30.5–40.5	21	60
41–50	40.5–50.5	25	85
51–60	50.5–60.5	20	105
61–70	60.5–70.5	18	123
71–80	70.5–80.5	11	134
N		134	134

Table 15.8
Median of Years of Schooling

	White	Black
Males:		
Residents of city center	12.1	8.7
Residents of suburbs	12.1	9.7
Residents of rural areas	12.3	8.9
Females:		
Residents of city center	12.1	10.5
Residents of suburbs	12.3	10.7
Residents of rural areas	11.8	8.0

An example of the application of the median is given in Table 15.8, which describes the education of 12 groups. The investigators compared the median education of each group. The medians reflect the educational characteristics of 12 different populations, each represented by one single value. For instance, 50 percent of the white rural males completed at least 12.3 years of education; such extended schooling was enjoyed by a smaller ratio of the equivalent black population, whose median was only 8.9 years.

Other Measures of Location

The median is a special case of a more general set of measures of location called *percentiles*. The nth percentile is a number such that n percent of the scores fall below it and $(100 - n)$ percent fall above it. The median is the $n = 50$th percentile; that is, it is a number that is larger than 50 percent of the measurements and smaller than the other 50 percent.

At times it is useful to identify values that divide the distribution into three, four, or ten groups. For example, the admissions office of a university that has decided to accept one-fourth of its applicants will be interested in finding the 25 percent with the highest scores in the entrance examinations. That is, it will locate the seventy-fifth percentile, also called the upper quartile (Q_3), which is the point above which 25 percent of the scores lie.

Equation (15.1) can be adjusted to find positional values such as the seventy-fifth percentile, the twenty-fifth percentile (also called the lower quartile, or Q_1), or the tenth percentile (D_1). The only adjustment required is multiplying the total number of cases by the required proportion and locating the interval where the measure is located. Equations (15.2) to (15.4) define Q_1, Q_3, and D_1.

$$Q_1 = L + \left[\frac{N(.25) - cf_{below}}{f} \right] w \qquad (15.2)$$

$$Q_3 = L + \left[\frac{N(.75) - cf_{below}}{f} \right] w \qquad (15.3)$$

$$D_1 = L + \left[\frac{N(.1) - cf_{below}}{f} \right] w \qquad (15.4)$$

To illustrate the calculation of other measures of location, we employ the data contained in Table 15.7 to find the tenth percentile.

$$D_1 = 10.5 + \left[\frac{134(.1) - 10}{12} \right] 10 = 10.5 + \left(\frac{3.4}{12} \right) 10 = 10.5 + 2.8 = 13.3$$

Arithmetic Mean

The **arithmetic mean** is the most frequently used measure of central tendency. It is suitable for representing distributions measured on an interval level and lends itself to mathematical calculations; it also serves as a basis for other statistical measures. The arithmetic mean is defined as the sum total of all observations divided by their number.

In symbolic notations, the mean is defined as

$$\bar{X} = \frac{\sum X}{N} \qquad (15.5)$$

where $\bar{X}$ = the arithmetic mean

$\sum X$ = the sum of total observations

N = the number of observations

According to this equation, the mean $(\bar{X})$ of the series 6, 7, 12, 11, 10, 3, 4, 1, is $54/8 = 6.75$.

When the mean is to be computed from a frequency distribution, it is not necessary to add up all the individual observations. Instead, each category can be given its proper weight by multiplying it by its frequency. The following equation can be used:

$$\bar{X} = \frac{\sum fX}{N} \qquad (15.6)$$

where $\sum fX$ = the sum total of all categories multiplied by their respective frequencies.

Table 15.9 presents data on the amount of schooling received by 34 individuals. The mean education of this group can be calculated by using Equation (15.6). To calculate the value of $\sum fX$ (column 3), each category (col-

Table 15.9
Distribution of Years of Study

(1) Years of Study	(2) f	(3) fX
2	3	6
3	2	6
6	5	30
8	10	80
10	8	80
12	4	48
14	2	28
Total	$N = 34$	$\Sigma fX = 278$

umn 1) is multiplied by its frequency (column 2), and the products are added up. The mean number of years of schooling is therefore

$$\bar{X} = \frac{278}{34} = 8.18$$

Equation (15.6) can be easily applied to grouped frequency distributions, where the midpoint of the class interval is taken to represent x. For example, in the calculation of the mean family size for a group of respondents presented in Table 15.10, only the midpoint is entered in the calculations:

$$\bar{X} = \frac{51}{18} = 2.83$$

Unlike the mode and the median, the arithmetic mean takes into account all the values in the distribution, making it especially sensitive to extreme values. For example, if one person in a group of ten earns $60,000 annually and each of the others earns $5,000, the mean income of the group would be $10,500, not a good representation of the distribution. The mean

Table 15.10
Family Size for a Group of Respondents

Family Size	Midpoint	f	fX
0–2	1	10	10
3–5	4	5	20
6–8	7	3	21
Total		$N = 18$	$\Sigma fX = 51$

will thus be a misleading measure of central tendency whenever there are some observations with extremely high or low values.

Comparison of the Mode, the Median, and the Mean

The three measures of central tendency just analyzed can be used to represent univariate distributions. However, each has its own characteristics, which both prescribe and limit its use. The mode indicates the point in the distribution with the highest density, the median is the distribution's midpoint, and the arithmetic mean is an average of all the values in the distribution. Accordingly, these measures cannot be applied mechanically. How, then, does one know when it is preferable to use which? There is no simple answer to the question; it depends on the objective of the study. For example, if the researcher is investigating the average level of income of a group so as to establish how much each person would receive if all incomes were distributed equally, the mean would be most pertinent, as it reflects the highest as well as the lowest income. If, by contrast, the information is needed to estimate the eligibility of the group to receive financial aid, the mode would be appropriate, for it shows the most typical income and is unaffected by extreme values.

The application of any measure of central tendency also depends on the level of measurement of the variable being analyzed. The mode can represent the distribution of party affiliation, which is a nominal variable. The median can be applied to ordinal variables such as political attitudes. The arithmetic mean is used with interval variables such as income and age.

Basic Measures of Dispersion

Measures of central tendency identify the most representative value of the distribution. However, a complete description of the distribution requires that we measure the extent of dispersion about this central value. (In the following discussion, the terms *dispersion, scatter*, and *variation* are used interchangeably.) The actual observations are distributed among many values, and the extent of their spread varies from one distribution to another. For example, two classes may have the same average grade; however, one class may include some excellent students as well as some very poor ones, whereas all the students in the other may be of average ability. Similarly, income distributions with an identical mean may present different patterns of dispersion. In some distributions, most incomes are clustered around the mean; in others, the incomes are widely dispersed. The description of the extent of dispersions about the central value is obtained by several measures designated as measures of dispersion. We shall discuss the measure of qualitative variation, the range, the mean deviation, the variance, the standard deviation, and the coefficient of variation.

Measure of Qualitative Variation

The extent of dispersion in nominal distributions can be assessed by means of an index of heterogeneity designated the **measure of qualitative variation**. This index reflects the number of differences among the categories of the distribution and is based on the number of categories and their respective frequencies. In general, the larger the number of categories and the greater the overall differences among them, the greater the degree of variation. Likewise, the smaller the number of categories and their differences, the smaller the variation within the distribution. Consider the racial composition of several communities. In an all-white community, there are no racial differences, but in racially mixed communities, there will be smaller or larger degrees of variation. The amount of variation will depend on the composition of the community. When most belong to a single racial group, the number of racial differences among the members of the community will be relatively small. Conversely, when most members are divided among several racial groups, the number of differences will be large.

Calculating the Total Number of Differences. The measure of qualitative variation is based on the ratio of the total number of differences in the distribution to the maximum number of possible differences within the same distribution. To find the total number of differences in the distribution, the differences between each category and every other category are counted and summed. For instance, in a group of 50 whites and 50 blacks, there would be $50 \times 50 = 2{,}500$ racial differences. Similarly, with 70 whites and 30 blacks, one would count $70 \times 30 = 2{,}100$ differences, and with 100 whites and no blacks, there would be $0 \times 100 = 0$ racial differences.

The procedure for calculating the total number of differences can be expressed in the following equation:

$$\text{Total observed differences} = \sum f_i f_j, \; i \neq j \qquad (15.7)$$

where f_i = frequency of category i

f_j = frequency of category j

For example, in a group of 20 Catholics, 30 Jews, and 10 Muslims, there would be $(20 \times 30) + (20 \times 10) + (30 \times 10) = 1{,}100$ religious differences.

Calculating the Maximum Possible Differences. The total of observed differences is meaningful only in relation to the maximum possible number of differences, for each distribution has a different number of categories and frequencies. Relating the observed differences to the maximum possible differences has the effect of controlling for these factors. The maximum number of differences occurs when each category in the distribution has an identical frequency. Thus the maximum number of frequencies is computed by finding the number of differences that would be observed if all frequencies were equal. Symbolically,

$$\text{Maximum possible differences} = \frac{n(n-1)}{2}\left(\frac{F}{n}\right)^2 \qquad (15.8)$$

where n = the number of categories in the distribution

F = total frequency

In the example of 20 Catholics, 30 Jews, and 10 Muslims, the maximum possible differences are

$$\left(\frac{3\times2}{2}\right)\left(\frac{60}{3}\right)^2 = 1{,}200$$

The measure of qualitative variation is the ratio between the total observed differences and the maximum possible differences. In other words,

$$\text{Measure of qualitative variation} = \frac{\text{Total observed differences}}{\text{Maximum possible differences}}$$

Symbolically, the measure is expressed in the following equation:

$$\text{Measure of qualitative variation} = \frac{\sum f_i f_j}{\dfrac{n(n-1)}{2}\left(\dfrac{F}{n}\right)^2} \qquad (15.9)$$

The measure of variation for our example is thus

$$\text{Measure of qualitative variation} = \frac{1{,}100}{1{,}200} = .92$$

The measure of qualitative variation varies between zero and one. Zero indicates the absence of any variation, and one reflects maximum variation. The measure will be zero whenever the total observed differences are zero. It will take the value of one when the number of observed differences is equal to the maximum possible differences.

One interesting application of the measure of qualitative variation is the Nachmias and Rosenbloom work on representative bureaucracy.[1] The investigators used the measure to compare the degree of social integration in selected federal agencies in 1970. Their results are presented in Table 15.11, where selected federal agencies are ranked according to the degree of integration in their general schedule work force. The table contains information that clearly indicates the utility of the measure. If an agency were proportionally representative of the social composition of the society as a whole, its measure of variation would be about .30. Thus more than half of the agencies in Table 15.11 are more integrated in terms of their social composition than the society at large.

---

1. David Nachmias and David H. Rosenbloom, "Measuring Bureaucratic Representation and Integration," *Public Administration Review,* 33 (1973): 590–597.

Table 15.11

The Social Integration of the General Schedule Work Forces of Selected Federal Agencies, 1970

Agency	Black	Spanish-surnamed	American Indian	Oriental	Other	Total	Measure Variation
EEOC	49.9%	9.5%	.8%	.9%	38.9%	748	.71
Government Printing Office	53.6	.4	.2	.3	45.6	1,548	.63
State	31.5	2.2	.3	.9	65.1	5,810	.60
Labor	25.7	1.7	.4	.5	71.7	10,535	.52
GSA	24.1	1.6	.2	1.0	73.2	18,931	.51
Health, Education and Welfare	21.3	1.5	2.4	.7	74.1	94,502	.51
CSC	23.0	2.3	.2	.7	73.8	5,216	.50
Veterans Administration	22.0	1.8	.2	1.0	75.1	115,997	.48
Housing and Urban Development	18.6	1.5	.3	.7	78.9	14,721	.43
Interior	4.0	1.7	12.7	.8	80.9	50,725	.41
Post Office	17.9	.6	.1	.6	80.7	2,775	.40
Small Business Administration	11.6	5.4	.4	.5	82.0	4,272	.39
Commerce	14.5	.6	.1	.8	84.0	29,115	.34
Treasury	12.3	1.5	.1	.7	85.4	82,318	.32
General Accounting Office	13.6	.6	.1	.4	85.3	4,598	.32
Justice	9.6	2.4	.1	.4	87.5	36,947	.28
Army	8.7	2.2	.2	1.0	87.9	237,914	.27
Defense (entire)	7.8	2.4	.2	1.0	88.7	600,044	.26
Navy	8.0	1.3	.2	1.3	89.3	158,986	.25
Air Force	4.6	4.3	.3	.7	90.1	151,217	.23
Agriculture	5.5	1.3	.3	.5	92.3	81,437	.18
Transportation	5.4	1.1	.3	.5	92.8	58,690	.17
National Aeronautics and Space Administration	2.7	.6	.1	.6	96.0	27,278	.10

From U.S. Civil Service Commission, *Minority Group Employment in the Federal Government* (Washington, D.C.: U.S. Government Printing Office, 1970).

Range and Interquartile Range

The **range** measures the distance between the highest and lowest values of the distribution. For example, in the following set of observations

$$4, 6, 8, 9, 17$$

the range is the difference between 17 and 4; that is, 13 $(17 - 4 = 13)$. This measure requires that observations be ranked according to size; thus it can be applied in cases where the distribution is at least on an ordinal level of measurement. The range has a special significance when a dearth of information produces a distorted picture of reality. For instance, two factories with annual average wages of $15,000 have different pay ranges: one has a range of $2,000, and the other has a range of $9,000. Without the additional information supplied by the range, one would get the impression that the wage scales in both factories were identical. The range is a useful device for gaining a quick impression of the data. However, it is a crude measure of dispersion because it takes into account only the distribution's two extreme values. Thus it is sensitive to changes in one single score.

An alternative to the range is the **interquartile range**, which is the difference between the lower and upper quartiles (Q_1 and Q_3). It measures the spread in the middle half of the distribution and is less affected by extreme observations. The lower and upper quartiles will vary less from distribution to distribution than the most extreme observations. To illustrate the interquartile range, consider the data in Table 15.7. The lower quartile (Q_1) for these data is 27.76, and the upper quartile (Q_3) is 58.75. These values were calculated with Equations (15.2) and (15.3). The interquartile range is thus $58.75 - 27.76 = 30.99$. The range can be calculated for other measures of location. For example, one can calculate the range between the tenth and ninetieth percentiles to measure the dispersion of the middle 80 percent of the observations.

Limitations. The major drawback of the range and the interquartile range is that based on two values alone, they reflect only the dispersion in some defined section of the distribution. Some measure must be devised that will reflect the aggregate dispersion in the distribution. However, to measure aggregate dispersion it is necessary to establish the deviation of all the values in the distribution from some criterion. In other words, some norm is to be decided on that will permit one to determine which value is higher or lower than expected. For example, the evaluation of income as "high" or "low" is meaningful only in relation to some fixed criterion. Income evaluated as high in India would be considered low in the United States.

Any of the measures of central tendency analyzed so far can be chosen as a norm. It is possible to measure deviations from the mode, the median, or the arithmetic mean; the mean is the most widely employed.

Measures of Dispersion Based on the Mean

The simplest way to obtain a measure of deviation is to calculate the average deviation from the arithmetic mean:

$$\text{Average deviation} = \frac{\Sigma (X - \bar{X})}{N}$$

where X = each individual observation

$\bar{X}$ = the arithmetic mean

N = the total number of observations

However, the sum of the deviations from the mean is always equal to zero; thus the average deviation will be zero, for its numerator will always be zero. This property of the mean can be bypassed in two ways: by ignoring the signs and taking the deviations' absolute values or by squaring the deviations. The mean deviation is obtained with the first method; the standard deviation, with the second.

Mean Deviation

The **mean deviation** makes use of every observation in the distribution. It is computed by taking the difference between each observation and the mean, summing the absolute value of these deviations, and dividing the sum by the total number of observations. Symbolically, the measure is expressed in Equation (15.10), in which the vertical lines stand for "absolute difference":

$$\text{Mean deviation} = \frac{\Sigma |X - \bar{X}|}{N} \tag{15.10}$$

where X = each individual observation

$\bar{X}$ = the arithmetic mean

N = the total number of observations

For example, to compute the mean deviation of the scores

$$2, 4, 6, 8, 10$$

we first calculate the mean

$$\bar{X} = \frac{2 + 4 + 6 + 8 + 10}{5} = \frac{30}{5} = 6$$

We then subtract the mean from each score and obtain the following deviations:

$$-4, -2, 0, +2, +4$$

These deviations are summed by ignoring the signs and dividing by the number of scores:

$$\text{Mean deviation} = \frac{4+2+0+2+4}{5} = \frac{12}{5} = 2.4$$

This figure indicates that the mean difference between each score and the arithmetic mean is 2.4.

The advantage of the mean deviation is that it takes into account all the observations in the distribution. However, absolute values are not amenable to arithmetic manipulations; thus the mean deviation, which is based on such values, cannot be applied when further mathematical calculations are required.

Variance and Standard Deviation

The computation of the variance and the standard deviation is similar to that of the mean deviation, but instead of taking the deviation's absolute values, they are squared, summed, and then divided by the total number of observations. The definitional formula for the **variance** is

$$s^2 = \frac{\sum (X - \bar{X})^2}{N} \tag{15.11}$$

where s^2 = variance. In other words, the arithmetic mean is subtracted from each score; the differences are then squared, summed, and divided by the total number of observations. The numerical example of Table 15.12 illustrates the various steps involved in the computation of the variance. Applying Equation (15.11) to the data, we get

$$s^2 = \frac{200}{5} = 40$$

In a simpler computational formula of the variance, the squared mean is subtracted from the squared sum of all scores divided by the number of observations; that is,

$$s^2 = \frac{\sum X^2}{N} - (\bar{X})^2 \tag{15.12}$$

Equation (15.12) is applied to the same data of Table 15.12:

$$s^2 = \frac{605}{5} - (9)^2 = 121 - 81 = 40$$

The variance expresses the average dispersion in the distribution not in the original units of measurement but in squared units. This problem is bypassed by taking the square root of the variance, thereby transforming the variance into the standard deviation. The **standard deviation** is a measure

Table 15.12
Computation of the Variance

X	$X-\bar{X}$	$(\bar{X}-\bar{X})^2$	X^2
3	−6	36	9
4	−5	25	16
6	−3	9	36
12	3	9	144
20	11	121	400
Total		200	605

$\bar{X}=9$

expressing dispersion in the original units of measurement. Symbolically, the standard deviation is expressed in Equations (15.13) and (15.14), corresponding to Equations (15.11) and (15.12), respectively:

$$s = \sqrt{\frac{\sum (X-\bar{X})^2}{N}} \qquad (15.13)$$

$$s = \sqrt{\frac{\sum X^2}{N} - (\bar{X})^2} \qquad (15.14)$$

where $s=$ standard deviation. For our earlier example, the value of the standard deviation, using Equation (15.13), is

$$s = \sqrt{\frac{200}{5}} = \sqrt{40} = 6.3$$

Variance and Standard Deviation for Grouped Data

If data are grouped, as they often are, a different procedure for computing the variance and the standard deviation must be employed. Equation (15.15) can be applied to grouped data where the interval's midpoint is represented by X and f stands for the corresponding frequencies:

$$s^2 = \frac{\sum fX^2 - (fX)^2/N}{N} \qquad (15.15)$$

This formula is applied to the data of Table 15.13:

$$s^2 = \frac{1,094 - (136)^2/20}{20} = \frac{1,094 - 18,496/20}{20} = \frac{1,094 - 924.8}{20}$$

$$= \frac{169.20}{20} = 8.46$$

Table 15.13
Age Distribution of 20 Respondents

Age	Midpoint X	f	X^2	fX^2	fX
1–3	2	4	4	16	8
4–6	5	3	25	75	15
7–9	8	10	64	640	80
10–12	11	3	121	363	33
Total		20		$\Sigma fX^2 = 1{,}094$	$\Sigma fX = 136$

We can now obtain the standard deviation by simply taking the square root of 8.46. Thus

$$s = \sqrt{8.46} = 2.91$$

Standard Deviation: Advantages and Applications

The standard deviation has various advantages over other measures of dispersion. First, it is more stable from sample to sample (on sampling, see Chapter 8). Second, it has some important mathematical properties that enable the researcher to obtain the standard deviation for two or more groups combined. Furthermore, its mathematical properties make it a useful measure in more advanced statistical work, especially in the area of statistical inferences (discussed in Chapters 8 and 19).

The application of the standard deviation as a research device is illustrated in the following example. Table 15.14 compares differences in feelings of life satisfaction among persons of several countries, using the mean and standard deviation of the variable "life satisfaction" in each country. The mean scores are almost identical, implying that satisfaction with life is similar in the countries studied. However, there are differences in the standard deviations of each country. The relatively low standard deviations in England, Germany, and the United States indicate that these countries are homogeneous as far as satisfaction is concerned; that is, people have a satisfaction score that is close to their group's mean score. In Italy, however, the dispersion is greater, suggesting that the degree of satisfaction reflected by the mean is not common to all the Italians in the group studied.

Table 15.14
Mean and Standard Deviation on an Index of Life Satisfaction in Four Western
Nations (Hypothetical Data)

	England	Germany	Italy	United States
Mean	6.7	6.7	6.6	6.5
Standard deviation	1.0	1.2	3.2	1.3

Table 15.15

Attitudes toward Federal Support for Abortion in Four States (Hypothetical Data)

	Wisconsin	Illinois	Alabama	Massachusetts
Mean	5.48	4.82	3.67	5.82
Standard deviation	2.9	2.9	2.8	2.7

Coefficient of Variation

Standard deviations cannot be compared in absolute magnitudes in instances where the distributions compared have very different means. A standard deviation of 2, for instance, would convey a different meaning in relation to a mean of 6 than to a mean of 60. Therefore, the degree of dispersion must be calculated relative to the mean of the distribution. This principle is reflected in the **coefficient of variation,** which reflects relative variation. Symbolically, the coefficient of variation is defined as follows:

$$V = \frac{s}{\bar{X}} \tag{15.16}$$

where V = the coefficient of variation

s = the standard deviation

$\bar{X}$ = the arithmetic mean

To illustrate the application of the coefficient of variation, consider the data in Table 15.15 on federal support for abortion. Presented are the means and standard deviations. In absolute magnitudes, there are no significant differences among the standard deviations in the four states. However, there are substantial differences between the means, indicating varying degrees of support for abortion in each state. In Alabama, for example, the mean is much lower than in the other states, but the degree of dispersion is almost identical. Intuitively, however, it seems that a deviation of 2.8 has a greater significance in relation to a mean of 3.67 than to a mean of 4.82 or 5.48. To correct for these discrepancies, the standard deviations were converted into coefficients of variation. The results are displayed in Table 15.16. Note that, indeed, the relative deviation from the mean is higher in Alabama than in other states, reflecting the lower degree of homogeneity of attitudes toward abortion.

Table 15.16

Means of Attitudes toward Federal Support for Abortion and Coefficient of Variation in Four States

	Wisconsin	Illinois	Alabama	Massachusetts
Mean	5.48	4.82	3.67	5.82
Coefficient of variation	.53	.60	.76	.46

Types of Frequency Distributions

Our discussion of univariate distributions has so far been limited to descriptive measures reflecting central tendencies and dispersion. The next step in describing a distribution is to identify its general form. Distributions may have distinctive forms with few low scores and many high scores, with many scores concentrated in the middle of the distribution, or with many low scores and few high scores. The simplest way to describe a distribution is by a visual representation. Examples of different forms are presented in Figure 15.1.

The values of the variable are represented along the baseline, and the area under the curve represents the frequencies. For example, in distribution *a*, the frequency of the interval 25–35 is represented by the area under the curve in that interval. The distribution (Figure 15.1*a*) is a symmetrical distribution; that is, the frequencies at the right and left tails of the distribution are identical, so if the distribution is divided into two halves, each will be the mirror image of the other. This usually means that most of the observations are concentrated at the middle of the distribution and that there are few observations with very high or very low scores. An example of a symmetrical distribution is the height of men. Few men are very short or very tall; most are of medium height. Many other variables tend to be distributed symmetrically, and this form of distribution plays an important role in the field of statistical inference.

In nonsymmetrical distributions, there are more extreme cases in one direction of the distribution than in the other. A nonsymmetrical distribution in which there are more extremely low scores is referred to as a negatively **skewed distribution** (Figure 15.1*b*). When there are more extremely high scores, the distribution is positively skewed (Figure 15.1*c*). Most income distributions are positively skewed, with few families having extremely high incomes.

Skewness can also be identified according to the positions of the measures of central tendency. With symmetrical distributions, the mean will co-

Figure 15.1
Types of Frequency Distributions

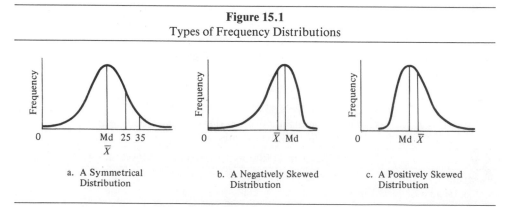

a. A Symmetrical
   Distribution

b. A Negatively Skewed
   Distribution

c. A Positively Skewed
   Distribution

incide with the median and the mode; with skewed distributions, there will be discrepancies between these measures. In a negatively skewed distribution, the mean will be pulled in the direction of the lower scores; in a positively skewed distribution, it will be located closer to the high scores. This property of skewed distributions makes the choice of an average value a critical issue. Since the mean is pulled in the direction of the extreme scores, it loses its typicality and hence its usefulness as a representative measure. In such instances, it might be advisable to employ the median or the mode instead.

Normal Curve

One type of symmetrical distribution is called the **normal curve**; it has great significance in the field of statistics. A normal curve is shown in Figure 15.2. Its principal properties are as follows:

1. It is symmetrical and bell-shaped.
2. The mode, the median, and the mean coincide at the center of the distribution.
3. The curve is based on an infinite number of observations.
4. A single mathematical formula describes how frequencies are related to the values of the variable.

The fifth property of the normal curve is its most distinct characteristic: *in any normal distribution, a fixed proportion of the observations lies between the mean and fixed units of standard deviations.* The proportions can be seen in Figure 15.2. The mean of the distribution divides it exactly in half; 34.13 percent of the observations fall between the mean and one standard deviation to the right of the mean; the same proportion fall between the mean and one standard deviation to the left of the mean. The plus signs indicate standard deviations above the mean; the minus signs, standard deviations below the mean. Thus between $\bar{X} \pm 1s$ fall 68.26 percent of all obser-

Figure 15.2
Proportions under the Normal Curve

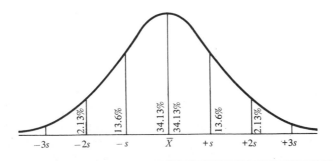

vations in the distribution; between $\bar{X} \pm 2s$, 95.46 percent of the observations; and between $\bar{X} \pm 3s$, 99.73 percent of the observations.

In any univariate distribution that is normally distributed, the proportion of observations included within fixed distances of the mean can be determined. For example, in a distribution of intelligence quotients with a mean of 110 and a standard deviation of 10, 68.26 percent of all subjects will have an IQ of $110 \pm 1s$—that is, between 100 and 120—and 95.46 percent will have a score that is not below 90 and does not exceed 130.

Standard Scores

To evaluate the proportion of observations included within an interval desired, one must express observations in standard deviation units. For instance, to find the proportion of cases that have an IQ between 110 and 130, one has to determine how many standard deviations away from the mean the score of 130 is located. Observations are converted into standard deviation units by means of Equation (15.17):

$$Z = \frac{X - \bar{X}}{s} \tag{15.17}$$

where Z = number of standard deviation units

X = any observation

$\bar{X}$ = the arithmetic mean

s = the standard deviation

Z, sometimes referred to as a **standard score**, expresses the distance between a specific observation (X) and the mean in terms of standard deviation units. A Z of 2 means that the distance between the mean of the distribution and X is two standard deviations. For example, in a distribution with a mean of 40 and a standard deviation of 5, the score of 50 is expressed as follows:

$$Z = \frac{50 - 40}{5} = \frac{10}{5} = 2$$

The score of 50 lies two standard deviations above the mean. Similarly, 30 is two standard deviations below the mean:

$$Z = \frac{30 - 40}{5} = \frac{-10}{5} = -2$$

To determine the proportion of observations that lie between the mean and any observation in the distribution, special tables have been constructed for the standard form of the normal curve (see Appendix E for an example of such a table). The table shows proportions for various Z values. The first two digits of Z are listed in the left-hand column; the third digit is shown

Figure 15.3
Proportion of Population Earning between $11,000 and $15,000

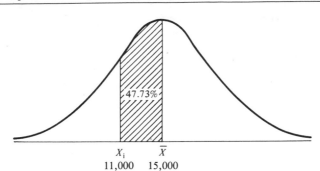

X_i $\bar{X}$
11,000   15,000

across the top. Thus, for example, the proportion included between the mean and a Z of 1 is .3413, or 34.13 percent; the value of a Z of 1.65 is .4505. Only half of the curve's proportions are given because the curve is symmetrical. Thus the distance between the mean and a Z of -1.0 is identical to the area between the mean and a Z of 1.0. To use the table, find the appropriate Z score for any particular observation by Equation (15.17), and then consult Appendix E.

To illustrate the use of the standard normal table, suppose that the distribution of income in a particular community is normal, its mean income is $15,000, and the standard deviation is $2,000. We want to determine what proportion of the people in this community have an income between $11,000 and $15,000. First, $11,000 is converted into standard deviation units:

$$Z = \frac{11,000 - 15,000}{2,000} = -2$$

Next, we consult Appendix E to determine that .4773 of all observations are included between the mean and a Z of 2. In other words, 47.73 percent of all people in the community earn between $11,000 and $15,000 a year. This is shown in Figure 15.3.

What proportion of the community earns between $16,000 and $20,000? Both figures are converted into standard scores:

$$Z_1 = \frac{16,000 - 15,000}{2,000} = 0.5$$

$$Z_2 = \frac{20,000 - 15,000}{2,000} = 2.5$$

Appendix E indicates that .4938 is included between the mean and 2.5 standard deviation units and .1915 between the mean and 0.5 units. Therefore,

Figure 15.4
Proportion of Population Earning between $16,000 and $20,000

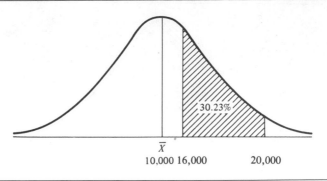

30.23%

$\overline{X}$
10,000 16,000   20,000

the area included between $16,000 and $20,000 is .4938 − .1915 = .3023 (30.23 percent). This is shown in Figure 15.4.

Summary

1. The preliminary stage of analysis consists of quite ordinary methods designed to provide a straightforward description of the data. Once coded, each item is summarized in some tabular form, and measures such as averages and percentages are calculated to describe its main characteristics. It is common to begin the analysis by showing how the respondents are distributed on all the items of the investigation. A distribution might show, for instance, that 20 of the 80 respondents included in a sample are males and the rest are females; that 46 are Democrats, 20 are Republicans, and 14 do not identify with either party. Such listings of the number of observations that fall into each of several categories are termed *frequency distributions*. Frequencies are often converted into proportions or percentages; these are helpful in assessing the weight of a single category in relation to other categories of the distribution or in relation to other distributions.

2. Often it is useful to obtain some average value that is representative of the distribution. For example, one may need to answer such questions as "What is the most typical political orientation of this group of respondents?" or "What is their average income?" These questions can be answered by using measures of central tendency. The three most commonly used statistical measures of central tendency are the mode, the median, and the arithmetic mean.

3. Measures of central tendency can be misleading if they are not accompanied by measures that describe the amount of dispersion in the distribution. Whereas the measures of central tendency reflect the most typical or average characteristics of the group, the measures of dispersion indicate how many members of the group deviate from it and the extent of the deviation. A small deviation denotes that most responses are clustered around the measure of central tendency; a large deviation indicates that the measure is a poor representation of the distribution.

4. One of the important steps in examining a distribution is the identification of its general form. Certain forms are characteristic of different empirical phenomena. For instance, many income distributions have few extremely high incomes; most incomes are concentrated in the middle or lower ranges. Such distributions are skewed toward the higher values. In contrast, intelligence distributions are typically symmetrical; most scores are concentrated in the middle range, with very few extremely high or extremely low scores.

Key Terms for Review

descriptive statistics	interquartile range
inferential statistics	mean deviation
frequency distribution	variance
mode	standard deviation
median	coefficient of variation
arithmetic mean	skewed distribution
measure of qualitative variation	normal curve
range	standard score

Study Questions

1. The table describes the employment status of women in two communities. What conclusions can be drawn from the absolute numbers? From the percentages?

	Community A		Community B	
In labor force:				
Professional	10,000	2%	10,000	5%
Skilled	30,000	6	16,000	8
Semiskilled	50,000	10	20,000	10
Unskilled	150,000	30	20,000	10
Not in labor force:	260,000	52	134,000	67
Total	500,000	100%	200,000	100%

2. Give two examples of problems in which (a) the mean is the best measure of central tendency; (b) the mode is the best measure of central tendency; (c) the median is the best measure of central tendency.
3. Give the mean, median, and mode of the following distribution:

$$22, 41, 43, 56, 33, 22, 20, 37$$

4. The following is the income distribution of a group of workers:

Income	Frequency
$ 5,000	6
6,010	3
6,500	3
7,000	2
24,000	1
	$N = 15$

   a. Which measure of central tendency would you use to represent the income of this group?
   b. Compute the measure.
5. On the curve shown here, what would be the approximate position of the mean? The median? The mode? Define the curve with respect to skewness.

6. Suppose that you obtain a set of scores of attitudes toward legal abortion from a group of respondents and that the standard deviation of this set of scores is zero. What does this imply about the group?
7. Attitudes toward authority often can be treated as an interval variable. Suppose that this variable is normally distributed with a mean score of 60 and a standard deviation of 10.
   a. What proportion of cases have scores between 60 and 63?
   b. What proportion have scores of less than 48?
   c. What proportion score between 72 and 83? Between 52 and 55?

Additional Readings

Agresti, Alan, and Barbara Finlay. *Statistical Methods for the Social Sciences.* San Francisco: Dellen, 1986.

Anderson, T. W., and Stanley L. Sclove. *The Statistical Analysis of Data.* Palo Alto, Calif.: Scientific Press, 1986.

Bohrnstedt, George W., and David Knoke. *Statistics for Social Data Analysis.* Itasca, Ill.: Peacock, 1988.

Hickey, Anthony A. *An Introduction to Statistical Techniques for Social Research.* New York: Random House, 1990.

McCall, Robert B. *Fundamental Statistics for Behavioral Sciences.* 4th ed. Orlando, Fla.: Harcourt Brace Jovanovich, 1986.

Witte, Robert S. *Statistics.* 2d ed. Fort Worth: Holt, Rinehart and Winston, 1985.

CHAPTER 16

Bivariate Analysis

*In this chapter, we explore the concept of relationships be-
tween two variables and discuss a number of measures of bivariate relationships.*

O NCE SINGLE VARIABLES HAVE BEEN
summarized and their pattern of distribution
described, the researcher confronts the next
task in the analysis of data: examining the pattern of relationship between the variables under investigation.
This chapter examines different methods for measuring
bivariate relationships between variables. The first section discusses the concept of relationship; the second
section describes nominal measures of relationship; the
third section deals with ordinal measures of relationship; and the last section presents interval measures of
relationship.

The Concept of Relationship

Each of us, scientist or layperson, knows what relationships are. We know that in the world around us, things
go together. We observe that as children grow, their
weight increases; that cities tend to be more polluted
than rural areas; and that the crime rate is higher in central cities than in suburbs. Each of these observations is
a statement of a relationship: between age and weight,
between degree of urbanization and pollution, and between living conditions and crime.

To say that people who live in poverty are usually unskilled is to describe a relationship between living conditions and occupation. This statement can be made only if it is known that people who have better living conditions are more likely to be trained for skilled work. In other words, to state a relationship between X and Y is to say that certain categories of the variable X go with certain categories of the variable Y. This principle of *covariation* is basic to the notion of association and relation, and it recognizes that observations can be placed in several categories simultaneously. For example, working-class people are also often Democrats, and highly educated individuals have higher incomes.

The first step in examining a relationship between two variables is the construction of a bivariate table.

How to Construct a Bivariate Table

In a bivariate table, two variables are cross-classified. Such a table consists of rows and columns; the categories of one variable are labels for the rows, and the categories of the second variable are labels for the columns. Usually, the independent variable is the column variable (listed across the top), and the dependent variable is the row variable (listed at the left side of the table).[1] As an illustration of how a bivariate table is constructed, observe the data we present in Exhibit 16.1. Sixteen individuals have been listed by their gender and their job satisfaction scores. These observations have been tallied and classified by their joint position on gender and job satisfaction into the appropriate cells in Table 16.1. The table is a 3×2 table because it has three rows and two columns, each representing a category of either the variable "gender" or the variable "job satisfaction." The fourth row represents the column totals; the third column, the row totals.

Principle of Covariation: An Example

The principle of covariation is demonstrated in Tables 16.2, 16.3, and 16.4. These tables summarize information on two variables: religious denomination and social class.[2] Table 16.2 illustrates a pattern of perfect covariation of the variables. It is observed that all the Catholics are classified into the low social-class category, that all Jews belong to the middle class, and that the Protestants occupy the high social-class category. The two variables covary because specific categories of the variable "religious denomination" go with specific categories of the variable "social class."

1. Herman J. Loether and Donald G. McTavish, *Descriptive and Inferential Statistics: An Introduction* (Boston: Allyn & Bacon, 1980), pp. 175–183.

2. John H. Mueller, Karl F. Schuessler, and Herbert L. Costner, *Statistical Reasoning in Sociology* (Boston: Houghton Mifflin, 1970), pp. 242–248.

Exhibit 16.1
Constructing a Bivariate Table

Gender	Job Satisfaction
Male = M	High = H
Female = F	Medium = M
	Low = L

ID Number	Gender	Job Satisfaction
1	M	H
2	M	H
3	F	H
4	M	M
5	F	L
6	F	L
7	F	L
8	M	M
9	M	H
10	F	M
11	M	H
12	M	H
13	M	L
14	F	M
15	F	L
16	F	H

Table 16.1
Job Satisfaction by Gender

Job Satisfaction	Gender		Row Totals
	Male	Female	
High	5	2	7
Medium	2	2	4
Low	1	4	5
Column totals	8	8	16

The same pattern recurs in Table 16.3, but to a lesser extent because not all members of a given religious denomination belong to the same class. Yet it can still be said that most members of a particular religion belong to a particular social stratum.

When variables are not related, we say that they are independent of each other; that is, they do not "go together." Table 16.4 illustrates this point. There is no clear pattern for any of the religious groups in the table. Catholics can be in the upper, middle, and lower classes; the same goes for Jews and Protestants. One cannot say anything about a person's socioeconomic status on the basis of the person's religion.

Table 16.2
Social Class by Religious Denomination (Perfect Covariation)

Social Class	Religious Denomination			Total
	Catholic	Jewish	Protestant	
Upper	0	0	8	8
Middle	0	8	0	8
Lower	8	0	0	8
Total	8	8	8	24

Tables 16.2, 16.3, and 16.4 are examples of bivariate distributions arranged in tabular form. The bivariate distribution consists of the categories of two variables and their joint frequencies. Its components are displayed in the bivariate tables of our example. Each table has two dimensions, one per variable. The variables are divided into a number of categories; for example, the variable "social class" has been divided into the categories "upper," "middle," and "lower" and the variable "religious denomination" into "Catholic," "Jewish," and "Protestant." The cells of the table constitute an intersection between two categories, each of one variable. The frequencies in each cell are of observations that have two traits in common. For example, Table 16.4 shows two Catholics from the upper class, three from the middle class, and three from the lower class. The Jews have three members of the upper class, two members in the middle class, and three in the lower class; finally, there are three Protestants in the upper class, three in the middle class, and two in the lower class.

The bivariate table can also be visualized as a series of univariate distributions.[3] By splitting each table down its columns and taking each column separately, we will have divided each bivariate distribution into three univariate distributions, representing the class standing of Protestants, Catholics, and Jews. In a comparison of the three univariate distributions derived from, say, Table 16.3, it is seen that each distribution differs from the others in its pattern of dispersion. In the Protestant distribution, most of the re-

Table 16.3
Social Class by Religious Denomination (Moderate Covariation)

Social Class	Religious Denomination			Total
	Catholic	Jewish	Protestant	
Upper	0	2	6	8
Middle	1	6	1	8
Lower	7	0	1	8
Total	8	8	8	24

3. Theodore R. Anderson and Morris Zelditch, Jr., *A Basic Course in Statistics* (Fort Worth: Holt, Rinehart and Winston, 1968), Chapter 6.

Table 16.4
Social Class by Religious Denomination (Near-Zero Covariation)

Social Class	Religious Denomination			Total
	Catholic	Jewish	Protestant	
Upper	2	3	3	8
Middle	3	2	3	8
Lower	3	3	2	8
Total	8	8	8	24

spondents tend to cluster at the upper extremity of the distribution, the Jews are lustered in the center, and the Catholics tend toward the lower section. This is even more pronounced in Table 16.2, where the tendency becomes absolute (that is, all Protestants are upper-class, and so on). In Table 16.4, by contrast, there is practically no difference among the three distributions, the dispersion being identical in each. Thus the amount of covariation in a bivariate table can be determined by a comparison of the univariate distributions that constitute the table. The larger the difference, the higher the degree of covariation of the two variables.

Percentaging Bivariate Tables

A useful way of summarizing a bivariate table and comparing its univariate distributions to assess relationship is by expressing its frequencies as percentages. Percentaging tables is appropriate whenever the variables are nominal, but the use of percentages is predominant even when the variables being analyzed are ordinal or interval. In Table 16.5, gender and marital status among public officials have been cross-tabulated to examine the hypothesis that the private life situation of women in elective office differs from that of their male counterparts. The table has been set up in the conventional way: "gender" (the independent variable) is at the top of the table, and "marital status" (the dependent variable) is on the left-hand side.

Table 16.5
Distribution of Marital Status by Gender among Public Officials

Marital Status	Gender	
	Women	Men
Married	49	59
Single, never married	2	2
Divorced, separated	10	5
Widowed	11	—
Total	72	66

Source: Susan J. Carroll, "The Personal is Political: The Intersection of Private Lives and Public Roles among Women and Men in Elective and Appointive Office," *Women and Politics*, Vol. 9, 2 (1989).

Table 16.6
Distribution of Marital Status by Gender among Public Officials
(in Percentages)

	Gender	
Marital Status	Women	Men
Married	68.1%	89.4%
Single, never married	2.8	3.0
Divorced, separated	13.9	7.6
Widowed	15.3	—
Total	100.0	100.0
	(N = 72)	(N = 66)

Each gender group can be visualized as a univariate distribution, and its frequencies can be transformed into percentages by using the total number of cases in each distribution as a base for percentaging (that is, 72 women and 66 men each represent 100 percent). The percentages are presented in Table 16.6. The next step is a comparison of the univariate distributions to determine the extent of correlation between gender and marital status among public officials. Whereas the computation of percentages goes down the columns, the comparison cuts across the rows. The proportion of women who are married is compared with the proportion of married men (68.1 percent and 89.4 percent, respectively). Table 16.6 displays a clear pattern of correlation: gender is associated with marital status among public officials. The two univariate distributions differ in their pattern of distribution: women in public office are less likely than their male counterpart to be married and more likely to be divorced or widowed.

Whenever one variable is considered the independent variable and the other the dependent one, the percentages should be computed in the direction of the independent variable. If gender were considered a dependent variable and marital status the independent variable (which seems unlikely in this example), percentages would be computed across the rows instead of along the columns.

For further details on reading tables, see Exhibit 16.2.

Median and Mean as Covariation Measures

When the variables of a bivariate distribution are ordinal, the medians of the various univariate distributions can be used as measures of covariation, as the survey data in Table 16.10 illustrates. Some 307 individuals were classified according to religion and their evaluation of the quality of community life. The dependent variable "quality of life" is on the left-hand side, and each religious group is assumed to be a univariate distribution. The variable "quality of community life" is ranked from 1 (excellent) to 4 (somewhat poor). The appropriate summary measure for ordinal data is the median which can be utilized to summarize each of the three distributions—Catholic, Jewish, and Protestant. By examining the cumulative percentages for each distribution, we can see that, for Catholics, the median is 2; among Jews, it is 1; and among Protestants, it is 2. Thus the data from this survey indicate that Jews have a higher evaluation of the quality of their community life than Catholics or Protestants. These differences indicate a relationship or covariation between religion and quality of community life.

Exhibit 16.2
The Principles of Table Reading

Social scientists make considerable use of statistical tables as a way of presenting research results. The following discussion may be useful as a quick guide to table reading.

1. *Look for the title.* The title describes the information that is contained in the table. In Table 16.7, the title tells about differences in preferred sports between socioeconomic strata.

2. *Examine the source.* The source of the data is usually written at the bottom of the table, as is shown in Table 16.7. Identifying the source will help in assessing the reliability of the information as well as in finding the original data in case further information is needed.

Table 16.7
Socioeconomic Differences in the Designation of Spectator or Participant Sports as Favorites by Metropolitan Residents

Favorite Sport	Socioeconomic Stratum			Totals
	Upper	Middle	Lower	
Spectator	35.6%	57.1%	54.7%	48.8%
Participant	64.4	42.9	45.3	51.2
	100.0	100.0	100.0	100.0
	$(N=188)$	$(N=175)$	$(N=172)$	$(N=535)$

Adapted from Gregory P. Stone, "Some Meanings of American Sport: An Extended View," in *Sociology of Sport: Proceedings of the C.I.C. Symposium on the Sociology of Sport*, ed. Gerald S. Kenyon (Chicago: Athletic Institute, 1969), p. 10.

3. *Determine in which direction the percentages have been computed.* This step is crucial and should be carefully observed. It is important to examine whether the percentages have been computed down the columns, across the rows, or on the basis of the whole table. Or is the table an abbreviated one, in which the percentages, as presented, do not add up to 100 percent? Determine the direction by examining where the 100 percent or total cases have been inserted. In Table 16.7, the percentages have been computed down the column. By contrast, in Table 16.8, the percentages have been computed in the opposite direction, across the rows.

Exhibit 16.2 (*continued*)

Table 16.8
Level of Education in Relation to Social Class

Social Class	Did Not Finish High School	Graduated from High School but Did Not Enter College	Entered College but Did Not Finish	Completed a Four-Year College Program	Total
Upper and upper middle	5	15	10	70	100 (N = 600)
Lower middle	3	12	36	49	100 (N = 420)
Working	16	23	41	20	100 (N = 510)

4. *Make comparisons.* Comparing the percentage differences in the table is a quick method for assessing the extent of a relationship between the variables. Comparisons are always made in a direction opposite to the one in which the percentages have been computed. If the percentages have been computed down the column, as in Table 16.7, then we compare percentages across the rows. The proportion of members in the upper stratum who favor spectator sports is compared to the proportion of the middle and lower strata who favor spectator sports (35.6 to 57.1 to 54.7). The proportion of each of the socioeconomic strata who favor participant sports can also be examined (64.4 to 42.9 to 45.3). There are social-class differences in the designation of spectator or participant sports as favorites. Individuals from the upper class are more likely to favor participant sports than those from the middle and lower strata.

Often, for the sake of simplicity, only part of the table is presented. Table 16.9 is an example. It is important to observe that the two percentages in this table do not add up to 100 percent and that they are to be compared directly. They represent the different proportion of individuals in the two categories of the independent variable (race) who belong to one response category of the dependent variable (family status).

Based on Roberta G. Simmons, "Basic Principles of Table Reading," in Morris Rosenberg, *The Logic of Survey Analysis* (New York: Basic Books, 1968), pp. 251–258.

Table 16.9
Family Status of Black and White College Students

Race	Percentage of Each Group with High Family Status	
Black	10.0	(N = 872)
White	32.2	(N = 6,403)

Based on Gail E. Thomas, "The Influence of Ascription, Achievement and Educational Expectations on Black-White Postsecondary Enrollment," *Sociological Quarterly*, 20 (1979): 209–222.

Table 16.10
Quality of Community Life by Religion

Quality of Community Life	Catholic		Jewish		Protestant	
	Percent	Cumulative Percent	Percent	Cumulative Percent	Percent	Cumulative Percent
1 Excellent	20	20	67	67	22	22
2 Good	55	75	17	84	43	65
3 Average	22	97	16	100	29	94
4 Somewhat poor	3	100	—	—	6	100
Total	100		100		100	
	(N=151)		(N=6)		(N=150)	

Source: *Social and Political Survey: Winter, 1989.* Social Science Research Facility, University of Wisconsin, Milwaukee (unpublished).

With interval variables, the arithmetic mean can be used as a comparative measure. Table 16.11 is a bivariate distribution of intelligence test scores by age. Each age group can be visualized as a distribution and summarized by the arithmetic mean. Table 16.12 presents the arithmetic means of the distribution. Each pair of means can be compared. It is noted that average scores rise with age, a fact that permits one to deduce that the variables "age" and "intelligence" covary.

Measurement of Relationship

So far, the extent of covariation of two variables has been assessed by comparing the univariate distributions that constitute the bivariate table. However, there are various statistical techniques that allow the researcher to assess the extent to which two variables are associated by a single summarizing measure. Such measures of relationship, often referred to as **correlation coefficients**, reflect the strength and the direction of association between the variables and the degree to which one variable can be predicted from the other.

Table 16.11
Intelligence Test Scores by Age (Hypothetical Data)

IQ Test Scores	Age				Total
	6–10	11–15	16–20	21–25	
0–4	10	6	4	1	21
5–9	8	10	3	2	23
10–14	6	7	8	8	29
15–19	4	3	3	10	20
Total	28	26	18	21	93

Table 16.12
Mean IQ Test Scores in Four Age Groups

Age Group	Mean
6–10	7.7
11–15	8.3
16–20	9.8
21–25	13.4

The notion of prediction is inherent in the concept of covariation. When two variables covary, it is possible to use one to predict the other; when they do not, information about one will not enable the prediction of the other. Consider Tables 16.2, 16.3, and 16.4 again; assume that no information is available about the religious denomination of the 24 persons and that the social status of each one is to be guessed. Generally, the best guess will be the most frequent category. However, since in all three tables the frequencies of all the categories are identical, any category can be arbitrarily selected. Suppose that the middle class is chosen as the best guess. Since only eight cases in each table do in fact belong to the middle class, there will be 16 errors out of 24 guesses in each of the three tables.

Religious denomination can be used to predict social class only if it is likely to reduce the number of errors in prediction. Suppose that it is predicted that all Protestants are upper-class, all Jews are middle-class, and all Catholics are lower-class. In Table 16.2, this prediction is accurate in each of the 24 cases; in Table 16.3, there are 5 errors; in Table 16.4, there are 16 errors.

The advantage of employing religious denomination to predict social class can be calculated by subtracting the new number of errors from the previous total. In Table 16.2, the advantage is absolute because the reduction in the number of errors is the greatest ($16 - 0 = 16$). In Table 16.3, a considerable advantage is gained since the number of errors is reduced by 11 ($16 - 5 = 11$). In Table 16.4, there is no change in the number of errors, despite the employment of religious denomination ($16 - 16 = 0$).

Proportional Reduction of Error

The strength of the association between social class and religious denomination can be assessed by calculating the proportional reduction in prediction error when using one variable to predict another. The **proportional reduction of error** is defined as follows:[4]

---

4. Mueller et al., *Statistical Reasoning in Sociology,* p. 248.

$$\frac{b-a}{b} \qquad\qquad (16.1)$$

where b = the original number of errors (before employing the independent variable as a predictor)

a = the new number of errors (after employing the independent variable as a predictor)

Using Equation (16.1), you can calculate the proportional reduction in errors of prediction from Tables 16.2, 16.3, and 16.4.

For Table 16.2: $\dfrac{16-0}{16} = \dfrac{16}{16} = 1$

For Table 16.3: $\dfrac{16-5}{16} = \dfrac{11}{16} = .69$

For Table 16.4: $\dfrac{16-16}{16} = \dfrac{0}{16} = 0$

The proportional reduction of error is absolute in Table 16.2, as reflected in the magnitude of the coefficient of 1, expressing a perfect relationship between the variables "religious denomination" and "social status." The number of errors in Table 16.3 has been reduced by almost 70 percent, following the employment of religious denomination as a predictor. This is expressed by the coefficient of .69. In Table 16.4, there is no advantage in using religious denomination. The coefficient of 0 expresses the absence of any association between the two variables.

Any measure of association can be developed along similar logic, provided that it is based on two kinds of rules: (1) a rule that allows the prediction of the dependent variable on the basis of an independent variable and (2) a rule that allows the prediction of the dependent variable independently of an independent variable.[5] On this basis, any measure of association can be defined as in Equation (16.2):

$$\text{Measure of association} = \frac{\text{error by rule 1} - \text{error by rule 2}}{\text{error by rule 2}} \qquad (16.2)$$

Most of the measures of relationship introduced in this chapter will be analyzed according to this definition. We shall discuss lambda, which measures the relation between nominal variables; gamma and Kendall's tau-b, which are ordinal coefficients; and Pearson's r, an interval measure of relation.

5. Herbert L. Costner, "Criteria for Measures of Association," *American Sociological Review*, 30 (1965): 344.

Nominal Measures of Relationship

Lambda, the Guttman Coefficient of Predictability

The correlation **lambda** (λ), also known as the **Guttman coefficient of predictability**, is suitable for calculating relationships between nominal variables.[6] To illustrate its calculation, suppose that one is interested in predicting the party identification of nonsouthern whites in a local election during the 1990s. One possibility is to use the distribution of party identification during 1990, thereby making use of prediction rule 2. The univariate distribution of party identification is presented in Table 16.13.

The most effective way of guessing the party identification of each of these 300 voters, on the basis of the distribution given earlier, is to use a measure of central tendency that will yield the smallest number of errors in prediction. As party identification is a nominal variable, the mode is the most appropriate. Since Democrats are in the most frequent category ($f = 126$), the best guess is that each voter identified with the Democratic party, for the number of errors will not exceed 174 (78 independents and 96 Republicans). Any other guess would magnify the number of errors. When guessing voters' party identification on the basis of the dependent variable alone, the most frequent category is chosen. According to this rule 2, the number of errors is 174 out of 300 guesses, that is, 58 percent.

The percentage of error might be reduced if another variable, "1986 party identification," is used as a predictor. Information is available on each of the 300 voters regarding their party identification in 1986. On this basis, it is possible to construct a bivariate table (Table 16.14) where all voters are classified according to two variables: their party identification in 1986 and in 1990. With this additional information, one can predict the party identification of nonsouthern whites prior to the elections of 1990 on the basis of their 1986 party identification. First, take those who declared themselves Democratic in 1986; there were 108 respondents, 93 of whom gave the same identification in 1990. As this is the most frequent category, it

Table 16.13
1990 Party Identification among Nonsouthern Whites
(Hypothetical Data)

Party Identification	f
Democrat	126
Independent	78
Republican	96
Total	300

6. Louis Guttman, "An Outline of the Statistical Theory of Prediction," in *The Prediction of Personal Adjustment,* ed. Paul Horst (New York: Social Science Research Council, 1941).

Table 16.14

1986 and 1990 Party Identification among Nonsouthern Whites (Hypothetical Data)

Party Identification, 1990	Party Identification, 1986			1990 Overall
	Democrat	Independent	Republican	
Democrat	93	27	6	126
Independent	15	48	15	78
Republican	—	15	81	96
1986 overall	108	90	103	300

is assumed that anyone who identified with the Democratic party in 1986 did so again in 1990. With this assumption, 15 errors of predictions are made because 15 of the 108 identified themselves otherwise in 1990.

Ninety voters identified themselves as independents in 1986; 78 of them did so again in 1990. It can therefore be assumed again that whoever identified themselves as independents in 1986 did so in 1900 as well. With this assumption, the number of errors is $27 + 15 = 42$, the number who did not identify themselves as independents. Finally, for the 102 who identified with the Republicans in 1986, it is assumed that their preference patterns did not change; as a result, $15 + 6 = 21$ errors are made.

The total number of errors made by using the new rule 1 is $15 + 42 + 21 = 78$ errors out of 300 predictions, or 26 percent. Using an independent variable as a predictor leads to a decrease in the error of prediction, as expressed in the magnitude of the correlation, which can now be calculated:

$$\text{Error stemming from rule 2} = 174$$

$$\text{Error stemming from rule 1} = \ \ 78$$

$$\lambda = \frac{174 - 78}{174} = .55$$

Thus 55 percent of the errors of prediction concerning party identification in 1990 were eliminated by using the identification pattern during the 1986 elections.

Lambda is an asymmetrical coefficient, as it reflects relationships between variables in one direction only. In practice, it is often represented as λ_a, a indicating that it is asymmetrical. The coefficient .55 expresses the relationship between party identification in 1986 and 1990, with that of 1986 serving as an independent variable. The correlation coefficient can also be calculated in the opposite direction, with 1990 serving as the independent variable. The method of calculation is identical: we compute the number of errors made when estimating 1986 identification patterns without reference to 1990 data and then calculate the advantage obtained by gauging the 1986 data from those of 1990.

Alternative Procedure for Computing Lambda.   Lambda can also be computed by a slightly simpler procedure using Formula (16.3).[7]

$$\lambda_a = \frac{\sum f_i - F_d}{N - F_d}$$ (16.3)

where f_i = the modal frequency within each category of the independent variable

F_d = the modal frequency in the marginal totals of the dependent variable

N = the total number of cases

We can now repeat our calculation of the correlation between the data from 1986 and those from 1990, with the 1986 party identification serving as an independent variable.

$$\sum f_i = 93 + 48 + 81 = 222$$
$$F_d = 126$$
$$N = 300$$
$$\lambda_a = \frac{222 - 126}{300 - 126} = \frac{96}{174} = .55$$

To summarize, the magnitude of lambda expresses the proportional reduction in error of estimate when switching from rule 2 to rule 1. The strength of the association between the two variables reflects the improvement in prediction attainable with the aid of a second variable. Lambda may range from zero to one; zero indicates that there is nothing to be gained by shifting from one prediction rule to another, whereas one reflects the fact that the use of an independent variable permits the dependent variable to be predicted without error at all.

Limitations of Lambda.   Lambda has a limitation in situations where the modal frequencies of the independent variable are all concentrated in one category of the dependent variable. In such a case, lambda will always be zero, even in instances where the two variables are in fact related. For example, in the bivariate distribution presented in Table 16.15, it can be seen

Table 16.15
Place of Residence and Self-esteem

Self-esteem	Place of Residence		Total
	Rural Areas	Urban Areas	
High	300	200	500
Low	100	100	200
Total	400	300	700

7. Linton C. Freeman, *Elementary Applied Statistics* (New York: Wiley, 1965), p. 74.

that place of residence is associated with self-esteem. More residents of rural areas (75 percent) have high self-esteem than residents of cities (66 percent). However, because the sum of all modal frequencies of the variable "place of residence" ($\Sigma f_i = 300 + 200$) is equal to the modal frequency of the marginal totals of the variable "self-esteem" ($F_d = 500$), lambda will take on the value of zero. Such a pattern of distribution is likely to occur when the marginal totals of the dependent variable are extremely uneven. Lambda would then be inappropriate.

Ordinal Measures of Relationship

When both variables of a bivariate distribution are ordinal, the construction of a measure of relationship is based on the principal property of the ordinal scale, by which observations can be ranked in relation to the variables being measured. With a single variable, one is generally interested in evaluating the relative position of the observations on the variable. For example, professions can be ranked according to the amount of prestige they command, and students can be ranked according to their relative degree of political tolerance. The same principle can be applied with two variables. Here the interest is in examining whether the ranking of observations on each of the variables is identical, similar, or different. Every two observations are compared, and it is noted whether one that is ranked high on one variable is as high with regard to the other. For instance, one can examine whether the ranking of professions by their prestige in the 1950s resembles their ranking in the 1990s or whether persons with a conservative orientation on foreign affairs show a similar tendency on domestic issues.

When observations display the same order on both variables, the relationship is said to be positive; when the order is inverse, so that the observation ranking highest on one variable is the lowest on the second variable, the relationship is negative. When there is no clear pattern in the relative position of the observations on both variables, the variables are said to be independent. Consider the following example: If all military personnel with high rank are also more liberal on political issues than lower-ranking officers, one may say that military rank and political liberalism are positively related. If, however, the high-ranking officers are less liberal, the association is negative. If some high officers are liberal and others are not, rank and liberalism are independent of each other.

The Pair Concept

Most ordinal measures of relationship are based on the *pair* as a unit of analysis and its relative ranking on both variables. For example, we can compare every pair of officers in terms of their rank and liberalism. The number of pairs that can be formed out of N cases is obtained by Formula (16.4):

$$\binom{N}{2} = \frac{N(N-1)}{2} \tag{16.4}$$

Suppose that six officers are classified according to their rank and degree of liberalism. The observations are presented in Table 16.16. According to Formula (16.4), 15 pairs can be formed out of six observations:

$$\binom{6}{2} = \frac{6(5)}{2} = 15$$

Table 16.17 lists the 15 pairs according to cell number and rank on each of the variables. The first column designates the pair's number; the second column, the cell number (with a designating the first member of the pair and b the second member); and the third and fourth columns, their rank and liberalism. The last column describes the relative position of the pair on the two variables.

For instance, the first pair, designated as tied on X and Y, consists of two officers, both classified in cell 11. These officers have the same rank and share the same political views. Pairs tied on Y are officers of different ranks sharing the same political views; pairs tied on X are officers of the same rank but of different political views; pairs designated as "same" are officers who have the same relative position on both variables, so the officer with the higher rank would be the more liberal as well. Pairs designated as "inverse" have a different relative position on both variables, so the officer with the higher rank would be the less liberal of the pair.

Types of Pairs

From the total number of pairs that can be constructed from N observations, the following groups can be distinguished:

1. Pairs that display the same order on both X and Y; they will be denoted as Ns.

Table 16.16
Liberalism by Rank (Hypothetical Data)

Liberalism (Y)	Rank (X)		
	Low	High	Total
Low	$2_{(11)}$	$1_{(12)}$	3
High	$1_{(21)}$	$2_{(22)}$	3
Total	3	3	6

The numbers in parentheses designate the cell numbers, with raw numbers designated first and column numbers second.

Table 16.17
Relative Position of Officers in Rank and Liberalism

Pair	From Cell	Rank of Officer (X)	Degree of Liberalism (Y)	Order
1	a 11	L	L	Tie on X and Y
	b 11	L	L	
2	a 11	L	L	Tie on Y
	b 12	H	L	
3	a 11	L	L	Tie on Y
	b 12	H	L	
4	a 11	L	L	Tie on X
	b 21	L	H	
5	a 11	L	L	Tie on X
	b 21	L	H	
6	a 11	L	L	Same
	b 22	H	H	
7	a 11	L	L	Same
	b 22	H	H	
8	a 11	L	L	Same
	b 22	H	H	
9	a 11	L	L	Same
	b 22	H	H	
10	a 12	H	L	Inverse
	b 21	L	H	
11	a 12	H	L	Tie on X
	b 22	H	H	
12	a 12	H	L	Tie on X
	b 22	H	H	
13	a 21	L	H	Tie on Y
	b 22	H	H	
14	a 21	L	H	Tie on Y
	b 22	H	H	
15	a 22	H	H	Tie on X and Y
	b 22	H	H	

2. Pairs that display an inverse order on X and Y; they will be denoted as *Nd*.
3. Pairs tied on X, denoted as *Tx*.
4. Pairs tied on Y, denoted as *Ty*.
5. Pairs tied on X and on Y, denoted *Txy*.

1. To find *Ns* in the general bivariate table, the frequency in every cell is multiplied by the total of all the frequencies in the cells below it and to its right, and the products are added up. In Table 16.16, the number of pairs displaying the same ranking on both variables is $2 \times 2 = 4$.

2. To calculate *Nd* in the general bivariate table, the frequency in each cell is multiplied by the total of all the frequencies in the cells below it and to its left, and the products are added up. In Table 16.16, the number of pairs displaying different rankings on the two variables is $1 \times 1 = 1$.

3. To find the number of pairs tied on X (Tx), the frequency in every cell is multiplied by the total of all the frequencies in the cells in that column, and the products are added up. The number of pairs tied on X is $(2 \times 1) + (1 \times 2) = 4$.

4. To find the number of pairs tied on Y(Ty), the frequency in each cell is multiplied by the sum of the frequencies in the cells in that row, and the products are added up. The number of pairs tied on Y in Table 16.16 is $(2 \times 1) + (1 \times 2) = 4$.

5. To work out the number of pairs that are tied on X and Y (Txy), all the pairs that can be created from every cell, by means of Formula (16.4), are added up. In Table 16.16, the ties on X and Y are as follows:

$$\text{Cell 11:} \quad \frac{2(1)}{2} = 1$$

$$\text{Cell 12:} \quad \frac{1(0)}{1} = 0$$

$$\text{Cell 21:} \quad \frac{1(0)}{1} = 0$$

$$\text{Cell 22:} \quad \frac{2(1)}{2} = 1$$

The total number of pairs of all kinds that can be constructed out of N observations is

$$\binom{N}{2} = Ns + Nd + Tx + Ty + Txy$$

In our example,

$$\binom{6}{2} = 4 + 1 + 4 + 4 + 2 = 15$$

Gamma

Gamma (γ or **G**), a coefficient used for measuring the association between ordinal variables, was developed by Leo Goodman and William Kruskal.[8] It is a symmetrical statistic, based on the number of same-order pairs (*Ns*) and the number of different-order pairs (*Nd*). Tied pairs play no part in the definition of gamma.

---

8. Leo A. Goodman and William H. Kruskal, "Measure of Association for Cross Classification," *Journal of the American Statistical Association*, 49 (1954): 732–764.

Table 16.18
Political Tolerance of College Students by Class Standing

	Class Standing						
	Fresh-man	Sopho-more	Junior	Senior	Graduate Student (Full-Time)	Graduate Student (Part-Time)	Total
Less tolerant	30	30	34	33	40	15	182
Somewhat tolerant	66	75	79	79	120	45	464
More tolerant	28	51	59	63	151	34	386
Total	124	156	172	175	311	94	1,032

The coefficient is defined by Formula (16.5):[9]

$$\gamma = \frac{0.5(Ns + Nd) - Minimum\ (Ns,\ Nd)}{0.5(Ns + Nd)} \tag{16.5}$$

To illustrate the calculation of gamma, consider the data presented in Table 16.18 on class standing and political tolerance of students. If these two variables are associated, it will be possible to predict students' political tolerance on the basis of their class standing with a minimum of error.

First, the number of pairs that can be constructed from 1,032 observations is counted. With tied pairs excluded, the overall number of pairs that can be constructed from a bivariate table is $Ns + Nd$. Ns and Nd are calculated according to the definitions presented previously.

$$
\begin{aligned}
Ns = \ & 30(75 + 51 + 79 + 59 + 79 + 63 + 120 + 151 + 45 + 34) \\
& + 66(51 + 59 + 63 + 151 + 34) \\
& + 30(79 + 59 + 79 + 63 + 120 + 151 + 45 + 34) \\
& + 75(59 + 63 + 151 + 34) \\
& + 34(79 + 63 + 120 + 151 + 45 + 34) \\
& + 79(63 + 151 + 34) + 33(120 + 151 + 45 + 34) \\
& + 79(151 + 34) + 40(45 + 34) + 120(34) \\
= \ & 157{,}958 \\
Nd = \ & 15(120 + 151 + 79 + 63 + 79 + 59 + 75 + 51 + 66 + 28) \\
& + 45(151 + 63 + 59 + 51 + 28) \\
& + 40(79 + 63 + 79 + 59 + 75 + 51 + 66 + 28) \\
& + 120(63 + 59 + 51 + 28) \\
& + 33(79 + 59 + 75 + 51 + 66 + 28) \\
& + 79(59 + 51 + 28) + 34(75 + 51 + 66 + 28) + 79(51 + 28) \\
& + 30(66 + 28) + 75(28) \\
= \ & 112{,}882
\end{aligned}
$$

9. Mueller et al., *Statistical Reasoning in Sociology,* p. 282.

The total number of pairs (tied pairs excluded) is $Ns + Nd = 157,958 + 112,882 = 270,840$.

Next the relative political tolerance of the students is determined on the basis of the dependent variable alone—rule 2. To find the relative position of each of the 270,840 pairs, some random system can be used. (As the univariate distribution of the variable "political tolerance" does not provide information about the relative political tolerance of the students, it cannot be used as a basis of prediction.) For example, one can label members of each pair as heads or tails and by flipping a coin decide which member is more tolerant. When this process is repeated for each pair, it can be expected that in the long run, 50 percent of the guesses about the relative position of the students will be accurate, whereas the other 50 percent will be erroneous. Hence prediction rule 2 will produce $(Ns + Nd)/2 = 135,420$ errors.

Prediction rule 1 states that if there are more pairs displaying the same order (Ns), this order will be predicted for all other pairs as well. In that case, the number of errors will be Nd, that is, the number of pairs whose ranking is different on the two variables. In the same way, should the number of inverted pairs (Nd) be greater, this order would be predicted for all remaining pairs, whereupon the number of errors will equal Ns.

The calculations based on the information in Table 16.18 indicate that the number of pairs with the same ranking is greater than the number whose ranking is inverted $(Ns > Nd)$. Hence the relative position of political tolerance for each pair will be predicted on the basis of its member's class standing, meaning that the student with the greater seniority exhibits greater tolerance. If Mary is a sophomore and John is a freshman, Mary will be more tolerant than John. As not all pairs display the same order, the number of errors made by such a prediction rule is $Nd = 112,882$.

The relationship between class standing and political tolerance can now be asserted, using the general formula for measures of association:

$$\frac{b-a}{b}$$

where $b = (Ns + Nd)/2$ and $a = (Ns, Nd)_{min}$. Accordingly,

$$\gamma = \frac{(Ns + Nd)/2 - Nd}{(Ns + Nd)/2} = \frac{135,420 - 112,882}{135,420} = \frac{22,538}{135,420} = .17$$

A value of .17 for γ reflects the advantage gained by using the variable "class standing" in predicting political tolerance. By the use of this variable, 17 percent of the total number of errors were eliminated.

Another Formula for Gamma.   Gamma can also be calculated by using Formula (16.6):

$$\gamma = \frac{Ns - Nd}{Ns + Nd} \tag{16.6}$$

This formula reflects the relative predominance of same-order or different-order pairs. When same-order pairs predominate, the coefficient is positive; when different-order pairs predominate, it is negative. When all pairs are same-order pairs, Nd will be zero and gamma will then equal one:

$$\gamma = \frac{Ns - 0}{Ns + 0} = \frac{Ns}{Ns} = 1.0$$

A coefficient of 1.0 indicates that the dependent variable can be predicted on the basis of the independent variable without any error. When $Ns = 0$, the coefficient will be negative, but prediction is still accurate:

$$\gamma = \frac{0 - Nd}{0 + Nd} = \frac{-Nd}{Nd} = -1.0$$

When the number of different-order pairs is equal to the number of same-order pairs, gamma is zero:

$$\gamma = \frac{Ns - Nd}{Ns + Nd} = \frac{0}{Ns + Nd} = 0$$

A gamma of zero reflects that there is nothing to be gained by using the independent variable to predict the dependent variable.

Limitations of Gamma. The main weakness of gamma as a measure of ordinal association is the exclusion of ties from its computation. Hence it will reach a value of ± 1 even under conditions of less than perfect association. For example, a perfect relationship was described early in the chapter as in the following table:

50	0
0	50

$$\gamma = 1$$

However, because gamma is based on untied pairs only, it becomes 1 under the following conditions as well:

50	50
0	50

$$\gamma = 1$$

In general, in marginal distributions that are uneven, with a concentration of many observations in few categories, there will be many tied pairs, and gamma will be based on a smaller proportion of pairs. This is especially acute in 2×2 tables, where the proportion of untied pairs will be small, even when all marginal frequencies are equal.

Kendall's Tau-*b*

With many ties, a different measure that handles the problem of ties can be used. It is **Kendall's tau-*b*,** defined as follows:

$$\tau b = \frac{Ns - Nd}{\sqrt{(Ns + Nd + Ty)(Ns + Nd + Tx)}} \qquad (16.7)$$

Tau-*b* varies from -1 to $+1$ and is a symmetrical coefficient. It has the same numerator as gamma but has a correction factor for ties in its denominator (Ty and Tx). For example, for the following bivariate distribution

	X		
Y	30	70	100
	30	20	50
	60	90	150

we get

$$Ns = \quad 600 \qquad Ty = 2{,}700$$
$$Nd = 2{,}100 \qquad Tx = 2{,}300$$

Therefore,

$$\tau b = \frac{600 - 2{,}100}{\sqrt{(600 + 2{,}100 + 2{,}700)(600 + 2{,}100 + 2{,}300)}} = \frac{-1{,}500}{5{,}196} = -.29$$

Note that under the same conditions, gamma gives a considerably higher figure than tau-*b*:

$$\gamma = \frac{600 - 2{,}100}{600 + 2{,}100} = \frac{-1{,}500}{2{,}700} = -.56$$

Gamma will always exceed tau-*b* when there are tied pairs. With no ties, its value will be identical with tau-*b*. Tau-*b* is difficult to interpret as a measure that designates a proportional reduction of error in prediction. In this respect, it is less satisfactory than gamma.

Interval Measures of Relationship

At lower levels of measurement, the ability to make predictions is restricted, even when the variables considered are associated. At most, one can point out an interdependence of certain categories or properties, such as the fact that Catholics tend to vote Democratic, or one can expect the same relative position of observations on two variables, for instance, that military rank is associated with liberalism. However, predictions of this type are imprecise, and there is frequently a need for more accurate predictive statements, as, for example, when one wishes to predict individuals' future income on the basis of their level of education or a city's crime rate from its racial composition.

Prediction Rules

When the variables being analyzed are at least interval, one can be more precise in describing the nature and the form of the relationship. Precise prediction rules are quite frequently made in the natural sciences in the form of prediction functions. For instance, there are functions that express the relationship between acceleration distance and time in the form $K = PV/T$; or between voltage resistance and current in the form $C = V/R$.

In the social sciences, however, prediction functions are expressed in much simpler terms. Most relationships can in fact be formulated in terms of a linear function rule. A function is said to be linear when pairs of (X, Y) values fall exactly into a function that can be plotted as a straight line. All such functions have rules of the form $Y = a + bX$, where a and b are constant numbers.

For example, there is a perfect linear relationship between the distance and the time that a car travels at a fixed speed (Table 16.19). If its speed is 60 miles per hour, it will go 60 miles in one hour, or X miles in Y time. The linear function expresses the relationship between the time and the distance that the car travels. Such a function takes the form of $Y = 1X$, reflecting the fact that a change of one unit of distance (miles) will bring about a change of one unit of time (minutes). The constant 1 preceding X in the formula is b, called the slope, expressing the number of units of change in Y accompanying one unit of change in X.

Linear Regression

This method of specifying the nature of a relationship between two variables is referred to as *regression analysis*. The task of regression is to find some algebraic expression by which to represent the functional relationship between the variables. The equation $Y = a + bX$ is a linear regression equation, mean-

Table 16.19
Distance by Time

X (Miles)	Y (Time in Minutes)
1	1
3	3
5	5
10	10
15	15

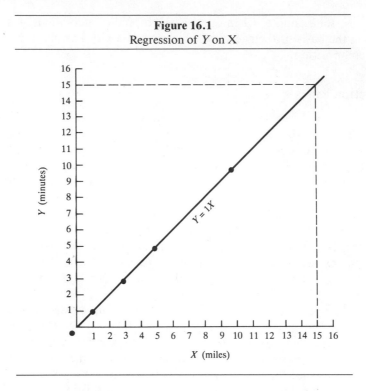

Figure 16.1
Regression of *Y* on X

The graph shows *Y* (minutes) on the vertical axis and *X* (miles) on the horizontal axis, with the line *Y* = 1X.

ing that the function describing the relation between *X* and *Y* is that of a straight line. Ordinarily, the observations of *X* and *Y*—and the **regression line** connecting them—are displayed in the form of a graph. The variables *X* and *Y* are represented by two intersecting axes. Each observation is entered as a dot at the point where the *X* and *Y* scores intersect. In Figure 16.1, we have entered the observations from Table 16.19 to illustrate the graphical presentation of bivariate observations and the functional form describing their interrelationship. The independent variable, *X*, is placed on the horizontal axis; *Y*, the dependent variable, is placed on the vertical axis; and each observation is plotted at the intersection of the two axes. For example, the last observation of Table 16.19 is plotted at the intersection of the two axes on the score 15, to represent its score of 15 on the two variables.

The regression line does not always pass through the intersection of the *X* and *Y* axes. When a straight line intersects the *Y* axis, there is a need for another constant to be introduced into the linear regression equation. This constant is symbolized by the letter *a* and is called the *Y* intercept. The intercept reflects the value of *Y* when *X* is zero. Each of the three regression lines in Figure 16.2 has different values for *a* and *b*. The three different values of *a* (6, 1, 2) are reflected in the three different intersections of the lines. The different values of *b* (− 3, .5, 3) reflect the steepness of the slopes. The

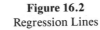

Figure 16.2
Regression Lines

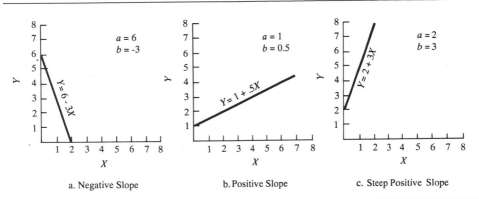

higher the value of *b*, the steeper the slope. Finally, the sign of *b* expresses the direction of the relationship between *X* and *Y*: when *b* is positive, an increase in *X* is accompanied by an increase in *Y* (Figure 16.2*b* and 16.2*c*); when *b* is negative, *Y* decreases as *X* increases (Figure 16.2*a*).

Most relationships in the social sciences can be fairly well expressed by the linear function. For example, the equation $Y = 5,000 + 1,000X$ could express the relation between income and education; *a* would stand for the initial yearly salary ($5,000) for individuals who had no education at all and *b* for an increment of $1,000 for each additional year of education. Using this prediction rule, we could expect individuals having ten years of schooling to make $15,000 $[Y = 5,000 + 1,000(10)]$.

Criterion of Least Squares

The regression equation, however, is only a prediction rule; thus there are discrepancies between actual observations and the ones predicted. The goal is to construct such an equation that the deviations, or **error of prediction**, will be at a minimum. If a specific criterion is adopted in determining *a* and *b* of the linear equation, it is possible to create a function that will minimize the variance around the regression line. This is the **criterion of least squares**, which minimizes the sum of the squared differences between the observed *Y*'s and the *Y*'s predicted with the regression equation. This prediction equation is

$$\hat{Y} = a + bX \tag{16.8}$$

where $\hat{Y}$ denotes predicted scores of the variable *Y*.

According to the least squares criterion, *a* and *b* can be calculated by the following formulas:

$$b = \frac{\sum (X - \bar{X})(Y - \bar{Y})}{\sum (X - \bar{X})^2} \tag{16.9}$$

$$a = \frac{\sum Y - b \sum X}{N} = \bar{Y} - b\bar{X} \tag{16.10}$$

A more convenient formula for computing b is

$$b = \frac{N\sum XY - (\sum X)(\sum Y)}{N\sum X^2 - (\sum X)^2} \tag{16.11}$$

An Illustration.   As an illustration of the construction of a precise prediction rule for interval variables, consider the series of observations in Table 16.20 on the number of robberies (per 100,000 population) and the percentage of the urban population living in metropolitan areas. These observations on ten states are presented with the aim of exploring the relationship between the degree of urbanization and the crime rate. The variable to be predicted (the dependent variable) is "robberies per 100,000 population," and the independent variable is "percentage of urban population."

To predict the number of robberies in any state, without any additional information, a value that will produce the smallest possible number of errors is chosen as an estimate for each state in the distribution. The arithmetic mean is the best guess for each interval distribution because the

Table 16.20
Robbery Rate and Percentage of Urban Population in Metropolitan Areas, 1986

State	Percentage of Urban Population (X)	Robberies per 100,000 Population (Y)	XY	X^2	Y^2
Massachusetts	91	193	17,563	8,281	37,249
Wisconsin	67	73	4,891	4,489	5,329
South Dakota	28	16	448	784	256
Virginia	72	106	7,632	5,184	11,236
South Carolina	60	99	5,940	3,600	9,801
Texas	81	240	19,440	6,561	57,600
Arizona	75	169	12,675	5,625	28,561
California	96	343	32,928	9,216	117,649
Arkansas	44	88	3,872	1,936	7,744
Hawaii	77	106	8,162	5,929	11,236
Total	691	1,433	113,551	51,605	286,661

Source: United States Bureau of the Census, *Statistical Abstracts of the United States: 1988* (108th edition). Washington, D.C., 1988.

mean of its squared distribution is lower than for any other value. The average robbery rate for 100,000 population, according to the data, is

$$\bar{Y} = \frac{\sum Y}{N} = \frac{1,433}{10} = 143.3$$

To assess the prediction error, subtract each observation from the mean (to calculate the deviations), and square the deviations. The sum of the squared deviations, referred to as total variation about $\bar{Y}$, is selected as an estimate of error of prediction—rule 2—because it produces the minimum of errors. The total variation about $\bar{Y}$ is defined as in Equation (16.12):

$$\text{Total variation} = \sum (Y - \bar{Y})^2 \tag{16.12}$$

The next step is to reduce the errors of prediction of number of robberies by employing a second variable, "percentage of urban," as a predictor. This can be accomplished by constructing a prediction rule in the form of a regression equation that will best describe the relationship between these two variables and that will allow us to predict the number of robberies in any state on the basis of percentage of urban population with a minimum of error.

The observations in Table 16.20 can be displayed in a scatter diagram, which is a graphic device providing a first approximation of the relationship between the two variables (Figure 16.3). Each letter or letters (representing the first letter of each state or its abbreviation) represents an observation that has a fixed X and Y characteristic. For example, point WI represents Wisconsin with 73 robberies per 100,000 population and 67 percent of its

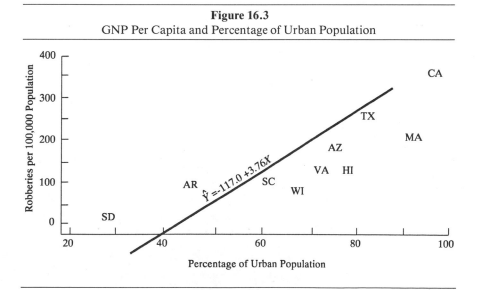

Figure 16.3
GNP Per Capita and Percentage of Urban Population

population in metropolitan areas. After all points have been plotted, a line that best approximates the trend displayed by the points is drawn. Obviously, several such lines can be drawn among the points, but only one—the line of least squares—comes as close as possible to all the individual observations. Before drawing this line, calculate the constants a and b:

$$b = \frac{10(113,551) - (691)(1,433)}{10(51,605) - (691)^2} = 3.76$$

$$a = 143.3 - 3.76(69.1) = -117.0$$

The resulting linear equation is therefore:

$$\hat{Y} = -117.0 + 3.76X$$

The estimated regression line can now be drawn and applied to predict the robbery rate for every level of urban population. For example, if a state had 50 percent of its population in metropolitan areas, its predicted robbery rate per 100,000 population would be

$$\hat{Y} = -117.0 + 3.76(50) = 71.0$$

Errors of Prediction

You can see from Figure 16.3 that most of the observations are spread around the regression line. The deviations of the actual observations from the predicted ones represent the errors produced when using the prediction rule specified for predicting the robbery rate based on the percentage of urban population (rule 1).

The error involved in predicting robberies based on the percentage of urban population can be estimated by measuring the deviations of the actual observations from the regression line. The predicted robbery rate for each state is subtracted from the actual observations recorded in Table 16.20. In Texas, for example, the predicted robbery rate per 100,000 population according to the prediction rule is $\hat{Y} = -117.0 + 3.76(81) = 187.56$. The actual robbery rate for Texas is 240; the error of prediction, therefore, is $240 - 187.56 = 52.44$.

The sum of the squared errors of prediction is the variation unexplained by the independent variable. It is defined in Formula (16.13):

$$\text{Unexplained variation} = \sum (Y_i - \hat{Y})^2 \qquad (16.13)$$

where Y_i = actual observations and $\hat{Y}$ = predicted observations.

Another measure of error that is widely used is the *standard error of estimate (Sy.x)*. It is based on the *unexplained variation* around the regression line and is defined as follows:

$$Sy.x = \sqrt{\frac{\sum (Y_i - \hat{Y})^2}{N}} \qquad (16.14)$$

The standard error of estimate closely parallels the standard deviation, discussed in Chapter 15.

Pearson's Product-Moment Correlation Coefficient (r)

There are two measures of variability for Y. The first, the total variation about $\bar{Y}$, is the error obtained when one predicts Y with no prior knowledge of X—rule 2. (Rule 2 is the total variation about $\bar{Y}$.) The second, the unexplained variation, as defined by Equation (16.13), is the error obtained when using linear regression as the prediction rule—rule 1.

These two estimates of error permit the construction of an interval measure of association that reflects a proportional reduction in error when one shifts from rule 2, the mean, to rule 1, the linear regression equation, to evaluate Y. This measure, r^2, is defined in Equation (16.15):

$$r^2 = \frac{\text{total variation} - \text{unexplained variation}}{\text{total variation}} \qquad (16.15)$$

The unexplained variation is subtracted from the original error of prediction to evaluate the proportional reduction in error. The proportional reduction in error is reflected by r^2 when X is used to predict Y.

Unexplained variation of zero means that the regression equation eliminated all errors in predicting Y, and r^2 then equals one, meaning that any variation in Y can be explained by X. Conversely, when the unexplained variation is identical to the total variation, r^2 is zero, indicating complete independence between X and Y.

Conventionally, the square root of r^2, r, designated *Pearson's product-moment correlation coefficient* or **Pearson's r**, rather than r^2, is used as a coefficient of correlation. Pearson's r ranges from -1.0 to $+1.0$, where a negative coefficient indicates inverse relations between the variables. A simple formula for computing r is

$$r = \frac{N\sum XY - \left(\sum X\right)\left(\sum Y\right)}{\sqrt{\left[N\sum X^2 - \left(\sum X\right)^2\right]\left[N\sum Y^2 - \left(\sum Y\right)^2\right]}} \qquad (16.16)$$

For our example the correlation coefficient will be:

$$r = \frac{10(113,551) - (691)(1,433)}{\sqrt{[10(51,605) - (691)^2]\,[10(286,661) - (1,433)^2}} = .82$$

Thus r^2 is $.82^2 = .67$ which indicates a proportional reduction of error of 67% when percent urban is used to predict robberies per 100,000 population. Another way to express this is to say that 67% of the variance in robbery rate is accounted for by percent urban.

The size of r^2 or r is determined by the spread of the actual observations around the regression line. Thus if all the observations are on the line, r will

Figure 16.4
Recognizing Trends from Scatter Diagrams

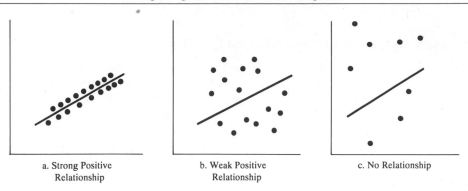

a. Strong Positive
Relationship

b. Weak Positive
Relationship

c. No Relationship

be 1.0; if they are randomly scattered, r will approximate zero. Figure 16.4 illustrates a hypothetical strong positive relationship, a weak positive relationship, and no relationship. However, when r or r^2 approximates or equals zero, one should not rush to the conclusion that the variables are not related. The relationship may be curvilinear—that is, it may not be described by a straight line—so that a coefficient based on the linear model would not give a correct picture of the statistical relationship. In general, careful scrutiny of the scatter diagram will give an indication as to the extent to which the observations display a linear or a curvilinear trend or none at all. When the data are clearly nonlinear, the *eta coefficient* can be employed instead of Pearson's r.[10]

Summary

1. This chapter focused on the nature of relationships between two variables and on the construction of measures of relationship. It was demonstrated that variables that are related vary together: specific categories of one variable "go together" with specific categories of the second or there is some correspondence in the relative position of the two variables. It is sometimes possible to describe the relationship between interval variables by employing specific functions that permit exact predictions.

2. A relationship between two variables can be assessed by comparing the univariate distributions that constitute the bivariate table, using summary measures such as the median or the mean. Alternatively, associations

10. It is beyond the scope of this text to discuss curvilinear relations. For further discussion, see George W. Bohrnstedt and David Knoke, *Statistics for Social Data Analysis* (Itasca, Ill.: Peacock, 1988).

can be described by special measures of relationships that reflect the relative utility of using one variable to predict another.

3. Measures of relationship usually correspond to the variables' level of measurement. Nominal relations can be assessed by lambda. Either gamma or Kendall's tau-*b* is used to calculate relations between ordinal variables. Finally, Pearson's *r* is an interval measure of relationship that reflects the proportional reduction of error when one shifts from the mean as a prediction rule to the linear regression equation.

Key Terms for Review

correlation coefficient
proportional reduction of error
lambda (Guttman coefficient of
   predictability)
gamma

Kendall's tau-*b*
regression line
error of prediction
criterion of least squares
Pearson's *r*

Study Questions

1. Discuss the concept of relationship between variables in terms of the proportional reduction of error.
2. Give an example of a bivariate nominal distribution for which lambda is not suitable as a measure of relationship. What measure would you use instead?
3. The following is a bivariate distribution of alienation by social status. By making a percentage comparison and by using a suitable measure of relationship, assess the following hypothesis: as status increases, the degree of alienation decreases. What other measures of relationship can be used to test this hypothesis?

	Social Status			
Alienation	Low	Medium	High	Total
High	93	41	10	144
Medium	77	78	46	201
Low	68	128	140	336
Total	238	247	196	681

4. Construct a 2 × 2 table based on 200 respondents of whom 69 percent are Democrats and 58 percent are for legalizing marijuana. Of the Democrats, 56 percent are for legalizing marijuana. With attitudes toward the

legalization of marijuana as the dependent variable, compute lambda. Discuss the relationship between the two variables.

5. Suppose that the correlation $r = .28$ exists between social class and college intentions. Analyze the meaning of this correlation.

6. Social scientists have been attempting to identify social variables that may be associated with economic variables. The following data can be used to investigate the relationship between unemployment rates and other variables. Which of the independent variables is most closely related to unemployment? Base your assessment on the following measures: b, r, r^2.

Country	Unemployment Rate	Political Stability	Level of Economic Development	Rate of Urbanization
United States	4.2	8.0	2.34	1.8
New Zealand	4.0	8.6	1.71	.8
Norway	3.1	8.6	1.41	1.2
Finland	3.6	8.1	.83	.7
Uruguay	6.2	3.2	.46	.9
Israel	4.8	8.1	.40	.9
Taiwan	5.8	7.2	.80	.6
Ghana	8.1	5.0	.02	.2
England	8.2	2.6	1.46	1.1
Greece	8.8	2.1	.09	.9

Additional Readings

Achen, Christopher H. *Interpreting and Using Regression.* Newbury Park, Calif.: Sage, 1982.

Bohrnstedt, George W., and David Knoke. *Statistics for Social Data Analysis.* Itasca, Ill.: Peacock, 1988.

Dietrich, Frank H., and Thomas J. Kearns. *Basic Statistics*: San Francisco: Dellen, 1989.

Kachigan, Sam K. *Statistical Analysis.* New York: Radius Press, 1986.

Levin, Jack, and James Allan Fox. *Elementary Statistics in Social Research.* New York: Harper & Row, 1988.

Lewis-Beck, Michael, S. *Applied Regression.* Newbury Park, Calif.: Sage, 1980.

CHAPTER 17

Control, Elaboration, and Multivariate Analysis

In this chapter, we investigate the analysis of three or more variables and the concept of statistical control. Multivariate cross-tabulation, multiple regression, and path analysis are described.

THE EXAMINATION OF A BIVARIATE relationship is but the first step in data analysis. Next one evaluates the substantive implications of the findings and draws causal inferences. The bivariate measure of a relation is limited to the establishment of covariation and its direction. To interpret the findings and to assess the causal priorities of the investigated variables, one introduces other variables into the analysis. Suppose that one finds a relationship between parents' age and child-rearing practices, that is, that older parents tend to be more restrictive with their children than younger parents. What interpretation can be given to this finding? One may claim that the variables are causally related and that increasing age of parents is associated with a shift from permissive toward restrictive attitudes. However, alternatively, it is possible that a difference in child-rearing practices is due not to a difference in age but rather to a difference in orientation: older parents were exposed to an orientation stressing restriction, whereas younger parents behave according to a more liberal orientation advocating more permissive practices. In other words, the relationship between parents' age and child-rearing practices is due to the fact that the variables "age" and "child-rearing practices" are both associated with a third variable, "orientation."

An observed correlation between two or more variables does not, of itself, permit the investigator to make causal interpretations. A bivariate relationship may be the product of chance, or it may exist because the variables are related to a third, unrevealed variable. Furthermore, the phenomenon under investigation can often be explained by more than a single independent variable. In either case, the introduction of additional variables serves the purpose of clarifying and elaborating the original relationship.

This chapter focuses on the analysis of more than two variables. The analysis of more than two variables serves three major functions in empirical research: control, elaboration, and prediction. The first function substitutes for the mechanism of experimental control when such is lacking. The second clarifies bivariate relationships by introducing intervening or conditional variables. The third is served by analyzing two or more independent variables to account for the variation in the dependent variable. This chapter discusses ways in which a third variable may enter into empirical research. First, we consider the strategy of controlling for a third variable and elaboration. Then we examine multivariate counterparts to the bivariate measures of relations. Finally, we examine the techniques of causal modeling and path analysis.

Control

An association between two variables is not a sufficient basis for an inference that the two are causally related. Other variables must be ruled out as alternative explanations. For example, a relationship between height and income can probably be accounted for by the variable "age." Age is related to both income and height, and this joint relationship produces a statistical relationship that has no causal significance. The original relation between height and income is said to be a **spurious relation**. Spuriousness is a concept that applies to situations where an extraneous variable produces a "fake" relation between the independent and dependent variables. It is essential that an investigation uncover the extraneous factors contaminating the data in this way. Thus in validating bivariate associations, an important step is to rule out the largest possible number of variables that might conceivably explain the original association. This is achieved by the process of *control*, a basic principle in all research designs. In experimental designs, control is accomplished by dividing research participants, by randomization, into experimental and control groups. The logic of controlled experimentation assures the researcher that all extraneous variables have been controlled for and that the two groups differ only with regard to their exposure to the independent variable. However, social scientists find it difficult to manipulate social groups and to apply experimental treatment prior to observations. Consequently, they lack control over numerous factors that throw doubt on any association between independent and dependent variables employed in the investigation.

In quasi-experimental designs, statistical techniques substitute for the experimental method of control. These techniques are employed during data analysis rather than at the data collection stage. There are three methods of statistical control. The first entails subgroup comparisons and is accompanied by the technique of cross-tabulation. The second technique, partial correlation, employs mathematical procedures to readjust the value of a bivariate correlation coefficient. The third is multiple regression, which enables us to estimate the effect of an independent variable on the dependent variable while controlling for the effect of other variables.

Methods of Control

Cross-tabulation as a Control Operation

The **cross-tabulation** method of control can be compared to the mechanism of matching employed in experiments. In both techniques, the investigator attempts to equate the groups examined with respect to variables that may bias the results. With matching, research participants are equated prior to their exposure to the independent variable. This is done by a physical allocation to the experimental and control groups, resulting in pairs that are identical with respect to the controlled factors. With cross-tabulation, research participants are allocated to the respective groups only during the analysis stage. Whereas matching is a physical control mechanism, cross-tabulation is a statistical operation.

Cross-tabulation involves the division of the sample into subgroups according to the categories of the controlled variable (called the **control variable**). The original bivariate relation is then reassessed within each subgroup. The division into subgroups removes the biasing inequality by computing a measure of relationship for groups that are internally homogeneous with respect to the biasing factor.

Generally, only variables that are associated with both the independent variable and the dependent variable can potentially bias the results. Thus only variables that show an association with the independent and dependent variables under investigation are selected as control variables.

An Illustration.   The following example illustrates the steps involved in controlling for a third variable through cross-tabulation. Suppose that a sample of 900 respondents is selected to test the hypothesis that people from urban areas are politically more liberal than rural dwellers. The data obtained are presented in Table 17.1. It is observed that 50 percent of urban residents are liberal, compared with only 28 percent of the respondents from rural areas. Thus it may be concluded that political liberalism is associated with place of residence. The question is whether this association is direct (in

Table 17.1
Political Liberalism by Urban-Rural Location

Political Liberalism	Urban Area	Rural Area
High	50%	28%
	(200)	(140)
Low	50%	72%
	(200)	(360)
Total	100%	100%
	(400)	(500)

which case the hypothesis may be supported) or is based on a spurious relation with another variable. One such additional variable might be education, which is associated with both place of residence and political liberalism, as reflected in the hypothetical bivariate distributions of Tables 17.2 and 17.3.

Partial Tables

To control for education, one divides the 900 persons into two groups according to level of education (high, low). Within each group, urban-rural location is cross-tabulated with political liberalism. The original bivariate association is then estimated in each of the subgroups. The controlled data are summarized in Table 17.4.

The resulting two bivariate tables of Table 17.4 are referred to as **partial tables** because each one reflects only part of the total association. Each pair of parallel cells in the two partial tables adds up to the corresponding cell in the original table (Table 17.1). For example, the 180 highly educated respondents who come from urban areas and are liberals plus the 20 respondents who are urban liberals with a low level of education together constitute the 200 respondents in the original bivariate table who are liberal and from urban areas.

Table 17.2
Education by Urban-Rural Location

Education	Urban Area	Rural Area
High	75%	20%
	(300)	(100)
Low	25%	80%
	(100)	(400)
Total	100%	100%
	(400)	(500)

Table 17.3
Political Liberalism by Education

| Political | Education | |
Liberalism	High	Low
High	60%	20%
	(240)	(100)
Low	40%	80%
	(160)	(400)
Total	100%	100%
	(400)	(500)

To assess the partial association, compute a measure of relationship for each of the control groups and compare it with the original result. Appropriate measures are selected in the same way as for regular bivariate distributions. Difference of percentages, gamma, or Pearson's r can be used, depending on the level of measurement.

The value of the partial association can be either identical or almost identical to the original one, it can vanish, or it can change. For the examination of spurious relationships, only the first two possibilities are relevant. When the partial association is identical or almost identical to the original one, one may conclude that the control variable does not account for the original relation and that the relation is direct. If it vanishes, the original association is said to be spurious. (A third variable may intervene between the dependent and independent variables, in which case the partial association will also vanish or approximate zero. An example will be considered shortly.)

If the partial association does not vanish but is different from the original one or if it is different in each of the partial tables, the independent and dependent variables are said to *interact*. We will return to interaction later.

Table 17.4
Political Liberalism by Urban-Rural Location, Controlling for
Education (Spurious Relationship)

| Political | High Education | | Low Education | |
Liberalism	Urban Area	Rural Area	Urban Area	Rural Area
High	60%	. 60%	20%	20%
	(180)	(60)	(20)	(80)
Low	40%	40%	80%	80%
	(120)	(40)	(80)	(320)
Total	100%	100%	100%	100%
	(300)	(100)	(100)	(400)

Figure 17.1

Overall Association of Variables in Table 17.4

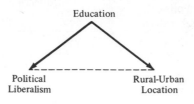

Education

Political   Rural-Urban
Liberalism   Location

Spurious Original Association.   In the example of Table 17.4, education completely accounts for the relation between residence and liberalism, for there is no difference between rural and urban residents in their degree of liberalism within either of the two education groups. Sixty percent of the highly educated rural residents, like 60 percent of the highly educated urban residents, are politically liberal. Within the low-education group, 20 percent are liberal wherever they reside. The overall association between the independent and dependent variables is completely accounted for by the association of each with education. This pattern can be presented graphically, as in Figure 17.1.

Education determines both political liberalism and place of residence. That is, people who are educated tend to live in cities and are generally politically liberal. There is no inherent link between political liberalism and place of residence, and the association between them is spurious.

Direct Original Association.   The control of a third variable may lead to entirely different results. In the hypothetical example of Table 17.5, the original bivariate association remains unchanged by educational level. In the total sample, as well as in each educational group, 50 percent of urban residents are liberal, compared with 28 percent of rural residents. This result

Table 17.5

Political Liberalism by Urban-Rural Location, Controlling for Education (Nonspurious Relationship)

Political Liberalism	High Education		Low Education	
	Urban Area	Rural Area	Urban Area	Rural Area
High	50%	28%	50%	28%
	(50)	(35)	(150)	(105)
Low	50%	72%	50%	72%
	(50)	(90)	(150)	(270)
Total	100%	100%	100%	100%
	(100)	(125)	(300)	(375)

indicates that the overall relationship between the two original variables is not accounted for by the control variable. The investigator can be confident that education is an irrelevant factor with respect to this particular association and that the association between the two original variables is direct.

In practice, the results are not as clear-cut as presented here. It is very rare for associations either to vanish or to remain identical with the original results. Often the partial tables show a clear decrease in the size of the original relationship; at times the reduction is slight. This is because of the numerous factors that can account for a bivariate association. In our example, other variables such as income, party identification, or religious affiliation might conceivably explain the relationship between urban-rural location and political liberalism. This characteristic of variables has been referred to as "block-booking."[1] It refers to the multidimensionality of human beings and of their social interaction. When a comparison is made between people in terms of social class, only one dimension is tackled. People may differ thoroughly from each other in a great many things, and all these other factors may enter into the phenomenon to be explained. The block-booked factors become our control variables; but when we control for only one or some of them, the rest may still explain the remaining residual in the dependent variable.

The procedure, then, is to hold constant all other variables that may be relevant to the subject of investigation. The selection of these variables is a logical and theoretical operation, the only statistical guideline being the requirement that the potential control factor be related to both the independent and dependent variables. Of course, one can never be completely sure that all relevant variables have been introduced into the analysis. However, the greater the number of relevant factors controlled for, the greater the confidence that the relationship is not spurious.

Elaboration

The mechanism of control is designed to uncover factors that might invalidate the original bivariate association. In that case, the investigators are likely to turn to other factors that can be employed as independent variables and repeat the process of validating the relationship. However, if the relationship observed is nonspurious, one can proceed to a more advanced stage of analysis and elaborate the bivariate association. **Elaboration** usually involves the introduction of other variables to determine the links between the independent and dependent variables or the specification of the conditions under which the association takes place.

1. Morris Rosenberg, *The Logic of Survey Analysis* (New York: Basic Books, 1968), pp. 26–28.

Let us illustrate the meaning of elaboration with some concrete examples. In the past decade, close attention has been paid to the effect of early childbearing on the life chances of adolescent parents. Investigators have discovered that early childbearers are more likely to experience economic hardship and family disruption in later life than later childbearers.[2] Early childbearing appears to be linked to school dropout, especially among adolescent mothers. Low educational attainment in turn makes it more difficult for teenage mothers to find stable and remunerative employment. These relationships may be represented schematically as follows:

Early childbearing→low educational attainment→economic disadvantage

In this scheme, low educational attainment provides a link between early childbearing and economic disadvantage. It is an **intervening variable** between the independent variable (early childbearing) and the dependent variable (economic disadvantage).

Although low educational attainment accounts for the economic disadvantage of many teenage mothers, there remains enormous variation in the life chances of these women. For instance, a recent study found that one fourth of early childbearers were on welfare while another fourth were relatively comfortable economically with a family income of more than $25,000 a year.[3] To account for these differences, a number of variables were controlled for. One of these variables was race. It was discovered that white mothers were more likely to attain a higher economic level than black mothers. In this example, the original bivariate association between early childbearing and economic disadvantage is pronounced only among one subgroup, black mothers. The control variable, race, is thus said to be a **conditional variable**, and the pattern is called **interaction**. Schematically, this pattern may be represented as follows:

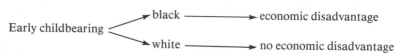

We shall examine empirical examples of both intervening variables and interaction.

Intervening Variables

Let us return to the first case, in which the controlled variable is said to intervene between the independent and dependent variables. Table 17.6 shows the relationship between childbearing and economic status. The data demonstrate that these two variables are associated: early childbearers are more

2. Frank F. Furstenberg, Jr., J. Brooks-Gunn, and S. Philip Morgan, *Adolescent Mothers in Later Life* (Cambridge: Cambridge University Press, 1987).
3. Ibid., p. 48.

Table 17.6
Childbearing and Economic Status (Hypothetical Data)

| Economic Status | Early Childbearing | | Total |
	Yes	No	
Low	54%	33%	(1,522)
	(869)	(653)	
High	46%	67%	(2,078)
	(731)	(1,347)	____
Total	100%	100%	
	(1,600)	(2,000)	(3,600)

likely to have low economic status. The investigators hypothesized that these differences could be explained by the variable "educational attainment." That is, that early childbearing effects economic status indirectly through educational attainment, with young mothers more likely to drop out of school than nonmothers.

As a means of testing this hypothesis, educational attainment was held constant, and the original relationship was reexamined. If, as suggested, childbearing has only an indirect influence on economic status, then when the intermediate link is controlled for, the association between childbearing and economic status should disappear. The results in Table 17.7 confirm the hypothesis: there are no differences in economic status between mothers and nonmother when the level of educational attainment is the same. The original relationship vanishes when educational attainment is controlled for.

The conditions for interpretation require that the control variable be associated with both the independent and dependent variables and that when controlled for, the original relationship should vanish (or diminish considerably) in all categories of the control variable. To the student who exclaims

Table 17.7
Childbearing and Economic Status by Educational Attainment
(Hypothetical Data)

| Economic Status | High Educational Attainment Early Childbearing | | Low Educational Attainment Early Childbearing | | Total |
	Yes	No	Yes	No	
Low	18%	18%	64%	64%	
	(90)	(216)	(704)	(512)	(1,522)
High	82%	82%	36%	36%	
	(410)	(984)	(396)	(288)	(2,078)
Total	100%	100%	100%	100%	
	(500)	(1,200)	(1,100)	(800)	(3,600)

that these were the identical conditions required for declaring the relationship spurious, we can confirm that this is indeed the case. The statistical tests in both cases are identical, but the interpretation is significantly different. With a spurious interpretation, the statistical results invalidate a hypothesis about the relationship between the independent and dependent variable; an intervening interpretation, by contrast, clarifies and explains such a relationship. How, then, can a distinction be made between the two?

Morris Rosenberg maintains that the difference is a theoretical issue rather than a statistical one and that it lies in the assumed causal relationship among the variables.[4] With a spurious interpretation, it is assumed that there is no causal relation betwen the independent and dependent variables; in the intervening case, the two are indirectly related through an intermediate link, the control variable.

Interaction

The second type of elaboration, interaction, involves a specification of conditions or contingencies necessary for the occurrence of the relationship. We will illustrate the meaning of interaction using the example of childbearing, economic status, and race. The bivariate association between childbearing and economic status already presented in Table 17.6 demonstrated that these two variables are associated. To gain further insight, race was controlled for, and the results are presented in Table 17.8.

The results clearly demonstrate an interactive relationship since the relationship between childbearing and economic status is different for white and black women; whereas for black women, early childbearing has a considerable impact on economic status (66% of the early childbearers have a low economic status compared to only 31% of women who are not early childbearers); among white women, there is no relationship between these

Table 17.8
Childbearing and Economic Status by Race
(Hypothetical Data)

Economic Status	Black Early Childbearing		White Early Childbearing		
	Yes	No	Yes	No	
Low	66%	31%	36%	38%	
	(594)	(372)	(252)	(304)	(1,522)
High	34%	69%	64%	62%	
	(306)	(828)	(448)	(496)	(2,078)
Total	100%	100%	100%	100%	
	(900)	(1,200)	(700)	(800)	(3,600)

4. Rosenberg, *Logic of Survey Analysis*, pp. 54–66.

two variables. A little over one-third in both groups (36% and 38%) are in the low-status group. Based on these results, it may be concluded that early childbearing and race interact in their effect on economic status; that is, the relationship between the independent and dependent variables is conditioned by race. One possible interpretation is that early childbearing has economic consequences only for women who are already disadvantaged.

Conditional relationships such as this one are quite common in social science research and can be inferred whenever the relative size or direction of the original bivariate relationship is more pronounced in one category of the control variable than in another. The presence of such differences between subgroups reflects the nature of social reality, where each variable can be broken down into various components. Indeed, many conditional factors are associated with almost any two-variable relationships. This makes the analysis of interaction one of the most important aspects of statistical analysis.

Interest and Concern as a Condition.   Herbert Hyman analyzed the various factors that are generally considered conditions for most bivariate association and classified them into three major groups.[5] The first class involves variables that specify relationship in terms of interest and concern. In many situations, interest and concern specify the conditions under which the effectiveness of an independent variable is more or less pronounced. For instance, consider the finding that self-esteem is associated with intensity of political discussion.[6] Adolescents with low self-esteem, who are more self-conscious, tend to avoid expressing their political views. Taking into account the level of political interest, it is observed that the relationship holds only among those who are interested in politics. Those who are not interested in politics also do not discuss politics, even though they might have a high degree of self-esteem. Thus the use of the conditional factor helps to clarify the original findings. People tend to differ in their interests, which in turn affect their attitudes and behavior patterns. Thus social stimuli are likely to have differential effects on them, and the identification of these differing patterns may prove to be essential to the social scientist.

Time and Place as a Condition.   The second class of factors specifies associations in terms of time and place. A relationship between two variables can vary according to the time and place at which it is studied. Studies in comparative politics typically introduce ''place'' as a control variable. The effect of class, gender, and race on voting, for example, differs from one country to another.

Specification by time is meaningful too. Often a relationship that holds at one time will be dismissed or changed at another. For example, there is a growing body of research documenting gender difference in support of

5. Herbert H. Hyman, *Survey Design and Analysis* (New York: Free Press, 1955), pp. 295–311.
6. Morris Rosenberg, ''Self-esteem and Concern with Public Affairs,'' *Public Opinion Quarterly,* 26 (1962): 201–211.

women in politics, with women more likely than men to reject stereotypical notions that "politics is for men."[7] A number of studies comparing the effect of gender on attitudes toward women in politics over time hypothesize that time will reduce gender differences because of the presence of more female political role models. Another example is the general process of development and socialization. The family is known to affect various behavioral patterns in children. This effect is pronounced, especially at the early stages, when the child is more exposed and more vulnerable to his or her family. At later stages, however, other aspects of socialization play an important role, and the family's influence diminishes. Thus a relationship between family characteristics and behavioral orientations would not stay constant if examined at different times.

Background Characteristics as a Condition.   The last class of factors is background characteristics of the units of analysis. Often associations are likely to differ for persons or groups that do not share the same characteristics. Thus the relation between class position and voting behavior is different for men and for women, and the effect of teachers' encouragement on self-esteem is not identical for black and white children. These distinctions are perhaps the most common among the types of specifications employed in the social sciences. In fact, some researchers employ such control variables as "social class," "level of education," "gender," and "age" almost automatically, reexamining all relationships obtained.

Partial Correlation as a Control Operation

The cross-tabulation control operation is quite popular in empirical research, and it is applied to all levels of measurement. However, it has a drawback that limits its use when the number of cases is relatively small. The cross-tabulation method of control entails a subdivision of the sample into progressively smaller subgroups, according to the number of categories of the controlled factor. This reduces the number of cases serving as a basis for computing the coefficient, thus rendering its validity and reliability questionable. This is particularly acute when several variables are controlled simultaneously.

A second method of control, not limited by the number of cases, is the **partial correlation**. This a mathematical adjustment of the bivariate correlation, designed to cancel out the effect of the control variable on the independent and dependent variables. The logic underlying the calculation of this measure of association is similar to that of cross-tabulation. The original association between the independent and dependent variables is reassessed so that it reflects a direct association, independent of the variables' association to a third extraneous factor.

Suppose that a correlation of $r_{12} = .60$ is found between self-esteem and

7. Diane Gillespie and Cassie Spohn, "Adolescents Attitudes toward Women in Politics: A Follow-up Study," *Women and Politics*, 10 (1990): 1-16.

educational expectation. To test the nature of this association, it is reasonable to introduce an additional variable, "social class," which is related to both self-esteem ($r_{31} = .30$) and educational expectation ($r_{32} = .40$). Partial correlation can be used to obtain a measure of association with the effect of social class removed. The formula for calculation of the partial correlation coefficient is

$$r_{12.3} = \frac{r_{12} - (r_{31})(r_{32})}{\sqrt{1 - (r_{31})^2} \sqrt{1 - (r_{32})^2}} \tag{17.1}$$

where X_1 = independent variable (in our example, self-esteem)

X_2 = dependent variable (educational expectation)

X_3 = control variable (social class)

The symbol to the right of the dot indicates the variable to be controlled. Thus $r_{12.3}$ is the correlation between variables X_1 and X_2 controlling for variable X_3. Similarly, a partial coefficient between variables X_1 and X_3 controlling for X_2 would be denoted $r_{13.2}$. A partial with one control is referred to as a *first-order partial* to distinguish it from a bivariate correlation, often denoted as a zero-order correlation. A partial with two controls is referred to as *second-order partial*, and so on. When more than one variable is controlled for simultaneously, their numbers are added to the right of the dot. Thus controlling for variables X_3 and X_4 would be expressed as $r_{12.34}$.

The partial correlation for self-esteem and educational expectation can now be calculated:

$$r_{12.3} = \frac{.60 - (.30)(.40)}{\sqrt{1 - (.30)^2} \sqrt{1 - (.40)^2}} = \frac{.48}{\sqrt{.7644}} = \frac{.48}{.87} = .55$$

The squared partial correlation reflects the proportion of variation left unexplained by the control variable and explained by the independent variable. Thus about 30 percent [$(.55)^2 \times 100$] of the variation in educational expectation was explained by self-esteem after removing the effect of social class.

In contrast to the cross-tabulation method of control, the partial correlation yields a single summarizing measure that reflects the degree of correlation between two variables controlling for a third. Thus variation in the partial associations in different categories of the controlled variable is not reflected in the partial correlation because it averages out the different partials. This property of the measure is its main disadvantage, as it might obscure otherwise essential information. In cases where the investigator suspects that there are significant differences between the partials of the various subgroups, it is advisable to use the cross-tabulation technique instead.

Multiple Regression as a Control Operation

Another method that allows us to assess the relationship between two variables while controlling for the effect of others is **multiple regression.** Multiple regression is a simple extension of bivariate regression, which was discussed in Chapter 16. A multiple regression equation, as in Formula (17.2), describes the extent of linear relationships between the dependent variable and a number of other independent (or control) variables:

$$\hat{Y} = a + b_1 X_1 + b_2 X_2 \tag{17.2}$$

where $\hat{Y}$ is the dependent variable and X_1 and X_2 are the independent variables. Designated as partial regression coefficients, b_1 and b_2 are the slope of the regression line for each independent variable, controlling for the other. Thus b_1 reflects the amount of change in Y associated with a given change in X_1, holding X_2 constant; b_2 is the amount of change in Y associated with a given change in X_2, holding X_1 constant; and a is the intercept point on the Y axis for both X_1 and X_2.

As with bivariate regression, the constants of the multiple linear regression equation are estimated so as to minimize the average square error in prediction. This is accomplished by using the least squares criterion to obtain the best fit to the data. The least squares estimates of a, b_1, and b_2 are shown in Equations (17.3), (17.4), and (17.5):

$$b_1 = \left(\frac{s_Y}{s_1}\right)\frac{r_{y1} - r_{y2}r_{12}}{1 - (r_{12})^2} \tag{17.3}$$

$$b_2 = \left(\frac{s_Y}{s_2}\right)\frac{r_{y2} - r_{y1}r_{12}}{1 - (r_{12})^2} \tag{17.4}$$

$$a = \bar{Y} - b_1\bar{X}_1 - b_2\bar{X}_2 \tag{17.5}$$

To illustrate the computation of the multiple regression constants using Equations (17.3), (17.4), and (17.5), we shall attempt to estimate the effects of self-esteem and education on political liberalism.

Designating liberalism as Y, education as X_1, and self-esteem as X_2, the following are the hypothetical means, standard deviations, and bivariate correlation coefficients for these variables:

$$\bar{Y} = 6.5 \qquad s_Y = 3 \qquad r_{y1} = .86$$
$$\bar{X}_1 = 8.9 \qquad s_1 = 4.1 \qquad r_{y2} = .70$$
$$\bar{X}_2 = 5.8 \qquad s_2 = 2.2 \qquad r_{12} = .75$$

For this problem, b_1 stands for the effect of education on liberalism controlling for self-esteem and b_2 for the effect of self-esteem on liberalism controlling for education.

Substituting the data into the formulas for b_1 and b_2, we have

$$b_1 = \left(\frac{3}{4.1}\right)\frac{.86 - (.70)(.75)}{1 - (.75)^2} = .56$$

$$b_2 = \left(\frac{3}{2.2}\right)\frac{.70 - (.86)(.75)}{1 - (.75)^2} = .17$$

The intercept for the multiple regression equation is

$$a = 6.5 - (.56)(8.9) - (.17)(5.8) = .53$$

With the obtained values of b_1, b_2, and a, the complete multiple regression equation for predicting liberalism on the basis of education and self-esteem would therefore be

$$\hat{Y} = .53 + .56X_1 + .17X_2$$

It indicates the extent of political liberalism that would be expected, on the average, with a given level of education and a given level of self-esteem. For example, for a person with ten years of schooling and a self-esteem score of 8, the expected level of liberalism would be

$$\hat{Y} = .53 + (.56)(10) + (.17)(8) = 7.49$$

As the b coefficients reflect the net effect of each variable, they can be compared so as to denote the relative importance of the independent variables. However, since each variable is measured on a different scale in different units, b *must be standardized to be comparable*. The standardized equivalent of the b coefficient is called the *beta weight* or *beta coefficient*; it is symbolized as β. The beta weights are obtained by multiplying b by the ratio of the standard deviation of the independent variable to the standard deviation of the dependent variable. Thus β_1 and β_2 would be expressed as follows:

$$\beta_1 = \left(\frac{s_1}{s_Y}\right) b_1$$

$$\beta_2 = \left(\frac{s_2}{s_Y}\right) b_2$$

For our example, we get

$$\beta_1 = \left(\frac{4.1}{3}\right)(.56) = .765$$

$$\beta_2 = \left(\frac{2.2}{3}\right)(.17) = .125$$

The intercept for a standardized regression equation is zero. Therefore, we have

$$\hat{Y}_z = X_{1z} + X_{2z}$$

The subscript z indicates that the variables have been standardized.

The standardized regression equation shows that for every increase of one standard deviation in education, political liberalism increases by .765 standard deviation, and with an increase of one standard deviation in self-esteem, liberalism increases by .125 standard deviation. One main advantage to using the standardized regression equation is that it translates the variables to a uniform scale that lets us easily compare the relative strength of education and self-esteem in their effect on liberalism. It is evident that education contributes more to liberalism (.765) than does self-esteem (.125).

Just as the partial correlation coefficient measures the effect of one independent variable on the dependent variable while controlling for another, the multiple regression coefficient measures the amount of change in the dependent variable with one unit change in the independent variable while controlling for all other variables in the equation.

In fact, beta weights and partial correlation coefficients are directly comparable, are usually similar in size, and always have the same sign.

Multivariate Analysis: Multiple Relationships

To this point, we have considered only situations in which one independent variable is said to determine the dependent variable being studied. However, in real situations, seldom is only one variable relevant to what is to be explained. Often numerous variables are directly associated with the dependent variable. Population change, for example, is explained by four variables: "birth rate," "death rate," "immigration rate," and "emigration rate." Similarly, differences in support for legal abortion are often explained by differences in "religion," "gender," and "race." Thus there are often several independent variables, each of which may contribute to the prediction of the dependent variable.

In a typical research problem, say, in which one attempted to explain differences in voting behavior, one would use a number of independent variables, for example, "social class," "religion," "gender," and "political attitudes." One would attempt to look at the effects of each independent variable while controlling for the effects of others, as well as at the combined effect of all the independent variables on voting.

The technique of multiple regression introduced earlier in this chapter is most appropriate for problems involving two or more independent variables. We have seen that the standardized regression coefficient—the beta weights—allows us to assess the independent effect of each variable in the regression equation on the dependent variable.

To examine the *combined* effect of all the independent variables, we compute a measure the *coefficient of determination,* denoted R^2.

Just as with simple bivariate regression, in multiple regression one needs to estimate how well the regression rule fits the actual data. In simple regression, the fit (or the relative reduction of error) was measured using r^2, which is defined as the ratio of the variation explained to the total variation in the dependent variable. Similarly, when the prediction is based on several variables, an estimate of the relative reduction of error is based on the ratio of the variation explained with several variables simultaneously to the total variation. This measure, R^2, designates the percentage of the variation explained by all the independent variables in the multiple regression equation.

The square root of R^2 indicates the correlation between all independent variables taken together with the dependent variable; it is thus the *coefficient of multiple correlation*.

For the three-variable case, the two formulas for R^2 are as follows:

$$R^2_{y.12} = \frac{r^2_{y1} + r^2_{y2} - 2r_{y1}r_{y2}r_{12}}{1 - (r_{12})^2} \tag{17.6}$$

or

$$R^2_{y.12} = \beta_1 r_{y1} + \beta_2 r_{y2} \tag{17.7}$$

As an example, let us calculate the percentage of variation in political liberalism (Y) using education (X_1) and self-esteem (X_2) as predictors. We will be using data generated earlier, presented on pages 000–000. We will use Equation (17.7) to calculate R^2.

$$R^2_{y.12} = (.765)(.86) + (.125)(.70) = .745$$

This means that almost 75 percent of the variation in political liberalism is accounted for by the combined effects of education and self-esteem.

Causal Models and Path Analysis

Our discussion has focused on methods of control that provide an interpretation of the relation between two variables. It was indicated that a direct relationship is one that does not prove to be spurious. This is determined by the time sequence of the variables and the relative size of the partial associations.

These two elements—the size of the partials relative to the original bivariate associations and the assumed time order between the variables—have been suggested by Paul Lazarsfeld as the kind of evidence required for inferring causation:

> We can suggest a clear-cut definition of the causal relation between two attributes. If we have a relationship between X and Y, and if for any antecedent test factor c the partial relationship between X and Y does not disappear, then the original relationship should be called a causal one.[8]

Although one can never directly demonstrate causality from correlational data, it is possible to make causal inferences concerning the adequacy of specific causal models.

Statistical methods that enable us to draw causal inferences involve a finite set of explicitly defined variables, assumptions about how these vari-

---

8. Paul F. Lazarsfeld, "The Algebra of Dichotomous Systems," in *Studies in Items Analysis and Prediction,* ed. Herbert Solomon (Stanford, Calif.: Stanford University Press, 1959), p. 146.

ables are interrelated causally, and assumptions about the effect of outside variables on the variables included in the model.[9]

Some Examples of Causal Diagrams

Hypothetically, there could be six causal connections between three variables X_1, X_2, and X_3, as follows:

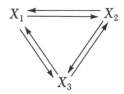

The causal order between two variables is represented by a single-headed arrow, with the head pointing to the effect and the tail to the cause. A simplifying assumption[10] rules out two-way causation either directly in the form $X_1 \rightleftarrows X_2$ or indirectly as in

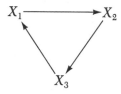

Furthermore, under this assumption a dependent variable cannot cause any of the variables preceding it in the causal sequence. Thus in a causal system where X_1 is the independent variable, X_2 the intervening variable, and X_3 the dependent variable, X_2 cannot cause X_1, and X_3 cannot cause X_2 or X_1.

With these assumptions, some possible models explaining relations between X_1, X_2, and X_3 are presented in Figure 17.2.

These diagrams display direct, indirect, and no effect between the variables. Diagram *a* shows a direct effect of X_1 on X_2, a direct effect of X_2 on X_3, and an indirect effect of X_1 on X_3 through X_2. Similarly, in diagram *b*, X_1 and X_2 affect X_3 directly and X_1 has no effect on X_2.

To illustrate how some of these ideas are applied, let us look at the following example on voting behavior and its determinants. It is hypothesized that voting behavior (X_4) is directly determined by party identification (X_1), candidate evaluation (X_2), and perception of campaign issues (X_3) and that candidate evaluation and campaign issues are directly determined by party identification. Furthermore, party identification influences voting behavior indirectly, through candidate evaluation and campaign issues. These ideas are presented in Figure 17.3.

9. Herbert A. Simon, *Models of Man: Social and Rational* (New York: Wiley, 1957).

10. Hubert M. Blalock, Jr., *Causal Inference in Nonexperimental Research* (Chapel Hill: University of North Carolina Press, 1964).

Figure 17.2
Models for Three Variables

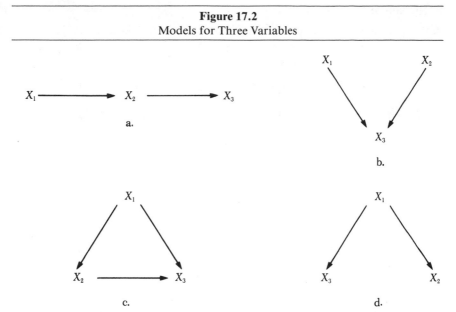

The variables *U, V,* and *W* are called *residual variables*; the arrows between them and each of the dependent variables in the model express the fact that variation in the dependent variables is not solely accounted for by variables in the model. Thus *W,* for example, would represent variation in voting behavior not accounted for by party identification, candidate evaluation, or perceptions of campaign issues.

Figure 17.3
A Path Diagram of Voting Behavior

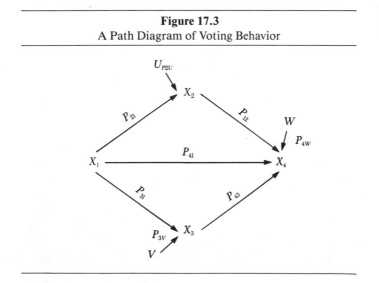

Path Analysis

Path analysis is a technique that uses both bivariate and multiple linear regression techniques to test the causal relations among the variables specified in the model. It involves three major steps:

1. The drawing of a path diagram based on a theory or a set of hypotheses.
2. The calculation of path coefficients (direct effects) using regression techniques.
3. The determination of indirect effects.

The first step of path analysis was exemplified in our illustration on voting behavior on pages 417–419. We will start with a discussion of step 2. You will notice that Figure 17.3 includes a set of coefficients identified as P_{ij}, i being the dependent variable and j the independent variable. These values are called **path coefficients.** For example, P_{31} is the path coefficient connecting X_1 with X_3, with X_3 being determined by X_1. Similarly, P_{4w} is the path coefficient linking X_4 with the residual variable W.

To estimate the path coefficients, we first write a set of regression equations that represent the structure of the model. We should have as many equations as we have dependent variables.[11] Thus to represent the model of Figure 17.3, we have

$$X_2 = P_{21}X_1 + P_{2u}U$$
$$X_3 = P_{31}X_1 + P_{3v}V$$
$$X_4 = P_{41}X_1 + P_{42}X_2 + P_{43}X_3 + P_{4w}W$$

You will notice that each equation includes as many terms as there are arrows leading to the dependent variable. Thus X_4 has four arrows, each representing a determining factor: X_1, X_2, X_3, and W.

To obtain estimates of the path coefficient, we simply regress each dependent variable on the independent variables in the equation. To estimate P_{21}, we regress X_2 on X_1. For P_{31}, we regress X_3 on X_1, and for P_{41}, P_{42}, and P_{43}, we simply regress X_4 on X_1, X_2, and X_3. Since the variables are standardized, the path coefficients are simply the beta weights for each equation; that is,

$$P_{21} = \beta_{21} \qquad P_{42} = \beta_{42}$$
$$P_{31} = \beta_{31} \qquad P_{43} = \beta_{43}$$
$$P_{41} = \beta_{41}$$

The residual path coefficient (P_{2u}, P_{3v}, P_{4w}) is the square root of the unexplained variation in the dependent variable under analysis. For the model presented in Figure 17.3, the residual paths are

$$P_{2u} = \sqrt{1 - R_{2.1}^2}$$

$$P_{3v} = \sqrt{1 - R_{3.1}^2}$$

11. Since variables in path analysis are typically standardized, we will follow the convention of analyzing Z scores.

$$P_{4w} = \sqrt{1 - R^2_{4.123}}$$

The estimation of the path coefficient results in an assessment of the direct effects on all variables in the model. Thus P_{21} expresses the direct effect of X_1 on X_2; P_{31}, the direct effect of X_1 on X_3; P_{41}, the direct effect of X_1 on X_4; and so on. However, as can be observed in Figure 17.3, X_1 affects X_4 indirectly as well, through X_2 and X_3.

To estimate the **indirect effects**, we multiply the path coefficients of paths connecting two variables via intervening variables. Thus for Figure 17.3, the indirect effect of X_1 on X_4 via X_2 would be expressed by $P_{21} P_{42}$, and the indirect effect of X_1 on X_4 via X_3 would be $P_{31} P_{43}$.

One interesting application of path analysis[12] is the Tompkins welfare expenditures model in the American states. Drawing on the theoretical literature, Gary L. Tompkins has constructed a path model that includes six variables: industrialization (X_1), income (X_2), ethnicity (X_3), interparty competition (X_4), voter turnout (X_5), and welfare expenditures (X_6).[13] Given the assumption of one-way causation, there are 15 possible path arrows be-

---

Figure 17.4

A Path Diagram with Path Coefficients and Residual Paths for Welfare
Expenditures in the United States

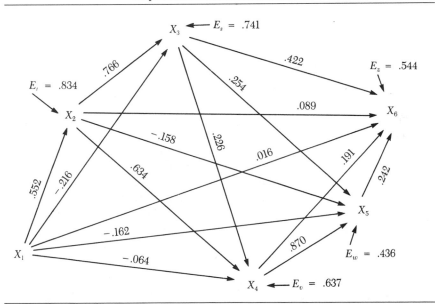

Adapted from Gary L. Tompkins, "A Causal Model of State Welfare Expenditures," *Journal of Politics,* 37 (1975): 406.

12. David Nachmias, *Public Policy Evaluation* (New York: St. Martin's Press, 1979).

13. Gary L. Tompkins, "A Causal Model of State Welfare Expenditures," *Journal of Politics,* 37 (1975): 392–416.

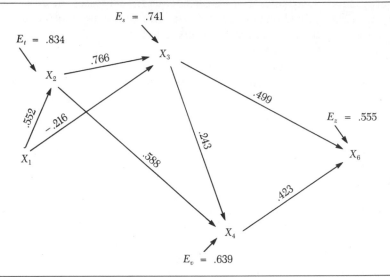

Figure 17.5

A Modified Path Diagram with Path Coefficients and Residual Paths for
Welfare Expenditures in the United States

Adapted from Gary L. Tompkins, "A Causal Model of State Welfare Expenditures,"
Journal of Politics, 37 (1975): 409.

tween the six variables, as illustrated in Figure 17.4. The values for the path
coefficients and those for the residual paths are also reported in this figure.
Although this path model accurately reflects the empirical relationships
among the six variables, Tompkins has developed a more parsimonious
model, obtained by eliminating weak path coefficients (coefficients with an
absolute value less than .200) and then recalculating the various estimates. By
eliminating six weak path coefficients, the more economical but nonetheless
powerful model shown in Figure 17.5 was developed. Now it is possible to
assess the direct and indirect effects of the variables on welfare expenditures.

Thus, for example, ethnicity (X_3) exerts a strong direct effect on the
level of welfare expenditure $(P_{63} = .499)$ and a relatively moderate indirect
effect via interparty competition: $P_{64}P_{43} = .102$. Income exerts no direct effect on welfare expenditures. However, income has a strong indirect effect
via ethnicity and interparty competition: $(P_{63}P_{32}) + P_{64} [P_{42} + (P_{43}P_{32})] =$
$(.499 \times .766) + .423 [.588 + (.243 \times .766)] = .710$.

Summary

1. Multivariate analysis has three basic functions: control, interpretation, and prediction. Statistical control is a substitute for experimental control and is accomplished through cross-tabulation, partial correlation, or

multiple regression. With cross-tabulation, one attempts to equate groups exposed to the independent variable with those not exposed, in all relevant matters. The selection of relevant control variables is based on theoretical as well as statistical considerations. It is required that the control variable be associated with both independent and dependent variables. The partial correlation is a method of statistically adjusting the zero-order correlation to cancel out the effect of the control variable on the independent and dependent variables. Multiple regression estimates the effect of one variable on another while controlling for the effect of others.

2. When the mechanism of control is applied to a bivariate association, it can either cancel out the original relationship or have no effect on it. In the first case, the association is either spurious or mediated by the control variable; in the second case, the association is considered direct and is subject to further analysis. Whereas a spurious interpretation invalidates a bivariate association, an intervening interpretation clarifies it and explains how the independent and dependent variables are related. A second class of interpretation specifies the conditions under which the association holds. Specification can be made according to interest and concern, time and place, and specific qualifications or characteristics.

3. Multiple regression and correlation comprise a technique for assessing the simultaneous effect of several independent variables on the dependent variable under study. In multiple regression, a prediction rule is estimated that evaluates the extent of change produced in the dependent variables by an independent variable, holding other relevant independent variables constant. The multiple correlation estimates the degree of fit of the prediction equation with the empirical data. R^2, the multiple correlation coefficient, measures the amount of variance in the dependent variable explained by the independent variables employed.

4. Path analysis is a multivariate technique that makes possible the testing of causal relations among a set of variables. It is based on linear regression analysis and involves the drawing of diagrams founded in theory and the determination of direct and indirect effects of variables.

Key Terms for Review

---

spurious relation	interaction
cross-tabulation	partial correlation
control variable	multiple regression
partial tables	path analysis
elaboration	path coefficient
intervening variable	indirect effect
conditional variable	

Study Questions

1. The first table shows the relationship between religion and life satisfaction. The second table shows the relationship between religion and life satisfaction when a third variable is held constant.

   a. Examine the relationship between the independent and dependent variables in the two tables by making a percentage comparison.
   b. Define the control variable. How does it affect the original relationship?

Life Satisfaction by Religion

	Religion	
	Protestant	Catholic
Satisfied	256	126
Not satisfied	258	139
Total	514	265

Life Satisfaction by Religion Controlling for a Third Variable

	Education					
	High		Medium		Low	
	Prot-estant	Cath-olic	Prot-estant	Cath-olic	Prot-estant	Cath-olic
Satisfied	89	13	116	35	51	78
Not satisfied	104	20	124	59	30	60
Total	193	33	240	94	81	138

2. The accompanying table shows the relationship between vote and social class, controlling for gender.

   a. Examine and describe (by making a percentage comparison) the relationship between the independent and dependent variables in the partial tables.
   b. Reconstruct the bivariate table showing the relationship between gender and social class.
   c. Reconstruct the bivariate table showing the relationship between gender and vote.
   d. Reconstruct the bivariate table showing the relationship between vote and social class.

Vote by Social Class Controlling for Sex

	Male			Female		
	Upper Class	Lower Class	Total	Upper Class	Lower Class	Total
Democratic	55	45	100	115	285	400
Republican	545	355	900	285	615	900
Total	600	400	1,000	400	900	1,300

3. Using the data from question 6 in Chapter 16:

   a. Obtain the partial correlation between unemployment and political stability controlling for economic development.
   b. Obtain the partial correlation between unemployment and economic development controlling for political stability.
   c. Obtain the multiple regression equation for these data taking unemployment as the dependent variable. Evaluate the relative effect of each independent variable on unemployment by comparing the beta weights.
   d. What percentage of the variance in unemployment is explained by the three independent variables taken together?

Additional Readings

Achen, Christopher H. *Interpreting and Using Regression*. Newbury Park, Calif.: Sage, 1982.

Blalock, Hubert M., Jr., ed. *Causal Models in the Social Sciences*. 2d ed. Hawthorne, N.Y.: Aldine, 1985.

Cohen, Jacob. "Multiple Regression as a General Data-analytic System." *Psychological Bulletin,* 70 (1968): 426–443.

Duncan, O. D. "Path Analysis: Sociological Examples," *American Journal of Sociology,* 72: (1966): 1–16.

Edwards, Allen L. *Multiple Regression and the Analysis of Variance and Covariance*. 2d ed. New York: Freeman, 1985.

Everitt, B. S., and G. Dunn. *Advanced Methods of Data Exploration and Modelling*. London: Heinemann, 1983.

Feinberg, Stephen B. *The Analysis of Cross-classified Categorical Data*. Cambridge, Mass.: MIT Press, 1980.

Johnson, Richard A., and Dean W. Wichern. *Applied Multivariate Statistical Analysis*. Englewood Cliffs, N.J.: Prentice-Hall, 1982.

Lewis-Beck, Michael S. *Applied Regression: An Introduction*. Newbury Park, Calif.: Sage, 1982.

CHAPTER 18

Index Construction and Scaling Methods

In this chapter, we trace the logic and practices of index construction and explore several scaling techniques, including arbitrary scales, Likert, and Guttman scaling techniques, as well as factor analysis.

I N CHAPTER 7, WE DEFINED MEASURE-ment as a procedure in which the researcher assigns symbols or numbers to empirical properties according to rules. We also discussed the structure of measurement, the idea of isomorphism, the four levels of measurement, and techniques for assessing validity and reliability. We are now in a position to discuss the more advanced topics of index construction and scaling.

Indexes and scales are measuring instruments. They are constructed to represent more validly the complexities inherent in human behavior. Indeed, concepts such as power, equity, freedom, intelligence, and bureaucracy are extremely difficult to measure because, among other things, they are composites of several empirical properties. Indexes and scales are means of measuring such complex phenomena.

Indexes and scales refer in most cases to composite measures constructed through the combination of two or more items or indicators. For example, socioeconomic status is a common index constructed by the combination of three indicators: income, education, and occupation.

Scales and indexes are employed in the social sciences for several reasons. First, they enable several variables to be represented by a single score that reduces the complexity of the data. Second, scales and indexes provide quantitative measures that are amenable to greater precision and statistical manipulation. Finally, indexes and scales increase the reliability of measurement. A score on a scale or an index is considered a more reliable indicator of the property being measured than a measure based on a response to one question or item alone. An example is something most students encounter daily. Students would not like to have an exam grade determined by their answer to a single multiple-choice or true-false question. First, the full universe of content of the material or topic being measured is not likely to be covered, and second, a misinterpretation or mistake on any one question is less likely to lead to a wrong conclusion about the student's knowledge of the topic if there are a larger number of questions. Multiple-item scales and indexes are therefore used to increase the reliability of the measurement and to obtain greater precision.

Scales differ from indexes by the greater rigor in their construction. Whereas indexes are constructed by the simple accumulation of scores, greater attention is paid in scales to the test of validity and reliability. Moreover, most scales involve the underlying principle of **unidimensionality.** This principle implies that the items comprising the scale should reflect a single dimension and belong on a continuum presumed to reflect one and only one concept.

Item analyses used in some scaling techniques identify questions or items that do not belong with the others in the set. Other scaling techniques permit us to rank items by level of difficulty or intensity. Also, some scaling methods produce interval-level scales, thereby avoiding the limitations imposed by nominal or ordinal data.

Before constructing a new scale, it is important to make a survey of the literature to ascertain if an appropriate scale is already available. The works listed in the additional readings at the end of the chapter constitute a comprehensive source of information on scales available in the social sciences.

We shall discuss the logic of index construction and present several techniques for constructing indexes. The Likert scaling technique will be discussed next. This scale is concerned with the measurement of attitudes on an ordinal and an interval level of measurement. Then we present and exemplify Guttman scaling, or scalogram analysis as a method for scaling. The Guttman technique can be applied to nominal and ordinal levels of analysis.

Index Construction

The combination of two or more items or indicators yields a composite measure, usually referred to as an **index.** For example, the consumer price index (CPI) is a composite measure of changes in retail prices. The retail prices that make up the index are divided into eight major groups: food, housing, apparel, transportation, medical care, personal care, reading and recreation, and other goods and services. The approximately 400 commodities and services that are included were selected as being representative of the price trends of subgroups of related items and include the cost of diverse commodities and services, such as rice, men's work gloves, women's wool suits, rent, mortgage interest, gasoline, and haircuts. The prices of the 400 commodities and services are collected in 50 urban areas selected to be representative of those cities' characteristics that affect the way in which families spend their money, such as city size, climate, population density, and income level. Within each city, price quotations are recorded where the families of wage and salary workers typically purchase goods and services. For each item, the prices reported by the various sources are combined and weighted appropriately to ascertain average price changes for the city. Index numbers are prepared monthly for the country and for each of five large cities, quarterly for the other cities.[1]

Four major problems are involved in constructing indexes: definition of the purpose for which the index is being compiled, selection of sources of data, selection of base, and selection of methods of aggregation and weighting.

Definition of Purpose

Essential to the process of index construction are two questions: what does one attempt to measure, and how is the measure going to be used? Logically speaking, if A is an index of X, A may be only one of several indexes of X. Thus some kind of supporting evidence is needed to make the case that the values of A correspond to the values of X. Most often, X is a broad concept like public welfare or political participation. Such concepts consist of a complex combination of phenomena and are subject to differing interpretations. Accordingly, no single indicator will cover all the dimensions of a concept, and a number of indicators have to be developed. Each indicator in turn serves a specific purpose that must be explained prior to construction of the index.

Selection of Data

Either obtrusive or unobtrusive methods of data collection (or both) may be used to construct indexes. Decisions as to which source of data to use depend on the purpose of the index and on the research design employed. In

---

1. The following discussion is based on U.S. Bureau of Labor Statistics, *The Consumer Price Index: A Short Description of the Index as Revised* (Washington, D.C.: U.S. Government Printing Office, 1964), and William H. Wallace, *Measuring Price Changes: A Study of Price Indexes* (Richmond, Va.: Federal Reserve Bank of Richmond, 1970).

all cases, the investigator must ascertain that the data pertain strictly to the phenomenon being measured. This involves issues of validity and reliability, which were discussed in Chapter 7.

Selection of Base

For comparative purposes, indexes are expressed in the form of a proportion, a percentage, or a ratio. A *proportion* is defined as the frequency of observations in any given category (f_i) divided by the total number of observations (N), or f_i/N. A proportion may range from zero to one. A proportion becomes a percentage when multiplied by 100 ($f_i/N \times 100$), and a *percentage*, by definition, may range from zero to 100. A *ratio* is a fraction that expresses the relative magnitude of any two sets of frequencies. To find the ratio between two frequencies, take the first frequency and divide by the second. For example, if a group consisted of 500 females and 250 males, the ratio of females to males is found by dividing 500 by 250, or 2/1.

To illustrate the use of these measures, consider Table 18.1, which reports the frequencies, proportions, and percentages of selected criminal offenses in a New Jersey city by sources of official data.[2] The first, crime in New Jersey (CNJ), is compiled annually by the office of the state's attorney general. The other source was compiled from the municipal court dockets (MCD) in the city.

An examination of the table reveals a serious ambiguity in the meaning of crime data. There are differences in the amounts of officially recognized crimes: CNJ reports more offenses than court dockets do. This is consistent with the fact that court dockets report information from a higher jurisdiction than CNJ. CNJ reports offenses that are known to police, whereas

Table 18.1
Selected Offenses and Source of Information

Selected Offenses	CNJ			MCD		
	f	Proportion	%	f	Proportion	%
Armed robbery	23	.04	4	0	.00	.0
Robbery	17	.03	3	5	.01	1.0
Atrocious assault	13	.02	2	2	.007	.7
Simple assault	223	.40	40	250	.89	89.0
Break and entry	206	.37	37	1	.003	.3
Larceny	78	.14	14	24	.09	9.0
Total	560	1.00	100	282	1.00	100.0

2. The frequencies are reported in W. Boyd Littrell, "The Problem of Jurisdiction and Official Statistics of Crime," in *Current Issues of Social Policy,* ed. W. Boyd Littrell and Gideon Sjoberg (Newbury Park, Calif.: Sage, 1976), p. 236.

Table 18.2
Changing the Base of an Index Number

Year	Values of Old Index (1986 = 100)	Values of New Index (1982 = 100)
1982	70	100.0
1983	80	114.3
1984	60	85.7
1985	95	135.7
1986	100	142.9
1987	115	164.3
1988	120	171.4
1989	118	168.6
1990	105	150.0

court dockets report cases in which offenders have been identified, arrested, and booked on official complaints. Given that many offenses occur for which offenders are not apprehended, one would expect attrition of cases as these move upward through the levels of jurisdiction. However, the data for the "Simple assault" category are most problematic because it appears that municipal courts heard more cases of specific offenses than were known to the police in a city where the courts and the police shared jurisdiction. This is indeed improbable, and an index based on such data would be misleading.

Shifting the Base. Often it is necessary to shift the base of an index number series from one time period to another. For instance, shifting the base is necessary if indexes of one series are to be compared meaningfully with those of another series. One method for shifting the base is to divide all the indexes in the original series by the original value of the index for the new base period and multiply by 100. This is illustrated with hypothetical data in Table 18.2. To obtain the new index (with base 1982) for 1982, we divide the original index (with base 1986) for 1982 by 70 and then multiply by 100. This results in $(70/70) \times 100 = 100$. The new index for 1983 equals $(80/70) \times 100 = 114.3$, and so on, until the complete new series is obtained.

Methods of Aggregation and Weighting

A common method for constructing indexes is by computing aggregate values. The aggregates can be either simple or weighted, depending on the purpose of the index.

Simple Aggregates. Table 18.3 illustrates the construction of a simple aggregative price index. The prices of each commodity (C_i) in any given year are added to give the index for that year. As noted earlier, it is convenient to designate some year as a base, which is set equal to 100. In this example, all the indexes are expressed in the last row as a percentage of the 1973 number, obtained by dividing each of the numbers by the value in the base period ($20.13) and multiplying by 100. Symbolically,

$$PI = \sum p_n / \sum p_o \times 100 \qquad (18.1)$$

where PI = price index

p = the price of an individual commodity

o = the base period at which price changes are measured

n = the given period that is being compared with the base

The formula for a particular year (for instance 1977, with 1973 being the base) is

$$PI_{73,77} = \sum p_{77} / \sum p_{73} \times 100 \qquad (18.2)$$

Thus,

$$PI_{73,77} = \frac{6.10 + 7.18 + 7.90 + 6.80}{3.21 + 5.40 + 6.62 + 4.90} \times 100$$
$$= \frac{27.98}{20.13} \times 100 = 139.00$$

Weighted Aggregates. Simple aggregates may conceal the relative influence of each indicator of an index. To prevent such misrepresentation, **weighted aggregates** are often used. To construct a weighted aggregative price index for the data in Table 18.3, take a list of the quantities of the specified commodities and calculate to determine what this aggregate of goods is worth each year at current prices. This means that each unit price is multiplied by the number of units, and the resulting values are summed for each period. Symbolically,

$$PI = \sum p_n q / \sum poq \times 100 \qquad (18.3)$$

where q represents the quantity of the commodity marketed, produced, or consumed, that is, the quantity weight, or multiplier. The procedure, using

Table 18.3
Construction of Simple Aggregative Index Numbers (Hypothetical Unit Prices)

Commodities	1973	1974	1975	1976	1977
C_1	$ 3.21	$ 4.14	$ 4.90	$ 5.80	$ 6.10
C_2	5.40	5.60	5.10	6.40	7.18
C_3	6.62	8.10	9.00	8.35	7.90
C_4	4.90	5.40	5.10	7.25	6.80
Aggregate value	$20.13	$23.24	$24.10	$27.80	$27.98
Index	100.00	115.45	119.72	138.10	139.00

Table 18.4

Construction of Aggregative Index Weighted by Consumption in 1973

Commod-ities	1973 Consump-tion	Value of 1973 Quantity at Price of Specified Year				
		1973	1974	1975	1976	1977
C_1	800	$2,568	$3,312	$3,920	$4,640	$4,880
C_2	300	1,620	1,680	1,530	1,920	2,154
C_3	450	2,979	3,645	4,050	3,758	3,555
C_4	600	2,940	3,240	3,060	4,350	4,080
Aggregate value		$10,107	$11,877	$12,560	$14,668	$14,669
Index		100.0	117.5	124.3	145.1	145.1

the quantities in 1973 as multipliers, is illustrated in Table 18.4. Because the total value changes while the components of the aggregate do not, these changes must be due to price changes. Thus the aggregative price index measures the changing value of a fixed aggregate of goods.

Index Construction: Examples

Let us first look at a simple index developed to evaluate statistics textbooks used in the social sciences according to students' instructional needs.[3] The index, the Statistic Textbook Anxiety Rating Test (START), uses seven factors keyed to aspects of statistic textbooks related to deficiencies in students' math backgrounds and corresponding anxieties:

1. Reviews basic algebraic operations.
2. Contains a section on notations.
3. Includes exercise answers.
4. Explains exercise answers.
5. Does not use definitional formulas.
6. Uses relevant examples.
7. Explicitly addresses student statistics or math anxiety.

The index works as follows: textbooks are given a score on each factor—1 if the book meets the criterion, 0 if it does not. Summing all the scores yields a composite score ranging from 0 to 7. When the index was used to evaluate 12 popular textbooks, the scores ranged from 0 to 4.

Another example is the Sellin and Wolfgang Index of Delinquency. Evaluating crime control policies requires at least three major types of information: data on the incidence of crimes, data on the response of the justice system, and data on social and demographic characteristics. With respect to the incidence of crimes, a major problem is that offenses vary in

3. Steven P. Schacht, "Statistics Textbooks: Pedagogical Tools or Impediments to Learning?" *Teaching Sociology*, 18 (1990): 390–396.

nature and magnitude. Some result in death, others inflict losses of property, and still others merely cause inconvenience. Yet the traditional way of comparing, say, one year's crime with another has been simply to count offenses, disregarding differences. Such unweighted indexes are misleading. A police report that shows an overall decrease or increase in the total number of offenses committed may be misleading if there are significant changes in the type of offenses committed. For example, a small decline in auto theft but a large increase in armed robbery would lead to a decline in an unweighted crime index because reported auto thefts are usually much greater in absolute numbers than reported armed robberies.

In a genuine attempt to tackle this problem in the area of delinquency, Thorsten Sellin and Marvin Wolfgang developed a system of weighting by describing 141 carefully prepared accounts of different crimes to three samples of police officers, juvenile court judges, and college students.[4] The accounts of the different crimes included various combinations, such as death or hospitalization of the victim, type of weapon, and value of property stolen, damaged, or destroyed; for example, "The offender robs a person at gunpoint," "The victim struggles and is shot to death," "The offender forces open a cash register in a department store and steals five dollars," "The offender smokes marijuana." Members of the samples were asked to rate each of these on a "category scale" and a "magnitude estimating scale," and their ratings were used to construct the weighting system. For example, a crime with the following "attributes" would be given the following number of points:

A house is forcibly entered.	1
A person is murdered.	26
The spouse receives a minor injury.	1
Between $251 and $2,000 is taken.	2
Total score	30

With such an index, comparisons over time and between different communities can be carried out more meaningfully, taking into account the seriousness of the crimes committed.

Attitude Indexes (Arbitrary Scales)

Attitude indexes, also referred to as *arbitrary scales*, involve a set of questions that are selected on an a priori basis. Numerical values are assigned arbitrarily to the item or question responses, and these values are summed to obtain total scores. These scores are then interpreted as indicating the atti-

---

4. Thorsten Sellin and Marvin E. Wolfgang, *The Measurement of Delinquency* (New York: Wiley, 1964).

tude of the respondent. Consider the following five statements designed to measure alienation:

1. Sometimes I have the feeling that other people are using me.
   - ☐ Strongly agree   ☐ Disagree
   - ☐ Agree   ☐ Strongly disagree
   - ☐ Uncertain
2. We are just so many cogs in the machinery of life.
   - ☐ Strongly agree   ☐ Disagree
   - ☐ Agree   ☐ Strongly disagree
   - ☐ Uncertain
3. The future looks very dismal.
   - ☐ Strongly agree   ☐ Disagree
   - ☐ Agree   ☐ Strongly disagree
   - ☐ Uncertain
4. More and more, I feel helpless in the face of what's happening in the world today.
   - ☐ Strongly agree   ☐ Disagree
   - ☐ Agree   ☐ Strongly disagree
   - ☐ Uncertain
5. People like me have no influence in society.
   - ☐ Strongly agree   ☐ Disagree
   - ☐ Agree   ☐ Strongly disagree
   - ☐ Uncertain

Suppose that we arbitrarily score responses in the following way: Strongly agree = 4; Agree = 3; Uncertain = 2; Disagree = 1; and Strongly disagree = 0. A respondent who answers "Strongly agree" to all five statements will have a total score of 20, indicating a high degree of alienation; a respondent who answers "Strongly disagree" to all five statements will have a total score of 0, indicating that that person is not alienated. In reality, most respondents will obtain scores between these two extremes, and the researcher has to work out a scoring system classifying respondents according to their degree of alienation. For example, respondents who score 0 to 6 are not alienated, respondents who score from 7 to 13 are somewhat alienated, and those who score between 14 and 20 are most alienated.

This index is also termed an *arbitrary scale* because there was nothing about the procedure to guarantee that any one statement or item tapped the same attitude as the other items. Is item 3 tapping the same aspect of alienation as item 5? Does item 4 correspond to the remaining item? Will another researcher who uses the index get the same findings? That is, is the index reliable? These central questions are addressed in our discussion of scaling methods.

Scaling Methods

Likert Scales

Likert scaling is a method designed to measure people's attitudes. Six steps can be distinguished in the construction of a **Likert scale**: (1) compiling possible scale items, (2) administering items to a random sample of respondents, (3) computing a total score for each respondent, (4) determining the *discriminative power* of items, (5) selecting the scale items, and (6) testing reliability.

Compiling Possible Scale Items. In the first step, the researcher compiles a series of items that express a wide range of attitudes, from extremely positive to extremely negative. Each item calls for checking one of five fixed-alternative expressions such as "strongly agree," "agree," "undecided," "disagree," and "strongly disagree." (Occasionally, three, four, six, or seven fixed-alternative expressions are used. Other expressions such as "almost always," "frequently," "occasionally," "rarely," and "almost never" are also used.) In this five-point continuum, weights of 1, 2, 3, 4, 5 or 5, 4, 3, 2, 1 are assigned, the direction of weighting being determined by the favorableness or unfavorableness of the item.

To measure attitudes toward employment of older people, Wayne Kirchner developed a 24-item scale using the Likert method. The following four items illustrate the scoring technique.[5]

1. Most companies are unfair to older employees.
   - ☐ Strongly agree ☐ Disagree
   - ☐ Agree ☐ Strongly disagree
   - ☐ Undecided
2. I think that older employees make better employees.
   - ☐ Strongly agree ☐ Disagree
   - ☐ Agree ☐ Strongly disagree
   - ☐ Undecided
3. In a case where two people can do a job about equally well, I'd pick the older person for the job.
   - ☐ Strongly agree ☐ Disagree
   - ☐ Agree ☐ Strongly disagree
   - ☐ Undecided
4. I think older employees have as much ability to learn new methods as other employees.
   - ☐ Strongly agree ☐ Disagree
   - ☐ Agree ☐ Strongly disagree
   - ☐ Undecided

5. Wayne K. Kirchner, "The Attitudes of Special Groups toward the Employment of Older Persons," *Journal of Gerontology,* 12 (1957): 216–220.

This scale was scored by assigning weights for response alternatives to positive items (acceptance of hiring older persons). The weights were assigned as follows: Strongly agree, 5; Agree, 4; Undecided, 3; Disagree, 2; Strongly disagree, 1. If negative items (that is, items indicating rejection of employment of older persons) had been included in the scale, their weights would have been reversed.

Administering All Possible Items. In the second step, a large number of respondents, selected randomly from the population to be measured, are asked to check their attitudes on the list of items.

Computing a Total Score. In this step, a total score for each respondent is calculated by summing the value of each item that is checked. Suppose that a respondent checked "Strongly agree" in item 1 (score 5), "Undecided" in item 2 (score 3), "Agree" in item 3 (score 4), and disagree" in item 4 (score 2). This person's total score is $5 + 3 + 4 + 2 = 14$.

Determining the Discriminative Power. In the fourth step, the researcher has to determine a basis for the selection of items for the final scale. This can be done either with the *internal consistency method*—that is, correlating each item with the total score and retaining those with the highest correlations—or with *item analysis*. Both methods yield an internally consistent scale. With either method, the problem is to find items that consistently separate those who are high on the attitude continuum from those who are low. With item analysis, each item is subjected to a measurement of its ability to separate the highs from the lows. This is called the **discriminative power (DP)** of the item. In calculating the *DP*, we sum the scored items for each respondent and place the scores in an array, usually from lowest to highest. Next we compare the range above the upper quartile (Q_1) with that below the lower quartile (Q_3), and the *DP* is calculated as the difference between the weighted means of the scores above Q_1 and of those that fall below Q_3, as illustrated in Table 18.5.

Selecting the Scale Items. The *DP* value is computed for each of the possible scale items, and those items with the largest *DP* values are selected. These are the items that best discriminate among individuals expressing differing attitudes toward the measured attitude.

Table 18.5
Table for Computing the DP for One Item

Group	Number in Group	1	2	3	4	5	Weighted Total*	Weighted Mean†	DP $(Q_1 - Q_3)$
High (top 25%)	9	0	1	2	3	3	35	3.89	
									2.00
Low (bottom 25%)	9	1	8	0	0	0	17	1.89	

*Weighted total = score × number who check that score
†Weighted mean = $\dfrac{\text{weighted total}}{\text{number in group}}$

Testing Reliability.   Reliability of the scale can be tested in much the same manner as in other measuring procedures. For example, we can select enough items for two scales (at least 100) and divide them into two sets, constituting two scales. The split-half reliability test can then be used (see Chapter 7).

Other Composite Measures

Various scaling procedures that incorporate some aspects of Likert scaling techniques have been developed. These procedures almost always include the initial compilation of possible scale items, administering the items to respondents, and some methods of selection of a set of items to be included in the final scale. The most common format for the items is a rating scale on which respondents are asked to make a judgment in terms of sets of ordered categories.

Most computer programs today include procedures and statistics that make it easier to select items for scales and evaluate how well the various items measure the underlying phenomena (see Appendixes A and B).

One of the simplest statistics to examine are the bivariate correlations (Pearson's *r*) linking each item with the whole scale. In general, items that have a strong association with other items will show higher overall correlations with the scales. Examining the bivariate correlation helps in deciding which items to include in the scale and which items to discard. Another helpful statistic is *Cronbach's alpha*, which is an estimate of the average of all possible split-half reliability coefficients. (For a discussion of reliability, see Chapter 7.) Alpha measures the extent to which the individual items comprising the scale "hang together."[6] A high alpha (.70 is an acceptable level) indicates that the items in the scale are "tightly connected."

Guttman Scaling

The **Guttman scale,** first developed by Louis Guttman in the early 1940s, was designed to incorporate an empirical test of the unidimensionality of a set of items as an integral part of the scale-construction process. Guttman suggested that if the items comprising the scale tap the same attitudinal dimension, they can be arranged so that there will be a continuum that indicates varying degrees of the underlying dimension. More explicitly, Guttman scales are unidimensional and cumulative. Cumulativeness implies that the items can be ordered by degree of difficulty and that the respondents who reply positively to a difficult item will also respond positively to less difficult items, or vice versa. If we take an example from the physical world, we know that if an object is 4 feet long, it is longer than 1 foot and longer than 2 feet and 3 feet. In the social world, we know that if a Hispanic father

6. See William Sims Bainbridge, *Survey Research: A Computer-assisted Introduction* (Belmont, Calif.: Wadsworth, 1989).

Table 18.6
A Hypothetical Perfect Guttman Scale

	Items in the Scale			
Respondent	Item 1: Admit to close kinship by marriage	Item 2: Admit to the same social club	Item 3: Admit as a neighbor	Total Score
A	+	+	+	3
B	−	+	+	2
C	−	−	+	1
D	−	−	−	0

+ indicates agreement with the statement; − indicates disagreement.

would not mind if his daughter married a black American, he would also not mind having this person belong to the social club he belongs to. Similarly, if he would not object to accepting this person as a member of his club, he would not mind having him live in his neighborhood. The scale that would result from administering these three items to a group of respondents is illustrated in Table 18.6. This scale is unidimensional as well as cumulative: the items are unidimensionally ranked on a single underlying dimension, and the scale is cumulative in that none of the respondents has a disagreement response before an agreement response or vice versa. Thus information on the position of any respondent's last positive response allows the prediction of all of his or her responses to the other scale items.

In practice, a perfect Guttman scale is rarely obtainable. In most cases, inconsistencies are present. Consequently, it is necessary to establish a criterion for evaluating the unidimensional and cumulative assumption. Guttman developed the **coefficient of reproducibility (CR)**, which measures the degree of conformity to a perfect scalable pattern:

$$CR = 1 - \frac{\Sigma_e}{Nr} \tag{18.4}$$

where CR = the coefficient of reproducibility

Σ_e = the total number of inconsistencies

Nr = the total number of responses (number of cases × number of items)

A CR of .90 is the minimum standard for accepting a scale as unidimensional.

Selecting Scale Items. In discussing the considerations involved in discovering and selecting items for a Guttman scale, Gorden lists three conditions that must be met, in the following order:[7]

---

7. Raymond L. Gorden, *Unidimensional Scaling of Social Variables* (New York: Macmillan, 1977), p. 46.

1. There must actually be an attitude toward the object (class of objects, event, or idea) in the minds of the people in the population to be sampled and tested.
2. A set of statements about the object must be found that have meaning to the members of the sample and elicit from them a response that is a valid indicator of that attitude.
3. The items in this set of statements or questions must represent different degrees along a single dimension.

Attitude scale items are selected by a variety of methods from all available sources: newspapers, books, scholarly articles, and the researcher's own knowledge of the problem. Interviewing experts as well as a subgroup of respondents will also help in securing good items. After a large set of potential items is compiled, a preliminary selection of items must be made. Items should be selected that clearly relate to the attitude being measured and cover the full continuum from strongly favorable to strongly unfavorable statements. Two to seven response categories may be constructed for each statement. The most common formats are Likert-type items with five-point scales, as in the following example:

> Please indicate how much you agree or disagree with the following statement: Nowadays a person has to live pretty much for today and let tomorrow take care of itself.
> *Strongly agree*   *Disagree*
> *Agree*   *Strongly disagree*
> *Undecided*

The items selected for Guttman scaling are usually included in a questionnaire and administered to a sample of the target population. Before the answers to the questionnaire are scored, items should be arranged so that higher numbers will consistently stand for either the most positive or most negative feelings. Items that do not correspond to this pattern should be reversed.

Calculating the Coefficient of Reproducibility. The coefficient of reproducibility is defined as the extent to which the total response pattern on a set of items can be reproduced if only the total score is known. This depends on the extent to which the pattern of responses conforms to a perfectly scalable pattern as was demonstrated in Table 18.6. When the obtained coefficient of reproducibility is below the required .90 criterion, the scale needs to be refined until the coefficient of reproducibility reaches the desired level.

Guttman Scale Application: An Example

After the development of the Guttman scale and its refinement, the results can be presented to describe the distribution of the variable measured. The scale can also be related to other variables in the study. An example of the development and application of a Guttman scale is Wanderer's study on riot

Table 18.7
A Guttman Scale of Riot Severity

Scale Type	% of Cities ($n = 75$)	Items Reported
8	4	No scale items
7	19	"Vandalism"
6	13	All of the above and "interference with firefighters"
5	16	All of the above and "looting"
4	13	All of the above and "sniping"
3	7	All of the above and "called state police"
2	17	All of the above and "called National Guard"
1	11	All of the above and "law officer or civilian killed"
Total	100	

Based on Jules J. Wanderer, "An Index of Riot Severity and Some Correlates," *American Journal of Sociology*, 74 (1969): 503.

severity in American cities.[8] This is a particularly interesting application of the Guttman scaling technique because it is based on behavioral indicators rather than on attitudes. The investigator analyzed 75 riots and civil criminal disorders reported to have taken place during the summer of 1967. Information used in the construction of the scale was provided by the mayors' offices at the request of a U.S. Senate subcommittee. The scale includes the following items of riot severity: killing, calling of the National Guard, calling of the state police, sniping, looting, interference with firefighters, and vandalism. These items are ordered from most to least severe or from least to most frequently reported. The coefficient of reproducibility of this Guttman scale of riot severity is .92. The scale and the distribution of the cities along the scale are presented in Table 18.7. Cities are organized into eight scale types according to the degree of severity, with 8 indicating the least severe and 1 the most severe riot activity.

At the second stage of the analysis, the researcher treated riot severity, as measured by the Guttman scale, as a dependent variable and examined a set of independent variables in terms of their relationship to riot severity. For example, a relationship was found between the percentage increase of nonwhites and riot severity as measured by the scale; that is, once a riot takes place, the greater the percentage increase of nonwhites, the greater the severity of the riot.

The Guttman scale of riot severity developed in this study suggests that the events that constitute riots and civil criminal disorders are not erratic or randomly generated. On the contrary, if one employs the property of Guttman scales, the sequence of events for levels of riot severity may be predicted.

8. Jules J. Wanderer, "An Index of Riot Severity and Some Correlates," *American Journal of Sociology,* 74 (1969): 503.

Factor Analysis

Factor analysis is a statistical technique for classifying a large number of interrelated variables into a limited number of dimensions or factors. It is a useful method for the construction of multiple-item scales, where each scale represents a dimension in a more abstract construct. Take, for example, community satisfaction. Many questions or items can be used to describe community satisfaction: satisfaction with public schools, shopping facilities, garbage collection, the local churches, the friendliness of the neighborhood, and so forth. However, the measurement of community satisfaction could be simplified if one were to identify a number of underlying dimensions of community satisfaction. This approach was taken by some studies dealing with this construct. Community or neighborhood satisfaction was divided into the following subconcepts: (1) satisfaction with service delivery, (2) satisfaction with community organization, (3) satisfaction with neighborhood quality, and (4) satisfaction with cultural amenities.

The relationship between the subconcepts and community satisfaction can be expressed as follows:

$$\text{community satisfaction} = S\,(\text{service delivery}) + S\,(\text{community organization}) + S\,(\text{neighborhood quality}) + S\,(\text{cultural amenities})$$

where S = satisfaction.

In this formulation, community satisfaction is a construct represented by few factors. In factor analysis, the factors are unobserved, each defined by a group of variables or items that constitute the factors. The research begins by selecting a large number of items that we assume define each of the factors. These items are then administered to the respondents included in the study.

The first step of factor analysis involves the computation of bivariate correlations (Pearson's r) between all the items. The correlations are then put in a matrix format. The correlation matrix is used as the input data in the factor analysis procedure. The extraction of factors is based on the common variation between a set of items. It is assumed the variables or items that can be represented by a single dimension will be correlated highly with this dimension. The correlation between an item and a factor is represented by a **factor loading.** A factor loading is similar to a correlation coefficient; it varies between zero and one and can be interpreted in the same way. For example, Table 18.8 presents the factor loadings of 14 items expressing community satisfaction on four factors. The items with the highest loading on each factor are underlined, and these items are the ones that are the best indicators for these factors. It can be seen that among the 14 items, only three have a high loading on factor 1. These items all refer to satisfaction with services; thus factor 1 can be identified as representing the dimension of *service delivery*. Similarly, factor 2 represents satisfaction with *community organization*; factor 3, *quality of life*; and factor 4, *cultural amenities*. Loadings of .30

Table 18.8
Factor Loadings of Community Satisfaction Items

Item Description	Factor 1	Factor 2	Factor 3	Factor 4
1. Neighborliness	.12361	.03216	.76182	.32101
2. Park and playgrounds	.62375	.33610	.32101	.02120
3. Public schools	.74519	.34510	.12102	.01320
4. Shopping facilities	.32100	.06121	.68123	.12356
5. Police protection	.90987	.12618	.21361	.01320
6. Local churches	.21032	.75847	.21362	.11620
7. Church groups and organization in the community	.01362	.83210	.01231	.11632
8. Community entertainment and recreational opportunities	.25617	.01320	.12341	.75642
9. Cultural activities	.16320	.12310	.32134	.82316
10. Quality of air	.02313	.11621	.83612	.32131
11. Noise level	.26154	.21320	.78672	.21368
12. Overcrowding	.24321	.02151	.91638	.02016
13. Racial problems	.08091	.11320	.82316	.16342
14. Neighborhood pride	.18642	.11218	.71321	.18321
Percentage of variance	18.2	5.6	40.1	2.4

or below are generally considered too weak to represent a factor. You can see that all items load on each of the factors but that most loadings are too weak.

The extent to which each factor is explained by the items' loadings is reflected by the percentage of explained variance. Generally, factors with the highest percentage of explained variance provide the most parsimonious representation of the items. You can see that the most parsimonious factor is quality of life (40.1 percent) and the least parsimonious is cultural amenities (2.4 percent).

In the final step in factor analysis, a composite scale is developed for each factor. For each case, a factor score (scale score) is calculated. A factor score is a case's score on a factor. It is obtained by using yet another type of coefficient, a **factor score coefficient**. To construct a case's factor score, we multiply the factor score coefficients for each variable by the standardized values of the variable for that case. For example, Table 18.9 represents the factor score coefficients for the items loading on factor 3. We may construct a case's factor score f_3, a composite scale representing factor 3, as follows:

$$f_3 = .6812Z_1 + .7234Z_{10} + .6916Z_{11} + .8162Z_{12} + .8110Z_{13} + .6910Z_{14}$$

Z_1 through Z_{14} represent the standardized values of items 1 through 14 for that case.

Table 18.9
Factor Score Coefficients

Item	Coefficient
1	.6812
10	.7234
11	.6916
12	.8162
13	.8110
14	.6910

Summary

1. An index is a composite measure of two or more indicators or items. An example is the consumer price index (CPI), which is a composite measure of changes in retail prices. Four major problems are involved in constructing indexes: definition of the purpose for which the index is being compiled, selection of sources of data, selection of the base, and selection of methods of aggregation and weighting.

2. Scaling is a method of measuring the amount of a property possessed by a class of objects or events. It is most often associated with the measurement of attitudes. Attitude scales consist of a number of attitude statements with which the respondent is asked to agree or disagree. Scaling techniques are applied to the problem of ordering the selected statements along some continuum. They are methods of forming a series of qualitative facts into quantitative series. All the scales discussed in this chapter are either assumed to be unidimensional or tested for unidimensionality. This means that the items comprising the scale should belong on a continuum, which is presumed to reflect one and only one concept.

3. One method of scale construction is the technique of summated rating or Likert scaling. The technique involves the compiling of possible scale items, administering them to a random sample of respondents, computing a total score for each respondent, determining the discriminative power of each item, and selecting the final scale items.

4. Another method of scaling is the Guttman scaling technique. This method was designed to incorporate an empirical test of the unidimensionality of a set of items as an integral part of the scale construction process. A Guttman scale is unidimensional as well as cumulative. The items are unidimensionally ranked on a single underlying dimension, and the scale is cumulative in that information on the position of any respondent's last positive response allows the prediction of all of that person's responses to the other items. To measure the degree of conformity to a perfect scalable pattern,

Guttman developed the coefficient of reproducibility. A coefficient of reproducibility of .90 is the conventional minimum standard for accepting a scale as unidimensional.

5. Factor analysis is a statistical technique for classifying a large number of interrelated variables into a smaller number of dimensions or factors. It is a useful method for the construction of multiple-item scales, where each scale represents a dimension in a more abstract construct.

Key Terms for Review

unidimensionality

index

weighted aggregate

Likert scale

discriminative power (*DP*)

Guttman scale

coefficient of reproducibility (*CR*)

factor analysis

factor loading

factor score coefficient

Study Questions

1. Why are scales and indexes used in the social sciences?
2. What is the difference between scales and indexes?
3. Develop an index to measure "popularity" among a particular subgroup of the population, such as college students. Use a method of aggregation with items of the type "How many times . . . ?" "How often . . . ?" "How many . . . ?" Consider and incorporate weighting as appropriate. Use about ten subjects to obtain the data for your scale. Discuss the problems of validity and reliability as they apply to your scale. On the basis of the results you obtain, submit a revised index of popularity.

Additional Readings

Beere, Carole A. *Gender Roles: A Handbook of Tests and Measures.* Westport, CT: Greenwood Press, 1990.

Bohrnstedt, George W., and Edgar F. Borgatta, eds. *Social Measurement: Current Issues.* Newbury Park, Calif.: Sage, 1981.

Brodsky, Stanley L., and H. O'Neal. *Smitherman Handbook of Scales for Research in Crime and Delinquency.* New York: Plenum Press, 1983.

Dawes, R. H., and T. W. Smith. "Attitude and Opinion Measurement." In *The Handbook of Social Psychology.* 3d ed., ed. Gardner Lindzey and Elliot Aronson. New York: Random House, 1985. pp. 507–566.

Kim, Jae-On, and Charles W. Mueller. *Introduction to Factor Analysis.* Newbury Park, Calif.: Sage, 1978.

Lodge, Milton. *Magnitude Scaling.* Newbury Park, Calif.: Sage, 1981.

Long, Scott J. *Confirmatory Factor Analysis.* Newbury Park, Calif.: Sage, 1983.

Maranell, Gary M. *Scaling: A Sourcebook for Behavioral Scientists,* 4th ed. Hawthorne, N.Y.: Aldine, 1974.

Miller, Delbert C. *Handbook of Research Design and Social Measurement.* White Plains, N.Y.: Longman, 1983.

Robinson, John P., Jerrold G. Rusk, and Kendra B. Head. *Measures of Political Attitudes.* Ann Arbor: Institute for Social Research, University of Michigan, 1968.

Robinson, John P., and Philip R. Shaver. *Measures of Social Psychological Attitudes,* Rev. ed. Ann Arbor: Institute for Social Research, University of Michigan, 1973.

Shye, Samuel, ed. *Theory Construction and Data Analysis in the Behavioral Sciences.* San Francisco: Jossey-Bass, 1978.

Straus, Murray A., and Bruce W. Brown. *Family Measurement Techniques: Abstracts of Published Instruments, 1935–1975.* Minneapolis: University of Minnesota Press, 1978.

Sullivan, John L., and Stanley Feldman. *Multiple Indicators.* Newbury Park, Calif.: Sage, 1979.

CHAPTER 19

Inferences

In this chapter, we examine the logic of statistical inference and hypothesis testing. Two major groups of statistical tests—parametric and nonparametric—are described.

I N CHAPTER 18, WE INTRODUCED THE general idea of inferential statistics, which deal with the problem of evaluating population characteristics when only the sample evidence is given. It was demonstrated that sample statistics may give good estimates of particular population parameters but that virtually any estimate will deviate from the true value owing to sampling fluctuations. The process of statistical inference enables investigators to evaluate the accuracy of their estimates.

A second use of inferential statistics is the assessment of the probability of specific sample results under assumed population conditions. This type of inferential statistics is called *hypothesis testing* and will occupy us throughout this chapter. With estimation, a sample is selected to evaluate the population parameter; with the testing of hypotheses, by contrast, assumptions about the population parameter are made in advance, and the sample then provides the test of these assumptions. With estimation, the sample provides information about single population parameters such as the mean income or the variance of education; with hypothesis testing, an inference is usually being made about relationships among variables—for example, the relationship between education and income or between occupation and particular political attitudes.

This chapter describes the strategy of hypothesis testing by focusing on concepts such as the sampling distribution, Type I and Type II errors, and the level of significance. We then consider several methods of testing hypotheses about the relationship between two variables: difference between means, Pearson's *r*, the Mann-Whitney test, and the chi-square test.

The Strategy of Testing Hypotheses

The first step in testing a hypothesis is to formulate it in statistical terms. We have already discussed how to draw a hypothesis from a theory or how to formulate a research problem as a hypothesis. However, in order to test the hypothesis, one must formulate it in terms that can be analyzed with statistical tools. For example, if the purpose of the investigation is to establish that educated individuals have higher incomes than noneducated individuals, the statistical hypothesis might be that there is a positive correlation between education and income or that the mean income of a highly educated group will be larger than the mean income of a group with a lower level of education. In both cases, the statistical hypothesis is formulated in terms of descriptive statistics (such as a correlation or a mean) as well as a set of specifying conditions about these statistics (such as a positive correlation or a difference between the means).

The statistical hypothesis always applies to the population of interest. If a population could be tested directly, no inferences would be necessary, and any difference between the means (or a positive correlation of any size) would support the hypothesis. However, sample results are subject to sampling fluctuations, which would account for the difference between the means or the positive coefficient. Thus a result in line with the hypothesis may imply either that the hypothesis is true or that it is false, with the results being due to chance factors. Conversely, a deviation between the sample results and the expected population value could mean either that the hypothesis is false or that it is true, with the difference between the expected and obtained values being due to chance. Table 19.1 illustrates these four possibilities.

Whether a sample result matches or deviates from expectation, either case can imply that the hypothesis is either *true* or *false*. Therefore, sample results cannot be interpreted directly; a decision rule is needed to enable the researcher to reject or retain a hypothesis about the population on the basis of sample results. The procedure of statistical inference enables the researcher to determine whether a particular sample result falls within a range that can occur by an acceptable level of chance. This procedure involves the following steps listed, which are discussed in some detail:

1. Formulate a null hypothesis and a research hypothesis.

Table 19.1
Alternative Interpretations of Sample Results

Hypothesis Status	Sample Results	
	According to Expectation	Deviation from Expectation
True	Results invalidate hypothesis	Results due to sampling fluctuation
False	Results due to sampling fluctuation	Results invalidate hypothesis

2. Choose a sampling distribution and a statistical test according to the null hypothesis.
3. Specify a significance level (α), and define the region of rejection.
4. Compute the statistical test, and reject or retain the null hypothesis accordingly.

Null and Research Hypotheses

Two statistical hypotheses are involved in hypothesis testing. The first is the **research hypothesis,** which is usually symbolized by H_1. The second, symbolized by H_0, is the **null hypothesis**; H_0 is determined by H_1, which is really what one wants to know; H_0 is the antithesis of H_1.

Suppose that the research hypothesis states that Catholics have larger families than Protestants. With the mean score for the size of family in the Catholic population designated as μ_1 and in the Protestant population as μ_2, the research hypothesis would be

$$H_1: \mu_1 > \mu_2$$

The null hypothesis would be

$$H_0: \mu_1 = \mu_2$$

The null hypothesis can be expressed in several ways. However, it is usually an expression of no difference or no relationship between the variables. Both the null hypothesis and the research hypothesis are expressed in terms of the population parameters, not in terms of the sample statistics. The null hypothesis is the one that is tested directly; the research hypothesis is supported when the null hypothesis is rejected as being unlikely.

The need for two hypotheses arises out of a logical necessity: the null hypothesis is based on negative inference in order to avoid the *fallacy of affirming the consequent*—that is, one must eliminate false hypotheses rather than accept true ones. For instance, suppose that theory A implies empirical observation B. When B is false, one knows that A must also be false. But when B is true, A cannot be accepted as true, because B can be an empirical implication of several other theories that are not necessarily A. Acceptance of A as true would be the fallacy of affirming the consequent.

Durkheim's theory of suicide may serve as an illustration. One of its propositions (A) is that people in individualistic situations are more likely to commit suicide. The empirical observation (B) derived from this proposition is that the suicide rate will be higher among single than married individuals. If B proves to be false (if there is no difference in the suicide rates of married and single persons), theory A is false. But what if B is true? A cannot be accepted as true; there are many other explanations for B that are not necessarily A. For instance, the higher suicide rate of single persons might be explained not by individualism but rather by excessive drinking, which may lead to depression and to suicide. Thus observation B might imply that A_1, another theory, is true.

Usually, many alternative theories might explain the same observations; the researcher has to select the most credible one. Thus the credibility of a theory can be established only by the elimination of all alternative theories:

> For any given observation which is an implication of A, say B_1, there will be *some of* the possible alternative theories which will imply not-B_1. If we then demonstrate B_1, these alternative theories are falsified. This leaves us with *fewer alternative possible theories* to our own.[1]

Sampling Distribution

Having formulated a specific null hypothesis, the investigator proceeds to test it against the sample results. For instance, if the hypothesis states that there is no difference between the means of two populations ($\mu_1 = \mu_2$), the procedure would be to draw a random sample from each population, compare the two sample means ($\bar{X}_1$ and $\bar{X}_2$), and make an inference from the samples to the populations. However, the sample result is subject to sampling error; therefore, it does not always reflect the true population value. If samples of the same size are drawn from the population, each sample will usually produce a different result.

To determine the accuracy of the sample statistic, one has to compare it to a statistical model that gives the probability of observing such a result. Such a statistical model is called a **sampling distribution**. A sampling distribution of a statistic is obtained by drawing a large number of random samples of the same size from the defined population, computing the statistic for each sample, and plotting the frequency distribution of the statistic. In Chapter 8, we saw an example of such a distribution: the sampling distribu-

1. Arthur L. Stinchcombe, *Constructing Social Theories* (Orlando, Fla.: Harcourt Brace Jovanovitch, 1968), p. 20.

tion of the mean. It is possible to construct a sampling distribution of any other statistic, for example, of the variance (s^2), of the standard deviation (s), of the difference between means ($\bar{X}_1 - \bar{X}_2$), or of proportions (p).

As an illustration, let us go back to Durkheim's theory on suicide. The hypothesis to be tested is that single people have a relatively higher suicide rate than the general population. One way of evaluating the proportion of suicide among single people is comparing the number of suicides in this group to the average proportion in the population at large. Suppose that the records of health centers indicate that the national suicide rate in the adult population is 20 out of every 100, or .20. The research hypothesis would then imply that the rate of suicide among single people is higher than .20. Thus

H_1: The proportion of suicides among single people > .20

The null hypothesis would state that the proportion of suicides among single people is the same as the national average:

H_0: The proportion of suicides among singles = .20

Suppose that a sample of 100 is drawn from the records on single persons' suicides and that the rate of suicide is .30. Is this result sufficiently larger than .20 to justify the rejection of the null hypothesis? To assess the likelihood of obtaining a rate of .30 under the assumption of the null hypothesis, it is compared to a distribution of suicide rates of the adult population. Let us assume that 1,000 random samples of 100 each are drawn from the records on suicide and that the suicide rate is computed for each sample. The obtained hypothetical sampling distribution[2] is presented in Table 19.2. This sampling distribution may serve as a statistical model for assessing the likelihood of observing a suicide rate of .30 among single people if their rate were equivalent to that of the adult population. The probability of observing any particular result can be determined by dividing its frequency in the distribution by the total number of samples. The obtained probabilities are displayed in the third column of Table 19.2. For example, the suicide rate of .38–.39 occurred five times; therefore, the probability that any sample of size $n = 100$ will have this suicide rate is 5/1,000 or .005; that is, we would expect to obtain such a result in approximately .5 percent of the samples of 100 drawn from the population. Similarly, the probability of obtaining a rate of .30–.31 is .015, or 1.5 percent. The probability of obtaining a rate of .30 or more is equal to the sum of the probabilities of .30–.31, .32–.33, .34–.35, .36–.37, .38–.39, and .40 or more; that is, .015 + .010 + .010 + .010 + .005 + .000 = .050. Thus we would expect 5 percent of all samples of 100 drawn from this population to have a suicide rate of .30 or more.

---

2. Such a distribution is often called an *experimental sampling distribution* because it is obtained from observed data.

Table 19.2

Hypothetical Sampling Distribution of Suicide Rates for 1,000 Random Samples ($n = 100$)

Suicide Rate	Number of Samples (f)	Proportion of Samples ($p = f/n$)
.40 or more	0	.000
.38–.39	5	.005
.36–.37	10	.010
.34–.35	10	.010
.32–.33	10	.010
.30–.31	15	.015
.28–.29	50	.050
.26–.27	50	.050
.24–.25	50	.050
.22–.23	150	.150
.20–.21	200	.200
.18–.19	150	.150
.16–.17	100	.100
.14–.15	100	.100
.12–.13	50	.050
.10–.11	15	.015
.08–.09	10	.010
.06–.07	10	.010
.04–.05	10	.010
.02–.03	5	.005
.01 or less	0	.000
Total	1,000	1.000

Level of Significance and Region of Rejection

Following the construction of the sampling distribution, the likelihood of the result of .30 (given the assumption of the null hypothesis) can now be evaluated. The decision as to what result is sufficiently unlikely to justify the rejection of the null hypothesis is quite arbitrary. Any set of extreme results can be selected as a basis for rejection of the null hypothesis. The range of these results is designated as the **region of rejection**. The sum of the probabilities of the results included in the region of rejection is denoted as the **level of significance,** or α. It is customary to set the level of significance at .05 or .01, which means that the null hypothesis is to be rejected if the sample outcome is among the results that would have occurred no more than 5 percent or 1 percent of the time by chance.

Figure 19.1 graphically represents the sampling distribution of Table 19.2 and the region of rejection with $\alpha = .05$. The region of rejection includes all the suicide rates of .30 and above. The sum of the probabilities of these results is equal to the level of significance, .05.

Figure 19.1
Sampling Distribution of Suicide Rates for 1,000 Samples ($n = 100$)

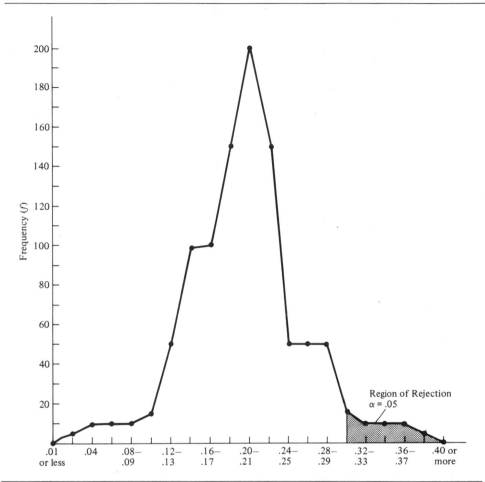

The obtained sample result of .30 falls within the region of rejection; thus the null hypothesis can be rejected at the .05 level of significance. The rejection of the null hypothesis lends support to the research hypothesis that the suicide rate of single people is higher than the rate in the general adult population.

One-tailed and Two-tailed Tests

In the preceding example, the set of extreme results was selected from the right tail of the sampling distribution. However, extreme sample outcomes are also located at the left-hand tail. In Table 19.2, the probability of a sui-

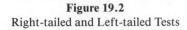

Figure 19.2
Right-tailed and Left-tailed Tests

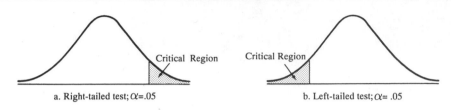

a. Right-tailed test; $\alpha=.05$ b. Left-tailed test; $\alpha=.05$

cide rate of .11 and below is equal to the probability of obtaining a rate of .30 and above; in both cases, it is .05.

A statistical test may be *one-tailed* or *two-tailed*. In a **two-tailed test**, the region of rejection is located at both left and right tails. In a **one-tailed test**, extreme results leading to rejection of the null hypothesis can be located at either tail.

The decision to locate the region of rejection in one or two tails will depend on whether H_1 implies a specific direction to the predicted results and whether it specifies large or small values. When H_1 predicts larger values, the region of rejection will be located at the right tail of the sampling distribution (as in the example of suicide). When H_1 implies lower values, the left tail is selected as a region of rejection. For instance, suppose that the research hypothesis had implied that single people have a lower suicide rate than the general adult population; that is,

H_1: The proportion of suicide in single population $< .20$

The results considered unlikely under this hypothesis are at the left tail of the distribution. At the .05 level of significance, the critical region will consist of the following rates: .10–.11, .08–.09, .06–.07, .04–.05, .02–.03, .01 or less. The sum of the probabilities of these results is $.015 + .010 + .010 + .010 + .005 + .000 = .050$. Figure 19.2 presents the right-tailed and left-tailed alternatives.

There are occasions when the direction of the research hypothesis cannot be predicted accurately. For example, we suspect that single persons have a different suicide rate but are unable to specify the direction of the difference. The research hypothesis would have been expressed as

H_1: The proportion of single persons' suicide $\neq .20$

When the direction of H_1 cannot be accurately specified, H_0 is rejected whenever extreme values in either direction are obtained. In such a case, the statistical test is designated as a two-tailed test, and the level of significance is divided in two. Thus a .05 level of significance would mean that H_0 will be rejected if the sample outcome falls among the lowest 2.5 percent or the

Figure 19.3
A Two-tailed Test

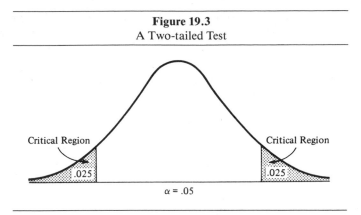

Critical Region   Critical Region

.025   .025

$\alpha = .05$

highest 2.5 percent of the sampling distribution. This alternative is diagrammed in Figure 19.3.

Let us select the .05 level of significance and make use of a two-tailed test in the suicide example. The critical region will consist of the alternatives .34–.35, .36–.37, .38–.39, .40 or more ($.010 + .010 + .005 + .000 = .025$) and .06–.07, .04–.05, .02–.03, .01 or less ($.010 + .010 + .005 + .000 = .025$). With a two-tailed test, a sample result of .30 is not in the region of rejection; thus the null hypothesis would not have been rejected in this case.

Type I and Type II Errors

In statistical hypothesis testing, the entire population is not measured directly, so the statistical test can never prove if the null hypothesis is true or false. The only evidence it provides is whether the sample result is sufficiently likely or unlikely to justify the decision to retain or to reject the null hypothesis.

The null hypothesis can be either true or false, and in both cases it can be rejected or retained. If it is true and is rejected nonetheless, the decision is in error. The error is the *rejection of a true hypothesis*—a **Type I error**. If the null hypothesis is false but is retained, the error committed is the *acceptance of a false hypothesis*; this error is designated as a **Type II error**. These four alternatives are presented schematically in Table 19.3.

Table 19.3
Alternative Decisions in Hypotheses Testing

Decision	Null Hypothesis Is True	Null Hypothesis Is False
Reject hypothesis	Type I error	No error
Accept hypothesis	No error	Type II error

The probability of rejecting a true hypothesis—a Type I error—is defined as the *level of significance*. Thus in the long run, an investigator employing the .05 level of significance will falsely reject 5 percent of the true hypotheses tested. Naturally, one would be interested in minimizing the error of rejecting a true hypothesis by making the level of significance as low as possible. However, Type I errors and Type II errors are inversely related: a decrease in the error of rejecting a true hypothesis leads to an increase in the probability of retaining a false one. Under these conditions, the selection of α is determined by (1) the type of problem one is investigating and (2) the consequences of rejecting a true hypothesis or retaining a false one. If, for example, the subject of investigation is the effect of an experimental teaching method on the achievement of disadvantaged children and the results of the study will determine the implementation of the method throughout the school system, the researcher should carefully consider the consequences of making a mistake. Suppose that the null hypothesis states that the new teaching method has negative effects. If the null hypothesis were to be rejected when it is actually true, the consequences could be very severe; hundreds of thousands of disadvantaged children would be harmed. If, conversely, it is not rejected when it is actually false, the implementation of the new method will be postponed until further evidence is available. Therefore, in this case it would be preferable to minimize α because the implications of rejecting a true hypothesis are more severe than those of retaining a false one.

When a study does not have practical implications, the selection of α will be arbitrary, but the choice will usually be governed by accepted conventions. The significance levels commonly used in social science research are .001, .01, and .05.

Parametric and Nonparametric Tests of Significance

We shall discuss the tests that are most common in social science research. They are divided into two major groups: parametric tests and nonparametric tests. A **parametric test** is a statistical test based on several assumptions about the parameters of the population from which the sample was drawn. Among the most important ones are the assumptions that (1) the observations must be drawn from a normally distributed population and (2) that the variables are measured on at least an interval scale.[3] The results of a parametric test are meaningful only insofar as these assumptions are valid.

A **nonparametric test** is one whose model neither specifies the normality condition nor requires an interval level of measurement. There are certain

---

3. Sidney N. Siegel, *Nonparametric Statistics for the Behavioral Sciences* (New York: McGraw-Hill, 1956), pp. 2–3.

assumptions associated with most nonparametric tests; however, they are weaker and fewer than those associated with parametric tests.

In practice, one need not go through the laborious procedure of constructing a sampling distribution. In many instances, sampling distributions have been constructed by previous researchers and are known in advance. Moreover, there are distributions that can be used as approximations of certain sampling distributions. For example, the sampling distribution of the mean closely approximates the normal curve distribution, which can therefore be used in testing hypotheses about means.

In the discussion of specific tests that follows, reference will be made to existing sampling distributions that have been constructed in advance or that approximate the desired distribution. The sampling distributions employed in this section are provided in Appendixes E through I.

Selected Parametric Tests

Difference between Means.   Many hypotheses in empirical research involve a comparison between populations. For example, to assess the relationship between social class and voting, one could compare different social classes with respect to their voting patterns. Similarly, in comparing Asian-Americans and Hispanic-Americans with respect to achievement, one is relating ethnicity to achievement.

When the dependent variable being investigated is measured on an interval scale, a comparison of means can be used to reflect the amount of relationship between two variables (see Chapter 16). To assess the significance of a difference between means, use the **difference-between-means test**.

To illustrate the testing of hypotheses about the difference between means, data are presented in Table 19.4, which shows scores on attitudes on women's issues for two samples: evangelical and nonevangelical women. The literature concludes that the evangelicals are less likely to take feminist positions than nonevangelicals.[4] This would lead to the following research hypothesis: H_1: $\mu_1 > \mu_2$ where μ_1 is the mean score of the population of non-

Table 19.4
Mean Scores of Attitudes on Feminist Issues for Evangelical
Women and Others (Hypothetical Data)

	Evangelicals	Others
n	126	101
$\bar{x}$	3.60	6.10
s	3.04	4.52

4. Clyde Wilcox and Elizabeth Adell Cook, "Evangelical Women and Feminism: Some Additional Evidence," *Women and Politics*, 9 (1989): 27–49.

evangelical women and μ_2 the mean of evangelical women. The null hypothesis could state that there is no difference in the mean score of the two populations; that is, H_0: $\mu_1 = \mu_2$.

Inspection of the data reveals a difference between the two sample means of 2.50 (6.10 − 3.60). Although this difference is in the expected direction, its probability of occurrence under the assumption of the null hypothesis has to be determined. If such a difference is unlikely to occur, assuming that the population means are identical, we must reject the null hypothesis.

The selection of the appropriate sampling distribution for testing the difference between means depends on the sample size. When each sample is larger than 30 ($n > 30$), the sampling distribution of the difference between means approaches normality, and thus the normal curve (Appendix E) can be used as the statistical model. The procedure is similar to the one employed in estimating population means (see Chapter 8). One can translate the difference between the means to standard Z scores and then determine its probability of occurrence according to the normal curve distribution. For a two-tailed test, using the .05 level of significance, the critical region expressed in Z scores includes all the positive scores of 1.96 and above or all the negative scores of − 1.96 and below, whose likelihood of occurrence is .025. For a one-tailed test, the critical region contains all scores of 1.65 and above or − 1.65 and below. Similarly, for the .01 level of significance, Z is ± 2.58 and ± 2.33, respectively.

To test the null hypothesis on difference in attitudes on feminist issues, we can select a right-tailed test because H_1 is a directional hypothesis implying larger values. The level of significance selected will be .01; any value larger than 2.33 will lead to rejection of the null hypothesis.

To determine the significance of the difference between the means using the normal curve, one must convert the difference to standard scores. This can be accomplished using a test statistic denoted as t, which is defined in Formula (19.1):

$$t = \frac{(\bar{X}_1 - \bar{X}_2) - (\mu_1 - \mu_2)}{\hat{\sigma}_{\bar{x}_1 - \bar{x}_2}} \tag{19.1}$$

where $\bar{X}_1 - \bar{X}_2 =$ the difference between the sample means

$\mu_1 - \mu_2 =$ the means of the sampling distribution of the difference between means

$\hat{\sigma}_{\bar{x}_1 - \bar{x}_2} =$ an estimate of the standard error[5] of the sampling distribution of the difference between the means

Like Z, t measures deviations from the means in terms of standard deviation units; $\bar{X}_1 - \bar{X}_2$ replaces X, $\mu_1 - \mu_2$ replaces $\bar{X}$, and $\hat{\sigma}$ replaces s. Z, how-

---

5. The standard error is the standard deviation of the sampling distribution; see Chapter 8 for a discussion of this concept.

ever, cannot be calculated when the variances of the two populations (σ_1^2 and σ_2^2) are unknown. That is, t substitutes for Z whenever sample variances (s_1^2 and s_2^2) are used as estimates of the populations' parameters. Because the populations' variances are almost never available, for all practical purposes, the t statistic is used to transform mean differences to standard scores. The t is normally distributed when $n > 30$; thus the normal distribution can be employed whenever each sample size is greater than 30. However, when $n \leq 30$, the normal approximation is not appropriate, and the sampling distribution of t has to be used.

The estimate of the standard error ($\hat{\sigma}_{\bar{x}1-\bar{x}2}$) can be obtained by two methods. The first assumes that the two population variances are equal—for instance, $\sigma_1^2 = \sigma_2^2$—and thus the variances of the two samples are combined into a single estimate of σ_1^2 or σ_2^2. The standard error under these conditions is as follows:

$$\hat{\sigma}_{\bar{x}1-\bar{x}2} = \sqrt{\frac{n_1 s_1^2 + n_2 s_2^2}{n_1 + n_2 - 2}} \sqrt{\frac{n_1 + n_2}{n_1 n_2}} \tag{19.2}$$

where n_1 and n_2 are the sample sizes of sample 1 and sample 2, respectively, and $s_1{}^2$ and $s_2{}^2$ are the variances of sample 1 and sample 2.

When there is no basis for assuming that the population variances are identical, it is not possible to pool the sample variance. In this instance, the estimation for the two variances is separate, and the obtained formula for the standard error is

$$\hat{\sigma}_{\bar{x}1-\bar{x}2} = \sqrt{\frac{s_1{}^2}{n_1 - 1} + \frac{s_2{}^2}{n_2 - 1}} \tag{19.3}$$

To calculate t for the data summarized in Table 19.4, we assume that $\sigma_1{}^2 = \sigma_2{}^2$ and estimate the pooled estimate of the standard error:

$$\hat{\sigma}_{\bar{x}1-\bar{x}2} = \sqrt{\frac{(101)(4.52)^2 + 126(3.04)^2}{101 + 126 - 2}} \sqrt{\frac{101 + 126}{(101)(126)}} = .50$$

As under the null hypothesis it has been assumed that $\mu_1 = \mu_2$, the definition of t reduces to

$$t = \frac{\bar{X}_1 - \bar{X}_2}{\hat{\sigma}_{\bar{x}1-\bar{x}2}} \tag{19.4}$$

We obtain the following result for our example:

$$t = \frac{6.1 - 3.6}{.50} = \frac{2.5}{.50} = 5$$

Referring to the normal curve table (Appendix E), we observe that the value of t is in fact greater than the value needed for rejection (2.33) at the .01 level of significance. In other words, the difference between the sample mean of mental patients and that of college students is not likely to be due to sampling error. Accordingly, we reject H_0 and conclude that the difference between the samples reflects different degrees of mental health and that the measuring scale is therefore valid.

The t Distribution.   When either or both of the sample sizes are less than 30, the normal curve does not approximate the sampling distribution of the difference between means. As a result, using the normal curve to determine the probability of H_0 will yield inaccurate conclusions, and the sampling distribution of t has to be used instead. The t is actually a family of curves, each determined by the sample size. Thus for a sample size of 7, t has a different distribution from that for a sample size of 10. The sampling distribution of t is reproduced in Appendix F. The values in this table are given in terms of the significance level (one tail and two tails) and the degrees of freedom.

Degrees of Freedom.   The concept of **degrees of freedom (df)** is a basic one that is used in other statistical tests. It refers to the number of free choices one can make in repeated random samples that constitute sampling distribution. If, for example, one is allowed to pick two numbers freely, there are two degrees of freedom. If, however, the two numbers must sum to 20, there is only one free choice or one degree of freedom, for after the first number has been freely chosen, the second number is determined by the sum total. The number of degrees of freedom of the t distribution is limited by the fact that for each sample, the population variance has to be estimated, and there are only $n-1$ quantities that are free to vary. The number of degrees of freedom is then equal to $n-1$ for each sample. Thus to test a hypothesis about difference between two samples, df is equivalent to $(n_1 - 1) + (n_2 - 1) = n_1 + n_2 - 2$.

To illustrate the use of the t table, we shall test the hypothesis that achievement is associated with assignment to tracks in a secondary school. The data are summarized in Table 19.5. The investigators hypothesized that achievement and track assignment were related so that a college preparatory track had more students that were high achievers than a noncollege track. The null hypothesis to be tested is that the means of the two populations are

Table 19.5
Mean Achievement of Students in College Preparatory and Noncollege Tracks

	College Preparatory Track	Noncollege Track
n	13	6
$\bar{x}$	48.3	20.5
s	23.6	12.2

identical, whereas the research hypothesis states that the mean achievement of the college preparatory track (μ_1) is higher than that of the noncollege track (μ_2):

$$H_0: \mu_1 = \mu_2$$
$$H_1: \mu_1 > \mu_2$$

We can follow the same procedure in calculating the standard error and the t ratio, using Equations (19.2) and (19.4):

$$\hat{\sigma}_{\bar{x}1 - \bar{x}2} = \sqrt{\frac{13(23.6)^2 + 6(12.2)^2}{13 + 6 - 2}} \sqrt{\frac{13 + 6}{(13)(6)}} = 10.8$$

$$t = \frac{48.3 - 20.5}{10.8} = \frac{27.8}{10.8} = 2.574$$

The obtained t can now be compared with the appropriate value in the sampling distribution of t. The number of degrees of freedom for sample sizes of 13 and 6 is 17 $(13 + 6 - 2)$. At the .01 level of significance with a one-tailed test (right tail), the t for which H_0 will be rejected is 2.567. A t larger than 2.567 is unlikely to occur if H_0 is true. As 2.574 is larger than 2.567, the null hypothesis is rejected, and the investigator can conclude that the difference in achievement between the two tracks is statistically significant.

A Significance Test for Pearson's r.   The correlation coefficient Pearson's r—like $\bar{X}$, Md, or b—is a statistic obtained from sample data; as such, it is just an estimate of a population parameter. Pearson's r corresponds to the population correlation denoted as ρ or rho. As a sample statistic, r is subject to sampling fluctuations; the test of its statistical significance is an assessment of the likelihood that the obtained correlation is due to sampling error. For example, a researcher may test the hypothesis that liberalism is correlated with income and draw a random sample of 24, obtaining an r of .30. It is probable that in the population these two variables are not correlated at all and that the obtained coefficient is a result of chance factors. In other words, is an r of .30 large enough to make the hypothesis of no relation unlikely?

The strategy of testing such a hypothesis is similar to that used in the difference-of-means test; the null hypothesis states that the correlation in the population is zero, and the research hypothesis, that it is different from zero:

$$H_0: \rho = 0$$
$$H_1: \rho \neq 0$$

Testing the Significance of r *When* ρ *Is Zero.*   When ρ is assumed to be zero under the null hypothesis, the statistical significance of r can be tested by converting r to a standard score using the t test statistic with $n - 2$ degrees of freedom. Thus t is defined as follows:

$$t = \frac{r\sqrt{n-2}}{\sqrt{1-r^2}} \tag{19.5}$$

To illustrate the use of t in testing the significance of Pearson's r, let us suppose that a correlation of .30 between income and years of schooling is obtained from a sample of $n = 24$ $(df = 2)$. The t is equal to

$$t = \frac{.30\sqrt{22}}{\sqrt{1-.30^2}} = 1.475$$

From the distribution of t in Appendix F, we see that at the .05 level of significance for a two-tailed test and with 22 df, the value of t required to reject the null hypothesis is 2.074. As the obtained t is smaller than this value, the null hypothesis cannot be rejected, and the relationship between income and political participation is said to be not significant.

The significance of r can also be tested by using a test statistic called F. The F statistic is based on the ratio of the explained (r^2) to the unexplained ($1 - r^2$) variance. It is defined in Equation (19.6), where $n - 2$ stands for the degrees of freedom:

$$F = \frac{r^2}{1-r^2}(n-2) \tag{19.6}$$

To use the data in our earlier example, we have

$$F = \frac{.30^2}{1-.30^2}(24-2) = 2.17$$

To evaluate the F statistic, we use the F distribution given in Appendix G. F values are given for $\alpha = .05$ (light numbers) and $\alpha = .01$ (bold numbers) and where the degrees of freedom for the explained variance is equal to 1 (across the top of the table) and the degrees of freedom for the unexplained variance is equal to $n - 2$ (left-hand column). H_0 is rejected when F is larger than or equal to the F value appearing in the table. Thus to find the significance of $F = 2.17$, we locate the F value corresponding to 1 (across the top) and 22 (left-hand column); there are two F values, $F = 4.30$ corresponding to $\alpha = .05$ and $F = 7.94$ corresponding to $\alpha = .01$. In either case, the obtained value of $F = 2.17$ is smaller than the F required to reject H_0.

Selected Nonparametric Tests

The Mann-Whitney Test.   The **Mann-Whitney test** is applicable whenever we wish to test the null hypothesis that two samples have been drawn from the same population against the alternative research hypothesis that the populations differ from each other.[6] The only assumptions required in

6. Siegel, *Nonparametric Statistics,* pp. 116–126.

making this test are that the two samples are independently and randomly drawn and that the level of measurement of the variables under investigation is at least ordinal.

Suppose that we have sampled 13 males ($n_1 = 13$) and 14 females ($n_2 = 14$) and have given each one a score reflecting their level of alienation:

Male sample: 5, 7, 10, 13, 19, 24, 25, 28, 30, 32, 33, 36, 37

Female sample: 1, 3, 4, 6, 9, 12, 14, 15, 17, 18, 20, 21, 22, 23

If we assume that the population of females is identical to the population of males with respect to level of alienation, we expect that the values in the two samples will be similiar. If the values have similar magnitudes, males will have larger alienation scores in approximately one half of the male-female pairs; in the rest of the pairs, the females' scores will exceed the males'. We can count the number of pairs in which the scores of males exceed the scores of females and designate it as U; the number of pairs for which the opposite is true is designated U'. If the null hypothesis of identical populations were true, we would expect U and U' to be approximately equal.[7]

To determine U, we can use the following equation:

$$U = n_1 n_2 + \frac{n_2(n_2 + 1)}{2} - R_2 \qquad (19.7)$$

where n_1 = the sample size of sample 1

n_2 = the sample size of sample 2

R_2 = the sum of ranks for sample 2

The ranks are obtained by arranging all the scores in order of magnitude. For instance, the first three females (1, 3, 4) head the scale, with rank 4 being the first male (score 5). Thus the ranks for males are 4, 6, 8, 10, 15, 20, 21, 22, 23, 24, 25, 26, 27, and the ranks for females are 1, 2, 3, 5, 7, 9, 11, 12, 13, 14, 16, 17, 18, 19. To determine U', we subtract U from the total number of pairs

$$U' = n_1 n_2 - U \qquad (19.8)$$

For our data,

$$U = (13)(14) + \frac{14(14 + 1)}{2} - 147 = 140$$

$$U' = (13)(14) - 140 = 182 - 140 = 42$$

To evaluate the significance of H_0, we compare the smaller of the two values U and U' with the significant values of the sampling distribution of

7. John H. Mueller, Karl F. Schuessler, and Herbert L. Costner, *Statistical Reasoning in Sociology* (Boston: Houghton Mifflin, 1970), p. 423.

U in Appendix H.[8] At the .05 level, we need a U of 50 or smaller when direction is not predicted or 56 or smaller when direction is predicted. In either case, the obtained value (42) is smaller and enables us to reject the null hypothesis.

The sampling distribution of U approaches normality when the samples' size increases. When either of the samples is larger than 20, we can compute standard scores and use the normal distribution. The mean of the sampling distribution would then be

$$\mu_u = \frac{n_1 n_2}{2}$$

and the standard error would be

$$\sigma_u = \frac{\sqrt{n_1 n_2 (n_1 + n_2 + 1)}}{12}$$

Z is obtained using the following formula:

$$Z = \frac{U - n_1 n_2 / 2}{\sqrt{n_1 n_2 (n_1 + n_2 + 1)/12}} \tag{19.9}$$

The Chi-Square Test (χ^2).   Chi-square is a general test designed to evaluate whether the difference between observed frequencies and expected frequencies under a set of theoretical assumptions is statistically significant. The **chi-square test** is most often applied to problems in which two nominal variables are cross-classified in a bivariate table. The data summarized in Table 19.6 are an example of a research problem to which the chi-square test is applicable. Table 19.6 is a bivariate table in which the religious denominations of wife and husband have been interrelated. When the frequencies are converted to percentages (in parentheses), it is observed that whereas 93

Table 19.6
Religious Denominations of Husband and Wife

Husband	Catholic	Protestant	Jewish	Total
		Wife		
Catholic	(93%) 271	(24%) 20	0	291
Protestant	(6%) 17	(74%) 61	0	78
Jewish	1	(2%) 1	(100%) 66	68
Total	289	82	66	437

From August B. Hollingshead, "Cultural Factors in the Selection of Marriage Mates," *American Sociological Review*, 15 (1950): 619–627.

8. For situations in which one of the samples is smaller than 9, another table of probabilities is used.

percent of the Catholic wives married Catholic husbands, only 24 percent of the Protestant wives, and none of the Jewish wives, had a Catholic husband. We want to examine whether such differences are statistically significant. Under the null hypothesis, we assume that there are no differences among the three groups of wives in their pattern of selection; that is, we would expect Catholic, Protestant, or Jewish wives to have the same proportion of Catholic, Protestant, or Jewish husbands. We then compute the frequencies, given this assumption, and compare them with the observed frequencies. If the differences between the observed and expected frequencies are so large as to occur only rarely (5 percent or 1 percent of the time), the null hypothesis is rejected.

The statistic used to evaluate these differences is chi-square (χ^2), which is defined as

$$\chi^2 = \sum \frac{(f_o - f_e)^2}{f_e} \tag{19.10}$$

where f_o = observed frequencies and f_e = expected frequencies.

To compute the expected frequencies for any cell, use the following formula:

$$f_e = \frac{(\text{row total})(\text{column total})}{n} \tag{19.11}$$

For Table 19.6, the expected frequency for the Catholic-Catholic pair is equal to

$$\frac{(289)(291)}{437} = 192$$

Table 19.7 is the reconstructed table containing frequencies we would expect if religious denominations of husband and wife were not related.

Calculating Chi-Square (χ^2).   To compute χ^2, subtract the expected frequencies of each cell from the observed frequencies, square them, divide by the expected frequency of the cell, and then sum for all cells. These calculations are summarized in Table 19.8. Note that χ^2 would be zero if the observed frequencies were identical with the expected frequencies. That is, the

Table 19.7
Religious Denominations of Husband and Wife: Expected Frequencies

Husband	Wife			
	Catholic	Protestant	Jewish	Total
Catholic	192	55	44	291
Protestant	52	14	12	78
Jewish	45	13	10	68
Total	289	82	66	437

Table 19.8

Calculation of χ^2 for the Data of Tables 19.6 and 19.7

f_o	f_e	$f_o - f_e$	$(f_o - f_e)^2$	$\dfrac{(f_o - f_e)^2}{f_e}$
271	192	79	6241	32.5
17	52	-35	1225	23.5
1	45	-44	1936	43.0
20	55	-35	1225	22.3
61	14	47	2209	157.8
1	13	-12	144	11.1
0	44	-44	1936	44.0
0	12	-12	144	12.0
66	10	56	3136	313.6
				$\chi^2 = 659.8$

larger the difference between what is observed and what would be expected were the hypothesis of no relations true, the larger will be the value of χ^2.

To evaluate the χ^2 statistic obtained, we need to compare it to the sampling distribution of χ^2 and to observe whether the value of 659.8 is large enough and thus unlikely if the null hypothesis is true. The sampling distribution of χ^2 is reproduced in Appendix I. Two factors determine the distribution: the level of significance (α) and the number of degrees of freedom. Thus χ^2 is really a family of distributions, each determined by different parameters. We shall select for this problem a level of significance of .01, which means that only if we obtain a χ^2 larger than what we would expect to find in no more than 1 out of 100 of our samples will the null hypothesis be rejected.

The number of degrees of freedom of the χ^2 sampling distribution is set by the number of cells for which expected frequencies can be selected freely. For any bivariate table, the cells that can be determined arbitrarily are limited by the marginal total of both variables. Thus in a 2×2 table, for instance, only one cell is free to vary, the three others being predetermined by the marginal totals. Generally, we can compute the number of degrees of freedom using the following formula:

$$df = (r - 1)(c - 1) \qquad (19.12)$$

where $r = $ the number of rows and $c = $ the number of columns. Thus

In a 2×2 table: $df = (2 - 1)(2 - 1) = 1$

In a 3×3 table: $df = (3 - 1)(3 - 1) = 4$

In a 4×3 table: $df = (4 - 1)(3 - 1) = 6$

The probabilities under H_0 are given at the top of each column in Appendix I, and the row entries indicate the number of degrees of freedom.

The sampling distribution of χ^2 is positively skewed, with higher values in the upper tail of the distribution (to the right). Therefore, with the χ^2 test, the critical region is located at the upper tail of the sampling distribution.

For our example, with 4 *df* and a .01 level of significance, the entry is 13.277, indicating that a value of 13.277 will occur in only 1 percent of the samples. Our obtained sample result of 659.8 is much larger than that and is obviously very unlikely under the null hypothesis. In fact, even higher levels of significance—of .001, for example ($\chi^2 = 18.465$)—calls for rejection of the null hypothesis.

Summary

1. Statistical inference refers to a procedure that allows the investigator to decide between two hypotheses about a population parameter on the basis of a sample result.

2. The first step in testing a hypothesis is to formulate it in statistical terms. The statistical hypothesis always applies to the population of interest. Two statistical hypotheses are involved in hypothesis testing. The first is the research hypothesis, symbolized by H_1. The second, symbolized by H_0, is the null hypothesis, which is set up for logical purposes. The null hypothesis is the one that is tested directly. The research hypothesis is supported when the null hypothesis is rejected as being unlikely.

3. The need for two hypotheses arises out of a logical necessity. The null hypothesis is based on negative inference in order to avoid the fallacy of affirming the consequent; that is, the researcher must eliminate false hypotheses rather than accept true ones.

4. After formulating a specific null hypothesis, the investigator proceeds to test it against the sample result; it is compared to a statistical model that gives the probability of observing such a result. Such a statistical model is called a sampling distribution. A sampling distribution of a statistic is obtained by drawing a large number of random samples of the same size from the defined population, computing the statistic for each sample, and plotting the frequency distribution of the statistic.

5. The sampling distribution allows us to estimate the probability of obtaining the sample result. This probability is called the level of significance, or α, which is also the probability of rejecting a true hypothesis (Type I error). When the likelihood of obtaining the sample result is very small under the assumptions of the null hypothesis, H_0 is rejected, and the rejection adds to our confidence in the research hypothesis.

6. Statistical tests are divided into two major groups: parametric tests and nonparametric tests. A parametric test is a statistical test based on several assumptions about the parameters of the population from which the sample was drawn. Among the most important ones are the assumption that the observations must be drawn from a normally distributed population and that the variables are measured on at least an interval scale. A nonparametric statistical test is one whose model does not specify the normality condition or require an interval-level measurement. The difference-between-means test and a significance test for Pearson's r are parametric tests. The Mann-Whitney test and the chi-square are nonparametric tests of significance.

Key Terms for Review

research hypothesis	Type II error
null hypothesis	parametric tests
sampling distribution	nonparametric tests
region of rejection	difference-between-means test
level of significance	degrees of freedom (df)
one-tailed test	t test
two-tailed test	Mann-Whitney test
Type I error	chi-square test

Study Questions

1. Discuss the role of the null hypothesis and the research hypothesis in the logic of hypothesis testing.
2. What is the difference between using a level of significance of .50 and using one of .05?
3. What is the difference between one-tailed and two-tailed tests?
4. Show in a diagram the difference between Type I and Type II errors.
5. Distinguish between parametric and nonparametric tests of significance.

Additional Readings

Anderson, T. W., and Stanley L. Sclove. *The Statistical Analysis of Data*. Palo Alto, Calif.: Scientific Press, 1986.

Blalock, Hubert M., Jr. *Social Statistics*. 2d ed. New York: McGraw-Hill, 1979, Chapters 8–15.

Bohrnstedt, George W., and David Knoke. *Statistics for Social Data Analysis*. Itasca, Ill.: Peacock, 1988.

Bradley, James V. *Distribution-free Statistical Tests*. Englewood Cliffs, N.J.: Prentice-Hall, 1968.

McCall, Robert B. *Fundamental Statistics for Behavioral Sciences*. 4th ed. Orlando, Fla.: Harcourt Brace Jovanovich, 1986.

Witte, Robert, S. *Statistics*. Fort Worth: Holt, Rinehart and Winston, 1985.

APPENDIX A Introduction to SPSS

Claire L. Felbinger and Stephen F. Schwelgien

This appendix is designed to assist students in preparing and executing computerized data analysis using one of the most widely available and used software packages, the Statistical Package for the Social Sciences (SPSS), Release 4.[1] SPSS was designed especially for the analysis of social science data and contains most of the routines employed by social scientists. Indeed, all the data analysis procedures described in this text can be executed by SPSS subprograms. Of particular interest to social scientists is the program's capacity to handle with ease the recurring needs of data analysis. For instance, SPSS enables the researcher to recode variables, to deal with missing values, to sample, weight, and select cases, and to compute new variables and effect permanent or temporary transformations.

Release 4 of the statistical package is a major revision of SPSS-X. For those of you familiar with SPSS-X, you will find that the commands were changed as little as possible. The greatest number of changes are in subprograms that allow you to explore data (EXAMINE), transpose data files (FLIP), perform logistic regression (LOGISTIC REGRESSION), and perform complex matrix manipulation (MATRIX). These functions are beyond the scope of this text. However, there are some other changes involving some OPTIONS and STATISTICS in subprograms such as CROSSTABS. Consult the *User's Guide* for those modifications. The procedural commands are similar to those of earlier versions. Where the commands you have been used to have been changed, every attempt was made to improve the function of the command. The *SPSS Reference Guide* provides a section, "Obsolete Specifications," to which you can refer for possible changes.[2] For the purposes of this appendix, we will limit ourselves to executing SPSS files with no reference to earlier versions. If you are concerned with the revisions and how they affect your earlier runstreams, refer to the new *User's Guide*. The *User's Guide* focuses on managing and analyzing data; the *Reference Guide* documents all commands and provides examples of output.

1. SPSS Inc., *SPSS Base System User's Guide* (Chicago: SPSS Inc., 1990).
2. SPSS Inc., *SPSS Reference Guide* (Chicago: SPSS Inc., 1990), pp. 891–902.

This treatment is intended to supply the novice analyst with the tools necessary to set up an SPSS file and execute basic analyses. It is not by any means an exhaustive display of either the variety of subprograms available or the intricacies of the more highly powered types of analyses possible with SPSS. Rather, the examples used are intended to parallel the work covered in this text. Refer to the SPSS *User's Guide* for information on other available subprograms and for a more detailed explanation of the ones covered in this appendix.

The data set used in the examples that follow is from Cleveland Poverty Survey of 1988.[3] A sample codebook containing the variables used is found in Exhibit A.1 at the end of this appendix (pages 497–500). We will use these data to build a permanent SPSS file, clean the data, and execute statistical procedures in much the same way as if we were actually involved in a research project. Hence we will assume that the data are prepared (as in Chapter 14) in machine-readable form, clean the data by examining univariate distributions (Chapter 15), perform bivariate (Chapter 16) and multivariate (Chapter 17) analysis with hypothesis testing (Chapter 19), and construct scales (Chapter 18).

Preparing the Data

We have prepared the data as discussed in Chapter 14. They can be prepared and stored on tape or disk. The particular data set we have assembled contains 528 cases with six 80-column lines of data called *decks* or *records* per case (although we will use information from only one record for our examples here). All the records associated with each case are together in order (case 1, record 1; case 1, record 2; and so on to case *n*, record *last*). To access SPSS at your particular research facility, you must supply commands known as *Job Control Language*, or JCL. These commands are unique to your mainframe computer system and to your facility. They grant access to the computer, initiate accounting procedures, assign disk or tape space, access the SPSS software, and perform other functions. It is advisable that you contact the consultants at your facility as to the proper JCL since site requirements vary from facility to facility.

Setting Up an SPSS System Data File

The language of SPSS is logical and quite simple. You will find a consistency in the language and patterns employed that match your expectations. There are a number of *files* that you must be familiar with in order to operate SPSS:

---

3. *Cleveland Poverty Study, 1988* (Cleveland: Northern Ohio Data and Information Service, Levin College of Urban Affairs, Cleveland State University, 1988).

1. *Command files* contain the SPSS commands you wish to execute in any particular run—the *runstream*. We will assume in this appendix that your commands will be stored in a file on your mainframe (and that you will not be using menus from the SPSS Manager).

2. *Input data files* contain your data. In this example, we will assume that your data are stored in 80-column lines on disk or tape on your mainframe. SPSS can accommodate virtually any form of stored data. However, since coding is traditionally done using the 80-column format, we will use that format here.

3. *Display files* contain the results of your executed procedures that were stored in a command file. This is the output that can be viewed on a screen or printed at a line printer.

4. *SPSS system files* contain the information about the data from the input file defined uniquely by the series of commands executed in the command file used to set up the system file plus any permanent transformations stored at a later time. As such, the system file contains a *dictionary* that defines variables and contains information concerning labels, missing values, and the like.

Data and File Definition.   Let us now describe the commands necessary to set up an SPSS system file. Commands are read from lines with command keywords beginning in column 1 of a line. (In this example, we will again use an 80-column line to define a line of text submitted in an SPSS run. This is the most common length of an input line; however, some systems will accept longer lines.) The specification of a command can continue for as many lines as necessary. However, specifications must not occupy column 1 of succeeding lines. In other words, continuations must be indented at least one column on lines following the command keyword. You may continue specifications on the next line provided that you begin in column 2 and that you do not break within a word or logical connector. Remember, a computer cannot read English and interpret your needs; it reads only signals (characters) for which it has been programmed. Therefore, be careful to key in command keywords and specifications exactly as designated. SPSS will accept commands in either upper- or lowercase.

The first step is to set up and save a file containing not only your data but also details about the type of information contained, where it is located, and what you plan to call it—this is the system file. Table A.1 lists command keywords in the order of their inclusion in the command file. The inclusion order is relatively flexible in SPSS; however, the one used here is an example of a successful run. One thing to keep in mind about inclusion order is that a variable must be defined before it is used. Table A.1 summarizes these commands and their structure.

Commands.   File definitions provide basic information about files handled in the process of setting up the system file—where the data are stored, where you want the resulting system file to be stored, and so on. Variable definitions provide information concerning the location, structure,

---

Table A.1
Format Specification for SPSS Data Definition Commands

Control Field (must begin in column 1)	Specification Field (no specifications or continuations appear in column 1)
TITLE*	Text up to 60 characters
FILE HANDLE	Handle/file specifications
[additional FILE HANDLES if necessary]	
DATA LIST	FIXED FILE = [handle]
	RECORDS = [N]
	/1 VARLIST₁ column number – column number, VARLIST₂ . . .
	[/2 . . ./N . . .]
MISSING VALUES*	VARLIST (value list)/[VARLIST (value list)]
VARIABLE LABELS*	VARNAME1 'label₁' [/VARNAME2 'label₂']
VALUE LABELS*	VARLIST₁ value₁ 'label₁' value₂ 'label₂'
	[/VARLIST₂ . . .]
[additional modifications and then procedures may be placed here]	
SAVE	OUTFILE = [handle]

*Optional commands.

---

and meaning of the data on your input file. Table A.1 lists the following file and variable definition lines:

1. TITLE. This optional feature allows you to label your run with a title of up to 60 characters that is printed across the top of each page of your output in the display file.

2. FILE HANDLE. The handle identifies a file already stored or to be stored as a result of the commands in your command file. File handles must not exceed eight characters and must begin with a letter of the alphabet or another symbol accepted at your facility. You will have enough FILE HANDLE lines to identify each file used in the process of the run, for example, raw data files or SPSS system files.[4] The "file specifications" refers to the facility-specific specifications that define files stored on the mainframe.

3. DATA LIST. This command, discussed in detail in the next section, describes the variable names, location, type of data, and number of records associated with your input file.

4. MISSING VALUES. This optional command defines which values (a maximum of three) for variables are designated as missing. By default, SPSS will automatically assign a system missing value for blank fields. The SET command allows blanks on the input file to be read as either system missing or as some other value you SET.[5] The ability to declare MISSING VALUES en-

---

4. Note that some operating systems use JCL to identify files and hence in some cases a FILE HANDLE is not necessary. Your facility's consultants can tell you when a FILE HANDLE is necessary.

5. *Reference Guide*, pp. 664–666.

ables the researcher either to include variables that contain missing values in statistical procedures or to exclude them.

5. VARIABLE LABELS. This optional command allows you to describe your variables further. It augments the variable names on the DATA LIST by associating a label with the name. This option is quite handy if you choose to assign v-numbers as variable names.

6. VALUE LABELS. This optional command allows you to associate a label with each value of a variable. For example, if the coded values 1, 2, 3 stand for the terms *low*, *medium*, and *high*, respectively, then when that particular variable is used in a procedure, its coded value will have its associated label next to it on the display file.

7. SAVE. This command saves your data and their labels or modifications as a permanent system file. We wish to save the file at this point since we know we will want to access this file at a later time for other purposes. Then we can eliminate many of the steps used to set up the file and begin with executing procedures via a FILE HANDLE and GET command. The GET command will be described shortly. The MAP specification on the SAVE command displays the order and complete list of variables SAVEd.

DATA LIST *Command.*   The DATA LIST command identifies your input file and indicates the format of the file and the number of records to be read per case from fixed-format data files. SPSS can read from a variety of data file types; this example follows the fixed-field format discussed in Chapter 14.

The FILE subcommand indicates the file handle of your input file as it was defined in an earlier FILE HANDLE command.

The keyword FIXED indicates that your data appear in a fixed-field format. FIXED is the format default in SPSS.

The RECORDS subcommand indicates the number of records, decks, or lines of input associated with each case for FIXED-format files.

The remainder of the specification refers to the variable definition. The number after the 1 refers to the number of the record on which SPSS is to find the variables described in the specification that follows. In the example

```
FILE HANDLE POVERTY/file specifications
DATA LIST FILE = POVERTY RECORDS = 2
   /1 IDNUMBER 1–5 Q2 6–11 Q3 12
```

the input file POVERTY has 2 RECORDS per case; the first variables are to be read from record number 1. Three variables, IDNUMBER, Q2, and Q3, can be found on record 1 in the fields containing columns 1 through 5, 6 through 11, and 12, respectively.

Each variable has a name designated in the DATA LIST command. Variable names have a maximum length of eight characters and must begin with a letter of the alphabet or with the character @, #, or $. Novices are cautioned not to use special characters if at all possible as these characters refer to special types of variables. Variable names must be unique. That is, a variable cannot be named twice. An attempt to do this will result in an ERROR message. You can select as names ones that reflect the nature of your variables, such as GENDER, AGE, and IDNUMBER, as long as the names are unique and they do not exceed eight characters. Otherwise, you can use a prefix (e.g., Q- for question number or V- for variable number). SPSS will then name your variables with the prefix and attach ascending numbers.

One of the easiest ways to identify the location of your variables on a record is to use the column numbers. In our example, SPSS expects to find the variable named IDNUMBER in columns 1 through 5 on the first record of each case, Q2 is found in columns 6 through 11 on the first record of each case, and so on. Our DATA LIST defines the first three variables in our codebook. Compare the DATA LIST with the information found in the codebook in Exhibit A.1.

Some data require the use of decimal points. For instance, you can have percentages rounded to one decimal place or have dollars and cents (two decimal points). You must specify in your DATA LIST whether decimals in your data set are implied or are directly keyed into your input file. Consider the following hypothetical specification:

```
DATA LIST FILE = POVERTY RECORDS = 2
    /1 IDNUMBER 1–5 Q2 6–11 Q3 12
    /2 PCTSPENT 1–3 (1) TOTSPENT 4–9 (2)
```

The parentheses following the column numbers on the second record indicate that the variable PCTSPENT has one implied decimal place in the field and TOTSPENT has two. Therefore, when SPSS encounters the following on the second record of a case

```
231028954
```

it will list the value for PCTSPENT as 23.1, while the value for TOTSPENT would be 289.54. If decimals are encountered on the input file, the number implied will be overridden.

SPSS can accommodate a number of methods to indicate the location of variables. For instance, FORTRAN-like formats can be used. If you feel comfortable using some method besides column locators, refer to the *User's Guide* for assistance.

SPSS also allows you to specify multiple adjacent variables with a shorthand notation. For example, if you have a list of ten adjacent variables, each with the same number of columns (two), you can name these contiguous variables

```
/3 Q1 TO Q10 1–20
```

SPSS will name these variables Q1, Q2, and so on to Q10 and identify each as being located in two-column fields beginning with the field 1–2 for Q1 and ending with the field in columns 19–20 for Q10. In other words, the columns allocated will be divided equally among the Q variables. The number of columns must be divisible by the implied number of variables. If you have five expenditure variables in a row, each with an equal number of columns to a field, you could also use the convention SPEND1 TO SPEND5 to name SPEND1, SPEND2, and so on, with SPSS allocating column fields if the number of columns you designated is divisible by 5. Note that you must know the final column number for the end of records when using this shorthand approach.

Data Modifications and Procedures. Once we have assembled the necessary JCL and SPSS data definition information, we are ready to take the final step in the process of setting up the file: instructing the computer to do something with the information we have supplied. The two generic processes we will be concerned with in this treatment are DATA MODIFICATIONS and PROCEDURES.

In general, when we wish to manipulate or transform our data in any way, we employ DATA MODIFICATIONS. PROCEDURES, by contrast, instruct the computer to calculate statistics for us. The DATA MODIFICATIONS available for our purposes are RECODE, COMPUTE, IF, SELECT IF, and LIST. The procedures are FREQUENCIES, CONDESCRIPTIVE, CROSSTABS, CORRELATIONS, SCATTERGRAM, PARTIAL CORR, and REGRESSION.

Initial Run. Our initial run should be executed with two goals in mind. First, we must determine whether the input data have been read into the SPSS system file exactly as we planned. Second, we must determine whether any stray or illegal codes were keyed in and not caught in the verification process. SPSS will print a table displaying the information contained on your DATA LIST lines that will include your list of variables, the record and columns on which each variable is found, the width of the field, and the number of decimal places the variable contains. This information should be checked carefully to ensure that you have properly transferred the data onto the system file. Assuming that the format is correct, we will insert a PROCEDURE to provide FREQUENCIES, or univariate distributions, for each variable. The output we get as a result of this procedure will enable us to determine the extent of cleaning (Chapter 14) necessary prior to generating statistical information.

The format of the FREQUENCIES command is

FREQUENCIES VARIABLES = VARNAME$_1$, VARNAME$_2$, . . . , VARNAME$_n$

where adjacent variables may be accessed by stating VARNAME$_{1st}$ TO VARNAME$_{last}$ and where all variables can be included by simply keying the word ALL after the equal sign. Table A.2 shows the actual setup of the poverty data set we are using in this appendix.

Subsequent Runs. Once you have created an SPSS system file, you can access it by beginning the runstream with appropriate JCL and FILE HANDLE commands followed by the GET command. The GET specifies the active SPSS

Table A.2
SPSS System File Setup for 1988 Cleveland Poverty Study

	[Insert initial JCL here]
TITLE	SETTING UP 1988 CLEVELAND POVERTY STUDY SYSTEM FILE
FILE HANDLE	DATA/[file specifications]
FILE HANDLE	POVERTY/[file specifications]
DATA LIST	FIXED FILE = DATA RECORDS = 1
	/1 IDNUMBER 1–3, Q1 TO Q4 4–7, Q5 8–11, Q6 12–13, Q7 TO Q32 14–39, Q33 40–45, Q34 46–47
VARIABLE LABELS	Q1 'HIGHEST GRADE COMPLETED'
	/Q2 'EMPLOYMENT STATUS'
	[additional labels here]
	/Q34 'AGE OF RESPONDENT'
VALUE LABELS	Q1 1 '1–8' 2 '9–11' 3 '12' 4 '13–15' 5 '16' 6 '17 + '
	/Q2 1 'EMPLOYED' 2 'UNEMPLOYED' 3 'RETIRED'
	4 'STUDENT' 5 'HOMEMAKER' 6 'OTHER'
	[additional labels here]
	/Q32 1 'YES' 2 'NO'
MISSING VALUES	Q7 TO Q19 (9)
FREQUENCIES	VARIABLES = ALL
SAVE	OUTFILE = POVERTY/MAP

system you want to perform the operations in your runstream. The format of the GET command is

GET FILE = [handle or file specification]

Cleaning the Data

Once we have verified that our DATA LIST is correct and that all the data were read in their intended formats, we will use the output generated from the FREQUENCIES procedure to determine whether there are any illegal responses listed for each of our variables. For example, if a variable was coded Q9: 1 = EXCELLENT, 2 = GOOD, 3 = FAIR, 4 = POOR, and 9 = DON'T KNOW and we find a 7 listed in the FREQUENCIES for that variable, we can either declare the 7 a MISSING VALUE on a subsequent run or replace the 7 with the actual value from the coding source. If we do not have the original coding source and cannot verify what a 7 is supposed to mean, we could use the following runstream to purge this inappropriate response:

GET FILE = [handle]
MISSING VALUES Q9 (7)
[insert remaining modifications, then procedures]
SAVE OUTFILE = [handle]

With this runstream, you make any modifications or permanent changes to your system file via the SAVE command. In this case, anytime you use Q9, SPSS will consider a 7 a MISSING VALUE and will treat it as you specify for MISSING VALUES. For example, it will not be used in any statistical calculations unless you directly specify to use it as such. Note that some facilities do not allow GET and SAVE on the same handle. Check with a consultant as to the most efficient way you can do this at your facility. The remainder of examples in this appendix will assume that the appropriate JCL, FILE HANDLE and GET commands are included in your runstream.

If you are setting up your own data and encounter an invalid response category, you can use the SELECT IF and LIST commands to identify and list the errant cases. Once you have the list, you can determine what the correct responses are and permanently change the values using the IF or RECODE command in combination with the SAVE command.

The SELECT IF command allows you to isolate a subset of cases for investigation. Often in the social sciences, we wish to look only at the responses of "women" or "old people" or "Democrats" who are included with persons having different attributes in the data set. The SELECT IF allows one to easily group respondents on the desired attribute. We can also use the SELECT IF while cleaning our data. Let's say that we found two responses of 7 to Q9. We can isolate those incorrect responses by using SELECT IF. The format of the SELECT IF command is

SELECT IF VARNAME [logical connector] value

where the logical connectors are

Connector	Meaning
EQ *or* =	equal to
LT *or* <	less than
LE *or* < =	less than or equal to
GT *or* >	greater than
GE *or* > =	greater than or equal to
NE *or* ≠ *or* < >	not equal to

and the value can be a number or another variable name. The SELECT IF may be made more complex by forming logical compound sentences connected by AND (meaning that all conditions must apply for case inclusion), OR (any condition can be met for case inclusion), or NOT (reverses the outcome of an expression).

Just isolating the errant cases for Q9 is not sufficient for cleaning the data. We can use LIST to list the cases selected and their values on a number of variables. In our example, all we need to identify and clean Q9 is the case IDNUMBER. Then we can consult our coding source to find the correct values. The general format of the LIST command is

LIST VARIABLE = [variable list]

The runstream to clean Q9 would be

SELECT IF Q9 EQ 7
LIST VARIABLES = IDNUMBER

Let's say that the output indicates that ID numbers 24 and 87 have the value 7 for Q9 and we find that the values should have been 1 and MISSING, respectively. We therefore need to change the 7 in the first instance to a 1 and to declare the 7 in the second instance as a MISSING VALUE. On a subsequent run, we could make the permanent transformations by using the IF command to isolate conditions that must exist for the transformation. The general format of the IF statement is

IF [logical condition] target variable = value

where the logical condition and value are the same as defined in the SELECT IF specification field and the target variable is the variable to which you wish to attach the value. The runstream to clean our two cases would be

```
IF IDNUMBER EQ 245 Q9 = 1
MISSING VALUES Q9 (7,9)
[any other permanent modifications]
SAVE OUTFILE = [handle]
```

When we are confident that all our variables are clean, we can generate a complete and up-to-date data definition description of our system file by a procedure called DISPLAY, keyed in the form

DISPLAY DICTIONARY

The more completely you define your data via the optional labeling, the better the DISPLAY functions as a revised codebook. Also, the more carefully you key in the raw data and data definition commands, the less time you will spend cleaning the data. At this point, we are ready to begin our analysis of the data.

Univariate Distributions (Chapter 15)

You recognized the output from FREQUENCIES as a univariate distribution of groups of responses for each variable. Now that the data are clean, you can repeat this procedure to generate summary statistics including the mean, standard error, median, mode, standard deviation, variance, kurtosis, skewness, range, minimum, and maximum values. If we wish to generate all of these statistics for a subset of our variables, the runstream would include

```
FREQUENCIES VARIABLES = Q2, Q4, Q6 TO Q12
    /STATISTICS = ALL
```

If you wish to select only some of the available statistics, thus saving some computer time, you may specify the name of the statistics you require in the field after the STATISTICS = specification.[6]

---

6. See *User's Guide*, pp. 90–91. You may also wish to construct histograms or vary the form of the output by using other specifications; see *User's Guide*, pp. 87–90.

You may wish to generate the same summary statistics on interval-level variables (e.g., age, salary, city populations) and not be concerned with seeing the actual frequency distribution. To examine all the statistics generated with the FREQUENCIES command, use the subprogram called DESCRIPTIVES. The DESCRIPTIVES procedure has this format:

```
DESCRIPTIVES VARIABLES = VARLIST
   /STATISTICS = ALL
```

A DESCRIPTIVES command without a STATISTICS subcommand will generate the mean, standard deviation, minimum, and maximum.

Bivariate Distributions (Chapter 16)

As you learned in Chapter 16, bivariate analysis enables us to see the association or relationship between two variables; we can observe how one variable covaries with another. Using bivariate statistics, we can determine not only whether a relationship exists at all (significance test) but also the strength and direction of such a relationship (measures of association).

Nominal and Ordinal Measures. The CROSSTABS procedure is specifically designed to generate bivariate tables and statistics for nominal and ordinal variables and takes the form

```
CROSSTABS TABLES = VARNAME₁ BY VARNAME₂ [BY VARNAME₃]
   /VARNAME₄ BY VARNAME₅ [BY VARNAME₆]
```

VARNAME$_1$ and VARNAME$_4$ will be treated as dependent variables (printed down the left-hand column, or Y axis, as has been the convention in this book) of individual tables; VARNAME$_2$ and VARNAME$_5$ and are the independent variables of their respective tables; and VARNAME$_3$ and VARNAME$_6$ function as control variables, generating one table for each value of the control. The use of controls is optional.

Suppose that we wish to examine the relationship between educational level and opinions regarding whether getting a good education is a good way to get ahead in life. The following command would be used:

```
CROSSTABS TABLES = Q8 BY Q1
   /CELLS = ROW, COL, TOT /STATISTICS = ALL
```

which would produce Table A.3. Let's look at the outlined cell. Here is how to interpret the numbers in the cell for persons with an eighth-grade education or less (Q1, value 1) who agree that education leads to getting ahead (Q8, value 2). The uppermost left-hand description cell (COUNT, ROW PCT, COL PCT, TOT PCT) tells the order of the numbers within each internal cell. The number 23 in the highlighted cell means that 23 respondents (count) have both of these characteristics. Of those who agree with the statement, 11.2 percent have an eighth-grade education or less (row percent), and 53.5 percent of those with less than an eighth-grade education agree with the state-

```
Q8  GOOD EDUCATION WAY TO GET AHEAD  by  Q1  HIGHEST GRADE COMPLETED
                      Q1
          Count   |
          Row Pct |1-8      9-11      12        13-15     16
          Col Pct |                                             Row
          Tot Pct |     1|       2|       3|       4|       5| Total
Q8        --------+--------+--------+--------+--------+--------+
              1 |    14 |   117 |    99 |    27 |     2 |   259
STRONGLY AGREE  |   5.4 |  45.2 |  38.2 |  10.4 |    .8 |  49.4
                |  32.6 |  50.0 |  51.0 |  57.4 |  33.3 |
                |   2.7 |  22.3 |  18.9 |   5.2 |    .4 |
                +-------+-------+-------+-------+-------+

              2     23       97 |    70 |    13 |     3 |   206
AGREE             11.2     47.1 |  34.0 |   6.3 |   1.5 |  39.3
                  53.5     41.5 |  36.1 |  27.7 |  50.0 |
                   4.4     18.5 |  13.4 |   2.5 |    .6 |
                +-------+-------+-------+-------+-------+

              3 |     5 |    10 |    16 |     4 |     1 |    36
SOMEWHAT AGREE  |  13.9 |  27.8 |  44.4 |  11.1 |   2.8 |   6.9
                |  11.6 |   4.3 |   8.2 |   8.5 |  16.7 |
                |   1.0 |   1.9 |   3.1 |    .8 |    .2 |
                +-------+-------+-------+-------+-------+

              4 |     1 |     1 |     2 |     2 |       |     6
SOMEWHAT DISAGRE|  16.7 |  16.7 |  33.3 |  33.3 |       |   1.1
                |   2.3 |    .4 |   1.0 |   4.3 |       |
                |    .2 |    .2 |    .4 |    .4 |       |
                +-------+-------+-------+-------+-------+

              5 |       |     7 |     7 |     1 |       |    15
DISAGREE        |       |  46.7 |  46.7 |   6.7 |       |   2.9
                |       |   3.0 |   3.6 |   2.1 |       |
                |       |   1.3 |   1.3 |    .2 |       |
                +-------+-------+-------+-------+-------+

              6 |       |     2 |       |       |       |     2
DISAGREE STRONGL|       | 100.0 |       |       |       |    .4
                |       |    .9 |       |       |       |
                |       |    .4 |       |       |       |
                +-------+-------+-------+-------+-------+
        Column      43     234     194      47       6     524
        Total      8.2    44.7    37.0     9.0     1.1   100.0
```

Chi-Square	Value	DF	Significance
Pearson	23.57048	20	.26166
Likelihood Ratio	24.47776	20	.22215
Mantel-Haenszel	.15428	1	.69448

Minimum Expected Frequency -   .023

Cells with Expected Frequency < 5 -   18 OF   30 (60.0%)

Statistic	Value	ASE1	T-value	Approximate Significance
Phi	.21209			.26166 *1
Cramer's V	.10604			.26166 *1
Contingency Coefficient	.20747			.26166 *1
Lambda :				
symmetric	.03063	.01486	2.02541	
with Q8 dependent	.03774	.02399	1.54655	
with Q1 dependent	.02414	.01834	1.30197	
Goodman & Kruskal Tau :				
with Q8 dependent	.01317	.00760		.02330 *2
with Q1 dependent	.01284	.00521		.13925 *2
Uncertainty Coefficient :				
symmetric	.02054	.00736	2.75055	.22215 *3
with Q8 dependent	.02176	.00775	2.75056	.22215 *3
with Q1 dependent	.01946	.00702	2.75056	.22215 *3
Kendall's Tau-b	-.04057	.03971	-1.02202	
Kendall's Tau-c	-.03151	.03083	-1.02202	
Gamma	-.06472	.06340	-1.02202	
Somers' D :				
symmetric	-.04053	.03967	-1.02202	
with Q8 dependent	-.03887	.03797	-1.02202	
with Q1 dependent	-.04234	.04153	-1.02202	
Pearson's R	-.01718	.04117	-.39246	.69488
Spearman Correlation	-.04439	.04417	-1.01521	.31048
Eta :				
with Q8 dependent	.05090			
with Q1 dependent	.11795			

*1 Pearson chi-square probability
*2 Based on chi-square approximation
*3 Likelihood ratio chi-square probability

Relative Risk Estimate cannot be computed

Number of Missing Observations: 4

ment (column percent). The N of 23 out of the total N of 524 accounts for 4.4 (total) percent of the respondents in the survey.

Notice that Table A.3 has six rows and five columns. We know that the value of our coefficients, for example, chi-square (χ^2), are a function of the number of cells in the table. There are only two people who strongly disagree with the "education to get ahead" statement. We can reduce the number of cells by excluding the "strongly disagree" respondents by using

    SELECT IF Q8 LE 5

or by collapsing the categories such that the "disagree strongly" respondents would be grouped with the "disagree" respondents since they all disagree. This collapsing can be done by using RECODE:

    RECODE Q8 (5,6, = 5)

We could go even further and collapse the categories such that all who agree are in one category and all who disagree are in the other:

    RECODE Q8 (1 THRU 3 = 1) (4 THRU 6 = 2)

Often in social science research, we wish to examine the relationships among a subset of our respondents. In CROSSTABS, this can be accomplished by including a third (control) variable in the TABLES = specification. However, if we are interested in only one category of the control variable (or if we are using a procedure that does not allow a method of control), SELECT IF is the handiest way to segregate such a subset. We can use SELECT IF and RECODE together to select cases and collapse categories. For example, the runstream

    SELECT IF Q3 EQ 1 AND Q4 EQ 2
    RECODE Q8 (0 THRU 3 = 1) (4 THRU 6 = 2)
    CROSSTABS TABLES = Q8 BY Q1
      /STATISTICS ALL

would produce a table of married female respondents only. (Note that the variables in the SELECT IF command need not appear in the PROCEDURE command.)

Interval Measures.   The subprogram CORRELATIONS calculates the Pearson product-moment correlation coefficient (Pearson's r), an association statistic appropriate for interval-level variables, and tests for significance using a one-tailed t test. In most cases, coefficients generated by CORRELATIONS are equivalent to the Spearman rank-order coefficients produced by NONPAR CORR as appropriate for ordinal-ordinal, ordinal-interval, and interval-interval variables. The series

    CORRELATIONS VARIABLES = HAPPY, WORK, Q5, Q6, Q20, Q33, Q34
      /STATISTICS = ALL

will produce one table showing the means and standard deviations of the variables, a variance-covariance table, and one table featuring the coefficients, the N on which the calculations were based, and the significance level. This is illustrated in Table A.4. (HAPPY and WORK are computed variables, to be discussed when we cover index construction.)

You may wish to plot a scatter diagram to visually assess the relationship between two of your variables. The subprogram GRAPH will plot these relationships for you if your SPSS installation has graphics capacity. The series

GRAPH /SCATTERPLOT = Q33 WITH Q6

will produce the output graphically, displaying the relationship between hours worked per week and annual income.

Multivariate Analysis (Chapter 17)

The three major functions of multivariate analysis, as we learned in Chapter 17, are control, interpretation, and prediction. Mechanically, the first two functions are covered by using control variables in the equations; the subprograms CROSSTABS and PARTIAL CORR can provide for these controls. Prediction is enhanced by REGRESSION.

Multivariate CROSSTABS.   The basic format of the CROSSTABS procedure has already been presented. The portion in brackets indicates the control variable(s). For instance, resultant output controlling for the variable "gender of respondent" would consist of two tables having the same dependent and independent variables but differing as to respondents' gender: for the first table, all cases reported will be men, and for the second, they will all be women.

PARTIAL CORR.   Partial correlations are conceptually similar to multivariate CROSSTABS in that the effects of other variables are controlled when analyzing the relationship between the original variables. Whereas CROSSTABS physically removes the effects by partioning the cases based on the values of the control, PARTIAL CORR statistically removes the effects. This difference can be very important when controlling for more than one variable because separation reduces the cell frequencies. Thus when the analysis involves interval-level variables, the use of PARTIAL CORR is indicated.

The following lines in your command file

PARTIAL CORR WORK WITH Q34 BY HAPPY, Q33 (1,2)
    /STATISTICS = ALL

would compute the zero-order, first-order, and second-order partial for each unique combination of the dependant variable (WORK) and the independent variable (Q34). The controls will be for HAPPY and Q33 individually and simultaneously. A maximum of five orders may appear within the parentheses. The order may not exceed the number of control variables. An example of PARTIAL CORR is presented in Table A.5.

Table A.4
Example of Correlation Output

Variable	Cases	Mean	Std Dev
HAPPY	496	27.6250	4.7047
WORK	528	8.9280	3.4126
Q5	343	2.9650	2.2358
Q6	356	35.2107	10.6222
Q20	471	1.0998	.6430
Q33	503	4360.5089	3682.5171
Q34	523	34.7667	12.2421

Variables		Cases	Cross-Prod Dev	Variance-Covar
HAPPY	WORK	496	951.2500	1.9217
HAPPY	Q6	340	-148.4412	-.4379
HAPPY	Q33	473	-340850.8161	-722.1416
WORK	Q5	343	-118.6181	-.3468
WORK	Q20	471	107.8004	.2294
WORK	Q34	523	-8865.3327	-16.9834
Q5	Q20	310	-3.8677	-.0125
Q5	Q34	339	2245.6018	6.6438
Q6	Q33	339	813777.5044	2407.6258
Q20	Q33	449	49996.8018	111.6000
Q33	Q34	499	1898444.3928	3812.1373
HAPPY	Q5	328	49.6433	.1518
HAPPY	Q20	442	-93.4887	-.2120
HAPPY	Q34	492	-4422.0427	-9.0062
WORK	Q6	356	-415.0281	-1.1691
WORK	Q33	503	-335632.1869	-668.5900
Q5	Q6	342	2650.4094	7.7725
Q5	Q33	328	681407.4085	2083.8147
Q6	Q20	322	179.6584	.5597
Q6	Q34	352	3030.6250	8.6343
Q20	Q34	466	-553.4807	-1.1903

- - Correlation Coefficients - -

	HAPPY	WORK	Q5	Q6	Q20	Q33	Q34
HAPPY	1.0000	.1207**	.0149	-.0092	-.0687	-.0416	-.1568**
WORK	.1207**	1.0000	-.0555	-.0378	.1075*	-.0536	-.4125**
Q5	.0149	-.0555	1.0000	.3246**	-.0089	.2443**	.2813**
Q6	-.0092	-.0378	.3246**	1.0000	.0825	.0580	.0744
Q20	-.0687	.1075*	-.0089	.0825	1.0000	.0497	-.1636**
Q33	-.0416	-.0536	.2443**	.0580	.0497	1.0000	.0863
Q34	-.1568**	-.4125**	.2813**	.0744	-.1636**	.0863	1.0000

* - Signif. LE .05   ** - Signif. LE .01   (2-tailed)

Table A.5
Example of Partial Correlation Output

VARIABLE	MEAN	STANDARD DEV	CASES
WORK	9.0554	3.2948	469
Q34	34.2708	12.1015	469
HAPPY	27.5906	4.6145	469
Q33	4385.5693	3712.5722	469

ZERO ORDER PARTIALS

	WORK	Q34	HAPPY	Q33
WORK	1.0000	-.4312	.1267	-.0493
	(0)	(467)	(467)	(467)
	P= .	P= .000	P= .003	P= .143
Q34	-.4312	1.0000	-.1584	.0935
	(467)	(0)	(467)	(467)
	P= .000	P= .	P= .000	P= .022
HAPPY	.1267	-.1584	1.0000	-.0450
	(467)	(467)	(0)	(467)
	P= .003	P= .000	P= .	P= .166
Q33	-.0493	.0935	-.0450	1.0000
	(467)	(467)	(467)	(0)
	P= .143	P= .022	P= .166	P= .

(COEFFICIENT / (D.F.) / SIGNIFICANCE)   (" . " IS PRINTED IF A COEFFICIENT CANNOT BE COMPUTED)

- - - - - - - - - - - - - - P A R T I A L   C O R R E L A T I O N   C O E F F I C I E N T S - - -

CONTROLLING FOR..   HAPPY

Q34

	Q34
WORK	-.4198
	(466)
	P= .000

(COEFFICIENT / (D.F.) / SIGNIFICANCE)   (" . " IS PRINTED IF A COEFFICIENT CANNOT BE COMPUTED)

Table A.5 *(continued)*

```
- - - - - - - - - - - - - - - PARTIAL   CORRELATION   COEFFICIENTS - - -

CONTROLLING FOR..    Q33

                Q34

WORK           -.4290
               (  466)
               P= .000


(COEFFICIENT / (D.F.) / SIGNIFICANCE)        (" . " IS PRINTED IF A COEFFICIENT CANNOT BE COMPUTED)



- - - - - - - - - - - - - - - PARTIAL   CORRELATION   COEFFICIENTS - - -

CONTROLLING FOR..    HAPPY    Q33

                Q34

WORK           -.4179
               (  465)
               P= .000


(COEFFICIENT / (D.F.) / SIGNIFICANCE)        (" . " IS PRINTED IF A COEFFICIENT CANNOT BE COMPUTED)
```

REGRESSION *(Multiple Relationships).*   Often there are a number of independent variables, each of which is hypothesized to contribute to the explained variance of a single dependent variable. Multiple REGRESSION is the SPSS subprogram that handles such simultaneous effects.

The commands for REGRESSION feature a declaration of the variables included in the analysis and a description of how the processing should take place. The following lines produced the output in Table A.6:

> REGRESSION /VARIABLES = HAPPY, Q5, Q34, Q20, Q6, WORK
> /DESCRIPTIVES /STATISTICS = ALL / DEPENDENT = Q5
> /METHOD = STEPWISE

In the sequence of lines, we asked for descriptive statistics to be computed for all the variables on the VARIABLES = list. Because REGRESSION is an asymmetrical statistic, we must state which of our variables is dependent so that we can regress Y on X. We chose a STEPWISE procedure so that we can see the results at each step. Notice that you receive an analysis of variance for the set of variables, the standard error, some summary statistics, the Pearson's *r* between each independent variable and the dependent variable, each *b*, beta, and the intercept *a*.

Measurement: Scale and Index Construction (Chapter 18)

In Chapter 18, we discussed methods for measuring respondents' attitudes. We tapped these attitudes by constructing scales and indexes with indicators of particular attitudes. SPSS has the facility to assist in a variety of ways in the construction of unidimensional and multidimensional scales. Students are encouraged to explore options in FACTOR analysis and COUNT operations as their expertise in methodology and statistics increases. However, for purposes of this treatment, we will only explore some options with the COMPUTE and IF commands.

Often in social science research, it is convenient to create or transform variables, for example, by weighting, percapitizing, or otherwise performing mathematical operations on existing variables. The COMPUTE transformation is probably the most useful and most universal facility in SPSS to satisfy these needs. The format of the command statement is quite simple in that you use logical mathematical expressions to create your composite measures. For instance, you can add (+), subtract (−), multiply (∗), divide (/), and exponentiate (∗∗N). It is also quite flexible in that the operands may be variable names, real numbers, or integers. The general format of the COMPUTE command is

COMPUTE COMPUTED VARNAME = ARITHMETIC EXPRESSION

If you COMPUTE new variables or indexes and use SAVE, the computed variables become permanent variables added to your system file. When new variables are computed, cases with missing data on any variable-operand will be assigned the system missing value.

For our REGRESSION procedure, we COMPUTED a new variable, "HAPPY," a scale that measures respondents' overall happiness. This variable is a combination of the responses to Q10 through Q19. In computing this variable, we assume that happiness is a unidimensional concept, that all of these variables contribute equally to the concept (i.e., that they are equally weighted). We can then place our respondents on a continuum between "not happy" and "very happy," with a low score on the scale indicating unhappiness and a high score happiness. First, we have to be sure that all the component variables are coded in the same direction, that is, that a high value on any one of the variables indicates a happy response. In our example, a low score on the variables identified on the RECODE line indicates happiness, while high scores on all the rest indicate alienation. Therefore, we have to use a RECODE to change the values on those variables to be consistent with the other component variables. The following lines were used to create "HAPPY":

RECODE Q10, Q11, Q17, Q18, Q19 (1 = 4) (2 = 3) (3 = 2) (4 = 1)
COMPUTE HAPPY = Q10 + Q11 + Q12 + Q13 + Q14
    + Q15 + Q16 + Q17 + Q18 + Q19

IF statements are especially useful when constructing typologies using nominal or ordinal variables (or both). The format of IF was discussed ear-

Table A.6

Example of Regression Output

**** M U L T I P L E   R E G R E S S I O N ****

Listwise Deletion of Missing Data

	Mean	Std Dev	Label
WORK	9.753	2.580	DESIRE AND AVAILABILITY TO WORK
Q5	2.893	2.206	WEEKLY TAKE HOME PAY CURRENT/LAST JOB
Q34	31.488	9.895	AGE OF RESPONDENT
Q20	1.144	.638	NUMBER OF TIMES ON WELFARE
Q6	35.027	10.574	HOURS WORKED PER WEEK CURRENT/LAST JOB
HAPPY	27.869	4.587	LEVEL OF SELF-HAPPINESS

N of Cases =   291

Correlation:

	WORK	Q5	Q34	Q20	Q6	HAPPY
WORK	1.000	-.063	-.224	.093	-.059	.114
Q5	-.063	1.000	.280	-.004	.302	.002
Q34	-.224	.280	1.000	-.100	.101	-.164
Q20	.093	-.004	-.100	1.000	.074	-.055
Q6	-.059	.302	.101	.074	1.000	.004
HAPPY	.114	.002	-.164	-.055	.004	1.000

* * * * M U L T I P L E   R E G R E S S I O N * * * * *

Equation Number 1   Dependent Variable..   Q5   WEEKLY TAKE HOME PAY CURRENT/LA

Block Number 1. Method: Stepwise   Criteria   PIN .0500   POUT .1000

Variable(s) Entered on Step Number 1..   Q6   HOURS WORKED PER WEEK CURRENT/LAST JOB

Multiple R   .30178
R Square   .09107   R Square Change   .09107
Adjusted R Square   .08793   F Change   28.95733
Standard Error   2.10711   Signif F Change   .0000

Analysis of Variance

	DF	Sum of Squares	Mean Square
Regression	1	128.56756	128.56756
Residual	289	1283.13003	4.43990

F =   28.95733   Signif F = .0000

AIC   435.76672
PC   .92151
CP   19.94521
SBC   443.11337

Table A.6 (continued)

Var-Covar Matrix of Regression Coefficients (B)
Below Diagonal: Covariance   Above: Correlation

```
              Q6

Q6        1.369E-04
```

XTX Matrix

	Q6	Q5	WORK	Q34	Q20	HAPPY
Q6	1.00000	-.30178	.05890	-.10121	-.07407	-.00363
Q5	.30178	.90893	-.04503	.24984	-.02609	9.33E-04
WORK	-.05890	-.04503	.99653	-.21799	.09740	.11462
Q34	.10121	.24984	-.21799	.98976	-.10777	-.16467
Q20	.07407	-.02609	.09740	-.10777	.99451	-.05511
HAPPY	.00363	9.33E-04	.11462	-.16467	-.05511	.99999

**** M U L T I P L E   R E G R E S S I O N ****

Equation Number 1   Dependent Variable..   Q5   WEEKLY TAKE HOME PAY CURRENT/LA

------ Variables in the Equation ------

Variable	B	SE B	95% Confdnce Intrvl B		Beta	SE Beta	Correl	Part Cor	Partial	Tolerance	VIF
Q6	.062966	.011701	.039936	.085996	.301783	.056081	.301783	.301783	.301783	1.000000	1.000
(Constant)	.687925	.428070	-.154604	1.530454							

------ in ------

Variable	T	Sig T
Q6	5.381	.0000
(Constant)	1.607	.1091

--------- Variables not in the Equation ---------

Variable	Beta In	Partial	Tolerance	VIF	Min Toler	T	Sig T
WORK	-.045184	-.047311	.996530	1.003	.996530	-.804	.4222
Q34	.252427	.263412	.989756	1.010	.989756	4.634	.0000
Q20	-.026235	-.027442	.994514	1.006	.994514	-.466	.6416
HAPPY	9.329E-04	.000979	.999987	1.000	.999987	.017	.9868

Collinearity Diagnostics

Number	Eigenval	Cond Index	Variance Proportions	
			Constant	Q6
1	1.95746	1.000	.02127	.02127
2	.04254	6.784	.97873	.97873

Table A.6 (continued)

* *

Variable(s) Entered on Step Number   2..   Q34   AGE OF RESPONDENT

Multiple R	.39261		
R Square	.15414	R Square Change	.06307
Adjusted R Square	.14827	F Change	21.47306
Standard Error	2.03622	Signif F Change	.0000

Analysis of Variance

	DF	Sum of Squares	Mean Square
Regression	2	217.59867	108.79934
Residual	288	1194.09892	4.14618

F =   26.24088   Signif F = .0000

AIC	416.84075
PC	.86348
CP	.64754
SBC	427.86072

**** M U L T I P L E   R E G R E S S I O N ****

Equation Number 1   Dependent Variable..   Q5   WEEKLY TAKE HOME PAY CURRENT/LA

Var-Covar Matrix of Regression Coefficients (B)
Below Diagonal: Covariance   Above: Correlation

	Q6	Q34
Q6	1.292E-04	-.10121
Q34	-1.397E-05	1.475E-04

XTX Matrix

	Q6	Q34	Q5	WORK	Q20	HAPPY
Q6	1.01035	-.10226	-.27623	.03661	-.08509	-.02047
Q34	-.10226	1.01035	-.25243	.22024	.10889	.16637
Q5	.27623	.25243	.84586	.01000	.00111	.04250
WORK	-.03661	-.22024	.01000	.94852	.07367	.07835
Q20	.08509	-.10889	.00111	.07367	.98278	-.07304
HAPPY	.02047	-.16637	.04250	.07835	-.07304	.97259

Table A.6 *(continued)*

------- Variables in the Equation -------

Variable	B	SE B	95% Confdnce Intrvl B	Beta	SE Beta	Correl	Part Cor	Partial	Tolerance	VIF	T	Sig T
Q6	.057636	.011366	.035265 .080006	.276234	.054474	.301783	.274816	.286300	.989756	1.010	5.071	.0000
Q34	.056286	.012147	.032379 .080194	.252427	.054474	.280385	.251131	.263412	.989756	1.010	4.634	.0000
(Constant)	-.897700	.536850	-1.954347 .158946								-1.672	.0956

------- Variables not in the Equation -------

Variable	Beta In	Partial	Tolerance	VIF	Min Toler	T	Sig T
WORK	.010541	.011162	.948521	1.054	.942073	.189	.8501
Q20	.001133	.001221	.982779	1.018	.978077	.021	.9835
HAPPY	.043698	.046857	.972590	1.028	.962640	.795	.4275

Collinearity Diagnostics

Number	Eigenval	Cond Index	Variance Proportions		
			Constant	Q34	Q6
1	2.88937	1.000	.00579	.01014	.00944
2	.07777	6.095	.00074	.59799	.50266
3	.03286	9.378	.99346	.39187	.48790

End Block Number 1 PIN = .050 Limits reached.

* *

Summary table

Step	MultR	Rsq	AdjRsq	F(Eqn)	SigF	RsqCh	FCh	SigCh		Variable	BetaIn	Correl	
1	.3018	.0911	.0879	28.957	.000	.0911	28.957	.000	In:	Q6	.3018	.3018	HOURS WORKED PER WEEK
2	.3926	.1541	.1483	26.241	.000	.0631	21.473	.000	In:	Q34	.2524	.2804	AGE OF RESPONDENT

lier. Let's say that you wish to construct a measure of the socioeconomic status of your respondents. We could use IF statements and VALUE LABELS thus:

```
IF Q1 EQ 1 AND Q33 LT 5000 SES = 1
IF Q1 GE 2 AND Q1 LT 4 AND Q33 LT 5000 SES = 2
[proceed until all combinations have been exhausted]
VALUE LABELS SES (1) LOWEST (2) LOW . . .
```

Note that you need to consider all possible combinations of your component variables. In other words, the typology must be mutually exclusive and exhaustive—every respondent must be able to be classified under a type, but in one category only. Also note that you can code different combinations into the same one, such as medium education and low income. In this case, both categories receive the same code.

Notes for PC Users

SPSS is available on PCs. Installation of the software requires a PC with a 10-megabyte or larger hard disk. The most recent full-purpose version is SPSS/PC+ Version 3.0.[7] Most of the commands in SPSS/PC+ are the same as in SPSS on the mainframe. All commands must end with a period (as when you are operating interactive SPSS on the mainframe). The REVIEW allows you to build runstreams either by using the available menu or by manually submitting your commands. Function keys are used to initiate runs.

The enhancements available in Version 3.0 mirror those of the newest mainframe version of SPSS. The expanded memory allows 500 variables (the same as the mainframe). The REVIEW has also been enhanced to allow you to work more efficiently.

A subset of SPSS/PC+ is available in a student-affordable package, SPSS/PC+ Studentware.[8] The Studentware package is available in both 5¼-and 3½-inch diskette format—a hard disk is not necessary. All of the statistics covered in this text can be performed in Studentware. However, there are a number of limitations. Studentware is limited to 21 user-created variables (plus two system variables). The menu-driven portion of REVIEW is available (although REVIEW functions as a text editor).

The Studentware manual provides a solid treatment of research methodology and statistics, also characteristic of Marija Norusis's earlier texts. Each chapter has a series of exercises that can be used to test understanding of the mechanics of statistical analysis and printout interpretation. Instructors' guides are also available.

---

7. The manuals needed to run SPSS/PC+ are Marija J. Norusis/SPSS Inc., *SPSS/PC+ V2.0 Base Manual for the IBM PC/XT/AT and PS/2* (Chicago: SPSS Inc., 1988), and *SPSS/PC+ V3.0 Update Manual* (Chicago: SPSS Inc., 1988).

8. Marija J. Norusis/SPSS Inc., *SPSS/PC+ Studentware* (Chicago: SPSS Inc., 1988).

Conclusion

The SPSS and other statistical package manuals may seem complicated and imposing on first inspection. This appendix was designed to assist you in taking that first big step into computerized data analysis. We hope that this treatment will encourage researchers to pick and choose portions of those packages that lend themselves to their data needs and methodological expertise. A package like SPSS has many capabilities and potentials that grow with the abilities of the individual researcher. Thus we encourage you to explore these potentials with the help of the manual as your skills increase.

Exhibit A.1
Cleveland Poverty Survey Codebook

Variable Name		Column Numbers
IDNUMBER	Interviewee Identification Number Code Actual Number (001-528)	1–3
Q1	Highest Grade Completed 1 = 1–8 2 = 9–11 3 = 12 4 = 13–15 5 = 16 6 = 17 +	4
Q2	Employment Status 1 = Employed 2 = Unemployed 3 = Retired 4 = Student 5 = Homemaker 6 = Other	5
Q3	Marital Status 1 = Married 2 = Widowed 3 = Divorced 4 = Separated 5 = Never Married	6
Q4	Gender 1 = Male 2 = Female	7
Q5	Weekly Take-Home Pay Current/Last Job Code Actual Dollars	8–11
Q6	Hours Worked Per Week Current/Last Job Code Actual Hours	12–13

Exhibit A.1 *(continued)*

Variable Name		Column Numbers
Q7	General Health Condition 1 = Excellent 2 = Very Good 3 = Good 4 = Fair 5 = Poor 9 = DK/NA	14
Q8	Good Education Way to Get Ahead 1 = Strongly Agree 2 = Agree 3 = Somewhat Agree 4 = Somewhat Disagree 5 = Disagree 6 = Disagree Strongly 9 = DK/NA	15
Q9	Reading Ability 1 = Excellent 2 = Good 3 = Fair 4 = Poor 9 = DK/NA	16
Q10	Playing Useful Part in Things 1 = Much More than Usual 2 = More than Usual 3 = Same as Usual 4 = Less than Usual 9 = DK/NA	17
Q11	Feeling Reasonably Happy 1 = Much More than Usual 2 = More than Usual 3 = Same as Usual 4 = Less than Usual 9 = DK/NA	18
Q12	Losing Confidence in Self 1 = Much More than Usual 2 = More than Usual 3 = Same as Usual 4 = Less than Usual 9 = DK/NA	19
Q13	Thinking You Are Useless Person 1 = Much More than Usual 2 = More than Usual 3 = Same as Usual	20

Variable Name		Column Numbers
	4 = Less than Usual	
	9 = DK/NA	
Q14	Constantly under Strain	21
	1 = Much More than Usual	
	2 = More than Usual	
	3 = Same as Usual	
	4 = Less than Usual	
	9 = DK/NA	
Q15	Feeling Unhappy and Depressed	22
	1 = Much More than Usual	
	2 = More than Usual	
	3 = Same as Usual	
	4 = Less than Usual	
	9 = DK/NA	
Q16	Unable to Concentrate	23
	1 = Much More than Usual	
	2 = More than Usual	
	3 = Same as Usual	
	4 = Less than Usual	
	9 = DK/NA	
Q17	Able to Face Up to Problems	24
	1 = Much More than Usual	
	2 = More than Usual	
	3 = Same as Usual	
	4 = Less than Usual	
	9 = DK/NA	
Q18	Able to Enjoy Day-to-Day Activities	25
	1 = Much More than Usual	
	2 = More than Usual	
	3 = Same as Usual	
	4 = Less than Usual	
	9 = DK/NA	
Q19	Capable of Making Decisions	26
	1 = Much More than Usual	
	2 = More than Usual	
	3 = Same as Usual	
	4 = Less than Usual	
	9 = DK/NA	
Q20	Number of Times on Welfare	27
	Code Actual Number of Times	
Q21	Willing to Work Full-Time	28
	1 = Yes	
	2 = No	
Q22	Willing to Work Part-Time	29
	1 = Yes	
	2 = No	

Exhibit A.1 (continued)

Variable Name		Column Numbers
Q23	Willing to Work as a Manager 1 = Yes 2 = No	30
Q24	Willing to Work at Home 1 = Yes 2 = No	31
Q25	Willing to Work for Self 1 = Yes 2 = No	32
Q26	Willing to Work for Others 1 = Yes 2 = No	33
Q27	Willing to Work in Group 1 = Yes 2 = No	34
Q28	Willing to Work Alone 1 = Yes 2 = No	35
Q29	Willing to Work for a Small Company 1 = Yes 2 = No	36
Q30	Willing to Work at Night 1 = Yes 2 = No	37
Q31	Willing to Work Weekends 1 = Yes 2 = No	38
Q32	Willing to Work Overtime 1 = Yes 2 = No	39
Q33	Total Annual Income—All Sources Code Actual Dollars	40–45
Q34	Age of Respondent Code Actual Years	46–47

APPENDIX B   Introduction to SAS

Claire L. Felbinger and Stephen F. Schwelgien

This appendix is designed to assist students in preparing and executing computerized data analysis using one of the most widely available and used software packages, SAS System, Version 6.[1] Designed to accommodate the analysis of social science data, the SAS System includes most of the routines employed by social scientists. Indeed, all the data analysis procedures described in this text can be executed with SAS programs. Of particular interest to social scientists is the system's capacity to handle with ease the recurring needs of data analysis. For instance, SAS enables the researcher to handle missing values and to create new character values; to rename variables, modify variable attributes, and compute new variables; to sample, weight, and select observations; and to create temporary or permanent data sets.

This version (6) and release (6.06) of the statistical package is a major revision of the last version (5) and release (5.18) of SAS. Most notably, the introduction of a processing superprogram called Multiple Engine Architecture makes accessible new means to produce SAS data sets and different enactments of the SAS data set. Other modifications are designed to make automatic recovery from some syntax errors possible and to provide greater ease and efficiency in data management, designing output, and performing more sophisticated analyses. For those of you familiar with earlier versions of SAS, the language of commands in this version was changed as little as possible. You will find the greatest number and the greatest effect of changes in the areas of file definition and data set organization. Nevertheless, you will be surprised, for example, to encounter a new procedure, SPELL, which can check the spelling in an external file and maintain dictionaries; you may also be impressed by the increased power and flexibility provided by several new options to old procedures. Changes made to commands of SAS procedures generally involved either the addition of new options or the improvement of command function. Fortunately, *SAS Language*

---

1. SAS Institute Inc., *SAS Language: Reference, Version 6* (Cary, N.C.: SAS Institute Inc., 1990).

and the *SAS Procedures Guide*[2] each provide a chapter of changes and enhancements to SAS in order to make the transition to the new version as painless as possible. For the purposes of this appendix, we will limit ourselves to executing SAS files with no reference to earlier versions. If you are concerned with the revisions and how they affect your earlier runstreams, refer to the aforementioned reference guides.

This treatment is intended to supply the novice analyst with the tools necessary to set up an SAS file and execute basic analyses. It is not by any means an exhaustive display of either the variety of subprograms available or the intricacies of the more highly powered types of analysis possible with the SAS System. Rather, the examples used are intended to parallel the work covered in this text. If you wish to explore a more extended introductory-level treatment of the SAS System, refer to the SAS usage guide.[3] Refer also to the *SAS Procedures Guide* for information on other available procedures and for a more detailed explanation of the ones covered in this appendix.

The data set used in the examples that follow is from Cleveland Poverty Survey of 1988.[4] A sample codebook containing the variables used is found in Exhibit A.1 at the end of Appendix A. We will use these data to build an SAS data set. Furthermore, we will clean the data and execute statistical procedures in much the same way as if we were actually involved in a research project. Hence we will assume that the data are prepared (as in Chapter 14) in machine-readable form, clean the data by examining univariate distributions (Chapter 15), perform bivariate (Chapter 16) and multivariate (Chapter 17) analysis with hypothesis testing (Chapter 19), and construct scales (Chapter 18).

Preparing the Data

We have prepared the data as discussed in Chapter 14. They can be prepared and stored on tape or disk. The particular data set we have assembled contains 528 cases or *observations* (SAS manuals use the keyword OBSERVATION) with six 80-column lines of data called *decks* or *records* (SAS manuals use the keyword RECORD) per case (although we will use information on only one record for our example here). All the decks associated with each case are together in order (case 1, record 1; case 1, record 2; and so on to case *n*, record *last*). To access SAS at your particular research facility, you must supply commands known as *Job Control Language*, or JCL. These commands are unique to your mainframe computer system and to your facility.

2. SAS Institute Inc., *SAS Procedures Guide, Version 6*, 3d ed. (Cary, N.C.: SAS Institute Inc., 1990).

3. SAS Institute Inc., *SAS Language and Procedures: Usage, Version 6* (Cary, N.C.: SAS Institute Inc., 1989).

4. *Cleveland Poverty Survey, 1988* (Cleveland: Northern Ohio Data and Information Service, Levin College of Urban Affairs, Cleveland State University, 1988).

They grant access to the computer, initiate accounting procedures, assign disk or tape space, access the SAS software, and perform other functions. It is advisable that you contact the consultants at your facility as to the proper JCL since site requirements vary from facility to facility.

Setting Up an SAS System Data File

The language of SAS is logical and quite simple. You will find a consistency in the language and patterns employed that match your expectations. There are, however, certain programming rules that must be observed in using the various elements of the SAS language. These rules concern both SAS statements and SAS names. For SAS statements, (1) all statements must end with a semicolon (;), (2) there is no limit—beyond space constraints—to the number of statements that can occur on a single line, (3) a statement can continue on a new line as long as no word is split, (4) statements can begin (and continue onto the next line) in any column, (5) statements may consist of lowercase, uppercase, or mixed characters, and (6) words are separated either by blanks or by special characters (such as the plus sign, minus sign, or equal sign encountered in arithmetic calculations). For SAS names (data set names, variable names, etc.), (1) the name must contain one but not more than eight characters, (2) no blanks can appear in a name, (3) the first character must be a letter or an underscore (_), (4) letters, numbers, or underscores must make up all additional characters in a name, and (5) variable names are unique; that is, a variable cannot be named twice.

There are a number of *files* that you must be familiar with in order to run the SAS System:

1. *Command files* contain the SAS commands you wish to execute in any particular run. Such commands include both DATA step statements, which define your data as an SAS data set (see item 4 on this list), and PROC (procedural) step statements, which typically act on the newly created data set.[5] We will assume in this appendix that your commands will be stored in a file on your mainframe (and that you will not be using the editing utilities found in the SAS Display Manager System or the menu-driven system of SAS/ASSIST software).

2. *External input data files* contain your raw data. In this example, we will assume that your data are stored in 80-column lines on disk or tape on your mainframe. SAS can accommodate virtually any form of stored data. However, since coding is traditionally done using the 80-column format, we will use that format here.

---

5. Although most SAS procedures require data on which to act, one procedure that we will use, PROC FORMAT, is employed merely to generate value labels. That is the only exception in this appendix.

3. *Procedure output files* contain the results of your executed PROCS (procedures) that were stored in a command file. This is the output that can be viewed on a screen or printed at a line printer.

4. *SAS data set files* occur as the outcome of your executed DATA step statements that were stored in a command file. They contain the information about the data from the input file as uniquely defined by your series of DATA step statements plus any transformations stored later. As such, the data file contains the data values logically organized in a rectangular pattern of columns and rows, descriptor information concerning the data set (number of observations, date of last data set modification, etc.) and its variables (name, type—such as numeric or character, format, label), and one or more indexes that allow the rapid location of observations identified with a data value or range of values through use of one or more specified key variables.

SAS Data Set Creation.   Let us now describe the statements and procedures necessary to set up an SAS data set. The object is to assist you in setting up and saving a file containing not only your data but also details about the type of information contained, where it is located, and what you plan to call it—this is your data set file. Table B.1 lists the SAS components we used to set up our SAS data set. The inclusion order is somewhat flexible in SAS; however, the one used here is an example of a successful run. One thing to keep in mind about inclusion order is that a variable must be defined before

Table B.1
Program Specification for Creation of an SAS Data Set

Item Number	Keyword	Specification Field	Delimiter
1*	TITLE	'Your Title Here'	;
2*	PROC FORMAT	[none]	;
	VALUE	valuename $range_1$ = 'label'	
		$range_2$ = 'label' . . .	;
	RUN	[none]	;
3	DATA	libref.dataname	;
4	INFILE	fileref	;
5*	MISSING	special-missing-character$_1$	
		special-missing-character$_2$ . . .	;
6	INPUT	varname$_1$ column#-column#	
		varname$_2$ column#-column# . . .	;
7*	FORMAT	varname$_1$ formatname$_1$.	
		varname$_2$ formatname$_2$. . . .	;
8*	LABEL	varname$_1$ 'your label$_1$ here'	
		varname$_2$ 'your label$_2$ here' . . .	;
9*		[other SAS statements may be placed here, each one separately delimited]	;
	RUN	[none]	

*Optional item.

it is used. Also, be careful to key in the SAS statement and procedural key-words (the capitalized words) precisely as indicated. Remember, however, that these keywords need not be keyed in uppercase, as they are here displayed. Table B.1 summarizes these components and their structure.

Components. The creation of an SAS data set requires, at minimum, one properly constructed and executed DATA step. This DATA step, as here tailored to our purposes,[6] requires, at minimum, the DATA, INFILE, and IN-PUT statements, in that order. Since, however, we desire to modify and customize our data set, we employ one optional SAS statement and an optional procedural step prior to the DATA step and we use several optional SAS statements within the DATA step. Table B.1 lists the model specifications of these SAS statements in this SAS procedure. Items 1 and 2 are optional but useful in customizing output. Statements 3, 4, and 6 are all essential to the DATA step and will be discussed further. The remaining items are optional.

1. TITLE. This optional feature allows you to label your run with a title that is printed across the top of each page of your output in the display file. The TITLE statement consists of the keyword TITLE followed by the title of your choice enclosed in single quotation marks (') and a semicolon (;). The maximum allowable length of this title depends on your host system (ask the consultants at your facility).

2. PROC FORMAT. The FORMAT procedure can be employed to create value labels to be associated with your variables. For instance, if you wish the terms *low, medium,* and *high* to stand for the coded values of 1, 2, and 3, you can format these three terms as value labels by this procedure. They will not, however, become associated with the values of the variable you wish them to represent until you refer to them with the FORMAT statement (item 7).

The FORMAT procedure step as it applies to value label creation consists of (a) the command PROC FORMAT followed by a semicolon (;); (b) the VALUE statement, consisting of the keyword VALUE followed by (i) the format name you choose,[7] (ii) the raw data value or range of values equated with the terms of the label in single quotes (range = 'label term'),[8] and (iii) a semicolon (;); and (c) the command RUN followed by a semicolon (;).[9]

---

6. That is, in accessing raw data stored in an external file. Other situations, for instance, entering data within the job stream, require different configurations of the DATA step. For information on how to compose an SAS DATA step to read instream data, refer to *SAS Language: Reference*, p. 28.

7. The name you choose must be a valid SAS name (see rules for SAS names), and it may not end in a number. If you are formatting a character variable, the first character of the name must consist of a dollar sign ($).

8. The terms of this label, which SAS manuals refer to as the FORMATTED VALUE, may be up to 40 characters in length. However, some SAS procedures employ only the first 8 or 16 characters of the value label.

9. The command RUN causes the PROC FORMAT step (or any other SAS step) and its attendant statements to execute. Although this step would execute automatically with the beginning of the next step—the DATA step—and hence is not necesssary, we include the RUN command as a boundary after each and every step in our programming to indicate clearly the limit of the step.

3. DATA. The DATA statement always begins the DATA step, which leads to the creation of an SAS data set. Essentially, this statement names the SAS data set. You can create a temporary or a permanent SAS data set, depending on the naming specifications following the keyword DATA. For our purposes, we will create a permanent set.

4. INFILE. The INFILE statement identifies the external file that contains your raw data and is stored in your facility's operating system. The specification 'THE-SELECTED-INPUT-FILE' refers to the facility-assigned name identifying this stored external file.

5. MISSING. This statement defines which numeric variables are designated by special missing values. By design, SAS automatically sets all variable values to MISSING prior to reading input. Once all data have been processed, any of these preset missing values that have not been transformed by the input remain missing in the data set. Numeric missing values are designated by a single decimal point (.), whereas character missing values are represented by a blank enclosed in single quotes ('). If any of the raw numeric data have been coded as missing with special designated characters such as, for instance, the letter M, they will not be read by default as missing but rather as invalid numeric variables. To avoid this error, use the MISSING statement followed by a list of single character values (possible range of A through Z) that you wish to designate as special missing values and then a semicolon (;).

6. INPUT. This statement identifies the fields to read from the raw data and names the variables you wish to define.

7. FORMAT. This statement associates the formatted value label created with PROC FORMAT (item 2) with your target variable or variables. By creating the value label *prior* to the DATA step (i.e., prior to commencing the DATA step with the DATA statement) and then associating it with the appropriate variable(s) in the DATA step, all data analysis procedural steps *after* the DATA step will output the value label where appropriate. To use the FORMAT statement, the format names *must* be previously defined, as was done in the PROC FORMAT step. The statement begins with the keyword FORMAT followed by the name of the variable whose values you wish to label, the format name you created in the VALUE statement of the PROC FORMAT step followed immediately (no space) by a period (.), and a semicolon (;).

8. LABEL. This statement allows you to describe your variables further. It augments the variable names from the input statement by associating a label with the name. This option is quite handy if you choose to assign Q numbers (Q1, Q2, Q3, etc.) as variable names. The statement consists of the keyword LABEL followed by the name of the variable you wish to label, a label of your creation up to 40 characters in length, enclosed in quotes ('), and a semicolon (;).

9. *Other SAS statements.* These permit you to modify the variables, compute new variables, and so forth. Included for our purposes later in this appendix are SAS statements used to clean the data, create subsets of the

data, recode the values of some variables, and compute new variables (and in so doing construct new scales). The last statement of the DATA step, which immediately precedes all subsequent procedural steps to analyze your data set, is the RUN statement.

A Closer Look at the DATA *Statement.*   The DATA statement consists of the keyword DATA followed by the name you select for your data set, which is in turn followed by a semicolon (;). The name you select for your data set may consist of any valid SAS name (following the rules discussed before); however, the convention you use in establishing this name will determine if the data set is temporary (i.e., existent only for the current session) or permanent (stored in an external file on your system as an SAS data set). A temporary data set is created when the data set name consists of only one SAS word. This is called a *one-level* name, and the form of the DATA statement becomes

   DATA dataname ;

A permanent data set, such as we intend to create here, however, requires a *two-level* name as displayed in the following example:

   DATA datalib.dataname ;

As you can see, this name actually consists of two SAS name components separated by a period (.). The second component serves the same naming function as the single name in the temporary data set. The first component, however, instructs the system to create a permanent data set. This component, which is called the *libref* (library reference), must be associated with an SAS data storage library in your operating system. Since this task of association is usually accomplished with JCL,[10] it is advisable to check with your system consultants to ensure that the libref you select corresponds properly to an SAS data library.

A Closer Look at the INFILE *Statement.*   The INFILE statement is used to identify an external input file that is not an SAS data file, as is the case with the file on which your raw data are stored.[11] This statement may be used either to identify the external file directly or to reference the external file indirectly with a file reference name called a *fileref*. The form of the statement when identifying the external file directly consists of the keyword INFILE followed by your input file name in quotes which is in turn followed by a semicolon (;):

   INFILE 'your-selected-input-file' ;

---

10. If JCL is not appropriate for this task on your operating system, an alternative way to associate the libref with the name of an SAS data library on your system is to use the LIBNAME command prior to the DATA step. For the specifications of this command, refer to *SAS Language: Reference*, pp. 431–443.

11. To reference an external file that *is* an SAS data file, use the SET statement (to be discussed shortly).

In this appendix, however, we use the convention of the fileref to reference our raw data. The form of the INFILE statement under this convention is

    INFILE refname ;

where REFNAME is the fileref consisting of any valid SAS name associated with the external input file. Like the libref used in conjunction with the DATA statement, this association is usually accomplished with JCL.[12] Hence we likewise advise that you check with your operating system consultants to ensure that the fileref you select corresponds properly to your external input file.

A Closer Look at the INPUT *Statement.*   The INPUT statement is used both to direct the SAS System how to read your raw data file and to define the variables for your SAS data set. Of the several styles of input SAS offers, we have selected column input. With column input, the SAS System recognizes that data values occupying the same columns within given records of all the observations are always to be identified with the same variables. Since your data were coded in just such a fixed-field format, the easiest way to identify the location of your variables on a record is to use the column numbers. In the following example, SAS expects to find the variable named IDNUMBER in columns 1 through 3 on the first record of each case, Q1 is found in column 4 on the first record of each case, and so on. Our INPUT statement defines the first three variables in our codebook. Compare this INPUT statement with the information found in the codebook in Exhibit A.1 (Appendix A).

    DATA libdata.poverty ;
    INFILE refname ;
    INPUT idnumber 1–3 q1 4 q2 5 ;

If your data contain more than one record for each observation, the second record is represented by a second INPUT statement immediately following the first:

    DATA libref.yourdata ;
    INFILE fileref ;
    INPUT idnumber 1–3 q1 4 q2 5 ;
    INPUT otherq1 1–4 otherq2 5 . . . ;

Each variable must be designated with a SAS name in the INPUT statement. Besides following the aforementioned SAS conventions for naming, all variable names must be unique within the data set. That is, a single variable name cannot be used twice within the INPUT statement to define data. You can select names that reflect the nature of your variables, such as GENDER,

---

12. If JCL is not appropriate for this task on your operating system, an alternative way to effect this association is to use the FILENAME statement prior to the DATA step. For the specifications of this statement, refer to *SAS Language: Reference*, pp. 353–359.

AGE, and IDNUMBER, as long as the names are unique and abide by the SAS naming conventions.

SAS can accommodate several other styles of input to read raw data and define variables. For instance, list input or formatted input can also be used. Although list input requires fewer specifications in the INPUT statement than column input, it is almost always inappropriate for handling fixed-field data formats. Formatted input merges column input with the capability to read data that contain such special characters as commas. If, for example, the data that comprise Q33 have been coded in with standard comma notation (i.e., commas separating every three digits from the right), our standard column input definition for this variable would fail when it encountered a comma. Instead, formatted input using a COMMAw.d format[13] is required to read such data into a data set and store them as valid numeric values without the commas. Consider the following hypothetical specification:

```
DATA libref.poverty ;
INFILE refname ;
INPUT idnumber 1–3 q33 40–45 COMMA6. ;
```

Since, in our scenario, the values for Q33 have been coded in with commas, let us say that the SAS System when reading the raw data encounters a numeric value of 6,000. The COMMA6. format specified in the INPUT statement and associated with Q33 instructs the SAS System to read six characters of data (including the comma), remove the comma from the data, and then write the standard numeric value without commas to the new data set. The raw data value of 6,000 then becomes a rectified stored data value of 6000, and we are able to perform further procedural analysis on the data. If, after performing analysis on this variable, we then decide that we would like it formatted in our output with commas, we can employ a FORMAT statement as follows:

```
FORMAT q33 COMMA6. ;
```

Including the FORMAT statement in the DATA step will create it as a permanent element of the data set; including this statement as part of a PROC (procedural) step will affect only the ouput for the PROC in which it was included.

If you feel comfortable using some method besides column input, refer to *SAS Language: Reference* for assistance.

---

13. COMMA is the keyword prefix; the w is a numeric specification that defines the width of the field of output, and the D is a value from 0 through 31 that specifies how many decimal digits to read. The default value of w is 1, and the default value of D is 0. This format, in addition to removing embedded commas, removes embedded periods, blanks, dollar signs, dashes, and right parentheses from the input. It transforms an embedded left parenthesis (at the beginning of a field) into a minus sign (−).

Data Modifications and Procedures.   Once we have assembled the necessary JCL and SAS data set definition information, we are ready to take the final step in the process of setting up the file—instructing the computer to do something with the information we have supplied. The two generic processes we will be concerned with in this treatment are data modifications and PROC (procedure) steps.

In general, when we wish to manipulate or transform our data in any way, we employ data modifications consisting of additional SAS statements within the context of a DATA step. PROC statements, by contrast, usually instruct the computer to calculate statistics for us. The data modifications available for our purposes are setting values to missing, creating a subset of the data, recoding the values of a variable, and computing a new variable from existent variables. The procedures are PROC CONTENTS, PROC FREQ, PROC PRINT, PROC UNIVARIATE, PROC CORR, PROC PLOT, and PROC REG.

Initial Run.   Our initial run should be executed with two goals in mind. First, we must determine whether the input data have been read into the SAS data set file exactly as we planned. Second, we must determine whether any stray or illegal codes were keyed in and not caught in the verification process. Placing a PROC CONTENTS step immediately after our DATA step (i.e., after the RUN statement whereby the data set is executed) will provide us with output that informs us of the number of variables and observations in our data set; the name, type, and length of each variable; the position of the variable in the observation; and the format and label for each variable, if existent. The PROC CONTENTS step, in its simplest implementation, consists of the keywords PROC CONTENTS followed by a semicolon (;). In the context of our model, this procedural step appears thus:

```
LABEL statement . . . ;
PROC FORMAT procedure . . . ; Value statement . . . ; RUN;
DATA statement . . . ;
INFILE statement . . . ;
MISSING statement . . . ;
INPUT statement . . . ;
FORMAT statement . . . ;
LABEL statement . . . ;
RUN ;
PROC CONTENTS ;
RUN ;
PROC FREQ ;
    TABLES idnumber q1 q2 q3 q4 q5 q6 . . . q34 ;
RUN ;
```

This information from the CONTENTS procedure should be checked carefully to ensure that you have properly transferred the data onto the system file. Assuming that the format is correct, we next prepare to determine whether any stray or illegal codes were keyed in and not caught. The output necessary for this determination is provided by the PROC FREQ step in our example. This procedural step consists, first, of the keywords PROC FREQ followed by a semicolon (;). Next comes a TABLES statement, which consists of the keyword TABLES followed by a list of all our variables and a semicolon (;). Finally, the procedural step is executed when the SAS System encounters the RUN command followed by a semicolon (;). The output in the form of frequencies that we get as a result of this procedure will enable us to determine the extent of cleaning (Chapter 14) necessary prior to generating statistical information. Table B.2 shows the actual setup of the poverty data set we are using in this appendix.

Table B.2
SAS Data Set File Setup for 1988 Poverty Study

	[inserted initial JCL here]
TITLE	'Cleveland Poverty Study, 1988' ;
PROC FORMAT ;	
VALUE	QA 1 = '1–8' 2 = '9–11' 3 = '12' 4 = '13–15' 5 = '16' 6 = '17 +' ;
VALUE	QB 1 = 'STRONGLY AGREE' 2 = 'AGREE' 3 = 'SOMEWHAT AGREE'
	4 = 'SOMEWHAT DISAGREE' 5 = 'DISAGREE'
	6 = 'DISAGREE STRONGLY' ;
RUN ;	
DATA	lib.poverty ;
INFILE	raw ;
INPUT	idnumber 1–3 q1 4 q2 5 q3 6 q4 7 q5 8–11 q6 12–13 q7 14 q8 15 q9
	16 q10 17 q11 18 q12 19 q13 20 q14 21 q15 22 q16 23 q17 24 q18 25
	q19 26 q20 27 q21 28 q22 29 q23 30 q24 31 q25 32 q26 33 q27 34
	q28 35 q29 36 q30 37 q31 38 q32 39 q33 40–45 q34 46–47 ;
FORMAT	q1 QA. Q8 QB. ;
LABEL	q1 'HIGHEST GRADE COMPLETED'
	q5 'WEEKLY TAKE-HOME PAY CURRENT/LAST JOB'
	q6 'HOURS WORKED PER WEEK CURRENT/LAST JOB'
	q8 'GOOD EDUCATION WAY TO GET AHEAD'
	q20 'NUMBER OF TIMES ON WELFARE'
	q34 'AGE OF RESPONDENT'
	happy 'LEVEL OF SELF-HAPPINESS'
	work 'DESIRE AND AVAILABLITY TO WORK' ;
ARRAY	recode {5} q10 q11 q17 q18 q19 ;
DO	count = 1 to 5 ;
	recode{count} = 5 − recode{count} ;
END ;	
	happy = q10 + q11 + q12 + q13 + q14 + q15 + q16 + q17 + q18 + q19 ;
ARRAY	generic{12} q21 q22 q23 q24 q25 q26 q27 q28 q29 q30 q31 q32 ;
DO	count = 1 to 12 ;
IF	generic{count} = 1
THEN	work = work + 1 ;
END ;	
RUN ;	

Subsequent Runs.   Once you have created an SAS data set file and quit the current session in which it was created, you can access it again by beginning the runstream with appropriate JCL and a DATA step consisting of the DATA statement followed by a SET statement. The SET statement specifies the SAS data set file you created and saved as a permanent data set. The model form of the SET statement is

SET libref.dataname ;

where LIBREF is the reference name of the SAS data library where you stored your data set and DATANAME is the name with which you designated your data.

Cleaning the Data

After we have examined the CONTENTS output and verified that all the data are in their intended input configuration, we will use the output from the PROC FREQ procedure to generate frequencies for each variable and to determine whether there are any illegal responses listed for each of our variables. For example, if a variable was coded Q9: 1 = EXCELLENT, 2 = GOOD, 3 = FAIR, 4 = POOR, and 9 = DON'T KNOW and we find a 7 listed in the output from the PROC FREQ for that variable, we can either declare the 7 a missing value or replace the 7 with the actual value from the coding sheets. If we do not have the original coding sheets and cannot verify what a 7 is supposed to mean, we can use the following runstream, incorporating an IF-THEN statement to purge this inappropriate response:

```
DATA tempdata;
SET libref.poverty;
If q9 = 7 THEN q9 = . ;
[insert remaining modifications]
DATA libref.poverty ;
SET tempdata ;
```

With this runstream, we first incorporate all our cleaning modifications (including those yet to be discussed) into a temporary SAS data file called TEMPDATA that prior to the modifications made an exact copy of our permanent data LIBREF.POVERTY with use of the first SET statement. With use of the second SET statement, we then remake LIBREF.POVERTY into an exact copy of the temporary and modified data set, except that we are storing all modifications permanently.[14] In this case, anytime we subsequently use Q9,

---

14. Instead of creating a temporary SAS data set as we did, you could directly create an additional permanent SAS data set—but this would require a different library reference (libref) and other JCL modifications. The model form of this DATA step would be

DATA newref.dataname ;
SET oldref.dataname ;

where OLDREF is the original libref for your first permanent SAS data set and NEWREF is an additional libref for your modified permanent data set.

the SAS System will consider a value of 7 a missing value (.). Whether or not this and other missing values appear in our procedure output files depends, however, on the particular procedure we use, since some procedures remove missing values from their analyses but others do not. The remainder of examples in this appendix will assume that the appropriate JCL and a DATA step consisting of DATA and SET statements are included in the runstream. Moreover, the remainder of the examples regarding cleaning the data will assume that the final runstream modifications are made in the context of the runstream model just given.

The subsetting IF statement allows you to isolate a subset of cases for investigation. Often in the social sciences, we wish to look only at the responses of "women" or "old people" or "Democrats" who are included with persons having different attributes in the data set. The subsetting IF statement allows one to easily group respondents on the desired attribute. We can also use the subsetting IF statement while cleaning our data. Let's say that we found two responses of 7 to Q9. We can isolate those incorrect responses by using the subsetting IF. The model form of the subsetting IF statement is

IF varname [logical connector] value ;

where the logical connectors are

Connector	Meaning
EQ or =	equal to
NE or ∧ =	not equal to
LT or <	less than
LE or < =	less than or equal to
GT or >	greater than
GE or > =	greater than or equal to
IN	equal to one value in a list

and the value can be a number or another variable name. The subsetting IF statement may be made more complex by forming logical compound sentences connected by AND (meaning that all conditions must apply for case inclusion), OR (any condition can be met for case inclusion), or NOT (reverses the outcome of an expression).

Just subsetting the errant cases for Q9 is not sufficient to allow us to clean the data. We next need to use the PROC PRINT procedure to list the cases selected and their values on a number of variables. In our example, all that we need to identify and clean Q9 is the case IDNUMBER. Then we can consult our code sheets to find the correct values. The model form of the PROC PRINT step is

PROC PRINT ;
VAR [variable list] ;
RUN ;

where VAR is the keyword of the VAR statement required in specifying this procedure.

The runstream to clean Q9, as such, is

```
DATA pretemp ;
SET libref.poverty ;
IF q9 EQ 7 ;
PROC PRINT ;
VAR idnumber ;
RUN ;
```

where the subsetting IF statement occurs in the context of a temporary DATA step executed in a run *prior* to the run of the previously mentioned runstream model that incorporates the final modifications and creates a final permanent SAS data set.[15] Let's say that the output indicates that IDNUMBERS 24 and 87 have the value 7 for Q9, and we find that the values should have been 1 and MISSING, respectively. We therefore need to change the 7 in the first instance to a 1 and to declare the 7 in the second instance as a missing value. In our final data set creation run, we can make the transformations by using the IF-THEN statement to isolate conditions that must exist for the transformation. The model form of the IF-THEN statement is

```
IF varname₁ [logical connector] value
THEN varname₂ = value ;
```

where the logical connector and first value are the same as defined in the subsetting IF statement specification field and VARNAME$_2$ is the variable to which you wish to attach the correct value. The runstream modifications to clean our two cases are

```
IF idnumber EQ 24 THEN q9 = 1 ;
IF idnumber EQ 87 THEN q9 = . ;
```

These modifications must occur in the final data step creation run.

---

15. Briefly, this run must precede the final data set creation run as such:

```
DATA pretemp;
SET libref.poverty;
IF . . .;
PROC PRINT;
VAR . . .;
RUN;
```

At this point, you examine the output of the PRINT procedure and decide on final modifications.

```
DATA tempdata;
SET libref. poverty ;
[modifications]
RUN ;
```

This way, the first temporary data set has utility but bears no continuing relationship (which is desirable) to the temporary data set that succeeds it and is used to make all final modifications permanent.

When we are confident that all our variables are clean and stored permanently either in a new or a revised permanent SAS data set, we can generate a final, complete, and up-to-date data definition description of our SAS data set file by repeating the previous PROC CONTENTS step. The more complete job you do at defining your data via the optional labeling and formatting, the better the CONTENTS output functions as a revised codebook. Also, remember that the more carefully you key in the raw data and data defining statements, the less time you will spend cleaning the data.

At this point, we are ready to begin our analysis of the data. Remember that all the subsequent procedural steps we will discuss should follow (in any order) a DATA step that sets your cleaned permanent data set.

Univariate Distributions (Chapter 15)

You recognized the output from PROC FREQ as a univariate distribution of groups of responses for each variable. Now that the data are clean, you can invoke another procedure, PROC UNIVARIATE, which can generate frequency tables and produce numerous simple descriptive statistics including moments, such as the mean, standard error, median, mode, standard deviation, variance, kurtosis, and skewness; quantiles, such as the median; details on a variable's extreme values; plots, such as a histogram, box plot, and normal probability plot; paired comparison test; tests of central location; and tests for normal distribution. If we wish to generate all of these statistics for a subset of our variables, the runstream should include the following procedural step:

```
PROC UNIVARIATE FREQ NORMAL PLOT ;
VAR q2 q4 q6-q12 ;
RUN ;
```

where FREQ, NORMAL, and PLOT are options providing, respectively, frequency tables, tests of normality, and various plots.

If you wish to select only some of the available statistics, thus saving some computer time, you may delete any of the options following the keywords PROC UNIVARIATE.

Bivariate Distributions (Chapter 16)

As you learned in Chapter 16, bivariate analysis enables us to see the association or relationship between two variables; we can observe how one variable covaries with another. Using bivariate statistics, we can determine not only whether a relationship exists at all (significance test) but also the strength and direction of such a relationship (measures of association).

Nominal and Ordinal Measures.   The PROC FREQ procedure is designed primarily to generate bivariate tables and statistics for nominal and ordinal variables and takes the form

```
PROC FREQ ;
TABLES [varname₃ * ] varname₁ * varname₂ ;
RUN ;
```

where VARNAME₁ is the dependant variable (printed down the left-hand column, as has been the convention in this book) of the table, VARNAME₂ is the independent variable, and VARNAME₃ functions as a control variable, generating one table for each value of the control. The use of a control is optional.

Suppose that we wish to examine the relationship between educational level and opinions regarding whether getting a good education is a good way to get ahead in life. The following procedural step can be used:

```
PROC FREQ ;
TABLES q8 * q1 ;
RUN ;
```

which produces Table B.3. Let's look at the outlined cell. Here is how to interpret the numbers in the cell for persons with an eighth-grade education or less (Q1, value 1) who agree that education leads to getting ahead (Q8, value 2). The uppermost left-hand description cell (FREQUENCY, PERCENT, ROW PCT, COL PCT) tells the order of the numbers within each internal cell. The number 23 in the highlighted cell means that 23 respondents (frequency) have both of these characteristics. This N of 23 out of the total N of 524 accounts for 4.39 percent of the respondents in the survey. Of those who agree with the statement, 11.17 percent have an eighth-grade education or less (row percent) and 53.49 percent of those with less than an eighth-grade education agree with the statement (column percent).

Notice that Table B.3 has six rows and five columns. We know that the value of our coefficients, for example, chi-square (χ^2), are a function of the number of cells in the table. There are only two people who strongly disagree with the "education to get ahead" statement. We can reduce the number of cells by excluding the "strongly disagree" respondents by using

```
IF q8 LE 5 ;
```

or by collapsing the categories such that the "strongly disagree" respondents would be grouped with the "disagree" respondents since they all disagree. This collapsing can be done by using an IF-THEN statement:

```
IF q8 = 6 THEN q8 = 5 ;
```

We could go even further and collapse the categories such that all who agree are in one category and all who disagree are in the other:

```
IF q8 = 1 OR q8 = 2 OR q8 = 3 THEN q8 = 1 ;
ELSE q8 = 2 ;
```

Often in social science research, we wish to examine the relationships among a subset of our respondents. In the PROC FREQ procedure, this can be accomplished by including a third (control) variable in the TABLES state-

Example of PROC FREQ (Cross-tabulation) Output

TABLE OF Q8 BY Q1

Q8(GOOD EDUCATION WAY TO GET AHEAD)   Q1(HIGHEST GRADE COMPLETED)

```
FREQUENCY       |
PERCENT         |
ROW PCT         |
COL PCT         |1-8     |9-11    |12      |13-15   |16      |  TOTAL
----------------+--------+--------+--------+--------+--------+
STRONGLY AGREE  |   14 | |  117 | |   99 | |   27 | |    2 | |    259
                |  2.67 | | 22.33 | | 18.89 | |  5.15 | |  0.38 | |  49.43
                |  5.41 | | 45.17 | | 38.22 | | 10.42 | |  0.77 | |
                | 32.56 | | 50.00 | | 51.03 | | 57.45 | | 33.33 | |
    ------------+--------+........+--------+--------+........+
AGREE             23        97 |    70 |    13 |     3 |    206
                4.39     18.51 | 13.36 |  2.48 |  0.57 |  39.31
               11.17     47.09 | 33.98 |  6.31 |  1.46 |
               53.49     41.45 | 36.08 | 27.66 | 50.00 |
    ------------+        .......+--------+--------+........+
SOMEWHAT AGREE  |    5 | |   10 | |   16 | |    4 | |    1 | |    36
                |  0.95 | |  1.91 | |  3.05 | |  0.76 | |  0.19 | |   6.87
                | 13.89 | | 27.78 | | 44.44 | | 11.11 | |  2.78 | |
                | 11.63 | |  4.27 | |  8.25 | |  8.51 | | 16.67 | |
    ------------+--------+--------+--------+--------+--------+
SOMEWHAT DISAGRE|    1 | |    1 | |    2 | |    2 | |    0 | |    6
                |  0.19 | |  0.19 | |  0.38 | |  0.38 | |  0.00 | |   1.15
                | 16.67 | | 16.67 | | 33.33 | | 33.33 | |  0.00 | |
                |  2.33 | |  0.43 | |  1.03 | |  4.26 | |  0.00 | |
    ------------+--------+--------+--------+--------+--------+
DISAGREE        |    0 | |    7 | |    7 | |    1 | |    0 | |    15
                |  0.00 | |  1.34 | |  1.34 | |  0.19 | |  0.00 | |   2.86
                |  0.00 | | 46.67 | | 46.67 | |  6.67 | |  0.00 | |
                |  0.00 | |  2.99 | |  3.61 | |  2.13 | |  0.00 | |
    ------------+--------+--------+--------+--------+--------+
DISAGREE STRONGL|    0 | |    2 | |    0 | |    0 | |    0 | |    2
                |  0.00 | |  0.38 | |  0.00 | |  0.00 | |  0.00 | |   0.38
                |  0.00 | |100.00 | |  0.00 | |  0.00 | |  0.00 | |
                |  0.00 | |  0.85 | |  0.00 | |  0.00 | |  0.00 | |
    ------------+--------+--------+--------+--------+--------+
TOTAL               43      234     194       47        6      524
                  8.21    44.66   37.02     8.97     1.15   100.00
```

FREQUENCY MISSING = 4

ment. However, if we are interested in only one category of the control variable (or if we are using a procedure that does not allow a method of control) the subsetting IF statement is the handiest way to segregate such a subset. We can use the subsetting IF and the IF-THEN statements together to select cases and collapse categories. For example, the runstream

```
IF q3 EQ 1 AND q4 EQ 2 ;
IF q8 = 0 OR q8 = 1 OR q8 = 2 OR q8 = 3 THEN q8 = 1 ;
ELSE q8 = 2 ;
PROC FREQ ;
TABLES q8 * q1 ;
RUN ;
```

will produce a table of married female respondents only. (Note that the variables in the subsetting IF command need not appear in the PROC FREQ procedure.)

Interval Measures.   The procedure PROC CORR, when no options are specified, calculates the Pearson product-moment correlation coefficient (Pearson's *r*), an association statistic appropriate for interval-level variables, and tests for the significance probability of the correlation. Its model form is

```
PROC CORR ;
VAR varname₁–varnameₙ ;
```

In most cases, these coefficients are equivalent to the Spearman rank-order coefficients produced by using the SPEARMAN option as appropriate for ordinal-ordinal, ordinal-interval, and interval-interval variables. If you desire both the Pearson correlations and the Spearman coefficients, you must specify both as options:

```
PROC CORR PEARSON SPEARMAN ;
VAR varname₁–varnameₙ ;
```

For our purposes, the following procedural step in our runstream:

```
PROC CORR ;
VAR happy work q5 q6 q20 q33 q34 ;
RUN ;
```

will produce a table showing the means, standard deviations, sums, minimums, and maximums of the variables and another table featuring the coefficients, the *N* on which the calculations were based, and the significance level. This is illustrated in Table B.4.

You may wish to plot a scatter diagram to visually assess the relationship between two of your variables. The procedure PROC PLOT will plot these relationships for you. The procedural step

```
PROC PLOT ;
VAR q5 * q6 ;
RUN ;
```

Table B.4
Example of PROC CORR (Correlation) Output

SUMS-OF-SQUARES AND CROSSPRODUCTS

	HAPPY	WORK	Q5	Q6	Q20	Q33	Q34
HAPPY	390435	124524	27497	336462	13415	57599808	466174
WORK	124524	48224	9660	119090	4772	19251774	154434
Q5	27497	9660	4725	38252	1013	4915438	34358
Q6	336462	119090	38252	481421	13000	53704812	404772
Q20	13415	4772	1013	13000	764	2159476	16842
Q33	57599808	19251774	4915438	53704812	2159476	1.6E+10	76521228
Q34	466174	154434	34358	404772	16842	76521228	710395

COVARIANCE MATRIX

	HAPPY	WORK	Q5	Q6	Q20	Q33	Q34
HAPPY	22.1121	1.92466	0.179322	-.394627	-.204641	-680.33	-8.98469
WORK	1.92466	11.6457	-.346836	-1.16909	0.229363	-668.59	-16.9834
Q5	0.179322	-.346836	4.99877	7.77246	-.012517	2083.81	6.64379
Q6	-.394627	-1.16909	7.77246	112.832	0.559683	2407.63	8.63426
Q20	-.204641	0.229363	-.012517	0.559683	0.413425	111.6	-1.19028
Q33	-680.33	-668.59	2083.81	2407.63	111.6	13560932	3812.14
Q34	-8.98469	-16.9834	6.64379	8.63426	-1.19028	3812.14	149.869

VARIABLE	N	MEAN	STD DEV	SUM	MINIMUM	MAXIMUM
HAPPY	497	27.63179074	4.70235393	13733.000000	12.00000000	40.00000000
WORK	528	8.92803030	3.41257446	4714.000000	0.00000000	12.00000000
Q5	343	2.96501458	2.23579347	1017.000000	1.00000000	14.00000000
Q6	356	35.21067416	10.62221953	12535.000000	4.00000000	80.00000000
Q20	471	1.09978769	0.64298172	518.000000	0.00000000	8.00000000
Q33	503	4360.50894632	3682.51708199	2193336.000000	300.00000000	38708.00000000
Q34	523	34.76673040	12.24209348	18183.000000	18.00000000	67.00000000

Table B.4 (*continued*)

PEARSON CORRELATION COEFFICIENTS / PROB > |R| UNDER H0:RHO=0 / NUMBER OF OBSERVATIONS

	HAPPY	WORK	Q5	Q6	Q20	Q33	Q34
HAPPY	1.00000	0.12105	0.01763	-0.00831	-0.06633	-0.03912	-0.15671
LEVEL OF SELF-HAPPINESS	0.0000	0.0069	0.7500	0.8785	0.1634	0.3954	0.0005
	497	497	329	341	443	474	493
WORK	0.12105	1.00000	-0.05555	-0.03782	0.10749	-0.05361	-0.41251
DESIRE AND AVAILABILITY TO WORK	0.0069	0.0000	0.3050	0.4769	0.0196	0.2301	0.0001
	497	528	343	356	471	503	523
Q5	0.01763	-0.05555	1.00000	0.32463	-0.00892	0.24433	0.28134
WEEKLY TAKE HOME PAY CURRENT/LAST JOB	0.7500	0.3050	0.0000	0.0001	0.8757	0.0001	0.0001
	329	343	343	342	310	328	339
Q6	-0.00831	-0.03782	0.32463	1.00000	0.08252	0.05801	0.07436
HOURS WORKED PER WEEK CURRENT/LAST JOB	0.8785	0.4769	0.0001	0.0000	0.1395	0.2869	0.1639
	341	356	342	356	322	339	352
Q20	-0.06633	0.10749	-0.00892	0.08252	1.00000	0.04972	-0.16362
NUMBER OF TIMES ON WELFARE	0.1634	0.0196	0.8757	0.1395	0.0000	0.2931	0.0004
	443	471	310	322	471	449	466
Q33	-0.03912	-0.05361	0.24433	0.05801	0.04972	1.00000	0.08632
TOTAL ANNUAL INCOME--ALL SOURCES	0.3954	0.2301	0.0001	0.2869	0.2931	0.0000	0.0540
	474	503	328	339	449	503	499
Q34	-0.15671	-0.41251	0.28134	0.07436	-0.16362	0.08632	1.00000
AGE OF RESPONDENT	0.0005	0.0001	0.0001	0.1639	0.0004	0.0540	0.0000
	493	523	339	352	466	499	523

will produce the output graphically, displaying the relationship between hours worked per week and take-home pay.

Multivariate Analysis (Chapter 17)

The three major functions of multivariate analysis, as we learned in Chapter 17, are control, interpretation, and prediction. Mechanically, the first two functions are covered by using control variables in the equations; the procedures PROC FREQ and PROC CORR can provide for these controls. Prediction is enhanced by the procedure PROC REG.

Multivariate Cross-tabulations. The basic format of the PROC FREQ procedure has already been presented. The portion in brackets indicates the control variable(s). For instance, when controlling for the variable Q4, "gender of respondent,'' the resultant output from an executed PROC FREQ step will consist of two tables having the same dependent and independent variables but differing as to respondents' gender: for the first table, all cases reported will be men, and for the second, they will all be women.

Partial Correlations. Partial correlations are conceptually similar to multivariate cross-tabulations in that the effects of other variables are controlled when analyzing the relationship between the original variables. However, whereas cross-tabulating with the procedure PROC FREQ physically removes the effects by partitioning the cases based on the values of the control, the procedure PROC CORR with an attendant PARTIAL statement statistically removes the effects. This difference can be very important when controlling for more than one variable because separation reduces the cell frequencies. Thus when the analysis involves interval-level variables, the use of PROC CORR with a PARTIAL statement is indicated.

The following lines in your command file:

```
PROC CORR ;
VAR work q34 ;
PARTIAL happy q33 ;
RUN ;
```

will produce output consisting of simple statistics and corrected sum-of-squares and cross-products for all four variables and partial corrected sum-of-squares and cross-products, a partial covariance matrix, and partial Pearson correlations for the variables ''work'' and ''q34.''

Regression (Multiple Relationships). Often there are a number of independent variables, each of which is hypothesized to contribute to the explained variance of a single dependent variable. PROC REG is the SAS procedure that handles such simultaneous effects.

The bare specifications for a PROC REG step consist of the keywords PROC REG followed by a semicolon (;); a MODEL statement wherein each dependent variable is specified, followed by an equal sign ($=$), the independent variable(s), and a semicolon (;); and the RUN command followed by a semicolon (;):

```
PROC REG ;
MODEL depvar = indvar₁ indvar₂ . . . indvarₙ ;
RUN ;
```

This sequence furnishes output that consists of an analysis-of-variance table, parameter estimates, and other statistics including the square root of the mean square error, the mean of the dependent variable, the coefficient of variation, R^2, and the adjusted R^2.

For our purposes, here is the actual procedural step used to produce the output in Table B.5. The variable ''happy'' used in the variable list was computed using a technique that will be described shortly.

Table B.5
Example of PROC REG (Regression) Output

DESCRIPTIVE STATISTICS

VARIABLE	SUM	MEAN	UNCORRECTED SS
Q5	998.00000	2.95266272	4598.0000
Q6	11858.00000	35.08284024	454174.0000
Q34	10862.00000	32.13609467	387548.0000
INTERCEP	338.00000	1.00000000	338.0000

VARIABLE	VARIANCE	STD DEVIATION
Q5	4.8998297	2.21355589
Q6	113.2394079	10.64140066
Q34	114.2010078	10.68648716
INTERCEP	0.0000000	0.00000000

SUMS OF SQUARES AND CROSSPRODUCTS

SSCP	Q5	Q6	Q34	INTERCEP
Q5	4598	37566	34323	998
Q6	37566	454174	384079	11858
Q34	34323	384079	387548	10862
INTERCEP	998	11858	10862	338

SEQUENTIAL PARAMETER ESTIMATES

```
INTERCEP  2.95266
Q6        0.605337 .0669081
Q34       -.968664 .0626821 .0535927
```

DEP VARIABLE: Q5   WEEKLY TAKE HOME PAY CURRENT/LAST JOB
ANALYSIS OF VARIANCE

SOURCE	DF	SUM OF SQUARES	MEAN SQUARE	F VALUE	PROB>F
MODEL	2	280.69455	140.34727	34.305	0.0001
ERROR	335	1370.54806	4.09´18823		
C TOTAL	337	1651.24260			

ROOT MSE	2.022669	R-SQUARE	0.1700
DEP MEAN	2.952663	ADJ R-SQ	0.1650
C.V.	68.5032		

PARAMETER ESTIMATES

VARIABLE	DF	PARAMETER ESTIMATE	STANDARD ERROR	T FOR HO: PARAMETER=0	PROB > |T|
INTERCEP	1	-0.96866436	0.48612665	-1.993	0.0471
Q6	1	0.06268211	0.01038613	6.035	0.0001
Q34	1	0.05359271	0.01034232	5.182	0.0001

VARIABLE	DF	TYPE I SS	TYPE II SS	STANDARDIZED ESTIMATE	TOLERANCE
INTERCEP	1	2946.75740	16.24415911	0	
Q6	1	170.83815	149.01460	0.30133664	0.99383445
Q34	1	109.85640	109.85640	0.25873204	0.99383445

VARIABLE	DF	VARIANCE INFLATION	VARIABLE LABEL
INTERCEP	1	0	INTERCEPT
Q6	1	1.00620380	HOURS WORKED PER WEEK CURRENT/LAST JOB
Q34	1	1.00620380	AGE OF RESPONDENT

COVARIANCE OF ESTIMATES

COVB	INTERCEP	Q6	Q34
INTERCEP	0.2363191	-0.0035134	-0.00314148
Q6	-0.0035134	0.0001078718	-.0000084345
Q34	-0.00314148	-.0000084345	0.0001069635

CORRELATION OF ESTIMATES

CORRB	INTERCEP	Q6	Q34
INTERCEP	1.0000	-0.6959	-0.6248
Q6	-0.6959	1.0000	-0.0785
Q34	-0.6248	-0.0785	1.0000

COLLINEARITY DIAGNOSTICS

NUMBER	EIGENVALUE	CONDITION NUMBER	VAR PROP INTERCEP	VAR PROP Q6	VAR PROP Q34
1	2.881175	1.000000	0.0060	0.0096	0.0113
2	0.084940	5.824095	0.0032	0.4363	0.6401
3	0.033885	9.221023	0.9908	0.5541	0.3487

```
PROC REG SIMPLE USSCP;
MODEL q5 = q6 q34 / SS1 SS2 STB TOL VIF COVB
                CORRB SEQB COLLIN;
RUN;
```

As you can see, several options were included in our step. On the first line, the option SIMPLE provides descriptive statistics for all variables used, and the option USSCP prints the uncorrected sums-of-squares and cross-products for all variables. In the MODEL statement, if options are specified, they must follow a slash (/) occurring after the required model specifications. The option ss1 prints the sequential sum of squares, ss2 prints the partial sum of squares, STB prints standardized regression coefficients, TOL prints the tolerance values of the estimate, VIF prints variance inflation factors, COVB prints the estimated covariance matrix, CORRB prints the correlation matrix of the estimates, SEQB prints a sequence of parameter estimates, and COLLIN prints collinearity diagnostics. Had we used the option ALL in the model statement instead of specifying individual options, the output would have consisted of all the options just cited (except VIF and COLLIN) plus many more.

Measurement: Scale and Index Construction (Chapter 18)

In Chapter 18, we discussed methods for measuring respondents' attitudes. We tapped these attitudes by constructing scales and indexes with indicators of particular attitudes. SAS has the facility to assist in a variety of ways in the construction of unidimensional and multidimensional scales. Students are encouraged to explore options in factor analysis (PROC FACTOR) as their expertise in methodology and statistics increases. However, for purposes of this treatment, we will only explore some options in computing, constructing, and recoding variables.

Often in social science research, it is convenient to create or transform variables, for example, by weighting, percapitizing, or otherwise performing mathematical operations on existing variables. The assignment statement is probably the simplest and most useful method in the SAS System to satisfy these needs. The model form of the statement is quite simple in that you use logical mathematical expressions to create your composite measures. For instance, you can add ($+$), subtract ($-$), multiply ($*$), divide ($/$), and exponentiate ($**N$). It is also quite flexible in that the operands may be variable names, real numbers, or integers. The general form of the assignment statement used for computing a new variable or recomputing an old one is

variable = arithmetic expression;

If you compute new variables or indexes and use them in the context of a permanent DATA step, the computed variables become permanent variables added to your data set file. When new variables are computed, cases with missing data on any variable-operand will be assigned a missing value (.).

For our regression procedure, PROC REG, we computed a new variable, "happy," a scale that measures respondents' overall happiness. This variable is a combination of the responses recorded in Q10 through Q19. In computing this variable, we assume that happiness is a unidimensional concept and that all of these variables contribute equally to the concept (i.e., that they are equally weighted). We can then place our respondents on a continuum between "not happy" and "very happy," with a low score on the scale indicating unhappiness and a high score happiness. First, we have to be sure that all the component variables are coded in the same direction, that is, that a high value on any one of the variables indicates a happy response. In our example, low scores on Q10, Q11, Q17, Q18, and Q19 but high scores on all the rest indicate happiness. Therefore, we have to use a sequence of statements to recode the values on Q10, Q11, Q17, Q18, and Q19 to be consistent with the other component variables. The following ARRAY statement, iterative DO loop, and assignment statements were used to create "happy":

```
ARRAY record{5} q10 q11 q17 q18 q19;
DO count = 1 to 5;
recode {count} = 5-recode{count};
END;
happy = q10 + q11 + q12 + q13 + q14 + q15 + q16 + q17 + q18 + q19;
```

Briefly, the ARRAY statement groups the selected variables for processing under a single name, in this case RECODE{N}, where RECODE{1} = Q10, RECODE{2} = Q11, and so on. The {N} in the ARRAY statement is called the subscript—here, 5 represents the number of variables that are being grouped under the RECODE{N} name form. The iterative DO loop causes all statements between the DO and END statements to be executed repetitively, in this case, five times (COUNT = 1 to 5). When COUNT = 1, RECODE{1}, or Q10, is recoded; when COUNT = 2, RECODE{2}, Q11, is recoded; and so forth. The arithmetic expression 5 – RECODE{COUNT} flips all the values of the variables being recoded (e.g., if the value of RECODE{N} is 1, the assignment becomes 4; if the value of RECODE{N} is 2, the assignment value becomes 3).

This programming sequence for recoding variables is rather sophisticated but extremely useful and timesaving when a large number of variables are being recoded identically. As an alternative (and one you should use if you are uncomfortable with the one just given), you can use as many IF-THEN statements as you need to accomplish the same recoding task:

```
IF q10 = 1 THEN q10 = 4;
IF q11 = 1 THEN q11 = 4;
IF q17 = 1 THEN q17 = 4;
. . .
IF q10 = 4 THEN q10 = 1;
IF q11 = 4 THEN q11 = 1;
IF q17 = 4 THEN q17 = 1;
. . .
```

IF-THEN statements are especially useful when constructing typologies using nominal or ordinal variables (or both). The form of the IF-THEN statement was discussed earlier. Let's say that you wish to construct a measure of the socioeconomic status of your respondents. You can use IF-THEN statements for this purpose:

```
IF q1 EQ 1 AND q33 LT 5000 THEN ses = 1 ;
IF q1 GE 2 AND q1 LT 4 AND q33 LT 5000 THEN ses = 2 ;
[proceed until all combinations have been exhausted] ;
```

where SES is the constructed measure of socioeconomic status and a value of 1 represents a lowest value, a value of 2 represents a low value, and so on. You can also assign labels to these values using the PROC FORMAT procedure and FORMAT statement as previously discussed.

Note that you need to consider all possible combinations of your component variables. In other words, the typology must be mutually exclusive and exhaustive—every respondent must be able to be classified under a type, but in one category only. Also note that you can code different combinations into the same one, such as medium education and low income. In this case, both categories receive the same code.

Notes for PC Users

SAS is available on PCs. It is recommended that you have an IBM AT, IBM PS2, or compatible to accept the software package. The most recent version is Release 6.03.[16] All the commands and procedures in PC SAS are the same as for SAS on the mainframe. You can build runstreams using either a front-end menu or a text editor. Function keys, as well as typed and entered commands, can initiate runs.

Conclusion

The SAS System and other statistical package manuals may seem complicated and imposing on first inspection. This appendix was designed to assist you in taking that first big step into computerized data analysis. We hope that this treatment will encourage researchers to pick and choose portions of those packages that lend themselves to their data needs and methodological expertise. A package like SAS has many capabilities and potentials that grow with the abilities of the individual researcher. Thus we encourage you to explore these potentials with the help of the manual as your skills increase.

16. The introductory manual supporting this package is SAS Institute Inc., *SAS Introductory Guide for Personal Computers, Release 6.03 Edition* (Cary, N.C.: SAS Institute Inc., 1988).

APPENDIX C Σ: The Summation Sign

In statistics, it is frequently necessary to make use of formulas involving sums of numerous quantities. As a shorthand substitute for writing out each of these sums at length, the Greek letter Σ (capital sigma), which means to summate or add, is used. As a rule, whenever Σ appears, it means that *all* quantities appearing to the right of it should be summed.

If we want to add ten scores, we can always write

$$X_1 + X_2 + X_3 + X_4 + X_5 + X_6 + X_7 + X_8 + X_9 + X_{10}$$

or the same expression can be shortened to

$$X_1 + X_2 + \cdots + X_{10}$$

which means the same thing. The three dots ($\cdot \cdot \cdot$) mean "and so on." This same instruction may be put in still another way:

$$\sum_{i=1}^{10} X_i$$

Σ instructs us to add up everything that follows (X_i), starting with the case specified below the symbol ($i = 1$) and ending with the case specified above (10). This example may be read as follows: add up (Σ) all the observations (X_i) ranging from the first ($i = 1$) through the tenth (10). If we want only to sum the observations 4 and 5 ($X_4 + X_5$), we can write

$$\sum_{i=4}^{5} X_i$$

and if we wish to indicate that all of some unspecified number of cases should be added together, we can use N to symbolize the unspecified number of cases and write

$$\sum_{i=1}^{N} X_i$$

This says to sum all the observations from the first to the Nth; it is a general instruction for the addition of all cases regardless of their number. When

527

this general instruction is intended, and when the range of values to be summed is obvious, it is customary to omit the notation of limits and write

$$\sum X_i$$

or even

$$\sum X$$

This indicates that the summation is to extend over all cases under consideration.

Rules for the Use of Σ

There are a number of rules for the use of Σ. For example,

$$\sum_{i=1}^{N} (X_i + Y_i) = \sum_{i=1}^{N} X_i + \sum_{i=1}^{N} Y_i$$

which says that the summation of the sum of the two variables (X and Y) is equal to the sum of their summations. It makes no difference whether one adds each X_i to each Y_i and then sums their total from 1 to N or sums all X_i and then all Y_i and adds their sums; the result is the same.

Another rule is expressed in the following equation:

$$\sum_{i=1}^{N} kX_i = k\sum_{i=1}^{N} X_i$$

A constant k may be moved across the summation sign. That is to say, if we are instructed to multiply each of a series of numbers by a constant

$$kX_1 + kX_2 + \cdots + kX_N$$

we can simply sum our numbers and multiply that sum by the constant; the result is the same.

A third rule is the following:

$$\sum_{i=1}^{N} k = kN$$

The summation of a constant is equal to the product of that constant and the number of times it is summed.

Another rule states that

$$\left(\sum_{i=1}^{N} X_i\right)^2 = (X_1 + X_2 + \cdots + X_N)^2$$
$$= X_1^2 + X_2^2 + \cdots + X_N^2 + 2X_1X_2$$
$$+ 2X_1X_3 + \cdots + 2X_{N-1}X_N$$
$$\neq X_1^2 + X_2^2 + \cdots + X_N^2$$

That is, we must distinguish between

$$\sum_{i=1}^{N} X_i^2$$

and

$$\left(\sum_{i=1}^{N} X_i\right)^2$$

APPENDIX D   Random Digits

Line/Col.	(1)	(2)	(3)	(4)	(5)	(6)	(7)	(8)	(9)	(10)	(11)	(12)	(13)	(14)
1	10480	15011	01536	02011	81647	91646	69179	14194	62590	36207	20969	99570	91291	90700
2	22368	46573	25595	85393	30995	89198	27982	53402	93965	34095	52666	19174	39615	99505
3	24130	48360	22527	97265	76393	64809	15179	24830	49340	32081	30680	19655	63348	58629
4	42167	93093	06243	61680	07856	16376	39440	53537	71341	57004	00849	74917	97758	16379
5	37570	39975	81837	16656	06121	91782	60468	81305	49684	60672	14110	06927	01263	54613
6	77921	06907	11008	42751	27756	53498	18602	70659	90655	15053	21916	81825	44394	42880
7	99562	72905	56420	69994	98872	31016	71194	18738	44013	48840	63213	21069	10634	12952
8	96301	91977	05463	07972	18876	20922	94595	56869	69014	60045	18425	84903	42508	32307
9	89579	14342	63661	10281	17453	18103	57740	84378	25331	12566	58678	44947	05585	56941
10	85475	36857	53342	53988	53060	59533	38867	62300	08158	17983	16439	11458	18593	64952
11	28918	69578	88231	33276	70997	79936	56865	05859	90106	31595	01547	85590	91610	78188
12	63553	40961	48235	03427	49626	69445	18663	72695	52180	20847	12234	90511	33703	90322
13	09429	93969	52636	92737	88974	33488	36320	17617	30015	08272	84115	27156	30613	74952
14	10365	61129	87529	85689	48237	52267	67689	93394	01511	26358	85104	20285	29975	89868
15	07119	97336	71048	08178	77233	13916	47564	81056	97735	85977	29372	74461	28551	90707
16	51085	12765	51821	51259	77452	16308	60756	92144	49442	53900	70960	63990	75601	40719
17	02368	21382	52404	60268	89368	19885	55322	44819	01188	65255	64835	44919	05944	55157
18	01011	54092	33362	94904	31273	04146	18594	29852	71585	85030	51132	01915	92747	64951
19	52162	53916	46369	58586	23216	14513	83149	98736	23495	64350	94738	17752	35156	35749
20	07056	97628	33787	09998	42698	06691	76988	13602	51851	46104	88916	19509	25625	58104
21	48663	91245	85828	14346	09172	30168	90229	04734	59193	22178	30421	61666	99904	32812
22	54164	58492	22421	74103	47070	25306	76468	26384	58151	06646	21524	15227	96909	44592
23	32639	32363	05597	24200	13363	38005	94342	28728	35806	06912	17012	64161	18296	22851
24	29334	27001	87637	87308	58731	00256	45834	15398	46557	41135	10367	07684	36188	18510
25	02488	33062	28834	07351	19731	92420	60952	61280	50001	67658	32586	86679	50720	94953

26	81525	72295	04839	96423	24878	82651	66566	14778	76797	14780	13300	87074	79666	95725
27	29676	20591	68086	26432	46901	20849	89768	81536	86645	12659	92259	57102	80428	25280
28	00742	57392	39064	66432	84673	40027	32832	61362	98947	96067	64760	64584	96096	98253
29	05366	04213	25669	26422	44407	44048	37937	63904	45766	66134	75470	66520	34693	90449
30	91921	26418	64117	94305	26766	25940	39972	22209	71500	64568	91402	42416	07844	69618
31	00582	04711	87917	77341	42206	35126	74087	99547	81817	42607	43808	76655	62028	76630
32	00725	69884	62797	56170	86324	88072	76222	36086	84637	93161	76038	65855	77919	88006
33	69011	65795	95876	55293	18088	27354	26575	08625	40801	59920	29841	80150	12777	48501
34	25976	57948	29888	88604	67917	48708	18912	82271	65424	69774	33611	54262	85963	03547
35	09763	83473	73577	12908	30883	18317	28290	35797	05998	41688	34952	37888	38917	88050
36	91567	42595	27958	30134	04024	86385	29880	99730	55536	84855	29080	09250	79656	73211
37	17955	56349	90999	49127	20044	59931	06115	20542	18059	02008	73708	83517	36103	42791
38	46503	18584	18845	49618	02304	51038	20655	58727	28168	15475	56942	53389	20562	87338
39	92157	89634	94824	78171	84610	82834	09922	25417	44137	48413	25555	21246	35509	20468
40	14577	62765	35605	81263	39667	47358	56873	56307	61607	49518	89656	20103	77490	18062
41	98427	07523	33362	64270	01638	92477	66969	98420	04880	45585	46565	04102	46880	45709
42	34914	63976	88720	82765	34476	17032	87589	40836	32427	70002	70663	88803	77775	69348
43	70060	28277	39475	46473	23219	53416	94970	25832	69975	94884	19661	72828	00102	66794
44	53976	54914	06990	67245	68350	82948	11398	42878	80287	88267	47363	46634	06541	97809
45	76072	29515	40980	07391	58745	25774	22987	80059	39911	96189	41151	14222	60697	59583
46	90725	52210	83974	29992	65831	38857	50490	83765	55657	14361	31720	57375	56228	41546
47	64364	67412	33339	31926	14883	24413	59744	92351	97473	89286	35931	04110	23726	51900
48	08962	00358	31662	25388	61642	34072	81249	35648	56891	69352	48373	45578	78547	81788
49	95012	68379	93526	70765	10592	04542	76463	54328	02349	17247	28865	14777	62730	92277
50	15664	10493	20492	38391	91132	21999	59516	81652	27195	48223	46751	22923	32261	85653

Appendix D (continued)

Line/Col.	(1)	(2)	(3)	(4)	(5)	(6)	(7)	(8)	(9)	(10)	(11)	(12)	(13)	(14)
51	16408	81899	04153	53381	79401	21438	83035	92350	36693	31238	59649	91754	72772	02338
52	18629	81953	05520	91962	04739	13092	97662	24822	94730	06496	35090	04822	86774	98289
53	73115	35101	47498	87637	99016	71060	88824	71013	18735	20286	23153	72924	35165	43040
54	57491	16703	23167	49323	45021	33132	12544	41035	80780	45393	44812	12515	98931	91202
55	30405	83946	23792	14422	15059	45799	22716	19792	09983	74353	68668	30429	70735	25499
56	16631	35006	85900	98275	32388	52390	16815	69298	82732	38480	73817	32523	41961	44437
57	96773	20206	42559	78985	05300	22164	24369	54224	35083	19687	11052	91491	60383	19746
58	38935	64202	14349	82674	66523	44133	00697	35552	35970	19124	63318	29686	03387	59846
59	31624	76384	17403	53363	44167	64486	64758	75366	76554	31601	12614	33072	60332	92325
60	78919	19474	23632	27889	47914	02584	37680	20801	72152	39339	34806	08930	85001	87820
61	03931	33309	57047	74211	63445	17361	62825	39908	05607	91284	68833	25570	38818	46920
62	74426	33278	43972	10119	89917	15665	52872	73823	73144	88662	88970	74492	51805	99378
63	09066	00903	20795	95452	92648	45454	09552	88815	16553	51125	79375	97596	16296	66092
64	42238	12426	87025	14267	20979	04508	64535	31355	86064	29472	47689	05974	52468	16834
65	16153	08002	26504	41744	81959	65642	74240	56302	00033	67107	77510	70625	28725	34191
66	21457	40742	29820	96783	29400	21840	15035	34537	33310	06116	95240	15957	16572	06004
67	21581	57802	02050	89728	17937	37621	47075	42080	97403	48626	68995	43805	33386	21597
68	55612	78095	83197	33732	05810	24813	86902	60397	16489	03264	88525	42786	05269	92532
69	44657	66999	99324	51281	84463	60563	79312	93454	68876	25471	93911	25650	12682	73572
70	91340	84979	46949	81973	37949	61023	43997	15263	80644	43942	89203	71795	99533	50501
71	91227	21199	31935	27022	84067	05462	35216	14436	29891	68607	41867	14951	91696	85065
72	50001	38140	66321	19924	72163	09538	12151	06878	91903	18749	34405	56087	82790	70925
73	65390	05224	72958	28609	81406	39147	25549	48542	42627	45233	57202	94617	23772	07896
74	27504	96131	83944	41575	10573	08619	64482	73923	36152	05184	94142	25299	84387	34925
75	37169	94851	39117	89632	00959	16487	65536	49071	39782	17095	02330	74301	00275	48280

76	11508	70225	51111	38351	19444	66499	71945	05422	13442	78675	84081	66938	93654	59894
77	37449	30362	06694	54690	04052	53115	62757	95348	78662	11163	81651	50245	34971	52924
78	46515	70331	85922	38329	57015	15765	97161	17869	45349	61796	66345	81073	49106	79860
79	30986	81223	42416	58353	21532	30502	32305	86482	05174	07901	54339	58861	74818	46942
80	63798	64995	46583	09785	44160	78128	83991	42865	92520	83531	80377	35909	81250	54238
81	82486	84846	99254	67632	43218	50076	21361	64816	51202	88124	41870	52689	51275	83556
82	21885	32906	92431	09060	64297	51674	64126	62570	26123	05155	59194	52799	28225	85762
83	60336	98782	07408	53458	13564	59089	26445	29789	85205	41001	12535	12133	14645	23541
84	43937	46891	24010	25560	86355	33941	25786	54990	71899	15475	95434	98227	21824	19585
85	97656	63175	89303	16275	07100	92063	21942	18611	47348	20203	18534	03862	78095	50136
86	03299	01221	05418	38982	55758	92237	26759	86367	21216	98442	08303	56613	91511	75928
87	79626	06486	03574	17668	07785	76020	79924	25651	83325	88428	85076	72811	22717	50585
88	85636	68335	47539	03129	65651	11977	02510	26113	99447	68645	34327	15152	55230	93448
89	18039	14367	61337	06177	12143	46609	32989	74014	64708	00533	35398	58408	13261	47908
90	08362	15656	60627	36478	65648	16764	53412	09013	07832	41574	17639	82163	60859	75567
91	79556	29068	04142	16268	15387	12856	66227	38358	22478	73373	88732	09443	62558	05250
92	92608	82674	27072	32534	17075	27698	98204	63863	11951	34648	88022	56148	34925	57031
93	23982	25835	40055	67006	12293	02753	14827	23235	35071	99704	37543	11601	35503	85171
94	09915	96306	05908	97901	28395	14186	00821	80703	70426	75647	76310	88717	37890	40129
95	59037	33300	26695	62247	69927	76123	50842	43834	86654	70959	79725	93872	28117	19233
96	42488	78077	69882	61657	34136	79180	97526	43092	04098	73571	80799	76536	71255	64239
97	46764	86273	63003	93017	31204	36692	40202	35275	57306	55543	53203	18098	47625	88684
98	03237	45430	55417	63282	90816	17349	88298	90183	36600	78406	06216	95787	42579	90730
99	86591	81482	52667	61582	14972	90053	89534	76036	49199	43716	97548	04379	46370	28672
100	38534	01715	94964	87288	65680	43772	39560	12918	86537	62738	19636	51132	25739	56947

Abridged from William H. Beyer, ed., *Handbook of Tables for Probability and Statistics*, 2d ed. (Cleveland: Chemical Rubber Company, 1968). Copyright © The Chemical Rubber Co., CRC Press, Inc. Reprinted with permission.

APPENDIX E   Areas under the Normal Curve

Fractional parts of the total area (10,000) under the normal curve, corresponding to distances between the mean and ordinates that are Z standard deviation units from the mean.

Z	.00	.01	.02	.03	.04	.05	.06	.07	.08	.09
0.0	0000	0040	0080	0120	0159	0199	0239	0279	0319	0359
0.1	0398	0438	0478	0517	0557	0596	0636	0675	0714	0753
0.2	0793	0832	0871	0910	0948	0987	1026	1064	1103	1141
0.3	1179	1217	1255	1293	1331	1368	1406	1443	1480	1517
0.4	1554	1591	1628	1664	1700	1736	1772	1808	1844	1879
0.5	1915	1950	1985	2019	2054	2088	2123	2157	2190	2224
0.6	2257	2291	2324	2357	2389	2422	2454	2486	2518	2549
0.7	2580	2612	2642	2673	2704	2734	2764	2794	2823	2852
0.8	2881	2910	2939	2967	2995	3023	3051	3078	3106	3133
0.9	3159	3186	3212	3238	3264	3289	3315	3340	3365	3389
1.0	3413	3438	3461	3485	3508	3531	3554	3577	3599	3621
1.1	3643	3665	3686	3718	3729	3749	3770	3790	3810	3830
1.2	3849	3869	3888	3907	3925	3944	3962	3980	3997	4015
1.3	4032	4049	4066	4083	4099	4115	4131	4147	4162	4177
1.4	4192	4207	4222	4236	4251	4265	4279	4292	4306	4319
1.5	4332	4345	4357	4370	4382	4394	4406	4418	4430	4441
1.6	4452	4463	4474	4485	4495	4505	4515	4525	4535	4545
1.7	4554	4564	4573	4582	4591	4599	4608	4616	4625	4633
1.8	4641	4649	4656	4664	4671	4678	4686	4693	4699	4706
1.9	4713	4719	4726	4732	4738	4744	4750	4758	4762	4767
2.0	4773	4778	4783	4788	4793	4798	4803	4808	4812	4817
2.1	4821	4826	4830	4834	4838	4842	4846	4850	4854	4857
2.2	4861	4865	4868	4871	4875	4878	4881	4884	4887	4890
2.3	4893	4896	4898	4901	4904	4906	4909	4911	4913	4916
2.4	4918	4920	4922	4925	4927	4929	4931	4932	4934	4936
2.5	4938	4940	4941	4943	4945	4946	4948	4949	4951	4952
2.6	4953	4955	4956	4957	4959	4960	4961	4962	4963	4964
2.7	4965	4966	4967	4968	4969	4970	4971	4972	4973	4974
2.8	4974	4975	4976	4977	4977	4978	4979	4980	4980	4981
2.9	4981	4982	4983	4984	4984	4984	4985	4985	4986	4986
3.0	4986.5	4987	4987	4988	4988	4988	4989	4989	4989	4990
3.1	4990.0	4991	4991	4991	4992	4992	4992	4992	4993	4994
3.2	4993.129									
3.3	4995.166									
3.4	4996.631									
3.5	4997.674									
3.6	4998.409									
3.7	4998.922									
3.8	4999.277									
3.9	4999.519									
4.0	4999.683									
4.5	499.966									
5.0	4999.997133									

From Harold O. Rugg, *Statistical Methods Applied to Education* (Boston: Houghton Mifflin, 1917), pp. 389–390. Reprinted by permission of the publisher.

APPENDIX F   Distribution of *t*

df	Level of significance for one-tailed test					
	.10	.05	.025	.01	.005	.0005
	Level of significance for two-tailed test					
	.20	.10	.05	.02	.01	.001
1	3.078	6.314	12.706	31.821	63.657	636.619
2	1.886	2.920	4.303	6.965	9.925	31.598
3	1.638	2.353	3.182	4.541	5.841	12.941
4	1.533	2.132	2.776	3.747	4.604	8.610
5	1.476	2.015	2.571	3.365	4.032	6.859
6	1.440	1.943	2.447	3.143	3.707	5.959
7	1.415	1.895	2.365	2.998	3.499	5.405
8	1.397	1.860	2.306	2.896	3.355	5.041
9	1.383	1.833	2.262	2.821	3.250	4.781
10	1.372	1.812	2.228	2.764	3.169	4.587
11	1.363	1.796	2.201	2.718	3.106	4.437
12	1.356	1.782	2.179	2.681	3.055	4.318
13	1.350	1.771	2.160	2.650	3.012	4.221
14	1.345	1.761	2.145	2.624	2.977	4.140
15	1.341	1.753	2.131	2.602	2.947	4.073
16	1.337	1.746	2.120	2.583	2.921	4.015
17	1.333	1.740	2.110	2.567	2.898	3.965
18	1.330	1.734	2.101	2.552	2.878	3.922
19	1.328	1.729	2.093	2.539	2.861	3.883
20	1.325	1.725	2.086	2.528	2.845	3.850
21	1.323	1.721	2.080	2.518	2.831	3.819
22	1.321	1.717	2.074	2.508	2.819	3.792
23	1.319	1.714	2.069	2.500	2.807	3.767
24	1.318	1.711	2.064	2.492	2.797	3.745
25	1.316	1.708	2.060	2.485	2.787	3.725
26	1.315	1.706	2.056	2.479	2.779	3.707
27	1.314	1.703	2.052	2.473	2.771	3.690
28	1.313	1.701	2.048	2.467	2.763	3.674
29	1.311	1.699	2.045	2.462	2.756	3.659
30	1.310	1.697	2.042	2.457	2.750	3.646
40	1.303	1.684	2.021	2.423	2.704	3.551
60	1.296	1.671	2.000	2.390	2.660	3.460
120	1.289	1.658	1.980	2.358	2.617	3.373
∞	1.282	1.645	1.960	2.326	2.576	3.291

Abridged from R. A. Fisher and F. Yates, *Statistical Tables for Biological, Agricultural and Medical Research*, 6th ed. (London: Longman, 1974), tab. III. Used by permission of the authors and Longman Group Ltd.

APPENDIX G   Critical Values of F

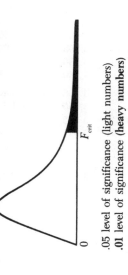

0   F_{crit}

.05 level of significance (light numbers)
.01 level of significance (heavy numbers)

Degrees of Freedom in Numerator

Degrees of Freedom in Denominator	1	2	3	4	5	6	7	8	9	10	11	12	14	16	20	24	30	40	50	75	100	200	500	∞
1	161	200	216	225	230	234	237	239	241	242	243	244	245	246	248	249	250	251	252	253	253	254	254	254
	4,052	4,999	5,403	5,625	5,764	5,859	5,928	5,981	6,022	6,056	6,082	6,106	6,142	6,169	6,208	6,234	6,258	6,286	6,302	6,323	6,334	6,352	6,361	6,366
2	18.51	19.00	19.16	19.25	19.30	19.33	19.36	19.37	19.38	19.39	19.40	19.41	19.42	19.43	19.44	19.45	19.46	19.47	19.47	19.48	19.49	19.49	19.50	19.50
	98.49	99.00	99.17	99.25	99.30	99.33	99.34	99.36	99.38	99.40	99.41	99.42	99.43	99.44	99.45	99.46	99.47	99.48	99.48	99.49	99.49	99.49	99.50	99.50
3	10.13	9.55	9.28	9.12	9.01	8.94	8.88	8.84	8.81	8.78	8.76	8.74	8.71	8.69	8.66	8.64	8.62	8.60	8.58	8.57	8.56	8.54	8.54	8.53
	34.12	30.82	29.46	28.71	28.24	27.91	27.67	27.49	27.34	27.23	27.13	27.05	26.92	26.83	26.69	26.60	26.50	26.41	26.35	26.27	26.23	26.18	26.14	26.12
4	7.71	6.94	6.59	6.39	6.26	6.16	6.09	6.04	6.00	5.96	5.93	5.91	5.87	5.84	5.80	5.77	5.74	5.71	5.70	5.68	5.66	5.65	5.64	5.63
	21.20	18.00	16.69	15.98	15.52	15.21	14.98	14.80	14.66	14.54	14.45	14.37	14.24	14.15	14.02	13.93	13.83	13.74	13.69	13.61	13.57	13.52	13.48	13.46
5	6.61	5.79	5.41	5.19	5.05	4.95	4.88	4.82	4.78	4.74	4.70	4.68	4.64	4.60	4.56	4.53	4.50	4.46	4.44	4.42	4.40	4.38	4.37	4.36
	16.26	13.27	12.06	11.39	10.97	10.67	10.45	10.27	10.15	10.05	9.96	9.89	9.77	9.68	9.55	9.47	9.38	9.29	9.24	9.17	9.13	9.07	9.04	9.02
6	5.99	5.14	4.76	4.53	4.39	4.28	4.21	4.15	4.10	4.06	4.03	4.00	3.96	3.92	3.87	3.84	3.81	3.77	3.75	3.72	3.71	3.69	3.68	3.67
	13.74	10.92	9.78	9.15	8.75	8.47	8.26	8.10	7.98	7.87	7.79	7.72	7.60	7.52	7.39	7.31	7.23	7.14	7.09	7.02	6.99	6.94	6.90	6.88
7	5.59	4.74	4.35	4.12	3.97	3.87	3.79	3.73	3.68	3.63	3.60	3.57	3.52	3.49	3.44	3.41	3.38	3.34	3.32	3.29	3.28	3.25	3.24	3.23
	12.25	9.55	8.45	7.85	7.46	7.19	7.00	6.84	6.71	6.62	6.54	6.47	6.35	6.27	6.15	6.07	5.98	5.90	5.85	5.78	5.75	5.70	5.67	5.65

8	5.32 / 11.26	4.46 / 8.65	4.07 / 7.59	3.84 / 7.01	3.69 / 6.63	3.58 / 6.37	3.50 / 6.19	3.44 / 6.03	3.39 / 5.91	3.34 / 5.82	3.31 / 5.74	3.28 / 5.67	3.23 / 5.56	3.20 / 5.48	3.15 / 5.36	3.12 / 5.28	3.08 / 5.20	3.05 / 5.11	3.03 / 5.06	3.00 / 5.00	2.98 / 4.96	2.96 / 4.91	2.94 / 4.88	2.93 / 4.86
9	5.12 / 10.56	4.26 / 8.02	3.86 / 6.99	3.63 / 6.42	3.48 / 6.06	3.37 / 5.80	3.29 / 5.62	3.23 / 5.47	3.18 / 5.35	3.13 / 5.26	3.10 / 5.18	3.07 / 5.11	3.02 / 5.00	2.98 / 4.92	2.93 / 4.80	2.90 / 4.73	2.86 / 4.64	2.82 / 4.56	2.80 / 4.51	2.77 / 4.45	2.76 / 4.41	2.73 / 4.36	2.72 / 4.33	2.71 / 4.31
10	4.96 / 10.04	4.10 / 7.56	3.71 / 6.55	3.48 / 5.99	3.33 / 5.64	3.22 / 5.39	3.14 / 5.21	3.07 / 5.06	3.02 / 4.95	2.97 / 4.85	2.94 / 4.78	2.91 / 4.71	2.86 / 4.60	2.82 / 4.52	2.77 / 4.41	2.74 / 4.33	2.70 / 4.25	2.67 / 4.17	2.64 / 4.12	2.61 / 4.05	2.59 / 4.01	2.56 / 3.96	2.55 / 3.93	2.54 / 3.91
11	4.84 / 9.65	3.98 / 7.20	3.59 / 6.22	3.36 / 5.67	3.20 / 5.32	3.09 / 5.07	3.01 / 4.88	2.95 / 4.74	2.90 / 4.63	2.86 / 4.54	2.82 / 4.46	2.79 / 4.40	2.74 / 4.29	2.70 / 4.21	2.65 / 4.10	2.61 / 4.02	2.57 / 3.94	2.53 / 3.86	2.50 / 3.80	2.47 / 3.74	2.45 / 3.70	2.42 / 3.66	2.41 / 3.62	2.40 / 3.60
12	4.75 / 9.33	3.88 / 6.93	3.49 / 5.95	3.26 / 5.41	3.11 / 5.06	3.00 / 4.82	2.92 / 4.65	2.85 / 4.50	2.80 / 4.39	2.76 / 4.30	2.72 / 4.22	2.69 / 4.16	2.64 / 4.05	2.60 / 3.98	2.54 / 3.86	2.50 / 3.78	2.46 / 3.70	2.42 / 3.61	2.40 / 3.56	2.36 / 3.49	2.35 / 3.46	2.32 / 3.41	2.31 / 3.38	2.30 / 3.36
13	4.67 / 9.07	3.80 / 6.70	3.41 / 5.74	3.18 / 5.20	3.02 / 4.86	2.92 / 4.62	2.84 / 4.44	2.77 / 4.30	2.72 / 4.19	2.67 / 4.10	2.63 / 4.02	2.60 / 3.96	2.55 / 3.85	2.51 / 3.78	2.46 / 3.67	2.42 / 3.59	2.38 / 3.51	2.34 / 3.42	2.32 / 3.37	2.28 / 3.30	2.26 / 3.27	2.24 / 3.21	2.22 / 3.18	2.21 / 3.16
14	4.60 / 8.86	3.74 / 6.51	3.34 / 5.56	3.11 / 5.03	2.96 / 4.69	2.85 / 4.46	2.77 / 4.28	2.70 / 4.14	2.65 / 4.03	2.60 / 3.94	2.56 / 3.86	2.53 / 3.80	2.48 / 3.70	2.44 / 3.62	2.39 / 3.51	2.35 / 3.43	2.31 / 3.34	2.27 / 3.26	2.24 / 3.21	2.21 / 3.14	2.19 / 3.11	2.16 / 3.06	2.14 / 3.02	2.13 / 3.00
15	4.54 / 8.68	3.68 / 6.36	3.29 / 5.42	3.06 / 4.89	2.90 / 4.56	2.79 / 4.32	2.70 / 4.14	2.64 / 4.00	2.59 / 3.89	2.55 / 3.80	2.51 / 3.73	2.48 / 3.67	2.43 / 3.56	2.39 / 3.48	2.33 / 3.36	2.29 / 3.29	2.25 / 3.20	2.21 / 3.12	2.18 / 3.07	2.15 / 3.00	2.12 / 2.97	2.10 / 2.92	2.08 / 2.89	2.07 / 2.87
16	4.49 / 8.53	3.63 / 6.23	3.24 / 5.29	3.01 / 4.77	2.85 / 4.44	2.74 / 4.20	2.66 / 4.03	2.59 / 3.89	2.54 / 3.78	2.49 / 3.69	2.45 / 3.61	2.42 / 3.55	2.37 / 3.45	2.33 / 3.37	2.28 / 3.25	2.24 / 3.18	2.20 / 3.10	2.16 / 3.01	2.13 / 2.96	2.09 / 2.89	2.07 / 2.86	2.04 / 2.80	2.02 / 2.77	2.01 / 2.75
17	4.45 / 8.40	3.59 / 6.11	3.20 / 5.18	2.96 / 4.67	2.81 / 4.34	2.70 / 4.10	2.62 / 3.93	2.55 / 3.79	2.50 / 3.68	2.45 / 3.59	2.41 / 3.52	2.38 / 3.45	2.33 / 3.35	2.29 / 3.27	2.23 / 3.16	2.19 / 3.08	2.15 / 3.00	2.11 / 2.92	2.08 / 2.86	2.04 / 2.79	2.02 / 2.76	1.99 / 2.70	1.97 / 2.67	1.96 / 2.65
18	4.41 / 8.28	3.55 / 6.01	3.16 / 5.09	2.93 / 4.58	2.77 / 4.25	2.66 / 4.01	2.58 / 3.85	2.51 / 3.71	2.46 / 3.60	2.41 / 3.51	2.37 / 3.44	2.34 / 3.37	2.29 / 3.27	2.25 / 3.19	2.19 / 3.07	2.15 / 3.00	2.11 / 2.91	2.07 / 2.83	2.04 / 2.78	2.00 / 2.71	1.98 / 2.68	1.95 / 2.62	1.93 / 2.59	1.92 / 2.57

Appendix G *(continued)*

Degrees of Freedom in Numerator

Degrees of Freedom in Denominator	1	2	3	4	5	6	7	8	9	10	11	12	14	16	20	24	30	40	50	75	100	200	500	∞
19	4.38	3.52	3.13	2.90	2.74	2.63	2.55	2.48	2.43	2.38	2.34	2.31	2.26	2.21	2.15	2.11	2.07	2.02	2.00	1.96	1.94	1.91	1.90	1.88
	8.18	5.93	5.01	4.50	4.17	3.94	3.77	3.63	3.52	3.43	3.36	3.30	3.19	3.12	3.00	2.92	2.84	2.76	2.70	2.63	2.60	2.54	2.51	2.49
20	4.35	3.49	3.10	2.87	2.71	2.60	2.52	2.45	2.40	2.35	2.31	2.28	2.23	2.18	2.12	2.08	2.04	1.99	1.96	1.92	1.90	1.87	1.85	1.84
	8.10	5.85	4.94	4.43	4.10	3.87	3.71	3.56	3.45	3.37	3.30	3.23	3.13	3.05	2.94	2.86	2.77	2.69	2.63	2.56	2.53	2.47	2.44	2.42
21	4.32	3.47	3.07	2.84	2.68	2.57	2.49	2.42	2.37	2.32	2.28	2.25	2.20	2.15	2.09	2.05	2.00	1.96	1.93	1.89	1.87	1.84	1.82	1.81
	8.02	5.78	4.87	4.37	4.04	3.81	3.65	3.51	3.40	3.31	3.24	3.17	3.07	2.99	2.88	2.80	2.72	2.63	2.58	2.51	2.47	2.42	2.38	2.36
22	4.30	3.44	3.05	2.82	2.66	2.55	2.47	2.40	2.35	2.30	2.26	2.23	2.18	2.13	2.07	2.03	1.98	1.93	1.91	1.87	1.84	1.81	1.80	1.78
	7.94	5.72	4.82	4.31	3.99	3.76	3.59	3.45	3.35	3.26	3.18	3.12	3.02	2.94	2.83	2.75	2.67	2.58	2.53	2.46	2.42	2.37	2.33	2.31
23	4.28	3.42	3.03	2.80	2.64	2.53	2.45	2.38	2.32	2.28	2.24	2.20	2.14	2.10	2.04	2.00	1.96	1.91	1.88	1.84	1.82	1.79	1.77	1.76
	7.88	5.66	4.76	4.26	3.94	3.71	3.54	3.41	3.30	3.21	3.14	3.07	2.97	2.89	2.78	2.70	2.62	2.53	2.48	2.41	2.37	2.32	2.28	2.26
24	4.26	3.40	3.01	2.78	2.62	2.51	2.43	2.36	2.30	2.26	2.22	2.18	2.13	2.09	2.02	1.98	1.94	1.89	1.86	1.82	1.80	1.76	1.74	1.73
	7.82	5.61	4.72	4.22	3.90	3.67	3.50	3.36	3.25	3.17	3.09	3.03	2.93	2.85	2.74	2.66	2.58	2.49	2.44	2.36	2.33	2.27	2.23	2.21
25	4.24	3.38	2.99	2.76	2.60	2.49	2.41	2.34	2.28	2.24	2.20	2.16	2.11	2.06	2.00	1.96	1.92	1.87	1.84	1.80	1.77	1.74	1.72	1.71
	7.77	5.57	4.68	4.18	3.86	3.63	3.46	3.32	3.21	3.13	3.05	2.99	2.89	2.81	2.70	2.62	2.54	2.45	2.40	2.32	2.29	2.23	2.19	2.17
26	4.22	3.37	2.98	2.74	2.59	2.47	2.39	2.32	2.27	2.22	2.18	2.15	2.10	2.05	1.99	1.95	1.90	1.85	1.82	1.78	1.76	1.72	1.70	1.69
	7.72	5.53	4.64	4.14	3.82	3.59	3.42	3.29	3.17	3.09	3.02	2.96	2.86	2.77	2.66	2.58	2.50	2.41	2.36	2.28	2.25	2.19	2.15	2.13
27	4.21	3.35	2.96	2.73	2.57	2.46	2.37	2.30	2.25	2.20	2.16	2.13	2.08	2.03	1.97	1.93	1.88	1.84	1.80	1.76	1.74	1.71	1.68	1.67
	7.68	5.49	4.60	4.11	3.79	3.56	3.39	3.26	3.14	3.06	2.98	2.93	2.83	2.74	2.63	2.55	2.47	2.38	2.33	2.25	2.21	2.16	2.12	2.10
28	4.20	3.34	2.95	2.71	2.56	2.44	2.36	2.29	2.24	2.19	2.15	2.12	2.06	2.02	1.96	1.91	1.87	1.81	1.78	1.75	1.72	1.69	1.67	1.65
	7.64	5.45	4.57	4.07	3.76	3.53	3.36	3.23	3.11	3.03	2.95	2.90	2.80	2.71	2.60	2.52	2.44	2.35	2.30	2.22	2.18	2.13	2.09	2.06
29	4.18	3.33	2.93	2.70	2.54	2.43	2.35	2.28	2.22	2.18	2.14	2.10	2.05	2.00	1.94	1.90	1.85	1.80	1.77	1.73	1.71	1.68	1.65	1.64
	7.60	5.42	4.54	4.04	3.73	3.50	3.33	3.20	3.08	3.00	2.92	2.87	2.77	2.68	2.57	2.49	2.41	2.32	2.27	2.19	2.15	2.10	2.06	2.03

df																								
30	1.62	1.64	1.66	1.69	1.72	1.76	1.79	1.84	1.89	1.93	1.99	2.04	2.09	2.12	2.16	2.21	2.27	2.34	2.42	2.53	2.69	2.92	3.32	4.17
	2.01	2.03	2.07	2.13	2.16	2.24	2.29	2.38	2.47	2.55	2.66	2.74	2.84	2.90	2.98	3.06	3.17	3.30	3.47	3.70	4.02	4.51	5.39	7.56
32	1.59	1.61	1.64	1.67	1.69	1.74	1.76	1.82	1.86	1.91	1.97	2.02	2.07	2.10	2.14	2.19	2.25	2.32	2.40	2.51	2.67	2.90	3.30	4.15
	1.96	1.98	2.02	2.08	2.12	2.20	2.25	2.34	2.42	2.51	2.62	2.70	2.80	2.86	2.94	3.01	3.12	3.25	3.42	3.66	3.97	4.46	5.34	7.50
34	1.57	1.59	1.61	1.64	1.67	1.71	1.74	1.80	1.84	1.89	1.95	2.00	2.05	2.08	2.12	2.17	2.23	2.30	2.38	2.49	2.65	2.88	3.28	4.13
	1.91	1.94	1.98	2.04	2.08	2.15	2.21	2.30	2.38	2.47	2.58	2.66	2.76	2.82	2.89	2.97	3.08	3.21	3.38	3.61	3.93	4.42	5.29	7.44
36	1.55	1.56	1.59	1.62	1.65	1.69	1.72	1.78	1.82	1.87	1.93	1.98	2.03	2.06	2.10	2.15	2.21	2.28	2.36	2.48	2.63	2.86	3.26	4.11
	1.87	1.90	1.94	2.00	2.04	2.12	2.17	2.26	2.35	2.43	2.54	2.62	2.72	2.78	2.86	2.94	3.04	3.18	3.35	3.58	3.89	4.38	5.25	7.39
38	1.53	1.54	1.57	1.60	1.63	1.67	1.71	1.76	1.80	1.85	1.92	1.96	2.02	2.05	2.09	2.14	2.19	2.26	2.35	2.46	2.62	2.85	3.25	4.10
	1.84	1.86	1.90	1.97	2.00	2.08	2.14	2.22	2.32	2.40	2.51	2.59	2.69	2.75	2.82	2.91	3.02	3.15	3.32	3.54	3.86	4.34	5.21	7.35
40	1.51	1.53	1.55	1.59	1.61	1.66	1.69	1.74	1.79	1.84	1.90	1.95	2.00	2.04	2.07	2.12	2.18	2.25	2.34	2.45	2.61	2.84	3.23	4.08
	1.81	1.84	1.88	1.94	1.97	2.05	2.11	2.20	2.29	2.37	2.49	2.56	2.66	2.73	2.80	2.88	2.99	3.12	3.29	3.51	3.83	4.31	5.18	7.31
42	1.49	1.51	1.54	1.57	1.60	1.64	1.68	1.73	1.78	1.82	1.89	1.94	1.99	2.02	2.06	2.11	2.17	2.24	2.32	2.44	2.59	2.83	3.22	1.07
	1.78	1.80	1.85	1.91	1.94	2.02	2.08	2.17	2.26	2.35	2.46	2.54	2.64	2.70	2.77	2.86	2.96	3.10	3.26	3.49	3.80	4.29	5.15	7.27
44	1.48	1.50	1.52	1.56	1.58	1.63	1.66	1.72	1.76	1.81	1.88	1.92	1.98	2.01	2.05	2.10	2.16	2.23	2.31	2.43	2.58	2.82	3.21	4.06
	1.75	1.78	1.82	1.88	1.92	2.00	2.06	2.15	2.24	2.32	2.44	2.52	2.62	2.68	2.75	2.84	2.94	3.07	3.24	3.46	3.78	4.26	5.12	7.24
46	1.46	1.48	1.51	1.54	1.57	1.62	1.65	1.71	1.75	1.80	1.87	1.91	1.97	2.00	2.04	2.09	2.14	2.22	2.30	2.42	2.57	2.81	3.20	4.05
	1.72	1.76	1.80	1.86	1.90	1.98	2.04	2.13	2.22	2.30	2.42	2.50	2.60	2.66	2.73	2.82	2.92	3.05	3.22	3.44	3.76	4.24	5.10	7.21
48	1.45	1.47	1.50	1.53	1.56	1.61	1.64	1.70	1.74	1.79	1.86	1.90	1.96	1.99	2.03	2.08	2.14	2.21	2.30	2.41	2.56	2.80	3.19	4.04
	1.70	1.73	1.78	1.84	1.88	1.96	2.02	2.11	2.20	2.28	2.40	2.48	2.58	2.64	2.71	2.80	2.90	3.04	3.20	3.42	3.74	4.22	5.08	7.19
50	1.44	1.46	1.48	1.52	1.55	1.60	1.63	1.69	1.74	1.78	1.85	1.90	1.95	1.98	2.02	2.07	2.13	2.20	2.29	2.40	2.56	2.79	3.18	4.03
	1.68	1.71	1.76	1.82	1.86	1.94	2.00	2.10	2.18	2.26	2.39	2.46	2.56	2.62	2.70	2.78	2.88	3.02	3.18	3.41	3.72	4.20	5.06	7.17
55	1.41	1.43	1.46	1.50	1.52	1.58	1.61	1.67	1.72	1.76	1.83	1.88	1.93	1.97	2.00	2.05	2.11	2.18	2.27	2.38	2.54	2.78	3.17	4.02
	1.64	1.66	1.71	1.78	1.82	1.90	1.96	2.06	2.15	2.23	2.35	2.43	2.53	2.59	2.66	2.75	2.85	2.98	3.15	3.37	3.68	4.16	5.01	7.12
60	1.39	1.41	1.44	1.48	1.50	1.56	1.59	1.65	1.70	1.75	1.81	1.86	1.92	1.95	1.99	2.04	2.10	2.17	2.25	2.37	2.52	2.76	3.15	4.00
	1.60	1.63	1.68	1.74	1.79	1.87	1.93	2.03	2.12	2.20	2.32	2.40	2.50	2.56	2.63	2.72	2.82	2.95	3.12	3.34	3.65	4.13	4.98	7.08

Appendix G (continued)

Degrees of Freedom in Numerator

Degrees of Freedom in Denominator	1	2	3	4	5	6	7	8	9	10	11	12	14	16	20	24	30	40	50	75	100	200	500	∞
65	3.99	3.14	2.75	2.51	2.36	2.24	2.15	2.08	2.02	1.98	1.94	1.90	1.85	1.80	1.73	1.68	1.63	1.57	1.54	1.49	1.46	1.42	1.39	1.37
	7.04	4.95	4.10	3.62	3.31	3.09	2.93	2.79	2.70	2.61	2.54	2.47	2.37	2.30	2.18	2.09	2.00	1.90	1.84	1.76	1.71	1.64	1.60	1.56
70	3.98	3.13	2.74	2.50	2.35	2.23	2.14	2.07	2.01	1.97	1.93	1.89	1.84	1.79	1.72	1.67	1.62	1.56	1.53	1.47	1.45	1.40	1.37	1.35
	7.01	4.92	4.08	3.60	3.29	3.07	2.91	2.77	2.67	2.59	2.51	2.45	2.35	2.28	2.15	2.07	1.98	1.88	1.82	1.74	1.69	1.62	1.56	1.53
80	3.96	3.11	2.72	2.48	2.33	2.21	2.12	2.05	1.99	1.95	1.91	1.88	1.82	1.77	1.70	1.65	1.60	1.54	1.51	1.45	1.42	1.38	1.35	1.32
	6.96	4.88	4.04	3.56	3.25	3.04	2.87	2.74	2.64	2.55	2.48	2.41	2.32	2.24	2.11	2.03	1.94	1.84	1.78	1.70	1.65	1.57	1.52	1.49
100	3.94	3.09	2.70	2.46	2.30	2.19	2.10	2.03	1.97	1.92	1.88	1.85	1.79	1.75	1.68	1.63	1.57	1.51	1.48	1.42	1.39	1.34	1.30	1.28
	6.90	4.82	3.98	3.51	3.20	2.99	2.82	2.69	2.59	2.51	2.43	2.36	2.26	2.19	2.06	1.98	1.89	1.79	1.73	1.64	1.59	1.51	1.46	1.43
125	3.92	3.07	2.68	2.44	2.29	2.17	2.08	2.01	1.95	1.90	1.86	1.83	1.77	1.72	1.65	1.60	1.55	1.49	1.45	1.39	1.36	1.31	1.27	1.25
	6.84	4.78	3.94	3.47	3.17	2.95	2.79	2.65	2.56	2.47	2.40	2.33	2.23	2.15	2.03	1.94	1.85	1.75	1.68	1.59	1.54	1.46	1.40	1.37
150	3.91	3.06	2.67	2.43	2.27	2.16	2.07	2.00	1.94	1.89	1.85	1.82	1.76	1.71	1.64	1.59	1.54	1.47	1.44	1.37	1.34	1.29	1.25	1.22
	6.81	4.75	3.91	3.44	3.14	2.92	2.76	2.62	2.53	2.44	2.37	2.30	2.20	2.12	2.00	1.91	1.83	1.72	1.66	1.56	1.51	1.43	1.37	1.33
200	3.89	3.04	2.65	2.41	2.26	2.14	2.05	1.98	1.92	1.87	1.83	1.80	1.74	1.69	1.62	1.57	1.52	1.45	1.42	1.35	1.32	1.26	1.22	1.19
	6.76	4.71	3.88	3.41	3.11	2.90	2.73	2.60	2.50	2.41	2.34	2.28	2.17	2.09	1.97	1.88	1.79	1.69	1.62	1.53	1.48	1.39	1.33	1.28
400	3.86	3.02	2.62	2.39	2.23	2.12	2.03	1.96	1.90	1.85	1.81	1.78	1.72	1.67	1.60	1.54	1.49	1.42	1.38	1.32	1.28	1.22	1.16	1.13
	6.70	4.66	3.83	3.36	3.06	2.85	2.69	2.55	2.46	2.37	2.29	2.23	2.12	2.04	1.92	1.84	1.74	1.64	1.57	1.47	1.42	1.32	1.24	1.19
1000	3.85	3.00	2.61	2.38	2.22	2.10	2.02	1.95	1.89	1.84	1.80	1.76	1.70	1.65	1.58	1.53	1.47	1.41	1.36	1.30	1.26	1.19	1.13	1.08
	6.66	4.62	3.80	3.34	3.04	2.82	2.66	2.53	2.43	2.34	2.26	2.20	2.09	2.01	1.89	1.81	1.71	1.61	1.54	1.44	1.38	1.28	1.19	1.11
∞	3.84	2.99	2.60	2.37	2.21	2.09	2.01	1.94	1.88	1.83	1.79	1.75	1.69	1.64	1.57	1.52	1.46	1.40	1.35	1.28	1.24	1.17	1.11	1.00
	6.64	4.60	3.78	3.32	3.02	2.80	2.64	2.51	2.41	2.32	2.24	2.18	2.07	1.99	1.87	1.79	1.69	1.59	1.52	1.41	1.36	1.25	1.15	1.00

From George W. Snedecor and William G. Cochran, *Statistical Methods*, 7th ed. © 1980 by the Iowa State University Press, 2121 South State Avenue, Ames, Iowa 50010.

APPENDIX H   Critical Values of *U* in the Mann-Whitney Test

Critical values of U at $\alpha = .001$ with direction predicted or at $\alpha = .002$ with direction not predicted.

N_1 \ N_2	9	10	11	12	13	14	15	16	17	18	19	20
1												
2												
3									0	0	0	0
4		0	0	0	1	1	1	2	2	3	3	3
5	1	1	2	2	3	3	4	5	5	6	7	7
6	2	3	4	4	5	6	7	8	9	10	11	12
7	3	5	6	7	8	.9	10	11	13	14	15	16
8	5	6	8	9	11	12	14	15	17	18	20	21
9	7	8	10	12	14	15	17	19	21	23	25	26
10	8	10	12	14	17	19	21	23	25	27	29	32
11	10	12	15	17	20	22	24	27	29	32	34	37
12	12	14	17	20	23	25	28	31	34	37	40	42
13	14	17	20	23	26	29	32	35	38	42	45	48
14	15	19	22	25	29	32	36	39	43	46	50	54
15	17	21	24	28	32	36	40	43	47	51	55	59
16	19	23	27	31	35	39	43	48	52	56	60	65
17	21	25	29	34	38	43	47	52	57	61	66	70
18	23	27	32	37	42	46	51	56	61	66	71	76
19	25	29	34	40	45	50	55	60	66	71	77	82
20	26	32	37	42	48	54	59	65	70	76	82	88

Critical values of U at $\alpha = .01$ with direction predicted or at $\alpha = .02$ with direction not predicted.

N_1 \ N_2	9	10	11	12	13	14	15	16	17	18	19	20
1												
2					0	0	0	0	0	0	1	1
3	1	1	1	2	2	2	3	3	4	4	4	5
4	3	3	4	5	5	6	7	7	8	9	9	10
5	5	6	7	8	9	10	11	12	13	14	15	16
6	7	8	9	11	12	13	15	16	18	19	20	22
7	9	11	12	14	16	17	19	21	23	24	26	28
8	11	13	15	17	20	22	24	26	28	30	32	34
9	14	16	18	21	23	26	28	31	33	36	38	40
10	16	19	22	24	27	30	33	36	38	41	44	47
11	18	22	25	28	31	34	37	41	44	47	50	53
12	21	24	28	31	35	38	42	46	49	53	56	60
13	23	27	31	35	39	43	47	51	55	59	63	67
14	26	30	34	38	43	47	51	56	60	65	69	73
15	28	33	37	42	47	51	56	61	66	71	76	82
16	31	36	41	46	51	56	61	66	71	76	82	87
17	33	38	44	49	55	60	66	71	77	82	88	93
18	36	41	47	53	59	65	70	76	82	88	94	100
19	38	44	50	56	63	69	75	82	88	94	101	107
20	40	47	53	60	67	73	80	87	93	100	107	114

Critical values of U at $\alpha = .025$ with direction predicted or at $\alpha = .05$ with direction not predicted.

N_1 \ N_2	9	10	11	12	13	14	15	16	17	18	19	20
1												
2	0	0	0	1	1	1	1	1	2	2	2	2
3	2	3	3	4	4	5	5	6	6	7	7	8
4	4	5	6	7	8	9	10	11	11	12	13	13
5	7	8	9	11	12	13	14	15	17	18	19	20
6	10	11	13	14	16	17	19	21	22	24	25	27
7	12	14	16	18	20	22	24	26	28	30	32	34
8	15	17	19	22	24	26	29	31	34	36	38	41
9	17	20	23	26	28	31	34	37	39	42	45	48
10	20	23	26	29	33	36	39	42	45	48	52	55
11	23	26	30	33	37	40	44	47	51	55	58	62
12	26	29	33	37	41	45	49	53	57	61	65	69
13	28	33	37	41	45	50	54	59	63	67	72	76
14	31	36	40	45	50	55	59	64	67	74	78	83
15	34	39	44	49	54	59	64	70	75	80	85	90
16	37	42	47	53	59	64	70	75	81	86	92	98
17	39	45	51	57	63	67	75	81	87	93	99	105
18	42	48	55	61	67	74	80	86	93	99	106	112
19	45	52	58	65	72	78	85	92	99	106	113	119
20	48	55	62	69	76	83	90	90	105	112	119	127

Critical values of *U* at $\alpha = .05$ with direction predicted or at $\alpha = .10$ with direction not predicted.

N_1 \ N_2	9	10	11	12	13	14	15	16	17	18	19	20
1											0	0
2	1	1	1	2	2	2	3	3	3	4	4	4
3	3	4	5	5	6	7	7	8	9	9	10	11
4	6	7	8	9	10	11	12	14	15	16	17	18
5	9	11	12	13	15	16	18	19	20	22	23	25
6	12	14	16	17	19	21	23	25	26	28	30	32
7	15	17	19	21	24	26	28	30	33	35	37	39
8	18	20	23	26	28	31	33	36	39	41	44	47
9	21	24	27	30	33	36	39	42	45	48	51	54
10	24	27	31	34	37	41	44	48	51	55	58	62
11	27	31	34	38	42	46	50	54	57	61	65	69
12	30	34	38	42	47	51	55	60	64	68	72	77
13	33	37	42	47	51	56	61	65	70	75	80	84
14	36	41	46	51	56	61	66	71	77	82	87	92
15	39	44	50	55	61	66	72	77	83	88	94	100
16	42	48	54	60	65	71	77	83	89	95	101	107
17	45	51	57	64	70	77	83	89	96	102	109	115
18	48	55	61	68	75	82	88	95	102	109	116	123
19	51	58	65	72	80	87	94	101	109	116	123	130
20	54	62	69	77	84	92	100	107	115	123	130	138

From D. Auble, "Extended Tables for the Mann-Whitney Statistic," *Bulletin of the Institute of Educational Research at Indiana University*, 1:2 (1953): tab. 1, 3, 5, and 7, with the kind permission of the publisher; as adapted in Sidney Siegel, *Nonparametric Statistics for the Behavioral Sciences* (New York: McGraw-Hill, 1956), tab. K.

APPENDIX I Distribution of χ^2

df	Probability													
	.99	.98	.95	.90	.80	.70	.50	.30	.20	.10	.05	.02	.01	.001
1	.0³157	.0³628	.00393	.0158	.0642	.148	.455	1.074	1.642	2.706	3.841	5.412	6.635	10.827
2	.0201	.0404	.103	.211	.446	.713	1.386	2.408	3.219	4.605	5.991	7.824	9.210	13.815
3	.115	.185	.352	.584	1.005	1.424	2.366	3.665	4.642	6.251	7.815	9.837	11.341	16.268
4	.297	.429	.711	1.064	1.649	2.195	3.357	4.878	5.989	7.779	9.488	11.668	13.277	18.465
5	.554	.752	1.145	1.610	2.343	3.000	4.351	6.064	7.289	9.236	11.070	13.388	15.086	20.617
6	.872	1.134	1.635	2.204	3.070	3.828	5.348	7.231	8.558	10.645	12.592	15.033	16.812	22.457
7	1.239	1.564	2.167	2.833	3.822	4.671	6.346	8.383	9.803	12.017	14.067	16.622	18.475	24.322
8	1.646	2.032	2.733	3.490	4.594	5.527	7.344	9.524	11.030	13.362	15.507	18.168	20.090	26.125
9	2.088	2.532	3.325	4.168	5.380	6.393	8.343	10.656	12.242	14.684	16.919	19.679	21.666	27.877
10	2.558	3.059	3.940	4.865	6.179	7.267	9.342	11.781	13.442	15.987	18.307	21.161	23.209	29.588
11	3.053	3.609	4.575	5.578	6.989	8.148	10.341	12.899	14.631	17.275	19.675	22.618	24.725	31.264
12	3.571	4.178	5.226	6.304	7.807	9.034	11.340	14.011	15.812	18.549	21.026	24.054	26.217	32.909
13	4.107	4.765	5.892	7.042	8.634	9.926	12.340	15.119	16.985	19.812	22.362	25.472	27.688	34.528
14	4.660	5.368	6.571	7.790	9.467	10.821	13.339	16.222	18.151	21.064	23.685	26.873	29.141	36.123
15	5.229	5.985	7.261	8.547	10.307	11.721	14.339	17.322	19.311	22.307	24.996	28.259	30.578	37.697
16	5.812	6.614	7.962	9.312	11.152	12.624	15.338	18.418	20.465	23.542	26.296	29.633	32.000	39.252

df														
17	6.408	7.255	8.672	10.085	12.002	13.531	16.338	19.511	21.615	24.769	27.587	30.995	33.409	40.790
18	7.015	7.906	9.390	10.865	12.857	14.440	17.338	20.601	22.760	25.989	28.869	32.346	34.805	42.312
19	7.633	8.567	10.117	11.651	13.716	15.352	18.338	21.689	23.900	27.204	30.144	33.687	36.191	43.820
20	8.260	9.237	10.851	12.443	14.578	16.266	19.337	22.775	25.038	28.412	31.410	35.020	37.566	45.315
21	8.897	9.915	11.591	13.240	15.445	17.182	20.337	23.858	26.171	29.615	32.671	36.343	38.932	46.797
22	9.542	10.600	12.338	14.041	16.314	18.101	21.337	24.939	27.301	30.813	33.924	37.659	40.289	48.268
23	10.196	11.293	13.091	14.848	17.187	19.021	22.337	26.018	28.429	32.007	35.172	38.968	41.638	49.728
24	10.856	11.992	13.848	15.659	18.062	19.943	23.337	27.096	29.553	33.196	36.415	40.270	42.980	51.179
25	11.524	12.697	14.611	16.473	18.940	20.867	24.337	28.172	30.675	34.382	37.652	41.566	44.314	52.620
26	12.198	13.409	15.379	17.292	19.820	21.792	25.336	29.246	31.795	35.563	38.885	42.856	45.642	54.052
27	12.879	14.125	16.151	18.114	20.703	22.719	26.336	30.319	32.912	36.741	40.113	44.140	46.963	55.476
28	13.565	14.847	16.928	18.939	21.588	23.647	27.336	31.391	34.027	37.916	41.337	45.419	48.278	56.893
29	14.256	15.574	17.708	19.768	22.475	24.577	28.336	32.461	35.139	39.087	42.557	46.693	49.588	58.302
30	14.953	16.306	18.493	20.599	23.364	25.508	29.336	33.530	36.250	40.256	43.773	47.962	50.892	59.703

For larger values of df, the expression $\sqrt{2\chi^2} - \sqrt{2df - 1}$ may be used as a normal deviate with unit variance, remembering that the probability for χ^2 corresponds to that of a single tail of the normal curve.

Reprinted from R. A. Fisher and F. Yates, *Statistical Tables for Biological, Agricultural and Medical Research*, 6th ed. (London: Longman, 1974), tab. IV. Used by permission of the authors and Longman Group Ltd.

GLOSSARY

Glossary terms are cross-referenced to text discussions, indicated by the boldface text page number following each term.

accretion measures Unobtrusive measures using deposited physical material **(303)**

actuarial records Public records concerning the demographic characteristics of the population served by the record-keeping agency **(305)**

ad hoc classificatory system A level of the theory with arbitrary categories constructed to organize and summarize empirical observations **(38)**

analytic induction A theoretical approach to field research where a researcher begins with a tentative hypothesis explaining the phenomenon observed and then attempts to verify the hypothesis by observing a small number of cases. If the hypothesis does not fit these cases, it is either rejected or reformulated so that the cases account for it **(284)**

anonymity The protection of research participants by separating specific identities from the information given **(86)**

arithmetic mean The sum total of all observations divided by their number **(348)**

attitude All of a person's inclinations, prejudices, ideas, fears, and convictions about any specific topic **(241)**

attitude index A series of questions selected on a priori basis, the scores of which are interpreted as indicating the attitude of the respondent **(434)**

authenticity The genuineness of private records **(310)**

axiomatic system A theoretical system that contains a set of concepts and definitions, a set of existence statements, a set of relational statements divided into axioms and theorems, and a logical system used to relate concepts to statements and to deduce theorems from axioms **(41)**

card sort Questionnaire format for measuring intensities of judgement whereby a respondent is handed a set of cards, each bearing a statement, and is asked to sort them into one of seven boxes, depending on his or her degree of agreement with the statement **(248)**

census tract A neighborhoodlike subdivision of a metropolitan area **(298)**

chi-square test (χ^2) A test statistic that allows one to decide whether observed frequencies are essentially equal to or significantly different from frequencies predicted by a theoretical model. The outcome of the test allows decisions as to whether or not frequencies are distributed equally among categories, whether or not a distribution is normal, or whether or not two variables are independent **(464)**

classic research design An experimental design format, usually associated with research in the biological and social sciences, that consists of two comparable groups: an experimental group and a control group. These two groups are equivalent except that the experimental group is exposed to the independent variable and the control group is not **(100)**

closed-ended question   A question that offers respondents a set of answers from which they are asked to choose the one that most closely reflects their views **(242)**

cluster sample   Type of probability sampling, frequently used in large-scale studies because it is the least expensive sample design, that involves selecting layer groupings (clusters) and selecting sampling units from the clusters **(173)**

code of ethics   Regulations developed by major professional societies that outline the specific problems and issues that are frequently encountered in the types of research carried out within a particular profession, and serves as a guide to ethical research practices **(88)**

codebook   A book compiled by the researcher identifying a specific item of observation and the code number assigned to describe each category included in that item **(326)**

coding   Assigning codes in the form of numerals (or other symbols) for each category of each variable in a study **(321)**

coding reliability   The extent of agreement between different coders when classifying their individual responses according to the coding scheme **(328)**

coding scheme   A system of categories used to classify responses or behaviors that relate to a single item or variable **(322)**

coefficient of multiple correlation   The correlation between a number of independent variabes with a dependent variable **(416)**

coefficient of reproducibility (*CR*)   A measure that indicates how precisely a score on a Guttman scale can be used to reproduce the scores on the items that compose the scale; the fewer the number of errors in predicted item scores, the higher the coefficient of reproducibility **(439)**

combined designs   The merging of two or more research designs into a single study to increase the inferential powers of that study **(139)**

comparison   The operational process required to demonstrate that two variables are correlated **(104)**

competence   The assumption that any decision made by a responsible, mature individual who is given relevant information will be the correct decision **(80)**

complete count census   The census of population and housing taken every ten years intended to reach every household in the country. Includes only basic demographic information on each member of the household plus a few questions about the housing unit **(297)**

complete participant   A role taken by the observer where the observer is wholly concealed; the research objectives are unknown to the observed, and the researcher attempts to become a member of the group under observation **(273)**

comprehension   An important element of informed consent that refers to the confidence that the participant has provided knowing consent when the research procedure is associated with complex or subtle risks **(82)**

computer-assisted telephone interviewing (CATI)   Type of telephone survey where the interviewer sits at a computer terminal and, as a question flashes on the screen, asks it over the telephone. Respondents' answers are typed and coded directly on a disk, and the next question comes up on the screen **(233)**

concept   An abstraction representing an object, a property of an object, or a certain phenomenon that scientists use to describe the empirical world **(27)**

conceptual definition   A definition that describes a concept by using primitive and derived terms **(30)**

conceptual framework   A level of theory in which descriptive categories are systematically placed within a broad structure of explicit and assumed propositions **(39)**

conditional variable   A contingency necessary for the occurrence of the relationship between the independent and dependent variable **(408)**

confidence interval   A measure that specifies the range of values within which a given percentage of the sample means falls **(187)**

confidentiality . Protection of the identity of research participants **(86)**

construct validity   A process that involves relating a measuring instrument to a general theoretical framework in order to determine whether the instrument is tied to the concepts and theoretical assumptions that are employed **(161)**

content analysis   The systematic, quantitative analysis of observations obtained from archival records and documents **(311)**

context of justification   Activities of scientists as they attempt logically and empirically to verify claims for knowledge **(21)**

contingency question   A question that applies only to a subgroup of respondents because it is relevant only to certain people **(244)**

continuous variables   Variables that do not have a minimum-sized unit **(57)**

contrasted groups   Comparison of groups that are known to differ in some important attributes **(128)**

control   A procedure designed to eliminate alternative sources of variation that may distort the research results. Methods of control include holding constant confounding variables under experimental conditions or during statistical analysis **(105)**

control group   The group in an experimental research design that is not exposed to the independent variable **(100)**

control-series design   A quasi-experimental design that attempts to control the aspects of history, maturation, and test-retest effects shared by the experimental and comparison groups **(138)**

control variable   A variable that is controlled for, or held constant, in order to examine whether it affects the relationship between independent and dependent variables **(56)**

correlation coefficient   A measure of linear association between two interval variables. Pearson's product-moment correlation coefficient (r) estimates the direction and magnitude of the association **(377)**

correlational design   The most predominant research design employed in the social sciences, most often identified with survey research, where data are used to examine relationships between property and dispositions, establish causal relations between these properties and dispositions, or to simply describe the pattern of relation before any attempt at causal inference is made **(112)**

cover letter   The letter that accompanies a mail questionnaire **(256)**

criterion of least squares   The criterion that minimizes the sum of the squared vertical distances between the regression line and actual observations **(393)**

cross-tabulation   A table showing the relationship between two or more variables by presenting all combinations of categories of variables **(127)**

data cleaning   A process that precedes analysis of collected information whereby data is proofread to catch and correct errors and inconsistent codes. Most data cleaning is performed by special computer programs that are designed to test for logical consistency set up in the coding specifications **(334)**

data editing   Process performed by coders both during and after the data coding phase of data processing that involves checking for errors and omissions, and making sure that all interview schedules have been completed as required **(334)**

deductive coding   Requires that data be recorded to some preconceived scheme that is constructed before the measurement instrument is administered **(323)**

deductive explanation   An explanation that accounts for a phenomenon by demonstrating that it can be deduced from an established universal generalization **(10)**

degrees of freedom (*df*)   A characteristic of the sample statistics that determines the appropriate sampling distribution **(460)**

demand characteristics   A bias that may occur when individuals know that they are in an experimental situation, are aware that they are being observed, and believe that certain responses are expected from them. Consequently, they may not respond to the experimental manipulation at face value but rather to their interpretation of the responses that these manipulations are intended to elicit **(208)**

dependent variable   The variable that the researcher wishes to explain **(54)**

descriptive statistics   Statistical procedures used for describing and analyzing data that enable the researcher to summarize and organize data in an effective and meaningful way and provide tools for describing collections of statistical observations and reducing information to an understandable form **(340)**

difference-between-means test   A test used to assess the significance of a difference between means to reflect the amount of relationship between two variables **(457)**

discrete variables   Variables with a minimum-sized unit **(57)**

discriminative power (*DP*)   A measure of each item's ability to separate the highs from the lows on an attitude continuum when selecting items for the Likert scale **(437)**

double-barreled questions   Questions combining two or more questions in one, thus confusing respondents who might agree with one aspect of the question but disagree with the other **(255)**

ecological fallacy   An error that results from analyzing groups but making inferences on the behavior of individuals **(53)**

elaboration   A method of introducing other variables to the analysis in order to determine the links between the independent and dependent variables **(407)**

empirical   Relying on perceptions, experience, and behavior **(8)**

epistemology   The study of the foundations of knowledge, especially with reference to its limits and validity **(6)**

erosion measure   An unobtrusive measure based on the wearing away of physical materials **(303)**

error of prediction   The deviation of the actual observations from the ones predicted by the regression line **(393)**

ethical dilemma   Arises when a decision is made to conduct research despite an ethically questionable practice **(78)**

experimental bias   A situation that occurs when an experimenter unintentionally communicates his or her own expectations onto the participants being studied. This behavior, though not intended to be part of the experimental manipulation, influences the participants **(209)**

experimental group   The group exposed to the independent variable in an experimental research design **(100)**

experimental mortality   Refers to the dropout problems that prevent the researcher from obtaining complete information on all cases. When individuals drop out selectively from the experimental or control group, the final sample on which complete information is available may be biased **(106)**

explanation   The systematic and empirical analysis of the antecedent factors that are responsible for the occurrence of an event or behavior **(10)**

extended time-series design   A research design that presents the data as part of a broadened time series and therefore controls for maturation **(135)**

external validity   The extent to which the research findings can be generalized to larger populations and applied to different settings **(111)**

extrinsic factors   Biases resulting from the differential recruitment of research participants to the experimental and control groups **(105)**

face validity   The investigators' subjective evaluation as to the validity of a measuring instrument. It concerns the extent to which the measuring instrument appears to measure according to the researcher's subjective assessment. **(158)**

factor analysis   A statistical technique for classifying a large number of interrelated variables into a smaller number of dimensions of factors **(442)**

factor loading   The correlation coefficient between a variable and a factor **(442)**

factor scores   A case's score and a factor obtained by multiplying the factor score coefficient for each variable by the standardized value of that variable for that case **(443)**

factorial design   A research design that allows one to examine simultaneously the effects of two or more independent variables on the dependent variable and also to detect interaction between the variables **(117)**

factual question   A question designed to elicit objective information from respondents regarding their background, environment, and habits **(240)**

fallacy of reification   The error of treating concepts as though they were the actual phenomena **(28)**

field research   Any research that is conducted in natural settings rather than in a laboratory. Established field research methodology in sociology emphasizes participation in the lives of those studied in order to share and better understand subjective perspectives **(272)**

filter question   In questionnaire design, the question that precedes a contingency question: the relevance of the contingency question is contingent on the response to the filter question **(245)**

focused interview   Type of personal interview (following an interview guide) that specifies topics related to the research hypothesis and gives considerable liberty to the respondents to express their views. The interview focuses on the subject's experiences regarding the situation under study **(224)**

follow-up   In mail questionnaires, a strategy used to secure an acceptable response rate (for example, sending a series of reminder postcards and/or a replacement questionnaire) **(219)**

frequency distribution   The number of observations of each value of a variable **(340)**

funnel technique   A technique of questionnaire construction in which the questionnaire begins with general queries and then "funnels down" to more specific items **(250)**

gamma   A coefficient of association indicating the magnitude and direction of the relationship between ordinal variables **(386)**

generalizability   Implies that what one really wants to know about a set of measurements is to what extent and with respect to what properties are they like other sets of measurement that one might have taken from a given universe of potential measurements **(166)**

grounded-theory approach   In field research, the development of a theory that is closely and directly relevant to the particular setting under study whereby the researcher first develops conceptual categories from data and then makes new observations to clarify and elaborate these categories. Concepts and tentative hypotheses are then developed directly from data **(284)**

Guttman scale   Scaling method designed to incorporate an empirical test of the unidimensionality of a set of items as an integral part of the scale-construction process. If the items comprising the scale tap the same attitudinal dimension, they can be arranged so that there will be a continuum that indicates varying degrees of the underlying dimension **(438)**

history   All events occurring during the time of the research study that might affect the individuals studied and provide a rival explanation for the change in the dependent variable **(106)**

hypothesis   A tentative answer to a research problem, expressed in the form of a relation between independent and dependent variables **(61)**

independent variable   The variable hypothesized to explain variations in the dependent variable **(54)**

index   A composite measure of two or more indicators or items **(428)**

indirect effects   When the effect of one variable on another is mediated through a third intervening variable **(421)**

inductive coding   When the coding scheme is designed on the basis of a representative sample, responses, or other kinds of data, and is then applied to the remainder of the data **(323)**

inferential statistics   Allows the researcher to make decisions or inferences about characteristics of a population based on observations from a sample taken from the population **(340)**

informed consent   The agreement of an individual to participate in a study after being informed of facts that would be likely to influence his or her willingness to participate **(79)**

instrumentation   A process that designates changes in the measuring instrument between the pretest and the posttest. To associate the difference between posttest and pretest scores with the independent variable, one must show that repeated mesurements with the same measurement instrument under unchanged conditions will yield the same result **(107)**

interaction   A difference in the relationship between two variables within different categories of a control variable **(408)**

interaction process analysis (IPA)   A set of 12 categories used to code interaction in groups. The analysis is a highly structured observational technique, using both structured observational categories and a structured laboratory setting **(202)**

internal validity   The evidence required in experiments to rule out the possibility that factors other than the independent variable are responsible for variation in the dependent variable **(105)**

interpretive approach Belief that the phenomena of focal concern to the sociobehavioral scientist are far less stable then those of interest to the natural scientists **(14)**

interquartile range The difference between the lower and upper quartiles (Q 1 and Q 3). It measures the spread in the middle half of the distribution and is less affected by extreme observations **(354)**

intersubjectivity A norm of scientific methodology that states that knowledge must be transmittable so that scientists can understand and evaluate the methods of other scientists and perform similar observations in order to verify empirical generalizations **(17)**

interval level The level of measurement achieved when each observation falls into exhaustive and mutually exclusive measurement categories, measurement categories can be ordered, and the intervals between adjacent categories are equal **(155)**

intervening variable An intermediate variable between an independent variable and a dependent variable; the independent variable affects the dependent variable through the intervening variable **(408)**

intrinsic factors Changes in units under study that occur during the study period, changes in the measuring instrument, and the reactive effect of the observation itself **(106)**

isomorphism Similarity or identity in structure **(150)**

Kendall's tau-*b* A coefficient of association between ordinal variables incorporating ties **(390)**

known-groups technique When a measuring instrument is administered to groups of people with known attributes, and the direction of difference is predicted **(161)**

lambda (Guttman coefficient of predictability) A measure of association indicating the magnitude and direction of the relationship between nominal variables **(380)**

leading question Question phrased in such a manner that the respondent believes that the researcher expects a certain answer **(253)**

level of measurement The degree to which typical numbers describe characteristics of the measured variable; the higher the level of measurement, the greater the number of applicable statistical methods **(151)**

level of significance The probability of rejecting a true null hypothesis; that is, the possibility of making a Type I error **(452)**

Likert scale A summated rating scale designed to assist in excluding questionable items **(436)**

linear relation A relation between two variables X and Y of the form $Y = a + bX$, where a and b are constant values; the graph of a linear relation is a straight line **(391)**

log A record of events, meetings, visits, and other activities of an individual over a given period of time **(309)**

magnitude of relation The extent to which variables covary positively or negatively **(60)**

mail questionnaire An impersonal survey method in which questionnaires are mailed to respondents, whose responses constitute the data on which research hypothesis are tested **(215)**

mainframe computer   A large computer that controls and coordinates activities of the computer system, such as executing the program instructions and monitoring the operation of the input and output devices **(335)**

manipulation   A procedure that allows the researcher in experimental settings to have some form of control over the introduction of the independent variable. This procedure allows for the determination that the independent variable preceded the dependent variable **(104)**

Mann-Whitney test   A nonparametric test that is applicable whenever researchers wish to test null hypothesis that two samples have been drawn from the same population against the alternative research hypothesis that the populations differ from each other **(462)**

matching   A method of control that involes equating the experimental and control groups on extrinsic variables that are presumed to relate to the research hypothesis **(108)**

matrix question   A method of organizing a large set of rating questions that have the same response categories **(248)**

maturation   Biological, psychological, or social processes that produce changes in the individuals or units studied with the passage of time. These changes could possibly influence the dependent variable and lead to erroneous inferences **(106)**

mean deviation   Computed by taking the differences between each observation and the mean, summing the absolute value of these deviations, and dividing the sum by the total number of observations **(355)**

measure of qualitative variation   An index of heterogeneity based on the ratio of the total number of differences in the distribution to the maximum number of possible differences within the same distribution **(351)**

measurement   The assignment of numbers or other symbols to empirical properties according to rules **(148)**

measures of central tendency   Statistical measures that reflect a typical or an average characteristic of a frequency distribution **(344)**

measures of dispersion   A family of statistics whose objective is to convey information, or the dispersion or spread of a distribution **(350)**

median   A measure of central tendency defined as the point above and below which 50 percent of the observations fall **(345)**

methodology   A system of explicit rules and procedures on which research is based and against which claims for knowledge are evaluated **(14)**

mode   A measure of central tendency defined as the most frequently occurring observation category in the data **(344)**

model   An abstraction that serves to order and simplify reality while still representing its essential characteristics **(43)**

multiple regression   A statistical technique that allows us to assess the relationship between an interval variable and two or more interval, ordinal, or nominal variables **(413)**

mundane realism   Refers to the extent to which the events that occur in a laboratory setting are likely to occur in the real world **(208)**

negative relation   An association whereby as the value of one variable increases, the value of another decreases **(58)**

nominal level   The level of measurement that requires that the measurement categories be exhaustive and mutually exclusive; it is the lowest level of measurement **(153)**

nondirective interview The least structured form of interviewing; no prespecified set of questions is employed, nor is an interview schedule used. The interviewer has a great deal of freedom to probe various areas and to raise specific queries during the couse of the interview **(225)**

nonparametric tests Statistical tests that require either no assumptions or very few assumptions about the population distribution **(456)**

nonresponse error Bias that occurs when persons do not respond to a survey and are therefore not represented in the total sample **(190)**

nonverbal behavior Body movements or expressions that convey a wide range of emotions, such as anger, surprise, and fear **(201)**

normal distribution A type of symmetrical distribution of great significance in the field of statistics. It is a mathematically defined curve. Under certain circumstances, it is permissible to treat frequency distributions of variables as close approximations of the normal distribution **(361)**

normal science The routine verification of dominant paradigms in any historical period **(18)**

null hypothesis A statement of no relationship between variables; the null hypothesis is rejected when an observed statistic appears unlikely under the null hypothesis **(449)**

one-tailed test A statistical test where extreme results leading to rejection of the null hypothesis can be located at either tail **(454)**

one-shot case study An observation of a single group or event at a single point in time, usually subsequent to some phenomenon that allegedly produced change **(141)**

open-ended question A question that is not followed by any kind of specified choice; the respondents' answers are recorded in full **(243)**

operational definition A set of procedures that describes the activities one should perform to observe a phenomenon empirically **(31)**

opinion The verbal expression of an attitude **(241)**

ordinal level The level of measurement achieved when each observation falls into exhaustive and mutually exclusive measurement categories and the categories can be observed **(152)**

ostensive definition A definition that conveys the meaning of a concept through examples **(30)**

panel A design in survey research that offers a close approximation of the before-and-after condition of experimental designs by interviewing the same group at two or more points in time **(133)**

parameter A specified value of the population **(170)**

parametric tests Hypothesis tests based on assumptions about the parameter values of the population **(456)**

partial correlation A statistical control that involves a mathematical adjustment of the bivariate correlation, designed to cancel out the effect of other variables on the independent and dependent variables **(412)**

partial tables Tables that reflect only part of the total association between the independent and dependent variables **(404)**

participant-as-observer Role most often assumed by contemporary fieldworkers, where the researcher's presence is made known to the group being studied, and the researcher becomes an active member and participants in the group being observed **(275)**

path analysis   Technique that uses both bivariate and multiple linear regression techniques to test the causal relations among the variable specified in the model. It involves three steps: drawing of a path diagram based on theory or a set of hypothesis, the calculation of path coefficients (direct effects) using regression techniques, and the determination of indirect effects **(419)**

path coefficients   A standardized regression coefficient that reflects the causal relationship between two variables in path analysis **(420)**

Pearson's *r*   The Pearson product-moment correlation coefficient, a statistic that specifies the magnitude and direction of relation between two interval-level variables, is the most commonly used statistic in correlational analysis **(397)**

physical location analysis   A simple observation that focuses on the ways in which individuals use their bodies in a social space **(304)**

planned variation   A research design involving the exposure of individuals to systematically varying values of the independent variable in order to assess the causal effects **(131)**

population   The aggregate of all cases that conform to some designated set of specifications **(170)**

positive relation   An association whereby as the value of one variable increases, the value of another also increases **(58)**

posttest   The measurement taken after exposure to the independent variable **(100)**

predictive validity   Validation of a measure by prediction to an external criterion **(159)**

pretest   The measurement taken prior to the introduction of the independent variable **(100)**

pretest-posttest design   A preexperimental design that compares the measures of the dependent variable before and after exposure to the independent variable **(100)**

primitive term   A concept so basic that it cannot be defined by any other concept **(30)**

probabilistic explanation   Accounting for a phenomenon by using generalizations that express an arithmetic ratio between phenomena or generalizations that express tendencies **(10)**

probability sample   A sample that permits specifying the probability that each sampling unit will be included in the sample **(174)**

probing   The technique used by an interviewer to stimulate discussion and obtain more information **(230)**

proportional reduction of error   A method used to measure the magnitude of the relations between two variables wherein one variable is used to predict the values of another **(378)**

quantifiers   The responses categories of the rating scale that reflect the intensity of the particular judgement involved **(247)**

quota sample   The selection of a nonprobability sample that is as closely as possible a replica of the population **(176)**

random-digit dialing (RDD)   Drawing a random sample of telephone numbers by selecting an exchange and then appending random numbers between 0001 and 9999 **(232)**

randomization   A method of control that helps to offset the confounding effects of known as well as unforseen factors by randomly assigning cases to the experimental and control groups **(109)**

range   Measure of the distance between the highest and lowest values of a distribution **(354)**

ranking   In questionnaire research, when researchers obtain information regarding the degree of importance of the priorities that people have given to a set of attitudes or objects. This procedure is a useful device in providing some sense of relative order among objects or judgments **(249)**

rating   A judgement made by the respondent in terms of sets of ordered categories such as "strongly agree," "favorable," or "very often" **(247)**

ratio level   The level of measurement that has a unique zero point **(156)**

rationalism   A school of thought that holds that the totality of knowledge can be acquired only by strict adherence to the forms and rules of logic **(5)**

region of rejection   The area under the sampling distribution specified by the null hypothesis that covers the values of the observed statistic that lead to the rejection of the null hypothesis. In a one-tailed test, there is one region of rejection; in a two-tailed test, there are two regions of rejection **(452)**

regression artifact   A threat that occurs when individuals have been assigned to the experimental group on the basis of their extreme scores on the dependent variable. When this happens, and measures are unreliable, individuals who scored below average on the pretest will appear to have improved upon retesting. Conversely, individuals who scored above average on the pretest would appear to have done less well upon retesting **(107)**

regression line   A line based on the least squares criterion which is the best fit to the points in a scatterplot **(392)**

relation   Joint occurrence or covariation between two or more variables **(57)**

reliability   The consistency of a measuring instrument **(107)**

replication   The repetition of an investigation in an identical way as a safeguard against unintentional error or deception **(16)**

representative sample   A segment of a population being studied chosen because it is as representative as possible of the population from which it is drawn. Said to be representative of the analyses made on its sampling units produce results similar to those that would be obtained had the *entire* population been analyzed **(174)**

research design   The program that guides the investigator in the process of collecting, analyzing, and interpreting observations **(98)**

research problem   An intellectual problem calling for an answer in the form of a scientific inquiry **(51)**

research process   The overall scheme of scientific activities in which scientists engage in order to produce verifiable knowledge **(61)**

response rate   The percentage of individuals who respond to a given questionnaire **(217)**

revolutionary science   The abrupt development of a rival paradigm that is accepted only gradually by a scientific community **(19)**

right to privacy   The freedom of individuals to choose for themselves the time, circumstances, and extent to which their beliefs and behavior are to be shared or withheld from others **(83)**

sample   Any subset of a population **(179)**

sampling distribution   A theoretical distribution that can be specified for any statistic that can be computed for samples from a population **(450)**

sampling frame   The list of the sampling units that is used in the selection of the sample **(172)**

sampling unit   A single member of a sampling population or, in cluster sampling, a collection of sampling units **(171)**

sampling validity   To what degree the content of the instrument adequately represents the content population of the property being measured **(159)**

schedule-structured interview   An interview in which the questions (their wording and their sequence) are fixed and identical for every respondent **(224)**

semantic differential   A rating scale that measures the respondent's reaction to some object or concept in terms of rating on bipolar scales defined with contrasting adjectives at each end **(249)**

sensitivity of information   Refers to how personal or potentially threatening is the information being collected by the researcher. The greater the sensitivity of the information, the more safeguards are called for to protect the privacy of the research participants **(84)**

simple observation   An unobtrusive measurement made in a situation in which the observer remains unnoticed by the observed **(303)**

simple random sample   A basic probability sampling design that gives each of the sampling units of the population an equal chance of being selected for the sample **(177)**

skewed distribution   A distribution in which more observations fall to one side of the mean than the other **(360)**

split-half method   A method of assessing the reliability of an instrument by dividing items into two equivalent parts and correlating scores in one part with scores in the other **(165)**

spurious relation   An apparent relation between the independent and dependent variables that is found to be false because both are caused by a third variable. When the third variable is controlled, the apparent relationship between the dependent and independent variables disappears **(56)**

standard deviation   A commonly used measure of variability whose size indicates the dispersion of a distribution **(356)**

standard error   The standard deviation of a sampling distribution **(185)**

standard score   An individual observation that belongs to a distribution with a mean of zero and a standard deviation of one **(362)**

stratified sample   A probability sampling design in which the population is first divided into homogeneous strata within each of which sampling is conducted **(179)**

systematic sample   A sample in which every *k*th case is selected (usually with a random start) where *k* is a constant **(177)**

t **test**   A hypothesis test that uses the *t* statistic and the *t* distribution to determine whether to reject or retain the null hypothesis **(461)**

taxonomy   A level of theory that consists of a system of categories constructed to fit the empirical observations so that relationships among categories can be described **(38)**

test-retest method   A method of assessing the reliability of an instrument by administering it twice to the same group of people and correlating the scores **(164)**

theoretical system   Systematic combinations of taxonomies, conceptual frameworks, descriptions, explanations, and predictions in a manner that provides structure for a complete explanation of empirical phenomena **(40)**

threatening questions   Questions that respondents may find embarrassing or sensitive **(254)**

time-series design   A quasi-experimental design in which pretest and posttest measures are available on a number of occasions before and after exposure to an independent variable **(134)**

topical autobiography   A private record that focuses on a limited aspect of a person's life **(309)**

two-tailed test   A statistical test where extreme results leading to the rejection of the null hypothesis will be located at both left and right tails **(454)**

Type I error   The rejection of a true null hypothesis **(455)**

Type II error   The acceptance of a false null hypothesis **(455)**

unidimensionality   Principle that implies that the items comprising a scale reflect a single dimension and belong on a continuum that reflects one and only one theoretical concept **(428)**

units of analysis   The entities to which concepts pertain that influence subsequent research design, data collection, and data analysis decisions **(52)**

unobtrusive measures   Any method of data collection that directly removes the researcher from the interactions, events, or behavior being investigated **(302)**

validity   The degree to which a measuring instrument measures what it is supposed to measure **(158)**

variance   A measure of quantitative variation reflecting the average dispersion in the distribution; it is the square of the standard deviation **(356)**

Verstehen   Understanding; the notion that social scientists can understand human behavior through empathy **(13)**

voluntarism   The freedom of participants to choose whether or not to take part in a research project and will guarantee that exposure to known risks is voluntarily undertaken **(80)**

weighted aggregate   Component in constructing an index specifying the relative influence of each indicator or item **(432)**

AUTHOR INDEX

SUBJECT INDEX

OVERCOMING OCD

OVERCOMING OCD

A Journey to Recovery

Janet Singer

with Seth J. Gillihan, PhD

ROWMAN & LITTLEFIELD
Lanham • Boulder • New York • London

Published by Rowman & Littlefield
A wholly owned subsidiary of The Rowman & Littlefield Publishing Group, Inc.
4501 Forbes Boulevard, Suite 200, Lanham, Maryland 20706
www.rowman.com

Unit A, Whitacre Mews, 26–34 Stannary Street, London SE11 4AB, United Kingdom

British Library Cataloguing in Publication Information Available

Library of Congress Cataloging-in-Publication Data

Singer, Janet, 1958–
Overcoming OCD : a journey to recovery / Janet Singer, with Seth J. Gillihan, PhD.
pages cm
Includes bibliographical references and index.
ISBN 978-1-4422-3944-9 (cloth : alk. paper)—ISBN 978-1-4422-3945-6 (electronic)
1. Gillihan, Seth J., 1975—Mental health. 2. Obsessive-compulsive disorder—Patients—United States—Biography. 3. Obsessive-compulsive disorder—Patients—United States—Family relationships. 4. Obsessive-compulsive disorder—Treatment—Popular works. I. Gillihan, Seth J., 1975– II. Title.
RC533.S62 2015
616.85'2270092—dc23
[B]
2014023225

Printed in the United States of America

For Dan,
whose courage to fight OCD
and willingness to share his journey
inspire and amaze me.
(Janet Singer)

For those determined to fight their OCD
and the loved ones who stand by them.
(Seth J. Gillihan)

CONTENTS

ACKNOWLEDGMENTS

JANET SINGER

When my son was in the throes of severe obsessive-compulsive disorder, my good friend Mark, who is a wonderful clinical psychologist, said, "You should write a book someday." When I responded that I'd thought about it but desperately wanted a happy ending, Mark assured me it could happen. He told me my son Dan's OCD was treatable, and in that moment he gave me and my family a great gift: *hope.*

Thank you, Mark, for encouraging me to pass that gift of hope to others, and for your support and confidence in me from the book's inception. I also want to thank Dr. Vogel, who played a major role in Dan's happy ending.

A special thank you to Seth Gillihan for agreeing to collaborate with me on this project. While your insight and expertise add an extra dimension to the book, it is your compassion for those who are suffering that truly stands out. It has been an honor to work with you.

Thank you to Arlene Robinson, my editor, whose combination of professionalism, honesty, and humor led me to produce a manuscript I could be proud of. I'd also like to express my gratitude to Suzanne Staszak-Silva, executive editor at Rowman & Littlefield, for believing in this book. Thank you also to Stephanie Sciuletti, Kathryn Knigge, and Naomi Burns, all of Rowman & Littlefield, who have been a pleasure to work with.

So many others have helped me on the road to publication. There are too many to name, but I'd like to acknowledge a few individually: Ellen Sawyer, whose commitment to helping those with OCD inspires me; Paulette Bates Alden, Diane Daniel, Keren G., Michael Lemov, Elizabeth Sunabee, and Brooke Warner, who all took the time to review my proposal, offer their insight, and cheer me on.

I am fortunate to have wonderful friends who not only supported my book but more importantly were there for me and my family throughout our ordeal: Mary Ann H., Kate K., Nancy K., Jacqui L., Ellen P., Karen R., Sheara S., Giselle S., and Phyllis S. I am grateful for all your friendships.

Mom, thank you for your unwavering faith in me; you and Dad supported me from day one, literally. Anita, thank you for always being there. A special thanks to each of my three children: you inspire me daily by the way you've chosen to live your lives. Finally, this book would not have been written without the love, support, and encouragement of my husband. Thank you for being with me every step of the way; this book is as much yours as it is mine.

SETH J. GILLIHAN

First of all, I'm deeply grateful to Janet for the opportunity to collaborate on this project. You are tireless in your efforts to connect OCD sufferers and their families with the help they need. Thank you for the trust you placed in me as your partner in this work. I also thank all the individuals with OCD whom I've worked with. It's a privilege to witness your courage as you face your greatest fears. Thank you to my colleagues from the Center for the Treatment and Study of Anxiety at the University of Pennsylvania, and in particular Drs. Edna Foa, Elna Yadin, David Yusko, Elyssa Kushner, and Steven Tsao; thank you also to Dr. Marty Franklin at COTTAGe. I could not have had better teachers and collaborators as I learned about OCD and its treatment. Special thanks also to Nyrah Madon for her gracious administrative assistance. Finally, I want to express my heartfelt gratitude to my wife and children—every day you're proof that nothing is stronger than the love of family.

AUTHOR'S NOTE

The decision to tell this story was not an easy one. But my son was brave enough to allow me to share it, so how could I not be brave enough to tell it? I found myself propelled forward by the belief that his journey could benefit and inspire others.

I kept a detailed journal throughout Dan's ordeal, mainly for my own sanity. The events in the book are true, as I remember them. All the names and places, however, have been changed. While I tell the story of Dan's journey, Dr. Seth J. Gillihan provides the expert commentary about obsessive-compulsive disorder.

OCD is a cruel, insidious illness with the potential to destroy lives. But it is also treatable. My hope is that this book will educate, enlighten, and motivate those whose lives have been touched by OCD and give them the strength to move forward and fight for the lives they deserve.

Janet Singer

INTRODUCTION

Countless families have been introduced to obsessive-compulsive disorder, or OCD, through their loved one's struggle with the condition. They have learned that OCD might not be what they thought, that it's a confusing and debilitating condition that affects the entire family, and that treatment that works can be frustratingly hard to find.

OCD has been called by many names, including the "doubting disease," and doubt is at the heart of OCD: Did I really turn off the stove? How can I know I won't impulsively hurt someone I love? What if wearing a certain shirt causes a plane to crash? Even if a person knows on some level that these worries are unreasonable, a lingering doubt makes it extremely difficult for the person not to focus on the terrible thing that might happen.

As a psychiatric diagnosis, OCD is fairly straightforward. In the American Psychiatric Association's *Diagnostic and Statistical Manual of Mental Disorders*,[1] which is used in the United States and other parts of the world for psychiatric diagnosis, OCD is defined by the presence of "obsessions," which are upsetting and intrusive thoughts or urges, and "compulsions," which are thoughts and behaviors meant to prevent the feared outcomes. These criteria should make it one of the simplest conditions to diagnose, yet it often goes unrecognized or is misdiagnosed.[2]

Over the past several years there has been an increased awareness of OCD. For example, TV shows such as "The OCD Project" and "Ob-

sessed" have shown real-life examples of what OCD looks like and how it's treated. However, the condition is still commonly misunderstood. For example, many people think OCD is just about repetitive hand washing, compulsive cleaning and organizing, or constant checking of locks and stoves. In reality, OCD has an impressive imagination and can attach to anything. Other depictions of OCD make it seem "cute" or "funny," or even helpful, as expressed in statements such as, "I wish I could be more OCD about keeping my apartment clean." No one with OCD wishes they were more OCD.

Cute, "harmless" forms of OCD are by definition not OCD, which has to get in the way of things a person cares about.[3] The irony of OCD is that while it drives OCD sufferers to try to protect what they most care about, it destroys those very things in the process. For instance, compulsive rereading and rewriting of school assignments can lead to failing grades from turning in work late. Untreated OCD can ruin every area of a person's life, from well-being to relationships, work, education, family harmony, and anything else a person holds dear.

Although much is known about OCD, we know relatively little about what causes it. There are several risk factors for the condition, including childhood abuse and other stressors, social isolation as a child, high levels of negative emotion, and a family history of OCD, among others. However, for any particular individual it is impossible to say with certainty what caused his or her OCD, and in many instances no specific risk factors can be identified. Research studies have also begun to identify which brain areas are linked to the disorder, with a focus on a "loop" involving parts of the frontal lobes, the thalamus (the brain's "switchboard"), and structures called the basal ganglia that are tucked deep inside the brain.[4] However, brain scans cannot tell whether an individual has the diagnosis or not.[5]

Fortunately we don't have to know what caused an individual's OCD in order to treat it effectively, and OCD is a highly treatable condition. The best-tested psychological treatment for OCD is exposure and response prevention (ERP),[6] a specific type of cognitive-behavioral therapy (CBT). The treatment, which is described in more detail in this book, can be summarized as "doing the opposite of what OCD tells you to do." OCD tells a person to avoid things that trigger obsessive thoughts, whereas ERP says to approach obsessive triggers; OCD says to do compulsive behaviors to prevent bad things from happening, while ERP says to resist

the urge to do compulsions. Over time the triggers stop being terrifying, and one learns that fear subsides even if a compulsion isn't performed.[7] ERP has been shown to lead to changes in brain areas that are implicated in OCD.[8]

There are also medications that have been shown to be helpful in treating OCD,[9] the most commonly prescribed of which are the selective serotonin reuptake inhibitors such as fluoxetine. Relatively high doses of these medications tend to reduce symptoms, at least for as long as the person takes the medication.

Even though there are very effective treatments for OCD, many OCD sufferers end up getting treatments that haven't been tested in research studies, or have been tested and shown not to work.[10] OCD is not like other conditions such as depression and panic disorder, which can respond to some degree to many forms of therapy and even to a pill placebo. OCD shows very little placebo response,[11] and general talk therapy tends to be ineffective.[12] Indeed, some well-intentioned approaches can even make the condition worse, by playing into the hands of OCD. For example, therapists often unwittingly fall into a pattern of providing their patients with reassurance, which only feeds the obsessive-compulsive cycle.[13]

OCD is a condition that is defined by conflict—conflict between one's rational mind and the doubt OCD creates. In a similar way, the current state of OCD treatment is defined by conflict: On the one hand, countless individuals can testify to the power of effective treatment to restore what OCD stole from them and to allow them to live a satisfying and fulfilling life. On the other hand, so many families continue to share their OCD experiences that involve missed diagnosis, wrong treatments, and a lack of access to treatments that work. Much work remains to be done to bring effective treatment to the millions of OCD sufferers who need it.

Seth J. Gillihan, PhD

I

EVERYTHING IS NOT FINE

His behavior was so bizarre that for a moment I thought he was joking. "Why are you taking tiny tippy-toe steps?" I asked, forcing a laugh. No response. This was my third time in three months flying down to Bridgeville to help my son out at college, and I was shocked at how much worse he seemed.

He'd just gotten himself out of my rental car by stiffly turning his whole body at once. Every movement had been slow and deliberate. Before putting his feet down on the pavement, he'd hesitated and then winced. I accompanied him on his silly, tiptoe walk and took his arm as we now stood at the bottom of the old motel's staircase. The night air was thick with heat and humidity, yet he was wearing long sleeves and shivering uncontrollably.

"Dan, what's going on?" I asked.

He stared straight ahead, eyes glazed. "I can't go up the steps," he whispered.

My stomach tightened, and I took a deep breath. "Sure you can, honey," I said, a little too cheerily. "I'll help you."

Still holding his arm, I stepped up onto the first cement step. Dan didn't budge. "Everything is all right," I said, wondering why I chose to say something that was so obviously not true. He lifted his foot and once again hesitated and winced as it touched the first step. His other foot followed. His body froze and he was still shaking.

"I can't do this," he said.

I looked up at his sallow face and saw it riddled with fear. As much as I wanted to spare my son, intuition told me to get him to my room. "Sure you can, honey," I said calmly. "I'm here to help you."

He made it onto the second step, and we continued the cycle: freezing, reassuring, coaxing, hesitating, wincing, and stepping. I have no idea how long it took, but we finally reached the top landing. It was as if we had climbed Mt. Everest.

But really it was just the second floor of the motel, and we now had to walk past four other rooms to get to mine. Again, I held on to Dan's trembling arm while we took slow, deliberate baby steps.

"See, you did it," I said when we found ourselves in front of my door. "Everything is fine."

Why did I keep saying that?

I unlocked the door and reached in to turn on a light. "Come on in," I said, stepping inside.

It was almost midnight, and the full moon lit up the outside corridor. I turned to look at Dan and wondered how someone six feet five could look so small, almost invisible.

"I'll just wait out here," he said. He was frozen again.

"No, you have to come in," I replied as the anxiety churned away at my stomach. "I'll help you."

I took his hand and tried to lead him into the room. He didn't seem physically capable of lifting his foot over the threshold.

"I can't come in, Mom," he whispered, with the desperate tone of someone who knew he was drowning yet couldn't quite reach the life preserver.

"I'll help you. You need to come inside."

No response. With a yank that felt strong enough to dislocate his shoulder, I pulled him into the room and closed the door.

And so our journey began.

Just a year earlier, all had been well. Sort of. There'd been a vague unrest deep inside of me for a while, a feeling that maybe something wasn't quite right. I'd like to think of it as mother's intuition, but really it was the accumulation of a lot of little signs. The "cereal incident" was one of them.

"Hey Mom, could you get the cereal out of the cabinet for me?" Dan had asked. He was standing a few feet from the cupboard, a strange look on his face.

"Dan, you're perfectly capable of getting it yourself," I said. "I'm not your maid." But that expression. What was that? Fear?

"No, Mom, really, please get it for me, okay? I can't go over there."

"What do you mean you can't go over there? What are you talking about?"

"Nothing. I just can't do it."

If it weren't for his obvious apprehension, I would've been sure he was joking. Why on earth would a healthy seventeen-year-old not be able to walk over to a cabinet, open the door, and remove a box of cereal?

"Come on, Dan, we'll do it together," I'd said. I tried to take his hand, but he resisted. "Did you see something scary over there?" My question seemed way off the mark, even to me, but I didn't know how to react to what was happening.

Eventually I got the cereal for him and mentally registered this event under the strange-but-true category, where there were other listings already: Dan had recently stopped eating ice cream and wouldn't go into our swimming pool. These and other changes were more subtle than the cereal incident, and I only became aware of them over time. I never thought of them as signs of a problem, just odd occurrences.

And there was the touching. "What's with your fingerprints all over the walls?" I'd asked. Dan was an artist and his hands were often covered in charcoal, so the walls were a mess.

"Oh sorry. I didn't realize I was doing that."

"Well, stop, okay?" I didn't think much of it. Still, I felt that vague unrest.

But the cereal incident was weird, and I'd relayed it to my husband Gary. "You know, I even thought of calling the doctor, but what would I say? My son won't open a cupboard door?" In retrospect, I should've called. But it didn't matter much, because soon after that, Dan, who had diagnosed himself with the help of the Internet, told me his secret. I had responded with, "Are you sure, Dan? You never even wash your hands!" Deep down, however, I knew if Dan said he had OCD, he had OCD. Dan knew his stuff. His diagnosis was confirmed by his longtime pediatrician, Dr. Wright, who prescribed a low dose of an SSRI (selective serotonin reuptake inhibitor). And the doctor somewhat alleviated my fear.

"Yes, Dan definitely has OCD. And he knows more about it than I do," Dr. Wright said between chuckles. He knew Dan well, and I found the doctor's lightheartedness comforting. He hadn't laughed when Dan was a baby and had a 105.8-degree fever, or when Dan was two and had a severe allergic reaction to a bee sting. Okay, he did laugh the time Dan plopped down on our couch and then had to have a pencil tip removed from his buttocks, but we all laughed at that one, even Dan. So how bad could OCD be? When Dr. Wright suggested Dan see a therapist, we found Dr. Thomas, who told us Dan's OCD was "no big deal." Dan then met with Dr. Thomas once every two weeks for four months until he left for his dream college fifteen hundred miles from home. We now knew that amounted to approximately ten sessions of the wrong kind of therapy, and come to find out, Dan's obsessive-compulsive disorder was a pretty big deal.

WHAT IS OBSESSIVE-COMPULSIVE DISORDER?

The essence of OCD is repeatedly worrying that something awful is going to happen and then doing something to try to prevent it. Usually when we think of OCD we imagine a "washer" or a "checker"[1]: individuals who wash their hands all the time so they don't catch a terrible disease, or who compulsively check and recheck the stove to be sure it's off. While "washers and checkers" make up a good number of the people with OCD, it's important to recognize the many different ways in which OCD can manifest itself.

Put simply, there is no limit to the kinds of things that OCD can make a person worry about. Relatively common areas of concern involve contracting an illness; being responsible for a fire, car accident, or other horrifying event; and behaving in a way that is illegal or immoral.

Regardless of the specific content, OCD involves a cycle of discomfort (triggered by an obsession) followed by an action or a thought (compulsion) to relieve that discomfort.[2] A person might worry that the stove was left on—which leads to a spike in worry and anxiety—followed by checking the stove to be sure it is off, which tends to give the person at least a brief feeling of "Ahh, it's

okay." This sense of relief feels good since it reduces the person's discomfort. OCD's trick, of course, is that it's impossible to be sure of anything, and uncertainty is fuel for OCD's fire. That sense of "It's okay" is soon enough followed by, ". . . or *is* it?" How do we *know* we've done something right, or seen correctly, or accurately remembered what we saw?

So people with OCD often get trapped in frustrating cycles of obsession-compulsion-obsession-compulsion. It feels good to get the little bit of relief that compulsions provide; when the obsessions inevitably return, the person will again resort to doing a compulsion. Now the person is playing OCD's game and may not know how to stop.

1. Jonathan S. Abramowitz, Martin E. Franklin, Stefanie A. Schwartz, and Jami M. Furr, "Symptom Presentation and Outcome of Cognitive-Behavioral Therapy for Obsessive-Compulsive Disorder," *Journal of Consulting and Clinical Psychology* 71, no. 6 (2003): 1049.
2. Ibid., 1055.

I'd picked him up earlier that evening at the Sculpture Garden, our usual on-campus meeting place. Amid the lights and shadows of the sculptures, I'd seen him from a distance and immediately knew something was terribly wrong. He was standing, and his tall frame seemed to hang limply. I sensed his fear, confusion, and defeat, even from afar, and a sense of panic had overwhelmed me. By the time I stood beside him, so debilitated he could barely climb steps, I'd walled off my emotions. I was there to help Dan, and if I fell apart there would be nobody to care for either of us. Still, the questions crept in. How could this be happening to my son? What *was* happening to my son? Surely we were now dealing with more than obsessive-compulsive disorder. More terrifying to me than these questions was the thought that I desperately tried to squelch: *This could be it.* Dan might be gone, beyond anyone's help, and I had no way of knowing if he'd ever be back.

He stuck close to the door and surveyed his surroundings, a typical drab motel room with two double beds. On the far right side of the room was a kitchenette with a refrigerator, a yellow-gold stove, and a microwave. A small drop-leaf table and two chairs completed the area. The bathroom was behind the kitchenette and not visible from where Dan was standing. The room had a mildly musty odor, not uncommon for the South.

"Want to lie down?" I said. "You must be exhausted."

"No, I don't want to," he replied, looking around the room nervously.

He stood for a while longer, seeming deep in thought, and then tiptoed past the beds so he could sit at the tiny kitchen table. He slouched over so much his head was practically touching its surface. I put my hand on his shoulder, and he flinched, which was unusual for him. He was always so affectionate.

"How about some food?" I offered in that cheery voice that was starting to annoy me. I rattled off some of his favorite things to eat.

He shook his head.

"Oh, I bought some of those smoothie drinks you like," I persisted. "I'll pour you one, okay?"

"No thanks," he replied softly.

"You have to have something," I pleaded. "You're probably dehydrated. At least have something to drink. Please."

"Okay, I'll have some water from the tap."

I poured the water and sat next to him. "You look so thin, honey. When was the last time you ate?"

"I don't know, probably five or six days ago."

I felt that tightness again. "You have to eat. I have a full refrigerator. Please let me give you some food."

"I just can't eat now, Mom. I'm sorry. I promise I'll eat tomorrow."

"Why haven't you been able to eat?" I asked, already knowing this simple question had a complicated answer.

"Well, I can't go into the dining hall," he said. Although undoubtedly relevant, there was obviously more. Here he was, sitting in front of a refrigerator stocked with all his favorite foods, and he couldn't eat?

"What about your medication, honey? Are you taking it?"

"Yup, every morning with a little water." He didn't seem to mind me asking questions, so I kept going.

"How about your classes? Are you still able to keep up with your work?"

"Yeah, pretty much, I guess, but it's really hard to concentrate."

"Oh, Dan, I'm sure not eating has a lot to do with that," I said, and then stopped. I didn't want to lecture him now, not tonight. "Did you have fun with your friends earlier?"

"I guess it was good, except I'm so anxious I can't enjoy myself."

At this point I realized Dan hadn't even touched the glass of water to his lips.

He lifted his head and looked at me. "But don't worry. I'm okay."

Of course I knew this wasn't true. Dan was obviously in rough shape; I just didn't know how to help him. His appointment with Dr. Vogel, a new therapist, was six days away, though I doubted he'd make it until then. My mind whirled as I tried to think clearly. I'd call Mark, a close friend who is a clinical psychologist, first thing in the morning.

"It's well after midnight, Dan. Why don't you just sleep here tonight?"

"No, thanks, I really want to go back to my room if you don't mind."

"Okay, as long as tomorrow we get you some food."

"Sure, that's fine."

We began our descent. Once outside the room, Dan's anxiety was palpable, and he froze briefly before we retraced our earlier steps, walking past the closed doors until we arrived at the top of the staircase. Then we did it all again: freezing, reassuring, coaxing, hesitating, wincing, and stepping. His eyes darted often, as if there were danger all around us. In the car, he tapped the window continuously during the three-minute ride back to his dorm.

"Thanks for driving me, Mom."

"You're welcome, honey," I said. "I hope you get a good night's sleep. By the way, how messy is your room?"

"Nothing like before. Don't worry."

I smiled at him. "Good night, I love you. See you tomorrow."

"Love you too, Mom."

He easily got out of the car. I watched him walk away, his gait interrupted now and then by a little skip, which in any other situation would have been cute. He walked into his dorm and out of my sight. Troubled and confused by his odd behavior, I consoled myself with the thought that tomorrow, he would eat.

Our meeting place was in the middle of the campus, and I arrived early. I sat in the midst of students scurrying to and from class, meeting up with friends, or just hanging out. Everyone seemed so . . . normal. Why wasn't my son one of them? From across the quad, Dan was walking toward me with his head down. He was wearing a long-sleeved

hooded sweatshirt, again in the heat, and he had the hood on. Every few steps he did a little shuffle.

"You on your way to rob a convenience store?" I asked, and he managed a little smile. "I figured we'd go to a restaurant, okay?"

"No, I really don't want to do that."

My anxiety from the day before had remained, and now I felt myself sweating. "You have to eat something today. You promised." When he didn't respond I said, "If you don't want to go to a restaurant, I'll make you something to eat at the motel."

He just shrugged. We drove back to the motel in silence. Panic erupted inside me over the real possibility Dan might not eat. I tried, unsuccessfully, to suppress this thought.

The stair climbing was tough, but at least this time I wasn't so shocked. Our audience was, though; it was now broad daylight, and there were several people milling about the motel.

Freezing, reassuring, coaxing, hesitating, wincing, and stepping; we did it all over again. I knew people were staring, but this wasn't a time to care about what others might be thinking. Plus, what other choice did I have? I had left my disappearing wand at home.

Once inside, Dan went right for the chair he sat in the night before, as if it were a safe haven amongst dangerous waters. I looked at my son closely. Hunched over once again, he was chewing on what was left of his hood strings. He was so thin, his cheekbones and jawbone protruded.

He stood up to use the bathroom, and his pants fell down. His belt, even on the tightest hole, couldn't keep them up. We burst out laughing, and for a moment all was well. Dan was still Dan, sense of humor and all.

If only he would eat. I offered him every food and drink combination I could think of. My son, whose zest for food had always paralleled his zest for life, wasn't capable of putting a morsel into his mouth.

"Nah, I don't want anything," he said.

"Dan, you promised you'd eat today."

"I know, but I can't eat today. I'll eat tomorrow."

"Did you even take your medication this morning?" I asked. I was annoyed now, and I needed to talk to Mark. Hopefully he'd return my call soon and remind me Dan wasn't in control; his OCD was.

"Yeah, I took it. Stop worrying. I'm okay."

"Dan, maybe you could tell me a little about what you're thinking, so I can understand better. Can you tell me why you can't eat today?"

"Because."

We sat in silence for a while.

"It's a beautiful day, honey," I said. "How about we go for a little walk just to get out of the room?"

"No thanks. I'd rather just sit here." He was shivering.

I took a blanket off one of the beds and wrapped it around his bony shoulders.

"Thanks," he said, and then proceeded to shift the blanket from his shoulders to his head, so now he was totally wrapped up in it, shaking and rocking back and forth slightly. He began moaning and mumbling, and wouldn't talk to me.

I sat on the bed, put my head in my hands and watched my son deteriorate.

A half hour later I broke the silence. "Honey, listen to me. I know a big part of your problem right now is physical, from not eating or drinking."

"No, I'm okay, I had something to drink this morning." He sounded eerily calm.

"Please, just have a little water."

"No, I'm fine. I think what I'll do is just sit here until midnight and then go back to my dorm and do some work or go to sleep, okay?"

"Midnight? You can't be serious." It was now four o'clock in the afternoon. My son wanted to stay in the exact same position, doing nothing but shaking, moaning, and mumbling, for the next eight hours. "No, you can't sit here until midnight."

He looked puzzled. "Why not?" he asked simply. "I do this all the time."

HOW DO I FIND AN OCD THERAPIST?

The good news for OCD sufferers is that cognitive-behavioral therapy (CBT), and in particular exposure and response prevention (ERP),[1] can be extremely effective. Unfortunately it can be difficult to find a therapist who specializes in this treatment, in large part because most therapists who treat OCD do not consistently use ERP.[2]

Many therapists who provide solid ERP are located in research and treatment centers within medical schools, such as the Obsessive-Compulsive and Related Disorders Research Center at Stanford University, the Center for Anxiety and Related Disorders at Boston University, and the Center for the Treatment and Study of Anxiety at the University of Pennsylvania. If you live close to this kind of academic center it can be an excellent place to start.

If, like most people, you don't have easy access to this type of center, there are other options available. The International OCD Foundation (IOCDF) website has a searchable database of providers (see below), so you can check if there is somebody close to you who provides ERP. The IOCDF also has helpful tips for figuring out if a therapist provides effective ERP; for example, if the clinician describes his or her approach as "eclectic," it's likely that you would receive a watered-down form of ERP.

If you don't live within easy driving distance to an outpatient ERP therapist, another option is to seek out intensive outpatient treatment for OCD. This option generally involves two-hour sessions of ERP five times a week for three to four weeks, and therefore a person generally stays in the city where the therapy is provided for the duration of the treatment. Again, the IOCDF website has a database of intensive treatment providers. Finally, there are a limited number of residential programs that offer inpatient ERP for individuals who require that level of treatment.

Although the task of finding a good OCD therapist can seem daunting, most people who have done so would say it was worth the time and effort to find the right treatment.

International OCD Foundation (IOCDF) Treatment Provider
    Search:
    http://www.ocfoundation.org/treatment_providers.aspx
Association for Behavioral and Cognitive Therapies (ABCT)
    CBT Therapist Search:
    http://www.abctcentral.org/xFAT

IOCDF Tips for Finding an ERP Therapist:
http://www.ocfoundation.org/treatment_providers.
aspx#Looking_for_therapist

1. Ana I. Rosa-Alcázar, Julio Sánchez-Meca, Antonia Gómez-Conesa, and Fulgencio Marín-Martínez, "Psychological Treatment of Obsessive-Compulsive Disorder: A Meta-analysis," *Clinical Psychology Review* 28, no. 8 (2008): 1311–12.
2. Stacy R. Freiheit, Christopher Vye, Rebecca Swan, and Mary Cady, "Cognitive-Behavioral Therapy for Anxiety: Is Dissemination Working?" *The Behavior Therapist* 27, no. 2 (2004): 28.

2

LOOKING FOR HELP

"**W**hat a smile!" strangers would say whenever I was out with my toddler son. Dan exuded joy. Not over anything in particular, just life. He was thrilled to be in the world and often couldn't contain himself, breaking into song or dance or twirl without warning. And always with that smile. From as far back as I could remember, he had that extra something that attracted people to him, and even as a young child he was caring and kind. Many a preschool girl would announce, "I'm going to marry Danny Singer." In elementary school, his good nature, nonjudgmental personality, and sharp sense of humor endeared him to his teachers and his peers. Everyone wanted him on their team. Parent-teacher conferences were a delight, hearing teachers gush over him and marvel at his vast knowledge and intelligence. He was interested in everything and read voraciously. At the age of eleven he was tackling philosophy books I couldn't even pretend to understand.

While Dan and his sisters Lainey and Ava had homeschooled off and on through the elementary school years, Dan continued on this path from seventh grade through high school (except for a five-month high school trial his freshman year, after which he declared he was leaving school so he could continue his education). Dan loved homeschooling and was more than willing to have the freedom to learn as he pleased. He honed in on the arts, specifically computer animation, and excitedly announced one day, "I'm going to be an animator."

His enthusiasm was contagious, and during a vacation to the Los Angeles area, we arranged an informational interview at California Institute of the Arts, a world-renowned college for animation started by Walt Disney. It went something like this:

Admissions rep: So you're interested in computer animation?

Dan: Yes.

Admissions rep: Did you bring your portfolio with you?

Dan: Oh, I need to have a portfolio?

Admissions rep: Yes, we need to evaluate your artistic skills. Do you draw or sketch at all?

Dan: No.

Admissions rep: Well, if you want to get into animation you need a portfolio, so start sketching, okay?

Dan: Okay.

Hmm. Well, that's that, I thought as we left the room. Dan would have to figure out something else to do with his life. He was never a doodler as a child and hadn't really done any drawing, though he did love art museums.

That was my take on the interview. Dan's only comment was, "I better start drawing."

And draw he did. From museum classes to painting classes to a figure-drawing co-op where he was the only one under forty years of age, Dan immersed himself in art. His teachers were impressed with his enthusiasm, maturity, and yes, talent. Four years later he entered Carson College, the number-one school for animation in North America.

Mark finally called. I left Dan in his chair and brought the phone outside, where I told Mark things that, even now, seemed unbelievable. How Dan could barely get out of the car and into the motel room, how

thin and sunken he looked, how he wouldn't eat or drink, and how he had just announced he wouldn't be moving for the next eight hours. I had to pretend I was talking about someone else, not my son.

"Janet," Mark asked, "does Dan realize how irrational his behavior is?"

"I honestly don't know."

"Well, people with OCD can have strange rituals," Mark explained. "But for the most part, they understand their behaviors are irrational; they just can't control them."

I knew what Mark was really asking: Are we dealing with more than OCD here? If Dan truly believed not eating made sense, then there was a chance he might be contending with an additional mental health disorder.

ODD BEHAVIOR IN OCD

It is not unusual for people with OCD to adopt behaviors that appear strange from the outside and that the individuals themselves may even recognize as being odd. For example, compulsions can involve tapping one's fingers together, repeating actions such as closing a door or turning off a light, or ritualized patterns of steps. At the extreme these behaviors can be mistaken for symptoms of schizophrenia.[1]

However, careful assessment can reveal the function of these odd-seeming movements. For example, individuals who tap repeatedly may have developed a compulsion to negate "wicked" thoughts by making a brief "cross" with their hands. Or, individuals might have developed a rule to repeat a step if while taking the step they thought about someone being hurt.

Most of the time a person with OCD will acknowledge that these apparently strange behaviors are not actually preventing bad things from happening. But when the person has an obsessive thought, it can be extremely hard to resist the urge to neutralize the thought with a ritualized behavior.

1. Spengler and Jacobi, "Assessment and Treatment," 100.

"Are you sure he's taking his medication?" Mark asked.

"Mark, at this point, I'm not sure of anything," I said, letting out a heavy sigh. Since arriving in Bridgeville, I'd felt like Alice from *Alice in Wonderland*. Nothing was as it should be.

"Well, regardless, you need to get him to the emergency room as soon as possible."

Of course! Consumed by anxiety, I hadn't even been able to come up with the most logical thing to do. "But what if he won't go with me?"

"You need to be firm with him and just tell him this is what you're going to do. If he doesn't cooperate, which I feel is unlikely knowing Dan, I'd call the police and have them escort you to the hospital."

Wow, wouldn't that be fun? My son, who has spent his life trying to do the right thing, might need to be carted away by the police. This image sparked an intense sadness that sat in me like lead.

I took a deep breath and went back into the motel room. Dan was still on the chair, moaning and shivering. I knelt next to him.

"So what did Mark say?" he asked.

I was glad he had the wherewithal to even ask. "He said we need to get you to the hospital."

"Really?" He didn't sound upset, just surprised.

"Yes, honey, you need help."

He didn't respond.

"Dan, do you realize how unreasonable your thinking has become? Do you really think something horrible will happen if you move from your chair before midnight, or if you have something to eat?"

"I know it doesn't make any sense," he replied, "but I also really believe it."

My heart sank. I didn't know what his response meant so I tried not to concentrate on anything except getting my son to the nearest hospital.

Once again we began the ordeal of getting from the motel room to the car, though this trip down the steps was a little easier than the last. Dan perked up a bit once we got into the car. "So what do you think they'll do to me at the hospital?" he asked.

"I'm guessing you're dehydrated so they'll probably give you some IV fluids," I said. "And they'll do some blood work."

"That sounds okay," he said, nodding. "What else?"

"Well, I hope there will be a psychiatrist or psychologist on call to speak with us." I turned into the parking lot and took the last available space.

He got out of the car eagerly. It occurred to me he might actually be glad to be at the hospital, to hopefully get some help. Hey, it beat sitting in a kitchen chair for eight hours. As for me, I was relieved to be among professionals who would know how to treat him. I felt, at the very least, that we were in the right place.

As pleased as Dan might have been to be getting help, he still wore his sweatshirt hood up and was chewing, no, chomping on the hood strings.

"Dan, please don't do that," I requested several times. He'd stop for a few minutes, but somehow those strings always ended up back in his mouth. I tried to ignore his chewing and surveyed the waiting room. There were many parents with sick children. Sitting next to us was an elderly couple, looking amazingly well put-together and healthy for being in an emergency room.

"Not too busy tonight," the man said, as if he were there every night and could compare.

I smiled half-heartedly.

"So what is he here for?" he asked, jutting his chin toward Dan. I guess it was obvious that Dan was the patient, not me.

"He has some health problems," I said, and wondered if he could tell by looking at Dan that he had some *mental* health problems. I quickly surmised he could. What he saw was a disheveled young man chewing on the strings of his hooded sweatshirt, hood on head. His foot was twitching uncontrollably, his anxiety evident. Perhaps the polite thing to do at this point would've been to ask what he or his wife was there for, but instead I turned away.

"Daniel Singer, right this way please," the admitting nurse called an hour later. I followed a few steps behind as she led us past some drawn curtains to the last open cubicle.

"Just sit up there," the nurse said, motioning to the exam table, "and someone will be in shortly." She turned and left.

"You do all the talking," Dan said, looking nervous.

"If you can't explain what's going on, then I'll try."

A few minutes later another nurse entered. "Well hello there," she said as she drew the curtain. "I'm Michelle and I'll be helping you out, okay?" She looked like Cameron Diaz and gave Dan a big smile. He smiled back.

"So what's been going on with you?" she asked him, as if she were talking to an old friend.

Dan shrugged and turned his head toward me. His eyes pleaded for me to speak.

"Dan has OCD," I said. "He hasn't eaten in about a week. He has an appointment with a clinical psychologist coming up but really needs help now."

Our eyes met and I knew Michelle sensed my desperation. "I'm going to draw some blood from you and then hook you up to an IV, okay?" she said to Dan.

He nodded.

"Just put on this johnny and I'll be back in a few minutes."

"Would you mind staying outside the cubicle for a while so I can have some privacy?" he asked me.

"Of course not, honey," I replied and then stepped out of the cubicle. "No problem." But there was a problem, and I already knew what he was trying to hide from me. "Dan, you should feel free to talk to the nurse and doctor about anything, okay?" I said through the curtain. "They're here to help you."

"Okay, Mom, I know."

Michelle smiled at me as she went around the curtain. There was some conversation going on as she hooked Dan up to the IV, but I couldn't hear what they were saying. It certainly wasn't from lack of trying. When she left, I was invited back in.

"So what's been going on here?" I asked.

"Well, Michelle took my blood and hooked me up to this IV," Dan explained.

He had a blanket wrapped around him. He tried to cover his arms, but I could see: razor-thin horizontal stripes from his wrists up to his shoulders, too many to count. Some were scarred over and others looked fresh. My eyes welled. I couldn't help it. The thought that my beautiful son had done this to himself on purpose was more than I could handle. I'd been devastated when the psychiatrist Dan saw a week earlier told us he'd been self-injuring, but now, witnessing it with my own eyes, I was heartbroken.

SELF-INJURY IN OCD

It is important to distinguish between harm-related obsessions, self-injury, and suicidality in OCD. Many individuals with OCD have a fear that they might harm themselves, with no actual desire to do so.[1] For example, a woman might fear she will impulsively drive her car off a bridge, or will jump off a tall building. Exploring the nature of these thoughts will reveal that these individuals have zero desire to injure or kill themselves and that the thoughts are obsessive concerns not based on a real risk.

In other cases individuals might actually harm themselves without any intention of dying,[2] for example, by making cuts on their skin that are unlikely to result in serious harm. People harm themselves for different reasons; some people experience a release of tension from cutting themselves, whereas other people might feel extraordinarily guilty and will cut themselves as a form of punishment.[3] Nonsuicidal self-injury is a serious concern not only because of the suffering that it signals but also because individuals who self-injure are at a much higher risk for making suicide attempts.[4]

Actual suicide attempts are not infrequent in OCD,[5] particularly among individuals with OCD plus depression.[6] These suicide attempts underscore the degree of suffering associated with OCD and the crucial need for effective treatment.

1. Monnica T. Williams, Beth Mugno, Martin Franklin, and Sonya Faber, "Symptom Dimensions in Obsessive-Compulsive Disorder: Phenomenology and Treatment Outcomes with Exposure and Ritual Prevention," *Psychopathology* 46, no. 6 (2013): 369.
2. Jose A. Yaryura-Tobias, Fugen A. Neziroglu, and Steven Kaplan, "Self-Mutilation, Anorexia, and Dysmenorrhea in Obsessive Compulsive Disorder," *International Journal of Eating Disorders* 17 , no. 1 (January 1995): 36.
3. Matthew K. Nock, "Self-Injury," *Annual Review of Clinical Psychology* 6 (2010): 352.
4. Matthew K. Nock, Thomas E. Joiner Jr., Kathryn H. Gordon, Elizabeth Lloyd-Richardson, and Mitchell J. Prinstein, "Non-suicidal Self-Injury among Adolescents: Diagnostic Correlates and Relation to Suicide Attempts," *Psychiatry Research* 144 (2006): 68.
5. Prakash Kamath, Y. C. Janardhan Reddy, and Thennarasu Kandavel, "Suicidal Behavior in Obsessive-Compulsive Disorder," *Journal of Clinical Psychiatry* 68, no. 11 (November 2007): 1744; Albina R. Torres, Ana Teresa A. Ramos-Cerqueira, Ygor A. Ferrao, Leonardo F. Fontenelle, Maria Conceicao do Rosario, and Euripedes C. Miguel, "Suicidality in Obsessive-Compulsive Disorder: Prevalence and Relation to Symptom Dimensions and Comorbid Conditions," *Journal of Clinical Psychiatry* 72 , no. 1 (January 2011): 19.
6. Kamath, Reddy, and Kandavel, "Suicidal Behavior," 1744–45.

It was Mark who'd eased my mind somewhat. "While I know it's upsetting to you, Dan's cutting himself is not as big a deal as it seems, and certainly not the worst of his problems," he'd explained.

"Really?" I'd responded. "It seems pretty bad to me."

"Dan cutting himself isn't about him wanting to hurt himself. In fact, it's just the opposite. The act of cutting actually jolts him out of his obsessive thinking and makes him feel better. You could compare it to someone being slapped in the face when he or she is out of control. It brings the person back to reality."

"Geez, can't he just splash some water on his face?" I'd asked.

"Good point," Mark replied. "Of course, cutting is a maladaptive behavior, and he'll need to learn better coping skills. But for right now, his OCD is the bigger problem."

I tried to take Mark's words to heart while Dan and I chatted and the IV fluids dripped into his veins. In just a few minutes, there was a noticeable change in his demeanor. He perked up. His eyes looked brighter, and his voice sounded stronger.

"How do you feel, honey?" I asked, wondering if he felt what I noticed.

"Actually, much better," he said. "Isn't it amazing what a little fluid can do?"

The curtain opened and a tall, spectacled man entered the cubicle. "I'm Dr. Snyder," he said, extending his hand to Dan and then me. He looked down at his clipboard. "Okay, let's see here. Not only are you dehydrated, young man, but you also have hypokalemia; that's low potassium. Both of these conditions can cause many physical and mental symptoms, including confusion, depression, and lethargy. That's the bad news. The good news is they're also easily remedied through eating and drinking properly. So you need to eat and drink, okay?"

"Okay," Dan said.

"Great. Now why don't you just rest a little more, and I'll talk to your mom out here." Dr. Snyder motioned me to follow him.

When I spoke with Mark, he had prepared me for the real possibility that Dan would be hospitalized. That's where I thought Dr. Snyder was heading when he spoke.

"Why hasn't Dan eaten in a week?" he asked me, once we were out of earshot.

"I just arrived yesterday, and all I know is that it's related to his OCD," I answered. Did I just say I arrived yesterday? I felt as if I'd been in Bridgeville a month.

"Does Dan have a health-care provider in the area?"

"Well, we're meeting with someone new in about a week," I answered.

Dr. Snyder nodded. "Okay, we'll discharge him as soon as the IV is done."

It took a few seconds for me to process what he was saying. "Wait," I called out as the doctor started to walk away. "I'm afraid I won't be able to get Dan to eat, and his appointment isn't for another week."

"I've spoken with Dan and told him he has to eat," Dr. Snyder replied. "What else do you want me to do?"

Did I hear correctly? What else did I want him to do? Wasn't he the doctor? Wasn't he supposed to know, or at least pretend to know, what to do? Did he really think just telling Dan he had to eat would do the trick?

"Is there a psychiatrist or psychologist on call who I could speak with?" I asked.

"There's no one here now. It's after hours," Dr. Snyder said. "But I'll have someone call you in the morning."

With that he walked away. And I never received a call from anyone.

Back in the cubicle, Dan had really connected with Michelle. When she arrived with his discharge papers, she hung around for a few minutes to chat.

"You know, you're a great guy," she said. "You keep following your dreams, okay? Because I have a hunch they'll all come true."

Dan was smiling. Apparently I'd missed a lot on the other side of the curtain.

"Maybe your medication just needs adjusting, but you're going to be fine," Michelle said, looking Dan right in the eye. "And don't forget what else we talked about, okay?"

"I won't," he replied, looking right back at her.

I wanted to take Michelle with us.

"Thanks for everything," he said sincerely.

"My pleasure. Good luck, Dan. Now go home and have something to eat." She smiled warmly, drew back the curtain, and was gone.

We both took a deep breath of fresh air once we were outside. Our ride back to the motel was quiet, each of us lost in our own thoughts. I had no

idea what he was thinking, but I was still processing the fact that not only had Dr. Snyder no idea how to help my son but he also didn't seem to really care. Of course I knew Dan needed to see a mental health professional, but I'd also naively imagined the hospital staff crowding around him, all the while assuring me gently that he'd be fine. Disappointment turned into fear as I realized for now anyway, we were on our own. At least I could call Mark and hoped he'd guide me in getting Dan to eat.

There was another thought that had been creeping into my mind, though I tried hard to shut it out. What if I hadn't come back to Dan? What would have happened to him? I imagine he would have collapsed eventually. What if he had been alone when it happened?

Don't waste your energy thinking about what could have been, I told myself. *It's hard enough having to deal with what really is.* I wasn't aware of it at the time, but learning to not dwell on "what-ifs" would be a critical component of Dan's therapy to get well.

It was close to two o'clock in the morning when we pulled into the parking lot across from Dan's dorm. "You can come back to the motel with me if you want," I said, breaking the silence.

"No, I'd really like to go back to my dorm," he replied. "I'm feeling so much better after that IV."

"Okay, that's fine. But first things first. Do you want to go home?"

"No, Mom, I really want to try to finish the semester," he said without hesitation. He sounded determined, yet the confidence in his voice wasn't mirrored in his face. He looked worried.

"All right, you know I'll help you in any way possible, but there are some stipulations."

"Like what?"

"You have to eat. And that means three meals a day."

He nodded.

"We have to contact Dr. Moore and let her know what's been going on."

He nodded again.

"And you have to meet with Dr. Vogel, and you have to let me into your room."

"Wow. You've certainly given this all some thought. I think I can do all of those things."

"That's great, honey. Get some sleep now and we'll meet in the afternoon. And we'll have a meal, okay?"

"Okay."

I gave him a big hug and he didn't flinch.

He got out of the car, closed the door, and leaned back in through the open window. "Thanks for a fun night," he said with a grin.

I watched him walk, with an occasional little hop, into his dorm.

3

TIME TO EAT

If you are going to have a mental health crisis in your family, I recommend having a close friend who is an amazing clinical psychologist. I called Mark first thing in the morning.

"Obviously our main focus now is getting him to eat," Mark said. "Do you have any idea what his reasons are for not eating?"

"I honestly don't know," I answered. "Maybe he feels he isn't worthy of eating, that because there are so many starving people in the world, why should *he* get to eat? He's always been so caring and empathetic, so that's a possibility. I don't know. I'm just guessing. Or maybe he just thinks something terrible will happen to himself or his loved ones if he allows himself to eat." I was just learning about obsessive-compulsive disorder and knew that many of Dan's obsessions centered on fear of harm coming to those he loved. I speculated that not being able to eat or drink was a compulsion Dan needed to perform to keep everyone "safe."

"We really don't know what he's thinking," Mark said, "but let's talk about some strategies you can use to help him."

I listened, took notes, and went off to meet Dan.

My goal was for Dan to eat, and I let him know this right away. "You know this isn't negotiable. You have to eat today."

He winced. "Okay, but not until six o'clock tonight."

My first inclination was to argue with him. After all, I'd insisted he eat three meals a day. But after speaking with Mark, it was clear that forcing

Dan to refrain from his compulsions would be torture for him. I'll admit I caved, not only to delay his suffering but to delay mine as well.

"Okay, you can wait until six o'clock, but no more negotiating."

"I can't go into a restaurant," he said.

"That's fine, honey," I said. "Whatever and wherever works for you."

Our plan was to order takeout from one of his favorite Mexican restaurants, but that wouldn't happen for hours. "I'll get some work done in your room," he said as we drove back to the motel. Once there, however, he went straight for his chair and wouldn't budge. He just sat there, thin, exhausted, and anxious.

It seemed like a good time to try to reason with him, and I embarked on a monologue. "You know, Mark and I were talking about how your reasoning related to eating is warped. You think you're stopping bad things from happening by starving yourself, but really, you're doing just the opposite. You're hurting yourself tremendously, and that's upsetting to those who love you. Eating isn't selfish. You need to eat to survive. You can't contribute to society, or function at all, unless you take care of yourself."

He seemed to be listening but didn't respond.

"You're not as powerful as you might think," I continued. "There's no real connection between your behaviors and what happens in the world. As much as we all like to think we have this kind of control over the universe, we don't. Not at all."

While I didn't expect him to openly agree with me, I was hoping for some sort of acknowledgment. All I got was a glazed look. I know he heard me, but his OCD was too entrenched at that point for my words to matter. I doubted I could help him alone and sadly resigned myself to the likelihood we'd be heading home soon.

"It's almost six o'clock, Dan. Let's get going."

By the look on his face you'd think I'd told him he was about to face a firing squad. We made our arduous way down to the car and drove to the restaurant.

"Why don't you come in and pick out what you want?" I suggested. All my anxiety had settled in my stomach, and I wondered how *I* would be able to eat.

"I can't go in, Mom," he answered quietly. "Just pick something out for me. You know what I like. Anything will be fine."

"Okay, honey," I said. "I'll be out soon."

Within minutes, I was back in the car with two bags full of white Styrofoam containers.

"Wow, that smells great," he said, surprising both of us.

"So we'll take the food back to the motel like we talked about, okay?" I said.

"Would you mind if we just ate in the car, Mom?"

You can eat in the trunk if you want—as long as you eat. To him I said, "Sure, that's fine."

"There's a really pretty spot near campus where we can park the car," he suggested.

This would have been a lovely idea in any other situation, but I sensed he was stalling. "Okay, I'll drive there but then you have to eat. We don't want the food to get cold."

"I will. I'll eat."

It was only a short drive to a side street where there was a magnificent view overlooking the bay. A few people were sitting on benches, eating and enjoying the beauty.

"Want to get out?" I asked.

"No thanks, I'd rather stay in the car," he answered. He'd been doing a lot of touching and tapping since I got the food, and now it was worse.

I divvied up the plastic silverware and handed him his food. He was shaking and couldn't open his container.

I pretended to be excited about my taco salad, hoping it would rub off on him. It didn't work. His container remained closed. Looking at him, unable to eat, I desperately wanted to understand. What on earth happened to my son?

"I know this is so hard for you," I said, "but I'm going to have to make airline reservations for us to go home tomorrow."

"No, you don't have to do that. I'll eat later."

"No, Dan, there's no more 'later.' You have to eat now. This is the time we agreed upon and you need to eat now, or we'll have to go home."

I took a deep breath and started my monologue again. "You controlling your own actions, like eating, has no effect whatsoever on what happens in the world. You can't cause bad things to happen by eating. In fact, as I said before, it's just the opposite."

I knew I was already sounding like a broken record, but I was hoping that hearing this continually would somehow be helpful. Besides, I had no idea what else to do.

Forty-five minutes later we were still sitting in the car. I'd been taking little bites of my food, but he still sat with the closed Styrofoam container on his lap. It was heart wrenching for me to see my son in this condition and not be able to help him.

He finally spoke. "I want to be alone when I eat. I'm going to sit on a bench."

Of course my first thought was that he'd unload his food on the first dog that walked by, so I said, "Okay, but I need to be able to see you from here."

He took his food and got out of the car, walked slowly toward the imaginary firing squad, hesitated, and then sat by himself on a bench. Even though I could only see him from the back, I could tell he was shaking badly. He stayed there, hunched over, trying to get himself to eat, for almost an hour.

I resigned myself that it just wasn't going to happen, got out of the car and walked toward him. Motion caught my eye. His fork was going from his food to his mouth in a mechanical, rhythmic way. I stopped and watched. Yes, it was true. Dan was eating. He was still shaking and it looked as though he was on automatic pilot, as if he couldn't think about or acknowledge what he was doing. But he was eating.

Once he forced himself to take that first bite, each subsequent bite seemed to be a little easier. *What a huge step. He did it! Maybe it would be possible for him to get through the semester after all?* I walked back to the car and waited for him to finish.

"I'm so proud of you," I gushed when he returned.

He seemed dazed, as if he couldn't believe what he'd just done. He got into the car and sat quietly for a minute before he spoke. "Boy that was really good. Guess I was kind of hungry."

Though he made me smile, there was a strange disconnect between the levity of his words and the magnitude of the situation. I wasn't sure if he meant to be funny. Either way, it was okay. He'd eaten. I said, "I have no idea what you're going through, but I know what you just did took a lot of courage and determination, and you should be very proud of yourself."

Who knew watching my son eat a burrito could overwhelm me with such pride?

We decided to call Gary and fill him in on the good news. Turns out my husband had some news of his own. "Dan got into St. Joseph's," he said. "The letter came today."

St. Joseph's Hospital has a world-renowned residential treatment program for OCD, and when I last visited Dan, he'd completed the extensive application, hoping to be admitted for the upcoming summer. That would be perfect for him, since he was determined not to miss any school. Not only did the program have a great reputation; it was also less than an hour's drive from our home.

"That's great," Dan said upon hearing the news. "Pretty impressive, huh? Do you think it was my essay or my recommendations that won them over?"

Ah, that sense of humor warmed my heart. Though he really did have to submit an essay and recommendations, there had been no doubt he was a "qualified" candidate. But Dan's admission came with one stipulation: he had to stop self-injuring immediately. We hadn't yet spoken about his cutting, and now was the time to do that. "Do you think you'll be able to stop cutting yourself?" I asked, as nonchalantly as anybody could sound asking a question like that.

"Yeah, that won't be a problem," he said. I could tell he was ashamed, and my heart broke for him. After what he'd just gone through, I wanted to focus on the positive, so we talked some more about St. Joseph's. What a relief to know he'd be spending the summer at this intensive program. Help was on the way!

"Thanks for everything, Mom," he said when I dropped him at his dorm. He gave me a hug.

A wave of exhaustion came over me. It had been an emotionally draining day, but at least I was starting to feel we were moving, however slowly, in the right direction.

For breakfast the next morning, Dan and I sat at a table in the beautiful courtyard of Carson's campus. I had brought him some yogurt and a bagel. He was trying so hard, but he just couldn't do it. We sat there for over an hour while he struggled to get that spoon into his mouth.

This pattern would be repeated often over the next few weeks. I'd mistakenly thought because he'd been able to eat once, it would just get easier and easier for him. Instead, eating was a new ordeal each day.

There were times when he was adamant about when he could eat. "I'll eat at six o'clock; I'll eat after my class; or I'll eat at midnight," he'd say. I often gave in to these demands. But when he'd announce, "I can't eat today. I'll eat tomorrow," that's when I got tough.

"No, you have to eat today," I'd say. "We'll just sit here until you do." Sometimes I'd embark on my monologue. At times we'd sit for hours. Though it was torturous and tedious, our goal of nourishing him daily was happening.

"I thought eating would just get easier for him," I said to Mark during one of our almost daily conversations. "I mean, he *has* eaten, and nothing bad has happened, so shouldn't eating the next time be less difficult? It just doesn't make sense to me."

"You're exactly right there," Mark said. "OCD doesn't make sense. But think of it this way. There's a constant battle going on between Dan and his OCD, and the OCD is extremely powerful. Sometimes Dan prevails, and he's able to eat. Other times, the forces of his OCD are just too strong to overcome, and he's not able to eat. That's why his progress hasn't been linear."

Mark was a godsend, my own private, patient consultant. "Since he's been forcing himself to eat, his anxiety levels seem even higher than before." I said. "Is that because he's constantly going against his OCD?"

"Absolutely. He's way out of his comfort zone."

"No question about that," I said with a sigh. "I don't even think he *has* a comfort zone."

There were times when Dan was able to push himself and go to a restaurant with me and other times when he couldn't put a morsel of food into his mouth. It was so helpful for me to remember Mark's explanation regarding Dan versus his OCD. I came to realize that who won each battle wasn't nearly as important as the fact that Dan kept fighting.

After finally eating breakfast that Monday morning, Dan just made it to class on time, and I headed off to his dorm for my agreed-to visit. Taking deep breaths while I climbed the three flights of stairs, I wondered

if his room would be as it was on my last trip, when I could barely open the door wide enough to get inside. *Something must've fallen and blocked the door*, I remembered thinking. I'd squeezed inside, looked around, and immediately felt dizzy at the sight of papers and artwork, sketchbooks, schoolwork, clothes, art supplies, paints, books, towels, and food, all completely covering the floor. I'd steadied myself by holding on to the doorknob and took a sweeping glance downward, which revealed an un-plugged clip-on lamp, a bar of soap, some open toothpaste, shampoo, paper clips, pens, broken pencils, and money.

As I'd stood there, ankle deep in the mess and overwhelmed, I realized there was something else buried under all the rubble: Dan's mattress. His bed was nothing more than a frame with coils. *Where, and how, has he been sleeping?* I'd wondered. It was at that point, two months ago, when the severity of Dan's illness began to reveal itself. My gut feeling back then was that we were on the brink of something huge, but beyond that I had no idea what was going on, or what to do about it.

That day, it took ten hours and six loads of laundry to make his room habitable. In that time, I saw glimpses of how Dan had lost control over his life: unwashed cereal bowls, lots of change, and his credit card in the rubble. His coveted computer speakers, which he'd handled with loving care at home, had been thrown onto the floor next to his broken clock radio and a razor covered with shaving cream. A care package of brown-ies and cookies I'd baked for him weeks before, still wrapped in tinfoil, were squished underneath his bed frame. His prized animation and draw-ing books, some dirty, some with ripped covers, and some with broken bindings, were strewn about the floor.

When he had refused to go to the counseling center on campus, we insisted he at least have a phone meeting with his therapist at home. The therapist told us Dan was fine; he just needed to keep his room clean. I knew Dan wasn't fine, and for the first time Gary and I discussed forcing him to come home. But he was doing well in his classes and wanted to be at Carson, so I tried to convince myself that having a really messy room wasn't that big a deal and certainly not a reason to leave college.

Now here I was, poised to enter that same room again. I braced myself as I turned the doorknob and pushed. No resistance. Cautiously optimis-tic, I kept going. The door easily swung open, and my hopes were instant-ly shattered. It was as bad as last time, except his mattress wasn't on the

floor. Disheartened, I suppressed my emotions and focused on the job ahead of me.

While I surveyed the room, trying to decide where to begin, it became clear this mess differed from the last. Countless pieces of torn paper lay on the floor, as if a ticker tape parade had just passed through. A credit card was broken in half, near a dollar bill ripped in two. It dawned on me that this tearing must be a compulsion. So much for suppressing my emotions. This concrete evidence of how difficult life had become for my son overwhelmed me, and the tears flowed.

After regaining my composure, I began my search for the main thing I'd come looking for. I peered into the top drawer of his dresser, thinking this was a good place to start. Not only was his medication in there; the pill bottle was almost full as well. And there were loose pills scattered throughout the drawer, most broken in half.

Dan had been so insistent he'd been taking his medication. Of course by now I'd had my doubts, but I was still shocked to see the full bottle. As I stood there trying to process this new information, something on the floor caught my eye. More broken pills, maybe thirty of them, were mixed in with the handmade confetti.

MEDICATION FOR OCD

Along with cognitive-behavioral therapy, certain medications are considered a first-line approach for treating OCD. In some cases, medication may provide initial symptom relief that makes it easier to engage in psychotherapy.

The most recent treatment guidelines suggest starting with a selective serotonin reuptake inhibitor (SSRI), such as fluoxetine (Prozac), paroxetine (Paxil), or sertraline (Zoloft).[1] The tricyclic medication clomipramine (Anafranil) may also be used, although it tends to have more pronounced side effects than the SSRIs.[2]

Effective treatment with SSRIs generally requires relatively high doses. For example, the typical target dose for sertraline is two hundred milligrams a day, with doses as high as four hundred milli-

grams a day occasionally prescribed. In contrast, the usual sertraline dose for major depression is as low as fifty milligrams a day and generally not more than two hundred milligrams a day. A small dose is initially prescribed and is gradually increased.[3]

Once the person starts taking medication, it generally takes at least four to six weeks before he or she feels much better.[4] For some, improvement isn't felt until they've been on a medication for ten to twelve weeks. It is understandable, given how long it can take for medication to start working, that some patients choose to stop taking their medication—even more so in light of the significant side effects that can accompany these drugs. For example, the SSRIs have been associated with headaches, weight gain, insomnia, and difficulty achieving orgasm, among others.[5] For these reasons it is important for patients who choose to take medication to work with a physician who is well versed in treating OCD and in managing issues that arise, such as uncomfortable side effects.

1. American Psychiatric Association, "Practice Guideline for the Treatment of Patients with Obsessive-Compulsive Disorder," 2007, http://www.psych.org/psych_pract/treatg/pg/prac_guide.cfm, 11.
2. Naomi A. Fineberg, Samar Reghunandanan, Angus Brown, and Ilenia Pampaloni, "Pharmacotherapy of Obsessive-Compulsive Disorder: Evidence-Based Treatment and Beyond," *Australian and New Zealand Journal of Psychiatry* 47, no. 2 (February 2013): 122.
3. Michael H. Bloch, Joseph McGuire, Angeli Landeros-Weisenberger, James F. Leckman, and Christopher Pittenger, "Meta-analysis of the Dose-Response Relationship of SSRI in Obsessive-Compulsive Disorder," *Molecular Psychiatry* 15, no. 8 (August 2010): 854.
4. Lorrin M. Koran, Gregory L. Hanna, Eric Hollander, Gerald Nestadt, and Helen B. Simpson, "Practice Guideline for the Treatment of Patients with Obsessive-Compulsive Disorder," *American Journal of Psychiatry* 164, no. 7 (July 2007): 12.
5. Mayo Clinic, "Selective Serotonin Reuptake Inhibitors (SSRIs)," accessed April 26, 2014, http://www.mayoclinic.org/.

Anger surged in me. *How could he lie to me like that?* Just as quickly, I remembered Dan was dealing with forces larger than himself, and hope replaced the anger.

I called Mark, even though I knew he was at work. "I know for sure now that Dan hasn't been taking his medication! *That's* why he's doing so poorly."

"That's very good news," Mark said. "It's what we've been suspecting all along. Just take the meds out of his room so you can be in charge of them yourself. Start with twenty milligrams and work your way up to sixty. And remember, it's going to take a good week or two to notice any positive effects."

Buoyed by that conversation, I was ready to clean Dan's room. Feeling like a pro, this time it only took a few hours to make it livable. But items I'd come across last time now stopped me in my tracks. Dan's X-Acto knife and razor blades, always innocuous possessions, were now tangible reminders of my son's illness and suffering. I kept repeating what Mark told me. *It isn't as terrible as it seems. Dan's cutting isn't nearly as big an issue as his obsessive-compulsive disorder.*

When Dan saw his cleaned room, he gave me a big hug. "Thanks so much, Mom. I really appreciate all your help."

Remembering Mark's suggestion, I was ready. "I know you do, honey. And because this is such a tough time for you, I'll be in charge of your pills for now."

"I really don't want to take those, Mom," he pleaded, pointing to the almost full bottle. "I've read a lot about the different meds, and I'm willing to take anything else."

"What's the problem with this medication?" I said, confused.

"I just don't think it's the one I should be taking," he insisted.

It was difficult to know if he was thinking rationally or if the OCD was controlling him. I agreed to contact a doctor at St. Joseph's to discuss medication options and received a reply that Dan should continue taking the SSRI. The doctor felt it was the best drug for treating OCD, with fewer side effects than other choices.

So, we had another struggle. This one was not as bad as with food, but occasionally Dan would say he couldn't take the pill until midnight, or it would take hours for him to be able to put it in his mouth and swallow it. Other times, it wasn't an issue. Dan versus OCD.

"One of the most frustrating things for me is seeing how much time Dan spends doing nothing," I said to Gary during one of our phone calls. "He sits for hours at a time until it's okay for him to work, eat, or take a bath. He isn't even able to use the shower."

Gary's reply became our mantra over the next several weeks: "Thank goodness he'll be going to St. Joseph's soon."

Dan's extremely high anxiety levels, coupled with the knowledge that he hadn't been taking his medication, led me to call Dr. Wright, Dan's longtime pediatrician. "I'm going to prescribe a mild tranquilizer for

Dan," Dr. Wright explained. "He can take it as needed. It'll curb some of his intense anxiety right away and should help while we're waiting for the SSRI to take effect."

I filled the prescription and drove Dan back to his dorm. He'd spent the evening in my room, doing nothing.

"You seem really anxious, Mom," he said as I pulled into his parking lot.

"You think?" I said, surprised I could smile. I'd arrived in Bridgeville a few days ago to discover that my son hadn't eaten in a week. We spent a night in the emergency room where I saw his arms covered with self-inflicted cuts. I sat with him for hours each day just to get him to eat and spent even more time than that watching him do nothing. He was thin and wan and was tapping, touching, and grimacing almost constantly. I had no idea what the future, even the next day, would bring. Yeah, I'd say I was a little stressed. But the last thing I wanted was for Dan to feel badly about it. He did, though; I could tell.

"I think you need something to calm yourself down," he teased.

Now I'm someone who rarely takes any medication, even for a headache. But I'd barely slept since arriving at the motel, and I couldn't seem to shake my anxiety.

So that night, my son and I did drugs together for the first and only time. We split a tranquilizer and both got a good night's sleep.

A few days later, we were on our way to Dr. Vogel.

"I don't see the point in going to another doctor now," Dan argued. "I'd rather just wait for St. Joseph's."

"We both need all the help we can get," I insisted. "Let's just meet him. If you aren't comfortable with him, we'll find someone else. The receptionist raved about him and said people come from all over to see him. I bet he's great."

I was trying to convince myself as well as Dan. Since his diagnosis, we'd come across some not-so-great doctors, most recently Dr. Snyder in the emergency room. We were due a good one.

As we approached the street-level office and saw the list of staff names, Dan and I giggled. "No wonder the receptionist raved so much about him," I whispered as we went inside. "She's his wife!"

The waiting area was empty, since it was after office hours. We were still smiling when Dr. Vogel, who'd stayed late just to meet with us, entered the room. I liked him immediately. He had a calm, gentle demeanor, and something about his caring face reminded me of Mark.

"Why don't you tell me whatever you want to tell me and then I'll meet with Dan alone," Dr. Vogel said, motioning for us to follow him. His office was warm and inviting, and we settled right in.

"Okay," I began, taking a deep breath. I could've talked for hours, but wanting to keep it short, I focused mainly on relaying the events of the past couple of weeks while Dan sat quietly, knee bouncing. I then left them alone.

When they returned to the waiting area, Dr. Vogel said, "I could see Dan once, twice, or even three times a week when he comes back to school in the fall."

The tension in my neck dissipated. "That's wonderful. Thank you."

"You're welcome," Dr. Vogel replied. "Dan has a sizable case of OCD, but I think I can help him. I'm also happy to hear he'll be going to St. Joseph's Hospital this summer. They have a world-renowned program, you know."

I nodded.

"Please keep in touch and let me know how things are going while Dan is there," he added.

"I will," I promised. Then the words, unplanned, just flowed. "You know, Dr. Vogel, the way your wife talked on the phone about you, with such love and admiration? Well, that's how I feel about my son. He's a great kid, and I appreciate all your efforts to help him." I tried, unsuccessfully, to hold back my tears.

"I understand," Dr. Vogel said, touching my arm, and I could tell by the look in his eyes that he really did.

Once outside I immediately said to Dan, "I'm sorry, honey, I didn't mean to embarrass you."

"That's okay," he replied, looking right at me. "I understand too."

4

GOING HOME

While our main goals were to get Dan through the semester successfully and keep him physically healthy (I had already given up on his mental health), there were also things that had to be done to prepare for the fall semester.

There was a difference of opinion as to where he should live. He hated the food at school, though at this point that didn't matter, since he wasn't even able to enter the campus dining hall.

"I really want to live off campus with some friends who've found a house," he announced one day while he tapped his fingers on the wall.

I was pleased he'd somewhat reconnected with friends after isolating himself so much, but his plan concerned me. He'd have to drive to school and was currently too anxious to get behind the wheel. He'd have to be responsible for all his meals, and goodness knows how that would work out. He'd be away from campus and disconnected socially. These were all negatives in my book.

"Why not put your name on the waiting list for an on-campus apartment?" I suggested. He'd missed the deadline to apply for housing. "You'd be on campus, but you wouldn't have to have a meal plan."

"I'll be fine," he insisted. "I really want to live off campus with Steve and Adam."

This was another case of my not knowing how much Dan's OCD played a part in his reasoning, or lack thereof. I argued with him a bit, but

it was half-hearted. The truth was, Dan came alive whenever he talked about living in this house. It made me so happy to see him so happy I probably would've agreed to let him live on the moon.

The other big item on the agenda was registering online for sophomore classes, and this process evoked intense anxiety in Dan. He was shaking, touching and tapping, and chewing on the strings of his hooded sweatshirt as if they were gum. I also noticed some new facial twitches. I'm not sure if Dan's OCD was dictating what courses he could take, or if it was the unspoken question causing so much anxiety: would he be well enough to take these classes?

With the deadline fast approaching, and Dan obviously not able to handle it, we turned to his academic advisor, Dr. Moore, for help. Dr. Moore was incredibly patient with Dan as it took him forever to make decisions.

"Throughout the school year, Dan, you've proven yourself to be a successful and motivated student, and I'll help you any way I can," she told him while they picked out courses together. But she was realistic as well. "Sophomore year is extremely difficult and intense, as the steepest learning curve occurs at this time. Now you've registered for five courses, which is a full course load. If you find that's too much for you, you can drop an elective. What you can't do, however, is drop any of your CA [computer animation] courses, of which there are three."

Dan nodded; he already knew this. The CA program at Carson is very intense and sequential, and all CA majors must successfully complete specific courses each semester to continue on. We had no way to know if Dan would be able to deal with the pressure.

We planned for the future anyway. "I have an idea," I said to Gary during our next phone call. "What if we moved to Bridgeville for the year?"

"Wow," Gary said. "That's some idea. Are you serious?"

"Well, I think it's worth discussing," I said. "We've talked about doing something different for a while now. You're working from home, so we really can live anywhere. I'd have to leave my part-time job, but I'm willing to do that and we'll be okay without my income."

"There's so much involved," he said.

"I know. The biggest question is, would it be a good thing for Ava?" Our daughter Ava was graduating eighth grade and poised to attend the local public high school, though we weren't convinced it would be a good

fit for her. She was also passionate about swimming, and her current team
was disbanding.

"Well, as long as you're there," Gary said, "why don't you look
around at some schools and see what you think? No harm in doing that.
We certainly don't have to make any decisions right now."

"Okay, I will."

Though our conversation ended, the idea kept swirling around in my
head. Is this something we could, or should, do? I wavered between "this
could be great" and "this is crazy." At the least, the thought was a diver-
sion for me, something to relieve the stress I'd been dealing with since
arriving in Bridgeville. When I wasn't caring for Dan, I talked with
people and researched schools.

It seemed it was meant to be: I found a school and a competitive swim
team that seemed perfect for Ava.

"We're just in the talking stages," I said to Dan, "but we're looking
into the possibility of moving to Bridgeville for the upcoming school
year."

"Really?" he said. "Ava and Lainey too?"

"Well, Ava, of course, but not Lainey." Our older daughter was on her
own, working and living in the city.

"I guess it's okay, as long as you stay away from me," Dan joked.

"Not a problem." That was the extent of our conversation, but at least
the seeds had been planted, and the discussion could continue once we
got home.

Ever since Mark asked me if Dan understood how irrational his thinking had become, that question had hovered in my mind, waiting to be
answered. I now felt reassured that, yes, Dan did realize how irrational his
behavior was; he just couldn't control it.

THE IRRATIONALITY OF OCD

It's usually hard for people without OCD to understand how some-one who seems mostly rational can also have such irrational fears and behaviors. Even the OCD sufferer will often feel frustrated with himself for not being able to dismiss senseless concerns. For exam-ple, an infectious disease specialist might know full well that she can't get HIV from a toilet seat and yet may be deathly afraid of public bathrooms and the possibility of contracting AIDS. Or an avowed atheist might have obsessions about having "sold his soul to the devil."

The natural response from family members is to give reassu-rance: "You know you can't get HIV from casual contact"; "You don't even believe in the devil, so you couldn't have sold your soul to him." Family members can feel confused, saying things such as, "I don't understand—he *knows* he didn't touch that spot of blood so why is he worried about it?"

I often tell people I work with clinically that "if it made sense, it wouldn't be OCD." OCD doesn't operate according to the rules we normally use, and it doesn't understand logic. We can deliver per-fectly sound and reasonable arguments for why obsessions are un-founded and compulsions are futile, and OCD will not be the least bit moved. Why? Because OCD is satisfied by only one thing: cer-tainty. And no matter how irrational the obsessive fear is or how cleverly we might reason against it, OCD can trump any logic with three words: are you sure? And the only rational answer is "no"—we can't be 100 percent certain of anything, not even that the sun will rise tomorrow.

The only way to beat OCD is to play a different game, one that isn't about guaranteeing that nothing bad will happen. Beating OCD means getting better at living with life's uncertainties, which is exactly what exposure and response prevention (ERP) is designed to do.

Just the night before he was in my hotel room, talking about all the schoolwork he needed to do, yet he'd insisted he couldn't work until midnight.

"Why, Dan?" I asked.

"I can't explain it," he said, "because it makes no sense. Don't even try to reason with me."

Other times Dan would give me orders. "Make me go to a restaurant," or "Make me go to the supermarket tomorrow," he'd say. Both of these events elicited intense anxiety, but he pushed himself. He knew his OCD wasn't logical and needed to be confronted. Neither of us realized it at the time, but Dan was instinctively engaging in exposure and response prevention therapy, the frontline treatment for OCD.

These actions and snippets of conversation were a comfort to me. Somewhere among the obsessions, compulsions, anxieties, and cutting, there was sanity.

Two and a half weeks after I stood with my son at the bottom of the staircase, we were on our way home. Though still a very sick young man, he'd made a lot of progress. He successfully completed all his courses and maintained his academic scholarship. He registered for sophomore year, connected with a therapist with whom he felt comfortable, and was taking his medication. Eating was still difficult, but he was doing it.

And most importantly he wanted help, which was only a month away at St. Joseph's Hospital.

On the plane ride home I tried to envision the upcoming month. Mark warned me the transition would be difficult, and the lack of structure awaiting Dan could make things even worse. He needed a schedule, and aside from an upcoming weekend trip to the city with extended family, we had nothing planned. Still, I was pleased to move on to this next chapter, as it meant we were that much closer to his starting treatment.

"Glad to be home?" I asked, once we'd unpacked.

"Yeah, it's great to be home with the cats," he said, and then chuckled when he realized he hadn't mentioned his dad or sister. "But I would've preferred to have gone directly to St. Joseph's."

I understood what he was saying. To Dan, home was just a holding tank, a stop on the way to getting help. Unfortunately he'd brought his OCD home with him, which went directly against my fantasy of him leaving it behind at Carson.

I tried to create structure for him, but it wasn't easy. I was working a few days a week, and on those days he was really on his own.

"So what did you do today?" I asked him one day.

"Some sketching, and then I was on the computer for a while," he said. "And I did all those chores you asked me to do."

That was a good day.

But as the days went by, there were fewer good days and more not-so-good days. The not-so-good days consisted of Dan being tied to the clock for all activities of daily living: eating, showering, dressing, going outside, and coming inside. At times, he'd lie on the floor for hours.

"There's just no rhyme or reason to his behavior," Gary said to me. "I mean, he went golfing with me the other day, and today he can't get off the floor."

"I think there's a lot of rhyme," I said, "just no reason. He's totally controlled by his OCD. Sure, he golfed with you. But the outing had to be thought out and planned. You told me he couldn't walk into the snack shack on the course, remember? His OCD is calling all the shots."

The hard-earned progress Dan had made during those last weeks of school dissipated. "The last few days you've only eaten peanut butter sandwiches, at midnight," I said. "How about trying to push through the OCD like you did at Carson?"

"I'm totally exhausted from fighting, Mom. It's so hard, and I really need a break. I'll just wait for St. Joseph's." He sounded as weary as an old man.

It occurred to me his lack of motivation right now was directly related to the absence of consequences for not fighting his OCD. At school, he fought his OCD because if he hadn't, he would've been forced to leave the school he loved. What was his motivation now? There was none.

MOTIVATION FOR OCD TREATMENT

One of the most crucial factors in recovery from OCD is the motivation to do the necessary work. When someone with OCD comes to treatment, the motivational stance should be assumed to be ambivalent. On the one hand, the individuals almost certainly recognize

that OCD is destroying their lives and on some level know the exaggerated fears and the rituals don't make any sense. On the other hand, OCD is persistent and persuasive, and is virtually impossible to ignore.

What leads to the motivation to change? As the saying goes, we're driven to change when the pain of staying the same is greater than the pain of changing. Therefore, motivation to do OCD treatment should be high when holding on to the OCD hurts more than getting rid of it. In the early stages of OCD it's common for a person to think that OCD is an ally—that the excessive concerns are in fact helping the person to stay safe, prevent harm, and so forth. As the condition progresses and more and more is given up for OCD, it's easier to see how OCD is life stealing, not life giving. This recognition alone can increase a person's motivation for treatment.

Does it matter where the motivation comes from? For example, does it make a difference if people come to treatment because they want to reclaim their lives versus coming to treatment because their parents are making them? As an OCD therapist I've worked with individuals under both conditions, and treatment outcomes tend to be better when the person is internally motivated to do the work. It shouldn't be surprising that being "sentenced" to treatment is usually less effective than when a person chooses to seek treatment. Research studies have backed up these observations.[1]

At the same time, there are ways to encourage people to seek treatment that can tap into their intrinsic motivation, particularly by explicitly connecting OCD recovery with things the person values. For example, a parent can point out in a very straightforward and nonpunitive way that a teenager is not well enough to participate in certain activities until the OCD is dealt with.

It's hard to make progress when people flatly state that they are not willing to change their OCD behavior.

1. Christopher M. Spofford, "The Role of Motivation to Change in the Treatment of Obsessive-Compulsive Disorder" (PhD diss., Graduate School of the University of Massachusetts Amherst, 2009), Open Access Dissertations (Paper 132).

Despite Dan's lack of motivation, his spirits were good, and this made sense to me. Surrendering to his OCD meant lower stress levels for now. He was an obedient slave, doing whatever it was OCD commanded.

Gary and I had no idea how to help him, and our lack of knowledge was evident in our behavior. As his parents, we instinctively wanted to keep his anxiety levels down, but as we later learned, following your instincts when it comes to OCD is rarely a good idea. One night, when Gary repeatedly reported the basketball game's score to Dan because Dan couldn't bring himself to watch television, it finally hit me: we were enabling our son, hurting him instead of helping.

"You want to know the score, Dan?" I shouted into the other room. "Then come watch the game." This was my first attempt to willingly not accommodate him. I say "willingly" because it was often hard to know what was OCD related and what wasn't. When Dan insisted on doing errands at 1:00 p.m. instead of 11:00 a.m., for instance, was it really because he was so busy, or was his OCD calling the shots?

ENABLING OCD

At some point almost every family member of an OCD sufferer realizes, "I've been feeding the OCD!" We do it unwittingly and with the best of intentions, of course. What loving family member wants to withhold reassurance from a scared child? And what good parent would not go to great lengths to make his or her child more comfortable?

Enabling in OCD comes in many forms. Providing reassurance is one of the most common—for example, a person with fear of germs might repeatedly ask whether she can get sick from touching certain things. Every time a family member says, "No, it's okay, you're not going to get sick," the OCD feels at least a little relief. That sense of relief then leads the person to continue to ask for reassurance in the future, and keeps the OCD going.[1]

Other kinds of OCD enabling can involve "OCD by proxy,"[2] that is, "doing OCD" for the individuals. Family members might remove their "contaminated" clothes at the door to prevent the OCD sufferers from feeling distressed. Similarly parents might do their children's laundry because it's "too upsetting" for them to do the laundry, it "takes forever," and they are out of clean clothes.

These kinds of enabling behaviors not only reinforce the cycle of OCD but also, perhaps more perniciously, can decrease motivation for treatment.[3] As noted above, change is more likely when the pain of staying the same is great. By providing reassurance and doing OCD for the person, the pain of staying the same is minimized. The discomfort of having OCD is distributed across the entire family, and the person with OCD thus does not feel its full effect. In this situation it actually *makes sense* that the person not seek treatment, because treatment is likely to be harder than the status quo.

When family members learn how to stop enabling, with sensitivity, they can play an invaluable role in their loved one's recovery from OCD. Although it's hard to do things that temporarily increase a child's, parent's, sibling's, or spouse's distress, in the long run it can be the most loving thing a family member can do.

1. Gillihan et al., "Common Pitfalls," 255–56.
2. Ibid., 256.
3. Ibid., 256.

The following weekend was our trip to the city and was meant to be a wonderful celebration of both my parents' birthdays, especially meaningful because my father seemed to be recovering well from surgery for esophageal cancer.

"I think I'll stay home," Dan said.

"No, that's not an option," I said. "We're all going." Dan had always loved spending time with his grandparents, but now he was too drained and anxious to enjoy anything.

To break up the long drive we stopped at a shopping mall, and everyone scurried out of our van, except for Dan.

"I'm fine," he said. "I'll just wait in the car."

It was obvious to us all that he *couldn't* get out of the car, but I tried to make light of the situation. I also walled off my own emotions, a trick that had served me well in Bridgeville. Still, we couldn't ignore Dan's condition. "This is the worst I've seen him physically," Gary said. "All those facial contortions, and some whole-body ones as well. It's actually frightening."

He wasn't the only one who noticed these disturbing changes. My father took me aside and asked what was going on. While we'd told Dan's grandparents he had obsessive-compulsive disorder, we'd given

them as few details as possible. There wasn't much to tell them; we had little understanding of it ourselves.

"It's all OCD related, Dad," I said. "He'll be going to St. Joseph's soon. They'll help him."

The next night we gathered in our hotel room to play some cards. "Dan, you're all scratched up. What happened to you?" My mother asked this as she pointed to his arm.

"Oh, the cats scratched me," Dan said, not missing a beat. I made a mental note of what a convincing liar OCD could be.

St. Joseph's couldn't come fast enough.

Carol Lucas, the program manager at St. Joseph's Hospital, suggested we come to the OCD clinic to familiarize ourselves with it before Dan actually arrived, so the next week Gary, Dan, and I took the forty-five-minute drive from our home to St. Joseph's. We were quiet during the car ride; I was thinking I never imagined myself going to tour the mental institution my son would be attending. What parent does?

We drove up the hill leading to the hospital, and as soon as those old state-hospital buildings appeared, my heart sank and I felt sick to my stomach. I imagined the olden days, with patients in johnnies clutching the jail-like bars that covered the windows. I could practically hear them screaming to get out. Forcing myself back to the present I saw, while the bars had been removed, nothing else had changed.

We parked the car and silently walked to the three-story red-brick building that housed the OCD clinic. Dan stood for a minute, staring at it. *I hope he doesn't change his mind*, I thought as I waited for him to speak.

"Great architecture!" he exclaimed, and proceeded to point out the Tudor style of this late nineteenth-century structure. Thank goodness for my artistic son. The three of us entered the clinic, and I felt my shoulders relax. What a pleasant surprise! Though much smaller than I'd imagined, it had obviously been renovated recently and was light and airy, the complete opposite of the outside.

Dan didn't say anything but was taking it all in. We'd entered the common room complete with televisions and computers, where patients, or clients as they are known, gathered. We walked through this room and down a corridor, which had a big sign-in board on the wall to keep track

of the clients who were allowed to leave the premises. I counted twelve double rooms off the corridor. At the very end of the hall were the kitchen and a dining room with a table large enough to seat all twenty-four clients. The whole clinic was housed on the first floor.

Aside from the nurse's station in the middle of the corridor, it looked like a small college dormitory. Another difference, though, was that the bathrooms were always locked. Since so many people with OCD have issues with germs and cleanliness, this proved a necessity. Dan seemed unfazed by the realization he'd need to ask someone to unlock the bathroom whenever he needed one.

Carol Lucas's office was at the end of the hall, and though we'd spoken on the phone many times, this was our first meeting. She was upbeat and personable, and after we chatted, she spoke with Dan privately for a few minutes while Gary and I walked outside. Like the inside, the premises could've easily been mistaken for a college. "I hope this place is as great as everyone says it is," I said.

"I'm sure it is," Gary said. "Why wouldn't it be? It's a great setup, and they obviously know their stuff. We're lucky to have such a world-renowned clinic so close to us."

"I guess you're right. This is where he needs to be." I was trying to convince myself, but I was feeling unsettled.

"Dan and I had a nice conversation," Carol said when we reunited a few minutes later. "I'll see you all again in a couple of weeks." She spoke with an air of excitement, as if Dan would be coming to summer camp.

And that's just how he felt. "I think it'll be great," he said on our way home. "I just wish I didn't have to wait two more weeks."

It turned out Dan had to wait even longer than that. A few days after our meeting we got a call from Carol. "I hate to have to do this to you. I know Dan is so ready to be here, but we're going to have to move his admission back a week, to the beginning of June. We just won't have a bed open until then."

"It's only seven extra days," Gary said. He was trying to bolster my spirits.

"I know," I said, "but when you've been counting the days, and anticipating help for so long, a week can seem like a year."

Dan took the news better than I did and was able to look at one positive aspect. "Well, at least now I'll be home for my nineteenth birthday."

I did have one concern I voiced to Carol. "I'm worried this delay might mean he won't be well enough to return to school."

"Even with Dan's formidable case of OCD," she said confidently, "that shouldn't be an issue."

Dan spent a good part of the next two and a half weeks lying on the floor; we were all relieved when moving day finally arrived. Around midmorning, Gary, Dan, and I pulled into St. Joseph's, and once again, those old state-hospital buildings loomed large. While we carried his stuff into the clinic, it was easy for me to slip into denial and imagine we were dropping him off at college. The procedure was the same, including setting up his room and meeting Dan's roommate.

"Hi, I'm Ryan," he said, extending his hand. They looked around the same age, and I found myself trying to figure out Ryan's OCD. He'd shaken hands with Dan, so he probably wasn't afraid of germs. His side of the room was neat, but not too neat, so that didn't seem to be an issue. He was friendly and composed, not what you'd expect from someone in intensive treatment for an anxiety disorder. As a matter of fact, most of the clients walking around appeared as "normal" as Ryan. There were some, however, whose anguish was apparent, either by the looks on their faces or by their obvious rituals.

I left Dan and Gary and went to retrieve a few things that were left in the car. On my way out I walked through the common area and noticed some therapists working individually with clients. One pair sat at a small table with a pile of coins between them.

"Okay, Missy, I know you can hold this quarter in your hand."

"No, no, I can't," Missy replied adamantly, shaking her head and looking panic stricken.

"Remember yesterday you were able to touch a nickel, and the day before that you touched a dime?" the therapist said.

What a strange disorder this OCD is, I thought as I walked past.

I got Dan's things and on the way back in walked past the big sign-in board we'd seen on our first visit to the clinic. This time I stopped and examined it closely. There were about ten first names listed, and when anyone on the list left the campus, they had to sign out and then sign back in when they returned. Just seeing this board boosted my spirits. Dan would eventually be able to come and go as he pleased during his free time. *It's not as if he's being locked up in a mental hospital*, I told myself; *he's just visiting.*

"Thanks, Mom," Dan said when I returned to his room with the rest of his stuff. I looked at my son; intense anxiety was etched on his face. He'd been through so much already, with a lot more to come. Even though he wanted to be at St. Joseph's, it was still terrifying for him. He knew he'd be asked to face his worst fears as part of his therapy to get well.

There was no way I could truly understand how he felt. Still, I imagined myself in a situation that would provoke intense anxiety: I'm on my way home, cruising down an almost deserted highway and singing along to the radio. Out of nowhere, a massive eighteen-wheeler appears. It's traveling at high speed in the wrong direction and is heading right toward me. I swerve, narrowly avoid a collision, and end up spun around on the side of the road as the truck barrels by me. I thought about how I'd feel: pounding heart, rapid breathing, sweating, and thinking I might die. I knew Dan would feel this way, over and over again, as he battled his obsessive-compulsive disorder. But I couldn't dwell on that now; there were too many other things to do.

The next task on our agenda involved going to the billing department. Gary was still setting up some electronics in Dan's room, so Dan and I walked over to the office, which was located in St. Joseph's main hospital building.

What struck me immediately when we entered was how eerily quiet and deserted it was. Usually when you walk into any hospital, the hallways are bustling with doctors, nurses, staff, and visitors. Dan noticed it too. "Where *is* everybody? It's empty."

"I know," I said. I wondered about the silence. Were the inpatients all locked up and drugged? Where were the doctors? I was glad this wasn't where we'd be leaving Dan; I didn't think I could have done that. We found our way to the bursar's office, filled out paperwork, and went back to the OCD clinic, which in comparison was bright and full of life.

"Time to meet with the social worker," Gary said. "Her office is on the third floor."

The three of us decided to walk instead of taking the elevator. On the door that entered the second floor, I noticed two signs: "Doors Always Locked" and "Authorized Personnel Only." It was troubling to know this floor was directly above the OCD clinic, even though I knew nothing about the patients past those intimidating signs—just one more thing to try to put out of my mind.

We continued on to the third floor, where there were administrative offices and no unsettling signs. The social worker waited for us in the hallway. "You must be the Singers. I'm Sharon Walsh. Please come in." She gestured toward her office. She appeared to be in her midfifties, petite, with shoulder-length blond hair. She told us she'd been working at St. Joseph's for "many years."

"I'll be the liaison between you and the rest of the staff at St. Joseph's," she said, addressing Gary and me. "You can always contact me with any questions or concerns you might have."

We sat and listened as she talked. Her speech was automatic, no doubt from saying these exact words to many families over the years. Just the names were changed. "Dan's psychiatrist is Dr. Parker, and he'll prescribe his medication. His clinical psychologist is Dr. Scott Stone. Together Scott and Dan will develop a program that should help Dan conquer his OCD."

I was feeling overwhelmed, and as I struggled to remember all the names and information, Sharon turned to Dan.

"You'll attend group sessions as well as individual sessions daily," she said. "The program will be extremely anxiety provoking at first, as you fight your demons head on. I'm sure you must've discussed this, at least a little, with Carol Lucas."

Dan nodded. He looked dazed. If I was feeling stressed and confused, I couldn't even imagine what was going through his mind. One thing was for sure. As advertised, it appeared to be a well-run, intensive program.

"What can Gary and I do to help Dan now?" I asked Sharon when she came up for air.

"Give yourselves a break." She smiled. "Let us worry about him for a change."

Considering what our family had been through the last few months, it was tempting to take her advice. Dan was at one of the finest institutions in the world. We could relax a little—but not just yet.

"I'm concerned about Dan's health," I said. "He's a good twenty-five pounds below his normal weight, and if his eating isn't supervised, he'll lose even more. You can see how thin he is." I knew I might be embarrassing Dan, but it was too important an issue to ignore.

Dan seemed disinterested in the whole conversation. "Don't worry," Sharon assured me. "The staff will work with Dan at mealtimes, and his weight will be monitored regularly." Her comment should have com-

forted me, but because it sounded as automatic as her introductory speech, it didn't.

"Just a couple more things before I let you go," Sharon said. "One of the most common issues that arise here is that clients call their families too often, usually to complain or to ask to go home."

"I don't see that being a problem," I said. "Do you, Dan?" I looked over at him.

"No," he said. I could tell he was even more anxious than before.

"Dan's OCD prevents him from using his cell phone," I told Sharon, "and I know the two phones in the hallway only accept incoming calls. Also, he rarely complains, and he is so ready to be here, I just can't imagine him asking to come home."

"Okay then," Sharon said, "let's talk about visiting. Because you live less than an hour away, you have the option of coming here for weekly meetings with me and Dan."

Of course we agreed to that. Tuesday would be our designated meeting day.

"And you can also visit Dan on weekends, as long as there aren't any conflicts with his therapy," Sharon added as our meeting ended.

We left her office and saw a young woman, obviously distressed, walking down the corridor. She stopped to knock lightly on each door she passed, not waiting or even expecting anyone to answer. Our eyes met knowingly, and she gave me a shy smile.

"There's nothing left for us to do," Gary said when we got back to Dan's room. "I guess we should go."

"Good luck, honey, I love you," I muttered, and then hugged my son. "You're finally here." I didn't know what else to say.

Dan nodded. "Yeah, I'm here." His words were filled with dread. "I'm really tired. I think I'll take a nap. See you next week."

As Gary and I were leaving, a counselor headed toward Dan's room.

"I'm going to get him started in one of the group therapy sessions," she said.

My eyes welled with tears at the realization that my son's torturous fight against OCD was beginning. I wished he didn't have such a difficult struggle ahead of him. "I'm so proud of Dan," I said as we got into the car.

"I know, me too," Gary said softly.

Emotionally drained, we drove home in silence.

5

ERP TO THE RESCUE

We didn't hear from Dan at all that first week. When I couldn't hold back any longer, I gave Sharon a call.

"Dan is settling in well, and he and Scott have really clicked," she said. "I knew they'd work well together. They have similar temperaments." Some of the stress of the last few months finally started to dissipate, and once again, I was thankful Dan was getting the help he needed.

Tuesday arrived quickly, and it was time for our first family meeting.

I was so excited to see my son I barely noticed the state-hospital buildings that had previously looked so daunting. Gary and I climbed the stairs to Sharon's office, past the dreaded second floor. Dan hadn't arrived yet, so we chatted with Sharon. By all accounts, he was adjusting well and already working intensely with Dr. Stone.

A few minutes later, he came in. I'm not sure what I was expecting but definitely not what I saw. He'd lost more weight. His jawbone was protruding, he had black circles under his eyes, and his anxiety was palpable.

"Hey Dan," I said. I embraced him and it was like hugging a skeleton. Though I smiled and tried to appear relaxed, I'm not sure I pulled it off; I was shocked at how he looked.

"Why don't you tell your parents a little bit about what you've been doing?" Sharon said.

Dan shrugged. Sharon urged him to talk, but he was unusually quiet. So she did all the talking. He spoke a few words here and there but overall was subdued.

Questions bombarded my mind. How could he have lost more weight? Why was he so uncommunicative? Was it medication related? How come he had big black circles under his eyes? Was he sleeping at all?

It was difficult, but I tried to attend to Sharon. "I'm surprised you didn't talk to your family at all during the week, Dan," she said.

Why? I thought. *We told you he couldn't use his cell phone.* I couldn't keep quiet. "I'm wondering why Dan has lost more weight."

"Oh, do you think he has?" Sharon said. "He looks about the same to me."

I knew every inch of my son's chiseled face. He had lost more weight. "Has he been weighed since he arrived last week?" I asked.

"Well, let's see," Sharon said while she thumbed through his records. "He was weighed when he arrived, but it looks as if that's it. Let's go down the hall and he can step on the scale." The four of us gathered around the scale, which revealed a weight loss of six pounds in one week.

"Okay, we're going to put a plan into action where Dan will eat five times a day, supervised, until he's full," Sharon said. "Additionally, he'll be given high-calorie milkshakes several times daily."

Why wasn't this plan introduced immediately upon Dan's arrival? His issues with food were well documented on his application. I'd also made a point of addressing the problem when he arrived at the hospital.

When I asked Sharon, she said, "We didn't realize how bad the situation was."

But I told you. Maybe she thought I'd been exaggerating?

"Let's talk about communicating with your parents," Sharon said when we settled back into her office. "What do you think about your mom and dad calling you a couple of times a week on the hall phone, to chat?"

"That's fine," Dan said. He didn't seem to care one way or the other.

It sounded good to me. The more contact the better.

Though we spent an hour with Dan, I felt less connected than ever; we barely communicated. And while we knew he'd feel worse before getting better, it was still tough to see. It was hard leaving him in this condition. "I'm wondering how his medication is affecting him," Gary said as we

walked to the car. Dan had told us he was now taking eighty milligrams of his SSRI daily.

My reprieve from worrying was over. "You know, if I hadn't brought up his weight, nobody would've even realized he wasn't eating."

We saw Dan several more times over the next couple of weeks: We took him out for lunch, and he and Gary even played golf once. We talked on the hall phone but not as much as originally planned. And, of course, there were our Tuesday family meetings, where I'd put Dan under my mental microscope: He was gaining weight and, more importantly, was becoming more comfortable eating. Some of his rituals, such as having to tap and touch, were noticeably reduced. But he was always on "high alert": nervous, jittery, and anxious. His hands were shaky, and he still had those same dark circles under his eyes. He was now taking a benzodiazepine in addition to the selective serotonin reuptake inhibitor (SSRI). We were told little about his therapy.

During one of our infrequent phone calls, Dan was unusually talkative. "I'm feeling terrible, but that's good," he said. He knew his heightened anxiety was an important part of his exposure and response prevention (ERP) therapy. "I'm making progress and learning lots of useful skills. My therapist, Scott, is amazing, and we've really connected. He's the best. And I'm comfortable here, too."

"That's great, honey," I said. What a relief to hear how pleased he was with the program. Even with all his anxiety, his spirits were good.

WHAT IS ERP?

Exposure and response prevention, or ERP, is the psychological treatment of choice for OCD. As the name suggests, there are two main parts that make up the treatment. First, "exposure" simply means approaching the things a person with OCD has been avoiding. For example, someone with OCD fears about stabbing a family member may begin to use knives again. The response prevention (or "ritual prevention") part of ERP means stopping the compulsions.[1]

Through repeated practice of exposure and response prevention, the thoughts and situations that trigger obsessions become less upsetting. Also, individuals with OCD learn that their distress in expo-

sure situations goes down over time even if they don't give in to the urge to do compulsions. Research studies have shown that both exposure and response prevention are needed for the treatment to work well.[2]

Treatment starts with a thorough psychological evaluation, including identifying the person's main obsessions and compulsions. In the first two treatment sessions, the therapist works with the OCD sufferer to develop a customized plan for how to tackle the person's OCD. The plan includes building a list of exposure exercises and gauging how difficult each one will be.

Exposure exercises generally begin in the third session and are done gradually, starting with things that the OCD sufferer can do now with some discomfort and working up systematically to things that are more challenging.[3] This approach is a lot like climbing a ladder: we start at the bottom, right where the person is. The initial exposure exercises are completed in session with the therapist and then are repeated as homework between sessions.[4] Response prevention also begins at the third session.

Sessions are often ninety minutes long to provide adequate time to practice exposures, but sometimes can be shorter. A typical course of outpatient ERP is around fifteen sessions—most often weekly, although sessions can be as frequent as five to six times per week in intensive treatment.

1. Gillihan et al., "Common Pitfalls," 251.
2. Rosa-Alcázar et al., "Psychological Treatment," 1315.
3. Foa, Yadin, and Lichner, *Exposure and Response*, 84–85.
4. Ibid., 97–98.

During our next visit, he took me for a walk around a pond near the hospital. It was a wooded setting on a beautiful summer day, and I felt peaceful and full of hope for Dan. He was quiet and pensive for most of our walk, but when we were almost back to the hospital he said, "I'm very lucky I only have OCD. There are so many people here who are worse off than I am. Sometimes I hear yelling and banging coming from the second floor."

I was so proud of my son. He was able to put his own illness in perspective, something I wasn't sure I could've done if I were in his

shoes. "You're amazing, Dan. Even though you're suffering, you realize how fortunate you are."

He gave Gary and me a tour of the campus as if showing us his home. He pointed out each clinic, telling us whom it housed. Nestled among the large state-hospital buildings was a smaller structure, possibly some kind of storage facility. As we walked by it, he said, "That's the claustrophobia clinic. I hear it's overcrowded." Warmth came over me as I looked up and saw him smile. He still had his sense of humor, and that made everything okay.

While we knew nearly nothing about his therapy, whatever they were doing at St. Joseph's was working. On several occasions Gary and I witnessed Dan doing things that had previously been too difficult for him, such as going into a store and making a purchase. With each success, Dan announced, "Scott would be so proud of me." I wasn't sure why, but this comment always made me uneasy.

Gary and I continued to discuss the pros and cons of relocating to Bridgeville for a year. "Unless there are some major objections from the kids, I think we should go for it," I said.

Gary agreed, adding, "It feels right."

We talked with Ava about the possible move, since she would be most affected. "There's a really neat high school in Bridgeville, and a great swim team as well," I said. "You should see those pools!"

"Let me think about it," she said. Five minutes later she was onboard. It would be an adventure.

"Now listen," I said. "Don't say anything to anybody yet. We haven't even told Lainey."

"Okay, I won't—."

The phone rang. "So were you ever planning on telling me you're moving to Bridgeville?" It was Lainey, upset.

I was dumbfounded. "Honey, how could you possibly know that? We literally just made the decision."

"Ava posted it on Facebook."

Clearly, there had been a breach in our "security system," and thanks to modern technology, millions of people now knew our plans. "I'm sorry

you had to find out that way, honey. Honestly, Dad and I were just going
to call you."

"That's okay," Lainey said. She was calming down. "Can I live in the
house while you're gone?"

Living at home would save Lainey a lot of money, even though she'd
have almost an hour commute to work. She could also take care of our
two cats. We agreed to let her house-sit for the year, even though finan-
cially it would be a strain not to rent out our home.

I called one of the hall phones at St. Joseph's and was able to track
down Dan to tell him our plans. "How do you feel about it, honey?" I
asked.

"It doesn't matter to me one way or the other." As was often the case,
he sounded preoccupied. Goodness knows he was dealing with lots of
thoughts. I believe it really didn't matter to him, that he was just trying to
get through each day.

Soon after our decision was made, Gary, Ava, and I took a whirlwind
trip to Bridgeville. In three days we rented a condo, had a tour and
interview at Ava's prospective school, and met with her future swim
coaches. Though I was still worried about Dan, I was feeling optimistic
since he was working so hard to get well.

On our way home from the airport, we stopped at St. Joseph's and
took him out to dinner. Though his anxiety levels were still quite high, he
was obviously more comfortable eating. He always hesitated before taking that first bite but then seemed to enjoy his meal. After the eating
struggles we'd been through at Carson, this was a pleasure to see.

He was chattier than usual at dinner. "You know, some clients who've
been at St. Joseph's for a while go home on weekends."

"Is that something you'd like to do, honey?" I asked.

"Sure," he said. "Maybe you could talk to Scott about it."

Even though we planned to meet Scott at the next family meeting, we
decided I'd e-mail him about our idea. Our hope was that Dan could join
some friends and us at a Fourth of July concert. "I've been at St. Joseph's
almost three weeks now, so maybe they'll let me." There was a hint of
anticipation in Dan's voice, and the thought of him coming home, even
for just one night, buoyed my spirits. I contacted Scott as soon as we
arrived home. He replied quickly but not with the response I wanted. He
expressed concern over the fact that Dan seemed to still isolate himself
from his peers. Because part of Dan's treatment required him to do things

he feared would put others at risk, it was crucial he not segregate himself. Only by interacting with others would he be able to feel connected to them and proceed with this part of his therapy. For this reason, Scott advised against any overnight trips in the near future, as well as limited weekend visits from us. Specifically he asked we not visit at all during the upcoming weekend and informed us he would meet with the "treatment team" regarding our Fourth of July request. He ended the e-mail by conveying hope for Dan's recovery, while also acknowledging our son was struggling with a severe and devastating illness.

As disappointed as I was with this response, I understood what Scott was saying and, of course, wanted to do what was best for Dan. I reread the e-mail several times and found myself obsessing over the phrase "severe and devastating illness."

"What's with our family and obsessions?" I asked Gary. "Why can't I just focus on the hope Scott has for Dan instead of the most negative phrase?"

Gary shrugged. "It's disappointing. Maybe Dan isn't making as much progress as we'd thought."

Mark reassured me. "Don't make too much of the phrase 'severe and devastating illness.' Dan has a good-sized case of OCD, but he's going to have a good life, accomplish wonderful things, fall in love, and have lots of fun and excitement. He has work to do, but he'll get there. I have no doubt of that."

What would I do without Mark?

"St. Joseph's has a good program, but it's tough," Mark said. "I think it makes sense for them to push the social issues with Dan."

My response to Scott was supportive, though I did request the staff make sure Dan interacted with peers over the weekend. Weekends at the clinic weren't as structured as weekdays, and Dan had, on occasion, spent the days in his room by himself. Scott assured me the staff would be aware of the situation and would make sure Dan didn't isolate himself.

We had no Tuesday meeting that week because Sharon was on vacation, so we spoke with Dan on the phone instead. "How was your weekend, honey?" I asked.

"Saturday I was depressed, so I just spent the day in my room," he said. "Sunday was better. I went on a group trip."

"He spent Saturday alone and depressed?" I said to Gary once we hung up. I was angry. "The main reason he didn't come home was be-

cause he was supposed to interact with his peers. He would've been better off at home with us." The thought of Dan, curled up on his bed the whole day, made me feel sick. Still, I didn't complain to Scott or Sharon about the botched weekend plans and instead set my sights on our next Tuesday meeting, where we'd talk about our plans for the Fourth of July.

Our Tuesday meetings had somehow evolved into stilted question-and-answer sessions, and they were often stressful as well. Though Dan had finally begun to contribute a little more, our conversations were never genuine. How could they be, having a moderator to talk to our own son?

OCD RESIDENTIAL TREATMENT CENTERS

The frequency of outpatient OCD treatment falls on a continuum from one to five (or more) times weekly. Although outpatient ERP helps the majority of individuals who complete it, OCD can be "treatment refractory," that is, it doesn't improve with typical treatment.[1] In these situations a residential treatment center (RTC) that provides intensive inpatient treatment might be helpful.

Treatment at an RTC usually involves several hours of daily ERP, evaluation, and (if necessary) treatment by a psychopharmacologist with expertise in treating OCD. There are also meetings with a counselor or social worker and group psychotherapy.

Fortunately, these programs tend to reduce OCD symptoms. One of the RTCs in the United States provided treatment outcome data from about four hundred individuals; the average OCD severity score at the beginning of treatment was in the severe range and by the end fell in the moderate range (an eight-point reduction on the Yale-Brown Obsessive Compulsive Scale, or Y-BOCS[2]). The average length of treatment was just over two months.

When considering whether to seek residential treatment, it's important to consider both the strengths and drawbacks of RTCs. Strengths include the intensive treatment focus and the support of a multidisciplinary team, usually including psychiatrists, psychologists, and social workers. The highly structured and supervised setting of the RTC can increase the likelihood that the OCD sufferer will engage in treatment, compared to outpatient treatment in which

the therapist generally sees the person only one to three hours per week; even in intensive outpatient treatment the therapist and OCD sufferer are typically together for ten hours or less per week. The RTC setting also allows the therapist and psychiatrist to work closely together.

On the other hand, RTC programs tend to be expensive, and even individuals with insurance often end up paying a significant amount out of pocket. Also, being in a residential center removes the person from his or her normal environment, including the support of family and friends and perhaps many of the most troublesome OCD triggers. Careful discharge planning, ideally in collaboration with the OCD sufferer's family, is essential to help the individual transition back to the home environment and hold on to the gains made during treatment.

1. Deborah Osgood-Hynes, Bradley Riemann, and Thröstur Björgvinsson, "Short-Term Residential Treatment for Obsessive-Compulsive Disorder," *Brief Treatment and Crisis Intervention* 3, no. 4 (2003): 414.

2. S. Evelyn Stewart, Denise Egan Stack, Colleen Farrell, David L. Pauls, and Michael A. Jenike, "Effectiveness of Intensive Residential Treatment (IRT) for Severe, Refractory Obsessive-Compulsive Disorder," *Journal of Psychiatric Research* 39, no. 6 (November 2005): 606.

Tuesday came, and Gary and I once again made our way up the stairs, past the second floor, to Sharon's office. Each time we walked by that second-floor door, with all those warning signs, I thought not of the patients behind the door but of their parents and the heartache they were likely experiencing. For now though, I tried to concentrate on our upcoming meeting, where we'd finally meet Scott.

Sharon was still on vacation so we met with her substitute, Mort, who was a semiretired social worker. It was nice to see a different face; maybe he'd perk things up. "Come on in," he said. He seemed like a genuinely happy person and gave us both warm pats on the back. Dan was already in the room, and we hugged. I'd become adept at scrutinizing him quickly. He was more jittery and anxious than usual, and the black circles under his eyes looked worse. Weight, stable.

"I've had the pleasure of chatting a couple of times with Dan already," Mort said, "and it's great to meet the two of you. Dan's a great kid."

I smiled and nodded. *Yes, Dan is a great kid.*

That was always the consensus. Dan was polite, personable, and always eager to work hard and do the right thing. He was a people pleaser, and I'd later realize this personality trait probably exacerbated his OCD.

"I understand Dan will be spending the Fourth of July with you," Mort continued. I looked at Dan, who was nodding. "He just needs to be back the next morning for a group meeting."

"No problem," I said. "We'll have him back early."

Yay! Dan was coming home. Sure, it'd be a quick visit, but at least there'd be no moderator. I'd take whatever time I could get with my son. I started to plan a menu in my head of all his favorite foods.

My thoughts were interrupted by Scott's entrance. "Nice to finally meet you," I said as Gary and I stood to shake his hand. He was tall and lanky, with red hair and freckles. *He's not much older than Dan!* I thought, and searched his face for signs of a wrinkle. Nothing. He couldn't have been more than thirty. *That doesn't mean he's not a good therapist*, I assured myself as he took a seat. At the very least, Dan thought the world of him.

"Dan, why don't you tell your parents about some of the things you've been doing?" Scott said. I liked that idea, as we'd never been given any details of Dan's therapy.

DOES ERP WORK?

ERP is recommended as the first-line psychological treatment for OCD by many professional bodies, including the American Psychiatric Association, the International OCD Foundation, and the Society of Clinical Psychology of the American Psychological Association.[1] These recommendations are based on many rigorous studies showing that ERP works.[2]

For example, in a large study of adults with OCD published by Edna Foa and colleagues, 86 percent who completed ERP were rated as "much improved" (29 percent) to "very much improved" (57 percent) at the end of treatment. The average symptom score for people who did ERP started in the "moderate-to-severe" range and at the end of treatment fell in the "mild" range.[3] Similar results have been reported among children and adolescents who received ERP.[4]

Many reviews have been written about the effectiveness of ERP for OCD, and two things stand out from these reviews. First, the "effect sizes"—standard ways that researchers measure how big of an impact a treatment has—are big for ERP.[5] In other words, the average person in ERP can expect to get a lot of benefit from it. Second, ERP tends to help with other difficulties that exist alongside the OCD, such as depression, general anxiety, and social difficulties.[6]

Given its effectiveness, ERP offers hope to OCD sufferers who want to reclaim their lives.

1. American Psychiatric Association, "Practice Guideline," 11; International OCD Foundation, "Cognitive Behavior Therapy," accessed April 25, 2014, http://www.ocfoundation.org/CBT.aspx; Society of Clinical Psychology (American Psychological Association, Division 12), "Exposure and Response Prevention for Obsessive-Compulsive Disorder," accessed April 25, 2014, http://www.div12.org/PsychologicalTreatments/treatments/ocd_exposure.html.
2. Rebecca E. Stewart and Dianne L. Chambless, "Cognitive-Behavioral Therapy for Adult Anxiety Disorders in Clinical Practice: A Meta-analysis of Effectiveness Studies," *Journal of Consulting and Clinical Psychology* 77, no. 4 (August 2009): 600; Hofmann and Smits, "Cognitive-Behavioral Therapy," 626.
3. Foa et al., "Randomized, Placebo-Controlled Trial," 156.
4. POTS Team, "Cognitive-Behavior Therapy, Sertraline, and Their Combination for Children and Adolescents with Obsessive-Compulsive Disorder: The Pediatric OCD Treatment Study (POTS) Randomized Controlled Trial," *JAMA* 292, no. 16 (2004): 1973; Shirley A. Reynolds, Sarah Clark, Holly Smith, Peter E. Langdon, Ruth Payne, Gemma Bowers, Elisabeth Norton, and Harriet McIlwham, "Randomized Controlled Trial of Parent-Enhanced CBT Compared with Individual CBT for Obsessive-Compulsive Disorder in Young People," *Journal of Consulting and Clinical Psychology* 81, no. 6 (2013): 1024.
5. Rosa-Alcázar et al., "Psychological Treatment," 1320–22.
6. Ibid., 1315.

"Well, I went off campus the other day and had some Mexican food," Dan said.

"Oh, you had Mexican food?" Scott interrupted. "You do realize that most of those ingredients were harvested by migrant workers, in terrible conditions, and their children are probably neglected, hungry, and overworked? But you still ate it?"

What? Wait a minute. Did I actually hear that? My mouth hung open in surprise. I looked at Dan, still a nervous wreck, and saw him nod. I then realized this was therapy.

No wonder Dan's anxiety was so high. I was shaken up myself. Dan continued to tell us about his afternoon in town, and thankfully, Scott went easy on the "therapy." Our meeting was almost over when Scott announced that Dan had something he wanted to tell us. I looked at my

son, and he was literally shaking. After what seemed like forever he spoke.

"I'm worried about going back to school, and I don't think I'll be able to deal with the work and the stress at Carson. I'm considering other options, like getting a job or going to a community college near Bridgeville."

Wham. I felt as if I'd just been punched in the chest. Of course the issue of Dan being well enough to go back to school was on all our minds. That was one of the main reasons he wanted to attend this intensive program in the first place, to help him get back on track without having to miss any school. Questions began forming and swirling in my head. My son's motivation to fight his OCD had been fueled by his strong desire to follow his dreams, and now he was giving those dreams up? Just like that? Instead of working on alternate plans, why couldn't more energy be spent on figuring how to get Dan back to school successfully? There were seven weeks left before school started, so why make a decision now? Was coming to St. Joseph's a big mistake? Overwhelmed, I couldn't respond.

Mort was the first to speak. "Dan, I have to say I'm stunned. When we spoke earlier you told me becoming an animator was your dream, and you'd been really happy at Carson until the OCD took over. Why don't we all think this through."

Gary and I nodded in agreement. I took a deep breath and spoke, surprised at how calm I sounded. "I'm glad you told us how you feel, honey. Obviously we have a lot to talk about." Unfortunately, or fortunately from my perspective, we were out of time, so further discussion would have to wait. I gave Dan a hug. "Don't worry, everything will work out," I said, though I was far from believing that myself.

Dan walked down the stairs with Gary and me. "Oh," he said. "I forgot to tell you I'm on another medication now."

My heart plummeted. "You mean instead of the SSRI and benzodiazepine, or in addition?" Gary asked.

"In addition. And I had a little problem with it."

"What do you mean?" I asked, not really wanting to know.

"Well I had double vision for a little while, but it went away. It's a side effect, but I'm fine now."

"What's the medication?" I already hated whatever it was.

"I forget the name of it," Dan said. "You can talk to Dr. Parker if you want to know why I'm on it."

He didn't want to tell us himself. I felt heavy with sadness as we said our good-byes. At this point, I was more than ready to go home; I don't think I could've handled any more news. It was only late morning, but I felt as if I'd been at St. Joseph's the whole day. I needed to get out of there.

6

MAKE ME DO THIS

On the car ride home I thought of how, over the last few years, Dan had immersed himself in art and animation, with the goal of attending Carson College. I smiled as I remembered the first time I'd dropped him off at his figure-drawing co-op. He knew he'd be the only teenager there, since it was during the day when other kids were in school. "I don't mind," he'd said, smiling. "You know I like old people."

Of course there was the issue of a fourteen-year-old boy being comfortable in that situation. The models, both male and female, were usually nude. "Are you going to be okay with that?" I asked him.

Dan gave me the same look I usually gave him when he said something that made no sense. "Mom, it's all about the art."

Gary was skeptical. "He's going to come home from that first class with a glazed look on his face and drool all over his sketchpad," he said. I wasn't sure what to think. I knew Dan could be serious and mature, but this was asking a lot from an adolescent boy.

Dan was gung ho. "This is going to be great," he said, practically jumping out of the car as we pulled up to the co-op building.

"I'll just come in this first time to introduce myself," I said. Together, we carried all his supplies.

We were greeted by Bill, the facilitator of the group. "Glad to have you," he said cheerily as he and Dan shook hands. He was an older gentleman with white hair and twinkling blue eyes, and he seemed almost

as excited as Dan. Out of the corner of my eye, I caught a glimpse of a woman in a white terry cloth wrap starting to disrobe. I said my good-byes and practically ran out of the room. Obviously Dan was much more comfortable with this situation than I was.

He loved the co-op and looked forward to it every week. He fit right in with the older crowd. "Maybe I can invite some of my new friends over for a play date," he joked. "Ethel is so much fun." Dan always made me laugh. I chuckled at the thought of him spending the afternoon with a middle-aged woman.

But he took his art seriously. "It's annoying when you and Dad make off-color jokes about my sketches," he said one evening. Gary and I had been known to giggle at some of the naked pictures.

"Gee, honey, I'm sorry," I said. "We won't do that anymore. I didn't realize it bothered you."

That confirmed it. Dan was surely an artist. Who else could take this all so seriously? I'm embarrassed to admit when Dan went to sleep at night, Gary and I would still occasionally sneak a peek at his sketches for a laugh. Clearly, we weren't artists.

The co-op was only one way Dan pursued his passion. He enrolled in art class after art class, snagged internships, and attended summer programs. He read, researched, and watched anything and everything that had to do with animation. I thought of the positive feedback he received from teachers and mentors as it became evident that Dan was not only driven but talented as well. I thought of the awe on his face as we toured a major animation studio, courtesy of a friend of a friend. I thought of how happy and excited he was to be at Carson, surrounded by friends who shared his passion and enthusiasm. And I thought of the end of this past school year when he was so debilitated but still insisted on staying at school and finishing his coursework. That was the real Dan, not the young man who now was more than willing to give up his dream. We needed to get the real Dan back.

"You know, Gary," I said, breaking the silence in the car, "this school issue is a huge decision, and Dan shouldn't be making it by himself. We need to be involved. The staff at St. Joseph's has only known him a few weeks, and in a weakened condition to say the least. He's our son, and nobody knows him, cares about him, or loves him as much as we do."

Gary nodded. He seemed too worn out to speak.

I called Mark when we arrived home.

"I think Dan should at least try to go back to Carson," Mark said. "I also feel there's a very good chance he'll be successful there. Scott has done a great job of relating to Dan and forming a relationship, but he's certainly not in a position to be making the more crucial life choices that should be the domain of your family. OCD typically waxes and wanes. It really will get better. I know how hard it is to feel positive in the middle of this, but I'm confident things will improve dramatically."

I wanted so badly to believe Mark.

"As you know, the program at St. Joseph's is very OCD-centric," Mark continued. "They feel that Dan's OCD has to be completely under control before he can continue on with his life, and they're letting him know that. That's where we disagree. I believe the best therapy for Dan is to get on with his life as best as he can and continue therapy at the same time. Of course, this gives him less time to actually concentrate on his OCD. And that's probably the best therapy of all for him. His life is more than OCD."

Mark made sense. Dan didn't need to be—indeed he shouldn't be—focused only on his OCD.

"We need to let Scott know how we're feeling," Gary said, "so we can all work together to support Dan." I agreed, and we sent Scott this e-mail.

Hi Scott,

It was nice to finally meet you today, and we're glad Dan was able to tell us some of what he has been thinking.

Obviously we all want what is best for Dan. We feel strongly that the best thing for him would be to try and go back to school. We have a two-page list of reasons why we feel this way, and would very much like to be involved in discussions (with you and him) about the issue. We know that making decisions himself is important, but this is huge, and we have a feeling that his reasons for feeling that he may not be able to go back are very complicated (we guess we don't have to tell you that).

Becoming an animator has been an almost lifelong dream of Dan's, and he has worked very hard over the last four to five years pursuing his dream. He has told us that his first semester at Carson was one of the happiest times of his life. It is the right place for him, not only academically, but socially. He has made extremely close friends there, which has been great for him. This school is not like a typical college, where you can take a semester off and then just jump right back in. It is

all very sequential and specific, and if he doesn't go back this year, there is really no guarantee that he will get the chance again. And even if he does, we doubt it will be easier for him having taken time off. In fact, we feel it will be harder in many ways.

It seems as if Dan is putting some time and energy into coming up with alternate plans to going back to Carson. We would like to support him by redirecting that energy into figuring out the best way for him to go back to school successfully. The school does have support services, and they are now aware of Dan's OCD. He has a therapist who he feels he could work with in Bridgeville. We will be there for whenever we are needed. He can reduce his course load by at least one course if necessary.

We would like to have conversations with Dan regarding school but want your opinion regarding that. At the very least we would like to be included in whatever discussions there are regarding Carson.

Thanks a lot. We hope to hear back from you soon.

Janet and Gary

P.S. Please feel free to share this e-mail with Dan if you think it would be helpful.

Scott replied promptly, saying he agreed with us completely that Dan shouldn't leave school. He hoped a much reduced course load might be an option. However, he also stressed that because of the severity of Dan's illness, we needed to be realistic about our expectations for Dan. Perhaps returning to Carson, or even pursuing animation, might not be feasible for our son.

My heart sank as I read this reply. Scott agreed with us completely but not really. I was disheartened to read he anticipated Dan having to lower his standards in reference to his goals.

"I know Scott's goal is to get Dan's OCD under control," I said to Gary. "I get that. But when Dan entered the OCD clinic, *his* goal was to learn how to manage his symptoms so he could get back to his life and follow his dreams. It wasn't to abandon or even alter them. He went into St. Joseph's knowing what he wanted. Then something changed, and I'm afraid he is slipping away from us. He's becoming nothing more than his OCD."

"I have the same feeling," Gary said. "We don't need to lower the bar for Dan. In fact, I think we need to keep it high. I'm not ready to accept that his life plans have to be modified. I'm not ready to let the OCD win."

I agreed with Gary, and said, "It's also confusing reading about 'the severity of Dan's illness,' yet we're always being told how great he's doing with his therapy."

I sent Scott another e-mail asking for clarification, and he replied, confirming that yes, Dan was indeed going in the right direction. But Scott was still concerned because he knew Dan barely made it through the previous school year and he didn't want him to be put into that situation again.

I was surprised Scott brought up Dan's condition at the end of the school year as a valid argument for keeping him from going back to Carson.

"I don't get it," I said to Gary. "I'm thankful for Dan's progress at St. Joseph's, but it seems as if Scott isn't taking any of his improvement into account."

"Really," Gary said, agreeing, "hasn't this past month counted for anything?"

I continued our e-mail exchange:

> In my mind, there is a huge difference between how Dan was feeling at the end of the semester compared to now.
>
> He was in trouble physically because he could not eat (and barely drank for a week or so). He was dehydrated and his potassium was low, which further clouded his thinking. He was not taking his medication and was receiving no therapy or support of any kind at all (until I arrived and he had two meetings with Dr. Vogel). I know his OCD was running wild.
>
> But even during this incredible low point, he managed to complete all five of his courses with something like a 3.3 GPA. Of course I never want to see him in that condition again, but with all the support we will have in place, Gary and I believe he has the potential to succeed, hopefully with a reduced course load.

Scott never replied, and as the days passed I felt more unsettled about Dan's situation. What was most upsetting was our isolation from him. We hadn't been asked to contribute to any school-related conversations that might have been happening. Gary and I both felt we couldn't talk freely

at our weekly meetings, which now reminded us of supervised prison visits. Discussions on the phone were difficult, since it was hard to reach Dan. Gary and I were deeply frustrated.

This state of affairs upset me so much I couldn't sleep; I scheduled a meeting with Mark for the following week. Meanwhile, a thought kept creeping into my mind that I tried to ignore: was Dan intentionally being kept away from us?

I was excited about Dan's Fourth of July visit, and though I really wanted to have a conversation with him about school, I decided not to. He was only going to be home for a short time, and I felt the most important things were for him to enjoy himself and for us to be together as a family.

"It'll be great to be home and see the cats," Dan said as we walked out of the clinic. We both laughed even though we already knew, for Dan, the cats always took precedence over the humans in the family. Overall he was in good spirits, though he was still exhausted and shaky.

"Four of the six people who started the program with me are being discharged this weekend," he said. "But not me. And I'll be in lockdown the next few weeks." This was his way of saying he wouldn't be allowed to come home at all.

Seeing his peers leave while he remained was obviously discouraging for him. "Oh, you'll be out before you know it," I said, trying to remain upbeat.

"That's okay. I really don't mind," he said. "Even though the therapy is really hard, everyone is so nice, and I'm comfortable there." He paused. "I could stay there forever."

Ouch. Even though he'd said it jokingly, I knew there was some truth to it. St. Joseph's was safe, with people who understood what he was going through. His remark troubled me, but I tried to shift my thoughts to the here and now and concentrated on spending quality time with my son.

Our Fourth of July trip was a success. The outdoor concert was in a beautiful venue surrounded by mountains. I was with my entire family, a rare occurrence those days, and we were joined by good friends, whom Dan interacted with minimally but comfortably. There was a long line to enter the grounds, so to pass the time, Gary, Dan, and Ava threw a football around. I looked over at Dan, thinking how normal he looked

now, compared to those days at Carson when he was slouched over, chewing his hood strings.

We entered the concert grounds and staked out a small portion of lawn with our blankets and folding chairs. Dan chose to lie on a blanket. The concert was great, and when they finally threw in some classical music to offset the folk music, he smiled and said, "Finally, some *real* music."

On the way home we chatted in the car. "That was fun," Dan said, "but I've always wanted to go to our city's Fourth of July celebration."

"Well, maybe you can go with some friends next summer," Gary said.

"I don't know. I may want to work at Carson next summer and be with my friends there." Students often worked at the school's pre-college summer program.

This was music to my ears, and it felt like my son speaking. Obviously he had mixed emotions about returning to Carson, but I think being away from St. Joseph's, even for a short time, steered him toward school. Perhaps it's easier to think about real life when you're in the real world. When you're in an intensive, institutional program it's all about the disorder and treatment.

As we drove up the hill to St. Joseph's early the next morning, I asked Dan if he wanted to talk about school. His answer was automatic. "No. We'll talk on Tuesday, at our meeting." Sharon was back from her vacation, and now Scott was away.

I watched as Dan disappeared into the building. "I wish we had more time with him."

"Me too," Gary said. "It's hard watching him go through those doors."

Once Dan informed us he was taking a third medication, I tried to get in touch with Dr. Parker, his psychiatrist. It took two weeks to finally connect with him on the phone. He was businesslike and got right to the point. "Dan is maxed out on eighty milligrams of his SSRI. You know he's also taking a benzodiazepine for social anxiety. We just need to watch out for sedation with that one. And he is on an atypical antipsychotic. It helps the SSRI work better, and we'll be increasing the dosage on that one a couple of times. Dan had been feeling discouraged and overwhelmed, and was having thoughts of self-injuring again. This medicine helps with those 'popping-up' thoughts."

ANTIPSYCHOTICS FOR OCD

Even with a therapeutic dose of well-established first-line medications for OCD such as fluvoxamine (Luvox) or sertraline (Zoloft), many people with OCD won't improve or will still have lots of symptoms.[1] These observations led to the search for other medications that might augment the effect of SSRIs on OCD.

Many studies have suggested that antipsychotic medications—drugs such as quetiapine (trade name Seroquel), risperidone (Risperdal), and olanzapine (Zyprexa)—provide additional benefit for OCD sufferers on SSRIs. A review of these studies in 2006 concluded that antipsychotics did indeed help individuals whose OCD hadn't responded to an SSRI alone: on average, an additional 22 percent of individuals showed a treatment response when an antipsychotic medication was prescribed, compared to placebo.[2]

However, many of the studies that were included in the review were small, with none of the medication groups having more than twenty-two participants, and some as few as ten.[3] A larger study from 2013 with forty individuals in the risperidone augmentation group found no benefit of risperidone over placebo.[4] Furthermore, a more recent Cochrane review from 2010 found limited evidence for the efficacy of olanzapine, possible efficacy for quetiapine, and significant effects of risperidone on anxiety and depression but no advantage versus a placebo on OCD scores. The authors also noted the sedation and profound weight gain that are often associated with antipsychotic use; the average weight gain after a year on risperidone is about twenty pounds.[5]

Many individuals report finding antipsychotic medications helpful, but research studies have produced mixed results. People with OCD who have not responded to ERP and a therapeutic dose of SSRIs need to weigh the risks and possible benefits of trying an antipsychotic medication.

1. Katja Komossa, Anna M. Depping, Magdalena Meyer, Werner Kissling, and Stefan Leucht, "Second-Generation Antipsychotics for Obsessive Compulsive Disorder," *Cochrane Database of Systematic Reviews* 12 (2010): 3.
2. M. H. Bloch, A. M. Landeros-Weisenberger, B. Kelmendi, V. Coric, M. B. Bracken, and J. F. Leckman, "A Systematic Review: Antipsychotic Augmentation with Treatment Refractory Obsessive-Compulsive Disorder," *Molecular Psychiatry* 11, no. 7 (July 2006): 626.

3. Ibid., 624–25.
4. Helen Blair Simpson, Edna B. Foa, Michael R. Liebowitz, Jonathan D. Huppert, Shawn Cahill, Michael J. Maher, Carmen P. McLean, James Bender Jr., Sue M. Marcus, Monnica T. Williams, Jamie Weaver, Donna Vermes, E. Van Meter, Carolyn I. Rodriguez, Mark Powers, Anthony Pinto, Patricia Imms, Chang-Gyu Hahn, and Raphael Campeas, "Cognitive-Behavioral Therapy vs. Risperidone for Augmenting Serotonin Reuptake Inhibitors in Obsessive-Compulsive Disorder: A Randomized Clinical Trial," *JAMA Psychiatry* 70, no. 11 (2013): 1190.
5. Komossa et al., "Second-Generation Antipsychotics," 2, 69.

"What about that double vision he was having?" I asked Dr. Parker.

"I wouldn't worry about that. It appears to have been a one-time thing. You know, this is a very difficult time for Dan. His therapy is extremely anxiety provoking. These meds aren't necessarily all long term, and it's hard to know what's working anyway."

That's how the conversation ended.

Never a big fan of medication, I had to be more open minded once Dan became ill. But to end the conversation with the admission that nobody knew what worked or didn't work didn't help my already fragile comfort level. I knew from researching and talking with Mark that these drugs, especially the atypical antipsychotic, came with some heavy-duty side effects.

"My big question," I said to Gary, "is why give Dan more medication to help him get through this difficult time when the difficult time was purposely created as part of his therapy? Isn't he *supposed* to feel horrible? Doesn't he *need* to feel horrible?" I was just learning the basics of exposure and response prevention (ERP) therapy and knew that feeling anxiety, particularly when refraining from ritualizing, was an integral part of the therapy.

Our Tuesday meeting arrived quickly. Although she'd been on vacation for two weeks, Sharon was well informed of Dan's situation. The communication among Dan's health-care providers (Sharon, Scott, and Dr. Parker) was excellent, and they seemed to really work as a team regarding all aspects of his treatment. They agreed on everything.

Dan was already in Sharon's office when we arrived. He looked worse than he had a few days ago, when he was home. The black circles under his eyes were darker than ever, and he seemed unable to control his nerves. I'd never seen him so jittery.

Sharon immediately guided the conversation toward school, and I began by speaking directly to Dan. "Honey, I can't even begin to imagine how difficult your life has been over this past year. I'm so proud of you

and the way you've handled yourself during this time. You're an amazing young man."

My eyes were tearing already. "You must know Dad and I only want what's best for you. As your parents, that's all we've ever wanted. We feel strongly you should at least try to go back to Carson this year. You have caring teachers who already think the world of you, and there are also special support services there. Dr. Vogel said he'd see you two, even three, times a week if needed. If you don't go back now and are lucky enough to get the opportunity to reenroll next year, we feel it'll be even harder to return after being away for so long."

Our eyes met. "Dan, this is your dream. You worked so hard to get to Carson and you were so happy there before you got sick. If you go back and it doesn't work out, you're no worse off. The only negative is that we'll lose money, but Dad and I are willing to take that risk."

Sharon asked Dan if he wanted to respond. I think it was hard for him not having Scott by his side, but he was able to speak, and speak he did. He acknowledged that much of what I said made sense, and that going back to school was a remote possibility, but he didn't want to commit to anything at this point. "I still think I should just take a couple of community college courses and concentrate on my OCD," he said.

DOING OCD TREATMENT PERFECTLY

Individuals with OCD don't "check their OCD at the door" when they come to treatment, and so it's not surprising that OCD can attach to the treatment itself.

For example, people with OCD generally have a really hard time living with uncertainty.[1] When they're told that ERP *tends* to be very helpful for treating OCD, they may want assurance that it will be helpful to them. In some cases people may have a hard time starting the treatment without knowing for certain that they're going to get better. Once treatment starts, OCD sufferers may try to do the treatment perfectly in order to guarantee their recovery.

For example, the individuals might:

- feel compelled to tell the therapist about every obsession they've had because the treatment will be compromised if the therapist "doesn't have all the information";
- keep excessive records about obsessions and rituals;
- be hypervigilant for any possible signs of OCD;
- spend an exorbitant amount of time on exposures; and
- want to continue treatment as long as there are any remaining OCD symptoms.

Some of these behaviors can look like positive signs of being committed to the treatment, but in fact they can be subtle manifestations of OCD. As with any OCD domain, the person needs to get used to living with uncertainty—in this case, uncertainty about OCD recovery. Since perfect is impossible, the goal in ERP is to do the treatment well and imperfectly.

1. David F. Tolin, Jonathan S. Abramowitz, Bartholomew D. Brigidi, and Edna B. Foa, "Intolerance of Uncertainty in Obsessive-Compulsive Disorder," *Journal of Anxiety Disorders* 17, no. 2 (2003): 237.

Hmm. If the whole college situation wasn't so upsetting, it might be amusing. I knew Dan meant he needed time for his therapy, but his thinking was warped. He shouldn't be revolving his life around his OCD. I thought back to the end of last semester, when he was in such bad shape. He still forged ahead and did what he had to do, all the while talking positively about coming back sophomore year. It was almost as if he didn't realize how debilitated he was until he arrived at St. Joseph's.

He had more to say. "How can I stay up until three o'clock in the morning working on projects, when I can barely shower and brush my teeth without ritualizing? I don't feel the OCD is at a point where I can handle it all. Last semester some of my rituals involved *not* doing my work. And I'm afraid I'll start cutting myself again."

I was overwhelmed. Not so much because of *what* Dan said but because of *how much* he said. The words just seemed to pour out of him. I was pleased he was expressing himself, and it was interesting that his thoughts seemed to jive with Mark's explanation of St. Joseph's philosophy.

"You say you can't brush your teeth without ritualizing, honey," I said. "I think that's okay. You don't have to be ritual free to get on with your life. Go back to school, ritualize when you brush your teeth if you have to, and work on it with Dr. Vogel."

I knew I was oversimplifying things, but I was trying to make my point. "I feel that if we support your decision to *not* go back to school, we'd be enabling you in avoiding a difficult situation. I'm sure you're afraid of the work, of seeing your close friends, and maybe even of doing something you really want to do. Supporting you in that decision is like letting the OCD win, and we can't do that."

Time was up again, but that was okay. I felt drained and exhausted from our meeting, and I'm guessing Dan did as well.

Sharon ended by saying, "I'd like to talk with Dan's advisor at Carson about the possibility of him taking a much lighter course load."

Once Dan had expressed reluctance about returning to Carson, she and Scott had brought up this alternative. Dan and I continually explained that their suggestion wasn't feasible at Carson. Dan could drop one course, but his animation courses were sequential, and they had to be taken next semester. So I was surprised when Sharon brought this up yet again.

"You can't do that at Carson," Dan and I said, almost in unison.

"Oh, I've been doing this for many years," Sharon said. "The schools always say that, but often they'll make exceptions."

Dan and I exchanged glances. We knew what the outcome would be, but I gave her Dr. Moore's contact information anyway. "I'll call her tomorrow," Sharon said, "and let you know what she says."

My appointment with Mark was the next day, and I updated him on our recent meeting. I remarked how Dan was uncharacteristically effusive with his words, and Mark said, "That's most likely from the atypical antipsychotic."

It never occurred to me that a drug could affect Dan that way.

Mark remained steadfast in his belief we should strongly encourage Dan to go back to school. "You know," he said, "they're very good at St. Joseph's with the mechanics of OCD. There's no question they know their stuff. But they're overlooking the big picture, that is, 'Who are you and what do you want to do with your life?' They're OCD about OCD," he added, referring to the fact that it was all about conquering the disorder.

He didn't speak again for a moment, and I sensed he was trying to choose his words with care.

"Here's what I think," he said. "For lack of a better word, the program has become like a cult for Dan. It's time for you to seriously consider removing him. In the business, we call it termination. I think Dan is way too attached to Scott, and the longer he's there, the more this will become a problem and the harder it'll be for Dan to leave. This isn't uncommon when patients are institutionalized. There's no way Dan will be able to think clearly or make the right decisions while he's still at St. Joseph's."

Wow. I didn't see that coming and tried to analyze the situation aloud. "You know, I've been feeling ambivalent about Dan still being at St. Joseph's. There's no question they've helped him deal with his OCD, but his overall state of mind is worse. He says he's working really hard to get better, and I know that's why his anxiety levels are so high, but he has almost no self-confidence in what he can achieve right now. In his thinking, his life is on hold until he conquers his OCD. Maybe their job is done and it's time for us to do ours. I mean, Dan once said that he could stay there forever. I'm afraid he could! It just never occurred to me that we could, or should, initiate the process of him . . . leaving." It was hard for me to use the word *terminate*.

Suddenly my mind began to whirl, and I was caught in a ball of anxiety. "I'm afraid of him coming home, Mark. What if he's no different from before he went? When he'd lie on the floor all day and not eat until midnight, we'd comfort ourselves by saying he was going to St. Joseph's soon. But what if he does that again? Where do we turn? I don't know how he'll be, or if we'll be able to take care of him, and it really scares me."

I couldn't stop talking. It was as if *I* were the one on the atypical antipsychotic. "And I don't think I told you Dan said he's afraid he'll start cutting himself again if he goes back to school. And what if he's so angry with us for making him leave that it ruins our relationship forever?"

I was all over the map with my thoughts, and Mark patiently waited until I calmed down before he spoke. "First of all, I think you'll be pleasantly surprised how much better he is once he leaves St. Joseph's. Even if he isn't, he'll be continuing his therapy in Bridgeville. As far as cutting himself, as I've said before, it's not the end of the world, and avoidance is not the answer."

I listened to Mark, but to me cutting was still such an awful, unnatural thing to think about.

"And your relationship with Dan won't be permanently damaged," Mark said, "because, well, he's Dan. I'd advise you to shift your focus from talking with the staff and Dan about returning to school to talking about Dan's termination. Once he's out, you can have real conversations with him regarding school. At this point, those conversations are just not possible. I think it makes sense to talk about Dan needing some time to adjust to life outside the program before you move and that it's getting expensive for him to remain at St. Joseph's. If it gets a bit sticky, I'd add that you have some concerns he's regressing a bit and becoming dependent on the staff to function. It's going to take a couple of weeks for Dan to adjust to life without Scott. I think he's going to be sad for a while without him. But I think it's important to begin the process of life after St. Joseph's."

I left Mark's office with a new sense of purpose: to get Dan out of St. Joseph's Hospital. Though still confused about some things, I felt better emotionally because at least I felt I was *doing* something to help my son.

On my drive home, my thoughts wandered back to those last few weeks in Bridgeville, when Dan was doing so poorly. He'd often say, "Make me do this," referring to eating, working, going into the supermarket, or whatever he was struggling with at that moment. Sometimes he was able to follow through, and sometimes he couldn't, but at least he always tried.

In my heart I knew the best thing for him now was to try to go back to Carson, and I could almost hear his voice saying, "Make me do this."

7

A POTHOLE IN THE ROAD

With Gary easily on board, I e-mailed Sharon and Scott, stating we wanted to begin the process of termination (there, I'd said it). Seconds after I hit the send key, Sharon called. Our cordial relationship had become strained, and there was tension when we spoke. "I was surprised to get your e-mail," she said. "What brought this on?"

"Well, Dan's been at St. Joseph's for nearly six weeks. We know leaving takes preparation, so we don't want to just yank him out. We're moving to Bridgeville in early August, and it's time for Dan to continue on with his life."

I'd wanted to keep the conversation short, but with Sharon's prodding, I rambled on about Dan's growing dependency on Scott, my fear he was regressing, our differing philosophies as to what was best for him, and even my concern that Gary's and my opinions weren't taken seriously. As I'd later tell Mark, Sharon had a knack for making me talk. "Of course she does," he said. "That's what she does for a living."

The one topic I hadn't brought up was school, and not surprisingly, Sharon did. "Do you still expect Dan to return to school?"

"That's a decision we'll make as a family after he's home with us," I said, cringing at the way it sounded. I already sensed the staff thought I was an overbearing, controlling mother who wanted her son to return to Carson at any cost. Imagine! I was even willing to uproot my family to get what I wanted. In contrast, our family and friends knew our actions

were motivated by love and the desire to support our son. I was getting antsy and wanted to end the conversation, so I got right to the point. "When can Dan be terminated?"

"Well, judging by the notes I have here, I'd say by the end of July."

I calculated mentally. The end of July was approximately three weeks away, and that would give Dan at least a week at home before we were scheduled to leave for Bridgeville—not ideal, but it seemed doable. We wanted to arrive in Bridgeville a couple of weeks before school started so Dan could settle in as well as hopefully meet with Dr. Vogel.

The next step was to talk with Dan about leaving St. Joseph's. Even though Scott had requested we not spend time with him on weekends, Gary and I were determined to communicate freely with our son. Scott was still on vacation, and Sharon didn't seem to know we weren't supposed to visit him, so we planned to see him that weekend. I felt a little sneaky, but it was worth it to see Dan. He looked well, and his spirits were good. As we drove to a nearby restaurant, I contemplated the best way to bring up his termination. Dan gave me a lead. "I hope they don't throw me out of the program," he said. "I clogged the toilet this morning." We laughed, and then I told him about my conversation with Sharon.

"The end of July?" he said. His mood darkened immediately. "I won't be ready by then." More to himself than us he said, "Maybe I could see Scott as an outpatient until we leave for Bridgeville."

"Oh, is that allowed?" I asked.

"I think some clients have done that. Maybe it could work for me."

Since it would only be for a short time, I didn't pursue this conversation. However, his comment gave me some insight as to how attached he was to Scott. His mood for the rest of our visit was subdued, and I felt personally responsible for this change. We talked briefly about his termination, and I tried to be upbeat and positive.

"There's a big, wonderful, world out there waiting for you."

"I know, I see it for three hours every Sunday (referring to his planned outings), and that's enough for me." Our eyes met, and even though he'd been half joking, I knew he realized it didn't sound right, that being so comfortable at St. Joseph's and not wanting to leave weren't good feelings to have. Still, during lunch he kept saying, "I'm really going to miss everyone, especially Scott."

"Of course you will, honey," I said, "but it's important to get on with your life."

Dan nodded. We dropped him back at St. Joseph's and once again watched him walk through the doors of the clinic. *He'll be home soon*, I assured myself as we slowly drove away.

I settled into my chair at our next Tuesday meeting, eager to discuss details of Dan's termination. "Well, I spoke with Dr. Moore at Carson, who told me Dan could only reduce his course load by one," Sharon said. "And he has to take all his computer animation courses to remain in that major."

No surprises there. Dan and I already knew this. "Did she say anything else?" I asked, remembering how concerned and supportive Dr. Moore had always been.

"Just that the program is extremely demanding and that sophomore year has the steepest learning curve."

Good one, Janet. You had to ask.

Dan spoke. "I feel I'm going in the right direction with my therapy, but it's very slow. I want to continue with intensive therapy, and I know at this point Carson will be way too stressful and I won't be able to cope with it, and I will regress and cut myself and I won't be able to do the animation because sometimes I can't even turn on my computer and did you know I have a panic attack every time I get dressed [because he forced himself to not do his rituals]?"

He came up for air and then continued. "Animation isn't as important to me as getting my life back together. Maybe I can take some classes at a community college and get a part-time job. I feel like I've been trapped inside my OCD forever, and I'm excited to get my life back. But I have to continue with intensive therapy or that won't happen. Do you remember how my room looked last semester? That's a metaphor for my life."

Wow. So many thoughts bombarded my mind. First, I had no doubt his atypical antipsychotic dosage had been increased, which I later found out was true. And though I really felt for him, and knew he was truly suffering, something about his words seemed scripted. He didn't sound genuine.

Sharon interrupted my thoughts. "So how do you feel about what Dan said?"

In the back of my mind I heard Mark's voice. *Don't talk about school. Just focus on his termination.* I opened my mouth but somehow all the wrong words came out. "You think you have to be all better to go back to school, Dan, but Dad and I see school as part of your therapy to get well. So we disagree. Also, I think there are flaws in your reasoning. How can you take courses at a community college and get a part-time job when you're not able to drive now? You'd have to live with us, and I'd have to take you everywhere. I'm guessing that's not what you want. I hear everything you're saying, and we'll discuss it as a family once you're home."

I stopped myself even though there was a lot more I wanted to say. One thing that really bothered me, and this wasn't the first time it had come up, was Dan's reference to suffering "forever." He had no recollection of ever being happy, and believe me, he was a happy child until the OCD took over. I was there. His thinking was distorted because he was depressed. I recalled at our last Tuesday meeting, I'd said, "We had a really nice time with Dan on the Fourth of July."

Dan had looked at me, puzzled, and said, "Maybe that's what it seemed like to you, but for me it was torture."

As I'd mentioned to Mark earlier, the other fact obvious to me was Dan's total lack of self-confidence. He was so convinced he'd fail at school, he couldn't bear to try. I know the thought of regressing must have been terrifying to him; I understood that. But I felt he still needed to forge ahead.

"Well, that's all the time we have today," Sharon said, bringing me back to the present. "See you next week."

I gave Dan a hug and was pleased to feel some meat on his bones. "I love you," I said, looking right at him.

"Love you too, Mom."

I left St. Joseph's with a heavy heart. As Gary and I walked to the car, it occurred to me: we hadn't discussed Dan's termination at all.

I e-mailed Sharon as soon as we got home and asked for the exact date of Dan's release. She replied a couple of days later, saying she was

waiting to hear back from our insurance company to get a better sense of what they would authorize moving forward.

Huh? I didn't understand at all. "Why would Sharon have to contact the insurance company to authorize Dan to leave?" I asked Gary. "I'd think the only reason she'd contact them is to find out how long he could *stay*."

"I don't get it either," he said. "Our insurance company pays for a portion of Dan's treatment in two-week intervals, as do we. Once he leaves, they just stop paying."

Instead of letting my thoughts run wild, I decided to call the insurance company to find out what was going on. After maneuvering my way through their automated system, I finally connected with a human being. And guess what? Because Dan was over eighteen the representative couldn't give me any information whatsoever. We could *pay* for Dan's treatment; we just couldn't know anything about it.

I had a bad feeling about what was happening, even though I had no idea what actually *was* happening. Because Dr. Vogel, who'd be Dan's therapist in Bridgeville, had asked to be kept up to date on what was going on with Dan, I gave him a call. I also wanted his unbiased opinion regarding Dan's situation. "I know we've only met briefly," I said, "and you don't know me well, but I'll try and fill you in, as honestly as I can, on everything that's been happening." I took a long, deep breath, and it all came pouring out. As my story unfolded, especially the part about us relocating to Bridgeville, I wondered if Dr. Vogel would also see me as a pushy, overbearing mother.

"Well," Dr. Vogel said once I was done, "I think there's no question it's time to get him out." He concurred with all the advice Mark had given us and also reiterated that he'd see Dan three times a week if needed.

"Let's also keep in mind Dan is only nineteen," Dr. Vogel said. "While he's technically an adult, he absolutely needs your guidance in this decision-making process. My goodness, his frontal lobe development won't even be complete until he's twenty-four."

While that was interesting news about Dan's frontal lobe, I was mainly pleased that Dr. Vogel, Mark, Gary, and I were all in agreement. My conversation with Dr. Vogel strengthened my conviction that we needed to get Dan home.

Next I called Dr. Moore, Dan's academic advisor, who'd also asked that we stay in touch; I updated her on everything.

"I just received an e-mail from Dan yesterday," she said. "You must know about that."

"No, I don't. What was it regarding?" I knew it wouldn't be good news. My heart was racing and I braced myself.

"Well, he said he was making slow progress," Dr. Moore said, "and that he and his therapists decided he wouldn't be returning to school. Instead he'll stay another month at St. Joseph's."

What? I needed to sit down. Was this really happening? I tried to process Dr. Moore's words. How could Dan have sent this e-mail without even consulting us?

Surely, the staff at St. Joseph's had to know about this correspondence. Yet nobody asked our opinion, or even told us about the letter. I was hurt and angry, not with Dan but with the staff, and I felt betrayed. Dan wasn't to blame. He'd been influenced by others and was unable to think clearly for himself. I remembered Mark saying St. Joseph's had become like a cult for Dan and now realized how accurate that analogy was. Dan's announcement he'd be staying another month at St. Joseph's shocked me for another reason: shouldn't that decision be made, in part, by the people who'd be paying for it?

CONTINUING LIFE WHILE RECOVERING FROM OCD

When does it make sense to reduce the intensity of OCD treatment? In an ideal world, individuals with OCD would receive treatment until their OCD was no longer bothering them. In the real world, few people have the luxury of putting the rest of their lives on hold indefinitely while pursuing treatment—parents need to work and parent, students need to go to class, and intensive therapy (inpatient or outpatient) can cost a lot of money. On the other hand, when OCD is in full force it's hard for many individuals to work full time, excel in coursework, or be one's best self in relationships. So how does a person balance these competing concerns: getting sufficient treatment while maintaining a life?

There's no simple or one-size-fits-all answer to this question. That said, there are important principles to keep in mind that can provide some guidance.

First, we don't want to reduce treatment intensity if there's a good chance that the person is going to regress. It's important to consider in this regard where the person is in her or his recovery. I often use the metaphor of climbing a mountain. When a person is climbing a very steep mountain—which the beginning of therapy can feel like—it's pretty easy to slip backward. As treatment progresses and the person's symptoms go down, the slope of the mountain flattens out so it's easier to hold on to the ground one has gained and to continue to make progress. If a person's recovery seems to be tenuous, then it's not a good idea to cut back on the level of treatment.

One of the best indicators of whether treatment is going well and is likely to be helpful is whether a person is diligently doing exposures and not doing rituals.[1] The ability to do self-directed exposures (without the presence of a therapist) is a particularly important predictor of whether the person can stay on track with less frequent treatment.[2] From a clinical perspective we would want to see that a person is making steady progress before considering reducing the level of care.

Encouragingly, there's good evidence that progress doesn't have to stop once treatment is over. In one of the longest follow-up studies to date, individuals who had completed nine weeks of ERP were contacted six to eight years after their treatment ended. OCD severity scores were slightly *lower* at the follow-up assessment, showing that treatment gains tend to be maintained long term following ERP for OCD. Depression scores actually *improved* significantly from the end of treatment to follow-up.[3]

In the end it's important to learn to manage life while continuing in recovery from OCD. After all, OCD tends to be a chronic condition and will need to be managed for the long haul. Returning to life when clinically appropriate also sends a strong message to oneself that life consists of more than OCD and of more than OCD treatment. Building a life of meaning and purpose that's not focused on OCD is an essential part of recovery from the illness.

1. Helen B. Simpson, Michael J. Maher, Yuanjia Wang, Yuanyuan Bao, Edna B. Foa, and Martin Franklin, "Patient Adherence Predicts Outcome from Cognitive Behavioral Therapy in Obsessive-Compulsive Disorder," *Journal of Consulting and Clinical Psychology* 79, no. 2 (April 2011): 249–50.
2. Luiz A. De Arayjo, Ligia M. Ito, and Isaac M. Marks, "Early Compliance and Other Factors Predicting Outcome of Exposure for Obsessive-Compulsive Disorder," *British Journal of Psychiatry* 169, no. 6 (December 1996): 747–52.

3. Michael Rufer, Iver Hand, Heike Alsleben, Anne Braatz, Jürgen Ortmann, Birgit Katenkamp, Susanne Fricke, and Helmut Peter, "Long-Term Course and Outcome of Obsessive-Compulsive Patients after Cognitive-Behavioral Therapy in Combination with Either Fluvoxamine or Placebo," *European Archives of Psychiatry and Clinical Neuroscience* 255, no. 2 (April 2005): 126–27.

While I sat in disbelief, I suddenly remembered Dr. Moore was still on the telephone. It wasn't easy, but I tried to contain my emotions and continue the conversation.

"Please disregard that e-mail," I said. "As you can see, the staff at St. Joseph's hasn't been totally candid with us. We're in the process of removing Dan from the program, and he'll be back at school. My husband and I believe with all the support he'll have this coming year, he can be successful. If he isn't, then we'll deal with it. At the very least he deserves the chance to pursue his dream. As you well know, even during that horrible time at the end of last semester, he was able to pull it together and complete his courses successfully."

"Of course I remember that," Dr. Moore said. "That's what I told the social worker when she called to ask about a reduced course load for him."

"Oh, Sharon? She didn't mention you spoke about last semester."

"Well," Dr. Moore said, "I told her I was so impressed with what Dan was able to do last year. Obviously I don't have an inkling of what he was going through. But what I saw was a young man with determination, resolve, strength, passion, and desire, even in the most dire of circumstances."

Tears welled in my eyes. I'm not sure if they were from hearing Dr. Moore speak so highly of Dan or from the realization that most of those words no longer described my son. "So you told all this to Sharon?" I wanted to be certain I understood her correctly.

"Yes, of course."

I thought back to yesterday's meeting, when I'd asked Sharon if Dr. Moore had said anything else. Sharon replied that Dr. Moore had mentioned how difficult sophomore year was, but she hadn't told us all the wonderful things Dr. Moore said about Dan. Why not? My anger was coming back full force, but at least this time I hadn't forgotten Dr. Moore was still on the telephone.

"Thanks for taking the time to talk with me," I said. "And you'll disregard Dan's e-mail?"

"Absolutely. I'm really looking forward to seeing him next month."

I hung up the phone, still shocked. I felt deceived by the staff at St. Joseph's. I sat for a few minutes, trying to regain my composure. As upset as I was, I knew we needed to do what was best for Dan.

"Let's say for argument's sake Dan stays at St. Joseph's another month," I said to Gary. "He's feeling better, or maybe he isn't, but either way he realizes not going back to school was a big mistake. What will happen then, when he's depressed, living with his parents, and floundering without any structure or direction?"

"Nobody from St. Joseph's will be around to help him then," Gary said.

I thought back to the evening before, when Gary and I had called Dan on the hall phone. We'd asked about visiting over the weekend, and he'd answered, "I don't know, I'll have to check with Scott." He'd sounded down and defeated, and I attributed it all to our meeting.

Now, of course, I realized there'd been a lot more going on. It wasn't like him to be deceitful, and I'm sure the fact he'd gone behind our backs weighed heavily on him. He'd been put into a no-win position, feeling pressured to make major life decisions while trying to please those he cared about, all the while still very much struggling with his OCD.

I updated Mark on the events of the past two days. "This reinforces what we talked about," he said. "It's time to focus all your energy into getting Dan out of St. Joseph's."

Gary and I decided to be proactive and sent the following e-mail.

Hi Sharon and Scott,

We understand Sharon was contacting the insurance company today though we're not really sure why.

We don't want to wait until Tuesday the twenty-second to discuss Dan's release date. When I spoke with you, Sharon, you told me Dan would be released by the end of July. We'd like to know the exact date and want to begin the process of transitioning.

We're getting the feeling there is some stalling going on and want to make it clear we want Dan home by the end of July.

We're concerned about him, as it seems he is regressing in certain ways. He is becoming institutionalized and has become too dependent on the program. We think it's fair to say the longer he stays at St. Joseph's the harder it will be for him to adjust to the outside world.

We realize Dan has significant OCD and will need continued treatment. We just feel at this time the best thing for him is to come back into the real world and be with his family and friends.

Please reply with the date of his release.

Thank you.
Janet and Gary

While there was no mention of Dan going back to school, it was the proverbial elephant in the living room. We all knew the issue of him returning to Carson was a major factor in our wanting him home. He might not end up going back to school, but he wouldn't even have that option if he stayed at St. Joseph's much longer. Fall semester at Carson began in mid-August.

Scott replied and assured me that Dan was spending more time each day outside of St. Joseph's and that he would continue this trend. He stressed that while Dan was receiving a lot of support from the program, the very core of his treatment plan required him to act independently.

"Scott appears to be addressing my concerns regarding Dan's dependency on the program," I said to Gary, "but I don't understand his reasoning. Just because he's able to leave the four walls of the clinic doesn't mean he's not dependent on it."

"What stands out for me is there's no mention of a termination date," Gary said. He sounded weary.

"Of course not. They're planning for Dan to stay another month. It's mind boggling to me that nobody has discussed this with us." I was becoming increasingly agitated and was still upset when Scott and Sharon called a few minutes later. I didn't want to talk with them but knew we had to. Gary got on the other line.

"We want to discuss your e-mail," Sharon said. That was all I heard as her voice became muted by the thought in my head I couldn't shake. *They know about the e-mail Dan sent to Dr. Moore, yet they're saying nothing about it.* I tried to understand the situation from their point of view but always came back to the fact that these major life decisions were being made behind our backs. I forced myself to tune back in to the conversation as Scott said, "So we feel it's important for Dan to make his own decisions." I had no idea what this had to do with my e-mail, but I knew he was talking about school.

I was surprised to hear the edge in my voice. "It's funny," I said. "When Dan was having difficulties with food, you and I had a conversation. You said that because of his OCD he wasn't even capable of making decisions of when, what, and how much he should eat. We all needed to make those decisions for him. But now you have no qualms about letting him make major life decisions on his own."

There was silence for a moment and no direct response to my comment. "Well, Dan and I have been doing some brainstorming," Scott said, "and we think he might just need to go a different route to find happiness. For example, he could be an art teacher."

If I wasn't so drained from the events of the morning, I probably would've gone into a tirade. Instead, I just held the phone and shook my head. *That's ridiculous*, I said to myself, only to realize I'd actually spoken the words aloud. Woops.

"While there's certainly nothing wrong with being an art teacher," I said, trying hard to remain calm, "it's nothing Dan has ever expressed even the most remote interest in. His lifelong dream is to be an animator." I remembered Mark's advice. "All we want is the date he'll be terminated."

They dodged our request, and that was the end of our conversation. As soon as we hung up, we looked at each other and knew: if they wouldn't give us a date, we'd give them one.

"How about August 1?" Gary said.

"Sounds good to me." I was relieved to be making some progress. "That's less than two weeks away, it coincides with the end of a payment period, and it gives the staff some time to help him with the pending transition." We decided to tell everyone about our decision at the next Tuesday meeting.

I had plans to take Dan to lunch over the weekend and called him on a hall phone to confirm. He sounded sad and irritated. "Are you okay?" I asked.

"No."

"What's wrong?"

"I have OCD."

This snide response was out of character for him, and I attributed it to all the stress he was under. "He'll do better once he leaves St. Joseph's," Mark said, "but the transition could be tough. At some level, and maybe this isn't the right wording, but he loves it there. It's a haven with people

he cares about and admires. It's almost as if he has Stockholm syndrome."

I kept Mark's words in mind when I picked Dan up for lunch that Sunday. He looked okay; I'd certainly seen him look a lot worse. But he seemed extremely tired and his voice sounded flat. I wondered how much his medication was affecting him.

"Want to walk a little before we eat?" I asked.

"Sure."

We walked for a while and I realized that, except for one little skip, there was no noticeable ritualizing. But he was all doom and gloom. While he spoke I thought back to another walk we'd taken earlier in the summer, when we were by the pond and he had commented that he felt so lucky to only have OCD. He'd done a complete turnaround.

I tried to give him the same pep talk Mark so often gave me. "Honey, I know this is hard for you to believe right now, but this really is just a bump in the road for you. You have a wonderful life ahead of you."

"This isn't a bump in the road," he said in his monotone voice. "It's a huge pothole, and I've felt so awful for so long. I still have so much anxiety, it's hard to function."

OCD AND DEPRESSION

For OCD sufferers, depression is a common co-occurring condition; about a third of individuals with OCD are currently depressed, and another third will experience depression at some point.[1] More often than not the OCD comes first and may be a contributing factor to the development of depression. For example, the loss of hope associated with extended bouts of OCD can lead to major depression, as can the loss of important activities and relationships due to OCD's interference.

When depression is added to OCD it changes the clinical picture. OCD tends to be more severe among depressed persons (with severity scores generally around 15 percent higher) and is associated with greater impairment.[2] Depression also raises the likelihood of hospitalization and, not surprisingly, puts the OCD sufferer at increased risk for attempting suicide.[3]

Unfortunately, severely depressed OCD sufferers are not as likely to benefit from treatment. For example, one study found that the treatment response rate with ERP (with or without medication) fell from 88 percent for nondepressed individuals to 45 percent among those with severe depression; the rate was 77 percent for individuals with both mild and moderate depression.[4] Thus there was not a marked decrease in treatment response until individuals were *severely* depressed, and even among this group approximately half of those who received treatment significantly benefited from it. The decrease in treatment efficacy probably happens because it's hard to engage in treatment when depression is really bad.

Clearly it's important to determine if a person with OCD is depressed. With severe depression it may be necessary to focus on treating the depression in order to allow the person to fully participate in treatment for OCD.

1. Stefano Pallanti, Giacomo Grassi, Elisa D . Sarrecchia, Andrea Cantisani, and Matteo Pellegrini, "Obsessive-Compulsive Disorder Comorbidity: Clinical Assessment and Therapeutic Implications," *Frontiers in Psychiatry* 2, no. 70 (2011): 2; R. Tükel, A. Polat, Ö. Özdemir, D. Aksüt, and N. Türksoy, "Comorbid Conditions in Obsessive Compulsive Disorder," *Comprehensive Psychiatry* 43, no. 3 (May–June 2002): 206.
2. Jonathan S. Abramowitz, Martin E. Franklin, Gordon P. Street, Michael J. Kozac, and Edna B. Foa, "Effects of Comorbid Depression on Response to Treatment for Obsessive-Compulsive Disorder," *Behavior Therapy* 31, no. 3 (2000): 522–25.
3. Kamath, Reddy, and Kandavel, "Suicidal Behavior," 1747.
4. Abramowitz et al., "Effects of Comorbid Depression," 523–24.

Once again, his depression prevented him from remembering even one happy moment in his life. "Obviously you've suffered a long time without us knowing," I said, "but you've also had a lot of good times. I know. I was there. It's as if they've been erased from your memory. I know you've had some enjoyable times, even in the past few months."

"When? Name one time."

"Well, how about that basketball game you went to with Dad for his birthday?"

"Oh yeah. That *was* a great day."

We ended up at a diner. When the waiter botched my order for the third time, I complained.

"Wow, that was assertive of you," Dan said, impressed. "Scott would be so proud of you."

I cringed. "I can be assertive when I need to be."

Lunch was pleasant and his mood lightened a bit, but I was worried about the conversation to come. When we were done eating, I took his hand and calmly said, "I know about the letter you and Scott sent Dr. Moore. I spoke with her on the telephone, and she told me about it."

Dan seemed genuinely confused. "Letter? What letter? We didn't send any letter."

"Okay then, the e-mail. The one where you said you weren't returning to school."

"Oh, *that*. Yeah, I sent it. But it's not 100 percent definite. We still have to talk about it."

While I was trying to figure out whom the "we" referred to, he smiled. "It's not that I don't want to go back to school; it's just that I need to do the opposite of what *you* want." He appeared to be joking, but I had no doubt there was some truth to that comment. Could it be that Dan asserting himself against his mother would surely make Scott proud of him? Was this part of his therapy?

"We can talk about this school stuff on Tuesday," he said.

"I'm happy to listen to anything you have to say, now or on Tuesday, but *I* won't be discussing school anymore until you leave St. Joseph's. Actually, I don't want you to worry about school now, either. Just concentrate on your treatment and getting well."

I wasn't sure why, but my comment really bothered him, and he persisted in trying to convince me we should discuss school on Tuesday. It didn't work, and he got annoyed. "But I have a whole list of other reasons why I shouldn't go back."

It had taken me a while, but I'd finally learned my lesson. The more I kept my mouth shut, the more everyone else talked. And now I knew that Dan, most likely as part of his therapy, had already been preparing for Tuesday's meeting. I didn't tell him I knew about his decision to stay at St. Joseph's for another month. We had plenty of other issues to deal with. One thing at a time.

"I'm sorry I didn't tell you about that e-mail, Mom." He looked sincere.

"That's okay, honey. These are tough times for all of us. I just want you to know that I love you very much and I'd do anything for you. Whatever happens, you know I'm always here for you."

"Really?" Dan said. He was totally surprised, almost shocked.

My heart dropped as I realized that, somehow, my son had stopped believing what he'd always known as true. Why didn't he know that anymore? Was he, for lack of a better word, brainwashed? "Dan," I said, looking into his eyes. "It's me. Mom. When in your life have I ever *not* been there for you?"

"Yeah, I guess you're right," he said, but I'll never forget that look of astonishment on his face. As we talked on the way back to the car, a lilt replaced his monotone. "I can't wait to get back to Bridgeville and see all my friends," he said.

Even though I knew I'd be seeing him two days later at our Tuesday meeting, it was hard to watch him walk through those doors. While his stay at St. Joseph's had been somewhat of a godsend, it had also affected him in ways we could not have imagined. We never expected his life course to be questioned and altered, or his dreams to be shattered. At the very least, one thing was clear from the hour and a half I'd just spent with my son. He was as confused and ambivalent as ever.

8

ST. JOSEPH'S TO THE RESCUE?

The next morning Sharon called. "Good news from the insurance company." She sounded cheery. "Dan has unlimited benefits and can stay here as long as needed."

Huh? What about the conversation she and I had recently, when she said he'd be terminated by the end of July? Did she think we'd forgotten about that? Neither the staff nor Dan knew we were aware he planned to stay another month.

I probably should have kept my mouth shut, but I couldn't. "Thanks for the information, but we're taking Dan home on August 1."

Silence. "This isn't what he's expecting," she said. I could sense her suspicion about our motive. Our conversation ended abruptly with terse good-byes.

Dan was outside when Gary and I arrived for our Tuesday meeting; it was the first time we'd seen him on the grounds by himself. "I'm doing some exposures," he said. "I'll be upstairs in a minute." He looked worn out and exhausted. I wondered whether anyone had told him about his upcoming termination, but I didn't ask.

"Okay, see you upstairs, honey," I said lightly. Inside I was a wreck.

Once we were all settled in Sharon's office, I brought up Dan's termination immediately. "Thank you for everything you've done for Dan," I said. "He's made a lot of progress, but now it's time for him to come home. He's been here more than seven weeks, is showing signs of be-

coming institutionalized, and is too dependent on the staff. The longer he stays the harder it will be to reacclimate to the outside world. We also sense our relationship with the staff is becoming destructive and adversarial, and I'm sure no one wants that."

Nobody stopped me so I kept talking. "We feel Dan has regressed in some ways." I spoke directly to Dan. "Honey, you seem more confused than ever about your life. You're dependent on Scott to figure out how you feel. Sometimes I can't tell if it's you talking or him. It's time to leave St. Joseph's so you can think for yourself. Your reasoning has become distorted because you've been here so long. You're only seeing the world from the standpoint of OCD. You need to come home so you can just live your life. Then whatever will be will be."

SIDE EFFECTS OF RESIDENTIAL TREATMENT

For many OCD sufferers, residential treatment is a lifesaver. The intensive focus on treatment and being supported by a team of experts can mean the difference between staying sick and getting well. At the same time, an extended stay on an inpatient ward might have less desirable effects that are important to keep in mind.

One problematic effect of an inpatient stay is seen when the hospital setting starts to feel more like "home" than home does. While it's good for the person to feel comfortable in the residential facility, the goal of treatment is to help individuals thrive in their normal settings. A related concern is when a person begins to feel apathetic about events outside of the ward, as though what happens within the walls of the hospital is all that matters. These tendencies have been labeled "institutionalism syndrome" and also include a lack of initiative and a desire to stay in the hospital.[1]

Some aspects of inpatient settings are relatively unavoidable, such as loss of autonomy and restriction of options. Hospital staff can emphasize the control and choices that a person does have on an inpatient unit, yet realistically it's hard to compare the highly struc-

tured and bounded nature of residential treatment to the endless options that life on the outside affords: where to go, whom to see, what to avoid, and so forth. The longer a person exists in these conditions, the more difficult it might be to reenter the world.

All treatments for OCD have pros and cons, and residential treatment is no exception. Individuals with OCD and their family members can collaborate with treatment team members to determine when the point of diminishing returns has been reached and when it's time to transition to a less intensive form of treatment.

1. Gary L. Wirt, "Causes of Institutionalism: Patient and Staff Perspectives," *Issues in Mental Health Nursing* 20, no. 3 (May–June 1999): 259–62.

I sat back, pleased I'd gotten through my little speech. *That wasn't so bad.* I had no idea what was coming.

I looked over at Dan, who was shaking more than at the previous week's meeting, if that was possible. He started talking, his voice trembling. "I want to stay at St. Joseph's as long as possible so I can take advantage of their intensive therapy. This is the best place in the world, with the best people, and I'm just really starting to make progress. Don't you want me to be happy? Don't you want me to have a good life? I need to stay here now if that's ever going to be a possibility. Please let me stay."

My heart was breaking. Never before had our son begged us for anything. My mind was muddled as I struggled to trust my instincts. They were nowhere to be found. I looked over at Gary and could see the pain etched on his face.

"Of course we want you to have all that, Dan." I didn't know what else to say.

Once again, this conversation was about returning to Carson, without anyone actually mentioning school. If we allowed Dan to stay at St. Joseph's longer, he wouldn't have the option of returning this year. He'd have to reapply for the next year if he wanted to go back, and there was no guarantee of readmission into his program. Part of me wanted to say, "Sure Dan, stay as long as you like," because he was begging us to do so, and all we wanted, really, was for him to be happy and healthy. But I couldn't say yes to his plea, and I took that as a sign that staying at St.

Joseph's, for all the reasons we'd previously discussed, was the wrong thing to do.

I glanced at Gary. His anguish was still visible. "Dan," I said, trying to keep my voice from shaking, "you can continue your therapy in Bridgeville, but you need to come home by August 1."

"But you have no idea what I've been through, or how bad things were for me," Dan said, not giving up and more emotional than he'd been in a long time. "There were times at school when I stood in the same place outside for four hours, or the time I stayed in a bathroom stall for even longer, because my OCD wouldn't let me move."

"I understand what you're saying, honey," I said, hoping the heartache I felt wasn't showing on my face. I don't know why his confession shocked me so much. This was the very condition I'd found him in when I arrived in Bridgeville three long months ago. Before I took him to the hospital, he was prepared to sit in a chair in my motel room for eight hours. It's just that I tried not to think of those days; it was too hard. And it was even more difficult for Dan, I'm sure. I think he was so terrified of relapsing he just couldn't go on with his life. It was easier to stay at St. Joseph's.

I turned toward my trembling son and said, "It's time to come home. The program is starting to have some negative effects on you."

"Like what?" he demanded, agitated.

"Well, for one thing," I said, feeling a little annoyed myself, "the real Dan wouldn't have sent that e-mail to Dr. Moore behind our backs."

"Well," Dan said, "I haven't been the real me my whole life. I've been controlled by my OCD. That was the real me who sent that e-mail."

I gave him a look that said, "C'mon Dan, give me a break."

Sharon spoke, addressing me patronizingly. "Why is it so hard for you to believe this is the real Dan now? His OCD notwithstanding, people do change you know."

"I know that." I was trying to remain calm, though I felt as if I might explode. "But I also know my son. Some of his thoughts and actions over the years may have been dictated by his OCD, but the essence of Dan, who he is, is still the same. Nobody, not even Dan, can convince me otherwise."

There was nothing left to say. Dan let me hug him good-bye, but he was still visibly upset. I felt sick to my stomach, and as Gary and I walked

to our car, I was already second-guessing myself. "I sure hope we're doing the right thing."

"We want to give him a chance to go back to school, so it's the right thing," Gary said. "But it's heartbreaking to see him like this."

"Yeah." I got into the car and the tears flowed. It felt good to cry, and when I'd finished, Gary and I tried to make sense of everything.

"Even if we were completely happy with the way things were going at the clinic," Gary said, "I still don't think it's worth an extra month at St. Joseph's to jeopardize his chances of returning to Carson."

"But it was so hard to see him like that, begging us to let him stay."

"I know," Gary said, his tone gentle. "I think a big part of the problem is Dan will miss Scott terribly, as Mark said. Isn't that all the more reason he should leave?"

I nodded, thankful for the support we'd gotten from Mark, Dr. Vogel, and Dr. Moore. If it hadn't been for them, we might well have left Dan at St. Joseph's. When the experts are telling you one thing, it's difficult to contradict them, even if your heart tells you otherwise. We needed to remind ourselves that as Dan's parents, we knew him better than anyone, and our thoughts, feelings, and opinions deserved consideration.

That very afternoon I sent an e-mail to Sharon confirming Dan's termination date of August 1. I wanted it in writing. I also wanted to shift our focus to how we could help him transition once he left the program. I asked her for suggestions.

She sent me a long reply, detailing how important it was for Dan to develop a daily regimen and stick to it. He needed to continue doing self-directed exposure and response prevention (ERP) therapy daily and maintain a consistent eating and sleeping schedule. She stressed the importance of Dan making time for friends, family, and leisure activities. If we noticed him ritualizing, Sharon recommended we encourage him to use the tools he learned at St. Joseph's to push through and not give in to his compulsions. Residents often see an increase in their symptoms once they are discharged, she said, and may need to work extra hard to stay on track and maintain their gains. Sharon made it clear we should have normal expectations for Dan; he should make his own decisions when appropriate and be able to participate in spontaneous activities. She ended by saying if Dan relapsed or wasn't responding to our support, we should contact his new treatment providers immediately.

It all seemed straightforward enough, yet this e-mail provoked intense anxiety in me. Were we really doing the right thing? What condition would Dan be in? Would he be able to function? Would *we* be able to function? I decided to arrange another telephone meeting with Dr. Vogel, since he'd be Dan's therapist in Bridgeville.

"I think we can expect Dan to regress a little once he's home, as he adjusts to life outside of St. Joseph's," he said. "Now what's going on with school?"

"Well, we really feel he should go back, but we'd never force him to do anything he truly doesn't want to do. Right now he's saying it'll be too hard for him. We're hoping he'll change his mind once he's home."

"It really would be best for him to get back to school, or else it will be just him, his OCD, and his treatment, and that's not healthy," Dr. Vogel said. "You'll have to play it by ear, and you don't want to come on too strong, but you should definitely convey a message of confidence, letting him know that one way or the other, things are going to work out."

Dr. Vogel's words were refreshing to me: none of that "us against them" attitude.

"The other thing that's really important," he said, "is to involve you and Gary, at least in the beginning, in Dan's therapy. He needs support and structure, especially if he's not in school, and a vital part of treatment involves family."

"I feel so much better after talking with Dr. Vogel," I later said to Gary. "What he's recommending for Dan is the exact opposite of what's been happening at St. Joseph's. I also scheduled an appointment for the three of us to see him on August 18."

"So Dan will be going from daily therapy at St. Joseph's to seventeen days with no therapy," Gary said.

"That's right. But who's counting?"

We planned to take Dan out to lunch his last Sunday at St. Joseph's. When we arrived we were told he didn't have to be back until nighttime, so we decided to head home for the day. He seemed fine; I was relieved he wasn't angry with us after Tuesday's meeting.

"So what do you want to do once we get home?" I asked him.

"I don't know. Just hang out with the cats I guess."

I realized Dan hadn't relaxed in his own home for eight weeks now, so I was glad he had this opportunity. Ava was away at summer camp, and Lainey hadn't moved back home yet, so there was nobody there except the cats and us.

Once home, however, Dan seemed out of sorts and anxious. "I'm going to rest," he said. I peeked into his room a few minutes later and saw him sleeping peacefully under the same blue and yellow comforter he'd used for years. I remembered my happy little boy and ached to have him back. For now he was gone, but I vowed to do everything in my power to bring my son back to himself. He slept until early evening and then sheepishly confessed, "Guess I was really tired. We're not supposed to sleep on weekends." On the ride back to St. Joseph's, I felt mixed emotions. On one hand I was thrilled he'd be home in five days, and on the other hand, I was terrified he'd be home in five days.

9

TERMINATION DAY

At our final Tuesday meeting, Sharon said, "We need to talk with your parents about what happened last night." Dan nodded.

I hate when you know something bad is unfolding before you and there's nothing you can do about it. That's not to say I haven't tried at times: *I'm done. I'm out of here. Stop time.* But it never works.

Sharon kept talking. "Dan was having thoughts of cutting himself, so he did the right thing by telling the staff. They brought him some ice to hold, which is often helpful. The cold is painful and often relieves the urge to harm."

"Any idea what brought that on, Dan?" I asked. I was almost certain I knew the answer. He just shrugged; he'd never felt comfortable discussing his cutting with us.

"Well, I know he's anxious about leaving," Sharon said. "We've also talked about stress that comes with feeling better and getting on with your life." She looked at Gary and me. "Don't be afraid to ask questions. Ask him how he's feeling. If he has the urge to cut there are things he can do, and giving him ice is one of them."

I felt overwhelmed and took some deep breaths to keep my mind from spinning. *One step at a time.*

Dan spoke. "I'm not going back to school. It's my decision and I've made it on my own. I'll get a job at a supermarket, maybe take some courses, and work on 'general living.' I'll also do lots of animation on my

own. Or I could get a job at Carson. Maybe I could work for the admissions office and give tours."

I immediately conjured up a picture of Dan walking backward on campus, leading a tour of prospective students and their parents. They're following him, listening intently. I imagined their conversation. "So what's your major?" they'd ask him.

"Oh, I'm not a student here anymore. I had some health problems so I dropped out, and now I'm afraid to come back. But it's a great place."

Yeah, that would go over big. I'm sure admissions would love to have him as a tour guide. I felt guilty for mocking his idea, even just to myself, but I was so tired and stressed over school, I needed comic relief.

Dan was waiting for a response. "We'll definitely talk more about this when you're home," I said, proud of my self-control. But then my mouth took over. "But just think about it, honey. When you feel better in a couple of weeks, or even a couple of months, do you think you might regret not giving school a try?"

Without hesitation he said, "I won't feel better in a couple of months." A pause. "So if I don't go back to school, can I still live with my friends?"

"Of course not."

Gary spoke. "For one thing, it's too expensive. I'm also concerned it'll be too stressful. If you go back to school we can discuss it. If you don't go back, there's no question you have to live with us."

"If you think living in that house will be too stressful for me, I can tell you going back to school would be much worse," Dan said, annoyed. "Anyway, I have some money saved, and I can use it to live in the house. I need to be independent. I want my freedom."

TRANSITIONING FROM A RESIDENTIAL PROGRAM TO THE OUTSIDE WORLD

Leaving a residential program presents many challenges under the best of circumstances, and careful planning is needed to ensure a smooth transition.

One of the most important considerations is that the step down in treatment should not be too big. For example, it most likely would not be wise to go from residential treatment to once-weekly outpa-

tient exposure and response prevention (ERP). The residential treatment team will make recommendations about the level of follow-up care—for example, intensive outpatient or partial hospitalization program—whether it happens at the same facility or elsewhere. The step-down treatment needs to be in place *before* the person leaves the residential facility so the transition can be as seamless as possible. The individual with obsessive-compulsive disorder (and often family members) should be in contact with the new therapist (and psychiatrist, if applicable) and know when the first treatment session will be—ideally within a day or two of discharge. Communication between the residential facility and outpatient providers is also strongly recommended.

In most cases family involvement can be a crucial part of the process. Family members often have a perspective on their loved one that the treatment team cannot have and can provide crucial input into the transition planning. For example, parents may know about specific situations or activities that are likely to help or hinder their loved one's recovery.

Thoughtful and collaborative planning can allow treatment progress to continue as individuals leave residential treatment, giving them the best chance to succeed in the next step of their recovery.

"Believe me," I said, "there's nothing I want more than for you to be independent. But how will you live there if you can't use your cell phone, drive, or go into the supermarket? I think the best way for you to work toward independence is to stay in school so you can graduate and get a good job you'll enjoy, all the while continuing therapy and moving forward. You think your plan will make you independent, when in reality all it's doing is extending your dependency on us as you avoid pursuing your life's goals."

"Well maybe that's why I should stay at St. Joseph's, because I still can't do all the things you just mentioned," he said. Now he was angry.

I'd rarely seen him this upset and was annoyed that I'd allowed the conversation to go this far. "We'll talk about everything when you come home," I said. In the months to come, I'd review this conversation in my head numerous times before I truly understood. While Dan had spoken

about wanting freedom from his family, that's not what he really meant. What he desperately wanted and needed was freedom from his OCD.

That evening, Dan e-mailed and asked me to call him. "I want to talk to you because I feel you weren't taking me seriously or really listening to me today," he said. He was calmer and sounded more like himself. "I want to go back to school more than anything, but I know if I do, I'll go back to ritualizing and I absolutely don't want that. I still do some now, but it's so much better than before. The stress of school would be too much for me. I'm not saying that to be negative. I'm just being realistic. As much as I want to go back, it's not worth the toll it'd take on my health. And I hate to even think about it or say it, but I'd probably start cutting myself again. I know I'll have to live with you, and I'm okay with that."

"I'm so glad we talked, Dan," I said. "I want to hear more of what you're thinking."

"My anxiety levels are as high now as they were last semester because I'm doing so much less ritualizing," he said. "I can barely walk from point A to point B without having a panic attack. What I really want to do is put all my efforts into therapy. I know I can't do that and schoolwork. If I go back to school I won't have time to concentrate on my OCD."

OCD VERSUS PANIC DISORDER

People with OCD by definition feel really upset when they encounter obsession-related stimuli. Not uncommonly these upsetting feelings can be so intense that they trigger a panic attack, which is a bout of fear that usually involves physical symptoms such as a rapid heartbeat, shortness of breath, and dizziness, among others. Panic attacks also frequently involve feeling "out of one's body" or other altered senses of reality.

Having a panic attack does not necessarily mean that a person has panic disorder, a type of anxiety disorder. In fact, the majority of people who have a panic attack do not have panic disorder, which

is experienced by about 4 to 5 percent of people in their lifetime.[1] In order to meet criteria for panic disorder, a person has to have other symptoms such as worrying about when the next panic attack will occur and fearing that the attacks mean something terrible—such as the person is having a heart attack. People with panic disorder also often avoid places where panic is likely, such as bridges and elevators.[2]

Existing research suggests that about one out of five individuals with OCD will also meet criteria for panic disorder.[3] So how do we tell if a person with OCD warrants an additional diagnosis of panic disorder, versus having panic attacks that are accounted for by the OCD-related fear responses?

The key question is whether the person's fears are about having panic attacks themselves or simply about the situations that trigger the panic. If the panic is just a manifestation of the person's extreme fear of OCD-related things, then an additional diagnosis of panic disorder is unlikely. However, if the panic attacks are a concern in and of themselves, and if they are triggered by situations that are unrelated to the person's OCD, then a panic disorder diagnosis is likely.

This diagnostic question has very important implications for treatment. If OCD fully accounts for the panic attacks, then exposure and response prevention alone is probably the right treatment choice. If panic disorder and OCD are both present, then the treatment plan may need to address the panic disorder directly. For individuals who choose to take medication, fortunately both panic disorder[4] and OCD tend to respond to selective serotonin reuptake inhibitors (SSRIs).

1. Ronald C. Kessler, Patricia Berglund, Olga Demler, Robert Jin, Kathleen R. Merikangas, and Ellen E. Walters, "Lifetime Prevalence and Age-of-Onset Distributions of DSM-IV Disorders in the National Comorbidity Survey Replication," *Archives of General Psychiatry* 62, no. 6 (June 2005): 596.
2. American Psychiatric Association, *DSM-5*, 208–10.
3. Ricardo C. Torresan, Ana Teresa A. Ramos-Cerqueira, Roseli G. Shavitt, Maria Conceicao do Rosario, Maria Alice de Mathis, Euripedes C. Miguel, and Albina R. Torres, "Symptom Dimensions, Clinical Course and Comorbidity in Men and Women with Obsessive-Compulsive Disorder," *Psychiatry Research* 209, no. 2 (2013): 190.
4. Abraham Bakker, Anton J. L. M. van Balkom, and Philip Spinhoven, "SSRIs vs. TCAs in the Treatment of Panic Disorder: A Meta-analysis," *Acta Psychiatrica Scandinavica* 106, no. 3 (2002): 165.

There it is again. That flawed thinking that he has to put his life on hold until his OCD is totally controlled. It seemed he wanted to re-create St. Joseph's out in the real world. That was what he'd become comfortable with.

"I'm so sorry you felt we weren't listening to you today," I said. "And I do understand what you're saying. I hope you know we'd never make you do anything you truly didn't want to do. How do you feel about talking with Dr. Moore and Dr. Vogel about the situation?"

"That'd be fine, but I'd say I'm 90 percent sure this is what I should do. I'm just wondering, have you spoken with Dr. Vogel lately?"

"Yes, I updated him on everything."

"What did he say?"

"He feels strongly you should go back to school."

"Oh, that's only because he doesn't realize how bad off I really am. What did Dr. Moore say?"

"She was incredibly complimentary." I told him what she'd said. "She wants you to come back."

There was silence for a few moments. "Can you call again tomorrow?" he said. Of course I agreed.

I relayed the conversation to Gary and then said, "It was the most genuine talk I've had with him in a long time. The other conversations we've had about school seemed scripted and rehearsed, and they never really sounded like Dan. Tonight, I felt like I was really talking to *him*."

That discussion with Dan quelled my anxiety, and I spent the next day happily preparing for his arrival home. I went grocery shopping and cooked some of his favorite foods. I cleaned his room and put fresh sheets on his bed. It had been a long time since I'd felt such excitement; it was as if we were expecting the king! My worries over him leaving St. Joseph's dissipated, and I was thrilled he was coming home. There was still the issue of him returning to school, but I felt we were ready to face the next chapter, whatever that might bring.

That afternoon, Dr. Parker, Dan's psychiatrist at St. Joseph's, called us. He'd never phoned us before, and we'd only spoken once in the nine weeks Dan had been at the clinic, when I'd asked about Dan's medications.

My first thought was something must've happened to Dan.

"I understand Dan's being terminated this Friday," Dr. Parker said. His tone was quite serious. "I want to talk with you regarding his medications."

What a relief! "Oh great, thanks for calling. I'm sure that'll be helpful." I grabbed a pencil and pad of paper so I could take notes.

"Well, it's Wednesday and Dan's leaving Friday, so what are you going to do?" Dr. Parker demanded. He was suddenly antagonistic.

"Excuse me? What?"

"I know you want Dan to go back to school. Don't push him. I'm warning you. He isn't ready, and things will take a turn for the worse if you make him go back."

It wasn't so much *what* Dr. Parker said that was so shocking; it was *how* he said it. He was actually yelling at me. This man I'd never even met was attacking me over the phone. Stunned, I listened as he continued, his voice escalating. "Dan needs to take this year off. I know what I'm talking about. I've seen it over and over again, and you're asking for trouble."

By this time, Gary had walked over to me and mouthed, "Who is it?"

I looked at him with my mouth literally hanging open and, shaking my head, mouthed back, "I can't believe this."

Dr. Parker kept going. "Dan was probably a lot worse off than you realized at the end of the last school year."

If I were able to get a word in edgewise, I would've explained that I knew exactly what condition Dan was in then because I was there, with him, for three weeks.

But he had no intention of coming up for air, and while he continued his ranting, I decided his behavior wasn't worthy of a response anyway.

"I know Dan really well, and I recommend you allow him to live in that house with his friends," he was saying. "The social interaction will be good for him. And you don't have to worry about him partying or anything like that. He's not like that." Then he repeated, "Today is Wednesday, and Dan's being terminated on Friday. What are you going to do?"

Then, for the first time during his diatribe, he paused. That gave me the opportunity to speak, though I was still shocked and could barely respond. "We haven't made any final decisions yet," I muttered, though in retrospect I should've just hung up the phone once the yelling started.

"Well, just keep in mind Dan doesn't want to disappoint you." He was still yelling but not quite as loudly. "He thinks you won't love him if he doesn't do what you want."

"What? That's ridiculous." The shock abated and now I was angry. "Why would you say such a thing? Our son absolutely knows we love him unconditionally."

Surprisingly, Dr. Parker had nothing else to say; we said our awkward good-byes, and I hung up the phone. I was still holding the pencil and paper, with not a word written down, and I was shaking.

I called Mark immediately, and Gary listened in as I relayed the conversation to both of them. "He was way out of line, unbelievably so, as you already know," Mark said. "I think there are a few things going on here. First, there are staff meetings regarding Dan, and everyone's in agreement over the course of his treatment. We're dealing with some pretty big egos here, and the truth is, they're not used to families standing up to them. Usually what they say goes. You're really crossing the line here, and it's riling them up."

I was still trembling. I understood what Mark was saying, but Dr. Parker's words hit a nerve, and they'd play over in my mind often once Dan left St. Joseph's.

"The other thing is," Mark said, "St. Joseph's does follow-up surveys on their 'success' rates. Now the way they measure success is by severity of symptoms. So if Dan's symptoms are 90 percent gone, but he's not in school, that would be considered great, because his symptoms are 90 percent gone. It doesn't matter what else is or isn't going on in his life. However, if he's in school, and his symptoms are only 50 percent gone, then that's not so great for their statistics. So that's where I think they're coming from, and they're letting you know how they feel. When Dan comes home and you discuss the program, you should acknowledge all the good things about it and how much it has helped him, but it really has been all about the symptoms. I feel you should be honest about the fact they haven't done a good job of helping him think about his life and what he wants from it."

"So much of what Dr. Parker said couldn't possibly have been thought through," I said. "That comment about Dan living in the house with his friends even though he won't be in school? How could that possibly be good for him? Everyone else will be in school, busy with classes and their own lives. What will he do all day? Work on his driving? Sketch a little?

He'll be alone most of the time, with no structure. Just him and his OCD."

"That's absolutely true," Mark said. "So try not to let this all bother you, and focus on the positive: Dan will be home in a couple of days."

Two hours after the infamous phone call, I was still shaking. "I think what's bothering me most now," I said to Gary, "is the realization that if it's that easy for me to be affected by one phone call, imagine what it's been like for Dan the last nine weeks. I know they probably weren't yelling at him, but they've certainly gotten him to see things their way."

The phone rang again. I just stared at it. Not having caller ID, I was hesitant to answer. I decided if it was Dr. Parker, I'd hang up. "Hello?" I said gingerly.

"Hi Mom." It took me a second to process the voice.

"Dan, where are you calling from?"

"My cell phone."

This was amazing news. I couldn't remember when Dan was last able to use his cell phone. "Good for you, honey."

"I want to live in the house with my friends and try to go back to school."

What? Did I really just hear that? I was still trying to grasp this information when Dan spoke again. "If I end up dropping out, can I still stay in the house?" He sounded nervous.

"Well, glad you're feeling confident," I joked. "No, you'd have to live with us."

"Okay. Do you think I should e-mail Dr. Moore?"

"Yes, I think you, or we, should talk to everyone we can at Carson." Was I really having this conversation?

"Okay, see you Friday. We can talk more then."

"Okay, see you soon, honey." It was that quick.

Gary came into the room and said, "Did the phone just ring?"

"Yeah, it was Dan. He called to tell us he's going back to school."

Gary gave me a quizzical look. "Are you serious?"

"Yes." We broke into big smiles and hugged.

"TWO MINDS" IN OCD

Most important life decisions—whom to marry, where to go to college, what job to take, and so forth—involve a lot of uncertainty, and OCD sufferers often struggle with uncertainty. For this reason it shouldn't be surprising that individuals with OCD are often "of two minds" and can have a hard time making decisions. They might delay making decisions until they believe they have "all the information," or might forego making a decision altogether.

Being of two minds is a hallmark of OCD and is represented in the diagnostic criteria, which state that the person has to experience obsessions as "intrusive and unwanted," at least at some point during the course of the illness.[1] Many OCD sufferers can say on the one hand, "I know these fears make no sense!" On the other hand they say, "I can't stop worrying about them, and doing rituals to prevent them from happening."

In exposure and response prevention (ERP) for OCD we often make a distinction between these two minds, calling one of them "you" and the other one "your OCD." This distinction seems to resonate with most people who receive ERP. As treatment progresses the sense of separation between oneself and one's OCD tends to increase. It gets easier for the person to recognize what is a realistic concern and what is OCD, and to see that serving one's OCD is a disservice to oneself. Treatment can also directly address the decision-making difficulty as part of exposure. For example, the individual with OCD might commit to making decisions in a fixed amount of time and when anxiety about the decision is still high. Over time individuals can get better at tolerating not knowing if they're making the "perfect" choice.

Therapists and family members should expect OCD sufferers to bring their ambivalence to treatment. They clearly want to get better, which is why they came for treatment. At the same time, getting better means giving up behaviors that have been relied upon to feel safe, which is a scary prospect. This ambivalence is likely a big part of why a good number of OCD sufferers who start ERP either drop

> out before treatment is over or don't fully commit to the treatment. Anticipating ambivalence can help the therapist and OCD sufferer to support the side that's determined to get better, even when the road is difficult.
>
> 1. American Psychiatric Association, *Diagnostic and Statistical Manual of Mental Disorders,* 5th ed. (*DSM-5*) (Arlington, VA: Author, 2013), 237.

Termination day finally arrived.

"I don't think I'll really believe he's coming home until he's in the car with us," I said as we drove to St. Joseph's Hospital for the last time.

Gary nodded. "It's been a long road."

We entered the area of the clinic we hadn't been in since dropping Dan off nine long weeks ago. The big blackboard that kept track of clients' whereabouts was filled with different names. I also noticed six or seven pieces of lined notebook paper randomly taped on the walls of the hallway. In double-spaced, perfect handwriting, each page had the same sentence written repeatedly: "I have cancer." It was exceptionally quiet, and I realized all the clients were probably in therapy sessions. The only sign of life came from a staff member who was standing outside a closed bathroom door.

"Your twenty minutes are up, Gwen," she said kindly but firmly. "You have to get out of the shower now."

Gwen tried to negotiate, but I didn't pay attention. I was focused on one thing only: finding Dan and bringing him home.

He was in his room, packing up some last-minute things. "All I need to do is check out and get my medications," he said. He was tapping, something I hadn't seen him do in a while.

At the nurse's station, he picked up several bottles of pills and written instructions. "Good luck with everything, Dan," the nurse on duty said.

It sure would've been helpful if Dr. Parker had actually talked with us about Dan's medications, I thought. "Anybody else you want to say good-bye to, honey?"

"Nope, I saw everyone yesterday. I'm ready to go."

It only took a minute to walk past the blackboard, the handwritten "I have cancer" papers, and the common area where I'd witnessed a young

client struggling to touch a quarter when Dan first arrived. I wondered how she was doing. We brought his stuff outside and loaded up the car, which Gary had driven right up to those doors we'd so often watched Dan walk through. I looked around and realized it was a beautiful, sunny day. As we pulled away from St. Joseph's, Dan smiled. "Thanks for paying for my summer vacation. It was great!"

10

BACK TO BRIDGEVILLE

We had a fun ride home, all of us in good moods. Dan seemed genuinely happy, and we talked about our upcoming plans. We had one week before driving down to Bridgeville.

"I have to do at least one exposure a day," he said, and I could see he was eager to get started. An exposure in exposure and response prevention (ERP) therapy involves facing one's fears. Dan needed to expose himself to anxiety-provoking situations over and over again until he eventually became more comfortable with them. This process is known as habituation. And he needed to do this without performing any compulsions. That very day he asked me to drive him to Borders bookstore for his first exposure; I was so proud of him for taking charge of his recovery.

Going to a bookstore might not seem like a big deal to most people, but before arriving at St. Joseph's, he couldn't enter that store. What made it more upsetting was that he used to spend hours at this particular store when he was homeschooling. We'd joke that it was his home away from home, and some of the staff and customers actually thought he worked there. Now, when I pulled up to the main entrance, he got out of the car easily, hesitated briefly, and walked inside.

He stayed an hour and a half. "I bought a book," he said as he got into the car. "I can't remember the last time I read for pleasure." He was

obviously pleased with himself. I sighed in relief. Things were going well.

The next week brought a whirlwind of activity, but Dan continued doing at least one exposure daily. He drove, shopped at the supermarket, and used his cell phone. He cooked for us, making vegetarian burritos one night. He packed for school and also helped move Lainey out of her apartment and back into our house. Our home was lively as many friends and relatives dropped by to say good-bye and wish Dan a successful year at school. While family and close friends knew Dan was struggling with obsessive-compulsive disorder, most of them knew little about his time at St. Joseph's.

Though he was doing better than we'd anticipated, evenings were hard. It was typically quieter then, with more time to think. The first night he was home, he came downstairs with a glazed look. "I need some ice," he said in that monotone voice I'd come to hate. He stuck his hand into a plastic bag full of ice cubes, and we talked.

"Dan, I think overall you're doing great."

"Yeah, I guess so," he said. "But nights are tough."

While I knew his cutting himself wasn't about suicide, I always imagined it happening while being in the depths of despair. He didn't seem "that bad" when he needed the ice, and that confused me. When I spoke to Mark, he explained that cutting was actually about feeling better.

"When someone is stressed or anxious, or has any other unpleasant emotion, cutting can get rid of these feelings. It's not that Dan wants to die or feels life isn't worthwhile. He just wants to feel better. Of course, most people are so bothered by the idea of self-injury that it freaks them out. As I've said before, it's just a maladaptive habit used for coping, and it works well and fast. Needless to say, Dan will need to learn better ways to deal with negative emotions."

Once again, I felt lucky to have Mark as a friend and advisor. I wished we could've taken him to Bridgeville with us.

Gary and I went to visit Ava at her overnight camp during Dan's first week home, and he stayed alone for the entire day.

"You want to come along?" I asked. "It'll be fun."

"Not really. I have so much organizing and packing to do."

I was hoping he'd come with us, since I felt uneasy about him being alone for such a long time. I considered asking my parents to stay with him but remembered Sharon's advice about treating him normally. Getting a babysitter for a nineteen-year-old is not normal.

It was great to see Ava enjoying herself at camp, away from the stress at home. It was also our last chance to see her before Gary, Dan, and I drove down to Bridgeville. Gary would fly back to get her once camp was over, a couple of weeks later.

I called home a few times (okay, four to be exact) to see how Dan was doing and left a message each time. He never called back.

"This brings back memories," I said to Gary, "of when we were constantly trying to get in touch with him last year. It's just as stressful now as it was then."

"You've got to calm down," Gary said. "You know using the phone has been an ongoing problem for him. I'm sure he's fine."

I worried the entire car ride back. Dan was awake when we arrived home, even though it was well after midnight. "So how was your day?" I asked.

He shrugged. "Okay, I guess." But he didn't seem okay. "I did some laundry and watched the baseball game, but that was about it."

I knew it was hard for him to be alone all day, and remembered Dr. Parker's recommendation that we let him live in a house with friends while not attending school. Seeing the way Dan felt now made that suggestion seem even more absurd. We didn't talk about it, but I sensed Dan might have realized spending a year focusing only on his OCD would be lonely and depressing.

A few days later we hugged Lainey good-bye. Though I knew I'd see her over the course of the year, it was still tough to leave. "Have a safe trip," she said as we pulled out of the driveway. With our loaded van, I felt like the Beverly Hillbillies, except we were Bridgeville bound, and we hadn't struck any oil.

We had twenty-four hours of driving ahead of us and hoped to do it in three days. Our first break was at the same mall we'd stopped at three months earlier on the trip with my parents. We'd left Dan alone in the car because he hadn't been able to get out. At the time I thought, *Thank goodness he'll be at St. Joseph's soon.*

This time he hesitated for a moment, did some touching and tapping, and then got out of the car relatively easily. We smiled at each other as

we entered the mall. While I knew his touching and tapping were rituals, that was okay. He was a work in progress. The rest of our trip was a combination of quiet times, reading, laughing, sleeping, and conversation. Not surprisingly, most of our talk revolved around going back to school and the logistics involved.

"It's really important that I live in the house with my friends," Dan said.

"I understand honey, but here's what I'm thinking," I said. "Going back to school isn't going to be easy. Our goal is to put you in the best possible position for success. I feel living in this house, with all the additional responsibilities, will add unnecessary stress. If you get a dorm room, you don't have to worry about driving, preparing your meals, or being isolated from campus life."

"I think it'll be good for me to have to do all those things." While I was pleased with Dan's newfound can-do attitude, I really believed it would be too much for him. But I also knew there was a fine line between being negative and being realistic.

"Do you think you'll be able to use your cell phone, drive, and grocery shop, for starters?" I asked him. "Because you have to do all those things if you're going to live in that house."

"Yeah, I think I can do all those things."

"Well, we have two weeks before school starts. If you're able to do everything by then, you can live in the house."

"But if that arrangement proves too much for you," Gary said, "you'll have to stay in school and live with us the rest of the semester."

"Sounds good to me," Dan said.

"Another concern is you'll forget to take your medications," I said. When he came home from St. Joseph's, we'd discussed it was his responsibility to take his medications. He'd agreed but never remembered; I often had to give him the pills myself.

Obviously this would be an issue if Dan lived on his own. While it was hard to know how much, or even if, his medications were actually helping him, he seemed to be on the right track now, and we wanted to keep it that way.

"Yeah, I guess I need to work on that," he said.

Three days after leaving home, we pulled into the garage of our rented condo. It had been a good trip, and though things were far from perfect, I marveled at how well Dan was doing. Only two weeks earlier he was

distraught, pleading with us to let him stay at St. Joseph's. Now here he was, poised to go back to school. While understandably nervous, he seemed eager and willing to accept the challenge. A wave of gratitude engulfed me. My son was back.

The next week was filled with meetings and appointments, the first with Dr. Moore. While Dan and I walked through the Carson campus courtyard, I experienced a flood of anxiety. To my left was the picnic table we sat at for three hours one day while I tried to get him to eat lunch. We passed one of our usual meeting spots, where I'd often find him with his sweatshirt hood on, chomping on the strings. It was as if we'd returned to the scene of the crime. For every memory I had, there was no doubt Dan had ten more.

"Is it hard for you to be back?" I asked as we headed to Dr. Moore's office.

"I'm okay."

I noticed his fingers moving, as if he was counting to himself. While I'd anticipated his return to campus would be anxiety provoking, I also knew avoidance wasn't the answer. As we walked through that courtyard together, I hoped all Dan's bad memories would soon be replaced by good ones.

Dr. Moore seemed genuinely happy to see him. "I hope you know you're already a cherished and valued member of the Carson community," she said. "I'm so glad you're back. Your work last year wasn't just good; it was very good, even with all those obstacles you faced. I'm confident you'll do well this semester."

Her upbeat tone was a refreshing contrast to what he'd been hearing at St. Joseph's. I might have imagined it, but I thought Dan sat up a little straighter, as though her words boosted his confidence. She believed in him; maybe now he could believe in himself. We then met with Marilyn Lambert, the head of Academic Support Services, and gave her a brief update on Dan's situation.

She was eager to help and had questions for Dan. "In relation to your studies, can you tell me some specific things that were difficult for you last year?"

"Well, there were times I couldn't check e-mail or even go on my computer," Dan said. Thinking about the past year was making him nervous; he was tapping the wall. "Entering the library was a problem too."

"We can have your teachers give you handwritten notes instead of sending you e-mail," she said. "And professors can bring you books so you don't have to go into the library."

I was uncomfortable with the direction this was going. "While I appreciate your trying to accommodate Dan," I said, "I'm worried it's the wrong thing to do. We don't want to enable him."

COLLEGE SUPPORT AND ACCOMMODATIONS

The transition to college is a big challenge for most students and perhaps even more so for individuals with OCD. College life is filled with things that provoke obsessions. For example, having a roommate, sharing a dormitory bathroom, and eating in the cafeteria can trigger contamination concerns. Similarly, exams and papers might be torturous for students whose OCD involves perfectionism and fears of making mistakes.

Most colleges are required to provide accommodations to students with a documented disability, which can include OCD. For example, students with extreme fear of contamination by a roommate who might be "unclean" might be allowed to have a single room as a freshman, even if the school's policy is to reserve single rooms for nonfreshmen. Or students who struggle to finish exams on time due to excessive correcting and rewriting might be allowed 50 percent additional time on exams.

It's important to consider that academic accommodations for OCD can be a two-edged sword. On the one hand they can play an essential role in allowing students to perform in line with their abilities. On the other hand, accommodations can be a form of enabling OCD behaviors and as a result can perpetuate the problem. For example, a student who is allowed to avoid having a roommate

misses out on a valuable form of everyday exposure to others' germs. In this way academic accommodations aren't unlike accommodations that well-meaning families make to their loved one's OCD.

A reasonable compromise in the college setting might include allowable accommodations while the person is going through treatment. The therapist can then work on a plan with the student and the school's administrators (with the student's permission) to decrease the reliance on accommodations as part of treatment. In this way the individual isn't unfairly disadvantaged by the OCD-related disability while symptoms are still high and accommodations are phased out to ensure maximal treatment success.

Dan slouched forward, put his head in his hands, and turned toward me. "That's what I was trying to tell you when I said I wasn't ready to go back to school." The confidence he showed in Dr. Moore's office had morphed into frustration and anxiety.

Marilyn came to the rescue. "I understand what you're both saying, and I think what we need to do is find the right balance for Dan. Hopefully you won't need any accommodations, but it's best to be prepared for the worst-case scenario."

The three of us then spent an hour composing a letter explaining Dan's OCD and outlining some things that might be difficult for him. He needed to give a copy to each of his teachers so they were aware of his disorder. Ongoing communication, along with flexibility when needed, was requested.

"I think this is great," I said after we left Marilyn's office. "The more support the better."

"Whatever," Dan said. "I still have to be able to do all the work."

I could tell he was drained though I wasn't fazed by his attitude. He'd been doing so well it almost hadn't seemed real. This was real.

"Of course you have doubts, honey," I said. "That's to be expected. But you're doing great so far. Let's take one day at a time, okay?"

He was about to respond when someone shouted, "Dan!" A girl with a huge smile was running toward him, arms open. "It's so good to see you," she said, giving him a big hug. I said a quick hello and left them alone to talk.

"That was quite a greeting you got," I said when he found me ten minutes later.

"Yeah, it was great to see Laura. She told me there's a get-together tonight, so maybe I'll go. I've really missed my friends."

It warmed my heart to see him smiling. "Oh, you should definitely go."

"I think I will. It'll be a good time to tell everyone I'm coming back."

That night, while I reviewed the day's happenings with Gary, I said, "Do you realize everything Dan did today? We had two meetings at school. He got his hair cut, used his cell phone, and went grocery shopping with me. He got together with his friends and told them he was returning to school. It's amazing when you think that not too long ago, he spent entire days lying on the floor. I'm so proud of him."

"Me too," Gary said. "And pretty soon, I bet, he'll be driving himself around." Our condo was a half-hour drive from Carson, and Gary had become Dan's personal chauffer. He wouldn't be able to keep that up for too long.

"We both know what the big test will be," I said, and Gary nodded. "Going back to classes, handling the stress, and doing the work."

A few days later Dan had his first appointment with Dr. Russell, a psychiatrist who'd been recommended by Dr. Vogel's wife, Sandy. Dr. Russell would manage Dan's medications and monitor him physically. His waiting room was warm and inviting, and the receptionist was pleasant. Dr. Russell, who came out to greet us, turned out to be a soft-spoken man around fifty years old, with a kind face. After our experience at St. Joseph's, where I felt deliberate distance from staff, I was pleased to be invited into his office with Dan.

We spent a good half hour discussing Dan's history, including his childhood illnesses, with me doing most of the talking. Then he spoke with Dan privately and gave him a physical examination. "His resting heart rate's a little high, so we'll keep an eye on that," Dr. Russell said. He also commented on Dan's tremors, which had been present since being at St. Joseph's, and requested some blood work. He was surprised Dan's blood had never been tested at St. Joseph's.

"How's Dan's weight?" I asked.

He glanced at Dan's file. "191 pounds."

"Gee, that's a six-pound weight gain in two weeks." When he left St. Joseph's, I knew Dan was back to his regular weight of 185 pounds, and

he'd been eating normally since then. Dr. Russell wasn't concerned, but I made a mental note of it; I knew weight gain could be a side effect of Dan's medication.

"Let's stay on the same meds for now," Dr. Russell said. "That's one milligram of the atypical antipsychotic, eighty milligrams of the SSRI, and the benzodiazepine as needed. I'll see you in a month, but don't hesitate to call if any issues arise. That's why I'm here."

"So what do you think of him?" I asked Dan as we walked to the car.

"He's good. I like him."

"Me too," I said, pleased we'd found another good health-care provider. "He didn't rush us, and I liked that he said as long as you're feeling well, the goal is to be on the least amount of medication that will still benefit you."

Dan wasn't listening to me. "My lease starts today," he said. "I'd really love to move into the house now. Can I?"

I was caught off guard. "I thought you'd wait until your housemates arrived in the next few days."

"No, I'm really excited to set up my room and organize all my stuff."

It was great to see him gung ho, so I agreed to help him, even though I felt the churn of anxiety. He'd kept his end of the bargain, mostly; he was able to use his cell phone (usually) and grocery shop. Taking his meds was a work in progress, but he promised to contact us every day, so I could always remind him. Driving was the one task he'd yet to do.

"It won't be a problem," he assured me. "I'll drive today." Though it was only a few minutes from his house to school, his confidence impressed me.

We packed most of his things and drove the half hour to his new home. It was in a lovely family neighborhood near Carson, was totally furnished, and had just been renovated. Dan's room was in the finished attic area, and he'd be sharing it with his friend, Steve. Another friend, Adam, would be in the attic's second, smaller bedroom. A living room and bathroom completed the area. Two other people would live downstairs. The steps to the attic were narrow and steep, and as we carried up boxes and bags, my anxiety rose. Everything was happening so fast; were we really going to leave him here? I thought of Dan cutting himself, forgetting to take his medication, and not answering his phone. And what about his fast heart rate? I took a deep breath and gave myself a good talking-to. *You should be proud of him and excited about his progress,*

not focusing on the negatives. I *was* proud of him. I really was. But I was also scared.

We spent the afternoon unpacking and setting up his room, and he kept bumping his head on the sloped ceiling. "There should be a height restriction here," I said. "Nobody who's as tall as you should be allowed to live in an attic."

Dan laughed. "Yeah. I have to remember to slouch and duck, or maybe I should wrap some foam rubber around my head." His humor relaxed me, and we actually had fun setting up his room together. "I'd like to stay here tonight," he said, once we'd finished.

"Oh honey, you'll be all alone." Anxiety surged in me, eating away at my stomach.

"I'm a big boy now," he said, and smiled. "And I like to be alone. You can pick me up in the morning to go to Dr. Vogel."

"We'll see. Why don't we go eat, and then you can drive from here to school. Remember, you still have to do that." I'm ashamed to admit part of me hoped Dan wouldn't be able to drive. Then he'd have to live with us and it would be less stressful for me—selfish but true.

"Sure, no problem, I'll drive now."

He got behind the wheel and sat for a minute but then easily drove to Carson. It was settled. He'd worked hard for the privilege of living in the house with his friends. We'd take one day at a time and hope for the best.

"Don't forget to take your pills tonight," I said after we had lunch. I gave him a hug. "And call anytime, okay?"

"Mom, I'll see you tomorrow morning."

"I know." I forced a smile because as the afternoon progressed, I'd noticed him getting more anxious, which in turn made me reluctant to leave him.

"You sure you don't want to hang out with us tonight?" I was almost pleading.

"I'll be fine. I'll probably just read and listen to music."

The drive back to the condo seemed longer than a half hour. "Guess he decided to stay," Gary said. There was a hint of anxiety in his voice.

"Yes." I sighed. "Do you realize this is the first time he's been on his own since he crashed at school last semester?"

Gary nodded. "I guess we should get used to it."

I arrived at Dan's house the next morning, fifteen minutes early. "How was the night, honey?" I asked, looking him over as I used to do when he was at St. Joseph's.

"Fine," he answered, and indeed he did seem fine. "I'm ready to go to Dr. Vogel."

Even though we'd only met Dr. Vogel a couple of times, I felt as if we were going to visit an old friend. It took a half hour to get there from Dan's house, since Dr. Vogel's office was on the other side of town. Until Dan felt comfortable driving that far, I'd be taking him back and forth to his appointments. I was happy to do that; it would give me some guaranteed time with him once classes began.

Dr. Vogel smiled and welcomed us into his office. He was genuinely pleased to see Dan, and they'd start out meeting twice a week. With both of us there, Dr. Vogel felt it was a good time to discuss communication. "Typically, most nineteen-year-olds are breaking away from their parents." Turning to me he said, "If you have concerns regarding Dan, I don't think you should e-mail or call me directly, unless it's an emergency, of course. Instead, bring your concerns up with him and he can convey them to me."

BOUNDARIES OF FAMILY INVOLVEMENT IN OCD TREATMENT

Family members can play an invaluable role in the recovery of their loved one with OCD. Many OCD sufferers say that their family's support meant everything during their treatment—even when their family was at times bewildered and frustrated by their OCD behaviors. Therapists often appreciate the family's involvement as well, for the support it provides the OCD sufferer and for the family's role in reinforcing the treatment principles between sessions.

Although family involvement can be extremely helpful, is more involvement always better? That is, where are the boundaries of family involvement in OCD treatment? While there are no absolute rules about these boundaries, there are some general principles.

First, a family's involvement tends to decrease with increasing age of the OCD sufferer. For example, parents of school-aged children are typically directly involved in their child's treatment, often being included in the therapy sessions. As children become teenagers, it's more common for parents to talk with their teenager and the therapist for a few minutes at the end of each session. It is relatively rare for adults to have a family member in each treatment session. After a certain age (depending on the state), therapists cannot share information with family members without the consent of the OCD sufferer.

In addition to developmental differences, families might need to be more involved when it's likely that the OCD sufferer is not always an "accurate reporter" in ways that are likely to affect the treatment. For example, individuals in treatment might not be forthcoming about how much they are ritualizing, and it is essential for the therapist to have this information.

Family members can talk up front with the therapist and their loved one about the degree of their involvement that will work best *for their loved one*. At times what is best for the OCD sufferer might not be what family members prefer. For example, a spouse might want updates from the therapist after every session—satisfying, in a way, his or her own "need to know"—whereas the person in treatment might feel that such updates are unnecessary and even intrusive. The crucial question regarding family involvement is what will help the OCD sufferer recover.

After being shut out of all conversation at St. Joseph's, I likely overreacted to Dr. Vogel's recommendation, but the proverbial alarms went off in my head and red flags appeared. "Well, Dan hasn't exactly been a typical nineteen-year-old over the last six months, so we had to be involved in his life." I immediately regretted saying this, especially in front of Dan, since the last thing I wanted was for him to feel embarrassed over needing his parents.

Dr. Vogel spoke. "Of course, I totally understand that. I'm just trying to establish boundaries and confidentiality as to how we'll all communicate."

Our experience at St. Joseph's had made me wary of trusting healthcare providers. Dr. Vogel had stressed the importance of family involve-

ment, and more importantly, I'd had a good feeling about him from the beginning. Moreover, I realized our situation now was quite different from when Dan was at St. Joseph's. We had access to our son and could speak with him whenever we wanted. He was no longer out of our reach. So I needed to take a leap of faith.

We rarely saw Dan during that last week before school started. He had some ups and downs but overall was doing really well, adjusting to living on his own and spending time with his friends. I'd been so worried about seventeen days without therapy, but he'd been doing great without any therapy at all.

"How do you explain that?" I asked him. He'd managed to carve out some time for lunch with me.

"It's all because of St. Joseph's," he said. "I learned so much there; I've been able to be my own therapist."

With all our complaints about St. Joseph's, one fact was undeniable: they knew how to treat obsessive-compulsive disorder. Treating the whole person was a different story, but because of them, Dan now had the insight and skills to help him deal with his disorder. And while I hoped his toughest times were over, I knew the real test would begin soon, when classes started.

The next day I drove him to an art store to buy supplies. While he was comfortable driving to Carson and the nearby supermarket, he still had difficulty driving anywhere else. I didn't mind; I missed spending time with him.

"How are you doing?" I asked as he got into the car.

"I'm okay," he said, "except I feel so fat."

He'd definitely put on weight, and after being so thin for so long, he felt it. I'd read about how serious weight gain from atypical antipsychotics could be, and I was concerned. The weight increase wasn't from overeating. It was metabolic in nature and had the potential to lead to diabetes.

"You aren't fat," I said. "You've just gained some weight. It's probably from the medication so we'll keep an eye on it."

"I'm also really achy all the time."

"Really?" He'd never mentioned that before.

"Yeah, I've been told it's from anxiety," he said, though I wondered if this could be another side effect of medication.

"I've noticed you're drinking a lot," I said, as long as we were bringing up symptoms.

"Yeah, I'm always thirsty."

"Well, make sure you tell Dr. Russell about all these symptoms when you see him in a few weeks," I said. I'd try to put these worries out of my mind until his next appointment.

It was fun being with Dan at the art store and seeing him so excited about purchasing his supplies. He then easily did some shopping at a supermarket before I dropped him at his house. All in all, it was a good day.

As he got out of the car, he turned toward me and smiled. "I can't wait for school to start."

A wave of gratitude enveloped me and I smiled back. "Good luck tomorrow, honey," I said. How I wished I could freeze this moment in time. *I must figure out how to do that.*

11

TRIAL AND ERROR

Dan promised he'd call the next day, but by eight o'clock at night I still hadn't heard from him. I gave him a call.

"I'm working in the animation labs," he said, his tone flat.

"Okay, I won't keep you, honey. Just tell me quickly how the day went."

"Fine," he said. "I've got to get back to work."

He sounded overwhelmed already, and a flood of anxiety washed over me. Dan's ordeal had left me frazzled, and I was always struggling to contain my nerves.

"It's going to take a while for him to settle in," Gary said. "You've got to calm down. He's in the labs already. That's a good sign."

"I guess so."

I didn't tell Gary I couldn't get Dr. Parker's voice out of my head: "I know you want Dan to go back to school. Don't push him. I'm warning you." Over and over again. I wondered if what I was experiencing mirrored what Dan dealt with all the time. *I should ask him for some good therapy tips.*

The next couple of weeks were a roller-coaster ride for Dan. On the upside, he was going to classes and working hard. He was living on his own and taking care of himself, though I continually helped him out with food, laundry, and reminders to take his medications.

On the downside he was overwhelmed and seemed to be hanging on by a thread. His comments ranged from "I'm a mess; I can't do this" to "Things are going pretty well." His living situation wasn't great. His roommates weren't around much, leaving him alone most of the time. And he was always tired.

I felt one of the biggest obstacles for Dan was his disorganization; he was constantly losing things such as his glasses, watch, cell phone, and wallet. While he'd always tended this way, it had gotten worse. It was obvious to me that every ounce of his energy went toward making it through the day; there was none left to be organized. Things were going poorly enough that even though he was seeing Dr. Vogel twice a week, Dan and I agreed he should meet with Dr. Russell earlier than planned. "I think it's time to try some medication changes," Dr. Russell said after talking with Dan privately. "Timing is very important in situations such as these, and although Dan is stable, he could certainly be doing a lot better. We want to try to reduce his obsessions and not have every little thing be so difficult for him. There's no reason he can't get to the point where his life is actually enjoyable."

He made it sound so easy. Change the meds, and Dan will be happy. Realistically I knew even if new meds were to help Dan, it would likely be a few weeks before he noticed a difference. But the prospect of Dan being able to enjoy his life was certainly something to aspire to. There were actually a few times after Dan left St. Joseph's and before he started school that I'd describe him as happy. Now, it seemed like a lofty goal.

"What changes will you make?" I asked.

"Well, for now, we'll wean him off the atypical antipsychotic he's taking and switch to a different one."

Dr. Frey, Dan's first psychiatrist and the one who'd told us about his self-injuring, had previously prescribed the medication Dr. Russell wanted to switch to. Dan had taken one pill and decided not to take any more. That was five months ago. I relayed this information to Dr. Russell, who confirmed with Dan that he'd be willing to take the drug now. "And there may be other changes down the road as well," Dr. Russell said, addressing Dan. He explained what we already knew: only through trial and error would we (hopefully) find the right combination of drugs. I wasn't comfortable with Dan being a human guinea pig, but he wanted to make the medication switch, and we both trusted Dr. Russell. Maybe this would be the combination that would work?

I updated him on Dan's physical symptoms: the thirst, the achiness, and the tremors. A quick physical exam revealed another five-pound weight gain over three weeks. His heart rate was still rapid. "Nothing to worry about," Dr. Russell said. "We'll keep an eye on things."

"I've read about the side effects of the meds he's taking," I said. "Couldn't they be contributing to some of these problems?"

"Our goal is to have him on the least amount of medication that will still benefit him," Dr. Russell said. "He definitely needs these meds now, and of course we'll continue to monitor him."

He hadn't answered my question, and I was concerned. I'd assumed because Dr. Russell was a psychiatrist and therefore an MD, he'd monitor Dan's mental and physical health. Now I wasn't so sure. "Would you recommend he see an internist?" I asked.

"That's not necessary," Dr. Russell said. "I'll keep an eye on him. All his blood work came back normal, though his triglycerides were a little elevated. Everything is fine."

Over the next eight weeks, the above scenario played out three more times. Dan kept gaining weight and still had tachycardia, a fast heart rate. Several more medication changes were made; he was now weaned off his selective serotonin reuptake inhibitor (SSRI) and first atypical antipsychotic, and was taking an antidepressant and a different atypical antipsychotic instead. He still took a benzodiazepine as needed.

PSYCHIATRIC MEDICATION SIDE EFFECTS

Almost all medications have side effects, and psychiatric drugs are no exception. Fortunately newer psychiatric medications tend to have fewer side effects than older ones. However, serious side effects continue to be an important factor to consider when weighing the pros and cons of any medication.

While specific reactions to medications can vary tremendously, there are certain side effects that are most common for each class of medications. Some common side effects reported for specific drug classes include the following:

- **Benzodiazepines** (examples: Ativan, Klonopin, Xanax, Valium): Drowsiness and fatigue; memory problems, especially forming new long-term memories; slurred speech[1]
- **Second-generation ("atypical") antipsychotics** (examples: Zyprexa, Abilify, Risperdal, Clozaril): Extrapyramidal side effects (movement problems such as difficulty sitting still, slurred speech, and others that can resemble Parkinson's disease); profound weight gain; sedation[2]
- **Selective serotonin reuptake inhibitors (SSRIs)** (examples: Prozac, Paxil, Zoloft, Celexa): Insomnia; agitation; anxiety; dizziness; nausea; sexual side effects (loss of sex drive, difficulty reaching orgasm)[3]
- **Stimulants for attention deficit/hyperactivity disorder (ADHD)** (examples: Focalin, Vyvanse, Adderall, Ritalin): Insomnia; decreased appetite; elevated heart rate; elevated blood pressure; headaches[4]

Important questions to consider when deciding whether to take medication include the following:

- Has the medication been shown to be highly effective for the specific condition?
- How common are the side effects?
- How disruptive are the side effects? For example, sexual side effects may be less of a concern for someone who is not sexually active, whereas memory problems may be extremely problematic for a student.
- Are there effective treatment alternatives? For example, many individuals with obsessive-compulsive disorder choose to try exposure and response prevention (ERP) without medication.

In a perfect world there would be no tradeoff between a drug's desired effect and potential side effects. In reality, individuals with OCD need to decide—in collaboration with their doctors—whether the pros of a specific medication outweigh the cons.

1. B. Dell'osso and M. Lader, "Do Benzodiazepines Still Deserve a Major Role in the Treatment of Psychiatric Disorders? A Critical Reappraisal," *European Psychiatry* 28, no. 1 (2013): 14–15.
2. Komossa et al., "Second-Generation Antipsychotics," 3.
3. Mayo Clinic, "Selective Serotonin Reuptake Inhibitors (SSRIs)."

4. Mark D. Rapport and Catherine Moffitt, "Attention Deficit/Hyperactivity Disorder and Methylphenidate: A Review of Height/Weight, Cardiovascular, and Somatic Complaint Side Effects," *Clinical Psychology Review* 22, no. 8 (November 2002): 1122–27.

"Every time Dr. Russell makes a medication switch," I said to Gary, "I get my hopes up that it will be 'the one': the right mix that will make him noticeably better. But it hasn't happened."

"I know," Gary said. "If it's this frustrating for us, imagine how Dan feels."

"I don't know," I said. "Sometimes I think he's resigned himself to feeling this way forever."

Throughout all the medication changes, Dan was still riding that roller coaster. He was doing his schoolwork, but that was it. I don't think his OCD was in total control, but it was definitely calling most of the shots. By now, he'd isolated himself from his friends, which was upsetting to me since I knew how much they meant to him. I didn't realize at the time that Dan's avoidance of his friends was due to his sense of hyper-responsibility. In his mind he felt he was responsible for the well-being of those he cared about. If he wasn't with his friends, then he wouldn't have to worry about something bad happening to them under his "watch." Avoidance was a compulsion.

"Dan," I'd say to him, "how about moving in with us? It'd make your life so much easier, and maybe you'd be able to focus on other things like exercising, seeing your friends, or even just doing some fun stuff. It would really help your mood."

"I'm fine. I want to stay in the house," he'd always reply.

Every time he said "I'm fine," I cringed, because that's exactly what he used to say the previous semester when he was so *not* fine.

And so our lives continued. I still drove Dan back and forth to Dr. Vogel, now once a week, and to Dr. Russell every two to three weeks. As I mentioned before, this was a good thing; at least I got to see him. He'd been communicating less with us, and I reminded him of this part of our deal. But he was always misplacing his cell phone, and often he didn't have it with him, it wasn't charged, or the charger was lost. While there were good days, there were also many when he was on the brink of

despair. These times often coincided with him forgetting to take his meds, particularly the antidepressant.

"Dan's antidepressant can be an effective medicine," Mark had told us, "but missing doses can lead to quick negative feelings."

It was at this point I decided to start my own business called "Mother's Reminder Service," a nonprofit agency dedicated to helping Dan remember things. I sent him an e-mail every day and left him phone messages whenever I could connect to his phone, all the while trying to stress the importance of remembering his medications. Doing this was probably more for my benefit than Dan's, since I didn't really know if he took my advice. But I needed to feel I was doing *something* to help him. I was always on edge, never knowing what each day would bring.

The phone rang one day, and the caller ID flashed the name "Richard Parker." I stood there, staring at the phone, but couldn't bring myself to answer it. "Oh my God, Gary," I said, nearly hysterical. "Dr. Parker just called. Why is he calling us? Does he want Dan back? Do you think he is coming to get him? What could he possibly want?" I began formulating what I would say once Dr. Parker started yelling at me again. As I was writing down some notes, it hit me.

Dr. Parker's first name was Robert, not Richard. Richard Parker, I later found out, was the repairman we were expecting at the condo. Whoops. Never mind. It was then I realized I needed to calm down and get my own anxiety under control.

As always, I looked to Mark for advice. "The best thing you can do for Dan and yourself is to settle into a routine and have a positive attitude," he said. "He has gotten over the biggest hurdle already, but he needs your help in settling down and being less scared of OCD and possible failure. I know this is easy to say but hard to do. Just try to keep things as light as possible. I really believe Dan will do best if you all approach this situation with a sense of bemusement rather than despair."

Dan also seemed tired of all the doom and gloom. "Look at this bag full of leftover pills. It's like a mini drugstore," he said the next time he visited us. Holding up a plastic bag filled with half-empty bottles of assorted drugs in various dosages, he said, "I could sell them on eBay or use them for an animation project." We laughed at the thought of a bunch of standing capsules dancing in unison. Yes, we needed to keep things light whenever possible. I reveled in those moments of levity, when for a minute or two, everything seemed normal.

The change happened gradually, as in three steps forward, two and nine-tenths steps back, but eventually Gary and I both noticed some positive changes in Dan.

"That look of anxiety that's been etched on his face for so long goes away once in a while," I said. "Have you noticed?"

"Well," Gary said, "I'm aware he's driven a few places other than school, and he's grocery shopping more often. He even drove to the movies with his friends the other night."

"Yeah, I definitely see improvements," I replied, "but life in general still seems to be a struggle for him. I guess we need to be patient and focus more on the positive."

Dan's workload increased another notch as he neared midsemester. We were on our way to his weekly appointment with Dr. Vogel when he anxiously announced, "I can't do this anymore. I want to quit school."

While he'd never actually said these exact words before, he'd certainly alluded that the stress was too much for him. "Do you really mean that, Dan?"

"I mean it right now," he said. His leg was bouncing more than usual. "But it changes every hour."

"Honey," I said. "Just think of what you've done up until this point. The semester is halfway over and you're doing your work and living on your own, just as you wanted. I know it's been a struggle for you, but I'm so impressed by your strength and determination. I think you're a courageous young man who should be very proud of himself. And things are only going to get better." I wasn't sure how much he was even listening to me, but he mumbled in agreement and got out of the car.

I picked him up after his appointment. "How'd everything go, honey?"

He gave his standard reply. "I think Dr. Vogel's feeling better. I helped him out, but he still needs me so I'm going back next week."

We chuckled, and then he said, "Oh, Dr. Vogel thinks I might have ADD."

I was confused. "Attention deficit disorder? You? Why on earth would he think that?"

"Well, he knows I lose things all the time and I'm disorganized and I've certainly had trouble concentrating lately. Oh, and I guess it's not

unusual for people with OCD to also have ADD. I think he might be right."

I tried to make sense of it all. "What you've said is all true, but those symptoms alone don't mean you have ADD. We need to research this, but as I understand it, ADD appears early on, and your trouble concentrating is new. I think it's obviously related to your struggles with OCD."

"Maybe," Dan said, "but I've always been disorganized."

"A lot of people are disorganized, honey, but once again that doesn't mean they have ADD. What else did Dr. Vogel say?"

"He said he might call Dr. Russell and discuss it with him."

Great. More pills coming our way.

ATTENTION DEFICIT HYPERACTIVITY DISORDER (ADHD) AND OCD

Having OCD raises a person's chances of having attention deficit hyperactivity disorder (ADHD). Estimates vary widely for how common ADHD is in people with OCD, from less than 10 percent to as high as 50 percent.[1] Researchers have tried to figure out why these conditions might co-occur, as there are few apparent similarities between OCD and ADHD. For example, ADHD often involves making careless mistakes whereas OCD sufferers tend to go to great lengths to avoid making mistakes. One suggestion for their co-occurrence is that the two conditions seem to involve similar brain areas (in particular the basal ganglia).[2]

When an individual does meet criteria for both OCD and ADHD, the OCD tends to look very similar to OCD without ADHD. That is, ADHD does not seem to fundamentally alter the nature of OCD. Nevertheless, untreated ADHD can interfere with OCD treatment. For example, problems with attention can interfere with completing homework or retaining information discussed in session. Thus treating the ADHD might help with the OCD treatment, too.

It is important to point out the potential for misdiagnosis of ADHD in a person with OCD. In fact, data from a recent study that examined the connection between OCD and ADHD challenge the finding of high co-occurrence of these two conditions.[3] The study's

results suggest that among OCD sufferers, symptoms such as disorganization, trouble focusing, and frequent misplacing of things, while classic symptoms of ADHD, might actually be a byproduct of dealing with OCD. The authors of the article conclude that "clinicians ought to pay careful consideration to OCD symptoms in the diagnostic process of individuals suspected of having ADHD, and be mindful that [obsessive-compulsive] symptomatology has the possibility to manifest through ADHD-like symptoms."[4]

1. Amitai Abramovitch, Reuven Dar, Andrew Mittelman, and Avraham Schweiger, "Don't Judge a Book by Its Cover: ADHD-like Symptoms in Obsessive Compulsive Disorder," *Journal of Obsessive-Compulsive and Related Disorders* 2, no. 1 (2013): 53–54.
2. David Beck Schatz and Anthony L. Rostain, "ADHD with Comorbid Anxiety: A Review of the Current Literature," *Journal of Attention Disorders* 10, no. 2 (2006): 144–45.
3. Abramovitch et al., "Don't Judge a Book," 58.
4. Ibid., 59.

When I got back to our condo, I immediately searched the Internet to read about ADD/ADHD. In less than five minutes I determined Dan didn't have it. ADD is characterized by inattention, impulsivity, and (usually) hyperactivity, none of which pertained to Dan. Forgetfulness was often a symptom too.

"First of all," I said to Gary, "let's think back to Dan's elementary school days at Oakmont. He had five different teachers in six years, and each one of them only had praise for him. Nobody ever expressed any concerns. He was interested in everything, extremely focused, well behaved, attentive, and responsive in class."

"You're right," Gary said. "He was a teacher's dream."

"And even though we homeschooled after that, Dan still took some traditional classes at the local community college. Again, he had no trouble, received positive feedback, and got great grades. I'd think if he had ADD, there'd have been some problems or warning signs before now. Sure, he loses things and can be disorganized, but those are the only symptoms he has, and from everything I read, that doesn't warrant a diagnosis of ADD."

The next week Dan had an appointment with Dr. Russell. The receptionist was at lunch, so we were alone in the waiting room. Dan stood to browse the pamphlets displayed on the counter. "Just checking out some more drugs," he said jokingly. As I was noticing what a handsome young man he was, the music from *Swan Lake* came over the sound system. He

turned to me, flashed an impish grin, and proceeded to do a funny little ballet dance with his six-foot-five frame, arms over his head. He stood on his toes and twirled. The whole thing lasted five seconds at most but lingered in my mind for days. It was undoubtedly the best ballet I've ever seen.

Our meeting with Dr. Russell was upbeat. "I feel more motivated in general," Dan said.

"And overall I think your mood has been better too, Dan," I said.

He nodded.

"Well, now that Dan is on a therapeutic dose of the antidepressant, we're seeing the benefits of that medication," Dr. Russell said. "I think you should stay on it, and we'll reevaluate in four weeks."

I brought up Dr. Vogel's thoughts about Dan possibly having ADD.

"Well, ADD is quite prevalent among those with OCD," Dr. Russell explained. "I don't like to get caught up in the different diagnoses. Having OCD is similar to having a cold. What I mean by that is you can talk to ten different people with colds, and they can all have different symptoms. It's the same with OCD. Dan does have some disorganization, which might or might not be related to ADD. I just try to customize the treatment to each individual." The bottom line was Dr. Russell wasn't recommending additional medication, so I was happy.

As we were leaving, Dan said, "I'd really love to do some traveling during winter break. What do you think?"

"Wow, Dan," I said, surprised. "That's an interesting thought. What were you thinking?"

"I'm not really sure. I have some money saved. Maybe go to Europe?"

The idea unsettled me. I was just getting used to my son living on his own across town, and now he wanted to go to Europe? "To be honest with you, honey, I'm not really comfortable with you traveling alone at this point. How about going somewhere with a friend?"

"Okay. I'll ask around."

Back at the condo, I told Gary about our conversation. "The amazing thing," I said, "is that he's thinking and planning ahead. Up until this point he hasn't been able to plan more than a day or two in advance, and even that's been stressful. I can't remember the last time he was able to anticipate something good coming his way."

"Maybe the medication really is making a difference," Gary said.

Dan was determined to travel, and he and his friend Sara decided on a trip to Quebec City, a place he'd visited a few years earlier with his grandparents and had fallen in love with. Every time he spoke about their plans, his face lit up.

"We'll fly there and stay in youth hostels," he said. "There's so much to do, and I love the Old City and the art galleries. Maybe we'll even go dog sledding." It was great to see him so excited about going back there. By now he was only a few weeks away from the successful completion of the semester, and his mood was better than it had been in almost a year.

Dan had one more appointment with Dr. Russell before his semester break. Once the doctor saw how well Dan was doing, I was sure he'd keep all his medications the same.

That was not to be. He began by asking Dan many specific questions about his obsessive thoughts. I knew Dan felt uncomfortable with me there, and I was just about to offer to leave when the questions stopped. Basically, Dan's answers reflected the fact he was doing much better but there was definitely space for improvement.

I, once again, brought up the problem of Dan's shakiness, mostly tremors in his hands. "Dan's commented on this himself," I told Dr. Russell. "He finds it difficult to write. I've seen his handwriting, and it looks like scary script for Halloween. The tremors also affect his drawing, which is a problem, right Dan?"

Dan nodded.

"The tremors are likely from some of his medications," Dr. Russell explained, "and once those are reduced, the shakiness should go away."

"Great," I said. "Are you going to reduce those dosages?"

"Well, not yet," Dr. Russell said. "What I'm going to do is prescribe a stimulant for Dan."

"Oh." I said. "Aren't stimulants used for ADD/ADHD? I'm convinced he doesn't have ADD."

"Well, this medication should enhance the effects of the antidepressant."

"But he's doing so well now," I pleaded, thinking of Dr. Russell's original assertion that Dan should be on the least medication possible. "Can't we leave well enough alone?"

"Well, it seems there's definitely room for improvement, wouldn't you say, Dan?" Dan nodded.

"Well," I said, "if you're going to add a drug can you at least take one away?" I was only half joking.

"Actually," Dr. Russell said, "if this works as I hope, then in six months to a year I imagine it'll be Dan's only medication. The atypical antipsychotic will be the first to go and then the antidepressant. The benzodiazepine could be kept as needed, but Dan rarely even needs that now."

I didn't understand how or why a stimulant would eventually be the only drug Dan would be on, especially if its purpose was to enhance the antidepressant that he would no longer be taking. I didn't bother asking for clarification, though, since it seemed this wasn't an imminent issue.

While I was unhappy Dan was given yet another drug, I still trusted Dr. Russell. After all, the changes he'd made in Dan's medications so far appeared successful. The physical side effects, however, remained. His tremors, tachycardia, and unusual weight gain of twenty-five pounds kept me up at night. I was more concerned than Dan; he left the appointment happy.

"I love new drugs," he joked, though I'm sure there was some truth to his statement. Why wouldn't he? They seemed to be helping him.

On the way home he said, "I'm picking my courses for next semester today, and I'm trying to decide whether to take super-easy electives along with my tough animation courses or take a harder elective I'm actually really interested in."

Not knowing enough to offer a definitive answer, I suggested, "Why don't you talk with Dr. Moore about it?"

"Maybe I will."

I thought back to the end of Dan's last semester, when he was in such rough shape Dr. Moore had to guide him in choosing courses. A very different young man would be meeting with her this time.

Dan had come so far. Four long months ago, in the depths of despair, he pleaded with us to let him stay at St. Joseph's. Now he was eagerly planning for next semester. It didn't matter which electives he took. He was back at school, pursuing his dream, and feeling well. We'd made the right decision, and for the first time in a long time, I felt like a good mom.

12

THE CRASH

Dan began taking the stimulant as prescribed, increasing the dosage over a short time period. Problems quickly arose.

"I haven't slept in three nights," he said when I spoke to him on the phone. "I'm feeling lousy."

"How about I come and get you so you can stay with us tonight?" I said.

"That'd be great. Thanks. I haven't slept at all, but I still feel really awake."

The fact he agreed verified how poorly he was doing. Gary drove the half hour to Dan's house and brought him back, wide awake and jittery.

I called Dr. Russell the next morning and updated him. "Cut back from the fifty-four milligrams to thirty-six milligrams and then to eighteen milligrams and see if that helps," he said.

I hated this trial and error, especially with a drug I was not at all convinced Dan needed.

"You feel more productive with your work at all, Dan?" I asked, knowing the stimulant was supposed to help with productivity.

"Not really," he said, "just more awake." Not only was he no more productive than usual; he was also as disorganized as ever. Currently his cell phone was missing. We went back to Dr. Russell.

"Things aren't working with this stimulant," I told the doctor. "Dan's still up nights and sleeps when he can during the day. Not a good way to end the semester."

"I'd like to switch Dan to an amphetamine, which might work better than the stimulant he's taking now," Dr. Russell said.

POSSIBLE EFFECTS OF ADHD MEDICATIONS ON OCD

According to the American Academy of Pediatrics, the first-line treatment for attention deficit hyperactivity disorder (ADHD) is stimulant medication (for children older than six years).[1] Taking stimulants carries the risk for typical side effects such as insomnia and low appetite and for some OCD sufferers can increase the anxiety that drives obsessions and compulsions.[2]

While stimulant medications seem to work better than nonstimulants for ADHD, a psychiatrist might consider a nonstimulant when OCD is also in the mix. For example, atomoxetine (Strattera) is approved for treatment of ADHD and is a norepinephrine reuptake inhibitor rather than an amphetamine.[3] As such it is less likely to make the OCD symptoms worse. Nevertheless, as with all medications it carries a risk for side effects, most commonly nausea, dry mouth, loss of appetite, and insomnia.

In light of these complexities, medication for ADHD in a person with OCD should be handled by a doctor experienced in treating both conditions. He or she should be knowledgeable about a range of treatment options for co-occurring ADHD and OCD and can monitor how ADHD treatment affects the OCD.

1. Mark Wolraich, Lawrence Brown, Ronald T. Brown, George DuPaul, Marian Earls, Heidi M. Feldman, Theodore G. Ganiats, Beth Kaplanek, Bruce Meyer, James Perrin, Karen Pierce, Michael Reiff, Martin T. Stein, and Susanna Visser, "ADHD: Clinical Practice Guideline for the Diagnosis, Evaluation, and Treatment of Attention-Deficit/Hyperactivity Disorder in Children and Adolescents," *Pediatrics* 128, no. 5 (November 2011): 1015.
2. Daryl Efron, Frederick Jarman, and Melinda Barker, "Side Effects of Methylphenidate and Dexamphetamine in Children with Attention Deficit Hyperactivity Disorder: A Double-Blind, Crossover Trial," *Pediatrics* 100, no. 4 (1997): 664–66.
3. Wolraich et al., "ADHD," 1016.

More trial and error. Why couldn't we have left well enough alone? "Dan has only two weeks left in the semester, and I'd really like to wait until he's done with classes before trying this new medication," I said.

"No, he should really start taking it now," Dr. Russell replied, and then ended our meeting.

As we left his office, I said, "You know, Dan, sometimes I think we need to use our common sense. Why risk running into trouble with this new drug while you're finishing up the semester? I say you wait the two weeks."

"But Dr. Russell said I should start it now."

"I know, but it doesn't make sense. You're doing fine without it. Finish the semester and then start taking it."

"Maybe." He was hesitant.

"What if you ask Dr. Vogel what he thinks?" I said.

"Okay, that's a good idea."

Dr. Vogel agreed that Dan should delay starting the medication, and so Dan conceded. He'd just needed to hear it from an authority.

In the meantime, everything seemed to be coming together for Dan. He was now eating ice cream, wearing his new glasses (when they weren't lost), and going into the 7-Eleven, all everyday things he hadn't been able to do for a long time. And of course there was his biggest accomplishment: he completed the first semester of his sophomore year at Carson College with excellent grades.

Dan and his friends decided not to renew the lease on their house, which meant Dan would live on campus with a roommate the next semester. He moved in with us for his winter break, and I was surprised how anxious he seemed. I assumed once the semester was over, he'd be able to relax. "He seems more stressed tonight than he's been in a long time," I said to Gary. "He even had to take a tranquilizer, and I can't remember the last time he did that. Maybe it's because he's transitioning from so much work to a month of little to no structure."

"Could be," Gary said. "He does seem a little shell-shocked."

Dan began taking the prescribed amphetamine as soon as school ended. "I definitely feel more awake," he said, but again had trouble sleeping.

And I still felt uncomfortable with this additional medication. This time Gary called Dr. Russell, who said, "Let's keep him on the seventy milligrams and give him some more time to adjust."

Dan had a couple of weeks free before traveling to Canada. He golfed a few times with Gary and got together with some of his friends who were still in the area. I offered to drive him to the bookstore one day, and he became annoyed. "You're really enabling me by driving me everywhere."

"You're right, Dan," I said, pleased he'd brought this to my attention. "There's no reason you can't drive yourself."

And so he did. He started driving all around Bridgeville to meet up with his friends, which warmed my heart. And he seemed comfortable behind the wheel. The time passed quickly, and before we knew it, he was off to Canada.

"Remember our deal, Dan," I said. "You need to be in touch once a day by phone, text, e-mail, smoke signal, whatever. Just so we know you're okay and I can remind you to take your pills."

"I know, I know." He rolled his eyes. He was losing his patience with me, which I took as a good sign. He was acting like a normal nineteen-year-old.

Dan and Sara had a great time in Canada. He contacted us every day, except for one, which was a lot better than I'd anticipated, and he arrived back home happy. The next week we moved him into his dorm room. It was huge and meant for four students, but only he and his roommate Eric would live there. While Dan didn't know Eric personally, he'd gotten a friend of a friend's approval. I was relieved Dan would be on campus.

"This semester is going to be tough," Dan said after setting up his room.

"Try to take one day at a time, honey," I said. "I'm sure you'll be fine. And don't forget, Marilyn Lambert in Academic Support Services wants to see you at the beginning of the semester, okay?"

"I'll get around to it, I guess," he said. I could tell he was feeling overwhelmed and stressed.

A lot of kids are anxious at the beginning of a new semester, I told myself. *It's normal.*

I kept remembering Dan's condition in August, and it was easy to see how far he'd come. He'd be fine.

At his next appointment, Dr. Russell said, "I haven't seen you in six weeks, and it's obvious to me you're more relaxed and comfortable."

This was true. After the initial stress of beginning the semester, Dan seemed to be settling in well. I was waiting for Dr. Russell to say he was going to wean Dan off the atypical antipsychotic, but instead he said, "Let's stay on all your meds for another three months. They seem to be working well, and I think three more months will benefit Dan. Of course you can take a tranquilizer as needed, but as far as I understand, you've rarely had to."

Dan nodded. His physical exam again revealed a fast heart rate and a weight gain of three more pounds. He was still visibly shaky with tremors. Dr. Russell wasn't concerned, and I comforted myself with the fact that in three more months, the weaning off of at least some of these meds would begin.

Gary and I decided it was time to give Dan some space. "You don't have to be in touch every day," I told Dan. "Just check in a few times a week, okay?"

"Sure."

It was actually a relief not to expect to hear from Dan daily. He still wasn't reliable in that department, and as I've mentioned, he was often hard to track down. Now I could wait two, maybe even three days before I'd worry about why we hadn't heard from him.

Two weeks into the semester, when Gary and Ava were away visiting some of our friends for the weekend, Dan called. I heard his voice and immediately knew something was wrong.

"I'm all out of sorts," he said, and I could sense his restlessness. "I've been up at night and sleeping during the day. Can I spend the night there?"

"Of course. I'll be right over." Anxiety flooded through me. If Dan wanted to come home, that meant something was terribly wrong.

As I drove to his dorm, I repeatedly told myself I was overreacting.

He was waiting for me outside. "You have your medication?" I asked.

"Oh, no, I'll get it." We'd bought him a pill organizer to keep track of all his meds, and I looked at it when he returned. Then I looked up at him.

"You haven't taken your medication in two days, honey. What's going on?"

"I don't know."

He spent the weekend with me and got back on track with the medication. He said he felt a little better, but his sleeping was still out of whack and I noticed he was twitching and wincing a lot. I hadn't seen movements such as this since his days at St. Joseph's.

I was reluctant to bring him back to his dorm on Sunday, but he insisted on going. "Call if you need me, and I'll see you in a few days for your appointment with Dr. Vogel," I said.

"Okay, see you soon." He was lying on his bed already. It was hard to leave him.

When I picked him up a few days later, he looked and felt even worse. "Dan," I asked, "is your OCD getting worse?"

"No, that's not it at all."

Now I was really confused. "So what's going on?"

"I don't know. Everything's just so hard, from daily living to schoolwork. I'm so exhausted. I missed a couple of classes this week because I overslept."

"You have any idea why things are worse now? You'd been doing so well."

"No I haven't. I've pretty much been like this all along."

All along? I knew this wasn't true. I immediately thought back to when Dan was at St. Joseph's and couldn't remember any happy times from his childhood. His thinking was distorted then, and it was distorted now.

"Dan, you just came back from a wonderful trip to Canada."

"It wasn't so great," he said. "I was anxious the whole time."

While Dan met with Dr. Vogel, I called Gary. "Something's up with Dan, but I'm not sure what." I'd updated him on Dan spending the weekend with me, but he hadn't been concerned. Then again, he hadn't seen Dan.

"Really? He's been doing so well," Gary said. "Maybe you're overreacting and this is all part of those ups and downs we need to expect."

"I don't know. This seems different. And it's not even his OCD that's the problem. I wish he'd never started taking that amphetamine. It hasn't even helped with his disorganization."

"Let's see what Dr. Vogel says, and we'll take it from there."

I was annoyed at my husband's composure.

"Dr. Vogel thinks we should call Dr. Russell," Dan said as he got into the car after his appointment. He was twitching a lot.

I tried to appear relaxed, though I wasn't sure I was successful. "Okay, honey. What else did he say?"

He spoke in a monotone. "He said he thinks I'm depressed, and I agree. It might have to do with the amphetamine."

I stared at my son. He was slumped over in the passenger seat, wincing. He looked defeated. Hadn't he been through enough already? My eyes filled with tears. I immediately called Dr. Russell.

"Let's reduce the amphetamine to thirty-five milligrams (from seventy milligrams) right away," he said. "And I'll see him on Monday."

It was a long weekend, but Monday finally arrived.

"It's possible what's happening to Dan might be a cyclical thing," Dr. Russell said. He'd just met with Dan alone, and I was then invited into his office. "From everything you've told me, it was just about a year ago things started to fall apart for him."

"Yes, that's true."

"Well, sometimes the brain goes in cycles. We want to stay on top of the situation so he doesn't regress to where he was this time last year."

I'd never heard about the brain having this type of memory, but I didn't find Dr. Russell's theory far-fetched. In fact, I easily related to it. Twenty-one years earlier, I'd given birth to our daughter Leah. She was premature and struggled with all her being to survive, but she died at the age of six weeks. Never in my life had I experienced such profound loss: intense grief seared through me, tearing my heart apart and bruising my soul. For the past twenty-one years, as the month of March had gotten underway, sadness enveloped me. It wasn't an emotion that stemmed from remembering. It was rooted in my being and arrived before I was even consciously aware of the time of year. It was my brain, or more likely my heart, remembering. Thinking of this, Dr. Russell's words made sense to me.

"So here's what we're going to do," Dr. Russell said. "Stop the amphetamine altogether right now. Increase the atypical antipsychotic from 5 milligrams to 7.5 milligrams. We'll keep the antidepressant the same at 150 milligrams. And I want Dan to take his benzodiazepine (one milligram) twice a day. Hopefully he'll start to feel better in a few days, and I'd like to see you both again a week from today."

So many changes. Dr. Russell's comment about Dan regressing to last year's condition truly frightened me. If this plan could prevent that from happening, then so be it. But one thing didn't sit right with me. "I've

always thought you weren't supposed to stop amphetamines abruptly. Shouldn't Dan be weaned off it?"

"No, he can just stop it completely," Dr. Russell assured me.

I turned to Dan. "Okay, let's get back to your room and refill your pill organizer."

Two days later, Dan and I were on our way to Dr. Vogel. Dan was unusually quiet until we turned into the parking lot. "School's too hard," he said, becoming increasingly agitated. "Everything's too hard. I don't want to do this anymore, and I'm not even happy at Carson."

I felt as if I'd just traveled back in time seven months.

"Honey, things were going well the end of last semester," I reminded him. "You thought your teachers were great, you enjoyed your courses, and you were even talking about ideas for your senior project."

He looked at me as if I were making this all up.

Instead of picking him up outside as I usually did, I decided to sit in the waiting area. I was hoping to talk with Dr. Vogel, or at least examine his face for signs of worry. He and Dan entered the room together, and Dr. Vogel looked at me. His eyes were filled with concern.

"If you and Gary want to sit down and talk with me at any point, with or without Dan, that'd be fine," he said.

The heaviness in my chest that had finally lifted a couple of months earlier had returned. "Okay, thank you," I said.

I tried to sound upbeat as we walked to the car. "You feel any better after talking with Dr. Vogel, honey?"

"No."

"Well, we'll help you out as much as we can until you're feeling better so you can just concentrate on your schoolwork, okay?"

"No. That's enabling me. I shouldn't even be at Carson. I've been having panic attacks every single night, and I'm close to cutting myself again. I don't want to do this anymore. I should've stayed at St. Joseph's."

Dr. Parker's voice in my head was telling me the same thing.

"Dan, you need to give this some time," I said. "It seems this new drug has done a job on you, and your other medication dosages have changed as well. Obviously this is a tough time for you."

"You're not living up to the bargain we made," he said. "When I was at St. Joseph's you told me if school was too hard, you wouldn't make me go. Well, now it's too much for me to handle. You said you'd never make me do anything I really didn't want to do."

What I wanted to tell Dan was that I knew, when he was feeling well, he absolutely *did* want to be at Carson. But I didn't. "Dan, I hear everything you're saying. I really do. But you're in the middle of a crisis, so now isn't the time to make any major decisions such as leaving school. We need to get you back on track first and then we can make smart decisions. Also, I think you should stay with us a few days, until you're feeling better. And please consider talking with Dr. Moore as soon as possible, so she knows what's going on too."

"Okay, I guess. But I want to go back to my dorm now. I'll be fine."

I kept in close contact with him the next couple of days, hoping for the phone call telling me he was feeling better. Instead he sounded more anxious and depressed each time we spoke. He was dragging himself to classes, but that was about it.

"Did you speak with Dr. Moore?" I asked him, more than once.

"No, I just go to classes and sleep."

"Why don't you come back to our place after school on Friday?"

"Okay." He didn't even argue.

Gary picked him up from his dorm on Friday evening, and when they walked through our door I was taken aback at how tired and worn out Dan looked, almost like an old man. He gave me a hug and then immediately went to bed.

At noon on Saturday, he was still sleeping. I tried to wake him a few times but wasn't able to. He finally arose early afternoon on Saturday, ate a lot, and went right back to sleep. He literally couldn't keep his eyes open. I searched the Internet and found that heavy sleeping, hunger, and depression are all symptoms of withdrawal from the amphetamine he was taking. I also read that the drug shouldn't be stopped abruptly but weaned off gradually, which confirmed my earlier thought.

"I'm worried," I said to Gary. "What was Dr. Russell thinking? I specifically questioned him about stopping the medication cold turkey."

"I'm calling him right now," Gary said.

The conversation was quick, and my husband was visibly upset. "Dr. Russell said we should keep Dan awake and reduce the antidepressant from 150 milligrams to 75 milligrams. He actually said he doesn't believe

all the sleeping is related to amphetamine withdrawal, and he expects to see you both on Monday."

"You've got to be kidding me." A rare feeling of rage enveloped me, and I felt as if I'd lose control. "Not related to amphetamine withdrawal?" I realized I was shouting.

"Try to calm down, Janet," Gary said, but there was no stopping me.

"I just need to get this straight," I ranted. "Dan was on seventy milligrams of this amphetamine for seven weeks. Dr. Russell reduced his dosage to thirty-five milligrams for three days and then stopped the medication. Everything I've read says that's a recipe for disaster. And now the doctor's trying to tell us Dan's symptoms aren't related to withdrawal? Seriously?"

I called Mark, who said, "This amphetamine is relatively new so issues with it might not be known yet. It certainly seems related to his sleepiness and is likely relevant to his depression as well. You know, people can have strong dependency issues with amphetamines. They provide a boost in energy and a state of relative optimism, so when someone's taken off them, it's not unusual to crash. Some patients need rehab to get off them. It sure seems as if Dan is having a strong reaction to stopping."

Yes, it did. By Sunday morning my rage had morphed into fear. Our efforts to keep Dan awake proved futile, and aside from a couple of eating binges, he slept until midafternoon on Sunday.

"I have to get back to school," he said. "I have work due tomorrow. I need to get to the labs."

"Let's talk with Dr. Moore tomorrow before your appointment with Dr. Russell," I said. "I don't think you're well enough to go to the labs."

"No, I have to go back," he insisted. Reluctantly, Gary drove him back to school. Dan slept the whole way.

I was worried about Dan's physical well-being as much as his mental health. All his sleeping had left him even more haggard. His body was being put through the wringer.

Shortly after Gary returned home, Dan called. His voice was barely audible. "Can you come get me? I can't stay awake." Once again, Gary drove to Carson and returned with Dan. We were able to talk for a few minutes before he fell asleep again. "I have a morning class, but I'm not prepared," he said.

"Don't worry about that, Dan. Your health is what matters now. How about if I talk to Dr. Moore in the morning while you tell your teacher what's been going on? Then we can see Dr. Russell in the afternoon." The thought of having to face Dr. Russell made me physically ill, but what choice did we have? The time to find a new doctor was not now. Dan agreed to that plan and within minutes was fast asleep again.

I was able to wake him in the morning, but he slept all the way to school. I parked in Carson's main lot and was able to nudge him awake. "Honey, I'll go see Dr. Moore now, and you'll go talk to your teacher, okay? Just as we talked about yesterday."

"Okay," Dan said. "But I'm a little early. I'll rest in the car until it's time for class."

"I'm afraid you'll fall asleep. Why don't you get out into the fresh air?"

"I'm fine," he insisted, speaking those two words I hated. Dan was not fine, physically or mentally. That would've been obvious to anyone. I was reluctant to leave him alone but decided to speak with Dr. Moore.

"Let's meet back here," I said, hoping he'd make it out of the car.

Being in Dr. Moore's office was always emotional for me. Dan and I were there when he was at his worst, and Dr. Moore was always so genuinely concerned about him that my guard automatically came down around her. Maybe it was because she had a son Dan's age. Somehow the feelings and concerns I always tried to hide were mirrored on her face. I took one look at her and began to cry.

"He's been trying so hard, but he's in rough shape," I said, and updated her on the last few days. "I'm not really sure what to do at this point."

"Do you know Chris over at the counseling center?" Dr. Moore asked. She handed me a tissue.

"No, I don't."

"Actually, I just saw him here. Let me see if I can find him. He's great."

Waiting in her office by myself, I vividly remembered Dr. Moore helping Dan choose his courses ten long months ago. He'd been chewing like crazy on his hood strings and was a bundle of stress, anxiety, and fear. He'd come so very far and was now sliding backward. *Just a temporary setback*, I thought, hoping with all my heart it was true.

Dr. Moore returned with Chris, who was all business. "Withdrawing abruptly from amphetamines can be dangerous, and from what Dr. Moore

just told me, it sounds as if Dan is being hit hard. If I were you, I wouldn't wait until his afternoon doctor's appointment. I'd take him over to Lakeview Center right now."

"Lakeview Center?"

"It's the mental health center of Bridgeville Memorial Hospital," Chris said. "It's a short-term facility, and they're good. They'll evaluate Dan and get him back on track, hopefully get him off some of these meds. He's going through severe withdrawal now and needs to be closely monitored." I could hear the concern in his voice. While I had been trying to not overreact to Dan's situation, Chris's obvious worry thrust me into panic mode.

"Thanks, I'll do that," I said, and hurried from Dr. Moore's office, promising to keep her posted.

I half ran, half walked back to my car, almost certain I'd find my son fast asleep in the front passenger seat. And there he was.

13

PICKING UP THE PIECES

I was almost frantic getting into the car and startled Dan when I shut the door. "How long was I sleeping?" he asked, groggy and disoriented.

"I left you almost an hour ago."

He lifted his heavy head and looked at me. "Mom, I really feel terrible." He sounded frightened.

I was scared too, but at least I had a plan. "Honey, we're going to Lakeview Center to see if they can help you, okay?" I didn't bother giving him any details about the clinic.

"Okay, that sounds good," he said, not bothering to ask any questions.

Even though I knew Lakeview Center was near Bridgeville Memorial Hospital, we had trouble finding it. Tucked away on a tree-lined side street, it was a nondescript three-story brick building that, to me, seemed purposely hidden. The parking lot was empty. Dan had been awake during the entire fifteen-minute drive, and I could tell by his expression he was troubled. Now that we'd arrived, neither of us knew what to expect.

"Am I staying here?" he asked. I got the impression he wouldn't have minded.

"I honestly don't know, honey. Why don't we take one thing at a time and hear what they have to say?" This was all happening so fast, for both of us. When Dan had gone to St. Joseph's Hospital we'd researched the program thoroughly and were still faced with surprises. Now here we were, about to cross the threshold into a mental health facility we knew

nothing about. My biggest fear was once Dan was in he'd never get out. But what were our options? He needed help now, and if we went to the emergency room at Bridgeville Memorial Hospital, they'd only refer him to Lakeview.

I looked at my son's face, etched with pain, and felt so proud of him for his continued willingness to accept help. I shuddered to think how much worse off we would've been if he'd been resistant to the therapy that had truly benefitted him. Still, I was ambivalent about what was to come.

RECOVERY AVOIDANCE

There are many obstacles to effective treatment for people with obsessive-compulsive disorder. For example, many people don't know that effective treatment exists, don't live close to an exposure and response prevention (ERP) therapist, or can't afford treatment. For some OCD sufferers, the final barrier is their own willingness to seek treatment, which has been termed "recovery avoidance."

Why would a person who is suffering from a debilitating condition refuse effective treatment? There are many possible reasons. Some people say it feels as if their OCD is an integral part of themselves, and the idea of giving it up is scary. They may say things such as, "I don't know who I am without my OCD." (The answer is usually "a happier and more productive version of you.") Part of the fear can come from the belief that the OCD has been keeping them safe, and giving up OCD may be a risk they're not yet willing to take.

Another common and related fear is that the exposures in ERP will be too hard. It's difficult for people to imagine not only doing what they've been avoiding but also not doing their rituals. These fears can be addressed in part by letting the individuals know that exposures will happen gradually and at their own pace, and that they will be "in the driver's seat." Some media depictions of "extreme" exposures such as licking toilet seats might be responsible in part for these fears about the treatment.

Family accommodation (discussed earlier) can also contribute to recovery avoidance. If treatment is seen as difficult and painful and family members are making it less painful to have OCD (for example, by doing rituals for the person), then the balance might be tipped in favor of recovery avoidance.

It can be painful for family members to see their loved one suffering and not getting help, especially when treatment is available. As family members we can do things that encourage treatment seeking, and yet we can't force a person to get help. The best we can do is to provide our love and support (which doesn't mean accommodating the OCD). In the end, the decision to seek treatment rests with the OCD sufferer.

We can always leave, I thought, as we opened the door and stepped inside of Lakeview Center. We found ourselves standing in an empty waiting room. Straight ahead was a glass receptionist's window. It was closed. As we walked toward the window, a young woman slid it open.

"What can I do for you?" she asked curtly, looking Dan and me over.

"My son's a student at Carson, and a counselor there recommended we talk with someone here."

"Julie," the receptionist yelled toward another room. "Screening for a possible admission!"

I took a deep breath, and Dan took a seat on a folding chair. Moments later, a middle-aged woman approached us. "Hi, I'm Julie, one of the admitting nurses. Let's go into a consultation room where we can talk."

She led us into a room barely big enough for the three of us, and we sat on metal chairs at a round table. Julie smiled at me kindly. "Why don't you tell me what's going on."

"Well, Dan has OCD and is on various medications. The problem now is he was taking an amphetamine and he became depressed. His doctor took him off it completely, and he's barely been awake for three days. He feels lousy also. I'm worried about his mental and physical health."

While that was quite a condensed version of Dan's story, I figured it'd be enough to work with. Part of me expected her to be incensed as she exclaimed, "The doctor did what?" but instead she showed no emotion while taking notes.

"Would you mind if I spoke with Dan alone?" she asked.

Of course I minded, but I went out to the waiting area anyway. I felt numb. If I'd allowed myself to think about what was unfolding before me, I knew I'd cry. A few minutes later, Julie came out and sat beside me. "I spoke with Dan, and we agree he needs to stay here," she said gently. My eyes welled with tears.

"I know, I know," she said, patting my arm. "We're going to try to get him back on track. Do you know he's been having suicidal thoughts?"

Bam. I felt as if I'd just been hit by a truck, which then landed on my chest. I struggled to catch my breath. "What?" I could not have possibly heard correctly.

"He says he doesn't feel he'd act on them, but he's been having these thoughts over the last few days."

"Could this all be from medication withdrawal?" I asked. I wished I'd still felt numb.

"Maybe," Julie replied, "but he also has urges to cut himself as I'm guessing you know."

"Yes."

"Let's go in and talk with Dan together," she said, "and I'll explain what to expect the next few days."

This was one of those rare times in my life when I felt I was on the sidelines watching a movie unfold. I mean, this couldn't be happening to *me*, or to *Dan*. I told myself I didn't want to watch this movie anymore. *I'm done. I want to leave now.* But a moment later I realized that wasn't possible. I was one of the main characters in the film, and the rest of the story had to be played out. So I stood and followed Julie, with that truck still sitting on my chest.

The conference room door had been left open, presumably so the nearby nurses could watch Dan. I saw him from the back, slumped forward in the chair with his head in his hands.

He's going to be okay. Just pull yourself together. He needs you.

Julie and I walked into the room and sat on either side of him.

"Okay, then," Julie said, addressing both of us. "We have a lot of paperwork to do. The usual stay here is three to five days. Dan will have a physical checkup, attend some group therapy meetings, and meet with a psychiatrist, who will likely adjust his meds. The idea is to get back on track and then follow up with your own health-care providers."

"How will the psychiatrist here make medication changes without knowing what meds Dan's previously been on?" I asked.

"Well, the doctor will contact Dan's psychiatrist, but if you could summarize his medication history yourself, that'd be great," Julie said. "You can bring it back tonight. Visiting hours are from six-thirty to seven-thirty every evening."

"Okay," I said. "Dan and I can go home, get his stuff, and come back this evening."

"No," Julie said. "We're admitting him now so he has to stay."

I was apprehensive about the whole situation so when Julie left to get the paperwork, I whispered to Dan, "You don't have to stay here. We have other options." I had no idea what other options there were, but I said it anyway.

"It's okay, Mom," Dan said. "I want to stay. I need to stay. I can't continue the way I am." He was shaking and looked as if he'd just climbed a mountain, yet he was the voice of reason.

"Okay, honey, if that's what you want." I hoped it was the right decision.

Julie came back in with a stack of papers. "What's the criteria for his discharge?" I asked.

"Well, as soon as the doctor feels Dan is stable and not a danger to himself in any way, he'll discharge him."

"What if that takes longer than five days?" I still imagined them keeping him forever.

"It shouldn't."

She sensed my discomfort and added, "If Dan decides he wants to leave at any point, he has the right to do that. He just has to sign a statement assuming complete responsibility for leaving against medical recommendation."

"Okay, thanks," I said, forcing a smile. We completed the paperwork, and Julie addressed Dan.

"You'll be assigned to the third floor, the adult ward with minimal supervision. There are people in similar situations as you, perhaps suffering from depression or other mental illness. Also substance abusers are on this floor. Clients who might be violent or need more supervision are on the second floor, and the first floor houses our children's ward." She paused. "The first twenty-four hours you're required to wear scrubs. You can put all your belongings in this bag, and you'll get them back when you leave."

It's like being in prison, I thought.

"You also need to give me the laces from your sneakers," Julie said.

No, more like a mental hospital.

Julie turned toward me. "When you come back tonight you can bring Dan loafers, or any shoes without laces. Feel free to bring him clothes and toiletries as well. Here's a list of prohibited items."

"Okay." I felt sad and overwhelmed. "I guess I'll go now. Dad and I will see you in a few hours, honey." I gave him a hug.

"Okay, Mom, see you soon." I could tell he was struggling to stay awake. I turned and left quickly; I didn't want my son to see me crying.

I walked outside and felt the sun on my face. It seemed like days ago that Dan and I were driving around looking for Lakeview. In reality it had been an hour. I got into the car, had a good cry, and called Gary. I had a lot to tell him, since the last thing he knew, we were going to check out Lakeview.

On my way home, I stopped at T.J.Maxx to look for sandals for Dan. Never in a million years would I have imagined myself on this shopping trip, and once again I felt as if I were in the audience watching a movie. The feeling only lasted a moment and then I wandered around the store in a daze, wondering, *What's appropriate footwear for a psychiatric facility?* By the time I arrived home, I was anxious and agitated. "There's so much to do before we go back tonight," I said to Gary. "But first I need to go online." I easily located several websites describing the amphetamine Dan was taking. Not only did they all list the withdrawal symptoms he had experienced, each one also had a variation of the same warning: the abrupt cessation of this medication could cause extreme fatigue as well as severe, even suicidal, depression in adult patients.

WITHDRAWAL FROM STIMULANTS

Psychiatric medications such as the stimulants used to treat ADHD have many effects on the body and the brain, and these effects can be seen quite vividly when a medication is suddenly stopped. As a rule of thumb, the effects of stopping a medication are the opposite of the effects of taking the medication. For example, benzodiaze-

pines (like Xanax) decrease anxiety; stopping a benzodiazepine can lead to increases in anxiety, irritability, and insomnia.[1] Similarly, stopping stimulants such as methylphenidate (Ritalin) and lisdexamfetamine (Vyvanse) can lead to fatigue and depression.[2]

Withdrawal symptoms are likely anytime the body has gotten used to the effects of a substance. In the case of amphetamines, the drugs cause more of the neurotransmitters dopamine and norepinephrine to be released, and also block the reuptake of these neurotransmitters. The result is increased levels of dopamine and norepinephrine, which has a stimulating effect and is probably responsible for the effectiveness of stimulants on ADHD. However, there are "downstream" effects of having more dopamine and norepinephrine available—for example, neurons that are constantly bathed in high levels of a neurotransmitter will tend to decrease the number of receptors for that chemical. Once the medication is stopped and neurotransmitter levels go back down, there are too few neurotransmitter receptors to support normal neuron firing, leading to the painful and potentially dangerous withdrawal symptoms.[3]

Many medications need to be stopped gradually and under a doctor's supervision in order to prevent serious, even grave, withdrawal symptoms. For example, someone who suddenly stops taking a benzodiazepine is at risk not only for feeling lousy but also for potentially lethal withdrawal symptoms like seizures. In the case of stimulants, a gradual taper will decrease the risk for incapacitating fatigue and depression (and the associated risk for suicide). Additionally, a doctor can work with the individual to plan the taper such that it's minimally disruptive for the person's life and can monitor for dangerous side effects, making adjustments to the plan as needed. A carefully planned and supervised schedule can make the withdrawal process as successful as possible.

1. Dell'osso and Lader, "Do Benzodiazepines Still Deserve a Major Role," 16.
2. Efron, Jarman, and Barker, "Side Effects," 663–64.
3. Zhihua Xie and Gregory M. Miller, "A Receptor Mechanism for Methamphetamine Action in Dopamine Transporter Regulation in Brain," *Journal of Pharmacology and Experimental Therapeutics* 330, no. 1 (July 2009): 316.

I felt sick. We'd trusted Dr. Russell, and he'd mistreated our son. There was no way we were going back to him. Anger was brewing inside of me,

but I knew this wasn't the time to dwell on the injustice of the whole situation. Instead, I focused on gathering Dan's clothes and toiletries. I looked at the list of prohibited items Julie had given me. There were the more obvious things, such as razors, knives, scissors, and belts. Also listed were pens, nail files/clippers, lip balm, and baby powder. No electronics were allowed, including cell phones and computers. I needed to remove all the drawstrings from Dan's pajama bottoms and make sure there was no alcohol in his toiletry items. I smiled when I realized there was one benefit to Dan gaining weight. His pants were more likely to stay up without the drawstrings. I put everything into a plastic bag and then realized my mistake and switched to paper. Plastic bags were forbidden.

I then typed out a detailed history of Dan's medications, beginning just about a year earlier, when he began taking an SSRI. I made sure to stress the most recent incident with the amphetamine. "Now that I see it in writing, I can't believe how many meds Dan's been on," I said to Gary.

"Yeah, lots of trial and error," Gary said. Our eyes met and we knew we were thinking the same thing. *Mostly error.*

"I hope Chris is right about Lakeview and they get Dan off some of these drugs," I said. "Who knows how else they're affecting him?"

Before we left for Lakeview, we updated Ava. "Dan's been having a rough time, honey, so he's in the hospital for a few days. He'll be okay. But kids can't visit, not even siblings, so Dad and I will be going to see him the next few nights." Even though Ava understood and seemed okay, I felt bad leaving her alone.

At six o'clock Gary and I took Dan's paper bag and medication history and headed to Lakeview. There were several other cars in the previously empty parking lot when we arrived. I couldn't wait to get up to the third floor to see Dan.

We entered the building through the same door Dan and I had walked through earlier in the day, but this time the waiting room was filled with people. I glanced around and saw an older couple, a couple likely in their forties, a few single adults, and a father with two young children. But children weren't allowed to visit; I wondered why they were there.

Not sure of the procedure, Gary and I stopped at the receptionist's window. This time an older man sat behind the glass. "We're here to see Daniel Singer," I said. The man looked shocked.

"Always use the ID number, never the name," he scolded. "We have privacy issues. Also you need to sign in here with the ID number of the person you're visiting."

I looked through all our papers, found Dan's ID number, and signed in.

"I'll need to look through that bag," the man said, pointing to our paper bag filled with Dan's stuff. He took it behind the counter, removed each item individually, put everything back into the bag, and then gave it back to me.

"Anything else we need to do?" I asked. I was feeling slightly violated.

"You need to empty your pockets and leave everything here until you leave the premises," he said, handing us a small tray. Gary and I were taken off guard. "What a lot of people do," the man said, "is leave everything in their locked cars except their car keys, which they drop off here."

"Thanks, we'll do that," Gary said. We gave Ava a quick call to let her know we wouldn't be accessible for a while and then left everything but the car keys in the car.

"I had no idea it'd be such an ordeal to see Dan," I said, "and we're not even upstairs yet." We went back into the clinic, wondering what would happen next.

At six-thirty exactly, a security guard came into the waiting room, and everyone stood and followed him. No words were spoken. He unlocked a door that led into a corridor with an elevator at the far end. Everyone walked silently behind the guard, and I noticed the children weren't there. The guard unlocked the elevator, and we all squeezed inside. Still, no one was talking. It was an express elevator to the third floor. The doors opened and we followed the group to the left. We ended up in front of what looked like a nurse's station.

There were some people milling around, and the crowd quickly scattered as visitors and patients found each other. I eagerly scanned the area looking for Dan but didn't see him.

"Who are you here to see?" one of the nurses asked kindly.

I wasn't even sure how to answer. Were we there to see Dan or 064? I made a split-second decision. "Dan Singer."

"Oh, Dan. He'll probably be down in a minute. I think he's in his room."

"Well, I have his medication history here," I said, thinking she might be a good person to give it to. Her name tag said, "Linda, Head Nurse."

"Great. Let's take a look at it."

She got to the part where I summarized the events of the past few days. "Yeah, that explains a lot," she said to me, rolling her eyes. This was the first of only two times during Dan's stay at Lakeview that there was any kind of acknowledgment of Dr. Russell's error.

"How's he doing?" I asked Linda.

"Let's look at his chart," she said. "The doctor prescribed ten milligrams of a new stimulant twice a day for Dan in addition to his other medications."

"More medication? I thought the idea was to get him off some of this stuff." I realized there was an edge to my voice, but I was exasperated.

"Why is he on that?" Gary, the calm one, asked.

"I'm guessing to help with his withdrawal symptoms, but I'm not really sure," Linda said. "While you're waiting for Dan, let's check the bag you brought for him."

"They already looked through it downstairs," I said.

"I know," Linda said, "but we have to go through it again and take inventory of everything."

"Okay." I was starting not to care who looked at what, but I didn't need to watch the staff count Dan's underwear. I turned around, hoping to see Dan, and noticed him at the far end of a long corridor. He was walking toward us, I assumed from his room. He was wearing blue scrubs and his laceless sneakers. His head was down as he shuffled along. It seemed to take a long time for him to reach us.

"Hi," he said with a forced smile.

"Hi, honey," I said. We each hugged him.

There was a big lounge area where all the patients and their visitors gathered. Everyone seemed to find their own little niche to have some privacy. The three of us settled into an area in the back left corner of the room. "So are you having fun?" I asked, trying to lighten the mood.

"What should I do about school?" he asked. He was nervous, jittery, and drawn.

"The most important thing is for you to get well, Dan, and then we can figure out school," I said. "Don't worry about it."

"I know," he said, "but we still have to make some decisions."

"Well, I figured I'd call Dr. Moore first thing in the morning, okay?"

"Yeah, that's a good idea," he said. "You know, there's no way I can miss a week of animation classes and still stay in those courses. It's too intense and I'd be too far behind. Not to mention, we're not allowed to miss any classes."

"I'll talk to Dr. Moore about it and get back to you. Whatever will be, will be," I said. I was glad when the talk shifted to sports; Gary and Dan both needed some lighter conversation, and I used the time to try to sort things out.

I knew Dan would have to drop out of his animation classes. He might even have to take a leave of absence from school. That was okay. The focus had to be on his physical and mental health. Everything else was secondary. It struck me how differently I felt now compared to when he was at St. Joseph's. Both situations involved Dan on the verge of not returning to school. Except now we were dealing with a crisis, not a difference in opinion as to how he should live his life.

Dan and Gary were still talking about sports, so I took a good look around the lounge. There was a young man around Dan's age talking quietly with his parents. Was he depressed, suicidal, addicted to drugs? There was no way to know. The older couple I'd seen in the waiting area was visiting with an elderly man. Why was he there? Had his wife of sixty years recently died and left him depressed? The loudest couple in the room was a woman and the man who'd left his two children downstairs. They were laughing and having a grand ol' time. What was she in for?

"Mom," Dan said, jolting me back, "you have to leave in a few minutes, so we thought we'd pay attention to you." He smiled.

"Thanks, I appreciate that." I smiled back. "When I talk to Dr. Moore, is there anything specific you want me to ask her?"

"Please be sure to thank her for all her help, okay?"

"I will."

"And I guess I need to know what my options are."

"Okay. You have any idea what you'd prefer to do?"

"I don't know. I might have to take a leave of absence this semester," he said. "It'd be great to just drop the animation courses and continue with my three other courses, but I don't know if that's allowed." He put his head in his hands. "I'm so sorry about all this."

"Sorry?" Gary said. "Dan, you've nothing to be sorry about. You didn't do anything wrong."

I agreed. "If anything, it's the other way around, honey. We thought you were getting good care, and I'm so sorry you weren't. That will change, I promise you."

Dan didn't seem to hear me. "Did you know the doctor prescribed a different stimulant for me?"

"Yeah, the nurse updated us when we arrived," I said. "Did the doctor say anything we should know about?"

"Not really, but he did some blood work."

Out of the corner of my eye, I noticed some visitors making their way to the elevator. It was 7:28 p.m.

"I guess we have to go," I said to Dan. I really didn't want to leave him there. I picked up the paper bag that now only had a pair of shoes. I had bought two pairs at T.J.Maxx for him to choose from.

"Tomorrow I get to wear real clothes," he said.

"Okay then, we'll see you tomorrow, same time, same place, in real clothes." I gave Dan a hug and he walked with us to the elevator.

"See you tomorrow," Gary said.

The security guard waited as the visitors crammed into the elevator. I waved to Dan as the door closed. Our trek back to the waiting area was exactly the same as earlier, only in reverse: the unlocking of doors, the walk down the long corridor, the silence, and the staying together as a group.

In the waiting room, the two children we'd left an hour ago were sitting quietly, waiting for their dad.

"They were fine," the receptionist said, and the dad thanked him.

Gary and I signed out and were handed our car keys. In the fresh air, away from the innards of Lakeview, this turn of events was hard to grasp. "I can't believe he's in there," I said to Gary.

"I know, it doesn't seem real. He'd been doing so well. I really thought he was on his way."

I nodded. "Me too, but now everything's a mess."

14

IT DIDN'T HAVE TO HAPPEN

I called Dr. Moore the next morning and told her Dan would likely be hospitalized all week. "As long as he gets well," she said. "That's the main thing."

"That's what I told him," I said, "but he's so concerned about school. He knows he'll have to drop his animation courses but was hoping to be able to catch up on the others."

"Yes, he will have to withdraw from his animation major," Dr. Moore said, "but continuing his other classes shouldn't be a problem." While I wasn't surprised that Dr. Moore confirmed Dan would have to drop out of his major, I'd secretly hoped she'd somehow make an exception for him. I knew it was a long shot, so why was I so disappointed? I cast my emotions aside and thanked her, sincerely, for her ongoing support.

Next, Gary and I decided to meet with Dr. Vogel during Dan's regularly scheduled appointment and discuss the situation with him. He knew what was going on, because someone from Lakeview had called and updated him. "Dan had really been doing well there for a while," he said. "I'm sorry this had to happen."

It didn't have to happen, I thought, but didn't say this aloud. I had a lot of pent-up anger but wanted to use our time with Dr. Vogel for Dan's benefit, not mine.

"Tell Dan to call me if he wants," Dr. Vogel said. "I do think he should continue with whatever courses he can. It's important for him to

be productive and have structure as well. And try to relax a little," he said, looking at me. "Lakeview's a good place."

That seemed to be the consensus: Lakeview was a good place. Meanwhile I had no idea what they actually did there. And because Dan was considered an adult, we'd had no contact with any of his doctors. We were, however, promised a meeting with a social worker prior to his discharge. Though we were totally disconnected from what was going on with Dan, I was okay with it. I certainly felt better than when he was at St. Joseph's, since I knew his stay at Lakeview would only be a few days. Still, a small part of me worried they'd want to keep him forever.

That evening, Gary and I arrived at Lakeview a little before six-thirty, and this time we were pros. There were familiar faces in the waiting room as well as some new, shell-shocked ones. We turned over our keys and signed in to visit 064. We hadn't brought anything for Dan so thankfully were able to bypass the degrading bag searches. Our trip to the third floor went exactly the same as the day before, and it would be that way for each subsequent visit.

"How are you feeling, honey?" I asked Dan as the three of us settled into our nook in the lounge area. His tremors were noticeable, his anxiety palpable.

"A little better," he said, "but I'm so hungry all the time."

"I'm guessing that's related to withdrawal," I said.

"Yeah. I got a new medication today."

"You're kidding." I regretted my words immediately.

"What is it?" Gary asked calmly.

"Some kind of sedative," Dan answered. "I take it as needed for anxiety."

"Oh, instead of the benzodiazepine?" I was hopeful.

"I'm not sure," he said. At this point he was taking so many medications he likely couldn't keep them straight.

USE OF BENZODIAZEPINES IN OCD TREATMENT

Obsessive-compulsive disorder often causes a tremendous amount of anxiety, which OCD sufferers understandably want to alleviate. One way to lower anxiety in the short term is to take medication

known as benzodiazepines; examples include familiar drugs such as Xanax (alprazolam), Klonopin (clonazepam), and Ativan (lorazepam). These medications work directly on the neurotransmitter system known as GABA—the same system through which alcohol and barbiturates have their calming effects.[1]

Do benzodiazepines work in the treatment of OCD? The answer based on several rigorous studies is "probably not." While they might take the edge off the anxiety in the short term (just as alcohol might), they don't effectively treat the obsessions or compulsions. The American Psychiatric Association does not recommend benzodiazepines for treating OCD, noting the lack of data showing that they work and the potential for bad side effects.[2] Common side effects of benzodiazepines include drowsiness and memory problems (as noted above) as well as dizziness, clumsiness, and nausea.[3]

Benzodiazepines may also lower the effectiveness of exposure and response prevention (ERP) for OCD. Exposure therapy typically requires some degree of anxiety during the exposures;[4] thus individuals who have their anxiety artificially reduced with drugs such as Xanax or Klonopin might not receive the full benefit of the exposures. When a person starts ERP while on a benzodiazepine, the therapist might work with the prescribing physician as well as the OCD sufferer to time the medication schedule so that the person is not taking the medication just before or after an exposure session.

Despite the reasons not to prescribe benzodiazepines for individuals with OCD, why do many doctors continue to do so? For one thing, the drugs do tend to relieve anxiety, at least in the short term, which might lead doctors to prescribe them for OCD. Additionally, some doctors might not be aware of the latest research in this area. An influential study from 1992 suggested that clonazepam might help individuals with OCD who hadn't responded to an antidepressant.[5] However, later studies found no advantage for clonazepam over placebo; for example, one study found that one of sixteen OCD sufferers improved on clonazepam, versus two of nine on placebo.[6]

The frequent prescribing of ineffective and risky medications for OCD again highlights the importance of finding a doctor who understands OCD and its effective treatment.

1. Dell'osso and Lader, "Do Benzodiazepines Still Deserve a Major Role," 7–8.

2. American Psychiatric Association, "Practice Guideline for the Treatment of Patients with Obsessive-Compulsive Disorder," 2007, http://www.psych.org/psych_pract/treatg/pg/prac_guide.cfm, 53.

3. Dell'osso and Lader, "Do Benzodiazepines Still Deserve a Major Role," 14–15.

4. Michael J. Kozak, Edna B. Foa, and Gail Steketee, "Process and Outcome of Exposure Treatment with Obsessive-Compulsives: Psychophysiological Indicators of Emotional Processing," *Behavior Therapy* 19, no. 2 (1988): 157.

5. Williams A. Hewlett, Sophia Vinogradov, and Stewart W. Agras, "Clomipramine, Clonazepam, and Clonidine Treatment of Obsessive-Compulsive Disorder," *Journal of Clinical Psychopharmacology* 12, no. 6 (1992): 424–25.

6. Eric Hollander, Alicia Kaplan, and Stephen M. Stahl, "A Double-Blind, Placebo-Controlled Trial of Clonazepam in Obsessive-Compulsive Disorder," *World Journal of Biological Psychiatry* 4, no. 1 (2003): 32–33.

He'll be out in a few days. Just stay calm. "Any discussion of when you might come home?" I asked.

"Probably not until Friday."

"Three days away," I said. "How do you feel about that, honey?"

"It's fine. I'm resting a lot, which is what I think I really need. They have some different kinds of therapy too. They're pretty good, though not as great as St. Joseph's. But some stuff's helpful."

"Okay, then, we'll set our sights on Friday," Gary said, "and in the meantime just try to take advantage of whatever you can here."

"How was your meeting with Dr. Vogel yesterday?" Dan asked. His knee was bouncing.

"I'm glad you asked," I said. "He said he'd be happy to talk with you about school if you want."

"No, I don't need to. I already know what he'd say. He'd tell me to continue with my three liberal arts courses since *it's good to have structure and be productive.*"

Gary and I chuckled. "That's *exactly* what he said," I admitted. "I guess you know Dr. Vogel pretty well by now."

"Yeah." Dan was smiling. "We spend a lot of time together. That's what I've been leaning toward doing anyway."

"Great," I said. "You'll still be in school, but we'll be able to focus more on your health. I'm looking into finding a new psychiatrist and a family doctor as well."

"Sounds good." He looked exhausted.

The crowd was beginning to gather near the elevator, so we headed in that direction with Dan.

"Any plans for the rest of the night?" I asked. I had no idea what his options were.

"They have some good snacks before bed," he said. "See you tomorrow."

We waved as the elevator door closed, and then settled into our group routine of leaving Lakeview.

Once Dan decided about his academics, I met with Dr. Moore. She said, "Because he's withdrawing from his major for medical, not academic, reasons, he'll be at the top of the list next year if there are openings."

"If?"

"Yes. There are no guarantees, but every year a few people drop out or fail. And as I said, Dan's at the top of the list." She noticed the concern on my face. "I spoke with Kevin, Dan's animation teacher, who told me Dan's quite talented. He's the type of student we don't want to lose, so just don't worry about next year now."

"Thank you." Of course she was right. Next year was a long time away. We had so many other things to worry about between now and then. And, most importantly, we needed Dan to get well.

At our next evening visit, Gary, Dan, and I agreed it'd be best for Dan to move in with us. Aside from the fact he was worn out and totally drained, both emotionally and physically, he really seemed to need some TLC. He wasn't going to get that from his roommate.

"You know, just keeping track of all your meds is a full-time job," Gary said to Dan.

"Yeah, I'm not up for that," he agreed.

"And with all the driving around you and Mom will be doing to various doctors, it just makes sense for you to stay with us."

Dan and I nodded. The truth was Gary and I were exhausted too, and having Dan with us would make our lives easier. He really couldn't live on his own at this point; he was still in rough shape.

The following morning, we headed over to Lakeview for our meeting with the social worker. Her name was Angela, and she was pleasant, perky, and young. Gary and I met her in the waiting area downstairs.

"I have all Dan's information right here," Angela said, patting her clipboard. A bunch of keys dangled from her wrist. "Let's go to the third-floor conference room so we can sit and talk."

We followed her as she led us on the familiar trek up to the third floor. It was odd to walk the halls and ride the elevator without the usual crowd, and I found myself actually missing them. There was something comforting about moving together in a group. It just took away the loneliness,

knowing we were all in the same situation. Each person on that trek had a loved one who was suffering. I realized how easy it was to find solace among others, even though we'd never even exchanged words.

We greeted Dan upstairs, and the four of us crowded into a small conference room. "One of our main goals today is to make sure continued care is in place for Dan once he leaves Lakeview," Angela said.

Gary and I nodded.

"I can set up appointments with Dan's doctors for you," she offered.

"Well, we'll be switching psychiatrists but haven't found a new one yet," I said. "Do you have any recommendations?"

"Not really. None of the doctors here accept outside patients. May I ask why you want to switch?"

I was surprised at this question, since I'd assumed all of Lakeview knew of the grave injustice done to my son. "Well, the short answer is Dr. Russell took Dan off the amphetamine he was taking cold turkey and then didn't admit that could've caused any of his recent problems."

"Oh dear," she said. "Sounds like he made a big mistake." That was the second and final time at Lakeview there was any acknowledgment an error in judgment had been made. Angela was likely too new and too young to realize you never blame the doctor.

"Let's talk about the meds Dan's on right now," she said.

This will take a while. My pent-up anger was at the surface.

"It says here Ritalin doesn't agree with Dan, right?"

Gary, Dan, and I looked at each other in confusion. "Unless he was given it here and nobody told us or him, he's never taken Ritalin," I said.

"*Hmm*, okay. I guess that's a mistake too." She crossed it off her paper.

Feeling impatient, I brought up the only issue that mattered to me. "Dan's being released tomorrow, right?"

"That's the plan," she said. "The doctor will see Dan this afternoon, and unless he sees a reason not to, he'll discharge him tomorrow." She returned to the medication discussion. "All Dan's meds have been listed here," she said. "It'll help you keep track of them."

I looked at the sheet of paper she laid before us and saw that the latest sedative had been prescribed in addition to the benzodiazepine, not instead, as we'd hoped. He was also taking calcium with vitamin D supplements twice a day. I knew that wasn't a big deal, but it still made the list longer. I remembered my brief conversation with Chris, the counselor at

Carson. He thought the staff at Lakeview would reduce Dan's meds. Instead, he was now poised to go home on more medication than ever. Studying the paper, I saw Dan was taking six different medications, four times a day. A benzodiazepine, an antidepressant, a stimulant, calcium, an atypical antipsychotic, and a sedative were ingested in different combinations at breakfast, lunch, dinner, and bedtime.

"I assume the new stimulant is temporary, to help with withdrawal symptoms?" I said, to nobody in particular.

"I don't think so," Dan said. "It helps me stay awake and focus."

I bet you'd be able to stay awake and focus if you weren't taking so many pills. Yup, add ornery and sarcastic to angry and impatient. I hated he was prescribed so many medications. Of course I knew he had problems, but I just couldn't believe all those meds were needed.

"I also want to talk about the results of Dan's blood work," Angela said. "Everything looks okay, except his triglycerides are very high."

"How high?" Gary asked.

"Well, normal levels are under two hundred. His are in the mid-three hundreds."

"I remember Dr. Russell said his triglycerides were slightly elevated before, but he never rechecked them," I said. "I know this could be a side effect of the atypical antipsychotic."

"Or it could be Dan's diet," Angela said.

"He's a nineteen-year-old vegetarian," I snapped, "and he's never had this problem before." I wanted to tell Angela I'd read about the potentially dangerous side effects of atypical antipsychotics and had spoken with Mark about it as well. But my orneriness had now turned into exhaustion. I felt like Dan looked. I was so drained, I couldn't continue the conversation. There was no point anyway. We needed to get our son out of Lakeview and find some good doctors.

We hugged Dan good-bye and planned to see him that evening for our (hopefully) last visiting hour. Angela took out her array of keys and led Gary and me into the elevator, down to the waiting area, and out of the building. I took a deep breath of fresh air. It always felt good to get outside after being at Lakeview.

On the drive back home Gary said, "How's the doctor hunt going?" He knew I'd been making many calls, trying to find doctors who were accepting new patients and who I thought might be a good fit for Dan. It was proving a more difficult task than I'd anticipated.

"I really liked one, but he's not taking new patients," I said. "Another one has immediate openings, but I didn't get a good feeling from him. Of course you never really know until you get started with them."

"Yeah," Gary said. "It's trial and error all over again, just like with his medication."

"There's one more doctor who seems promising," I said. "I'll call today and see if I can set up an appointment."

That evening we were back at Lakeview for our nightly visit. "You all packed and ready to go home tomorrow?" I asked Dan.

"Now it's not definite," he said. "The doctor wants to see me again tomorrow afternoon before making a final decision."

My heart sank. *They're going to keep him forever.* "Why?"

He shrugged.

I didn't press for more information, but I suspected the delay had to do with Dan's history of cutting himself. Was he having the urge again? They wouldn't release him if they felt he might hurt himself.

"I'll meet with the doctor tomorrow. I think he'll let me out," he said. "I'm so ready to leave now, even though the nighttime snacks are really good." He smiled.

Oh, how I loved that smile. "We have good snacks at home too," I assured him.

We got a call from him the next morning. "I really hope I can leave today. I have way too much time on my hands and there's nothing to do here. I can't believe we're not allowed to have computers or iPods or cell phones. Geez, you'd think this was a mental hospital or something."

I loved when he joked, yet the joking didn't cover the underlying dejection in his voice. "Well, let us know what's going on as soon as you know," I said.

I went about my day, trying not to dwell on the fact Dan might not be released. It was midafternoon when the phone rang.

"You can come and get me."

There was a lilt in his voice. The familiar weight on my chest lifted. "I'll be there within the hour."

Driving to Lakeview, I imagined having to complete lots of paperwork before I could take Dan home, but it turned out it was as quick to get discharged as it was to get admitted. Dan, with his paper bag in hand, was ready to leave when I arrived.

We walked outside and I encouraged him to take some deep breaths. "You've been cooped up for five days," I said. "You need to breathe some outside air."

"Maybe that's why I'm still so tired," he said.

"I don't know, honey. You're also taking so much medication. That could be the reason too. We'll use these next few months to really concentrate on your health."

"Sounds good. Did you find a new psychiatrist yet?"

"Yes, we have an appointment next week," I said. "His name is Dr. Marino, and everything I've read and heard about him is positive. We'll check him out and see what we think, okay?"

"Okay. What about all my stuff at the dorm?"

"We'll move you out in the next few days, as soon as you feel up to it, okay?"

"Sure. And what about going back to classes?" Obviously he had a lot on his mind. He was anxious and overwhelmed, and was tapping the window in the car.

"I spoke with Dr. Moore, and if there's any way you can go back early next week, that'd be great. That still gives you a few more days to rest and recover."

"Too much to think about right now," he said. "I just want to go home and sleep."

"He's so wiped out," I said to Gary later, while Dan slept. "It's hard to imagine him ever having energy again."

My concern increased over the next few days, when all Dan did was eat, sleep, take the pills I handed him, and occasionally listen to music.

"I'm glad he's seeing a new doctor," Gary said. "I think it'll be good to get a fresh perspective on what's going on."

"I think it'll be good to get him off these drugs."

15

SIDE EFFECTS TAKE OVER

On Monday, Dan and I drove to Carson to move him out of his dorm, and I was encouraged that he stayed awake the whole time. "I wonder if my roommate noticed I wasn't here for a week," he said. He was only half joking, since the two of them barely had time to get to know one another. The semester had only been underway for a couple of weeks when Dan crashed. I dropped him off at his room and found a parking spot. As I got out of the car, I noticed a woman riding a bicycle toward me. At first I thought she was a student, but as she got closer it was obvious she was older, maybe in her late thirties.

"Do you live here?" she said.

"No, these are college dorms."

She seemed confused and began to ramble, saying she wanted to live there and whom should she contact to make arrangements? I quickly realized she wasn't making any sense. I studied her face and saw something wasn't right. She wasn't making eye contact with me, and in fact, she now didn't even seem to know I was there. She was mumbling to herself and becoming increasingly agitated.

She's somebody's daughter, I thought. *Is her mother worried sick about her? Does she even have a family? Anyone?*

While I was trying to figure out how I could help her, she pedaled off. I watched her cycle away in a serpentine manner, until she was out of my

sight. I thought of her the whole time we packed up Dan's stuff and still sometimes wonder what happened to her.

The next couple of days were jam-packed. Dan returned to his liberal arts classes and seemed to settle in well. I drove him back and forth, but I was happy to spend that time with him. We also met his new psychiatrist, Dr. Marino, who invited me into his office as well. Score one point for Dr. Marino.

"I see you spent time at St. Joseph's Hospital," he said to Dan while he looked over his health history forms. "What'd you think of it?" He sounded as if he were inquiring about a vacation destination.

"It was great and very helpful," Dan said.

"Yeah, they know their stuff." Dr. Marino was nodding away. "I spent a lot of years affiliated with them, but most of my colleagues aren't there anymore." Dr. Marino appeared to be in his mid-to-late sixties, with kind but tired eyes. He was laid back, as if he had seen it all and nothing could surprise him. "Tell me about the events leading up to your stay at Lakeview," he said to Dan. My son gave me that look that said, *You talk.*

I tried to keep it brief, focusing mainly on all the various medications Dan had been, and was still, taking. When I got to the part about stopping the amphetamine abruptly, Dr. Marino interrupted me. "There's no doubt stopping that way can cause someone to crash the way Dan did." He looked at Dan. "I assume you have ADD?"

Dan shrugged, again looking at me. I said, "I never thought Dan had ADD, though there was some talk of it with his therapist and his last psychiatrist. How do you diagnose it anyway?"

"By doing what we're doing right now," he said. "Talking and getting a history."

After asking us a few questions, Dr. Marino determined Dan did not have ADD. "It's not something you just develop, and your history shows no indication of ADD whatsoever. Also, the drugs you took never helped with your organizational problems. If you had ADD, the meds would've helped."

MISDIAGNOSIS IN OCD

Obsessive-compulsive disorder can look like other conditions and so is misdiagnosed disturbingly often as something else.[1] For example, a person with somewhat bizarre obsessions and compulsions might be misdiagnosed as being psychotic; in fact, the revised OCD criteria in *DSM-5* are intended to clarify the distinction between OCD and psychosis, and to allow for an OCD diagnosis even when the OCD-related beliefs seem delusional.[2] A person's OCD may also resemble the pervasive worries seen in generalized anxiety disorder, or the fear seen in specific phobias. Tragically, some individuals with OCD related to being a pedophile have been treated as though they actually are sexually attracted to children, when in fact they're repulsed by their obsessive fears.

Misdiagnosis in OCD can work in the other direction as well. Some thoughts might be "obsessive" without signaling OCD, such as obsessive interests seen in individuals with autism spectrum disorder,[3] or obsessive thoughts about a love relationship that are not accompanied by compulsive thoughts or behaviors. Similarly, "compulsive" behaviors may not be of the sort that defines OCD, such as compulsive gambling or philandering.

Proper treatment requires appropriate assessment and diagnosis, so the importance of getting the right diagnosis in OCD cannot be overstated. Unfortunately, many OCD sufferers and their families don't know to seek out OCD experts; after all, how can sufferers look for "the right diagnosis" if they've been misdiagnosed and don't know it? Thankfully there are many individuals and organizations that are working to raise awareness about OCD. The Internet has been helpful in this regard, bringing information about OCD to countless people who need it. Getting the right diagnosis can be a life-changing, and even life-saving, experience.

1. Spengler and Jacobi, "Assessment and Treatment," 95.
2. American Psychiatric Association, *DSM-5*, 241.
3. American Psychiatric Association, *DSM-5*, 50.

I said to Dr. Marino, "When I told Dr. Russell I felt strongly Dan didn't have ADD, he said the amphetamine would also enhance the other meds he was taking."

Obviously perturbed yet trying not to show it, Dr. Marino rested his head in his hands. "The only reason these medications should be prescribed is to treat ADD or ADHD. I see he's on a different stimulant now. We need to wean him off it."

I, on the other hand, couldn't hide my delight. "Yes, he's on so many drugs. Anything else you can stop?"

"Well, I do have concerns about him taking an atypical antipsychotic for an extended period of time," he said. "Over the next couple of weeks, we'll wean him off that also, with the possibility of having to go back on it, depending on how he's feeling."

I wanted to leap over his desk and give him a hug. My excitement was quickly tempered when I remembered how pleased I'd initially been with Dr. Russell too. One of the many lessons I'd learned on this journey was if something doesn't sit right, question it until you're satisfied. But for now, everything was sitting great. Dan was getting off some of his medications, and Dr. Marino wasn't done.

"Now, this benzodiazepine can be addictive," he said to Dan. "Why don't you stay on one per day for now, but hopefully we'll be able to get you off those soon." Dan nodded, and Dr. Marino said to me, "Eventually I'd just like to see Dan on his antidepressant."

"That sounds great to me." I was almost giddy.

I told Dr. Marino about Dan's high triglycerides, and he recommended he see Dr. Amy Turco, an internist. "You won't find a more thorough doctor anywhere. I suggest seeing her as soon as possible."

I told him I'd call her later that day. We planned to see Dr. Marino again in three weeks, earlier if there were problems. As we did after meeting each new doctor, Dan and I had the "so what'd you think?" conversation. We both liked Dr. Marino, though I guessed for different reasons.

"I like him because he's getting you off a lot of the meds you might not need," I said.

"Yeah," Dan said, and then proceeded to fall asleep in the car. He was still so worn out. I glanced at my sleeping son and guessed the reason he liked Dr. Marino was because he hadn't pestered him with the same questions every other doctor had.

Three days later I sat in the waiting room while Dan met with Dr. Turco. He wanted to see her alone. "I'm a big boy now," he said, "and I can go into the doctor's office without my mommy." His joking around warmed my heart, and I was fine with not being included. It was just a routine checkup, and I assumed Dr. Turco would also address the triglyceride issue. While it would've been nice to meet her, I was just as happy to sit in a comfortable chair and read a magazine for a change.

The appointment took longer than I'd anticipated, and when I saw Dan at the checkout station, I motioned for him to hurry so he wouldn't be late for his class. "I need a consult with another doctor," he said, waving a piece of paper.

"Oh, okay." I walked over to him. "Well, we'll schedule it later. We're in a rush now."

"Mom." Dan was shaking his head. "You don't understand. I have to go right now." He looked serious.

"What are you talking about?"

"I need to see this doctor right away. He's a cardiologist."

He must've noticed the color drain from my face because he added, "It's okay. I'm going to be all right."

I turned toward the nurse sitting behind the glass window. "What's going on?" I said.

"Dr. Stein can see Dan right now," she said. "His office is only ten minutes from here."

"Okay, Dan, let's go," I said to him. I didn't press for more information. Why bother? It would come soon enough, I knew. I felt that familiar numbness, that pressure on my chest.

On the way to Dr. Stein's office, Dan updated me. "I told Dr. Turco about the palpitations I sometimes have, so she did an EKG and said I might have pericarditis and I should see a cardiologist. She's a great doctor; I really like her a lot."

"That's good, honey," I said. I'd been so surprised by this new development that we hadn't had the usual "so what do you think" portion of our conversation.

"Dr. Turco say anything else about your heart?" I said.

"Just that I should take ibuprofen, and it shouldn't cause permanent damage. I don't know. She said the cardiologist would figure it all out."

"Okay." I forced myself to breathe. "Let's see what this Dr. Stein has to say."

"Oh, I gained another six pounds since I was weighed at Lakeview," he said. I think he was trying to keep both our minds off this new heart issue.

"Gee, that was only a week and a half ago." I wasn't able to hide my concern. I was beginning to feel as if Dan was a ticking time bomb; in my mind, he couldn't get off all his meds fast enough. Even though I didn't know how he'd be affected mentally, I had a hunch he'd be no worse off. And I certainly knew they were hurting him physically.

"Oh yeah, she also gave me a prescription for niacin to help reduce my triglycerides. They're really high."

I nodded. Even though I knew niacin and ibuprofen were necessary additions to his regimen, I still wanted fewer pills, not more. I didn't think any more would fit into his pill organizer.

We had no problem finding Dr. Stein's office, which was located on a main street, much easier than Lakeview Center. "We've been expecting you," the receptionist said as she handed Dan a pile of forms to complete. We sat down in the comfortable chairs, and I surveyed the room while Dan filled out the forms. There were five other patients waiting, all elderly, and all staring at Dan.

"Mom," Dan said, "I need help listing all my medications."

Of course he did. I couldn't remember them myself but kept a list in my purse. I'd just finished squeezing the last med onto the form when Dan was called in, ahead of all the patients who'd been waiting longer. I didn't even ask if it was okay if I came along; I just followed him into the exam room.

"Take off your shirt and put on this gown," the nurse instructed. "Dr. Stein will be right in." Dan barely had time to change before the doctor entered.

"I'm Dr. Stein," he said, extending his hand toward Dan and then me. He was tall and thin and appeared to be in his fifties. What I noticed most about him was how rushed and pressured he seemed. A young woman not much older than Dan trailed behind him. "This is Dr. Kay, a resident in cardiology. Would you mind if she sat in on your exam?" He spoke directly to Dan.

"I guess not," Dan said.

Dr. Stein got right down to business. "Would you mind leaving the room so I can examine Dan privately?" he asked me.

"Of course not," I said, though I hated to leave. I waited right outside the closed door, annoyed Dr. Stein seemed so rushed. Then I remembered he fit Dan into his busy schedule, and I felt a little guilty. Maybe we were the reason he was harried.

While I was still pondering this, Dr. Stein came out of the exam room and closed the door behind him. "Dan has a lot of scars on his arms. Are they from self-injury?"

"Yes," I said, though I desperately wished I could've answered differently.

"Okay, come back in now so I can talk with both of you." He held the door open for me, and I gave Dan a weak smile as I entered.

Dr. Stein talked quickly, as if he were on one of those commercials where you have to say everything you need to in a minute. "Dan has tachycardia, a fast heart rate. He may have had pericarditis recently, but I don't think he does now. Just to be safe, we'll schedule an echocardiogram, a Holter monitor, and a stress test. Questions?"

I felt as if I needed to speak right away or he'd leave the room. "Yes. I assume the irregularities on Dan's EKG and the tachycardia are caused by his medications?"

"Let's take a look at what meds he's taking," Dr. Stein said, clearly not pleased with the extra time it'd take. He looked at the forms we'd just filled out. At the same time, Dr. Kay pulled out a pocket reference guide. "Check on these," he said to her, giving her the list of his meds. Then he logged onto his computer, saying, "This might be quicker," which it was. "Yeah, Dan's symptoms are likely from the atypical antipsychotic, or perhaps the antidepressant. It's possible there might be some lingering effects from the amphetamines as well."

He saw the worry on my face.

"But if he needs the meds, he needs the meds," he said. "Things will probably return to normal whenever he stops taking these medications."

"Probably?"

"There are no guarantees."

My heart felt heavy; this was so not acceptable. I looked at Dan, who seemed unfazed by this information.

"Okay then, if there are no other questions, schedule those tests on your way out," he said, and scurried out the door, Dr. Kay in tow, before we even had a chance to say good-bye.

On the way home, Dan's biggest concern was that he missed a class and an exam. My concern, of course, was his health. Looking at his haggard face and limp body, I could almost see his exhaustion. I think all his health problems from the past year or so had finally overtaken him. I desperately wanted my son back, in good health.

Back at the condo, I updated Gary on the day's events. Picking up Dan's medication organizer, stuffed with colorful pills, I felt queasy. "I can't bear to give him another one of these pills, knowing they're affecting his heart, triglycerides, weight, and goodness knows what else."

Gary nodded. "Why not call Dr. Marino?" He was obviously concerned, and I took his advice. Dr. Marino had planned to wean Dan off the atypical antipsychotic in the next couple of weeks anyway, so I asked about stopping the drug right away. After hearing about our day, he agreed Dan should discontinue that medication immediately.

"Just keep a close eye on him," Dr. Marino said.

We were practically tripping over each other in our small condo, so watching Dan closely would be easy. While I was pleased about reducing his meds, I'd certainly learned some lessons from everything he'd just gone through. I checked online to make sure stopping the atypical antipsychotic abruptly was acceptable protocol, and seeing that it was, I happily deposited the medication into the big plastic bag that held so many others.

As the days passed, it was clear Dan was no worse off without the atypical antipsychotic. But he was no better either and now had no desire to do anything. "I have to nag him about every little thing, even shaving," I told Gary. "It's so frustrating."

"I know," he said. "When he was at Lakeview Center, he talked about using this time to get his life back together. Remember he was going to connect with friends, exercise, and maybe even look for a part-time job? He hasn't done any of those things. He goes to classes, sleeps, and occasionally listens to music. That's it."

I tried to talk with Dan about his lack of motivation, but our conversations didn't get very far. "Do you think it's related to your OCD?" I asked him.

"Well, my OCD's pretty much nonexistent right now," he said.

Wow! Now *that* was a sentence I never expected to hear. While this was wonderful news, it made his behavior even more frustrating. It was time to meet with Dr. Vogel.

16

A TURNING POINT

The three of us filed into Dr. Vogel's office. I always felt comfortable and safe there, and did this time as well. "So what's going on?" the doctor said, looking at me.

"Well, I know it's been a rough few weeks for Dan and he's still adjusting to being off two of his meds, but he has no motivation for anything. All of his get up and go has got up and went."

Gary spoke. "Maybe Dan's physical issues are contributing to how he's acting? He's a good thirty-five pounds over his normal weight. He still has tremors and tachycardia. My guess is these are contributing factors to his lack of energy and motivation."

"I just don't know how to act toward him at this point," I said. I felt awkward expressing these thoughts with Dan sitting next to me.

"What do you mean?" Dr. Vogel said.

"Well, with everything he's been through the past year or so," I said, "I've gotten used to treating him with lots of patience and understanding, without expecting much from him. But now I have to admit, I just feel like yelling and screaming at him because his lack of motivation is so frustrating. He says his OCD is practically nonexistent, yet he seems to have no desire to do anything. Even the few times his friends have contacted him, he's gone out of his way to avoid them."

"You bring up an interesting point," Dr. Vogel said, "regarding how Dan should be treated." He looked at Dan. "We all know you've been

through a lot, and obviously there are still many issues that need address-ing. But what do you think about what your mother is saying? Do you feel you need to be handled with kid gloves, or is it okay for her to get annoyed with you and push you a little?"

How odd to ask a question like that, I thought. *Who'd want to get yelled at?*

Dan sat quietly for a moment before speaking. "Yeah, I think she really needs to push me. That's what I need now."

While I was surprised at his answer, I was even more taken aback by the fact it had never even crossed my mind to ask him that very question myself. Why hadn't I questioned my son about how he wanted to be treated? If he had a broken arm, or the flu, I would've asked what he needed to feel better. Why hadn't it occurred to me that the person who might just know what's best for Dan was Dan? In the past, he'd always been honest about what he needed. He'd even made sure we didn't enable him when he was working on exposure and response prevention therapy at home. Yet while I wracked my brain trying to figure out how I could help my son, I never once asked him.

"I'm sorry I never asked you what you needed, honey," I said. "Pre-pare to be nagged."

We smiled at each other. Dan had been doing so poorly, I hadn't bugged him about taking out the trash or helping with other chores. Without realizing it, I'd likely contributed to his lethargy. What he wanted, and what he needed, was to be treated as normally as possible. Pampering him did none of us any good, and now that I knew that, I was prepared to stop.

The atmosphere back at the condo gradually improved; everything felt a little lighter. Dan helped out a bit more with chores, but everyone, including me, hated my nagging, which often didn't even work. Still, Dan had little oomph for anything. For example, he'd missed the deadline to apply for on-campus housing for the next school year. "Yeah, whatever, I'll just live with you guys instead," he'd said. "I don't really care."

Gary and I had recently decided to remain in Bridgeville for a few more years. Ava's school was working out well, and while we were wholeheartedly hoping Dan wouldn't need us, we wanted to be there in case he did.

The next few weeks brought a whirlwind of activity, mostly revolving around doctors and medical tests. Dan had an echocardiogram, a stress

test, and a twenty-four-hour Holter monitor. There were some results that warranted more tests, at which point it was determined Dan's heart was okay. He didn't have pericarditis, or if he had, it had cleared up. This was all good news, except that the tachycardia remained.

His blood work revealed his triglycerides had plummeted from 341 to 178 in just two weeks. These results were attributed to his stopping the atypical antipsychotic and starting the niacin, which he was now able to discontinue. Dr. Turco's nurse also noted Dan was losing weight. "Keep up whatever diet and exercise program you've adopted," she said. "It's working."

Dan and I chuckled, since he was neither dieting nor exercising. He'd merely stopped taking the drugs that had caused the weight gain to begin with. In the weeks and months to come, his weight would return to normal with no effort on his part.

With Dan now completely off stimulants and the atypical antipsychotic, Dr. Marino continued down the list. "Let's stop this sedative and only take one benzodiazepine as needed," he directed. This was relatively easy to do, and so these medications joined the pile in the big plastic bag stored in the closet. It was around this time I noticed his hand tremors, while not gone, were markedly decreased. Gary had noticed also.

Slowly but surely, other positive signs emerged as Dan became more interested and engaged in the outside world. But he was still actively avoiding his friends and had turned down multiple invitations from them. I happened to be near him while he was on his laptop one afternoon. I heard the familiar *bada boomp* of an instant message and asked him who it was.

"Oh, I'm just ignoring it. It's a friend inviting me to go for ice cream with a bunch of people."

"Dan," I said, losing my patience, "*go!* Get out of the house. I bet you'd have a great time."

"Are you trying to get rid of me?" he said. He was actually grinning.

"Absolutely." And I wasn't joking.

"I don't know." He was obviously hesitant. "Maybe I'll go." Several more *bada boomps* later he headed out the door. I realized at that moment I'd just witnessed a turning point in his recovery, and a sense of peacefulness wafted over me. This was really happening.

He returned home several hours later. "It was great hanging out with my friends," he said. "How come you never suggested that before?"

I pretended to hit him over the head, while inwardly a feeling of joy was brewing. This was the beginning. More glimpses of the real Dan were revealed almost daily, and as the weeks went by, his sluggishness began to dissipate also.

"Have you noticed Dan's been going for long walks every day?" I asked Gary.

"Yup," he said. "And he's even come to the gym with me a few times. He says he feels so much healthier when he exercises and asked why we didn't suggest it sooner." Again, this was a joke, since we'd been nagging him to do all these things for months.

There was a new air of happiness in the condo. It wasn't until the heaviness lifted that I began to realize what a toll the past year had taken on our family. For the first time in a long time, I let myself truly feel my emotions, and I hugged Gary and cried. "When Dan was in such bad shape last year I really thought we'd lost him," I said. "And now, listen."

We stood silently for a moment, and heard Dan downstairs, laughing heartily at something. It didn't matter what. "Every time I hear that laugh," I said, "a wave of gratitude engulfs me."

The only medication left in Dan's pill organizer was the antidepressant, and he was doing great on it, just as Dr. Marino had hoped. Unfortunately his tachycardia remained, and the doctor was concerned. "This medication must be the cause of Dan's tachycardia," he said. "I'd like to wean him off it completely and see his heart rate return to normal. This will take a while. Then we'll try to find another medication without these side effects to keep his OCD under control."

ARE LONG-TERM MEDICATIONS ALWAYS NECESSARY IN OCD TREATMENT?

Many OCD sufferers take medications, usually SSRIs, as part of their recovery. How long does a person need to stay on medication once their OCD is in remission? The question is an important one—nobody wants to stay on medication longer than necessary, or risk a return of OCD by discontinuing medication too soon.

Several studies have shown high rates of relapse when medication is stopped, leading some experts to advise lifelong drug treatment for OCD as the "safest option." Current treatment guidelines by the American Psychiatric Association suggest continuing medication treatment for one to two years after the person has recovered.[1] If a person wants to stop medication after that period of time they suggest a slow taper of the medication, with careful observation for any return of symptoms.

Existing evidence suggests that exposure and response prevention (ERP) protects a person from relapse. For example, a large multisite trial compared the relapse rates after treatment with medication alone to treatment with ERP (with or without medication). Twelve weeks after treatment ended, 45 percent of those who got only medication had relapsed, versus 12 percent of those who had received ERP.[2] Thus ERP seems to have a protective effect when medication is withdrawn.

Additional studies are underway to further develop guidelines for long-term management of OCD. One such study is being conducted at Columbia University and the University of Pennsylvania. Researchers are comparing outcomes for patients on OCD medication who also receive ERP and have a good treatment response. After completing ERP, half of the participants will be tapered off their medication and the other half will continue to take medication; all patients will receive monthly sessions of ERP. The goal is to determine if medication can be discontinued for those who "achieve wellness" with ERP.[3]

This study and others are addressing crucial questions about how to safely stop medication for OCD once a person has recovered. The hope is that more individuals will be able to avoid the troublesome side effects that accompany medication, while continuing to enjoy a good quality of life.

1. Koran et al., "Practice Guideline," 13.
2. Ibid., 60.
3. New York State Psychiatric Institute, "Attaining and Maintaining Wellness in Obsessive-Compulsive Disorder," ClinicalTrials.gov, U.S. National Institutes of Health, last updated July 26, 2014, https://clinicaltrials.gov/ct2/show/NCT01686087.

While I was usually thrilled with any reduction in Dan's medication, I was hesitant about this one. He was doing so well; I hated to change anything. And the thought of having to start the whole process of trial and error with meds again was discouraging, to say the least. But I understood a fast heart rate over a prolonged time wasn't good either. He needed to come off the medication.

The antidepressant he was taking is notorious for being difficult to stop, and Dan was instructed to wean off it slowly. As the days turned into weeks, we saw even more positive changes in him.

"I'm really surprised," I said to Gary, "but believe me, I'm not complaining."

"It's pretty amazing," Gary said. "Did you know yesterday Dan went on to the Carson website to apply for some part-time jobs?"

I nodded. "As each drug has been withdrawn, it's almost as if another layer of crud has been chiseled off him. And now finally, the real Dan isn't covered up anymore."

"I know," Gary said. "It's almost too good to be true. He's happier and more relaxed than I've seen him in ages."

By the time Dan was almost completely weaned off that last medication, he was livelier, sharper, and more social than ever. He'd sing his way out the door on his way to school, often announcing he'd be home late because he was meeting friends. And then one day, out of the blue, he announced, "I feel great. I'm making a comeback." He proceeded to flash that amazing smile that once again lit up the room.

His comeback included a last-ditch effort to get on-campus housing. "There's a meeting tonight for kids still looking for rooms, so I'll be home late," he announced.

When he left, Gary chuckled. "I bet he woke up this morning in a panic, thinking, 'Oh my God, I'm living with my parents next year.'"

I laughed. "And now he finally has the desire and energy to get out of here."

I realized, in some convoluted way, Dan's stay at Lakeview Center had been a blessing in disguise: the impetus to change our course of action. He was almost medication free now and feeling better than ever. While we'd never really know if any of the drugs he took throughout his ordeal ever helped him, we did know, in the end at least, they hurt him. I was so thankful all those bottles of pills were now where they belonged: in that plastic bag on the floor of my closet.

17

HOPE

"Mom, my head's killing me," Dan said. He sounded scared. I'd just come home from grocery shopping to find him lying on the couch holding his head. "It feels like zaps of electricity, and I'm really dizzy too."

It only took a few seconds for me to realize what was happening. "You're having withdrawal symptoms from the antidepressant. It makes sense. You've been totally off it for a few days."

I immediately called Dr. Marino, who said Dan should go back on a low dose of the medication. An hour later he was fine. In order to avoid these brain zaps, as they're called, I set up a pharmacy on our kitchen table. Every few days, I'd open several capsules, push the tiny beads to one side with a toothpick, count them, and then refill the capsules by two fewer beads. Several days later I'd do the same thing again, only leaving out four beads, then six, and then eight. I always counted the beads, since often there'd be differing amounts in each capsule, and we needed to be precise. This routine went on for weeks, until there were only a few beads left in the capsules and finally Dan was weaned off the medication. The process was tedious and time consuming, and I often found myself mulling over Dan's experiences with medication as I maneuvered the tiny beads. The same questions repeatedly haunted me. When did all these pills stop helping and start hurting him? Indeed, did any of them actually ever benefit him? In my opinion, he had been overmedicated as well as

improperly medicated. No wonder he improved as much as he did once he was off all the medications.

While many people with obsessive-compulsive disorder seem to be helped by medication, things were not so clear cut for Dan. Instead we were left with some tough questions with no definitive answers. My son's journey through severe OCD was not a well-conducted experiment with easy-to-analyze results. We had no medication-free "control Dan" along-side our drugged one.

Looking back, it was hard to believe we'd allowed Dan to be so heavily medicated. But I understood how it happened. We were desperate, searching for that promised yet elusive "right combination" of meds to fix our son. And we trusted the doctors. Yet things were not always as they appeared. When Dan was taking so many pills and still doing poorly, I thought, *If he's in such bad shape now, I hate to think what he'd be like without his medication.* It had never occurred to me that maybe he was in such bad shape *because* of the meds.

And what about all those side effects? Dan's doctors were aware of them, yet their concern seemed minimal at best. When I asked Dr. Russell if Dan's depression could stem from his medication, he cocked his head and gave me a patronizing look that said, *Poor woman, stop being in denial over your son's illness.*

"As you know, it's always trial and error when switching medications," Dr. Marino said when we settled in for Dan's next appointment. He was off everything, and his tachycardia was going in the right direction; it was time to try something new.

I couldn't keep my mouth shut. "Dan's doing great now. Why bother with meds when he's doing so well without anything? How would we even know what's working if he has no symptoms? Dan himself has said his OCD is now practically nonexistent."

Dr. Marino looked thoughtful as he repeatedly tapped his pen on his desk. "*Hmm,* I guess there's no harm in watchful waiting for now. Once all the meds are totally out of his system we can reevaluate. I mean, he'll have to be on *something.*" He peered over his glasses and looked at Dan. "How do you feel now that you're off all meds?"

"I really don't notice much difference."

I was shocked by his answer. "Really, Dan?" I said. "Because there's a huge difference in how you're acting."

"How so?" Dr. Marino asked.

"To begin with, he sings around the house all the time now," I said, realizing I was probably embarrassing Dan. "He's more motivated, and he's active, alert, and happy."

I could've continued, but Dr. Marino interrupted me. "I get the picture," he said. The ordinarily serious doctor was smiling.

I was puzzled Dan couldn't see what was so obvious to his family and friends. Could he have been in such a fog on all those meds it was hard for him to remember how he felt? Perhaps that was a good thing. In any case, we left Dr. Marino's office without a prescription, and I couldn't have been happier.

"So how many kids you bringing for Thanksgiving?" Dan was over for a rare visit, since he was always so busy with school and friends. It was the fall of his senior year at Carson, two and a half years after we'd walked out of Dr. Marino's office. As it turned out, the "watchful waiting" went on for quite some time, and we never needed to go back to Dr. Marino. He himself got tired of waiting and retired. Dan was winding down his twice-monthly exposure and response prevention (ERP) therapy sessions with Dr. Vogel. Though he had been quickly reinstated into the animation program, we knew Dan would have to spend five, not four, years at Carson because of the sequential nature of his major. He was now in the home stretch of a long and successful college career.

RECOVERING FROM OCD: WHEN NORMAL FEELS WEIRDLY NORMAL

Many individuals with OCD live with their symptoms for so long that the obsessions and compulsions begin to feel normal. For example, washing one's hands for three minutes, checking the stove five times, or counting to a certain number all feel expected and familiar.

In the process of exposure and response prevention (ERP), OCD sufferers are required to do things that feel abnormal, even wrong. They may be asked to wash their hands "the wrong way," to not check the stove as they've grown accustomed to, or to count to the "wrong" number. This feeling of "wrongness" tends to cause a lot of distress; with continued ERP practice, the distress diminishes.

Some individuals with OCD experience a paradoxical form of anxiety once their obsessions and rituals are under control. If it gets easy to skip hand washing, stove checking, counting, or any other ritual, it's not uncommon for these individuals to suddenly feel as if something is missing. They might have gotten so used to practicing doing things "the wrong way" in exposure therapy that it feels strange for normal behavior *not* to feel strange. After walking away from the stove without rituals and without anxiety, individuals might have a thought such as, "Wait—it *can't* be that easy."

OCD sufferers might even worry about no longer being plagued by obsessions—that is, they might develop obsessions about not having the old obsessions. For example, a woman might worry that she will become cavalier in her actions since obsessive worries are no longer compelling her to be extremely cautious.

These fears are not unusual and in fact are quite understandable—how strange it must feel for normal behavior to finally feel normal! If the positive changes cause anxiety or obsessions, the best approach is to keep doing the same thing: let it feel weird to do normal behavior, and do it anyway. As with any obsessive thought, the instruction is to face it head-on without rituals or avoidance. Over time the fear should go down, and the person can continue to enjoy the extra time and freedom that come from conquering OCD.

"I'm guessing ten or so. Is that too many?" Dan said, regarding my inquiry about friends coming for Thanksgiving. We'd become the go-to home for major holidays, since most of Dan's friends lived out of state. I liked them all and loved spending time with them. There was always plenty of laughter and lots of energy, and of course seeing my son in the middle of it all always flooded me with gratitude.

"No, that's fine, honey. We'll just squish in, no problem."

It turned out this Thanksgiving was more subdued than usual, since these senior animation students, my son included, were exhausted and

stressed. There was lots of talk, and worry, over their thesis films, which were due in a month. "Every year they fail a few students without warning, and so we're all nervous wrecks," Dan said. His friends nodded. "And if you fail, you need to repeat senior year, or just not graduate."

"Without warning?" I said. "That doesn't make any sense. How, and why, would they do that? Don't you get feedback? Wouldn't you have an idea how you're doing?"

"You'd think so but no," Dan said. "They do it to scare us, to keep us on our toes, so we work hard to make the best movie possible." All I knew about Dan's film was that it was unconventional, which didn't surprise me.

"I think we're all in pretty good shape, though," his friend Amy said. Everyone nodded again and dug into their pumpkin pie. While I knew he and his friends were on top of things, I assumed they'd gotten it wrong. There *had* to be some sort of warning or notice given if you were in danger of not graduating.

The e-mail from Dan arrived right before winter break. He apologized for letting us down once again. He had indeed failed, apparently for neglecting to include certain elements in his movie. He was shocked, angry, hurt, and depressed. I was all those things too. Gary and I replied, telling him he, in fact, had *never* let us down, and we were going to fight this to the bitter end. We met that afternoon to discuss our plan. My biggest worry was that this stressful turn of events might cause Dan to relapse.

"I'm so sorry," Dan kept saying. "I've been so much trouble." While apologizing was a compulsion for Dan when his OCD was bad, that didn't seem to be the case here. He was genuinely sorry, and that broke my heart.

"Dan, you have nothing to feel sorry about. You've done nothing wrong. If anything, we should be apologizing to you, for all the mistreatment you've endured over these past few years. We're your parents, and we're supposed to take good care of you. You're not trouble. You're the best son in the world, and we'd do anything for you."

"Thanks, Mom." He hugged me, a little longer than usual.

I couldn't believe Carson College, the school that had kept Dan going when his OCD was severe, the place that had become like a second home to him, had betrayed him. "I think we're fighting a losing battle here, Mom," Dan said. "Nobody crosses the department head, Joe Sawyer, and he never changes his mind."

"We'll see about that." I was on a mission. My son had been wronged, and I wasn't about to let five years of hard work, and college tuition, go to waste. I sent Mr. Sawyer an e-mail detailing some of Dan's struggles, and we arranged a meeting with me, Dan, Gary, Amanda (Dan's animation teacher, who totally supported him), and Joe Sawyer.

Joe was a tall, dark, and handsome man, but the minute he opened his mouth, he became one of the most unappealing people I'd ever met. "Lots of kids have disabilities, and Dan won't get any special considerations. That's it in a nutshell," he said, leaning back in his swivel chair with his hands behind his head. You couldn't talk to this man, and even my mild-mannered son was close to exploding. It turned out Dan knew of another student who *had* been forewarned about failing, and Mr. Sawyer said that was because he was a slacker, not because of the quality of his work. Huh? So because Dan was a conscientious student, he got no warning? We also discovered not giving students proper feedback *was* against the school's grading policy, but somehow this didn't seem to matter.

Knowing we'd get nowhere with Mr. Sawyer, I set up meetings with anyone at the school who would listen to us. We met with Dr. Moore, and with Dan's new academic advisor as well. We connected with Marilyn Lambert, the head of Academic Support Services who'd been helpful to Dan in the past. Dan met with her at the beginning of every semester to assess his needs, which were minimal. He'd had some issues with balancing details within the big picture, which is common for those with OCD, and his teachers were expected to give him regular feedback. We even met with the president of the college, who informed us we were fighting an "uphill battle."

"Don't you have the final say?" I asked.

"No, that would be the dean of Academic Affairs, Dr. Tiffany Wales, and right now she's out with the flu."

Each morning for the next three days Dan and I arrived at Carson early, hoping to meet with Tiffany. She finally returned to work and agreed to see us right away. I was surprised to meet an attractive woman in her sixties, with kind eyes. With a name like Tiffany, I'd imagined her

much younger. As soon as our eyes met, I had hope. She'd been through something. I could tell. I wasn't sure what, but there was a gentleness about her and compassion within her.

"Why don't you tell me what's been going on, Dan?" she asked. As difficult as it was, I sat there quietly. I couldn't have been more proud of my son. Composed and confident, he explained he knew his movie was unusual, but he'd had a vision of what he wanted to do. He'd had the support of his teacher and felt he was on track with it. Only because he was so comfortable at Carson did he feel he could take a risk, and isn't that what creativity is all about? All he wanted was a chance to fix what they felt was wrong. Just a chance. That's all he asked for. Not once did he bring up the fact he had OCD.

"I have to tell you, Dan, it's been a pleasure to meet you. In my job, I rarely have direct contact with students, and if they're all like you, I'd say we're a lucky school."

Hope, there's hope.

"Anything you'd like to add?" Dr. Wales turned to me.

She'd already given us so much of her time, so I kept it short. I told her about Dan's OCD, his stay at St. Joseph's, his problems with medication, and his stay at Lakeview. "Being at Carson is a dream come true for Dan, and he's worked so hard toward recovery, always with the goal of returning to school." For the first time since he failed, I felt someone was truly listening to us, not just going through the motions.

"Wow, Dan, you've been through so much." At first I thought I'd imagined it, but I hadn't. There were tears in her eyes.

"The other thing I'd like to mention," I said, "is this isn't a case of a student who's just been squeaking by all these years and is now hoping to graduate. Dan has maintained his academic scholarship the entire time he's been at Carson and has also consistently had his work chosen for 'The Best of Carson' juried shows. And now, after five years, he can't graduate? That's not right." Now I was the one tearing up.

Dr. Wales was taking notes. "There's a judicial process that needs to be followed, and I'll call you Friday with a decision." The three of us walked outside together, and she continued to chat with Dan about school.

"Thank you for taking the time to really listen to me," he said. "That means a lot." So he'd felt it too. She really cared.

Friday was only two days away, though it felt as if we waited forever. Dr. Wales called in the evening to inform Dan a decision wouldn't be final until Monday morning. They were still conferring with Mr. Sawyer. On Monday morning, Dan got the call. He had two weeks to make the necessary changes to his film, and then it would be reevaluated.

He worked day and night during his winter break, resubmitted the movie, and passed.

18

TRIUMPH OVER OCD

"Everybody ready?" Gary asked. He, Ava, my mother, and I piled into our car and headed to the Class of 2012 Senior Animation Show, where all the graduates' movies would be showcased. I'd been to this event once before, for the Class of 2008. During my long stay in the old motel four years earlier, Dan had insisted on going, even though it was distressing for him to be in crowds, or even interact with his friends. He'd stuck close to me that whole night, visibly anxious and apprehensive. At the time, I had trouble focusing on the movies because I was too worried about how Dan was going to eat the next day. And it was painful for me to watch, knowing there was little chance I'd ever see my son's work on that screen. At point his dream of becoming an animator was way beyond reach.

And here we were, about to enter that same auditorium. Dan wasn't clinging to me this time; he was on the other side of the big hall, sitting with his girlfriend and laughing with his friends. Sure, he was nervous too, as were they all, anticipating the debut of their films in front of almost one thousand people.

While the atmosphere was one of fun and excitement, for me it was an experience of profound gratitude and emotion—almost surreal. *He made it. We're here.* He'd been on a journey few could imagine and, through sheer determination (and exposure and response prevention therapy), had arrived right where he wanted to be. While everyone else was caught up

in the celebration, I sat in my chair and cried, tears of relief and thankfulness.

The night before Dan's graduation, there was an outdoor reception in the school's quad. Our entire family was together, including Dan's grandmothers. In addition to Lainey and her boyfriend, a cousin and uncle had also made the long trip to celebrate with us. I missed my dad terribly that night. He'd passed away a couple of years earlier and had always hoped to "make it" to Dan's graduation. I don't know if he did it purposely or not, but Dan wore one of my dad's shirts that evening. As we led our family to the big white tent in the middle of the courtyard, we passed the table Dan and I used to sit at for hours while I'd coax him to eat a spoonful of yogurt. The table was empty, and we continued on to the festivities: a jazz band, lots of food, and small gifts for his class. Dan was already there and was now surrounded by friends and family. He was holding a plate of food, piled high, and he looked so happy.

"Thanks for everything, Mom," he said, and then hugged me tightly. I struggled to contain my emotions.

Graduation was the following night, and once again we all squeezed into the car. On the way to the ceremony, we drove by the old motel that I'd stayed in four long years ago. I gasped. It was in the process of being razed, and they'd started with those steps Dan could barely climb. They no longer existed.

My son had come so far. Dr. Vogel, whom Dan had stopped seeing six months earlier, classified his OCD as mild and described his recovery as remarkable. While Dan still had OCD, OCD didn't have him. There was a big difference. We now had our son back.

IS OCD CURABLE?

Conventional wisdom suggests that OCD is a lifelong illness with symptoms that wax and wane. Even with exposure and response prevention (ERP), the best psychotherapy for OCD, the average patient at the end of treatment still has some OCD symptoms. For example, a large research study found that after ERP the average OCD score fell in the "mild" range.[1]

However, averages hide individual differences in treatment outcomes. A closer look at existing studies on ERP shows that about one out of four OCD sufferers will be virtually symptom-free at the end of treatment. That is, for about a quarter of those who do ERP, the OCD will be gone when the treatment is over. The obvious question, of course, is whether this improvement lasts, and existing studies show very promising findings. For example, one study found that 39 percent of those who underwent ERP were still symptom-free about nine months after the end of treatment.[2]

While nine months is promising in terms of treatment durability, it doesn't tell us what happens over the long haul—five years, or fifty years, later. In a review of long-term follow-ups (average length of 5.7 years) for children and adolescents with OCD, a full 40 percent no longer met criteria for OCD.[3] Caution is needed in interpreting these findings, as it wasn't possible for the researchers to determine how much of the remission was due to ongoing treatment.

In short, it's still unknown how often OCD can be "cured." A related and perhaps even more important question is, *Can a person with OCD live a meaningful and rewarding life?* The answer is unequivocally "yes"—even for individuals who continue to battle symptoms of OCD. Countless OCD sufferers are a testament to this possibility.

1. Foa et al., "Randomized Placebo-Controlled Trial," 156.
2. Peter L. Fisher and Adrian Wells, "How Effective Are Cognitive and Behavioral Treatments for Obsessive-Compulsive Disorder? A Clinical Significance Analysis," *Behaviour Research and Therapy* 43, no. 12 (2005): 1554– 55.
3. S. E. Stewart, D. A. Geller, M. Jenike, D. Pauls, D. Shaw, B. Mullin, and S. V. Faraone, "Long-Term Outcome of Pediatric Obsessive-Compulsive Disorder: A Meta-analysis and Qualitative Review of the Literature," *Acta Psychiatrica Scandinavica* 110, no. 1 (July 2004): 10.

What did the future hold? The only answer to that question, for any of us, is *I don't know*. I did know we all need to accept the uncertainty of life, just as Dan learned to do through his therapy for OCD.

As I heard my son's name called and watched him cross the stage in his cap and gown, I marveled at his capacity to face his struggles head on and at his choice to embrace life to the fullest. Looking at him closely, I couldn't help thinking that this young man would go on to accomplish amazing things.

And then I remembered. He already had.

RESOURCES

AUTHORS' WEBSITES

Janet Singer: http://ocdtalk.wordpress.com/
Seth J. Gillihan: http://sethgillihan.com/

ORGANIZATIONS

Anxiety and Depression Association of America (ADAA)
8701 Georgia Ave. #412
Silver Spring, MD 20910
Telephone: (240) 485-1001
Website: http://www.adaa.org/

Association for Behavioral and Cognitive Therapies (ABCT)
305 7th Avenue, 16th Floor
New York, NY 10001
Telephone (212) 647-1890
Website: http://www.abct.org/

Beyond OCD
2300 Lincoln Park West, Suite 206B
Chicago, IL 60614

Telephone: (773) 661-9530
E-mail: info@beyondocd.org
Website: http://beyondocd.org/

International OCD Foundation, Inc. (IOCDF)
PO Box 961029
Boston, MA 02196
Telephone: (617) 973-5801
E-mail: info@iocdf.org
Website: http://www.ocfoundation.org/

Mental Health America (MHA)
2000 N. Beauregard Street, 6th Floor
Alexandria, VA 22311
Telephone: (800) 969-6642 (toll free)
Website: http://www.mentalhealthamerica.net/

National Alliance on Mental Illness (NAMI)
3803 N. Fairfax Dr., Suite 100
Arlington, VA 22203
Telephone: (703) 524-7600
Helpline: (800) 950-6264 (toll free)
Website: https://www.nami.org/

National Institute of Mental Health (NIMH)
6001 Executive Boulevard
Rockville, MD 20852
Telephone: (866) 615-6464 (toll free)
E-mail: nimhinfo@mail.nih.gov
Website: http://www.nimh.nih.gov/index.shtml

The Peace of Mind Foundation
PO Box 310296
Houston, Texas 77231
E-mail: info@peaceofmind.com
Website: http://www.peaceofmind.com/

TREATMENT CENTERS

Anxiety Behaviors Clinic
   Child and Adolescent Psychiatry and Behavioral Science
   Children's Hospital of Philadelphia
   34th Street and Civic Center Boulevard
   Philadelphia, PA 19104
   Telephone: (215) 590-7555
   Website: http://www.chop.edu/service/behavioral-health-center/progr
ams-and-services.html#abc

The Center for Anxiety and Related Disorders at Boston University
   648 Beacon St., 6th Floor
   Boston, MA 02215
   Telephone: (617) 353-9610
   Website: http://www.bu.edu/card/

Center for the Treatment and Study of Anxiety
   University of Pennsylvania
   3535 Market Street, 6th Floor
   Philadelphia, PA 19104
   Telephone: (215) 746-3327
   Website: http://www.med.upenn.edu/ctsa/

Child and Adolescent OCD, Tic, Trich and Anxiety Group
   University of Pennsylvania
   3535 Market Street, 6th Floor
   Philadelphia, PA 19104
   Telephone: (215) 746-1230
   Email: antinoro@mail.med.upenn.edu
   Website: http://www.med.upenn.edu/cottage/

CLA Child OCD, Anxiety, and Tic Disorders Program
   Semel Institute
   760 Westwood Plaza, 67-467
   Los Angeles, CA 90024
   Telephone: (310) 825-0122
   E-mail: ocdinfo@ucla.edu

Website: http://www.semel.ucla.edu/caap

Houston OCD Program
   1401 Castle Court
   Houston, TX 77006
   Telephone: (713) 526-5055
   E-mail: info@houstonocd.org
   Website: http://houstonocdprogram.org/

McLean Hospital
   OCD Institute
   115 Mill Street
   Belmont, MA 02478
   Telephone: (800) 333-0338
   E-mail: mcleaninfo@mclean.harvard.edu
   Website: http://www.mclean.harvard.edu/patient/adult/ocd.php

Obsessive-Compulsive and Related Disorders Research Center
   Stanford University
   Department of Psychiatry and Behavioral Sciences
   401 Quarry Road
   Stanford, CA 94305-5721
   Telephone: (650) 498-9111
   Website: http://ocd.stanford.edu/

Obsessive Compulsive Disorders Research and Clinic Unit
   Simches Research Building
   Massachusetts General Hospital
   185 Cambridge Street
   Boston, MA 02114
   Telephone: (617) 726-6766
   Website: http://www.massgeneral.org/psychiatry/services/ocd_home.
aspx

Pediatric Anxiety and Mood Research Clinic
   Columbia University
   1051 Riverside Drive
   New York, NY 10032

Telephone: (646) 774-5793
Website: http://columbiapsychiatry.org/pamrc

Rogers Memorial Hospital
Obsessive-Compulsive Disorder Center
34700 Valley Road
Oconomowoc, WI 53066
Telephone: (800) 767-4411
Website: http://rogershospital.org/

Rogers Behavioral Health—Tampa Bay
2002 North Lois Avenue
Tampa, FL 33607
Telephone: (844) 220-4411
Website: http://rogershospital.org/rogers-behavioral-health-tampa-bay

The Rothman Center for Pediatric Neuropsychiatry
University of South Florida
880 6th Street South
Suite 460, Box 7523
St. Petersburg, FL 33701
Telephone: (800) 456-4543, ext. 8230
E-mail: rothmanctr@health.usf.edu
Website: http://health.usf.edu/medicine/pediatrics/rothman/index.htm

UNC Anxiety and Stress Disorders Clinic
University of North Carolina at Chapel Hill
Department of Psychology
CB#3270, Davie Hall
Chapel Hill, NC 27599
Telephone: (919) 843-8170
Website: http://jonabram.web.unc.edu/anxiety-lab

Yale OCD Research Clinic
Connecticut Mental Health Center
34 Park Street, 3rd Floor—CNRU
New Haven, CT 06508
Telephone: 1-855-OCD-YALE

E-mail: ocd.research@yale.edu
Website: http://www.ocd.yale.edu/index.aspx

BOOKS

Baer, Lee. *The Imp of the Mind: Exploring the Silent Epidemic of Obsessive Bad Thoughts.* New York: Plume, 2002.

Bell, Jeff. *Rewind, Replay, Repeat.* Center City, MN: Hazelden, 2007.

———. *When in Doubt, Make Belief.* Novato, CA: New World Library, 2009.

Foa, Edna B., and Reid Wilson. *Stop Obsessing! How to Overcome Your Obsessions and Compulsions.* New York: Bantam, 2001.

Grayson, Jonathan. *Freedom from Obsessive Compulsive Disorder: A Personalized Recovery Program for Living with Uncertainty.* New York: Berkley Trade, 2014.

Murphy, Terry Weible, Edward E. Zine, and Michael A. Jenike. *Life in Rewind.* New York: William Morrow, 2010.

Schwartz, Jeffrey M., and Beverly Beyette. *Brain Lock: Free Yourself from Obsessive-Compulsive Behavior.* New York: Harper Perennial, 1997.

WORKBOOKS AND GUIDES

Abramowitz, Jonathan S. *Getting Over OCD: A 10-Step Workbook for Taking Back Your Life.* New York: Guilford Press, 2009.

———. *The Stress Less Workbook: Simple Strategies to Relieve Pressure, Manage Commitments, and Minimize Conflicts.* New York: Guilford Press, 2012.

Baer, Lee. *Getting Control: Overcoming Your Obsessions and Compulsions.* New York: Plume, 2012.

Hershfield, Jon, and Tom Corboy. *The Mindfulness Workbook for OCD: A Guide to Overcoming Obsessions and Compulsions using Mindfulness and Cognitive Behavioral Therapy.* Oakland, CA: New Harbinger Publications, 2013.

Hyman, Bruce M., and Cherlene Pedrick. *The OCD Workbook: Your Guide to Breaking Free from Obsessive-Compulsive Disorder.* Oakland, CA: New Harbinger Publications, 2010.

Tompkins, Michael A. *OCD: A Guide for the Newly Diagnosed.* Oakland, CA: New Harbinger Publications, 2012.

NOTES

INTRODUCTION

1. American Psychiatric Association, *Diagnostic and Statistical Manual of Mental Disorders*, 5th ed. (*DSM-5*) (Arlington, VA: Author, 2013), 237.

2. Paul M. Spengler and David M. Jacobi, "Assessment and Treatment of Obsessive-Compulsive Disorder in College Age Students and Adults," *Journal of Mental Health Counseling* 20, no. 2 (1998): 95.

3. American Psychiatric Association, *DSM-5*, 237–38.

4. Gordon M. G. Shepherd, "Corticostriatal Connectivity and Its Role in Disease," *Nature Reviews Neuroscience* 14, no. 4 (April 2013): 286.

5. Seth J. Gillihan and Erik Parens, "Should We Expect 'Neural Signatures' for *DSM* Diagnoses?" *Journal of Clinical Psychiatry* 72, no. 10 (2011): 1384.

6. Stefan G. Hofmann and Jasper A. J. Smits, "Cognitive-Behavioral Therapy for Adult Anxiety Disorders: A Meta-analysis of Randomized Placebo-Controlled Trials," *Journal of Clinical Psychiatry* 69, no. 4 (April 2008): 626.

7. Edna B. Foa, Elna Yadin, and Tracey K. Lichner, *Exposure and Response (Ritual) Prevention for Obsessive-Compulsive Disorder: Therapist Guide*, 2nd ed. (New York: Oxford University Press, 2012), 72–75.

8. Patricia Ribeiro Porto, Leticia Oliveira, Jair Mari, Eliane Volchan, Ivan Figueira, and Paula Ventura, "Does Cognitive Behavioral Therapy Change the Brain? A Systematic Review of Neuroimaging in Anxiety Disorders," *Journal of Neuropsychiatry and Clinical Neurosciences* 21, no. 2 (2009): 120–21.

9. American Psychiatric Association, *Practice Guideline for the Treatment of Patients with Obsessive-Compulsive Disorder* (Arlington, VA: Author, 2007), 23–24.

10. Caroline Schwartz, Sandra Schlegl, Anne Katrin Kuelz, and Ulrich Voderholzer, "Treatment-Seeking in OCD Community Cases and Psychological Treatment Actually Provided to Treatment-Seeking Patients: A Systematic Review," *Journal of Obsessive-Compulsive and Related Disorders* 2, no. 4 (2013): 453–54.

11. Edna B. Foa, Michael R. Liebowitz, Michael J. Kozak, Sharon Davies, Rafael Campeas, Martin E. Franklin, Jonathan D. Huppert, Kevin Kjernisted, Vivienne Rowan, Andrew B. Schmidt, H. Blair Simpson, and Xin Tu, "Randomized, Placebo-Controlled Trial of Exposure and Ritual Prevention, Clomipramine, and Their Combination in the Treatment of Obsessive-Compulsive Disorder," *American Journal of Psychiatry* 162, no. 1 (January 2005): 156.

12. Hofmann and Smits, "Cognitive-Behavioral Therapy," 626.

13. Seth J. Gillihan, Monnica T. Williams, Emily Malcoun, Elna Yadin, and Edna B. Foa, "Common Pitfalls in Exposure and Response Prevention (EX/RP) for OCD," *Journal of Obsessive Compulsive and Related Disorders* 1, no. 4 (October 2012): 254.

BIBLIOGRAPHY

Abramovitch, Amitai, Reuven Dar, Andrew Mittelman, and Avraham Schweiger. "Don't Judge a Book by Its Cover: ADHD-like Symptoms in Obsessive Compulsive Disorder." *Journal of Obsessive-Compulsive and Related Disorders* 2, no. 1 (2013): 53–61.

Abramowitz, Jonathan S., Martin E. Franklin, Gordon P. Street, Michael J. Kozac, and Edna B. Foa. "Effects of Comorbid Depression on Response to Treatment for Obsessive-Compulsive Disorder." *Behavior Therapy* 31, no. 3 (2000): 522–26.

Abramowitz, Jonathan S., Martin E. Franklin, Stefanie A. Schwartz, and Jami M. Furr. "Symptom Presentation and Outcome of Cognitive-Behavioral Therapy for Obsessive-Compulsive Disorder." *Journal of Consulting and Clinical Psychology* 71, no. 6 (2003): 1049–57.

American Academy of Pediatrics. "ADHD: Clinical Practice Guideline for the Diagnosis, Evaluation, and Treatment of Attention-Deficit/Hyperactivity Disorder in Children and Adolescents." *Pediatrics* 128, no. 5 (November 2011): 1007–22.

American Psychiatric Association. *Diagnostic and Statistical Manual of Mental Disorders*. 5th ed. (*DSM-5*). Arlington, VA: Author, 2013.

———. "Practice Guideline for the Treatment of Patients with Obsessive-Compulsive Disorder." (2007). http://www.psych.org/psych_pract/treatg/pg/prac_guide.cfm.

Bakker, Abraham, Anton J. L. M. van Balkom, and Philip Spinhoven. "SSRIs vs. TCAs in the Treatment of Panic Disorder: A Meta-analysis." *Acta Psychiatrica Scandinavica* 106, no. 3 (2002): 163–67.

Bloch, M. H., A. M. Landeros-Weisenberger, B. Kelmendi, V. Coric, M. B. Bracken, and J. F. Leckman. "A Systematic Review: Antipsychotic Augmentation with Treatment Refractory Obsessive-Compulsive Disorder." *Molecular Psychiatry* 11, no. 7 (July 2006): 622–32.

Bloch, Michael H., Joseph McGuire, Angeli Landeros-Weisenberger, James F. Leckman, and Christopher Pittenger. "Meta-analysis of the Dose-Response Relationship of SSRI in Obsessive-Compulsive Disorder." *Molecular Psychiatry* 15, no. 8 (August 2010): 850–55.

De Arayjo, Luiz A., Ligia M. Ito, and Isaac M. Marks. "Early Compliance and Other Factors Predicting Outcome of Exposure for Obsessive-Compulsive Disorder." *British Journal of Psychiatry* 169, no. 6 (December 1996): 747–52.

Dell'osso, B., and M. Lader. "Do Benzodiazepines Still Deserve a Major Role in the Treatment of Psychiatric Disorders? A Critical Reappraisal." *European Psychiatry* 28, no. 1 (2013): 7–20.

Efron, Daryl, Frederick Jarman, and Melinda Barker. "Side Effects of Methylphenidate and Dexamphetamine in Children with Attention Deficit Hyperactivity Disorder: A Double-Blind, Crossover Trial." *Pediatrics* 100, no. 4 (1997): 662–66.

Fineberg, Naomi A., Samar Reghunandanan, Angus Brown, and Ilenia Pampaloni. "Pharmaco-therapy of Obsessive-Compulsive Disorder: Evidence-Based Treatment and Beyond." *Australian and New Zealand Journal of Psychiatry* 47, no. 2 (February 2013): 121–41.

Fisher, Peter L., and Adrian Wells. "How Effective Are Cognitive and Behavioral Treatments for Obsessive-Compulsive Disorder? A Clinical Significance Analysis." *Behaviour Research and Therapy* 43, no. 12 (2005): 1543–58.

Foa, Edna B., Michael R. Liebowitz, Michael J. Kozak, Sharon Davies, Rafael Campeas, Martin E. Franklin, Jonathan D. Huppert, Kevin Kjernisted, Vivienne Rowan, Andrew B. Schmidt, H. Blair Simpson, and Xin Tu. "Randomized, Placebo-Controlled Trial of Exposure and Ritual Prevention, Clomipramine, and Their Combination in the Treatment of Obsessive-Compulsive Disorder." *American Journal of Psychiatry* 162, no. 1 (January 2005): 151–61.

Foa, Edna B., Elna Yadin, and Tracey K. Lichner. *Exposure and Response (Ritual) Prevention for Obsessive-Compulsive Disorder: Therapist Guide.* 2nd ed. New York: Oxford University Press, 2012.

Freiheit, Stacy R., Christopher Vye, Rebecca Swan, and Mary Cady. "Cognitive-Behavioral Therapy for Anxiety: Is Dissemination Working?" *Behavior Therapist* 27, no. 2 (2004): 25–43.

Gillihan, Seth J., and Erik Parens. "Should We Expect 'Neural Signatures' for *DSM* Diagnoses?" *Journal of Clinical Psychiatry* 72, no. 10 (2011): 1383–89.

Gillihan, Seth J., Monnica T. Williams, Emily Malcoun, Elna Yadin, and Edna B. Foa. "Common Pitfalls in Exposure and Response Prevention (EX/RP) for OCD." *Journal of Obsessive-Compulsive and Related Disorders* 1, no. 4 (October 2012): 251–57.

Hewlett, Williams A., Sophia Vinogradov, and Stewart W. Agras. "Clomipramine, Clonazepam, and Clonidine Treatment of Obsessive-Compulsive Disorder." *Journal of Clinical Psychopharmacology* 12, no. 6 (1992): 420–30.

Hofmann, Stefan G., and Jasper A. Smits. "Cognitive-Behavioral Therapy for Adult Anxiety Disorders: A Meta-analysis of Randomized Placebo-Controlled Trials." *Journal of Clinical Psychology* 69, no. 4 (April 2008): 621–32.

Hollander, Eric, Alicia Kaplan, and Stephen M. Stahl. "A Double-Blind, Placebo-Controlled Trial of Clonazepam in Obsessive-Compulsive Disorder." *World Journal of Biological Psychiatry* 4, no. 1 (2003): 30–34.

International OCD Foundation. "Cognitive Behavior Therapy." Accessed April 25, 2014. http://www.ocfoundation.org/CBT.aspx.

Kamath, Prakash, Y. C. Janardhan Reddy, and Thennarasu Kandavel. "Suicidal Behavior in Obsessive-Compulsive Disorder." *Journal of Clinical Psychiatry* 68, no. 11 (November 2007): 1741–50.

Kessler, Ronald C., Patricia Berglund, Olga Demler, Robert Jin, Kathleen R. Merikangas, and Ellen E. Walters. "Lifetime Prevalence and Age-of-Onset Distributions of DSM-IV Disorders in the National Comorbidity Survey Replication." *Archives of General Psychiatry* 62, no. 6 (June 2005): 593–602.

Komossa, Katja, Anna M. Depping, Magdalena Meyer, Werner Kissling, and Stefan Leucht. "Second-Generation Antipsychotics for Obsessive Compulsive Disorder." *Cochrane Database of Systematic Reviews* 12 (2010): 2–69.

Koran, Lorrin M., Gregory L. Hanna, Eric Hollander, Gerald Nestadt, and Helen B. Simpson. "Practice Guideline for the Treatment of Patients with Obsessive-Compulsive Disorder." *American Journal of Psychiatry* 164, no. 7 (July 2007): 7–70.

Kozak, Michael J., Edna B. Foa, and Gail Steketee. "Process and Outcome of Exposure Treatment with Obsessive-Compulsives: Psychophysiological Indicators of Emotional Processing." *Behavior Therapy* 19, no. 2 (1988): 157–69.

Mayo Clinic. "Selective Serotonin Reuptake Inhibitors (SSRIs)." Accessed April 26, 2014. http://www.mayoclinic.org/.

New York State Psychiatric Institute. "Attaining and Maintaining Wellness in Obsessive-Compulsive Disorder." ClinicalTrials.gov, U.S. National Institutes of Health. Last updated July 26, 2014. https://clinicaltrials.gov/ct2/show/NCT01686087.

Nock, Matthew K. "Self-Injury." *Annual Review of Clinical Psychology* 6 (2010): 339–63.

Nock, Matthew K., Thomas E. Joiner Jr., Kathryn H. Gordon, Elizabeth Lloyd-Richardson, and Mitchell J. Prinstein. "Non-suicidal Self-Injury among Adolescents: Diagnostic Correlates and Relation to Suicide Attempts." *Psychiatry Research* 144 (2006): 65–72.

Osgood-Hynes, Deborah, Bradley Riemann, and Thröstur Björgvinsson. "Short-Term Residential Treatment for Obsessive-Compulsive Disorder." *Brief Treatment and Crisis Intervention* 3, no. 4 (2003): 413–35.

Pallanti, Stefano, Giacomo Grassi, Elisa D. Sarrecchia, Andrea Cantisani, and Matteo Pellegrini. "Obsessive-Compulsive Disorder Comorbidity: Clinical Assessment and Therapeutic Implications." *Frontiers in Psychiatry* 2, no. 70 (2011): 1–11.

Perugi, Giulio, Hagop S. Akiskal, Chiara Pfanner, Silvio Presta, Alfredo Gemignani, Alessandro Milanfranchi, Patrizia Lensi, Susanna Ravagli, and Giovanni B. Cassano. "The Clinical Impact of Bipolar and Unipolar Affective Comorbidity on Obsessive-Compulsive Disorder." *Journal of Affective Disorders* 46, no. 1 (October 1997): 15–23.

Porto, Patricia Ribeiro, Leticia Oliveira, Jair Mari, Eliane Volchan, Ivan Figueira, and Paula Ventura. "Does Cognitive Behavioral Therapy Change the Brain? A Systematic Review of Neuroimaging in Anxiety Disorders." *Journal of Neuropsychiatry and Clinical Neurosciences* 21, no. 2 (2009): 114–25.

POTS Team. "Cognitive-Behavior Therapy, Sertraline, and Their Combination for Children and Adolescents with Obsessive-Compulsive Disorder: The Pediatric OCD Treatment Study (POTS) Randomized Controlled Trial." *JAMA* 292, no. 16 (2004): 1969–76.

Rapport, Mark D., and Catherine Moffitt. "Attention Deficit/Hyperactivity Disorder and Methylphenidate: A Review of Height/Weight, Cardiovascular, and Somatic Complaint Side Effects." *Clinical Psychology Review* 22, no. 8 (November 2002): 1107–31.

Reynolds, Shirley A., Sarah Clark, Holly Smith, Peter E. Langdon, Ruth Payne, Gemma Bowers, Elisabeth Norton, and Harriet McIlwham. "Randomized Controlled Trial of Parents-Enhanced CBT Compared with Individual CBT for Obsessive-Compulsive Disorder in Young People." *Journal of Consulting and Clinical Psychology* 81, no. 6 (2013): 1021–26.

Rosa-Alcázar, Ana I., Julio Sánchez-Meca, Antonia Gómez-Conesa, and Fulgencio Marín-Martínez. "Psychological Treatment of Obsessive-Compulsive Disorder: A Meta-analysis." *Clinical Psychology Review* 28, no. 8 (2008): 1310–25.

Rufer, Michael, Iver Hand, Heike Alsleben, Anne Braatz, Jürgen Ortmann, Birgit Katenkamp, Susanne Fricke, and Helmut Peter. "Long-Term Course and Outcome of Obsessive-Compulsive Patients after Cognitive-Behavioral Therapy in Combination with Either Fluvoxamine or Placebo." *European Archives of Psychiatry and Clinical Neuroscience* 255, no. 2 (April 2005): 121–28.

Schatz, David Beck, and Anthony L. Rostain. "ADHD with Comorbid Anxiety: A Review of the Current Literature." *Journal of Attention Disorders* 10, no. 2 (2006): 141–49.

Schwartz, Caroline, Sandra Schlegl, Anne Katrin Kuelz, and Ulrich Voderholzer. "Treatment-Seeking in OCD Community Cases and Psychological Treatment Actually Provided to Treatment-Seeking Patients: A Systematic Review." *Journal of Obsessive-Compulsive and Related Disorders* 2, no. 4 (2013): 448–56.

Shepherd, Gordon M. G. "Corticostriatal Connectivity and Its Role in Disease." *Nature Reviews Neuroscience* 14, no. 4 (April 2013): 278–91.

Simpson, Helen B., Michael J. Maher, Yuanjia Wang, Yuanyuan Bao, Edna B. Foa, and Martin Franklin. "Patient Adherence Predicts Outcome from Cognitive Behavioral Therapy in Obsessive-Compulsive Disorder." *Journal of Consulting and Clinical Psychology* 79, no. 2 (April 2011): 247–52.

Simpson, Helen Blair, Edna B. Foa, Michael R. Liebowitz, Jonathan D. Huppert, Shawn Cahill, Michael J. Maher, Carmen P. McLean, James Bender Jr., Sue M. Marcus, Monnica T. Williams, Jamie Weaver, Donna Vermes, E. Van Meter, Carolyn I. Rodriguez, Mark Powers, Anthony Pinto, Patricia Imms, Chang-Gyu Hahn, and Raphael Campeas. "Cognitive-Behavioral Therapy vs. Risperidone for Augmenting Serotonin Reuptake Inhibitors in Obsessive-Compulsive Disorder: A Randomized Clinical Trial." *JAMA Psychiatry* 70, no. 11 (2013): 1190–99.

Society of Clinical Psychology (American Psychological Association, Division 12). "Exposure and Response Prevention for Obsessive-Compulsive Disorder." Accessed April 25, 2014. http://www.div12.org/PsychologicalTreatments/treatments/ocd_exposure.html.

Spengler, Paul M., and David M. Jacobi. "Assessment and Treatment of Obsessive-Compulsive Disorder in College Age Students and Adults." *Journal of Mental Health Counseling* 20, no. 2 (April 1998): 95–111.

Spofford, Christopher M. "The Role of Motivation to Change in the Treatment of Obsessive-Compulsive Disorder." PhD diss., Graduate School of the University of Massachusetts Amherst, 2009. Open Access Dissertations (Paper 132).

Stewart, Rebecca E., and Dianne L. Chambless. "Cognitive-Behavioral Therapy for Adult Anxiety Disorders in Clinical Practice: A Meta-analysis of Effectiveness Studies." *Journal of Consulting and Clinical Psychology* 77, no. 4 (August 2009): 595–606.

Stewart, S. E., D. A. Geller, M. Jenike, D. Pauls, D. Shaw, B. Mullin, and S. V. Faraone. "Long-Term Outcome of Pediatric Obsessive-Compulsive Disorder: A Meta-analysis and Qualitative Review of the Literature." *Acta Psychiatrica Scandinavica* 110, no. 1 (July 2004): 4–13.

Stewart, S. Evelyn, Denise Egan Stack, Colleen Farrell, David L. Pauls, and Michael A. Jenike. "Effectiveness of Intensive Residential Treatment (IRT) for Severe, Refractory Obsessive-Compulsive Disorder." *Journal of Psychiatric Research* 39, no. 6 (November 2005): 603–9.

Tolin, David F., Jonathan S. Abramowitz, Bartholomew D. Brigidi, and Edna B. Foa. "Intolerance of Uncertainty in Obsessive-Compulsive Disorder." *Journal of Anxiety Disorders* 17, no. 2 (2003): 233–42.

Torres, Albina R., Ana Teresa A. Ramos-Cerqueira, Ygor A. Ferrao, Leonardo F. Fontenelle, Maria Conceicao do Rosario, and Euripedes C. Miguel. "Suicidality in Obsessive-Compulsive Disorder: Prevalence and Relation to Symptom Dimensions and Comorbid Conditions." *Journal of Clinical Psychiatry* 72, no. 1 (January 2011): 17–26.

Torresan, Ricardo C., Ana Teresa A. Ramos-Cerqueira, Roseli G. Shavitt, Maria Conceicao do Rosario, Maria Alice de Mathis, Euripedes C. Miguel, and Albina R. Torres. "Symptom Dimensions, Clinical Course and Comorbidity in Men and Women with Obsessive-Compulsive Disorder." *Psychiatry Research* 209, no. 2 (2013): 186–95.

Tükel, R., A. Polat, Ö. Özdemir, D. Aksüt, and N. Türksoy. "Comorbid Conditions in Obsessive Compulsive Disorder." *Comprehensive Psychiatry* 43, no. 3 (May–June 2002): 204–9.

Williams, Monnica T., Beth Mugno, Martin Franklin, and Sonya Faber. "Symptom Dimensions in Obsessive-Compulsive Disorder: Phenomenology and Treatment Outcomes with Exposure and Ritual Prevention." *Psychopathology* 46, no. 6 (2013): 365–76.

Wirt, Gary L. "Causes of Institutionalism: Patient and Staff Perspectives." *Issues in Mental Health Nursing* 20, no. 3 (May–June 1999): 259–74.

Wolraich, Mark, Lawrence Brown, Ronald T. Brown, George DuPaul, Marian Earls, Heidi M. Feldman, Theodore G. Ganiats, Beth Kaplanek, Bruce Meyer, James Perrin, Karen Pierce, Michael Reiff, Martin T. Stein, and Susanna Visser. "ADHD: Clinical Practice Guideline for the Diagnosis, Evaluation, and Treatment of Attention-Deficit/Hyperactivity Disorder in Children and Adolescents." *Pediatrics* 128, no. 5 (November 2011): 1007–22.

Xie, Zhihua, and Gregory M. Miller. "A Receptor Mechanism for Methamphetamine Action in Dopamine Transporter Regulation in Brain." *Journal of Pharmacology and Experimental Therapeutics* 330, no. 1 (July 2009): 316–25.

Yaryura-Tobias, Jose A., Fugen A. Neziroglu, and Steven Kaplan. "Self-Mutilation, Anorexia, and Dysmenorrhea in Obsessive Compulsive Disorder." *International Journal of Eating Disorders* 17, no. 1 (January 1995): 33–38.

INDEX

ABOUT THE AUTHORS

Janet Singer is an advocate for OCD awareness, with the goal of spreading the word that obsessive-compulsive disorder, no matter how severe, is treatable. In 2008, her son Dan suffered from OCD so debilitating he could not even eat. Thanks to ERP therapy, Dan made a remarkable recovery. Singer writes regularly for Psychcentral.com as well as Mentalhelp.net, and has been published on many other websites, including Beyond OCD, Anxiety and Depression Association of America, and Mad in America. She has also been an invited speaker at OCD conferences. She started her own blog, ocdtalk (www.ocdtalk.wordpress.com) in 2010, and it currently reaches readers in 166 countries. She uses a pseudonym to protect her son's privacy.

Seth J. Gillihan, PhD, is a clinical assistant professor of psychology in the Psychiatry Department at the University of Pennsylvania, and a visiting assistant professor of psychology at Haverford College. Dr. Gillihan was on the faculty at the Center for the Treatment and Study of Anxiety at the University of Pennsylvania from 2008–2012. His research publications include articles and book chapters on the effectiveness of cognitive-behavioral therapy (CBT) for OCD, anxiety, and depression, how CBT helps people to get better, and the use of brain imaging to study psychiatric disorders. Dr. Gillihan's clinical practice is located in Haverford, Pennsylvania.